QUEEN
OF THE DESERT

Georgina Howell began working in magazine journalism at the age of seventeen. She was fashion editor of the *Observer*, features editor of *Vogue*, deputy editor of *Tatler* and a principal feature writer for the *Sunday Times*. She lives in London and Brittany.

'One reads this richly rewarding book wishing that Britain had a shred of the esteem it had in the Arab world in the days of Gertrude Bell' *Daily Mail*

'Journalist Georgina Howell readily admits to being a fan of the intrepid Victorian Gertrude Bell even before starting her biography . . . Drawing extensively on Bell's writings and personal letters, Howell draws up a detailed picture of Bell's life and loves . . . In the current climate Bell's part in creating modern-day Iraq is particularly resonant' *Metro London*

'Riveting. Howell's mastery of an extremely complex network of events in the Middle East appears to be effortless; her portraits of the personalities involved, both British and Arab, are excellent . . . few women have had a life more worth reading about' *Literary Review*

'Her story is well known in the context of Middle-Eastern politics, but Georgina Howell humanizes the political woman by giving a full, engagingly written account of her privileged upbringing and frustrated love, while a young woman, for two men' *The Times*

GEORGINA HOWELL

QUEEN
OF THE DESERT

THE EXTRAORDINARY LIFE OF
GERTRUDE BELL

PAN BOOKS

First published 2006 by Macmillan

First published in paperback 2007 by Pan Books
This edition published 2015 by Pan Books
an imprint of Pan Macmillan
20 New Wharf Road, London N1 9RR
Associated companies throughout the world
www.panmacmillan.com

ISBN 978-1-4472-8626-4

10

A CIP catalogue record for this book is available from the British Library.

Typeset by SetSystems Ltd, Saffron Walden, Essex
Maps designed by Raymond Turvey
Printed and bound by CPI Group (UK) Ltd, Croydon CR0 4YY

For, with and also by Christopher Bailey

CONTENTS

Preface, ix
Acknowledgements, xiv
Maps, xix

1 GERTRUDE AND FLORENCE, 1
2 EDUCATION, 28
3 THE CIVILIZED WOMAN, 43
4 BECOMING A PERSON, 63
5 MOUNTAINEERING, 78
6 DESERT TRAVEL, 99
7 DICK DOUGHTY-WYLIE, 135
8 LIMIT OF ENDURANCE, 173
9 ESCAPE, 208
10 WAR WORK, 233
11 CAIRO, DELHI, BASRA, 256
12 GOVERNMENT THROUGH GERTRUDE, 295
13 ANGER, 326
14 FAISAL, 362
15 CORONATION, 395
16 STAYING AND LEAVING, 414

Notes, 455
Bibliography, 476
Note on Money Values, 485
Chronology, 487
Index, 505
Permissions, 519

PREFACE

It was summer, 1997. The contract writers for *The Sunday Times Magazine*, we had collected for dinner in a London restaurant at the invitation of the editor Robin Morgan, to hear his thoughts for the new winter features. Philip Norman, whose award-winning interviews have captured the magic and madness of rock 'n' roll, Vatican expert John Cornwell of Jesus College, Cambridge, Bryan Appleyard who can explain advanced science and make it gloriously readable, and others were tucking into our duck *en croûte* when each of us was invited to write a feature for a series to be entitled 'My Hero'. I returned home excited: I knew who 'My Heroine' would be, and I thought a reminder of her glorious life was overdue. The feature, published that October, provoked the biggest mailbag I'd had in thirty-six years of journalism.

At one time more famous than Lawrence of Arabia, Gertrude Bell chose to compete on male terms in a masculine world. She avoided all publicity. She would not have cared that in an opening sequence of the popular 1997 film *The English Patient*, her name was taken in vain by British soldiers poring over a map spread out on a folding table in a camouflage tent:

'But can we get through those mountains?'

'The Bell maps show a way.'

Then: 'Let's hope he was right.'

He!

When I started to write about Gertrude Bell I revered her as one of those heroines of the Wilder Shores who followed their romantic notions here and there about the world. I loved the way she dressed and the way she lived – so stylishly, a pistol strapped to her calf under silk petticoats and dresses of lace and tucked muslin, her desert table laid with crisp linen and silver, her cartridges wrapped in white stockings and pushed into the toes of her Yapp canvas boots. She was not a feminist; she had no need or wish for special treatment. Like Mrs Thatcher – admire her or despise her – she took on the world exactly as she found it. Only this was in the 1880s, when women were hardly educated or allowed to prove themselves outside the home.

The Bells were very rich: but it was not money that got Gertrude a First at Oxford, or helped her survive encounters with murderous tribes in the desert, or made her a spy or a major in the British army, or qualified her as poet, scholar, historian, mountaineer, photographer, archaeologist, gardener, cartographer, linguist and distinguished servant of the state. In each of these fields she excelled, even pioneered. She was many-faceted – in this respect comparable with those giants among mankind, Elizabeth I and Catherine the Great of Russia. T. E. Lawrence wrote that Gertrude was 'born too gifted'. But rigour was the real legacy that she was born with, and she was intensely proud of her family's pragmatism – their grasp of economics, the good management of their mighty steel business, and their public and private works of charity. When called upon, she dedicated herself to grinding, unglamorous office work: to the structuring and filing that transformed the wartime Wounded and Missing Office of the Red Cross from chaos to an efficiently functioning system; to the minutiae of administration and map-drawing; to the taking of hundreds of precise measurements at archaeological sites; and to the writing of reams of position papers in Basra and Baghdad.

Rising in three generations from artisan to high middle class, the Bells were beginning to marry into the aristocracy. They remained outside the great social networks of English life, those exclusive clubs that conferred inherited privilege and power and determined your prejudices, associates and affiliations. Gertrude enjoyed a rare freedom from the traps that imprison us in the grooves of social life. She met the great and the good on equal terms, but she knew something of what it meant to be working class, and of how those families stood on a knife-edge between survival and precipitation into the street and the workhouse. Her clear, unequivocal vision cut straight through political correctness, self-importance, status and fame. She gave no quarter to an opinionated bishop, a pompous statesman or a self-satisfied professor. At fifteen she decided that the unprovable did not exist, and told her scripture teacher so without prevarication. She would meet people head on – whether a patronizing don, a knife-waving dervish, a corrupt Turkish official or an effete English aristocrat. Her friends came from diverse walks of life, ranging from an Iraqi gardener to the Viceroy of India, from a *Times* correspondent to a battle-scarred tribal warrior, from a *mutjahid* to a servant from Aleppo. Once they had been admitted to her trust, she was the most loving, the most attentive and faithful of friends.

Of course she made enemies. She snubbed the modestly gifted wives of British officers – 'The devil take all inane women!' she once said; she was liable to attack anyone who menaced her, confronted villains and murderers and would denounce them face to face over the dinner table. It seemed to me at one point during my research that she might have been murdered by one of the latter, and there are students of her work and at least one recent member of the British Council who believe this to be the case. As if aware of constant threat, she always slept with her gun under her pillow, even at her family home in Yorkshire, where she preferred to spend her nights in a summer-house in the garden rather than in her own comfortable bedroom amongst her beloved family. Was she trying to protect them? While there were undoubtedly people who wished her dead, I found no evidence of murder, though facts are hard to come by. I do believe that, just as, full of curiosity and excitement, she had always courageously ventured out into the unknown on her expeditions, so she ventured out one last time.

She yearned to be married and to have a family of her own, but time and again, tragedy intervened to put an end to those hopes. She was, however, much loved, not least by that great family to whom she finally dedicated her life and work: the people of Arabia.

And they have not forgotten her. Recently, her name and her work
for Iraq were reinstated in the nationwide school syllabus. Lawrence
kick-started the Arab Revolt, but it was Gertrude who gave the
Arabs a route to nationhood. She cajoled and intruded, guided and
engineered, and finally delivered the often promised and so nearly
betrayed prize of independence. While she remained dedicated to
this mission through thick and thin, Lawrence agonized, faltered,
and finally abandoned the Arab issue and tried to escape from his
own tortured personality, to reappear in the nondescript persona of
one Aircraftsman Shaw.

Gertrude Bell stuck to her ambition for the Arabs with a
wonderful consistency. She showed her clever but floundering
colleagues of the Cairo Intelligence Bureau how to win their bit
of the Great War; she guided the fledgling British administration of
Mesopotamia to a thriving future, hand in hand with the Arabs and
to their mutual advantage. And she stuck to her guns when her
colonialist chief tried to have her sacked, when Churchill wanted to
pull the British out of Iraq altogether, when political machinations
in Europe brought all her achievements to the brink of disaster, and
when, playing her last card, she kept King Faisal from throwing it
all away in the name of Arab supremacy.

She established the public library and the Iraq Museum in
Baghdad, of which the principal wing was dedicated in 1930 to her
memory. The museum still guards the remaining treasures of a
country whose origins were those of the first civilizations. While
Iraq's future is desperately uncertain, one fact remains indisputable.
Dying in 1926, Gertrude Bell left behind a benevolent and effective
Iraq government, functioning without institutionalized corruption
and intent on equality and peace. In days when 'Empire' and
'colonialism' are dirty words, Britain has little to be ashamed of
in the establishment of Iraq, in which the promise of Arab independence was finally honoured. I have come to agree with her old
friend from Oxford, Janet Hogarth, who wrote of her: 'She was, I
think, the greatest woman of our time, perhaps amongst the greatest
of all time.'

As long as Faisal lived, Iraq was a place where all its people could carry on their daily lives without fear and suffering. His son Prince Ghazi — the little boy for whom Gertrude had bought toys at Harrods — inherited the crown in 1933 and continued to rule the country strongly, perhaps too strongly: in suppressing an Assyrian uprising for independence, he allowed the massacre of 1933. After Gertrude's death, the dynasty she had put in place continued for thirty-two more years, while Europe plunged into war again after only thirteen, dragging the rest of the world with it. What would America and Britain not give today for the promise of a peaceful and well governed Iraq for even four years?

Her prolific letters, diaries and intelligence position papers, no less than her eight books and her magnum opus *The Review of the Civil Administration of Mesopotamia*, make Gertrude Bell one of the best-documented women of all time. Her voice as it comes through in her writing, so personal, so visionary, so humorous and crystal-clear in its purpose, has guided me as to how to write this book. Although she lacked the narrative strain needed to set all she had to say in the context of her story, her voice ought to be heard and appreciated, it seemed to me — which is why I decided to use many more of her own words than would appear in a conventional biography and to give them a distinct typeface of their own. In parallel with her story, they give the immediacy and the sparkle of her ardent mind, vividly revealing her wit and character.

ACKNOWLEDGEMENTS

When this book was just a vague idea, it was Valerie Pakenham, one-time colleague and longtime friend, who said 'You must do it.' Simon Trewin of Peters Fraser and Dunlop has been more than encouraging. We have been immensely fortunate that Georgina Morley gave us the backing of Macmillan in London and has guided us with unfailing enthusiasm ever since. She took this slightly unusual style of biography in her stride, and with Sarah Crichton of Farrar Straus and Giroux in New York edited it in masterly fashion.

When first writing about Gertrude Bell for *The Sunday Times Magazine*, I was privileged to be helped by Lesley Gordon, the late Archivist of the Robinson Library of the University of Newcastle upon Tyne and custodian of the Gertrude Bell archive. It appears that she gave her life to the memory of Gertrude; writing the handbook and providing material for the British Council Gertrude Bell exhibition in 1994. Authors and historians alike must be forever grateful for her 'Gertrude Bell Project' through which she raised funds for Gertrude's diaries, letters and seven thousand photographs to be available on the Internet. When we wrote to tell her about the book, we were sad to discover that she had died. Nevertheless, we had the benefit of her help beyond the grave: her exhibition booklet *Gertrude Bell 1868–1926* is the best short guide you could hope to find.

Our searches for original documents were facilitated by the Robinson Library's patient librarians and archivists: Helen Arkwright together with Melanie Wood, Elaine Archbold, Frank Addison and Alan Callender. The erudite Jim Crow of the School of

Historical Studies at Newcastle University, another Gertrude enthusiast, helped us to grasp the essentials of Gertrude's contributions to archaeology and photography. In a very different field, Yvonne Sibbold of the Alpine Club and the climber Michael Westmacott kindly reviewed our chapter on Gertrude's climbs, an aspect of the book whose drama took some teasing from the detail of ledges and chimneys, arêtes and overhangs, in her writings. We are indebted to Timothy Daunt for guidance on the Gallipoli campaign, and to Patricia Daunt, who walks in Gertrude's footsteps through the wilderness of sites she studied and loved in Anatolia.

Gwen Howell read every chapter as it was written, made salient comments and found texts that had escaped professional researchers. Tom Buhler put at our disposal his grasp of the book-writing process at all stages, and developed the character of the book from the beginning. Charlotte Stafford's comprehensive understanding of book image also guided us from the first. Daniel Bailey contributed to our original conversations about the idea of a book on Gertrude, and has helped us with two years of encouragement, besides answering our occasional questions about military rank and practice. Alice Whittley has shown an enthusiastic interest and offered ideas throughout.

Gertrude's critics are quick to question her democratic credentials. We hope we confound them, but her attachment to the campaign against votes for women is hard to fathom some hundred years later. On both subjects, Joanna Morritt gave us well chosen texts.

Paul Miles placed Gertrude's Yorkshire garden schemes in the context of post-Victorian design, and explained the myth and legend of the mandrake.

While we were walking the overgrown site of the Bells' demolished Rounton Grange, by chance we met Gertrude's great-nephew Bob Richmond and his father Miles. Their help, then and subsequently, has been considerable. Susanna Richmond, daughter of Gertrude's half-sister Elsa, lived for a time with Gertrude's parents Hugh and Florence. She has given us many reflections and critical questions to consider. She still lectures about her aunt, and remembers a magical moment of empathy with her on her last trip to England. We have gained great pleasure from our visits to Patricia Jennings, Gertrude's niece, who remembers her with awe. At her home on the Trevelyan estate in County Durham, she showed us the family albums and the cedar of Lebanon that Gertrude brought home as a seed and planted on the lawn.

Sir John and Lady Venetia Bell, farming together the Yorkshire land acquired by Gertrude's grandfather, were extremely kind in showing us pictures and memorabilia. We are specially grateful to Venetia for introductions and guidance, photographs and permissions. Dr William Plowden kindly provided us with a wealth of anecdote and a valuable unpublished biography of Dame Florence Bell. We also appreciate the connections given to us by Nick Vester.

We would particularly like to thank the following: Jane Mulvagh and Anthony Bourne for wonderful hospitality and introductions; Anne-Françoise Normand for the historical identity of Iraq; Martin Brown, Secretary of Rounton Parish Council, for photography, and Terry Huck for showing us the Rounton festival displays. Malcolm Hamlyn of Edmund Carr has earned our gratitude for his professional advice throughout this project. When we stayed in Gertrude's childhood home, Red Barns, now a hotel, the proprietor Martin Cooper allowed us to crawl about in the cellars and attics where Gertrude played. While we were exploring the site of the Bell foundries at Clarence in Middlesbrough, Graham Bennet of the Bridge Museum showed us original footage of Sir Hugh and Lady Bell at the opening of the Transporter Bridge.

We are grateful to Mrs Jane Hogan at Durham University Library for helping us with collections including the all-important letters from Gertrude to Valentine Chirol. Gillian Robinson at the Imperial War Museum helped us find the last letter from Lieut.-Col. Doughty-Wylie about his wife.

Mrs Abu Husainy at the National Archives, Judy Hunton at Redcar Public Library, Brenda Mitchell of Tyne Tees Television, Diana Wright of the Literary and Philosophical Society in Newcastle, David Spooner in the Cabinet Office, Julie Carrington at the

Royal Geographical Society and and Helen Pugh of the Red Cross all earned our considerable thanks for their help. Jessica Stewart of Berkeley, California, did us a great service by sharing her transcripts of many of Gertrude's barely legible handwritten texts in the Bell Miscellaneous archive in the Robinson Library. Researcher Anita Burdett, a Middle East specialist, searched records in the National Archives, the Women's Library, the Red Cross archives and the Imperial War Museum.

For their help and suggestions we thank Editorial Manager Georgina Difford and Kate Harvey of Macmillan; Zoe Pagnamenta of PfD, our agent in New York; and Claire Gill and Emily Sklar of PfD in London. Our thanks to Emma Grey for the jacket artwork.

Amongst many lifelong friends in the world of books who have encouraged us with ideas and criticism we thank particularly Virginia Ironside, Jonathan Mantle, Jean Moore and Nicky Hessenberg. Fiona McCarthy elucidated a reference of Gertrude's to Byron's goose. Reflections on Gertrude's character have provided a continuing source of discussion with Betty Woodall. Peter and Anthea Pemberton have heartened us with their continuing interest, as well as their occasional criticism for not writing the book on the back of a camel.

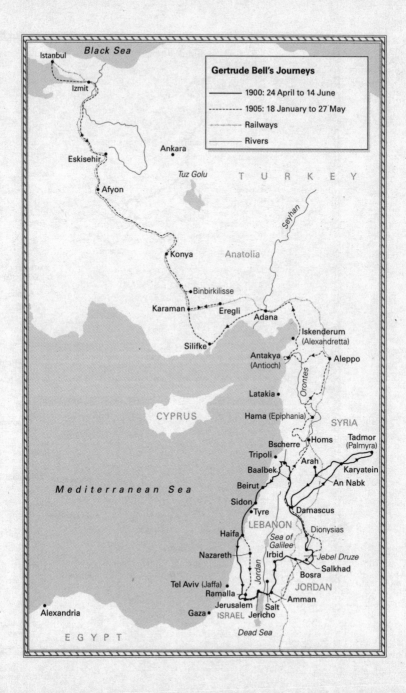

Gertrude Bell's Journeys

—— 1900: 24 April to 14 June
----- 1905: 18 January to 27 May
—·—·— Railways
—— Rivers

Black Sea

Istanbul

Izmit

Eskisehir

Ankara

Afyon

Tuz Golu

T U R K E Y

Seyhan

Konya

Anatolia

Binbirkilisse

Karaman   Eregli

Silifke   Adana

Iskenderum
(Alexandretta)

Antakya   Aleppo
(Antioch)

Orontes

Latakia

CYPRUS

Hama (Epiphania)   SYRIA

Bscherre   Homs   Tadmor
                                    (Palmyra)
Tripoli
              Arah   Karyatein
Baalbek
                                    An Nabk
Beirut

Sidon   Damascus
      Tyre

Mediterranean Sea   LEBANON   Dionysias

Haifa   *Sea of
                    Galilee*
Nazareth   Irbid   *Jebel Druze*
                                    Salkhad
              Jordan   Bosra
Tel Aviv (Jaffa)
Ramalla   JORDAN
         Jerusalem   Salt   Amman
Gaza   Jericho
         ISRAEL

Alexandria

Dead Sea

E G Y P T

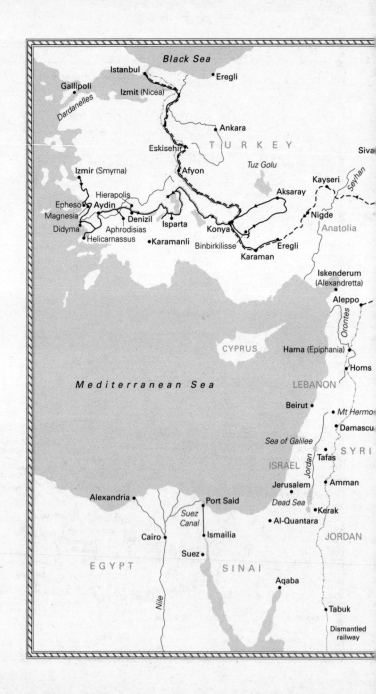

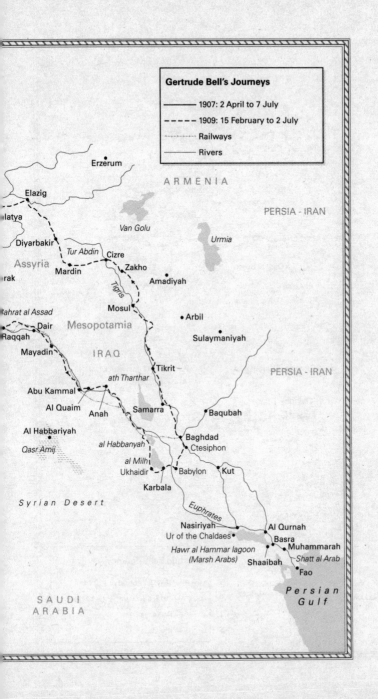

Gertrude Bell's Journeys

- —— 1907: 2 April to 7 July
- – – – 1909: 15 February to 2 July
- ········· Railways
- —— Rivers

Erzerum

ARMENIA

PERSIA - IRAN

Elazig

latya

Van Golu

Urmia

Diyarbakir

Tur Abdin   Cizre

Assyria   Mardin   Zakho

rak   Amadiyah

Tigris

Mosul   • Arbil

Bahrat al Assad   Dair   Mesopotamia   Sulaymaniyah

Raqqah

Mayadin   IRAQ

PERSIA - IRAN

Tikrit

ath Tharthar

Abu Kammal   Samarra

Al Quaim   Anah   • Baqubah

Al Habbariyah

Qasr Amij   al Habbanyah   Baghdad
Ctesiphon

al Milh
Ukhaidir   Babylon   Kut

Karbala

Syrian Desert

Euphrates

Nasiriyah   Al Qurnah
Ur of the Chaldaes•   Basra
Hawr al Hammar lagoon   Muhammarah
(Marsh Arabs)   Shaaibah   Shatt al Arab
Fao

SAUDI
ARABIA

Persian
Gulf

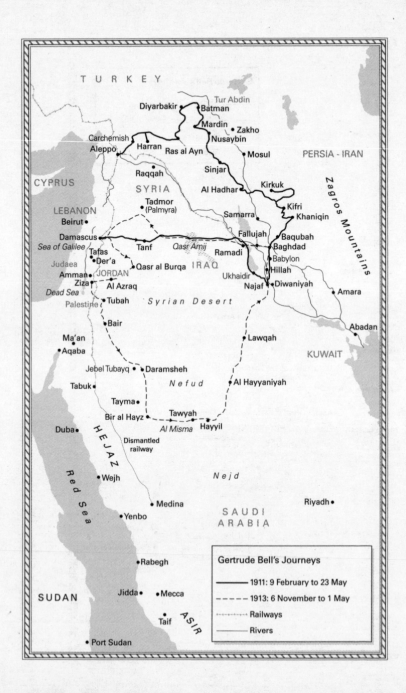

In February 1905 Gertrude Bell made camp in bad weather at Tneib, east of the Dead Sea near Madeba, and was joined by Bedouins of the Beni Sakhr tribe. She wrote: 'We made great friends, the Beni Sakhr and I. "Mashallah! Bint Arab" said they: "As God has willed: a daughter of the desert."'

We are all the more one because we are many
For we have made ample room for love in the gap where we
   are sundered.
Our unlikeness reveals its breath of beauty radiant with one
   common life,
Like mountain peaks in the morning sun.

RABINDRANATH TAGORE

1

GERTRUDE AND FLORENCE

It is 22 March 1921, the last day of the Cairo Conference and the final opportunity for the British to determine the postwar future of the Middle East. Like any tourists, the delegation make the routine tour of the pyramids and have themselves photographed on camels in front of the sphinx. Standing beneath its half-effaced head, two of the most famous Englishmen of the twentieth century confront the camera in some disarray: Colonial Secretary Winston Churchill, who has just, to the amusement of all, fallen off his camel, and T. E. Lawrence, tightly constrained in the pin-striped suit and trilby of a senior civil servant. Between them, at her ease, rides Gertrude Bell, the sole delegate possessing knowledge indispensable to the Conference. Her face, in so far as it can be seen beneath the brim of her rose-decorated straw hat, is transfigured with happiness. Her dream of an independent Arab nation is about to come true, her choice of a king endorsed: her Iraq is about to become a country. Just before leaving the Semiramis Hotel that morning, Churchill has cabled to London the vital message 'Sharif's son Faisal offers hope of best and cheapest solution.'

By what evolution did a female descendant of Cumbrian sheep farmers become, in her time, the most influential figure in the Middle East? She was as English as English can be, which is to say that she was bred in the wuthering heights of Yorkshire. These northern farmers have acquired a very particular character ever since the eleventh century, when, alone among the English, they refused to submit to William the Conqueror. Physically and mentally tough, they are given to few words, unvarnished and bluntly delivered.

Gertrude Bell's great-great-grandfather was a Carlisle blacksmith, and her great-grandfather began the first alkali factory and iron foundry at Jarrow. Her famous and powerful grandfather Sir Isaac Lowthian Bell, born in 1816, was a metallurgical chemist and perhaps the country's foremost industrialist. Manufacturing steel on a huge scale, he produced one-third of the metal used in Britain and much of that used for railtrack and bridge construction in the rapidly developing Empire. He became a Fellow of the Royal Society, Britain's most distinguished scientific institution. Educated first as an engineer, he studied at Edinburgh University and at the Sorbonne in Paris, then in Denmark and the south of France. Author of *The Chemical Phenomena of Iron Smelting*, he was looked upon as the 'high priest of British Metallurgy' and he was the first to identify the value of phosphorus fertiliser as a by-product of steel-making. Referred to as 'Sir Isaac' or more familiarly as 'Lowthian', in 1854 he was elected Lord Mayor of Newcastle upon Tyne, then later became Liberal Member of Parliament for Hartlepool and High Sheriff of County Durham. He was a contemporary and friend of Charles Darwin, Thomas Huxley, William Morris and John Ruskin, men to whom can be attributed seminal advances in evolution and science, art, architecture and social reform. Lowthian was president or vice-president of eight national engineering and chemical institutions, several of which he had founded. He was also the director of the North Eastern Railway.

With Lowthian's two brothers John and Tom, Bell Brothers owned collieries, quarries and iron ore mines; factories and foundries whose furnaces, burning twenty-four hours a day, regularly reddened the night skies. His company and its associates employed more than forty-seven thousand men, and the family boast was that they would make anything 'from a needle to a ship'. Besides the first iron and steel works in Newcastle, and the second at Port Clarence in Middlesbrough, he set up a chemical plant for the country's first manufacture of aluminium – until then, a metal as valuable as gold. On the factory's opening day, he was driven in his carriage through the streets of Newcastle in an aluminium top hat, which he doffed to the crowd. He was the first British ironmaster to own a machine for making steel rope.

Lowthian wrote several scientific books, but his most remarkable was a comprehensive and logical assessment of Britain's prospects for competing with the world in steel production. He invested heavily in research into the process of steel-making, and was determined to push Britain into developing new technological industries. In the hope that all of British industry would follow his example, he advocated government support for scientific research and technical development. But in this, after a lifetime's work, he failed. As he had forecast, other countries – and particularly Germany with its Krupps armaments and Thyssen steel – grew in technical competence and productivity, outstripping Britain and building the wealth and power they were to wield in the First World War.

A formidable giant of a man, a paterfamilias who would have almost sixty grandchildren – the number is disputed – Lowthian and his wife Margaret Pattinson set a pattern for the Bells of comfortable rather than lavish lifestyle. Considering the huge scale of his enterprises, and his position as the Bill Gates of his day, he did not live extravagantly. This may have had something to do with Margaret's influence: she came from a family of shopkeepers and scientists. His first house, Washington New Hall – four miles south of Newcastle-Upon-Tyne, a stone's throw from the home of the ancestors of George Washington – was not quite a mansion, and the house he built at the zenith of his power, Rounton Grange, was not quite a stately home. He toyed with Gothic, but settled for William Morris's humbler Arts and Crafts style, with its emphasis on traditional artisan skills as a panacea for the ravages wreaked by the Industrial Revolution. This would remain the characteristic style of the Bells' private houses and public buildings. Unlike many heirs to great fortunes, Lowthian's elder son Hugh, Gertrude's father, also lived modestly for a captain of industry. His own first house Red Barns, at the fishing village of Redcar on the Yorkshire coast, a short train journey from Clarence, reflected this. After Lowthian's death, the house he owned in London was sold, the money presumably divided between Hugh and his siblings – Charles, Ada, Maisie and Florence.

Lowthian was admired rather than loved, and appears to have been dictatorial and harsh towards his family. Gertrude and her sisters and brothers addressed him as 'Pater'. An illustrated family alphabet they drew up for Christmas at Rounton in 1877, when Gertrude was nine, reflects the feelings of the children towards their abrasive grandfather.

> *A for us All come to spend Christmas week*
> *B for our Breathless endeavours to speak*
> *C is the Crushing Contemptuous Pater . . .*

Elsa, Gertrude's younger half-sister, has added: 'Sir Isaac Lowthian Bell' in pencil, lest it be thought that this description referred to the gentler and kindlier Hugh.

A family story suggests the awe with which 'Pater' was regarded by the Bells. Lowthian forbade anyone to use his horses. When one of his granddaughters fainted one evening at dinner from a riding injury (a broken collarbone), everyone conspired to hide the truth: she had borrowed one of his horses and gone hunting with the gentry. The children's grandmother Margaret could be as scathing as Lowthian. A teatime visitor once said to her hostess: 'Your scones are lovely.' 'So I see,' retorted the old lady. 'Your hand has not been out of the dish since you arrived.'

Some previously unknown stories about Lowthian emerged recently from papers found in one of the Bell houses, Mount Grace Priory, the ruined medieval abbey where Gertrude's father and stepmother ended their days. English Heritage was renovating the house before opening it to the public when they found the papers hidden under the floorboards. Among them is a reference to a tragic event at Washington New Hall, where 'in 1872 a seven-year-old sweep was suffocated in the Hall chimney'. If the little boy met his end in Lowthian's chimney in 1872, the ironmaster had comprehensively broken the law. Parliament had forbidden the use of children as chimney-sweeps a full twenty-six years earlier. Sir Isaac may have known nothing about the presence of the chimney-sweep until it was too late; however, whether because he was deeply upset or because he wanted to escape a damaging association, he moved into the newly built Rounton Grange as soon as possible, and let Washington New Hall stand empty and unsold. Nineteen years later, he gave it away as a home for waifs and strays, on condition it was renamed 'Dame Margaret's Hall'; today, it is divided into pleasant apartments. Not perhaps unconnected with this story is the fact that many years later Hugh Bell successfully lobbied for a parliamentary bill to protect children from dangerous work. (In the 1860s, the Earl of Shaftesbury reported that children of four and five were still working in certain factories from six in the morning until ten at night.)

The papers found under the boards also contained the sentence, 'On one winter's night [Sir Isaac] came out of the Hall to find his coachman frozen stiff on the box-seat of his carriage.' The facts remain mysterious. The unfortunate coachman may have had a heart attack rather than dying of exposure, and yet it emerges clearly that consideration for others was not, perhaps, Lowthian's principal quality.

The author of these papers, which contain many confirmable facts about Lowthian's life and work, may have been Miss K. E. M. Cooper Abbs, a Bell relation who was the last tenant to live at Mount Grace. If she was moved to record Lowthian's life, it may be because she was incensed that, whether by accident or intent, so many family papers and archives were burnt by members of the family after his death. There is to this day no biography of the man who was as famous in his day as Isambard Kingdom Brunel.

A more lovable, more charming man, Gertrude's father Sir Hugh led the Bell industries and inherited a vast fortune. Like his father, he was educated in Edinburgh, at the Sorbonne and in Germany, where he studied mathematics and organic chemistry. He began work at eighteen at the Bell Brothers Ironworks in Newcastle, became director of the growing Port Clarence steelworks that dominated the grimy roofscape of Middlesbrough, and eventually ran the entire business and all its ramifications. He dug the ironstone from the Cleveland hills, worked the coal from Durham, brought the limestone from the backbone of England, lived on the Tees, and was a director of the North Eastern Railway, which brought the raw material to the steel foundry. His public works were second to none, especially after his second marriage to Florence Olliffe. He built schools and founded libraries, constructed meeting houses and workers' terraces, made a community centre for staff and labourers at Rounton and paid for a holiday home for worthy families needing a country break from life at the works. He also constructed the famous Transporter Bridge, which is still used to ferry workers and tourists quickly and cheaply over the River Tees. In 1906 he became Lord Lieutenant of the North Riding, welcoming royalty and other VIPs whenever they ventured into the windswept Yorkshire landscape; and was three times elected Mayor of Middlesbrough.

In supplying the Empire, the Bells brought a global view to British industry. Sir Hugh was an accomplished public speaker, delivering persuasive messages on such subjects as free trade, which he passionately endorsed, and home rule for the Irish, which he passionately opposed. You can hear in his published speeches the vigour and humour with which he captivated audiences of all types and classes. In his words:

> Free Trade is like the quality of mercy: it is twice blessed, for it blesses him that gives and him that takes, and I for one will do nothing to place any restriction upon it. The Free market is the greatest safeguard we have against the tyranny of wealth. I look forward with dread to the accumulation of great fortunes in single hands . . . There are millions of persons in this country depending upon weekly wages, upon work which may be discontinued at the end of any week. It is with them I am concerned, and about them that I am perturbed, and not about the class to which I belong.

He welcomed the rise of the new trade unions, while warning that the writings of Karl Marx could lead socialists into revolutionary movements that would destroy British industry and employment in the competitive world that he endorsed.

When Gertrude was born, Queen Victoria had been on the throne for thirty years. She was driven by Prince Albert's relentless determination to replace the louche self-indulgence of Georgian Britain with Victorian industry and propriety. Britain, and particularly England, led the world in technical superiority – as evinced in that paeon to the Empire, the Great Exhibition at the Crystal Palace in 1851. The British army, able to call on troops from around the world, represented what was probably the greatest military power of all time; the British navy held control of the oceans and the trade across them, and kept the peace. If those other empires, the Russian and the Ottoman, were still in a state of feudal serfdom and of institutionalized corruption at every level, the British example, inspired by Victoria and Albert, brought at least a concern for moderation, philanthropy and honest dealing. By the mid-nineteenth century, the concept of Empire was evolving from one of commercial exploitation to one capable of taking a pride in honest and benevolent government. Commercially aggressive but socially responsible, the Bells personified the new mood, and they enjoyed all the confidence of the right people in the right place at the right time.

Hugh married Mary Shield when he was twenty-three, choosing a local girl who was the daughter of a prominent merchant of Newcastle upon Tyne. They were married on the Scottish island of Bute on the Clyde, where the Shields kept a holiday home. Their first child, Gertrude, was born in 1868 at Washington New Hall, the home of Hugh's father. Family life centred on this larger-than-life industrialist who had made the Bells the sixth-richest family in England. He could not have been easy to live with, nor the house peaceful, and there are many intimations of his bombastic temperament and caustic wit. Although Hugh, his elder son, had an inclination for the political life, he had had it made brutally clear to him that his future lay in Middlesbrough, with the fastest-growing part of the iron business. Lowthian, based at the original works in Newcastle, would descend on the new Port Clarence steelworks at irregular intervals, to scrutinize and doubtless criticize every aspect of Hugh's work.

It would have been with great relief that Hugh and Mary moved with their two-year-old daughter out of Washington New Hall for a quieter domestic life of their own. It was not to last long. Beautiful but delicate, Mary survived only three weeks after the birth of their second child, Maurice, in 1871.

Hugh became for a time a poignant figure. When he had built Red Barns at Redcar, he had imagined a healthy and happy seaside life there for his family. Now, his sister Ada moved in to run the house and look after the children. Hugh was working six days a week at Clarence, and now had to share his Sundays with his sister, a wet-nurse and some half-dozen servants. His moments of freedom were spent on the beach or in the countryside hand-in-hand with his lively little daughter – Maurice being as yet too young for walks – talking to her and searching her candid face for a likeness to her mother. From these early days the closest of loving father–daughter relationships developed between them, one that would last all her life.

Hugh's situation was appealing. A charming young widower whose wife's death had left him with two motherless children, he would have been a catch even without being heir to a large fortune. His warm sense of humour and his mischievous yet kindly smile were particularly engaging. Nevertheless, daughters of the aristocracy would have regarded marriage to a Bell as a step down; and Hugh, in any case, was no snob. Maisie had overcome the resistance of Lady Stanley of Alderley in marrying her witty son Lyulph, later Lord Sheffield. This formidable woman was known for her habit of turning away from a conversation on one side to loudly remark to her neighbour on the other that 'Fools are so fatiguin'. She was the grandmother of Bertrand Russell, and had been one of the founders of Girton College, Cambridge. For allowing the marriage of her son to Maisie, Lady Stanley considered herself very broadminded: the Bells, after all, were 'trade'. 'As Sir Hugh was a multi-millionaire, I was not very impressed,' Bertrand Russell was to say later.

Ada, a pretty and gregarious young woman, missed London and doubtless resented being forced into the unappetizing role of spinster aunt, so well known to unmarried Victorian women. It was not long before she and her sister Maisie had someone in mind for Hugh, and they hatched a plot to bring the two together.

They met the twenty-two-year-old Florence Eveleen Eleanore Olliffe through their shared interest in music. She was studying at the Royal College and sang in the Bach Choir. She had moved to London in 1870 from Paris, where her father, the distinguished and agreeable Sir Joseph Olliffe, had been physician to the British Embassy. Her Easter holidays had been spent at the Surrey house of her grandfather, Sir William Cubitt, MP, sometime Lord Mayor of London. At other times she would stay with her great-uncle Thomas* at his Hampshire estate, Penton Lodge. Summer holidays had been spent at Trouville or Deauville, fashionable seaside resorts for wealthy Parisian families. When, at the onset of the Franco-Prussian War, her father had suddenly died, the family had had to leave France fast. Florence was nineteen when she said goodbye to Paris and went to live far less glamorously at 95 Sloane Street in London, in a narrow, dingy house, all dusty red velvet and heavy furniture, with a lingering smell of tomcat. English society of the time, once described as 'a series of shut doors', must have seemed a painful contrast with the brilliant cosmopolitan world she had just left.

Florence was tall and slim with blue, rather hooded eyes, and dark hair. She was very sociable, and spoke English with a slight and charming French accent. Maisie saw to it that when Hugh went up to London, Florence was included in family parties, while Ada invited her once or twice to visit her at Red Barns. After these visits the six-year-old Gertrude found herself under pressure from her aunt to write fond letters to Florence, signing herself 'Your affectionate little friend'.

Ada's and Maisie's plan almost misfired. They tried too hard to throw the two together, and it did not take Florence long to guess what they were up to. She would never marry an Englishman, she

* It was Thomas Cubitt who rebuilt Osborne Castle on the Isle of Wight for Queen Victoria and Prince Albert.

declared, and she said it with increasing force over the two years during which Hugh failed to propose. Hugh's reaction to his sisters' pressure to remarry was to tell Ada that he would never do so, and to dig himself deeper and deeper into his work. Yet Florence's description of her first sight of Hugh, framed in a tunnel of roses in Maisie's garden, suggests her heart was immediately engaged. She saw him 'looking beautiful, but very sad . . . with thick curly hair and a beard of a bright auburn colour'.

Part of Hugh's difficulty, as he grew more interested in Florence, was in imagining that a woman brought up in the most sophisticated milieu of the most beautiful city in the world could settle down near Middlesbrough. One biographer of Gertrude described her own impressions of the city at the same period, when for the first time she visited an aunt who lived there: 'The district round Middlesbrough and Tees side to the sea was caked with grime . . . For twenty miles the air smelt of chemicals and ash and soot, as the crowded houses smelt of cabbage, cheese and cat. Basements . . . were covered with black, gluey mud whenever it rained.' The term 'day-darkness' was coined to describe the smog of industry; and in particular, Middlesbrough and Cleveland were said by a contemporary to 'succeed in almost excluding daylight from the district'.

Redcar, a cobbled village raked by the storm-force sea winds of North Yorkshire and soon to develop into a small town, was the dormitory where many wealthy Middlesbrough industrialists were building their new family homes. (The big house next door to the Bells, for instance, belonged to an eminent metallurgist.) Here they raised their children away from the soot and polluted atmosphere, forming an elite milieu still lagging some way behind the society to which Florence had been used.

Life here was likely to be a daunting prospect for a young woman used to an *hôtel particulier* in the rue Florentin, its elegant courtyard secreted away behind decorative eighteenth-century gates. Born in 1851, the tumultuous first year of the Second Empire under Napoleon III, Florence had taken her daily walk with her nurse in the Jardin des Tuileries, where she could ride in decorated carriages, bowl her hoop, or buy barley-sugar twists and honey gingerbread from the stalls with their striped and scalloped awnings. Just around the corner from their house was the Place de la Concorde with its 'jewelled cascades springing and spurting hilariously'. Much later, she was to write: 'What a privilege to be born in Paris. To know Paris first, to know it all the time, to grow up in one of the most beautiful parts of it, to take it all for granted, to belong to it, and have it belong to me. Isn't that enough?' Despite civic upheavals, she had had a very happy childhood, settling contentedly at a little tutorial *cours* that provided an education somewhere between that of a personal governess and a small private school, without learning much more than good manners and music.

The woman that Ada and Maisie had picked for Hugh was, in fact, an extraordinarily appropriate choice. The daughter of a physician, Florence was neither 'trade' nor aristocracy, and she harboured a couple of passions that outweighed all the disadvantages of Middlesbrough: she adored children and domestic life. There was a dispossessed aspect to this recent immigrant, adrift in London and still homesick for Paris. She longed for the security of her own household, and had already formed dozens of opinions on the education of children and the right and wrong ways of running a home. Life could hold no greater excitement than the gift of her own domain, wherever that might be.

Hugh finally succumbed to his sisters' scheme, and to Florence, on the night of the private staging of an opera that she had written. *Bluebeard* was performed by friends and relations on 4 June 1876, at Lady Stanley's house in Harley Street. Ada and Maisie were to sing, and the pianist Anton Rubinstein was to play. Hugh afterwards asked if he might take Florence home. Descending from the coach at the front door of 95 Sloane Street, he escorted Florence into the drawing-room. 'Lady Olliffe,' he told her mother, 'I have brought your daughter home – and I have come to ask if I may take her away again.' In answer to this graceful speech, Lady Olliffe burst into tears.

On 10 August, after their quiet wedding in the small church in Sloane Street, they spent an urbane honeymoon in Washington DC as guests of Florence's much-loved sister Mary and her husband Frank Lascelles, then a secretary at the British Embassy. Returning to London, they took the train north. At this first homecoming Florence was trembling with emotion at what was to her, and perhaps would be to any new bride and stepmother, a truly momentous occasion. As the heirs of the director of the North Eastern Railway, the Hugh Bells were transport royalty. At Middlesbrough the stationmaster doffed his hat and ushered them on to the train to Redcar. Many years later, Florence's daughter Lady Richmond was to remember an occasion when she was seeing her father off from King's Cross, and he had remained on the platform so that they could talk until the train left. The packed train failed to leave on time. Remarking on its lateness, they continued to talk until they were approached by a guard. 'If you would like to finish your conversation, Sir Hugh,' he suggested, doffing his hat, 'we will then be ready to depart.' The train to and from Redcar had a personal Bell stopping place on a tiny platform inside the Red Barns garden. Hugh, returning from the works, could simply step out of the train and cross the rose garden by the fountain to reach his own back door. Gertrude, who was always waiting there, would greet him joyfully. When she was small, he carried her to the house on his shoulders, then when she was a little older she would seize his case of papers and run alongside him, talking at the top of her voice.

On the couple's return from their honeymoon, both children would have been washed and brushed and be waiting on the Bell platform to greet them. The staff would have been lined up behind them, ready to curtsy or bow. Florence, hoping to make a firm bond with them from the start, had intended, as soon as she arrived, to ask Gertrude and Maurice to show her into every corner of the house, from cellar to attic. However, to her dismay they had been joined at Middlesbrough by Hugh's brother Charles who, with the kindest of intentions but no sensitivity at all, accompanied them to Red Barns. Hugh, equally unromantic, went straight to his office on the ground floor and started to go through his papers. Abandoned with Charles in the drawing-room, and passionately wanting him to go, Florence made distracted conversation while her new brother-in-law sat solidly in an armchair, also stuck for something to say.

A contented Ada departed for London, and a new life began for eight-year-old Gertrude and five-year-old Maurice. Since children of that age do not naturally assume that their parents have a life independent of their own, they must have been shocked to hear that their father had married Florence. Talking about their new stepmother later, it was Maurice's guess that she was eighty, but his sister thought that she might be quite a bit younger. Perhaps, she suggested, Florence was sixty. Poor Florence was actually twenty-four, eight years younger than Hugh.

And so came into Gertrude's life the good-hearted woman who would influence and form her more than any other, sometimes in opposition but chiefly in fundamental and positive ways. Florence had many talents. She had a keen appreciation of music and literature, she wrote books, essays and plays; she was able to get on with all kinds of people, and was deeply interested in sociology and the education of children. Everything she did remained within the limits of the roles she considered the most important for a woman, those of wife and mother. She gave herself unstintingly to her family while achieving a body of work in the community that would earn her public recognition, and eventually make her a Dame of the British Empire. The drawing-room dramas and comedies she liked to write were initially for the children to perform at Christmas and other family gatherings. In time, through the intervention of theatrical friends, she would have three plays put on in the West End. Characteristically, she chose to remain anonymous.

Florence was nonplussed at first by northern manners. As soon as she met her neighbours, she began to institute an 'at home' on Tuesdays, when she hoped couples would drop in for light refreshments (non-alcoholic). She was mystified to discover that Yorkshiremen did not accompany their wives on this sort of occasion. Her biographer Kirsten Wang writes that when one lady turned up at the Bells' with her husband she disconcerted Florence by whispering: 'I managed to bring Mr T with me. I had *such* a work to make him come!' Apparently believing there was safety in numbers, the women would arrive together, then seat themselves as far apart as possible, after which a silence would fall. A desperate Florence, offering them chairs closer to the fire, would meet with the response: 'Thank you, I am very well where I am.' In one of her books Florence writes of her heroine, a teacher who had newly come north: 'The girl was ill at ease with the downright Yorkshire women who surrounded her . . . In that class of life when people have nothing to say they say nothing; their rough blunt manner, when they did speak, alarmed her still more. Nevertheless, the women after their fashion, were not unkind to her.' The new Mrs Bell persevered, and before long her 'entertainments' were obligatory events in the life of the town.

But Florence was far more interested in cementing her relationship with Hugh's children. The eight-year-old observed her in speculative fashion. This stranger who had burst into their family life had something about her that the child would not have recognized: a Parisian polish in both her manner and her dress. Although Florence was essentially serious and inclined to the moralistic, she never criticized an individual's interest in her appearance or derided a love of clothes as frivolous. Her carefully considered opinions on this and other subjects were often expressed obliquely. She was an intensely private person and preferred to give her views in the form of stories or essays. In one, she wrote of the heroine:

> Ursula had what the French call 'genre' . . . The nearest English equivalent to the expression is 'style', but that . . . suggests being dashing and assertive; 'genre' is a grace inherent in the wearer, and does not depend upon clothes, but upon the way they are put on. And the reason there is no word for it in English, is that the thing is so rarely found that it is unnecessary to have a term on purpose.

From Florence's example, Gertrude, in turn, would acquire *genre*, so that people meeting her for the first time would comment on her 'Mayfair manners and Paris frocks'. But Florence never followed fashion. She continued to wear Edwardian clothes all her life because she felt they suited her, even in the 1920s when every other woman was in a short skirt. Her granddaughter remembers being with Florence when she slipped and fell one day on a London pavement. The child was amazed to see that under Florence's skirts was a pair of normal legs. Tending to primness, Florence wore grey silk gloves most of the time, indoors and outdoors, and even to play the piano.

Gertrude was growing up fast, a wilful child used to competing with her aunt Ada, her governess, her brother and the numerous household staff for her father's attention. Florence could so easily have made an enemy of the child. On the contrary, she was an affectionate step-parent, always gentle, encouraging and sympathetic. She was attentive to both children, inquisitive and humorous. Lively herself, she liked them to be similarly busy: when they were not doing something active, she liked them to be reading and not 'loafing around'. She would always have a story or two ready to read aloud to the youngest. Maurice, who was rather deaf, cannot have had any memory of his own mother, but took to Florence immediately.

Gertrude was divided in her opinion of her new stepmother, whom she was encouraged to address as 'Mother'. Her father would undoubtedly have done his best to encourage her to make Florence feel welcome, and to do whatever she was asked; but the child must have smarted at the introduction into their close relationship of a woman that she must have seen initially as an interloper. Hugh and Gertrude's bond was extraordinary. They were all-in-all to each other, and would always remain so, even when living on other sides of the world. As Florence was to write, 'The abiding influence in Gertrude's life from the time she was a little child was her relation to her father. Her devotion to him, her whole-hearted admiration, the close and satisfying companionship between them, their deep mutual affection – these were to both the very foundation of existence until the day she died.' Florence's words about Gertrude also reveal the woman's noble and generous instincts: she never gave way to jealousy, never tried to divide the devoted father and daughter.

The artist Sir Edward Poynter, RA, painted a double portrait in 1876. The subject is not, as might be expected, a wedding portrait of Hugh and Florence, but the eight-year-old Gertrude, red curls falling on to the shoulders of her lace-trimmed pinafore, being ushered forward by a proudly smiling Hugh. Having had his first wife Mary painted at their marriage, Hugh may well have had the idea of commissioning a portrait of Florence when she became his second wife. It would have been typical of the thoughtful Florence to suggest the change of subject.

Whether Gertrude would have appreciated this tactful gesture is another question. Florence was too kind and discreet to betray the fact that she was having a difficult time with her stepdaughter, but there are plenty of clues that this was in fact the case. *Angela*, a play she published in 1926 – significantly, perhaps, after Gertrude's death – tells the story of the second marriage of a Yorkshire industrialist in which his new wife tries to cope with the exceptionally strong bond already formed between father and motherless daughter.

'Gertrude was a child of spirit and initiative,' wrote Florence in her introduction to *The Letters of Gertrude Bell*. Sometimes this spirit and initiative were too much for her:

> Full of enterprise, [Gertrude] used to lead her little brother, whose tender years were ill equipped for so much enterprise, into the most perilous adventures, such as commanding him, to his terror, to follow her example in jumping from the top of the garden wall nine feet high to the ground. She used to alight on her feet, he very seldom did.

On one occasion, a crash and an ominous tinkling brought Florence running from the drawing-room to the greenhouse. Gertrude had led Maurice on a climbing expedition along the ridge of the roof. She had made her way deftly and rapidly along while her little brother, sick with fear, had stumbled after her. Gertrude had clambered down safely, but Maurice had put his boot through the roof and followed it to the ground, landing in the broken glass. On another occasion, she played the garden hose down the laundry chimney and put the fire out. When Florence on this occasion lost her temper, Gertrude and Maurice collected all the hats from the hall and threw them at their stepmother. Gertrude only stopped when one of Florence's hats found its way into the fire. 'Even as a child, Gertrude took a great interest in clothes,' one of the family told me.

For most of her eight years, Gertrude had been used to bossing the servants and running rings around her governess. She bitterly resented discipline, and liked to goad people to distraction. Miss Ogle had departed in dudgeon, but Florence hoped for better from Miss Klug. This German lady stayed much longer, but Florence was periodically irked by having to placate the new governess over Gertrude's misdeeds.

The house where Mrs Bell was establishing her new domain was a raw brick Arts and Crafts building, an early and rather confused Philip Webb experiment with the local vernacular. Webb had designed William Morris's own Red House, and he copied many elements into this second commission, Red Barns. Morris had decorated the interior, and his charming botanical wallpapers were used throughout. The house was solid and small in comparison with the elegant homes of Florence's youth, but it would expand as the family expanded. There was a porch giving on to Kirkleathan Street, which led to a large square of terraced Georgian houses around a bleak green. It was a short walk from Red Barns to Redcar's long beach, stretching from Coatham southward to the Saltburn cliffs. Around its featureless crescent of sand, where the clinker-built fishing boats were beached at low tide, there were striped bathing huts in the summer, and donkeys for children's rides. The countryside around was flat, and not especially pretty. But Florence had always thought that children should be brought up in the countryside, and there was no doubt that Gertrude and Maurice loved the place.

Given a constant succession of ponies, the children virtually grew up on horseback. Gertrude's fearless exploits often led, inevitably, to Maurice coming home covered in bruises from trying to follow his sister's lead. Among her contemporaries, she became known as the most courageous of riders, and her letters to aunts and cousins were full of boasts about her prowess. 'My poney behaved like a brute, kicking all the time. If she does that with mother, I am afraid mother will come strait off,' she wrote to her cousin Horace.

Hacking about, galloping along the beach or out hunting, girls rode side-saddle in the appropriate habit, consisting of a black jacket and buttoned apron skirt over breeches. 'Yesterday I rode like a circus boy,' wrote Gertrude, meaning that she had that day ridden astride. The Bell children would trot along the sands under the supervision of the stable-boy, the nurse or the governess. If accompanied by the anxious Miss Klug, once out of sight of the house Gertrude would kick her pony into action and gallop off into the distance, leaving the governess to run hopelessly after her, calling her name. After taking the children for a beach walk one day, Miss Klug returned alone and burst into Florence's literary reverie in floods of tears. When she had told them to come back to the house for tea, she reported, they had run away and hidden among the fishing boats, from which she had been trying to chivvy them for an exhausting and fruitless thirty minutes.

Domineering and wilful, Gertrude was always demanding attention and expecting her father to spend his every domestic moment entertaining her. Hugh, preoccupied at the works, was often at home for only one day a week. Florence, naturally, wanted some time alone with her husband, and her Victorian insistence on domestic order and routine, though hardly onerous, was bound to interfere with the children's freedom. Gertrude found that she could not be sure of bending the will of her stepmother as she could her father's. The child's way of countermanding Florence's dictats was to wait until her father came home, and then try to cajole him to her defence.

It was not long until Florence's own children were born – Hugo in 1878, Elsa in 1879 and Molly two years later. A two-storey wing was added at Red Barns, with bedrooms, bathroom and schoolroom, as well as a stable block. Already an intrepid tree climber, Gertrude thought scaffolding a brilliant addition to the house. Once, when she used it as a climbing frame, Florence, spotting her from a window, came dashing into the garden and ordered her to come down at once. Gertrude chose not to hear, and so Florence ran for Hugh and sent him up after her. She returned to the house to watch from the window and was horrified to see her husband climbing a ladder to the upper floor to join his daughter – with a small child under each arm.

Hugh was a wonderful father and not too fastidious about the children hurting themselves. As Elsa was to remember late in life, he would accompany them on Sunday scrambles among the sandhills and 'suddenly crook his walking stick round our ankles so that we should fall off the top of a precipice'. She remembered him 'running along the hard sand with a child in each hand, and then clapping us together in front'. To Gertrude's questions he would provide ample answers to which she would attend closely. In this she was different from her siblings. If any of them should idly muse, 'I wonder what makes the tide come up' or 'What is bi-metallism?' they would immediately shout, 'Don't tell me!' Hugh would laugh and say, 'You naughty children!'

Life had gradually got better for Hugh, and there came a moment when he realized that he had a happy home again, that it had been no mistake to ask Florence to marry him. A revealing letter of Florence's to Molly tells of the occasion early in her life at Red Barns when she and Hugh reached the turning point.

I remember as if it were yesterday the coming at Redcar, when we were about your ages – when your father could have got in [to parliament] with almost a walkover at Middlesbrough and was frantically anxious to do it and go in for politics, for you know how much he cares and always has cared. That was all his head was in. His father (this is a very private letter!!) was against it and quite without sympathy in it – as always he was, and trade wasn't good, and we walked up and down the gravel path talking it over and finally decided to give it all up and do nothing but Middlesbrough. You know how he then threw himself into that. But it was . . . a lifelong renunciation and a lifelong regret and we knew it was at the time. And then he felt afterwards what it would have been to him if he had to do

it alone – and what a joy it was to care so much and be so close
to each other. What a huge difference it makes in the whole
aspect of life to be married – that there is some one who cares
as much for the thing that happens to one as one does oneself!

As far as Gertrude was concerned, life at Red Barns was perfect,
and she too came to realize that Florence's arrival had only
improved their family life. The children were outdoors all summer,
and had their own garden plots. Gertrude was finding that she
loved flowers and had a natural skill with plants. In an early diary
entry, in careful italic script, she writes: 'We now have out some
yellow crocus and primroses snodrops and primroses.'

Spelling, music – of which Florence was so fond – and cooking
were three fields in which she had no interest and therefore did not
excel, in spite of her stepmother's efforts. On the other hand,
Gertrude's nose was never out of a book. She would read anything
she could get hold of: *The Days of Bruce* by Aguilar was a favourite,
as was Green's *History of the English People*, which she perused every
day before breakfast. 'I am reading a very nice book called The Tower
of London . . . all full of murders and tortures.'

When Florence was mysteriously 'unwell' – in other words,
pregnant – Gertrude and Maurice were sent off to stay with large
groups of cousins, to a gentler southern seaside or to Scotland,
where they picnicked and learnt to climb rocks and to fish.

My dear Mamy,

We are having such fun here. Yesterday we caught an alive eel.
Every morning we go to the rocks in our wading suits, our game
is to jump off the rocks into the pool, we call it taking headers, it
is such fun. Give my love to Papa.

From your loving child, Gertrude

Her favourite companion was Horace Marshall, her first cousin
and the son of her mother Mary Shield's sister, Mrs Thomas
Marshall. Then there were the Lascelles boys and their sister
Florence, called after her stepmother, some years younger than
Gertrude but always one of her favourite friends. Gertrude used

her pocket money to buy birds' eggs for her collection, competing with Horace — '5 Jackdaws, 2 Golden Crested Wrens, 1 Greenfinch, 2 Brown Linnet,' she wrote in her diary — or to buy as many pet animals or birds as Florence would allow. In the garden shed lived the pet raven Jumbo, to be kept for ever out of the way of the excitable cat they called 'the Shah'. When, in the course of time, these died, Gertrude would assuage her grief by laying on lavish funerals, complete with cortège of family and staff, cardboard coffins, crosses and flowers.

Beyond the Red Barns garden and the railway track was a large enclosed private park (now turned into a public garden) in which the children could ride their ponies and play on their own, almost within view of the house. Laid out around a pond were pathways through the trees where they could ride, or walk on stilts, until the gong rang out for midday 'dinner', or 'teatime' (their last meal before bed). Sometimes on a Sunday, Hugh would take the two oldest children out into the country around Redcar or along the beach, all of them on horseback, with a picnic tea packed by Florence. Gertrude would lay out the sandwiches on a checked blanket, and play hostess to Hugh and Maurice.

For rainy days, Gertrude and Maurice had invented a game of hide-and-seek called 'Housemaids', a game that she would remember and that would come to have a very different significance for her in the desert, many years later. Beginning in the cellar, where the children could stand upright but the adults had to bend their heads, the object was to run silently along the many corridors and up the narrow, twisting stairs that led up to the maids' bedrooms, without being seen by the servants. If you were spotted, you screamed and went back, to begin again. Or you might begin from behind the water tank in the attic, which could be reached up a short ladder fixed to the wall, then scuttle down to the laundry and the housekeeper's room in the quiet semi-basement. Lined with cupboards painted cream, its William Morris wallpaper depicted singing blackbirds perched on a trellis wreathed in leaves and fruit against a dark-blue sky. A trace of it still remains today.

Gertrude was lucky to have a stepmother with Florence's sweet nature. A harsher regime could have dented her stepdaughter's confidence, or more likely turned her into the rebel she somehow never became. Florence's younger daughter Molly, later Lady Trevelyan, wrote of her mother: 'I cannot remember her speak in a harsh way to us, nor shout at us for wrong-doing. She was gentle and forbearing, full of tenderness to all children, unselfish and sympathetic to a degree that went far beyond any other person I have ever known . . . The security of her presence was an unfailing standby.'

Florence was also great fun. The children had turned the garden shed into a playhouse and named it the 'Wigwam'. They had a rubber stamp with the name on it, and would deliver stamped letters containing very formal tea or dinner invitations to their parents, the gardener or the governess. Florence, emerging from the house in response to one of these invitations, in her very best evening gown and with diamonds in her hair, had found the children waiting to wheel her to the shed in a goat-cart. On the way to the Wigwam they upset the cart on to the gravel but Florence, though scratched and dirtied, stayed on heroically through the afternoon programme, not only demonstrating her good nature but also providing a fine example of social poise.

Another invitation invited 'Mr and Mrs Hugh Bell to tea on Saturday August 13, 1892, at 5 pm' and added 'RSVP'. Florence, much teased by the children for her French accent, had accepted along similar lines. 'To Monsieur and Mesdames de Viguevamme, Red Barns, Coatham, Redcar' she wrote, 'The Marchioness de Sidesplitters will have much pleasure in dining this evening with Mr Prinketty, Miss Fiddlesticks, and Miss Pizzicato at 7.30', and – probably anxious not to sacrifice another evening dress – she had added: 'She regrets that the unfortunate delicate state of her health will not permit her to wear on this occasion her Court dress and feathers or to powder her hair.'

Entertaining and tolerant as Florence could be, she was rigorous about behaviour. She was forever writing essays with titles such as 'The Minor Moralist' or 'Si Jeunesse Voulait' ('If Only the Young Would . . .'). Her rules concerning good manners were not negotiable, whether she was ticking off a waiting coachman who had left his driving seat to shelter from the rain, or a child who had failed to greet guests correctly. Manners, she insisted, were as important for ourselves as for others. She might have been repeating a conversation with an older Gertrude when she wrote: 'However valuable the intellectual wares you may have to offer, it is obvious that if your method of calling your fellow man's attention to them is to give him a slap in the face at the same time, you will probably not succeed in enlisting his kindly interest in your future achievements.'

The impatient Gertrude had some difficulty with all of this. To her, a conversation was about finding out something or telling someone something. She could not feel very interested, she may well have retorted, in her fellow man's assessment of her achievements. But there were times when Florence was entirely on Gertrude's wavelength, as in her deploring 'the tendency displayed by many otherwise reasonable people to believe that their own race is of quite peculiar interest, their own family traits the most worthy of note, the school they have been to the only possible one, the quarter of London they live in the most agreeable, and their own house the best in it'; it was 'an insidious peril to be striven against'. Half-English and half-Irish herself, she was sensitive to the kind of slur that commonly figured in *Punch* cartoons about the French, their habits, hygiene, food and morals, all of which she knew in many cases to be superior to those of the British. This climate of receptiveness to other standards and ways of life was the best initiation to travel that Gertrude could have absorbed in her childhood. Later in life, she was to take it to its logical conclusion – and far further than Florence could ever have intended.

'Correct' as had been Florence's upbringing, the cosmopolitan society to which she had been exposed before her marriage to Hugh Bell had plunged her into an intellectual and artistic milieu that she would probably not have encountered if she had been brought up in England. Not until Edward VII came to the throne were actresses and artists and newly moneyed merchants routinely included in aristocratic circles, unless under the particular freedoms implied by patronage. Florence was to make great friends with actors in the course of her life, in particular Coquelin, a star of the French theatre, Sybil Thorndike and the American actress Elizabeth Robins. Florence met Robins, who introduced the plays of Ibsen to the English stage, soon after her own arrival in London. Despite the fact that Robins was an active member of the suffrage movement, with which Florence could never agree, they became intimates. Robins brought Florence's most famous play, *Alan's Wife*, to the West End in 1893, taking the lead in this tragedy of working-class life. She became one of the Bells' most frequent houseguests, adding much to the texture of the intellectual background in which Gertrude was to be raised. Liza, as they called her, would amuse the children by taking them into her bedroom and demonstrating a theatrical 'pratfall', flat on to her face on the carpet. Later, when Gertrude was older and after Florence had retired to bed, the two women would sit up late discussing the pros and cons of suffrage. Florence felt so strongly on this issue, and wrote so much in support of anti-suffrage, that she could not discuss it with Liza. Gertrude and Liza became lifelong correspondents, and the constant traveller was often to mention in the letters she wrote from her desert tents how much she missed their 'fireside chats'.

Florence told Gertrude and Maurice of her earliest acquaintance with Charles Dickens, whose daughter Kitty Perugine had been one of her first companions. Dickens was an intimate of her parents Sir Joseph and Lady Olliffe, as was his contemporary Thackeray. Dickens often visited them in Paris. Once, when he was about to give a reading at the British Embassy in support of a charitable fund started by her father, Florence remembered Dickens entering the salon and asking, 'And where is Miss Florence going to sit?' 'Florence is not going,' said Lady Olliffe firmly. 'She is too young.' 'Very well then,' he replied cheerfully, 'I shan't go either.' In the event, Florence sat in the front row and wept copiously at the melancholy death of Paul Dombey. Dickens wrote in a subsequent letter: 'Florence at the reading tremendously excited.'

Florence's educational ideas were advanced for her day and much influenced by her admiration for progressive new European theories. Long after her own children had grown up, in 1911 she went to Rome to study the work of the educational reformer Maria Montessori. Her preference, where a governess could be afforded, was for schooling girls at home. This was the education she chose for her own girls, Elsa and Molly. Molly wrote later:

> My mother's idea of the equipment required for her two daughters was that we should be turned out as good wives and mothers and be able to take our part in the social life of our kind. We must speak French and German perfectly, and be on friendly if not intimate terms with Italian. We must be able to play the piano and sing a bit, we must learn to dance well and know how to make small talk. The more serious side of education did not take any part in the plans my mother made for us. Science, mathematics, political economy, Greek and Latin — there was no need for any of these.

No girl they knew was trained for any profession, nor did 'girls of our class' go to school. That this worked well enough for the two sisters in their day is evident in the impression they gave of being delightful company. Less formidable than Gertrude, but with her erect bearing and good clothes sense, they became an attractive and entertaining couple, and much in demand. Virginia Stephen, later Virginia Woolf, mentioned them in a discursive letter about her first May Ball at Cambridge: 'It was the Trinity ball . . . Boo was there, and Alice Pollock and the Hugh Bells (If you know them — MAP calls them "the most brilliant girl conversationalists in London" — and Thoby [her brother] was much attracted by them and them by him).'

Florence subscribed to the then common medical theory that girls become overstrained if subjected to too much mental exertion. For adolescent girls in particular, education was supposed to be a serious health risk. As late as 1895, when Gertrude was twenty-seven, a Dr James Burnett, author of *Delicate, Backward, Puny and Stunted Children*, informed the world that a girl at puberty would always fall behind her brothers in academic achievement because of her 'disordered pelvic life', and assured readers that 'Not one exception to this have I ever seen.' A book by Elizabeth Missing Sewell, *Principles of Education, Drawn from Nature and Revelation*, had stated that a girl should always be guarded from study, for 'if she is allowed to run the risks, which, to the boy, are a matter of indifference, she will probably develop some disease, which, if not fatal, will, at any rate, be an injury to her for life'. Florence saw to it that all of the Bell girls had as active a life as their brothers, but was beginning to realize that when it came to education, her formula would not do for every girl. As she put it, 'There are a thousand of us who can walk along a level road and get to the end of it successfully, for one who can swim a river or scale a cliff which stands in the way.' Gertrude, she now speculated, was this exception.

When Maurice went to boarding school, the fifteen-year-old Gertrude missed him far more than she had expected. Her half-sisters and half-brother were much younger, and life became rather empty. She had long outstripped poor Miss Klug, who was constantly offended at the flat contradictions and dismissive behaviour of her troublesome charge. All her life Gertrude had trouble confining herself to armchairs, and could now be found at all times of day sprawled on the carpet flicking impatiently through a book, or thrashing away at knitting she had begun but would never finish. She would stalk about the house with a scowl on her face, airing her recently acquired views, arguing with anyone who would take issue with her and getting in the way of the maids. Invited to go and amuse herself in the garden, she invented a game called 'rackets', something like squash, which could be played on her own by smashing a ball as hard as she could against the coach-house doors. The constant banging and the cries of fury when she missed must have been a great irritation to Florence, perhaps trying to concentrate on some children's story or treatise on the nursery. Despite her father's remonstrations, Gertrude made a point of throwing her dog into the pond every day because 'he does hate it so much'.

Florence, with three younger children to cope with, was at her wits' end to know how to occupy the teenager. She was not the only member of the family sooner or later to find Gertrude difficult. Molly Trevelyan wrote: 'Gertrude is being rather thorny & I shall have to have another scene with her soon — she contradicts everything Mother says, and goes out of her way to be disobliging and snubby.' It was not hard for Florence to come to the decision that Gertrude was a special case and that a fifteen-year-old so confident, so able and thirsty for knowledge ought to be stretched.

Florence had made the best of beginnings with her stepdaughter, and her influence on Gertrude would be permanent. That influence would not always turn her in the direction that her stepmother wished, but in the things that mattered, however far she ventured, Gertrude would all her life follow Florence's lead. She always followed the conventions and observances of her upbringing. She would always be devoted to her family, and however far her life would take her from home, she never distanced herself from their interests or thought them less important than her own.

Now, breathless with excitement, Gertrude was told that she was going to be sent to school in London.

2

EDUCATION

My darling, dearest Mother,

I do so hate being here . . . if only you were in town. I couldn't be more desolate than I am now. Every day I want you more . . .

Will you please get me Gray's Elegy, also two brush-and-comb bags and a nightgown case. And a german book called Deutches Lesebuch by Carl Oltrogge.

And so Gertrude packed her trunk and went up to London with Florence on a third-class ticket — having had it pointed out to her that she would do herself no good if she was seen to be richer than the other pupils. In term time, during the first year, she would live with Florence's mother Lady Olliffe, in the imposing but still dingy premises of 95 Sloane Street. It was a staid house, relieved only by the visits of the reprehensible Tommy, Florence's brother, who when playing billiards with his young step-niece would routinely chalk his nose along with the cue. He was a tease skilled in goading little girls to fury, and with older girls a flirt whose intentions, as he once assured a straight-faced father, were 'strictly dishonourable'. His 'deaf and stupid' sister Bessie, who lived with their mother, once spotted him through the window flirting with a young lady on a bench in the garden. She opened the window and hurled a tennis ball at him. Narrowly missing the object of his affections it hit him squarely on the side of the head.

The choice of school for Gertrude had been made easier by the fact that a former friend of Florence's, Camilla Croudace, had recently become the 'Lady Resident' of Queen's College in Harley Street. Housed in an elegant Georgian four-storey, cream-painted block, it had been founded twenty years before Gertrude's birth by the educational reformer and Christian Socialist Frederick Denison Maurice. The birthplace of academic education and recognized qualifications for women, it had been granted the first royal charter for female education in 1853. It produced confident and self-assured young women capable of playing a valuable part in the nation's intellectual, business and public life. Later the school would number the writer Katherine Mansfield amongst its alumnae, but in 1884, when Gertrude enrolled, many of its graduates were destined to be governesses.

While this school was the best thing that could have happened for Gertrude, her excitement was soon overtaken by homesickness. This, for a young woman who had scarcely left her home town except for holidays in the company of sisters, brothers and cousins, was at first severe. Distance certainly made her heart grow fonder of her stepmother. She observed her classmates narrowly, and was soon writing to ask Florence to get her 'some stays' – the stiff laced whalebone corsets that she had discovered the other girls were wearing under their tightly buckled belts.

The pupils were taken to concerts and picture galleries, churches and cathedrals. Gertrude was quickly developing opinions about all things, and stating them forcibly, not least in her letters home: 'I *don't* like Rubens. I *don't* like him at all . . . The passage walls are papered with the most dreadful green paper you ever saw . . . How I do loathe and detest St Paul's . . . there is not a single detail which is not hideous not to say repulsive.'

The young ladies were scrupulously chaperoned wherever they went, and Gertrude, longing to see more of the sights of the city, chafed at not being allowed to go about on her own. 'I wish I could go to the National,' she told her parents. 'But you see, there is no one to take me. If I were a boy I should go every week!'

At Queen's College no less than at Red Barns, strict adherence to the conventions of the day was not negotiable. Gertrude must accept it, explained Mrs Croudace, as a condition of her increased freedom and independence. Florence responded to Gertrude's complaint only that she wished the child would not use abbreviations such as 'National' for National Gallery. A ruffled Gertrude replied angrily:

> I waded through [your letter] which I consider a great act of self-discipline – but I avenged myself by burning [it] promptly . . . The next letter I write to you, when I am not too cross to bother myself with finding words, my adjectives shall be as numerous as Carlyle's own . . . Would you have me say when talking of the sovereign: The Queen of England, Scotland, Ireland, Empress of India, Defender of the Faith? My life is not long enough to give everything its full title.

Receiving this somewhat smart letter, Florence may well have sighed. Hugh would have found it hard to suppress a smile at his daughter's spirit and powers of argument.

These outbursts would soon be followed by contrite messages to her parents that she had made new resolutions, and hoped that Florence would find her a better and more obedient daughter in future.

It had probably never occurred to Gertrude before to wonder whether people liked her or not. Now she had to acknowledge that she was not very popular at the school, and in response began to betray what might be a reciprocal emotion, the start of a lifelong haughtiness and aversion to the company of 'ordinary' women. Florence counselled her, as tactfully as she could, against her tendency to boastfulness, which brought another outburst. Her schoolmates, she said, were 'uninteresting' and then, finding a more diplomatic way to express her discomfiture, added: 'It's a very disagreeable process finding out that one is no better than the common run . . . I've gone through rather a hard course of it since I came to College and I don't like it at all.'

For the second year at Queen's College she became a boarder, and got on better with her peers. She was asked to stay for the weekend by a friend from Florence's youth, Thackeray's daughter Anne, Mrs Richmond Ritchie, and by the widow of the historian whose books she had devoured before breakfast, Mrs J. R. Green. But approaches from her new schoolfriends were heavily censored from Redcar. Invitations, she had to learn, were not to be accepted before Florence and Hugh had checked the suitability of the family through Mrs Croudace. Three invitations, already accepted, had to be turned down as a result, which did not help to make her better liked. It has been assumed that these families were 'not good enough' for the Bells because they were not important enough. This is unlikely. The homes that Florence would not allow Gertrude to visit were those where alcohol was consumed, where house parties were the excuse for extramarital activities, where girls were not strictly chaperoned – in other words, homes belonging to the often dissolute aristocracy, circles that might even include that of the Prince of Wales.

In the classroom, Gertrude shone. She was welcomed as an exceptional student who would volunteer for a higher class whenever she found the work easy. In her first year, in a class of some forty girls, she had come first in English history, her favourite subject, with marks of 88 out of 88. She had come second in English grammar, third in geography and fourth in French and ancient history. She had not done at all well in scripture. When the master had asked her why she had not done better when she was doing so well in all her other subjects, her response was robust: 'I don't believe a *word* of it!' Hugh and Florence only occasionally attended church, and no one could ever convince Gertrude that there was a God. She began to call herself an atheist.

She was just as resilient to criticism of her history work. When Mr de Soyres argued that an essay she had written on Cromwell did not merit his usual comment of 'Excellent' because she had assumed facts without proving them and ignored counter-arguments, she wrote home indignantly to justify herself to her father: 'The fault of my essay is that I tried to prove that Cromwell was *right* when I need only have proved that he was *not wrong*.'

She now had plenty to do, she felt, and begged Florence to let her give up embroidery and piano lessons. Her learning to play, she said, was a 'pure waste of time', craftily adding, 'Fancy the amount more books I could read in the practising hour.' Her stepmother, who believed that nothing was to be gained without persistence, did not succumb to this tempting prospect, and wrote that she must continue. Gertrude allowed a few weeks to pass, and then set to work on her father. Hugh interceded — as he always would intercede on her behalf — and she was at last allowed to give up the piano, if not the embroidery needle.

If she regarded those two skills as optional, she was falling in love with poetry, a pleasure that would endure throughout her life. At fourteen, she had snubbed her cousin Horace because he hadn't read Robert Browning's latest volume. Now she was writing home to say, 'I've done Milton most of today. I always feel I could stand on my head for want of a better outlet for my delight after Lycidas or Comus. It's very difficult to keep the knowledge of all that exquisite beauty to myself without discussing it with anyone.'

In her stream of letters home, the difference in her relationship with her father and that with her mother was becoming apparent. She still depended on her father's judgement on the larger questions, and now wrote to him specifically to ask his opinion of Home Rule for Ireland and the fate of Gladstone and the Liberal Party. She would write to Florence in a different vein when she wanted a new cotton dress, for instance, so that when she was taken to visit Maurice and her cousin Herbert Marshall at Eton she would look her best. She was now a very attractive young woman. Her green gaze was rather confrontational and her nose was a little sharp, but she had a strong, slim figure, a good carriage, and bundles of beautiful, untidy auburn hair.

Her two history teachers, Mr de Soyres and Mr Rankine, felt that she was a brilliant pupil, as did Mr Cramb, the history master. She had earned the right to go further with her education, they decided, and in her last term she wrote to ask her father if she might go to Oxford. Hugh and Florence had some way to go before they would be convinced. Florence might have given way on Gertrude's schooling, but Oxford she had never considered for a daughter. Having travelled up to London to discuss the issue with Mrs Croudace, though, it was finally agreed. Gertrude was enrolled at Lady Margaret Hall, one of the two women's colleges at Oxford, in 1886.

Meeting the alarming Lady Stanley, a founder of Cambridge's Girton College, Gertrude told Florence: 'I felt rather guilty when I shook hands with her – rather as if "I'm not going to Girton" were written on my forehead, but she didn't say anything!'

In 1885 she heard that her grandfather Lowthian had been made a baronet. She wrote to congratulate him, but told Hugh: 'I may say to you I suppose that I am very sorry indeed, it's a great pity. I think he quite deserves to have it only I wish it could have been offered and refused.' Unknown to her at the time, Hugh had not been informed. 'Imagine my astonishment at opening my Times', he had written to his mother, 'to see the announcement that the Pater is to be made a Baronet! Why have you none of you written to me?' Although he added, 'I am pleased that the dear clever Pater's merits should be recognised', the note of hurt feelings is clear. Hugh felt that he should have been consulted. He, after all, would inherit the title. Gertrude and Hugh appear to have agreed that it was questionable to inherit titles through birth rather than ability, an attitude to equality and plain living perhaps inherited from the Pattinsons' Quaker tradition. If so, that is probably the reason why Hugh chose to write to her rather than to his father.

The old lady was already ill when she became Lady Bell, and survived only another year. Within a short time of her death came another to sadden the family: Uncle Tommy, Florence's naughty brother, was killed when he was run over by a London bus.

Back in Redcar, Gertrude was drawn into Florence's social work, as she would always be if she stayed at home too long. Soon after marriage, her stepmother had begun an immense project which she dedicated to Charles Booth, who, a few years later, would begin to publish his voluminous study of poverty, *Life and Labour of the People in London*. Over a period of nearly thirty years she and her committee were to interview a thousand of the families employed at the Clarence steelworks, putting these working-class people's lives under the microscope. Gertrude joined the committee inter-mittently, interviewing the wives and in 1889 acting as treasurer for various works projects. Later, in Florence's absences, she would arrange teas, give lectures with lantern slides about her own adventures, and organize Christmas festivities for the workers.

The book that Florence eventually published in 1907, *At the Works*, was factually exhaustive, providing ample research material for those who had a mission to campaign for change. It is easy to regard Florence's work as incomplete. Having exposed the suffering endured by the poorer working families and especially when they struck hard times, it explores no further the deep fissures in Victorian society. It poses no remedies. Florence's position as the ironmaster's wife has been suggested as compromising. This is to ignore the extraordinary character of her husband and of the Bell enterprises. Capitalist and employer as Hugh was, he saw no conflict between masters and men – more, he saw them as mutually dependent. His men were well paid, enjoying comforts and pleasures denied to many industrial poor and to those who toiled on unenlightened agricultural estates. He carried on his father's mission to promote education, and it was a lack of education that lay behind much of the hardship in poorly run homes. He was not just a liberal in his thinking, but active in Liberal politics. He joined the debate about the duty of the state to care for the individual. He believed in the role of the new trade unions, and that employers should encourage them in a shared concern for the welfare of the workers. Socialism was already at the heart of the new political philosophy, if not accepted in its more Marxist extremes. Hugh was part of the thrust towards a welfare state, realized in his lifetime by Lloyd George and Churchill in legislation for benefits for the sick and unemployed and eventually in retirement. It was enough for Florence to display the workers' suffering and to show how it arose. Hugh's respect for her as a woman of intelligence and purpose no doubt lay behind her unique access to his men, their wives and homes.

To understand the importance of Florence's work, one has to bear in mind that at the time the commonplace middle-class view of the working classes was ill-informed and moralistic. Merchants' wives and ladies at London supper parties would be applauded for such sentiments as 'I cannot have any sympathy for the labouring classes because they don't look after their children properly, or keep their houses clean. The children die, and it is the mothers' fault.' What Florence did was to lay down the facts of the workers' and their families' lives so truthfully that no one who read *At the Works* could possibly make such a statement again. Florence's mission was one that could be properly promulgated even as the wife of the ironmaster whose fortune rested on the workers. Having established the facts, she analysed them. She succeeded in producing an impressive piece of social investigation and left the conclusions to the industrial sociologists and reformers who would follow. Equally, she left the emotional music to the family friend Charles Dickens, who had the God-given ability to put an unforgettable face and soul to the poorest of the poor.

Readers of *At the Works* learnt about the poorest of the workers and 'how terribly near the margin of disaster the man . . . walks, who has, in ordinary normal conditions, but just enough to keep himself on'.* Wages ranged from 18 to 80 shillings a week; readers learnt what proportion went on the absolute necessities – rent, coal and wood, clothes and locomotion, 'in a place where for many of the men the river lies between them and their work, and has to be crossed at a halfpenny a passage on a steam ferry-boat'. They learnt that the quantity of food expected to last a family of three for seven days would be consumed by a better-off family in only two. Working-class women were frequently reviled by the rich for their filthy skirts that dragged in the mud. Florence revealed the truth, which was that they did not choose to display the miserable state of their decaying footwear. She explained how teenage girls went into marriage full of hope and excitement, and how the arrival of one baby after another left them broken in health, depressed and unable to make the physical effort demanded by cleaning, mending and cooking: 'it is not so very surprising that she should leave the clothes unmended, that she should leave the floor unswept'. Florence describes the breakdown of marriages as the weary worker

* See 'Notes on Money Values', p. 485.

begins to look 'for comfort and enjoyment out of his own home'; his life is turned in the wrong direction by his wife 'not because she is ill-intentioned, but simply from her incapacity to deal with existence, however she may struggle, and above all from her failing health'. She drew the obvious comparison – with the middle-class woman who can rely on someone else to see to the cleaning and tidying. 'We shall understand better if we admit this and do not try to deceive ourselves; if we frankly recognize that . . . there is regrettably one code of conduct for the rich and another for the poor.'

As civic leaders and local benefactors, the Bells built assembly rooms, libraries, schools and offices. Florence recognized that a place of recreation was needed in Middlesbrough, where exhausted workers could go in the evening to escape their crying babies. She wanted to provide an alternative to the pub, where men were led into spending too much of their wage packet and where fights often broke out. In 1907 she would open the Winter Garden, a large, well warmed modern hall that was 'light and bright and cheerful . . . open to anyone and everyone who chose to pay one penny'. A cup of tea and a biscuit could be had for another penny, but alcohol was *not* served. At the opening, Hugh made his usual graceful speech: there was no position he would rather hold, he declared, than that of 'a fellow-worker, a captain of industry of such an army that I command'; he hoped the Winter Garden would make the lives of that army brighter and better. Women were welcome, although Florence acknowledged that most mothers had to stay at home in the evening to feed and look after their children; but, she noted joyfully on the first day, there were 'Lots of women!'

Hugh had borne the expense of clearing the site and erecting the building, and a further sum of £2,070 was raised locally. The finished hall was decorated with hanging flower baskets and supplied with billiard tables, rows of seats and tables with newspapers and magazines. During the week and at the weekend there would be brass band competitions, singers and buskers of all sorts. After working hours it was always crowded, and when Florence dropped in she was generally asked to play the piano and lead the songs. The

Winter Garden, later renamed the Dame Florence Bell Garden, was an immediate success, and continued to be so. On one of their wedding anniversaries, Hugh presented Florence with the title deeds of the building.

Gertrude was both part of this, and not part of it. Observing from close quarters what it took to devote yourself to the improvement of conditions for your fellow men and women, the constant efforts of sympathy to be made and the stamina to go on year after year without acknowledgement, she came to understand that this kind of work was not for her. Florence owned this particular territory. Tacitly acknowledging her stepmother's enormous achievements in the field, Gertrude began to look outward. Her own concerns would be international rather than local, her contributions on a world scale.

Her attitudes honed by long discussions with her father, Gertrude already took a strong line on many of the issues of the day. She itched for debate, and hoped to find it at the many lunches and dinners in which she was now included. When she met up with the 'normal' views of 'normal' people, though, she was often angered by their incomprehension and their failure to take her point. She wrote home from London: 'I have had enough of these dinners where people say "I think" all the time.' She wanted to talk to people who knew the facts, or were prepared to discover them. It is easy to imagine her at the dinner table, fidgeting in her seat between two kindly adults, doing her best to derail the lumbering train of the conversation winding its way slowly to the usual conclusions. If Free Trade were the subject, the discussion might have gone something like this:

NEIGHBOUR: 'If we relax the import tariffs there will be terrible unemployment, because we can't compete against cheap labour from abroad.'

GERTRUDE: 'Nonsense. How do you know?'

NEIGHBOUR: 'Because, my dear young friend, our factories would close.'

GERTRUDE: 'The factories might close, but there would not necessarily be widespread unemployment.'

NEIGHBOUR: 'And how do you reach that conclusion?'

GERTRUDE: 'Because if Britain can buy cotton more cheaply from India, the population will have more money to spend on other things made in Britain.'

NEIGHBOUR: 'And what about the poor crofter whose livelihood has vanished?'

GERTRUDE: 'He will come to Middlesbrough and learn to work pig iron at Clarence, and earn more money for a higher skill.'

As Florence's daughter no less than Hugh's, Gertrude would frequently have become entangled in discussions about the working classes. She was a Liberal and a Gladstonian, and she pursued her views on contemporary political controversies with logical reasoning and sound historical perspective. By the time she went up to university, she had become something of a social hand grenade.

In 1886, at Oxford, the undergraduates still drove dog-carts, Dr Jowett still presided at Balliol, and the figure of Lewis Carroll could occasionally be spotted crossing the quadrangle of Christ Church. Although there were two colleges for women at the university, it nevertheless managed to remain a bastion of misogyny. At the age of eighteen, Gertrude was joining an almost exclusively male world under the guidance of Lady Margaret Hall's first principal, Miss Elizabeth Wordsworth, grandniece of the poet. But even here, where it might have been expected that emancipation would flourish, she found that chaperones were required whenever the women entered men's colleges or entertained men or mixed in male society. Miss Wordsworth was cautious. Woman, she said, was designed to be 'Adam's helpmate' and must develop the 'minor graces'. Reluctantly, Gertrude submitted to being taught neat handwriting and 'the ways of opening and shutting doors'. On the other hand, she bicycled everywhere and ventured into every circle that would have her. She swam, she rowed, she played hockey, she acted, danced and spoke in debates, but she still had to spend precious hours doing needlework. She quickly learnt to compare the extraordinary freedoms of her own upbringing with the modes of conduct of the larger world. 'I am going to a teaparty of Mary's today to meet some sort of relation of hers who is Headmaster of

Wellington. She is so unhappy because Miss Wordsworth has pronounced that she had better entertain him in the drawing room! It isn't half the same thing giving a teaparty not in one's own room . . .' Her room was rather bleak, but soon the bed and the floor were covered with the familiar clutter of books and papers. She asked Florence to tell the gardener to put a pot of snowdrops on the train for her.

The presence of women spread dismay throughout the university. It would not admit women to full membership until 1919; Cambridge refused to do so even then. Most undergraduates of Gertrude's day saw university as a series of male-only clubs providing a wealth of contacts for future careers in the army, in parliament, the Church or the Empire. Women were no part of this, any more than they participated in the leisure pursuits of drinking, gambling, racing – or womanizing. It was a male society run for males and the presence of women was deeply disconcerting, as embarrassing for them as if their mothers and sisters had joined them at university, preventing them from behaving as men behave without women around.

It was the age when even piano legs were draped lest they should seem too provocative. At Oxford the idea that women were inferior was built into the teaching. Special applications had to be made for permission for women to attend lectures and to take certain exams. 'The overtaxing of [women's] brains,' wrote contemporary philosopher Herbert Spencer, would lead to 'the deficiency of reproductive power'. 'Inferior to us God made you, and our inferiors to the end of time you will remain,' Dean John Burgon had thundered from New College Chapel. When one tutor, a Mr Bright, made the women in the room sit with their backs to him, Gertrude's shoulders began to shake. The giggles quickly spread between the three women, and soon they were in a state of uncontrollable laughter. The problem, she wrote to Hugh, was Mr Bright's, not hers.

She put in seven hours' work a day, every day, but wrote home:

> The amount of work is hopeless. This last week for instance, I
> ought to have read the life of Richard III, another in two volumes

of Henry VIII, the continuous history of Hallam and Green from Edward IV to Ed. VI, the third volume of Stubbs, 6 or 7 lectures of Mr Lodge, to have looked up a few of Mr Campion's last term lectures, and some of Mr Bright's, and lastly to have written 6 essays for Mr Hassall. Now I ask you, is that possible?

And so Gertrude, wearing a loose black gown that swirled around her laced boots, rammed a tasselled mortar-board on her bundled-up hair and made her way in a crocodile with the rest of the LMH women across University Parks to Balliol College for their first history lecture. In the hall were two hundred men, already filling the benches. With amazing discourtesy they remained seated and refused to move up. Instead, the women were led up to the platform where they found chairs alongside the professor. At the end of his lecture, Mr Lodge turned to the women beside him and asked with an insufferably patronizing air: 'And I wonder what the young ladies made of that?' Green eyes flashing, Gertrude retorted loudly: 'I don't think we learned anything new today. I don't think you added anything to what you wrote in your book.' There was a roar of laughter, and perhaps the atmosphere relaxed a little.

Gertrude's self-confidence was extraordinary. Once, in the middle of an oral examination, she started an argument with a don about the position of a German town: 'I am sorry, but it is on the *right* bank. I have been there, and I *know.*' Another time, she offended the distinguished historian Professor S. R. Gardiner by interrupting his discourse with 'I'm afraid I must differ from your estimate of Charles I.' When informed of this, Miss Wordsworth shuddered, fretting 'Would she be the sort of person to have in one's bedroom if one were ill?' But Gertrude had no ambition to play nursemaid. She polished off her finals in two years instead of the usual three, declared the examinations 'delightful!' and went straight out to play a vigorous game of tennis. Then she went up to London to buy an emerald silk gown for the commemoration ball, and came back with an enormous straw hat covered in cabbage roses. Before long she was informed that she had taken a brilliant First.

A first-class degree is the pinnacle of intellectual qualification. A good second is awarded for diligence in acquiring copious knowledge and for supplying logical and discriminating answers to the examiner's questions. The first-class student must see beyond the accepted theories of the day, marshalling knowledge to explore new horizons of understanding, challenging the finest minds in the subject without faltering. Gertrude was the first woman to receive a First in Modern History, a measure of the outstanding quality of her mind.

There is an anonymous limerick of around this time that could well have been written about Gertrude by one of the male undergraduates she encountered.

> *I spent all my time with a crammer*
> *And then only managed a gamma,*
> *But the girl over there*
> *With the flaming red hair*
> *Got an alpha plus easily — damn her!*

Enterprising as Gertrude thought herself, the wife of one of her tutors described her as 'prim'. There are parallels at this age and stage with the fictional Lucy Honeychurch in E. M. Forster's *Room with a View* (published in 1908): she was intolerant, seeing herself as fascinatingly different, and full of elevated ideals. She loved the company of men, and had started what would become a lifetime habit of dismissing their wives as 'dull dogs'. On the other hand, she looked down her nose at male high spirits as though she were fifty, not nineteen. 'There's a reading party of Oxford men in the Inn with us ... Judging from the noise they make I should say they read very little indeed.'

The Oxford women she was meeting were far more to her taste than most of her earlier classmates, although one new friend, Edith Langridge, had come, like her, from Queen's College. She liked Mary Talbot, niece of the Warden of Keble, but her best friend was Janet Hogarth. Janet's brother, archaeologist and Arabist David Hogarth, would also become important to her later. Janet wrote a revealing portrait of the nineteen-year-old Gertrude:

She was, I think, the most brilliant creature who ever came amongst us, the most alive at every point, with her tireless energy, her splendid vitality, her unlimited capacity for work, for talk, for play. She was always an odd mixture of maturity and childishness, grown up in her judgement of men and affairs, child-like in her certainties, and most engaging in her entire belief in her father and the vivid intellectual world in which she had been brought up.

But it is Florence, the sweet woman to whom had been entrusted the extraordinary and clever child that was Gertrude, and who had broken her own rules so as to ensure that her stepdaughter had an education equal to a man's, who provides us with the clearest insight into Gertrude's soul. Florence had handled the difficult girl with great sensitivity, when a wrong move would have turned her into a rebel. She had directed her stepdaughter's life, watched it separate from hers in unforeseen but positive ways; and she would come to feel herself outstripped by Gertrude's adventures and her career. She never resented that Gertrude became more cosmopolitan, a better writer and administrator, more respected as an intellectual, more admired – if not more loved – more famous and influential. Gertrude in her turn began to love Florence, never as much as she loved her father but as someone with whom she would want to keep in close touch all her life, and someone whom she would occasionally protect from the knowledge of her own dangerous predicaments. Her letters to her father were usually more passionate and fond, just as Florence's letters to her own children, Elsa, Hugh and Molly, had a special intimacy. Warmed by affection but not blinded by love, Florence wrote of her stepdaughter after her death: ' . . . in truth the real basis of Gertrude's nature was her capacity for deep emotion. Great joys came into her life, and also great sorrows. How could it be otherwise, with a temperament so avid of experience? Her ardent and magnetic personality drew the lives of others into hers as she passed along.'

3

THE CIVILIZED WOMAN

On becoming the first woman to be awarded a First in Modern History, Gertrude and her triumph were featured in an announcement in *The Times*. Faced with the intellectually arrogant, occasionally self-important young woman who returned to Red Barns after Oxford, Florence told Hugh that they must now get rid of her 'Oxfordy manner', or no one would want to marry her. Florence determined to domesticate Gertrude, and teach her that life was about more than passing exams and winning arguments: but first, she deserved a holiday.

She would go to stay with Aunt Mary, Florence's sister, in Bucharest, where her husband Sir Frank Lascelles was British Minister to Romania. Mary was particularly fond of Gertrude, who amused her mightily, and her own daughter Florence, named after Florence Bell, was one of Gertrude's best friends. There were also the two Lascelles boys: Billy, who had just left Sandhurst and was waiting for his commission in the Guards, and his younger brother Gerald. Billy, the object of Gertrude's first 'fluctuating flirtation', would meet Hugh and Gertrude in Paris and escort her, otherwise unchaperoned, to Munich, where they would meet Gerald and continue to Eastern Europe.

Gertrude was wildly excited, and ready to be supremely happy. She had slimmed down over the last couple of years, and was no longer an untidy tomboy but a well groomed young woman whose soft auburn hair was her great beauty, her curls escaping from the pins to soften the effect of her penetrating gaze. It was Christmas, and Bucharest in 1888 was one of the smartest and most social capitals of Europe, its nucleus the Court and the legations. She travelled with trunks of ravishing new couture clothes for the four-month whirl of balls and dinners and evenings at the opera; fur-collared coats and laced white boots for ice-skating parties in the forest; Indian shawls, muffs and mittens for sledging expeditions in the hills with their medieval castles and brightly painted inns.

It was not long before she was presented by the Lascelleses to King Carol and Queen Elizabeth, and struck up a passing friendship with the rather sad and beautiful queen. Better known by her nom de plume of Carmen Sylva, the Queen was widely preferred to her austere and somewhat pedestrian husband. 'The King was so like every other officer,' Gertrude wrote to her cousin Horace, 'that I never could remember who he was and only merciful providence prevented me from giving him a friendly little nod several times during the evening under the impression that he was one of my numerous acquaintance . . . Billy and I waltzed over his toes once. "'Ware King" – whispered Billy, but it was too late.' Many debutantes meeting their first member of royalty would have been reduced to monosyllables, but here Gertrude displayed her ability to meet important people without becoming either obsequious or self-conscious:

You can't think how charming the Queen is. Yesterday we went to a charity ball . . . and she came and had a long talk with Auntie Mary and me and finally presented me with 10 francs and sent me off to buy tombola tickets . . . I had a long crack with the Queen whom I suddenly became conscious of immediately in front of me . . . However she need not have talked to me unless she liked. She told me how she spent her winters – it sounds dreary enough, poor lady.

The Lascelleses provided plenty of the improving sightseeing that Gertrude had been brought up to. She was entertained by the passionate, almost violent debates she was taken to listen to in the chamber of government, and the many late-evening entertainments and balls were all she had hoped. She was a good dancer, knew all the steps, and even taught the legation secretaries to do a new dance, the Boston. She wrote to Florence of the different Romanian way of taking a partner:

> You dance nothing through with one person. This is what happens: your dancer comes up and asks you for a turn. You dance three or four times round the room with him and he then drops you by your chaperon with an elegant bow and someone else comes up and carries you off . . . The officers all appear in uniform, of course, with top boots and spurs, but they dance so well that they don't tear one in the least . . . I can't attempt to tell you whom I danced with for it was impossible to remember them all.

After these evenings, when she danced without stopping until three in the morning, they went home in a pair of carriages through the moonlit snow, wrapped in blankets, the harnesses of the trotting horses jingling as they passed through the icy cobbled streets. Back at the legation they found sandwiches and hot drinks in the warm drawing-room, and would sit another hour or so by the fire, discussing everyone they had met. Here Gertrude was thrown into a more sophisticated, cosmopolitan circle than she had encountered under the watchful eye of Florence. She expressed her surprise at finding divorced women integrated into society. Unadorned with cosmetics, like all proper young ladies of the time, she was rather impressed by a flirtatious maid-of-honour to the Queen who powdered herself quite openly – and then proceeded to powder the faces of all the young men hanging round the door of the dressing-room. Among the throngs of counts and princes, secretaries and ambassadors, Gertrude met two men who would be of great importance to her: Charles Hardinge, from the British Legation in Constantinople, later Viceroy of India, and the thirty-six-year-old Valentine Ignatius Chirol, foreign correspondent of *The Times*. Chirol, already an intimate of the Lascelles, would become one of Gertrude's closest friends; she would write to him from all over the world, and their relationship would last to the end of her life. To her beloved 'Domnul' (Romanian for 'gentleman') she could reveal the emotions and dilemmas she could not expose even to her parents. It was the breadth of his international knowledge that first captivated her. He, in turn, was amused at the enquiring and confrontational style of her conversation, to which he quickly responded in kind. He had begun his career as a Foreign Office clerk; then, equipped with a dozen languages, he embarked on a lifetime of travelling, lecturing and writing, while passing sensitive information to Whitehall. He became an expert on all aspects of Britain's imperial power and the threats to it, and later, foreign editor of *The Times*.

Gertrude's independent mind sometimes got her into trouble. On one occasion, listening to a discussion her uncle was having with a foreign statesman concerning European problems, she broke into the conversation to tell the Frenchman: 'Il me semble, Monsieur, que vous n'avez pas saisi l'esprit du peuple allemand.' A ripple of disapproval ran round the group, except for Chirol, who turned away, smiling. A horrified Aunt Mary whisked Gertrude away and told her off. When she reflected on the incident some twenty-five years later, Florence agreed with her sister's response: 'There is no doubt that . . . it was a mistake for Gertrude to proffer her opinions, much less her criticisms, to her superiors in age and experience.' But she added: 'The time was to come when many a distinguished foreign statesman not only listened to the opinions she proffered but accepted them and acted on them.'

The end of the Romanian holiday came at last, and Gertrude's happy four months would end in a trip to Constantinople with the Lascelles. Adding to her pleasure, Chirol accompanied them, picking out many wonderful and exotic sights that tourists would normally have missed. Billy rowed her in a caique up the Golden Horn: 'It was perfectly delicious with a low sun glittering on the water, bringing back the colour to the faded Turkish flags of the men of war and turning each white minaret in Stamboul into a dazzling marble pillar,' she wrote home.

Gertrude was soon to 'come out' as a debutante in London – the ritual for well-heeled girls emerging from the schoolroom to join 'society' – and be presented to the Queen at a reception, called a 'drawing-room'. But back at Redcar, Florence now put into action her threat of domesticating Gertrude. For intelligent people like Florence and Hugh, men were not moral because they went to church, or women because they kept a clean and orderly house. But intellectual women who filled their lives with 'men's work' – political debate, meetings, campaigning – while neglecting their children, husbands and homes were quite definitely immoral. Charles Dickens had characterized this type unforgettably as Mrs Jellaby in *Bleak House*, written thirty years previously. She was a lady of 'very remarkable strength of character, who devotes herself entirely to the public' and especially to 'the African project'. Her dress was undone at the back and her hair unbrushed. Her dirty room was strewn with papers while her hungry children milled and whined around her, and the mild and silent Mr Jellaby, his virility in shreds from long exposure to this virago, sat in a corner with his aching head pressed against the wall. Gertrude might be a bluestocking, Florence thought, but she would not be a Mrs Jellaby.

Having some travelling of her own to do, Florence put her stepdaughter in charge of the three youngest children. She was to teach them history, run the house and the servants, balance the books and have everything in order when Hugh came home from Clarence each evening. Maurice was at Eton, where he would stay until he was nineteen. Gertrude, who enjoyed the company of children and was deeply fond of all her brothers and sisters, did her absolute best, scowling over the accounts, visiting Clarence wives and organizing events for them, attempting needlework and sending Florence bulletins of their daily activities. 'I went into the gardens to be cool, but presently came the babies who announced that they were barons and that they intended to rob me. I was rather surprised at their taking this view of the functions of the aristocracy . . . We all played at jumping over a string . . . Molly shocked Miss Thomson [the governess] dreadfully the other day by asking her what was the French for "This horse has the staggers"!'

Not a very distinguished cook herself, she taught Molly and Elsa to make scones and gingerbread. In between domestic duties she took dancing lessons, read Swinburne's *Jonson*, and occasionally left the children to the servants and travelled up to Lady Olliffe's in

Sloane Street for fittings for dresses for her London season. Her struggles with the accounts suggest the emphasis that Florence placed on home economy, and her insistence that her stepdaughter should learn the value of money. No one would have thought from Gertrude's letters at this time that they were from a scion of the sixth-richest family in Britain.

> About the little girls' frocks, Hunt [the nursemaid] would like to have one for Molly made of cambric matching the pattern of Elsa, 16d. a yard 40 in. wide; the other two of nainsook which will wash better, 13d. and 38 in. wide. There are two insertions, one at 6¼[d.] not so very pretty, one at 10½[d.] very pretty indeed. However it is 4d. a yd. dearer . . . Mr Grimston says that he cannot supply us with mutton at 9d. a pound, it is so dear now. I have asked the other butchers and find they are all selling it at 10d. or 10½[d.] a pound . . .
>
> I paid everything but the butcher with what you sent and had over one pound balance which I have kept for next time . . . I went to Clarence today and arranged about the nursing lecture to-morrow . . . Then I paid some visits and came home with Papa at 4.35. Molly and I have since been picking cowslips.

Having paid her family dues, Gertrude moved up to London for her 'coming out.' At the series of receptions, weekend house parties and balls to which they were invited, the young ladies would be presented with an array of eligible bachelors from an official list, from which it was assumed they would find husbands. In her obligatory white gown and train, with tall white feathers securely pinned in her red hair, Gertrude drove to Buckingham Palace with Florence and Hugh in a slow-moving line of carriages, and made her formal curtsy to the ageing queen. Heavily chaperoned, she attended assemblies at dozens of great houses, including the Duke of Devonshire's, the Londonderrys' and the Stanleys', stayed in Audley Square with Lord and Lady Arthur Russell, of whose many children Flora was her special friend; went to Ascot in a magnificent hat; attended the Eton and Harrow cricket match; and did the full round of country-house weekends. She wrote to Florence: 'Do you remember discussing what other girls do with their days? Well I have found out – they spend their entire time rushing from house to house for cricket weeks, which means cricket all day and dancing all night . . .'

She was enjoying talking to all kinds of people. 'Lord Carlisle came and sat by me and we discussed football and the Church! He was very surprised to find what a lot of ecclesiastical gossip I know, and I that he should know about football. I must tell you I had on a very pretty gown which had a great success.'

Just as Oxford had seemed restrictive after the freedoms she relished at home, now London society bound her to conventions that had not been so strictly enforced in Bucharest. Since aristocratic families such as the Cecils, the Howards, the Cavendishes and the Stanleys ruled society, the receipt or absence of invitations from these social arbiters determined the degree of a girl's acceptability. Most onerous for Gertrude, as it had been at school and at university, was having to be accompanied by a chaperone whenever she passed beyond the front door, even to visit a picture gallery or a church. Used to galloping about all over Yorkshire and leaping fences on the hunting field, at country-house weekends her riding was reduced to the sedate pace of a cavalcade, with fellow guests, grooms and family coachmen all lumbering along together. She had even to be careful which books she was seen to be carrying, and was reproved for reading Bourget's *Le Disciple*. The fact that she was reading it in French did not protect her from disapproval: the novel concerns a pupil who applies his master's naturalistic theories to everyday life.

Occasionally she broke away. Her good friend Mary Talbot from Lady Margaret Hall days, a saintly woman who would marry the future Bishop of Chichester, was devoting her tragically short life to working in the slums of the East End of London. No doubt reflecting on the different directions their lives were taking, one day Gertrude gave her chaperones the slip and incurred Florence's displeasure by going off by herself on the new underground railway to Whitechapel, where she spent a fascinated day accompanying Mary on her rounds.

Florence had expressed her disapproval of Gertrude's flirtation with Billy Lascelles. The fact that they were cousins, she said, did not permit Gertrude to waive the conventions, especially because Billy was much in London at the time and his family were abroad. Gertrude was on her honour to behave well, irritating as it often was. 'Billy and I sat in the garden and had a long talk . . . he wanted to take me with him to Paddington and send me back in a hansom, don't be afraid, I didn't go – what would have happened if I had, it was ten o'clock?' she wrote. There was another man, one Captain X, who took her to an exhibition and brought her home alone in a hansom: she told Florence, 'I hope that doesn't shock you.' If he had hoped for a flirtation, he was disappointed. 'I discussed religious beliefs all the way there and very metaphysical conceptions of truth all the way back . . . I love talking to people when they really will talk sensibly and about things which one wants to discuss.' When Florence wrote to reprimand her for this indiscretion, Gertrude disarmingly replied: 'I don't think many of our watchful acquaintances saw me on Sunday, it was a streaming afternoon. I felt sure you wouldn't like it, but you know, I didn't either!'

When in the course of time it was Gertrude's turn to chaperone Elsa and Molly to London dances, she immensely enjoyed helping them dress up in their finery, but soon became bored when required to watch over them from the sidelines. Remembering a remark of Florence's at the May balls about how old the function of chaperoning had made her feel, Gertrude wrote to her: 'I sat on a bench and watched them dancing round and knew just what you felt like at Oxford.'

What was Gertrude like in her early twenties? It is fascinating to think that we may have a partial description of her by that fine analyst of character, Henry James. The author was a good friend of Florence and of Elizabeth Robins, and Gertrude met him several times, sometimes as a guest of the Bells and more than once at a dinner party of the Russells, where he was also a frequent guest. Hearing him make fun of a novel of Mrs Humphry Ward's, she judged him 'the critic – so moderate, so just; and so contemptuous! Every sentence hit the nail right on the head, and every nail ran down into the coffin of Mrs Ward's reputation as a novelist.' Of the novel's protagonist James had remarked: 'A shadow, a character indefinitely postponed, he arrives nowhere.' It is hard to believe that Gertrude's guileless and very direct personality went unnoticed by James then or afterwards, and very tempting to compare her with the character of Nanda, the heroine of his novel *The Awkward Age*, published several years later in 1899. Gertrude may well have been one of the young ladies serving as his inspiration. Florence Bell was a strong supporter and confidante of James in his pursuit of success in the theatre, and in 1892 he based a leading character on her in his short story, 'Nona Vincent'.

The Awkward Age is drawn from a slightly earlier period of James's life when he was an inveterate diner-out in London society. It concerns 'the sometimes dreaded, often delayed, but never fully arrested coming to the forefront' of the debutante, and 'the "sitting downstairs", from a given date, of the merciless maiden previously perched aloft' – a situation that 'could easily be felt as a crisis [because of] the account to be taken, in a circle of free talk, of a new and innocent, a wholly unacclimatized presence'. His comedy shows the sophisticated circle of adults 'put about by having, of a sudden, an ingenuous mind and a pair of limpid searching eyes to count with'. In the Jamesian world of dim drawing-rooms and subtle subtexts, Nanda stands out as an uncompromising figure, questioning, characterful, honest to the point of awkwardness. 'Not so pretty' as the lovely little Aggie, she is 'self-possessed . . . downright . . . curiously wanting . . . in timidity and in levity . . . not easily abashed', and shows 'a crude young clearness' in conversation. From beneath a 'disposition . . . of fair hair', her eyes are fixed on her interlocutor with 'a mild straightness', which 'makes the beauty of the remainder'. She chooses, whenever possible, to walk rather than take the carriage.

Gertrude had reached the age of twenty-four without really falling in love – a state of affairs that could not be expected to continue. She had been out in society for three years, but her character was already too decided, her mind too sharp and her critical sense too finely tuned to mesh easily with the less developed personalities and intellects around her. So many people of her age were in awe of her, if not for her social standing then for her intellect, and in a manner often typical of daughters of powerful and famous fathers, she failed to hide a felt superiority to men who could not measure up to Hugh. She must have recognized this, and felt unable to release herself from a certain pressure of expectation from – and because of – her family. She was feminine, attractive, lively; she was ready to be happy; but Bucharest lived on in her mind as the place where she had had most fun and felt most admired. When Aunt Mary invited her to join the Lascelleses again, this time in Persia, she was ecstatic. It would be her first encounter with the East.

As soon as she heard that 'His Ex' Sir Frank was going to take up his ambassadorship in Teheran, she had begun to learn the language. Lord Stanley of Alderley – of the family into which Aunt Maisie had married – was her first teacher of Persian and afterwards she attended the London School of Oriental Studies. By the time she got to Persia, six months later, she was able to understand what she heard. Travelling with her cousin Florence, she took the train from Germany through Austria to Constantinople, then by Tiflis and Baku round the Caspian Sea. Her sense of escape and exhilaration increased with each country that she crossed, and from the moment she set foot in Persia, she felt reborn.

On her first day there, riding out of Teheran as the sun was rising, she was led by her guide to the crest of a mountain. She saw, spread out beneath her, the landscape she found more beautiful than any other. The moment is crystallized in a letter to her cousin Horace Marshall dated 18 June 1892, a moment of sheer delight, ecstatically described, in which, as her eyes travelled the limitless horizon, there is almost a note of mysticism as she ventured into the edges of the wilderness that would become her spiritual home:

Oh the desert around Teheran! Miles and miles of it with nothing, *nothing* growing; ringed in with bleak bare mountains snow crowned and furrowed with the deep courses of torrents. I never knew what desert was till I came here; it is a very wonderful thing to see; and suddenly in the middle of it all, out of nothing, out of a little cold water, springs up a garden. Such a garden! Trees, fountains, tanks, roses and a house in it, the houses which we heard of in fairy tales when we were little: inlaid with tiny slabs of looking-glass in lovely patterns, blue tiled, carpeted, echoing with the sound of running water and fountains . . .

Constrained and compartmentalized at home, in the East Gertrude became her own person. Her spirits soared and her receptiveness to nature and life expanded so that she was forced to recognize within herself two Gertrudes. Part of the sense of difference was that here there were few rules, few expectations. She had emerged from the shadow of the Bells into the light of independence. It had the effect of humbling her, and led her to conclusions and realizations that would not have occurred to her at home:

Are we the same people I wonder when all our surroundings, associations, acquaintances are changed? Here that which is me, which is an empty jar that the passer by fills at pleasure, is filled with such wine as in England I have never heard of . . . How big the world is, how big and how wonderful. It comes to me as ridiculously presumptuous that I should dare to carry my little personality half across it and boldly attempt to measure . . . things for which it has no table of measurements that can possibly apply.

Each enchanted day began with a two-hour ride into the countryside, followed by a cold bath scented with rosewater, then breakfast spread out in a tent in the embassy garden. Ahead lay a wealth of pleasure: expeditions and sightseeing, delicious long lunches, lying in a hammock with a book in her hand, games and entertainments, and heady evenings dancing and dining in fabulous palaces and pavilions until the cool early hours. Just riding or driving through the streets was a revelation:

In this country the women lift the veil of a Raphael Madonna to look at you . . . I felt ashamed almost before the beggars in the street – they wear their rags with a better grace than I my most becoming habit, and the veils of the commonest women (now the veil is the touchstone on which to try a woman's toilette) are far better put on than mine. A veil should fall from the top of your head to the soles of your feet, of that I feel convinced, and it should not be transparent.

And love came at last, in the form of an agreeable legation secretary, Henry Cadogan, the eldest son of the Hon. Frederick Cadogan and the grandson of the 3rd Earl Cadogan. Gertrude described him in her letters with a wealth of detail that might have given Florence an early warning of her interest. He was thirty-three, 'tall and red and very thin . . . intelligent, a great tennis player, a great billiards player, an enthusiast about Bezique, devoted to riding though he can't ride in the least . . . smart, clean, well-dressed, looking upon us as his special property to be looked after and amused'. He was well educated – scholarly, even – and his attentions to Florence and Gertrude soon focused particularly on the latter. He read and spoke the language, and brought her piles of books to get through. He found her a teacher who would continue her lessons in Persian.

It certainly is unexpected and undeserved to have come all the way to Tehran and to find someone so delightful at the end – he rides with us, he arranges plans for us – he shows us lovely things from the bazaars – he is always there when we want him . . . He appears to have read everything that ought to be read in French, German and English.

Aunt Mary, perhaps not entirely well during Gertrude's long visit, was easy-going where Florence would have been zealous. On their frequent rides and picnics, Gertrude and Henry would canter off on their own to sit by streams and in gardens, to read and talk. They searched for treasures in the bazaars and played backgammon with a merchant friend. They visited the treasure house of the Shah, fished for trout and hunted quail with falcons. When it became too hot in Teheran, the foreign legations moved to their summer quarters, to the cool of Gulahek, where meals were served under the trees in the gardens or in open tents. By then, their wandering through the bazaars had been curtailed by an outbreak of cholera. With the supreme confidence of youth, Henry and Gertrude continued to ride everywhere they wanted to go. Henry had decided views, and tended towards the didactic. He could hold his own against Gertrude, and on at least one occasion they had 'a serious difference of opinion and I sent him away goodnightless!' . . . 'Mr Cadogan and I went for a long walk on Sunday and talked vigorous politics. His views with regard to Home Rule leave much to be desired, but I think I have made him modify his opinions with regard to the Unionists!'

They were most alike in their fascination with Persia and its romance and mystery. Henry read Sufi poetry, and would produce a book from his pocket and read aloud to Gertrude the swooning stanzas of Hafiz, the fourteenth-century Sufi master and Persia's most famous poet, describing that yearning for the Beloved that filled the vacuum between the profane and the divine. One morning they got up before dawn and rode north to a desolate mountainside where stood the Citadel of the Dead. 'Before we had gone far,' Gertrude wrote, 'with a flash and a sudden glitter, the sun leapt up above the snow-peaks, and day rushed across the plain . . . A stony valley led us to the heart of desolation and the end of all things.' Here they found the Tower of Silence, gleaming white, the first stage in the journey of the afterlife, where the Zoroastrians used to leave their corpses for the sun and the vultures to purify and pick clean. 'Here they come to throw off the mantle of the flesh . . . before their souls, passing through the seven gates of the planets, may reach the sacred fire of the sun.'

The two travellers circled the tower, climbed to the platform at the top, and listened to the great silence of the wilderness. Then they descended, and giving the horses their heads, they raced each other across the barren landscape with all the exuberance and passion of youth. She describes the moment, expressing all the happiness and liberation of being in love:

> Life seized us and inspired us with a mad sense of revelry. The humming wind and the teeming earth shouted 'Life! Life!' as we rode. Life! life! the bountiful, the magnificent! Age was far from us

– death far; we had left him enthroned in his barren mountains, with ghostly cities and outworn faiths to bear him company. For us the wide plain and the limitless world, for us the beauty and the freshness of the morning!

One moonlit evening as they lay on the grass by a stream, the air scented with violets and roses, distant music mingling with the hooting of an owl, Henry proposed and Gertrude accepted. She wrote home immediately to tell Hugh and Florence that she and Henry were engaged, and waited for the reply. When, at length, it arrived, she was told that it was impossible. Not only must she break the engagement, she must come home at once – or at least, as soon as Gerald, Billy's brother, would be free to accompany her. It was the end of the happiest time of her life, she felt; and the end of her hopes of marriage to Henry. Hugh had made enquiries, of Sir Frank and others, and had concluded that Henry's income was 'entirely insufficient' to set up a household. As Hugh so devastatingly remarked, Henry's 'charm and intelligence had not prevented him from getting into debt'. Although Hugh did not say so to his daughter, he had heard worse – that Henry was a gambler.

Robust as the Bells' finances seemed to be, Hugh was still a salaried manager-director of the steelworks. His father and uncle held the reins as well as all the capital. Hugh maintained an expensive household of wife and five children in what was still a fairly modest house, Red Barns, and had one son at Eton and another soon to start. Lowthian lived in his five-storey country mansion, Rounton Grange, and maintained his London house at 10 Belgrave Terrace, largely for his own use. The iron industry, in company with other staple industries, had recently undergone a downturn, and profits had begun to fall. Late in 1889 Gertrude had been an interested eavesdropper on a conversation between two men on a train, discussing whether ironmasters were 'making a roaring fortune': she had remarked to Florence, 'They thought they must be, poor deluded wretches; I didn't undeceive them!' Now, in July 1892, her hopes dashed, a broken-hearted Gertrude wrote a most touching letter to Chirol:

Mr Cadogan is very poor, his father I believe to be practically a bankrupt, and mine, though he is an angel and would do anything in the world for me, is absolutely unable to run another household besides his own, which is, it seems to me, what we are asking him to do . . . I hope he will now see Mr Cadogan in London and arrive at least at some conclusion. Meantime, Henry Cadogan and I are not allowed to consider ourselves engaged and I'm afraid the chances of our eventual marriage are very far away somewhere in the future. I write sensibly about it, don't I, but I'm not sensible at all in my heart, only it's all too desperate to cry over – there comes a moment in very evil days when they are too evil for anything but silence . . . it's easier to appear happy if no one knows you have any reason to be anything else. And I care so much . . . I'm forgetting how to be brave, which I always thought I was.

There was nothing for Henry to do but stay on in Persia for a year or two, and try to work his way into a more remunerative post. A lesser soul than Gertrude might have rebelled against her father's decision, but she wrote a letter to Florence that is remarkable for its sense of honour, and even in its extraordinary sympathy for her parents:

Our position is very difficult, and we are very unhappy. We have not seen much of each other . . . since my father's letter we don't feel that we have any right to meet. The thing I can bear least is that you or Papa should ever think anything of him which is not noble and gentle and good. That is all of him I have ever known.

It's very horrid of me to write like this, it will only make you sorry quite uselessly and needlessly. You must not think for a moment that if I could choose I would not have it all over again, impatience and pain and the going which is yet to come. It is worth it all . . . Some people live all their lives and never have this wonderful thing . . . only one may cry just a little when one has to turn away and take up the old narrow life again – Oh Mother, Mother.

There could be no doubt that Gertrude was in love. And Henry may well have truly loved her in return. Perhaps they would have been happy together, he would have given up his gambling and she would have learnt to subject herself to the rigours of his modest career, following him from post to post. But they were not to have the chance. The painful goodbyes were somehow endured, and she returned to Sloane Street, where a loving Florence was waiting to comfort her. A day or two later, Hugh arrived from the north, to fold his beloved daughter in his arms and talk her through her tears.

Subdued for once in her life, Gertrude wrote few letters in the following months. Her feelings were deep, and she was slow to recover. Nonetheless, the spring found her in France, writing home of a romantic garden in Nîmes whose beauty reminded her of a certain garden in Persia, where she had once been so happy:

> Took a carriage and drove to the garden where lies the Temple of Nymphs. The frogs croaked and the little owls screamed in the trees, and the warm scented night with all its sounds was so like those other nights in a far away garden where the owls scream. I cried and cried in the Temple, and filled the Roman baths with tears which no one saw in the dusk.

Not a year after she left Persia, and from a brief illness caused by falling into an icy river while fishing, Henry Cadogan died of pneumonia. A tragic pattern in her love life had been set. Succeed as she might in so many extraordinary ventures, this was an event from which Gertrude would never entirely recover.

Partly to distract her, it was Florence's idea that her stepdaughter publish a travel book, making use of her diaries and almost daily letters home from Persia during the first happy months of her stay there. Gertrude was opposed to the idea, but it is probable that Florence approached the publishing house of Bentley, and in response to their letter Gertrude unenthusiastically capitulated. She wrote to her friend Flora Russell:

> Bentley wishes to publish my Persian things, but wants more of them, so after much hesitation I have decided to let him and I am writing him another six chapters. It's rather a bore and what's more I would vastly prefer them to remain unpublished. I wrote

them you see to amuse myself and I have got all the fun out of them I ever expect to have, for modesty apart they are extraordinarily feeble. Moreover I do so loathe people who rush into print and fill the world with their cheap and nasty work – and now I am going to be one of them. At first I refused, then my mother thought me mistaken and my father was disappointed and as they are generally right I have given way. But in my heart I hold very firmly to my first opinion. Don't speak of this. I wish them not to be read.

Her feelings were as emotional as they were rational, but still her own judgement was probably right. Denison Ross, head of the London School of Oriental Studies and a great admirer of his pupil, was to write the explanatory preface for a later edition. He admitted that in the chapters written in Persia there was 'a something . . . which is wanting from the later ones'. *Persian Pictures* was published anonymously in 1894, a compromise between Florence's wishes and Gertrude's reluctance, and was soon forgotten.

Persia had been made infinitely more interesting to her by her knowledge of the language. But as Florence wrote, 'She had not yet reached the stage in which the learner of a language finds with rapture that a new knowledge has been acquired, the illuminating stage when not the literal meaning only of words is being understood, but their values and differences can be critically appreciated. It was not long before Gertrude was reading Persian poetry by this light.'

Gertrude continued her lessons in London, with a particular view to studying the love poetry of Hafiz. Henry had introduced her to Hafiz's work, and had discussed with her its rhythms and mystical import. The work was begun as a way of keeping alive her love for him. She had determined to produce a book of real value this time: a collection of her translations into English of the poems of Hafiz, together with a biography of the Sufi poet set in the context of his contemporary history. It became, perhaps, a secret monument to Henry.

Denison Ross wrote a preface in which he modestly related that in teaching Gertrude he had had 'the healthy experience of realizing in the presence of such a brilliant scholar my own limitations'; to have pieced together the biography of Hafiz from manuscript sources, he said, was a tour de force, there being no history of Islamic Persia at the time.

The Divan of Hafiz, an anthology of his poems, was published by Heinemann in 1897, the year of the Queen's Diamond Jubilee – and, more sadly for the Bells, of the death of Aunt Mary, provider of so many welcome interludes in Gertrude's life. The book was published to as large an acclaim as a book of poetry can elicit. Edward G. Browne, the greatest authority on Persian literature of his day, said of her translations: 'though rather free, they are in my opinion by far the most artistic, and, so far as the spirit of Hafiz is concerned, the most faithful renderings of his poetry'; and, with the single exception of Edward FitzGerald's paraphrase of the quatrains of Omar Khayyam, 'probably the finest and most truly poetical renderings of any Persian poet ever produced in the English language'.

The intentional vagueness of Hafiz's poetry, the play on words and the musicality of the Persian language in its form, metre and rhyme, all make it almost impossible to translate. Her solution was to write free poetry which could be said to take off from the originals, capturing their essence and function – then soaring up and away. Denison Ross demonstrated the problem, and her solution, in his preface, offering a literal translation of the beginning of one of the poems for comparison with Gertrude's rendering.

The first four lines of his translation read:

> *I will not hold back from seeking till my desire is realized,*
> *Either my soul will reach the beloved, or my soul will leave its body.*
> *I cannot always be taking new friends like the faithless ones,*
> *I am at her threshold till my soul leaves its body.*

Gertrude wrote:

> I cease not from desire till my desire
> Is satisfied; or let my mouth attain

> My love's red mouth, or let my soul expire
> Sighed from those lips that sought her lips in vain.
> Others may find another love as fair;
> Upon her threshold I have laid my head . . .

Particularly poignant are her last lines of the poem, which depart rather noticeably from the original:

> Yet when sad lovers meet and tell their sighs
> Not without praise shall Hafiz' name be said,
> Not without tears, in those pale companies
> Where joy has been forgot and hope has fled.

She was fortunate in her teachers of Persian and Arabic: as well as Denison Ross, there was the eminent linguist S. Arthur Strong, whom she refers to as 'my Pundit'. 'My Pundit kept congratulating me on my proficiency . . . I think his other pupils must be awful duffers! . . . He brought me back my poems [her translations of Hafiz] yesterday – he is really pleased with them.'

All her life Gertrude read and reread both the classical and the modern poets, collecting every edition as it was published, and including poetry in her travelling library. To the surprise and disappointment of Florence and Hugh, after all the praise that was heaped on her as the translator of Hafiz, she appeared to consider her own gift of verse as a secondary pursuit and abandoned it altogether. 'That gift has always seemed to me to underlie all she has written,' said Florence. 'The spirit of poetry coloured all her prose descriptions, all the pictures that she herself saw and succeeded in making others see.' This spirit, thought her stepmother, was a strange and interesting ingredient in a character 'capable on occasion of a very definite hardness, and of a deliberate disregard of sentiment: and also in a mental equipment which included great practical ability and a statesmanlike grasp of public affairs'.

It is perhaps unreasonable to have expected Gertrude to produce more books of poetry as well as her stream of wonderful letters, diaries and books. On this unique occasion the yearning for the unattainable beloved, whether metaphysical or human, struck that chord in her aching soul capable of producing a superlative vein of poetry. It seems that the pure creative power ignited in her was a response to something already out there, but felt within her on a different level. All aspects of her life work were, in a sense, passionate responses: her travel books, her exploration, her archaeology; her learning, especially of languages; her mountaineering, her work for the British Empire; her ultimate wish to recreate an Arab civilization. Reading her translation of Hafiz's poem on the death of his beloved son, it is impossible not to hear the voice of Gertrude, or to draw comparisons with her own cruel loss.

> Good seemed the world to me who could not stay
> The wind of Death that swept my hopes away . . .
> Light of mine eyes and harvest of my heart,
> And mine at least in changeless memory!
> Ah! When he found it easy to depart,
> He left the harder pilgrimage to me!
> Oh Camel-driver, though the cordage start,
> For God's sake help me lift my fallen load,
> And Pity be my comrade of the road!

4

BECOMING A PERSON

In December 1897, at the age of twenty-nine, Gertrude set off with Maurice on the first of her round-the-world voyages. She was devoted to her brother, as were the whole family: he was much liked, too, by the steelmen at Clarence, before the army took over his life and carried him far from Cleveland. They travelled in style, taking state rooms on the Royal Mail steamship *City of Rio de Janeiro*. Maurice had soon asked the captain's permission to mark out a golf course on board, which was a great success with the other passengers. He was the life and soul of the captain's ball, while Gertrude made immediate friends with the children on board and organized a piquet tournament.

Maurice was a tease. He had brought with him a book for Gertrude entitled *Manners for Women*, and took much pleasure in reading improving passages to her while she sat in a deck-chair smoking and staring at the horizon. ' "The Englishwoman of today," ' he read ' "should be able to use a needle with the same skill as she can ride a bicycle" . . . so would Gertrude be sewing on his buttons for him during the journey?' At which she might well have plucked the book out of his hands and thrown it at him.

Back in Yorkshire in June the next year, she returned to her work with the Clarence women, giving travel lectures and arranging events. She played tennis and golf, hunted and fished. On visits to London, she and a group of friends would take long walks on moonlit nights, along the embankment to the Strand, through the City to Tower Bridge, then home to Sloane Street via Holborn

Viaduct and Oxford Street. She kept her old bicycle in the front hall, and rode across Hyde Park to the British Museum, to her Arabic lessons and the London Library, books piled into the basket on the handlebars. She cycled across Kensington Gardens to ice-skate at Prince's Rink, and to her fencing and dancing lessons. When she told her father what hard work it was, peddling against the wind, he sent her a cheque for a new machine. 'I went to the stores this afternoon, mounted my bicycle and rode away on it. It's a dream!' she wrote to him. 'I took it right to the other side of London . . . I have qualms because I feel I have far too many things that I want. It isn't good for me and I should like you to try a system of denial for the next few months.'

In 1901, after prolonged setbacks in the coal, steel and ship-building industries, the ailing Sir Lowthian, now eighty-five, took action to protect the Bell interests. He could see that despite all his efforts, Britain had not achieved the technical advances that Germany had; America and Japan were also surging ahead in the manufacture of iron and steel. He decided to amalgamate his companies with the longtime Bell competitor Dorman Long, in order to provide the necessary resources for the future. The sale of the shares and the chemical companies, together with the amal-gamation of the Bell rail interests with the North East Railway, released huge amounts of money into the family. The grand-children, nephews and nieces received £5,000 each. This good for-tune was no doubt a factor in Gertrude's and and her half-brother Hugo's decision to attend the once-in-a-lifetime event, Lord Cur-zon's durbar in Delhi, to announce the accession of Edward VII as Emperor of India. They would then extend their journey for a further six months: it would be Gertrude's second round-the-world trip.

The event, in January 1903 at the height of Empire, was something that no one who saw it would ever forget. In Delhi, Gertrude and Hugo met up with their party – the Russells, Valentine Chirol and a cousin, Arthur Godman – and everywhere they went, as Gertrude said, they met all the world. They stayed at the Viceroy's superb visitors' camp, and watched the spectacular procession from the best seats. She wrote in her diary:

> It was the most gorgeous show that can possibly be imagined . . .
> First soldiers; then the Viceroy's bodyguard, native cavalry; then
> Pertab Singh at the head of the Cadet Corps, all sons of Rajas;
> then the Viceroy and Lady Curzon, followed by the Connaughts,
> all on elephants; and then a troop of some hundred Rajas on
> elephants, a glittering mass of gold and jewels. The Rajas were
> roped in pearls and emeralds from the neck to the waist, with
> cords of pearls strung over their shoulders, and tassels of pearls
> hanging from their turbans; their dresses were shot gold cloth, or
> gold embroidered velvet. The elephants had tassels of jewels
> hanging from their ears.

But whether she was accepting the gift of a new bicycle or allowing herself the most fabulous of holidays, it often occurred to Gertrude to question how her time and resources should properly be used. She fluctuated between pursuing personal fulfilment and devoting her energies to serving the community for no reward. She would do this all her life. An avowed atheist, she was in the forefront of the new thinking that was looking afresh at man and society. Utilitarianism, expressed as a basis for moral philosophy by Jeremy Bentham, emphasized the pursuit of happiness and the avoidance of pain and distress as the fundamental aims of man. It recognized that only a free man could pursue these aims, but stated that freedom should not be enjoyed without a corresponding sense of personal, moral responsibility to his fellow man and the world around him. John Stuart Mill faced the practical issues of achieving responsible freedom, proposing possible forms of government that would enable society to develop cohesively while the individual remained free.

Questions concerning the way a human being should conduct himself in society were constantly being debated, and the conclusions arrived at applied as the moral dimension to all aspects of life. To what extent, for instance, should a person going out to play tennis worry about whether his time is well spent, about whether he should let his opponent win, or about whether it is right that he should be playing tennis while others are at work? Or should a game of tennis be just a game of tennis?

This was the core of the argument that raged intermittently between Gertrude and Hugo on their travels. At Redcar, before they left for India, they had been visited by the Trinity College don who had taught Hugo at Oxford and fostered his wish to go into the Church. This ambition had come as a surprise to all the Bells, who were what Gertrude called 'happily irreligious', and was a considerable disappointment to Florence, who had wanted Hugo to follow his talent for music and become a concert pianist or composer. Gertrude, rooted in scientific argument, found herself poles apart from Hugo in his religious convictions. Their visitor, the Revd Michael Furse, later the Bishop of Pretoria and of St Albans, was taken around the garden after lunch by Gertrude, who suddenly rounded on him with the question, 'I suppose you don't approve of this plan of Hugo going round the world with me?' 'Why shouldn't I?' asked the perplexed Furse. 'Well,' she replied, 'you may be pretty sure he won't come back a Christian.' 'Why?' 'Oh, because I've got a much better brain than Hugo,' she responded with her usual effrontery. 'A year in my company will be bound to upset his faith.' Furse burst into laughter, then told her that she should not be too sure of it.

It was a challenge she could not resist. Hugo told his parents:

Gertrude is an excellent person for a travelling companion, for besides the fact that she . . . takes a great interest in things Oriental, she also (which is of great interest to me) holds strong atheistic and materialistic views, the effect of which will be, as Michael Furse says, to put me on my mettle. She holds them sometimes aggressively: I think that aggression on her part will probably be met by aggression on mine and that we shall thereupon be rude and quarrel!

The debate was jocular at first, when Gertrude told a story about the former Bishop of London, Dr Temple. He had once taken a cab to Fulham and given a tip that had not satisfied the driver,

who said: 'If St Paul were here he would give me one and sixpence.'
'If St Paul were here,' the Bishop had responded with great dignity,
'he would be at Lambeth, and that is only one shilling to Fulham.'

She and Hugo talked about utilitarianism, Gertrude maintaining
that the pursuit of personal happiness was the most persuasive
motivation for mankind's actions — always remembering that it
must not compromise the happiness of others. People had to use
their brains. Poetry was a better pastime than croquet, she said,
because it was more likely to be of use to the community. To
Hugo, every action was either moral or immoral, and man must
struggle to follow the moral path. When she climbed a mountain,
Gertrude said, it was for her pleasure alone and it hurt nobody — it
was neither moral nor immoral. The debate grew warmer when
she declared that Christ ranked with Muhammad the Prophet and
the Buddha — all great men, but no more than men. Hugo became
upset, Gertrude flippant and more provocative. When she declared
that if the poor got hold of the idea that all men were equal there
would be no more servants, he stalked off, and for a while they
went their separate ways.

Gertrude was an avid sightseer. No temple, museum or ruin
within reachable distance went unviewed by her. Nor did she stop
working on her languages or reading. Denison Ross was startled
one day to receive a telegram from her on the Rangoon leg of the
journey, asking: 'Please send first hemistich of verse ending "a khayru
jalisin fi zaman kitabue".' In whatever distortion of telegraphese the
message arrived, he was able to reply, 'A'azz makanin fiddunya
zahru sabihin', and she was able to complete the verse:

> The finest place in the world is the back of a swift horse,
> And the best of good companions is a book.

Gertrude and Hugo ended their global travels in the United
States and Canada, where Gertrude spent a day or two climbing in
the Rocky Mountains before visiting Chicago. 'We went on a switch-
back that looped the loop. I can't say it was nice,' she wrote to her
parents, '. . . I only knew a rush and a scramble and my hat nearly off.'

*

On her grandfather Lowthian's death in 1904 when Gertrude was thirty-six, Hugh succeeded to the baronetcy and the family upscaled from Red Barns to Rounton Grange. This substantial country house with massive chimney-stacks set in its own 3,000-acre estate had been completed by architect Philip Webb in 1876 as a showpiece of Arts and Crafts architecture. The house, honey-coloured with red pantile roof – a Bell hallmark – was set amongst old trees that Lowthian had not permitted to be cut down. There was hardly a person in the two villages situated on those acres who was not employed at Rounton. The labourers were housed a short walk from the house in a terraced village development, also by Webb. Florence employed several of the daughters of the Clarence steel-workers, training them as housemaids and laundresses, and made sure that the 'rest house', built to give their families a break in the country, was always occupied.

The house, Webb's largest project so far, employed elements of post-medieval decoration and Gothic motifs. A broad staircase spiralled up from the hall, with its enormous fireplace, and an arched gallery ran down one entire side of the house. The drawing-room, with its Adam fireplace and two grand pianos, had a carpet so large that it took eight men to carry it out of doors for its annual beating. Groupings of chairs and tables were arranged across the room to accommodate the largest of house parties. The dining-room, richly decorated by William Morris, featured a tapestry frieze designed by Morris and Burne-Jones to illustrate Chaucer's *Romaunt of the Rose*, executed over several years by the first Lady Bell and her daughters, Hugh's sisters. There was accommodation for a butler, a housekeeper and a chief cook, plus a two-storey laundry and a servants' hall. Every quarter-hour the 'Rounton chimes' rang out from the stableyard. Hugh was soon to introduce a 'motor house' for the chauffeurs and the fleet of Bell cars.

A Christmas list of 1907 in Florence's writing registers twenty staff and their presents: handkerchiefs, brooches, belts, cardigans and hatpins for the women; tie-pins, handkerchiefs and knives for the men. For the family, purses and books, boas, scissor-cases, the *Larousse Encyclopaedia*, gloves and tool-cases, with little wheeled horses and rattles for the babies. In the same year, there are also presents noted for the permanent London staff of four. In 1900, after the death of Lady Olliffe, in whose house it appears the family had always preferred to stay when in the capital, Florence had taken over 95 Sloane Street and redecorated it from top to bottom, even altering the floors. Gertrude, who had her own suite of rooms there, wrote to Chirol on Christmas Day: '95 grows apace. When you come back you will find us established in the most beautiful house in London!' A month later, she was delighted to report that her friend Flora Russell was 'much impressed' by it.

Gertrude was thirty-six by the time the family moved into her grandfather's house. Her life was far from spinsterly, but Rounton expanded her world in two important ways. As co-hostess with Florence, she was able to invite large numbers of people to stay, and her spells in England were now punctuated with friends' and relations' house parties. The social round began in 1906 with a splendid New Year Ball for all their friends and acquaintances.

Immediately she took charge of the extensive garden with its sweeping lawns, daffodil wood, rose garden and two lakes – one of them big enough for boating. She took enormous pleasure in laying out new areas of special plant interest, working with Tavish the Scottish gardener and his team of a dozen assistants, and it was not long before she had turned Rounton into one of the show gardens of England.

Flowers had been precious to her since her ninth birthday, when she acquired her own plot and grew 'primroses and snodrops', her first diary revealing how often she 'went into the gardin' to look at flowers. Once she started writing travel books she gave free rein to her love of wild flowers and their effect in the landscape: describing an ancient wall, for instance, she would dwell on the knots of wild violets tucked into the crevices. The watered desert was astonishing to her, with its miracle of instant colour and scent. 'I pitched my camp in a grove of apricot trees, snowy with flowers and a-hum with bees. The grass was set thickly with anemones and scarlet ranunculus,' she would write; then:

When we reached the level of the Jordan plain, behold, the wilderness had blossomed like the rose. It was the most unforgettable sight . . . waist deep in flowers. I found the loveliest iris I have yet seen – big and sweet-scented and so dark purple that the hanging-down petals are almost black. It decorates my tent now.

Climbing in the Alps, she wrote home to ask her sister to send her a book on alpine flora, so that she could identify the 'entrancing' flowers she saw there. In a Swiss meadow at Glion, she wrote of 'meadows full – full of flowers. Whole hillsides were white as if snow had fallen on them – white with the big single narcissus. I never saw anything so beautiful . . . Isn't it odd how the whole flora changes from one valley to another . . .' Toiling up the lower slopes of the Schreckhorn in 1901, she was distracted by the scent of violets: 'I walked over the tiny alp botanizing while my guides cooked the soup. Every sort of Alpine plant grows on the cultivated alp; I found even very sweet pale violets under the big stones. I had it all to myself.'

When she was staying with her friends the Rosens in Jerusalem in 1899, she fell to 'gardening violently' at the consulate. In her letters to Chirol the frequency with which she mentions plants and gardening suggests they were a shared interest: 'My Japanese trees are coming into flower and all my Syrian roots are coming up finely – when you come home I will present you with a bundle of black irises from Moab!'

She brought back with her, sometimes sent back, the most sensational botanical specimens. Once it was cones of Lebanon cedars – one planted at Rounton, another still visible at Wallington Hall, the seat of the Trevelyan family into which her half-sister Molly married. Another time it was the mandrake, or mandragore, the mysterious plant whose tuberous and divided roots beneath a rosette of leaves resemble the human form. When pulled up the root was thought, from medieval times, to 'shriek' – a sound that was said to drive a man mad. Early drawings show men covering their ears while a dog is chained to the plant; when the mandrake was pulled up, it was the dog that would go mad. Rounton received its own mandrake: 'I am sending you a little packet of seeds,' she wrote home. 'They are more interesting for association's sake than for the beauty of the plant – it is the famous and fabulous mandrake. By the way the root of the mandrake grows to a length of 2 yards, so I should think somebody shrieks when it is dug up – if not the mandrake, then the digger.'

On her world trip with Hugo after the durbar in 1903, she stopped in Tokyo long enough to meet Reginald Farrer, 'who is a great gardener'. Farrer delighted in the restrained beauty of Japanese gardens, disparaging the popular English 'imitations' of the time. Born with a hare lip and having great difficulty in speaking, he covered this deformity with a large black moustache. He came from Clapham in North Yorkshire, not far from the Bells' family estate. He was destined to become one of the world's great plant collectors; he favoured a natural kind of gardening and wrote about it in Wildean prose. He had fallen in love at Balliol with Aubrey Herbert, son of the Earl of Carnarvon. Herbert was now attaché to the British Embassy in Tokyo, and Farrer was one of the Oxford friends he had invited to join him. Farrer had a house there, and travelled with Gertrude and Hugo into rural Japan and Korea. In a letter of 28 May she described him as coming down from Mount Fuji carrying a 'rose pink cyprodium [cypripedium]'. 'Reginald Farrer, the Colliers, and Mr Herbert all came to see us, and carried Hugo off to a tea house to spend the evening in the company of geisha! I wonder how he comported himself.'

The contrast between Gertrude and a geisha was very pronounced, and in his book published the following year, *The Garden of Asia*, Farrer includes a chapter on the lives of Japanese women – no doubt a subject for lively conversation between him and the Bells. The double standard applied to Japanese women – they were either geishas or wives – threw into sharp relief his conclusions about his own countrywomen, who were either boring, in which case suitable as wives, or not boring, in which case not suitable. Gertrude, unmarried at thirty-five, with all her radiant curiosity and energy, was perhaps the catalyst for this idea, with which he remained intrigued all his life.

Gardening before the twentieth century was rather different from gardening as we know it today. The emphasis was on the use of glasshouses, which forced thousands of plants into bloom and enabled the gardens of stately homes and municipal parks to be filled with brightly coloured blocks of flowers in geometric designs, living carpets in borders that could run to hundreds of feet long. In 1877 two million plants cultivated in glasshouses were planted out in London's parks. The champion of hardy-plant gardening – the more natural gardening of today – was the gardener and writer William Robinson, who set up a press for the denunciation of carpet bedding. Robinson, working with Gertrude Jekyll, filled borders with herbaceous perennials, and planted flowers in drifts: producing effects known to this day as 'English garden'.

Farrer was one of the first rock gardeners. Gertrude wanted a rock garden for Rounton, where she would set it around the lake and plant it with the Alpine flowers she had loved on her mountaineering trips. Farrer's and Gertrude's rock gardens were no suburban mounds of rubble with sickly, prickly plants struggling up between the stones. They had both been brought up around areas of limestone quarries, and conceived of something massive, like a natural rockface in whose fissures and crevices flowers blossomed as they did on mountains in the spring. Farrer's *My Rock Garden* was published in 1907, four years after their meeting, but Gertrude had established Rounton's two years previously. Using huge lumps of stone from the quarries in the Cleveland Hills, displaced in the collecting of iron ore, she must have commandeered the services of Rounton's entire garden and stable staff, village helpers included, to build a massive necklace of rocks around the little lake. She then planted them up with quantities of flowers interspersed with clumps of flowering bushes, in which azaleas are particularly apparent in the Bells' family album. She wrote to Chirol in April 1910: 'I have spent most of the afternoons in the rock garden which is a vision of beauty in spite of weather that passes belief for cold and rain. Still, the world is wonderfully beautiful and no matter what the weather I really think there is no such marvel in the world as England in Spring.'

A couple of years later, she was constructing a water garden at another part of the lake. 'If you look with the eye of faith you can see irises blossoming over the stones and mud heaps. It will be lovely,' she told him.

In the summer of 2004, London's National Portrait Gallery mounted an exhibition of portraits of pioneering women travellers called 'Off the Beaten Track'. Gertrude's corner contained a watercolour of her as a teenager by Flora Russell, a map, and the beautiful little theodolite given to her with the Gill Memorial Award by the Royal Geographical Society in 1913. She was the first woman ever to be awarded a prize by this august institution. It was given for her many expeditions and exploratory journeys. The short four-line caption – all that was devoted to her – stated: 'Despite her own achievements she actively opposed British women being given the right to vote.' Technically correct, the statement is nonetheless a crude assessment of her ultimate intentions and one that takes no account of the complex politics of the times, or her position as a daughter of the Industrial Revolution. This oversimplification is often levelled against her and has been partially responsible for the way in which her achievements have been undervalued.

Female suffrage was the moral and intellectual debate of the age, and from the moment of being allowed to join the adults for meals, Gertrude would have heard the issue being discussed passionately, and from all points of view. Hugh and Florence were opposed to it for cogent reasons, but some of their friends, and notably the actress Elizabeth Robins, were adamant in its support. All the Bells agreed with John Stuart Mill, the greatest proponent of women's emancipation of his time, that it was vital for a woman to be a 'Person': it became a family joke that the women seldom felt themselves to be quite enough of a Person.

Florence has been criticized for coming to no conclusions in her book *At the Works*. On the contrary, she arrived at one mighty conviction: 'There will never be more than a certain proportion of women who can carry the immense burden allotted to the workingwoman by the conditions of today.' By 'working-woman' she meant the wives of the working men, and in those twenty-six words lay much of her argument for anti-suffrage.

If Florence influenced Gertrude in anything, it was in the latter's endorsement, strange to us, of the movement against women getting the vote. She had seen for herself, as she accompanied her stepmother on her visits to the working families of Middlesbrough, that these women were already at the limit of their capabilities. Without wives who gave themselves unstintingly to the round-the-clock demands of home and family, that family, and the social structure, fell apart. Many women, as Florence and Gertrude saw, fell by the wayside, many families starved and died, and many men drank themselves to death. Weren't these issues, asked Florence, just as important as parliamentary bills and reforms? How could a Clarence wife leave her children in order to vote, or find the time to read – or, being illiterate, learn to read – so that she could understand the political questions of the day? What could a Clarence wife know of the issues on which she would be asked to vote – Free Trade, the Reform Bill, political corruption, penal reform, Home Rule? These were the questions with which the government of the day was concerned, and the vote, considered today to be a universal human right, was then judged to be a serious business requiring a degree of education and political acumen.

Matters such as health, schooling, men's leisure activities, social services, the Poor Laws, subsistence benefit, the workhouse and almshouses were dealt with by local government, and in these issues Florence and most of the middle-class women she knew were involved up to the hilt. They dreaded a reaction to the demands of the suffragists – who kept within the law – and the suffragettes – who broke it – that would bring swift retribution and destroy the advances that women had already made.

If anything tipped Gertrude into action, other than family pressure, it was the militancy of Christabel Pankhurst, who by 1904 was leading women against what she called 'the noxious character of male sexuality'. The suffragettes were engaged in a sex war, and employed methods tantamount to terrorism. Pankhurst's supporters attacked property, smashing windows and train carriages, trampled flowerbeds and slashed paintings of nude women in galleries. They denounced marriage as legalized prostitution, rioted, and worked in gangs, tearing the clothes off their male victims and horse-whipping them. They poured tar and acid into letter-boxes and sent packages of sulphuric acid to Lloyd George, later attempting to burn down his house. They assaulted men who happened to resemble the Prime Minister, Herbert Asquith. On 28 October 1908 Gertrude wrote: 'Last night I went to a delightful party at the Glenconners' and just before I arrived (as usual) 4 suffragettes set on Asquith and seized hold of him. Whereupon Alec Laurence in fury seized two of them and twisted their arms until they shrieked. Then one of them bit him in the hand till he bled . . . When he told me the tale he was steeped in his own gore.' She evidently regretted missing the drama, but perhaps it was providential. Disdaining violence though she did, one wonders whether she might have been tempted to join the fray and break a vase over the head of a suffragette. In any scuffle, the publicity could only have been damaging for her.

Apart from Florence's concerns about the strains on the wives of working men, and the damage being done to the women's cause by the militant suffragettes, there were sound reasons for the Bells to resist the demands of the noisy campaign for all women to have the vote. For all that the Reform Bill of 1832 and its successors had increased voters from a paltry 500,000 to 5 million by 1884, the vote was still limited to men of property, so that only a quarter of the men in Britain had the vote. When the franchise was denied to so many men, Parliament could not have contemplated giving the vote to all women.

The solution might seem to be clear – to give the vote to all adults, regardless of sex or property. But this would have swamped the system with voters who paid none of the taxes and would demand most of the benefits. There was much discussion about the possibility of giving the vote only to women of property, but under the current law, the possessions of wives automatically became their husband's property on marriage. So married women would be denied the vote, while much of the franchise would have been granted to widows, spinsters and prostitutes.

As independent and rational women such as Florence Nightingale felt, women's suffrage could not be addressed until the property laws were transformed. The sticks and stones of the suffragettes would be as nothing to 20 million working men marching to retain their property rights. To Liberal reformers such as the Bells, there were more pressing social issues than the lengthy battle to redress the franchise balance of the nation.

Gertrude joined the movement against women's suffrage in 1908 and became a member of the Anti-Suffrage League. This became her first work, and being the person she was, she could do nothing by halves. She entered the debate with the zest for winning the argument that she had exercised at Oxford, and given her talent for effective administration it is likely that it was Gertrude who organized the first collection of 250,000 signatures for the anti-suffrage petition of 1909. But she nonetheless betrays a lack of 'mission' in the affairs of the anti-suffrage movement that suggests she had taken on the work largely to please Florence. Of the first meeting of the League, she wrote:

> We have Lady Jersey as chairman ... I have been obliged to become honorary secretary which is most horrible ...
>
> Life was nearly wrecked for a month by arranging an Anti-Suffragist meeting in Middlesbrough on the largest scale. We did it and made a great splash ... It was very interesting but it took an appalling amount of time and meant hours of letter writing and canvassing.

Later in life, in Iraq, her work for Muslim women would be considerable. She helped found the first girls' school in Baghdad, led the fund-raising for a women's hospital, and arranged the first series of lectures for a female audience by a woman doctor. Gertrude was to look back on her anti-suffrage days with mixed feelings: her old friend Janet Hogarth commented that Gertrude was 'amused by her own attitude' at that former time.

Her involvement in the movement had played itself out by the end of the decade. New all-absorbing interests were about to take her over: she was becoming obsessed by archaeology as a motive for her desert adventures, and she would soon be deeply in love. The gauche student had become a supremely civilized and able woman; she was wealthy, she was single, she had no children to preoccupy her. Her abilities spanned the spectrum, from poetry writing to administration, from pioneering adventure and sportsmanship to archaeology. She possessed a rare grasp of world history and contemporary political debate alongside a love of pretty clothes. She spoke six languages, and could write a good letter or hold a discussion in any of them. And all of this was well grounded in the gentler human qualities: a deep sense of family, of landscape and architecture – a love of life itself. Few have rivalled her in the sheer range of her abilities. As a 'Person' she had come to fulfil the highest aspirations that John Stuart Mill had envisaged for women.

5

MOUNTAINEERING

From childhood, Gertrude had possessed an extraordinary vitality of both mind and body. Though small, she was strong and athletic; she needed quantities of exercise, the harder the better. She hunted, she danced, she bicycled, shot, fished, gardened and skated, and on holiday she was a tireless sightseer. She could not bear to be thought self-indulgent, and by the time she was thirty, with most of her contemporaries committed to marriage and motherhood, she was ready for a new challenge that would prove that she was not just drifting. And then she discovered climbing. Of her first important mountain ascent, in 1899, she wrote: 'It was awful – perfectly fearful! It was absolutely sheer down and I had practically never been on a rock before. I think if I had known exactly what was before me I should not have faced it . . . However, I didn't let on.'

On a family holiday in the French Alps two years previously, she had promised that she would come back to climb the Meije, whose snow-covered ridge towered above the village of La Grave and the little mountain inn where the Bells had been staying. The family had looked at her askance. The mountain was the reserve of serious climbers, a very different proposition from anything she had yet encountered. And when she came to ascend this 13,068-foot mountain, she found it most convenient to do so in her under-clothes. There were then no 'right clothes' for women mountaineers, and she would take off her skirt at the point where she and her guides roped up, then put it on again as soon as they descended back on to the glacier.

For wealthy late-Victorian families, a summer holiday in the Alps represented a romantic and exotic interlude comparable to today's winter break on a celebrity island such as Barbados or St Bart's. Healthy mountain walks, healthy meals, hard cycling, boat trips on the lakes and card games before bed were all on the agenda. The Bells, well travelled as they were, were no different from everyone else in this respect, and although Gertrude took mountain walking to its limits, that is all the Alps meant to her until almost the end of their fortnight at La Grave.

It was 1897, the Queen's Diamond Jubilee year, marked more solemnly for the Bells by the death of Mary Lascelles, Florence's sister. Mary had been a witness to every stage of Gertrude's adolescence, had attempted to feminize the 'Oxfordy' young woman in the intensely social milieu of Bucharest, and had been the worried observer of her love affair with Henry Cadogan. Her death came barely a month after Gertrude had been staying with them again, this time in Berlin, where Sir Frank was the British ambassador. Four months of mourning had scarcely transformed their distress into resignation, and Hugh and Florence decided they all needed a holiday. They would assemble in force in August. Florence had been in Potsdam visiting the Lascelles and would meet them in Paris. Hugh, Gertrude, Hugo, Elsa and Molly would gather in London, join Florence, and then they would all travel in carefully staged cultural steps to the Massif des Écrins in the Dauphiné, visiting the galleries of Lyon and the churches of Grenoble en route.

Once there, Hugh and Gertrude got up early and bicycled or walked. Florence at first retired to bed with a bad chill. The others liked to sit in the sun and drink hot chocolate. Father and daughter were ideally suited for the gentler excursions, enjoying the views and the flowers, talking and getting agreeably lost together. Hugh decided to join Gertrude in half-walking, half-climbing a local peak, the Bec de l'Homme. They scrambled up a steep, edelweiss-covered slope to the foot of the glacier, then roped themselves together and climbed for half an hour. They breakfasted on the arête, admiring the view, then descended. This was enough for Hugh, but Gertrude was soon venturing further and coming back later. She arranged her own expedition with the local mountain guides Mathon and Marius, up a minor peak (3,669 feet) about 400 feet below the Meije summit, and almost all of it a far easier climb than the Meije presented. Gertrude wrote in her diary on 7 August: 'Elsa and Papa stayed on the Col while the guides and I went up the Pic de la Grave, cutting steps in the ice for 3½ hours . . . Papa and Elsa started away back to the Refuge by themselves.'

Just before the end of the holiday she went over the Brèche, the guides steering her away from the extreme rock and ice route. She slept the night up at the mountain refuge, two hours' walk from the inn. The next morning, in high spirits, she ran down the last slope back into La Grave. 'She proudly strode back into the village . . . between her guides, well pleased with herself,' wrote Florence, wrapped in coats and shawls on the terrace on her first day up. At thirty, Gertrude had discovered the thrill and danger of climbing, and the die was cast. When the Bells followed their luggage out of the little hotel, she knew she would be back.

She fulfilled her promise a couple of seasons later, having been round the world in the meantime. She came on alone to La Grave from Bayreuth, where she and the musical Hugo had been joined by Frank Lascelles and his daughter Florence, as well as Gertrude's dear 'Domnul' from Romania, now Sir Valentine Chirol, who did his level best to dissuade her from her dangerous new adventures. It was not unusual at the time for male climbers, often British university students on holiday, to tackle the Alps without experience even of rock climbing at home, as long as they could find good guides. Crampons would not be in use for nearly a decade, and even then would be thought seriously unsporting. Karabiners had not been invented, any more than had nylon. Ropes, to be of any use, had to be thick and heavy (and grew heavier when saturated with water). Without any modern aids, and no interim climbing experience, Gertrude was as much of a novice as she had been in '97. Still, perhaps, in an operatic frame of mind, she met up with Mathon and Marius and committed herself to climb the Meije with them, weather permitting, on 29 August.

They spent the preceding couple of nights in the refuge, and the first day on a practice climb. As it was getting dark, a young Englishman called Turner joined them with his guide, Rodier. Gertrude went out to watch the sunset and gazed with some awe at the Meije rearing above them, a mass of sheer cliffs and forbidding shadows. By 8 p.m. all five were packed on to and under the sleeping shelf. With straw for a mattress and her cloak as a pillow, Gertrude declared herself 'very comfortable', but spent the four-hour night wide awake, no doubt speculating on her proximity to Turner, the two of them packed side by side 'as tight as herrings'. Soon after midnight she was washing in the tumbling river under the stars, and then she and Marius followed Mathon's lantern up to the snow line. At one-thirty the moonlight was bright enough for them to rope up and start over the Glacier du Tabuchet. At this point, Gertrude divested herself of her skirt. She still had no climbing trousers — 'I gave my skirt to Marius, Mathon having said that I couldn't possibly wear it. He was quite right, but I felt very indecent.'

Having crossed the Brèche from north to south, they reached the Promontoire, a table of rock on which they rested for ten minutes. After climbing — 'most pleasantly' — a long chimney, they were on the steep Grand Pic ridge. At a couple of places Mathon and Marius simply pulled Gertrude up like a parcel.

So far it had been fairly easy, but now came the moment of initiation. 'We had about two hours and a half of awfully difficult rock,' she wrote later, '. . . perfectly fearful. The first half hour I gave myself up for lost. It didn't seem possible that I could get up all that wall without ever making a slip . . . but presently it began to seem quite natural to be hanging by my eyelids over an abyss.'

By the time they reached the famously tricky Pas du Chat Gertrude was supporting her own weight and managing so well that she didn't realize she had completed one of the most difficult manoeuvres of the climb. They reached the Grand Pic at 8.45 a.m., which left just the Cheval Rouge to negotiate. Fifteen feet of almost perpendicular rock, its name derives from the necessity to climb it astride. That completed, there was a twenty-foot overhang, then the summit.

Mathon, ahead of her, suddenly snagged and broke the cord of the ice-axe that was tied to his wrist. Slicing the air as it flew past her, it winged its way into the eerie silence of the void below. And then they were on the summit of the 13,000-foot Meije in the hot sunshine, with an incomparable view all around them. There they were joined by Turner and Rodier.

In half an hour Mathon was shaking her awake. The way down was longer than the way up, and the going would be just as hard. This time they would all do it together. Halfway down the Grand Pic, the guides fastened a double rope to an iron bolt and let Gertrude and Turner down on to a small ledge. Here they sat, side by side, their boots dangling over a vertiginous drop. The next bit – 'very nasty', Gertrude thought – had to be done without the double rope. She was now at the Brèche, another part of which she had climbed two years before, and was not expecting what turned out to be the worst moments of the entire venture. Mathon, roped to her and going on ahead, suddenly vanished around a corner of rock. She waited, and presently she felt a tug on the rope and heard his voice: 'Allez, Mademoiselle.' In a letter to her parents: 'There were two little lumps to hold on to on an overhanging rock and there was La Grave beneath and there was me in mid-air and Mathon round the corner holding the rope tight – but the rope was sideways of course – that's my general impression of those ten minutes.'

Three more hours of unrelenting concentration and she was safely down on the glacier again, being handed back her skirt. Mr Turner, she slyly noted, was 'awfully done'. Only climbers know how a long day on the mountain can reduce one to a mixture of tears and exultation, how one can at the same time ache for sleep and want to relive every moment of the danger just past. Shaking, no doubt, in every limb, and feeling a tumult of emotions, she trudged down into the village with Mathon and Marius. There, to her surprise, Gertrude found the guests and staff of the inn stamping their feet on the frozen doorstep, waiting to congratulate her. They slapped her on the back and let off a fusillade of firecrackers to celebrate this, her first ascent. She fell into bed and slept for eleven hours, drank five cups of tea on waking and sent a telegram to Red Barns: 'Meije traversee'.

Gertrude always had to have a project. Now she had cut her teeth on the Meije, she went on, after a few days' practice on less challenging rocks, to tackle the highest summit of the southern French Alps, the Barre des Écrins. It was a huge challenge for a climber as inexperienced as she was, but she was sure she would prove herself on the 13,422-foot peak – officially categorized as *extrême*. As a concession to the risky endeavour, she had now acquired a pair of men's trousers, which she wore tightly belted under her skirt; so her diary account of each climbing day still started: 'Skirts off and up the rock!'

Gertrude and her guides spent the night of 31 August in the refuge, together with another climber, Prince Louis of Orléans – 'a nice little boy with a giggle' – and his porter, Faure, who cooked his dinner. She read Edward Whymper's account of his first ascent up the Écrins until it grew dark, then sat talking until bedtime with Prince Louis and some German late arrivals. They set off at 1.10 a.m. Accidents happened that day, perhaps due to the intense cold. Marius dropped his axe, and she sat on her hands to try to keep them warm while Faure went down to retrieve it. Once she slipped and fell on her back on to the ice, but was caught on the rope by Mathon: both cut their hands, he badly. She took some photographs, her numb fingers fumbling with the camera. Bitter winds drove clouds of snow around them at midday, delaying the descent from the peak. It was nearly three in the afternoon when they ate their lunch on the glacier – bread and jam, with sardines. On the way down from there, for a time, Mathon lost the way, and she twisted her foot painfully on some loose stones. She had ripped her trousers to bits on the climb, and by the time she got down she was frozen. 'I was now in rags, so I put on my skirt for decency – at least Mathon did, for I couldn't feel at all with my fingers.' When they got back to the inn, they had been nineteen hours on the Écrins – rather too long, even for her.

This was not the end of her climbing for that year, but her lack of interest in personal publicity has led to some confusion among her biographers about her precise programme. After days starting soon after midnight and ending in mountain huts late in the evening, it is unlikely that she kept her diary consistently or wrote letters home. If she did, some are missing, and even the Alpine Club, the oldest climbing club of all, has no very accurate record of her achievements.

For the climbing season of 1900, Gertrude chose the Swiss Alps. She spent happy hours in Chamonix with her two new guides, Ulrich and his brother Heinrich Führer, studying charts and talking their way through her new project. She had decided to tackle Mont Blanc, at 15,771 feet the highest summit in the Alps. Its white dome, she explained, mocked her from across Lake Geneva. Although not the most difficult climb, it is a serious proposition and physically demanding. To date, more than a thousand climbers have been killed in the attempt. She climbed it only a year after the Meije; a well known contemporary mountaineer was to confide to the Alpine Club that his most vivid recollection of his ascent of Mont Blanc was the effort required to follow Miss Bell. Her fame as a mountaineer was beginning to spread. As she wrote home at about that time, 'I am a Person! And one of the first questions everyone seems to ask everyone else is "Have you ever met Miss Gertrude Bell?"'

During the seasons 1899–1904 she became one of the most prominent women climbers in the Alps. In conquering the classic peak of Mont Blanc, she was following in the footsteps of an extraordinary Frenchwoman, Marie Paradis, who had climbed it almost a hundred years earlier, in 1808. In fact, the history of women mountaineers had begun as early as 1799, when a Miss Parminter made several Alpine ascents, but no others climbed Mont Blanc until the 1880s, when Meta Brevoort and Lucy Walker competed to bag the maximum number of peaks and passes. Gertrude's contribution in the field of mountaineering was to notch up many achievements in a total of only five seasons – especially remarkable given that climbing was just one interest among so many. Seen in the context of her whole life, it was little more than a brief craze, a hobby she took up for a while, less important to her than travelling, learning languages, archaeology or photography, but more important, perhaps, than her rock gardening, fencing and hunting.

With the Führers she went on that season to climb two other peaks in the Mont Blanc range, the Grépon and the Dru. And in spite of remaining aloof from journalists and photographers, she became rather boastful among her own circle, writing with over-weening confidence of her prowess in this new field: 'Ulrich is as pleased as Punch and says I'm as good as any man, and from what I see of the capacities of the ordinary mountaineer, I think I am . . . I rather hanker after the Matterhorn and must try to fit it in . . . Guess I can manage any mountain you like to mention.'

She was riding for a fall, but she was so natural and agile a climber, combining such strength and courage, that it would be some time before the reckoning. In 1901, she met Ulrich and Heinrich again, this time in the Bernese Oberland. At seventy miles, the longest range in the Swiss Alps, it offered the most complex concentration of major ice routes. And this time, according to the diaries of an admirer, one Lady Monkswell, Gertrude had acquired a blue climbing suit with trousers. She never wore it, however, off the mountain, and still decorously changed back into her skirt at the base hut. From a written request to Molly in London for 'two gold pins for my necktie, and thick black garters' it is clear that her trim and masculine appearance on the mountains set the fashion for the women skiers of the next couple of decades.

Her first ambition was to climb the Schreckhorn, which lifts its two streaming peaks against the sky like enormous waves just before they break. The high point on a long narrow ridge of crags, it is one of the most rugged and difficult of all 13,000-foot peaks in the European Alps, primarily due to the 2,000-foot rock tower that forms its ice-bound summit. It is dominated only by the immense razor of the Finsteraarhorn, and even with modern equipment is still considered too hard for most mountaineers.

At the mountain hut at the Baregg, where she and her guides spent the first night, she was joined by two cheerful young men, Gerard and Eric Collier, together with their guides, and much enjoyed the evening. They all started up the mountain together soon after midnight. She appears from a letter home to have vaulted up the first snow couloirs and small arêtes without turning a hair. Then: 'I was beginning to think that the Schreckhorn had an absurd reputation, but the hour of arête from the saddle to the top made me alter my opinion. It's a capital bit of rock climbing . . . a couple of very fine bits of climbing in it . . . thoroughly enjoyable!' She beat Gerard and Eric to the top by fifteen minutes, glissaded down in high spirits, and returned to the hut much looking forward to lunch, only to discover three Frenchmen burning her wood and drinking her tea. She gave them a piece of her mind, then dodged back outside to change into her skirt. After their rapid departure, she settled down to discuss with the Führers a wild ambition she had conceived: to climb the virgin north-east face of the Finsteraarhorn. It had been tried three times, unsuccessfully. They would work up to it, said Ulrich, probably swallowing hard, and for the moment they would keep this ambition a deadly secret.

Meanwhile, it was time to apply herself to the main purpose of the visit: to become the first mountaineer to climb, systematically, the peaks of the Engelhörner range. This, a romantic but horrendous skyline of small limestone peaks, is famous for its preponderance of perpendicular routes. Conan Doyle could find no wilder place to set the disappearance of Sherlock Holmes than the nearby Reichenbach Falls, where the torrent, swollen by melting snow, disappears in a cloud of spray into an abyss of black rock. She planned to apply herself methodically to one peak after another over the course of a fortnight. With the Führers as her guides, she would make several first ascents of what had hitherto been considered impossible challenges. She wrote home: 'I am enjoying myself madly!'

She met up with the jolly Collier family in her hotel at Rosenlaui, and joined them for a game of cricket using pine branches for stumps and their butterfly nets to fish the balls out of the river. Temporarily driven out of the higher mountains by a heavy snowfall, Ulrich took Gertrude through her paces, pitting her against the most difficult rockfaces he could find at the lower levels. He led her up awkward gullies and set her to hammer in nails, sling ropes and cut rock steps. She retained enough energy to climb a small crag that had not been climbed before, and to build a cairn on top. Ulrich was sufficiently impressed to agree to her daunting programme.

Over the course of those two weeks Gertrude climbed seven virgin peaks, one of them first-class, and two 'old' peaks, all of them new routes or first ascents. One of these was christened after her and remains in all the Engelhörner literature to this very day: Gertrudspitze – Gertrude's Peak – situated between Vorderspitze and Ulrichspitze. At her personal best and with those successes behind her, on 6 and 7 September she undertook the most difficult ascent of the year: the unclimbed first-class traverse of the Urbachthaler Engelhorn, the Great Engelhorn itself.

Gertrude and her two guides began the climb from the tiny valley on the west side, the Ochsental. At the north, east and south this desolate place is surrounded by precipitous walls of polished rock. They proposed to start at the southern end, a route that local guides and a couple of expert climbers had assessed as impossible. 'We decided on a place where the rock wall was extremely smooth, but worn by a number of tiny water channels, sometimes as much as 3 inches deep by 4 across. These gave one a sort of handhold and foothold.'

As they set off, the snow started to fall. It took them forty-five minutes to climb the first hundred feet, and in one place they came up against a six-foot wall without handholds. Standing on Heinrich's shoulders, Ulrich reached a more promising rockface, but in the meantime the snow had changed to thick sleet. By luck they found a deep cave and breakfasted, then carried on in the rain until they faced a smooth arête which gave no holds at all. They retreated, traversed and tried again in another place. Climbing cautiously up a narrow couloir and a chimney of broken rock, they found themselves at the top of the pass. On one side lay the row of four peaks they had climbed previously; on the other, two peaks – the first, the Klein Engelhorn, blocking the view of the highest, the Urbachthaler Engelhorn itself. The way up the Engelhorn, of which she could see the top half, was by a path used only by chamois deer. Neither the north nor the south side of the saddle ahead had ever been climbed. But now the weather turned against them, the snow came down thick and wet, and with great disappointment they decided they could do no more that day. They let themselves down the rockface in torrents of melting snow that ran into their collars, sleeves and boots. At dawn on the 7th, they started again, in perfect sunshine.

The Klein Engelhorn, which hid the ascent to the summit, was itself partly masked by a buttress of rock which they climbed easily enough. But when the lesser peak came into view it was as daunting a rock as she had yet seen.

> The lower third [of the Klein Engelhorn] was composed of quite smooth perpendicular rocks, the next piece of a very steep rock wall with an ill-defined couloir or two, the top of great upright slabs with deep gaps between them. The great difficulty of it all was that it was so exposed, you couldn't ever get yourself comfortably wedged into a chimney, there was nothing but the face of the rock and up you had to go.

They crawled their way forwards and upwards, scrabbled up a shallow crack, then halted. They were at the bottom of a perfectly smooth overhang. Their position was precarious in the extreme. Ulrich climbed on to Heinrich's shoulders and groped to the end of his reach without finding a single handhold. For a minute or two they must have hung there, motionless; then Gertrude offered to take Ulrich's place, standing on Heinrich's shoulders, and Ulrich could try again, standing on hers. The minutes ticked by as they manoeuvred themselves, inch by inch, into position, only their gasps and muffled exclamations breaking the frozen silence. Stacked one above the other, Ulrich's boots digging into Gertrude's shoulders, he reached up again – and still found no handhold. Gritting her teeth, she stretched every muscle and sinew of her five feet five and a half inches to give him another inch and a half. That fraction more height allowed him to find the smallest of cavities, and with all his formidable strength he began slowly to raise himself on his fingertips alone. It was the only move available to him, but with no foothold to help him lift his body, it should have been a fatal one. Gertrude, suffering silently below him, understood what was going to happen. As his foot left her shoulder she raised her arm, extended it and made a platform for his boot. Gertrude wrote: 'He called out, "I don't feel at all safe – if you move we are all killed." I said, "All right, I can stand here for a week."'

With the utmost care, Ulrich struggled up to a safe ledge, and then it was Gertrude's turn. Last on the rope but now in second place, she could not be lifted: the rope snaked down from Ulrich to Heinrich below her. She could, however, hold on to that rope for dear life, and by massive exertion she managed the next nine feet, to join Ulrich on the ledge above. Now Heinrich had to do the same, with two ropes but from five feet lower down. He could not manage it. 'The fact was, I think, that he lost his nerve, anyhow, he declared that he could not get up ... there was nothing to do but to leave him.'

After they had rearranged the ropes, Heinrich tied himself on to the rockface, and grimly waited for their return. Ulrich and Gertrude carried on up the next slab, but just a few feet from the top they reached a sticking place and could get no further. Ulrich, looking thunderous, came down past Gertrude and told her they must try again from lower down. They were now on the opposite side of the mountain from where Heinrich hung, waiting. They edged across a precipice and came to a chimney. Here she wedged herself in as tightly as she could, and Ulrich climbed from her shoulders. Then, suddenly, it was done. They had reached the top of the Klein Engelhorn. One more problem assailed them when the wet rope by which they were letting themselves down became trapped between rocks and Ulrich had to return to the top of the chimney to release it. Twice it stuck fast, and twice he climbed back. Finally he threw it down to Gertrude and came down without it. There was some complicated rope work to do when they reached Heinrich, but they got to the bottom of the buttress, back to where the serious climbing had begun. Looking back on four hours of the hardest climbing it is possible to do, she found it incredible that so much had been endured in so short a time.

With fingers numb from the morning's exposure, anyone else

would have called it a day. Gertrude, however, had decided to get to the highest peak, the Urbachthaler Engelhorn, and get there she would. Heinrich appears to have joined them, under duress; he had probably expected to be home by nightfall, and being trumped by Gertrude on the precipice cannot have been pleasant for him. The three of them ate their picnic lunch and then, bypassing the Klein Engelhorn, took the arête up to the summit used by the deer. 'This proved quite easy – it has not been done before, however,' Gertrude noted.

By 7 p.m. they were down at the foot of the rocks once more. It was too dark now to think of descending into the valley, so they decided to sleep at a shepherd's hut known to the Führers. It was for her a kind of idyll, an innocent and charming experience. The chalet, nestling in the mountainside, was surrounded by rushing cataracts. Inside, three taciturn, pipe-smoking shepherds shared the accommodation with a family of large pigs. A fire was lit and the climbing party were given the most delicious bread and milk that she had ever tasted. Afterwards she climbed up into the hayloft, wrapped herself in a blanket and a duvet of hay and slept for eight hours, until she was woken by the grunting of the pigs. She was almost reluctant to leave, staying to watch the safe arrival of some goats that had been out all night. At 7.30, she swung off down the mountain path with Ulrich — Heinrich having vanished at dawn — and they conversed with the intimacy that shared danger brings. At the village of Innertkirchen he took her home and introduced her to his seventy-year-old father. 'It was an enchanting house,' she wrote, 'an old wooden chalet dated 1749, with low rooms and long rows of windows, with muslin curtains and geranium pots in them. All spotlessly clean.'

They sat down to eat. Her appetite was enormous: she consumed bread, cheese, bilberry jam and eggs. She had never had two more delightful Alpine days, she told Hugh and Florence: 'What do you think is our fortnight's bag? Two old peaks. Seven new peaks – one of them first class and four others very good. One new saddle, also first class. The traverse of the Engelhorn, also new and first-class. That's not bad going, is it!'

And then, the fortnight over, it was back to Redcar and the autumn rain, the Mothers' Meetings, and her adventures relived to the accompaniment of magic lantern slides for the benefit of the Clarence wives.

She was in Switzerland again in 1902, to hold Ulrich to his promise to take her up the Finsteraarhorn. She discovered that her reputation had grown. To her great pleasure the guard on the train asked her if she were the same Miss Bell who had climbed the Engelhorn the previous year. Now, in the same Rosenlaui inn, she ran into a rival, and one who sharpened her ambitions. She wrote:

> There is another climbing woman here, Frl. Kuntze – very good indeed she is, but not very well pleased to see me as I deprive her of Ulrich Führer with whom she has been climbing. She has got a German with her, a distinguished climber from Berne, and I sat and talked to them this afternoon when they came in . . . They have done several things in the Engelhorn but the best thing hereabouts remains to be done.

The 'best thing hereabouts' was the Finsteraarhorn. Gertrude was so intent on its conquest that she took in her stride the first of the 'impossibles' that Ulrich had decided they would do together, the Lauteraarhorn–Schreckhorn traverse. It would be a first ascent. On 24 July they had climbed up to the high ridge when, somewhat comically, they came face to face with the formidable Fräulein Helene Kuntze, who had also determined to build her cairn on the top and get her name in the record books. It appears that there was an acrimonious exchange between the two ladies, but the laurels went to Gertrude. Amused and on her mettle, she achieved the first ascent without much difficulty, rather to her surprise. According to the *Alpine Journal*, it remains technically her most important climb.

Now she had truly earned her attempt on the Finsteraarhorn, the highest mountain in the Oberland. The first ascent had been made in 1812, but the north-east face had never been climbed, and it was this new and difficult route that she and Ulrich had cautiously been considering for two years. Sharp as a blade, this remote and bad-tempered mountain rises perpendicular to a razor ridge at

14,022 feet, its majestic steeple point visible for a hundred miles. Solitary and far from civilization, it is notorious for its bad weather and frequent avalanches. Experienced climbers had turned away from the challenge that this 35-year-old woman and her guide now set themselves. This was to be Gertrude's most dangerous mountain exploit. For the next twenty-five years, it would be regarded as one of the greatest expeditions in the history of Alpine climbing.

For practice, she and the Führers polished off the Wellhorn arête, with intense cold the only problem. Then she went with Ulrich for an inspection walk of the rock conditions on the Wetterhorn, an unconventional approach on to the Finsteraarhorn but one that he thought might get them off to a good start. This morning I started out at 5.30 to – well, Ulrich calls it examining the movement of rocks, it means that you go up and see if a stone falls on you and if it doesn't you know you can go up that way . . . We went under a glacier fall, where I examined the movement of a stone on my knee . . . it hurt.'

They lost twenty-four hours in trying this approach, and started again the next day. On a perfect evening, they arrived at the hut early, and Gertrude wandered off across the grass without a coat, turning over stones to admire the clumps of sweet pale violets. At 1.35 a.m. they left the hut, the first object being the unstable arête before them, rising from the glacier in a series of angled gendarmes and towers. The great points are continually over-balancing and tumbling down . . . they are all capped with loosely poised stones, jutting out and hanging over and ready to fall at any moment.' Putting her hand into a crack, she loosened a crumbling two-foot-square rock. It fell on top of her and knocked her skidding down the ice until she managed to arrest her fall at a tiny ledge. 'I got back on my feet without the rope, which was as well for a little later I happened to pass the rope through my hands and found that it had been cut half through about a yard from my waist.'

Now with a shorter rope, she toiled on up the arête, while the angle grew steeper, and below them, ominous black clouds began to boil up from the west. They could see the top of the arête still far above, and the summit of the mountain beyond. At first they were encouraged, but another hour passed without much progress, the weather getting worse by the minute. The snow began to fall, and they were still a thousand feet from the summit when the way narrowed to a single pinnacle, a terrifying prospect with a twenty-foot overhang. If they managed to climb the pinnacle, Ulrich thought, they should be able to make it from there to the summit. In any case, there was no alternative.

Meanwhile the wind strengthened, and a thick mist began to rise up from the valley. To get to the pinnacle, they had to creep along the knife edge of a col. Having managed that, they tied Ulrich's rope to a rock, then lowered him gingerly on to a sloping ledge below the overhang, from which he would attempt to climb. He tried for a few minutes and gave up in despair: not only did the rockface slope outwards as well as downwards, but it was brittle and flaky. Next they tried the far side of the tower, where an almost vertical couloir of glassy ice ran upwards from the foot. This way, too, proved impossible. Although only fifty feet from the top of the arête, they were now in a desperate situation. There was only one option left, and it was a grim one: to turn back down the precipice in what was now appalling weather. The wind was bringing down upon them a continual avalanche of thin snow, and half an hour into the descent the mist was so thick that they could see nothing beyond the rock in front of their faces. She wrote: 'I shall remember every inch of that rock face for the rest of my life.'

They successfully negotiated a vertical chimney, to emerge onto a narrow ledge sloping steeply downwards. From there, they roped themselves one by one to the rock, then tumbled down eight otherwise impassable feet on to sheer and slippery snow. They had the fixed rope to hold on to, but they were blinded by fog, and they felt as if they were plunging to their deaths. It was now nearly 6 p.m. They struggled on until eight, by which time a storm was raging.

We were standing by a great upright on the top of a tower when suddenly it gave a crack and a blue flame sat on it for a second.

My ice axe jumped in my hand and I thought the steel felt hot
through my woollen glove – was that possible? Before we knew
where we were the rock flashed again . . . we tumbled down a
chimney, one on top of the other, buried our ice axe heads in
some shale and hurriedly retreated from them. It's not nice to
carry a private lightning conductor in your hand.

They could go no further that night, and would have to spend
the hours of darkness halfway down a precipice in the thick of the
storm. They had no choice. They squeezed themselves into a crack
on the rockface, Gertrude finding just room enough to wedge
herself into the back of it. Ulrich sat on her feet, to keep them
warm, with Heinrich below, both of them with their feet in their
knapsacks. They tied themselves individually on to the rock above
their heads in case one or other of them should be struck by
lightning and fall out of the crack. They could shift their position
by only an inch or two, and discomfort soon became agony. The
golden rule is to take no brandy because you feel the reaction more
after. I knew this and insisted on it.' She fell asleep 'quite often', to be
woken by thunderclaps and flashes, impressed in spite of everything
by the power of the storm and the way the lightning made the
rocks crackle and fizz like damp wood igniting. 'As there was no
further precaution possible I enjoyed the extraordinary magnificence of
the storm with a free mind . . . and all the wonderful and terrible things
that happen in high places . . . Gradually the night cleared and became
beautifully starry. Between 2 and 3 the moon rose, a tiny crescent.'

They longed for the warmth of the sun, but the dawn brought a
blinding mist and a cutting, snow-laden wind. They emerged from
their crack crippled with cold. Gertrude ate five ginger biscuits,
two sticks of chocolate, a slice of bread and a scrap of cheese with
a handful of raisins; she now drank her tablespoon of brandy. For
the next four hours the three figures inched their way down blindly,
their ropes stiff and slippery with ice, in a gale-force wind that
whirled around them in spirals of snow. The couloirs were now
waterfalls. As soon as she cut a step in the ice, it filled with water.
Always, in situations of extreme danger, Gertrude could somehow

detach herself from her suffering and drive on. This extraordinary ability now allowed her to exercise the utmost courage. 'When things are as bad as ever they can be you cease to mind them much. You set your teeth and battle with the fates . . . I know I never thought of the danger except once and then quite calmly.'

That moment came later, after each one of the three had fallen at the same place, one after the other, spinning into the abyss and then brought up with a rib-cracking jerk as the rope held. They thought the worst was over, but they were wrong. Their nemesis came in a short slope of icy rock skirting the base of a tower. This had been difficult enough to climb when, aeons ago yet only yesterday, they had crawled their way up. Now it was covered with four inches of snow that hid every hold and crack. Beside it raced a cataract of watery snow. Both men − Ulrich beside her, Heinrich below − were too insecure to hold her, and the reaches of the next ten feet were too far apart. 'We managed badly . . . I had to refix the extra rope on a rock a little below me so that it was practically no good to me. But it was the only possible plan. The rock was too difficult for me. I handed my axe down to Heinrich and told him I could do nothing but fall.'

In this state of extreme tension, she acted precipitately. Heinrich did not have time to secure himself before she jumped. They both fell, tied together, head over heels down the ice corridor. But Ulrich, on hearing her say she was going to fall, had stuck his axe into a crack, hung on to it with one hand and held the two of them with the other. Afterwards, he could hardly believe he had done it. Gertrude wrote, 'It was a near thing and I felt rather ashamed of my part in it. This was the time when I thought it on the cards we should not get down alive.'

She felt excruciating pain in her shoulders and back, probably caused by a torn muscle. The three of them were shaking with the wet and cold. The day ground on. At 8 p.m. they still had to cross several crevasses and get down the serac before they reached safety. A serac, a barrier of ice at the lower edge of a glacier, is very dangerous to negotiate because of the constant shifting and breaking under the pressure being exerted on it. It should never be crossed at night. But they were desperate. For half an hour they tried to light their lantern with wet matches under the shelter of Gertrude's dripping skirt. Giving up on that, they began to grope forward in what was now pitch-black night, but straight away Heinrich fell into eight feet of soft snow. 'That was the only moment of despair,' she recalled.

Ahead of them was another night in the open on the glacier, in driving sleet. The men each carried a sack as a mattress of last resort, and Heinrich, gallantly and unusually, gave up his to Gertrude; while Ulrich put her feet, with his own, into the second sack. She passed the hours thinking of Maurice away at the front, fighting the Boers, commanding the Volunteer Service Company, Yorkshire Regiment. He had written of night after night spent sleeping out in the pouring rain, and assured her that he had been none the worse for it.

In the grey light of the second dawn, crippled from exposure, they could hardly walk. They staggered on and at last, barely comprehending that they had reached safety, came to the end of their ordeal. Arriving back in the village of Meiringen after fifty-seven hours on the mountain, they found her hotel buzzing with anxiety about their fate. After a hot bath and supper in bed, Gertrude slept for twenty-four hours. Her hands and feet were frostbitten – her toes were so swollen and stiff that she had to delay her return to London for days until she could put on her shoes again. Her fingers recovered quickly enough for her to write the longest letter to her father ever, acknowledging that Domnul's prognostications on the likelihood of her demise in the Alps had almost come true.

From the glacier to the summit of the Finsteraarhorn is three thousand feet. It was only the final few hundred that had cheated them of glory. Their fifty-three hours on the rope had nearly all been endured in the worst possible weather, with winds that could have blown them off the mountain, in cold so intense that the snow froze on them and on the ropes as it fell; and, at times, in a mist that prevented them from seeing where their next step might take them. While her traverse of the Lauteraarhorn–Schreckhorn was her most important ascent, she will always be remembered for the expedition on the Finsteraarhorn. The attempt had been a failure, but a glorious one. Their safe retreat under such conditions was a tremendous performance. 'There can be in the whole Alps few places so steep and so high. The climb has only been done three times, including your daughter's attempt, and is still considered one of the greatest expeditions in the whole Alps,' Ulrich Führer wrote to Hugh. 'The honour belongs to Miss Bell. Had she not been full of courage and determination, we must have perished.'

A year later, Gertrude took a couple of days out of a world tour to climb in the Rockies near Lake Louise. There, to her delight, she ran into three Swiss guides from the Oberland who teased her mercilessly, asking, 'How did the gracious Fräulein enjoy the Finsteraarhorn?'

Her last climb of note was the Matterhorn, in August 1904, from the Italian side and once more with Ulrich and Heinrich. Until she had notched up this last giant, she felt, she had unfinished business in the Alps. More than any other mountain in Switzerland, it is full of history. More fatal accidents have occurred on the Matterhorn than on any other Alpine peak. Gertrude had read and reread the account by Edward Whymper, the British climber who thirty-nine years previously had made the first ascent of the Matterhorn, of the appalling descent on which four members of the party slipped and fell, only the breaking of the rope saving Whymper and the two remaining guides from the same fate. The deaths of his companions undoubtedly ruined his life: 'Every night, do you understand, I see my comrades of the Matterhorn slipping on their backs, their arms outstretched, one after the other, in perfect order at equal distances . . . Yes, I shall always see them.'

Gertrude knew the mountain so well by hearsay that every step was familiar. After an unpromising dawn, the weather cleared and they made the whole climb in comfort. Near the summit, they encountered the famously difficult Tyndall Grat overhang. A rope ladder was usually to be found at this point, but it had broken and been partially replaced by a fixed rope. They took two hours to climb twenty feet. 'I look back to it with great respect. At the overhanging bit you had to throw yourself out on the rope and so hanging catch with your right knee a shelving scrap of rock from which you can just reach the top rung which is all that is left of the rope ladder. That is how it is done . . . and I also remember wondering how it was possible to do it.'

Poor Heinrich found it 'uncommonly difficult'. They reached the summit at 10 a.m. and came down the Swiss side, Whymper's original route, which was now hung with the ropes of recent climbers. Gertrude described the descent as '. . . more like sliding down the bannisters than climbing'.

The most recognizable of all mountain profiles, it is the Matterhorn that is portrayed in the memorial window to Gertrude in East Rounton church. At the top of the window, the mountain is pictured opposite a vignette of her on camelback, with palm trees behind. These two parts of her life were, indeed, in opposition, and her interests were now to focus on archaeology and the desert. The Matterhorn was her last great mountain. In 1926 Colonel E. L. Strutt, then editor of the *Alpine Journal*, wrote that in 1901–2 there had been no more prominent female mountaineer than Gertrude Bell:

> Everything that she undertook, physical or mental, was accomplished so superlatively well, that it would indeed have been strange if she had not shone on a mountain as she did in the hunting-field or in the desert. Her strength, incredible in that slim frame, her endurance, above all her courage, were so great that even to this day her guide and companion Ulrich Führer – and there could be few more competent judges – speaks with an admiration of her that amounts to veneration. He told the writer, some years ago, that of all the amateurs, men or women, that he had travelled with, he had seen but very few to surpass her in technical skill and none to equal her in coolness, bravery and judgment.

6

DESERT TRAVEL

'Miss Gertrude Bell knows more about the Arabs and Arabia than almost any other living Englishman or woman.' These were the words of Lord Cromer, a former High Commissioner in Egypt, in 1915, when, with no end to the First World War in sight, Gertrude's knowledge would become the key to unlocking the stalemate.

As a tourist in Jerusalem in 1900, she could not have known where and how far her arrival would lead her. It would be the beginning of her passion for the desert. Most of the world was profoundly ignorant about the territory that went by the all-encompassing name of 'Arabia', as if one race and one nation ruled all the uninhabitable deserts, fertile valleys and inhospitable mountains, tribal territories, regions, imamates, sheikhdoms and colonies that comprised its 1,293,062 square miles. Over two per cent of the global landmass, it reached in roughly rhomboid shape from the River Jordan near the eastern Mediterranean and the corner of the African continent, then south to the Indian Ocean, from the Red Sea to the Persian Gulf, and northwards along the border of Persia to the Russian front, with Turkey forming its great northern lintel.

This vast terrain was not given the name of 'Middle East' until 1902, when the phrase was coined by the American naval strategist Alfred Thayer Mahan. As far as the West was concerned, once the Suez Canal was cut in the 1860s, the desert routes formed by millennia of oriental camel trade became redundant. Once British steamships could conveniently reach India, before the days of the combustion engine and of oil, the great landmass ceased to be of

interest to anyone beyond its southern shores and northern mountains, except its Turkish rulers in remote Constantinople. The
countries known today as Syria, Lebanon, Israel, Palestine, Jordan,
Saudi Arabia and Iraq were at that time undifferentiated regions of
the Ottoman Empire.

For several hundred years the Turks had been infiltrating, then
taking over, the administration of the towns and the few large cities
that ringed the deserts at the heart of the Middle East. The Ottoman
Empire had systematically set about replacing the Sharia law, the
divine law of Islam, with their own Napoleonic laws, and had
introduced Turkish as the language of administration and education.
The Turks drew leading Arab figures into the Turkish web,
rewarding them for loyalty until its gentle hold on Arabia had
become a vice-like grip. All this was kept in place by systematic
corruption and the careful fostering of enmity between its peoples.
But, as Gertrude soon discovered, Ottoman power petered out
only a few miles into the wilderness: there the Bedouin sheikhs did
as they pleased, defending their precious wells, camel routes and
sparse grazing grounds against their neighbours and rivals. The
deserts remained lawless, only to be crossed, as Gertrude would so
courageously cross them, by arming herself with a mastery of the
language, politics and customs of the Bedouin tribes, until she was
welcomed to their tents.

For all that the religion of Islam predominated and the Arabs
were in the majority, the towns of Arabia were extraordinarily
cosmopolitan. The few Jews who survived the destruction of their
communities by the Romans in the first century AD had taken
shelter, continuing as traders, where they could. Greeks, Egyptians,
Persians, Armenians and Assyrians both Christian and Muslim had
thrived on the camel-borne trade between India, Europe and Africa.
They profited from the annual Muslim pilgrimage to Mecca and
Medina, and served the Turks as minor officials.

Most cosmopolitan of all was Jerusalem. Continually invaded
over the centuries since the Romans left, it had become ostensibly
an Arab town, being merged into the Ottoman Empire in 1840.
From then on it had been a focus for every European nation that

wanted to affirm its religious history. The French, British, Germans, Italians and Russians in particular had built churches, hospitals and colleges there. By the time Gertrude arrived, the Jewish community was gaining influence, with increasing numbers of refugee settlements. With a population of seventy thousand, Jerusalem was an axis of cultures and special interests at the entrance to Arabia.

Gertrude's career as a desert traveller did not begin until her thirty-second year, when she accepted a Christmas invitation from Nina Rosen, an old friend, now wife of the German Consul at Jerusalem.

The German consulate was small, having only three bedrooms. The two little Rosen boys shared one, and Nina's sister Charlotte was installed in the other. Gertrude intended to stay in Jerusalem several months. She booked herself into the Hotel Jerusalem, two minutes' walk from the consulate, where she would join the family for meals and expeditions. On 13 December she wrote home:

> My apartment consists of a very nice bedroom and a big sitting room, both opening on to a small vestibule which in its turn leads out on to the verandah which runs all along the first story of the hotel courtyard with a little garden in it. I pay 7 francs a day including breakfast . . . My housemaid is an obliging gentleman in a fez who brings me my hot bath in the morning . . . 'The hot water is ready for the Presence' says he. 'Enter and light the candle' say I. 'On my head' he replies. That means it's dressing time.

Settling into a Middle Eastern hotel, be it in Jerusalem, Damascus, Beirut or Haifa, would become a happy ritual, an almost sacred preliminary to the extensive organization required at the start of Gertrude's desert expeditions. At this particular moment she was wanting only to buy a horse and begin a new course of Arabic, but these initial arrangements set a pattern that would never vary. She would always book two rooms with a veranda or view, and turn one room into a work space for the campaign ahead; she would stipulate two armchairs and two tables, and banish all unnecessary furniture. Having unpacked her books and maps she would trail cigarette ash across the room as she tacked up her pictures with the small hammer and nails she had brought for the purpose. 'I spent the morning unpacking and turning out the bed and things out of my sitting room; it is now most cosy – two armchairs, a big writing table, a square table for my books, an enormous Kiepert* map of Palestine . . . and photographs of my family on the walls. There is a little stove in one corner and the wood fire in it is most acceptable.'

On this first visit, she at once engaged a teacher and set herself six Arabic lessons a week. The rest of the time before Christmas she would spend mainly riding, and joining with the Rosens and their children in festive activities such as painting walnuts gold to decorate the Christmas tree. On Christmas Eve they all attended high mass at the Franciscan church in Bethlehem, before joining a candlelight procession to the Grotto of the Nativity.

Gertrude already spoke French and Italian, her Persian was as good as her German, and she understood a little Hebrew. She would learn Turkish easily, but it would be the only language she did not retain. Arabic proved to be far more difficult than she had anticipated. Slow progress in this most difficult of languages, however, did not stop her reading verses of Genesis in Hebrew before dinner, for light relief. The first fortnight of her Arabic lessons brought her to the brink of despair:

> I may say in passing that I don't think I shall ever talk Arabic . . .
> It is an awful language . . . There are at least three sounds almost
> impossible to the European throat. The worst is a very much
> aspirated H. I can only say it by holding down my tongue with
> one finger, but then you can't carry on a conversation with your
> finger down your throat, can you? I should like to mention that
> there are five words for a wall and 36 ways of forming the plural.

She tried out a few horses before settling on a small and lively Arab stallion. She paid about £18 sterling, and hoped to sell him for the same when she left. She wrote home: 'a charming little horse,

---

* Engraver Heinrich Kiepert of Weimar was well known in the mid-nineteenth century for his precise maps.

a bay, very well bred with lovely movements, rather showy, but light and strong and delightful in every way . . . Will you order Heath to send me out a wide grey felt sun hat (not double, but it must be a regular Terai* shape and broad brimmed) to ride in, and to put a black velvet ribbon round it with straight bows.'

She was delighted by all she saw in and around Jerusalem. Riding down to the Jordan, then to the Dead Sea — 'very sticky!' — and the Virgin's Tomb — 'shut!' — she began to feel constrained by the stiff posture demanded by riding side-saddle. Amongst the varied local costumes, her habit seemed clumsy and obstructive. With Friedrich and Nina's encouragement, she started to ride astride. She tried out a 'masculine' saddle and liked it so much she bought one of her own. When the sisters at the nearby convent made her a divided riding skirt, the first of many, her sense of freedom was complete. Pulling away from the well-used tourist roads busy with Thomas Cook caravans and carriages, she would gallop off on her own, raising clouds of dust as she leapt stone walls, whooping for joy, one hand hanging on to the newly arrived Terai hat with its velvet ribbon:

> The chief comfort of this journey is my masculine saddle, both to me and to my horse. Never, never again will I travel on anything else; I haven't known real ease in riding until now. You mustn't think I haven't got a most elegant and decent divided skirt, however, but as all men wear skirts of sorts too, that doesn't serve to distinguish me. Till I speak the people always think I'm a man and address me as Effendim!†

Exploring the hills and valleys, she would dismount to pick hyacinths, bee orchis or cyclamen, sometimes squinting up at the Anchorites entering their caves high above, then drawing their rope ladders up after them. The Bible came alive to her: every time she

---

* A terai was a wide-brimmed felt hat, often with a double crown, worn by white men in subtropical regions. (The terai is a belt of marshy jungle between the Himalayan foothills and the plains.)

† A Turkish title of respect (usually, effendi) applied to government officials and members of learned professions — necessarily male.

wanted to buy butter and bread, her route led her past Herod's house and the Pool of Bethesda. She started to take her camera everywhere she went, photographing the gracefully robed women she passed in the streets. She watched a mass baptism of singing Russian pilgrims, amused at the way the monks seemed to take pleasure in holding them under water until they struggled for breath. On the outskirts of Jerusalem, she stopped to look at an encampment of black Bedouin tents, appearing out of the desert one evening, then gone without trace the next.

A telegram, then letters from Red Barns, interrupted her pleasure with sad news. Aunt Ada, who had helped bring up the motherless Gertrude and Maurice before Hugh remarried, had died. Her father was suffering from a painful rheumatic illness, and Maurice was preparing to depart for the Boer War. Her concern for the two men frequently breaks through her correspondence: she was 'much bothered' about her brother – it was 'an awful blow' to hear he had left for South Africa. 'Rode out in very bad spirits . . . very miserable,' she wrote in her diary.

It was March 1900. In spite of bad weather, Gertrude decided to make an expedition of ten days or so into the Moab hills, riding some seventy miles down the east bank of the Dead Sea. It would be her first journey with her own caravan and its crew of three – a cook and a couple of muleteers – none of whom could speak a word of English. She would pick up a guide along the route, probably a Turkish soldier travelling between garrisons.

As soon as she reached the Jordan plain, she found herself waist-deep in a wilderness of flowers. In the first of many letters home addressed 'From my tent' she described the scene before her:

> sheets and sheets of varied and exquisite colour – purple, white, yellow, and the brightest blue and fields of scarlet ranunculus. Nine-tenths of them I didn't know, but there was the yellow daisy, the sweet-scented mauve wild stock, a great splendid sort of dark purple onion, the white garlic and purple mallow, and higher up a tiny blue iris and red anemones and a dawning pink thing like a linum.

Beyond were great pale swathes of corn sown by the Bedouin as they passed, that would be reaped when they returned. Her Arabic improving by the day, she talked principally to Muhammad, the handsome Druze muleteer who ate only rice, bread and figs. She liked him, and everything he told her about his tribal homeland. She decided that one day she would ride into the Jebel Druze, the mountains to the south-west of Syria, to meet his kinsmen. Buying yoghurt from a family of the Ghanimat tribe, she stopped for a rudimentary conversation with the women and children, noting with surprise that they were eating grass 'like goats': 'The women are unveiled. They wear a blue cotton gown 6 yards long which is gathered up and bound round their heads and their waists and falls to their feet. Their faces, from the mouth downwards, are tattooed with indigo and their hair hangs down in two long plaits on either side . . . Isn't it a joke being able to talk Arabic!'

At the crusader fort of Kerak, where she should have turned back for Jerusalem, she changed her mind and added another eight days to her journey: she would go on to the Nabataean ruins of Petra. She wanted to see the famous 'treasury', a delicate two-storey façade carved out of pink sandstone, approached through a narrow chasm. When a Turkish official turned up to check on her caravan and its destination, she realized she would have to get authorization. Pretending to be German — 'for they are desperately afraid of the English' — she asked him to take her to the local governor, from whom she obtained permission to travel on south, with a soldier as her guide. Writing to her parents that she was doubling the anticipated length of her journey, she added that she would, naturally, have telegraphed them to ask their permission if only it had been possible. It was not the last time she would go through the pantomime of following English codes of conduct, while doing exactly what she liked.

Accompanied by the guide, the little party made their way through companies of storks picking off a cloud of locusts, soon finding themselves next to a camp of Beni Sakhr, the warrior tribe who had been last to submit to Turkish rule. As yet she was ignorant of the rules of the desert. She did not know that whenever she came upon an encampment she should immediately pay a courtesy visit to the sheikh in his tent. And with a Turkish soldier accompanying her instead of a paid local guide, she soon ran into trouble. Her caravan was threatened twice by several of the forbidding Beni Sakhr, armed to the teeth. Appearing out of nowhere, they suddenly sprang up on both sides, and only backed off when Gertrude was joined by the Turk, who was following behind. She was undeterred: 'Don't think I have ever spent such a wonderful day.'

Soon on the road to Mecca, the route of the annual Haj, she found that it was not a road at all. At one-eighth of a mile wide, it consisted of hundreds of parallel tracks trodden out by the immense caravan of pilgrims on their inward and outward journeys. She learnt the ABC of desert travel as she went. She found the maps full of errors and often underestimating distances. They had water, but soon ran out of barley, charcoal, and all food but rice, bread and a little pot of meat. They stopped at a village where she thought they might be able to buy a lamb, or failing that a hen, but drew a blank. 'What the people in Wady Musa live on I can't imagine. They hadn't so much as milk.'

By the time they reached Petra, her delight at the magical beauty of the Corinthian façade and the amphitheatre beyond was rudely interrupted by pangs of hunger: '. . . the charming façade . . . the most exquisite proportions . . . the tombs extremely rococo . . . but time has worn them and weather has stained the rock with exquisite colours – I wish the lamb had come!' Arriving back late at her tent at Wady Musa, she found 'a surprising lot of long black sort of slugs' on the ground, but, nonetheless, she appears to have slept well. From Petra she turned back north towards the Dead Sea, and that night pitched her tent alongside a camp of gypsies. She shared their supper of sour-cream cheese, eaten with the fingers, and a single cup of coffee passed from lip to lip. Darkness fell, a crescent moon appeared, and the music began. She wrote to Hugh:

. . . the fire of dry thorns flickered up – faded and flickered again and showed the circle of men crouching on the ground, their black and white cloaks wrapped round them and the woman in the middle dancing. She looked as though she had stepped out of an Egyptian fresco. She wore a long red gown bound round her waist with a dark blue cloth, and falling open in front to show a redder petticoat below. Round her forehead was another dark blue cloth bound tightly and falling in long ends down her back, her chin was covered by a white cloth drawn up round her ears and falling in folds to her waist and her lower lip tattooed with indigo! Her feet, in red leather shoes, scarcely moved but all her body danced and she swept a red handkerchief she held in one hand round her head, and clasped her hands together in front of her impassive face. The men played a drum and a discordant fife and sang a monotonous song and clapped their hands and gradually she came nearer and nearer to me, twisting her slender body till she dropped down on the heap of brushwood at my feet, and kneeling, her body still danced and her arms swayed and twisted round the mask like face . . . Oh, Father dearest, don't I have a fine time! I'm only overcome by the sense of how much better it is than I deserve.

Suddenly the weather changed, and it became excessively hot. Gertrude's face was burnt red, and when she rode back into the plain she found that the brilliant flowers she had passed earlier had all died and turned to hay.

It was the end of her first expedition. She had travelled 135 miles in eighteen days, and learnt one more lesson: to wrap up well against the sun. On future journeys into the Syrian desert she would wear the traditional white cloth, the keffiyeh, tied over her hat and wound over her lower face, and a fine blue veil with holes cut for her to see through. Her white linen divided skirt would be partly covered by a large masculine coat in khaki cotton, with deep pockets. Effectively, though unintentionally, she would disguise herself as a man.

The Rosens had promised Gertrude a week's expedition north to Bosra, at the edge of the Druze mountains, a Roman city with a castle and triumphal arches. By April, however, she had already

taken off alone into the desert for weeks at a time, and was
beginning to think of this scheme as a rather tame affair. When the
Rosens returned to Jerusalem, she said she would press on into the
mountains to meet some of Muhammad's fellow Druze, and perhaps
even aim for the Syrian desert as far as Palmyra, some two hundred
miles beyond. Her friends' reaction, if they expressed one, is
unrecorded. The fierce Druze, a closed Muslim sect, were considered by the Turks to be dangerous and generally regarded as
subversive. The Rosens must have had misgivings about Gertrude
travelling among them as a woman alone.

The journey began in comfort, with two cooks, Muhammad and
two other muleteers, plus five mules to carry the equipment. In her
diaries, written in her tent almost nightly, she noted every archaeological ruin passed and every tribal encampment: Abbad, Beni
Hassan, Adwan, Hawarni and Anazeh. There are few anecdotes
amongst the mass of information, but she records that when a small
boy stole her riding crop, she chased after him, boxed his ears and
took it back.

At Bosra, she walked around town in the way normal for many
Arab villages – on the rooftops – and began tiresome negotiations
with the *mudir*, the local Arab authority, about the rest of her
journey. The proper procedure was to request permission to enter
Druze territory, but she knew she was unlikely to get it. She
therefore pretended that her destination was Salkhad, to the north-
east, where she wished to look at the ruins. She was not the first
desert traveller to use archaeology as the ostensible motive for a
journey undertaken for quite different reasons, but it was the first
time she had done so. By now, her Arabic was good enough to
encompass the formality and high courtesies of the language. She
was beginning to speak it on two levels – a patois, and a purer
dialect. She re-enacted the scene for her parents:

'Where was I going?'

'To Damascus.'

'God has made it! There is a fine road to the west with
beautiful ruins.'

'Please God I shall see them! But I wish first to look upon Salkhad.'

'Salkhad! There is nothing there at all, and the road is very dangerous. It cannot happen.'

'It must happen.'

'There has come a telegram from Damascus to bid me to say the Mutussarif fears for the safety of your Presence.' (This isn't true.)

'English women are never afraid.' (This also isn't true!)

Her next interview, with the head of the town's military, went equally badly, partly because he was in his shirtsleeves, being shaved by an orderly throughout. He had his eyes nicely blackened with kohl, she remarked drily, but otherwise his toilet was incomplete.

She did not like the *mudir*, and she liked him even less when he turned up at her tent late at night. She hastily blew out her candle and told her cook to say that she was asleep. Eavesdropping on the conversation, she heard the man warn that she was to go nowhere without permission. Whenever she was threatened with any kind of restriction, she would act fast. She struck camp at two in the morning, shivering in her thin summer clothing, and by dawn was well on her way northwards, beyond Salkhad, where she knew the *mudir* might well have her followed.

She was the first woman ever to travel alone in this territory. Even her crew were alarmed at what might happen. But luck was on her side, and her idyll with the Jebel Druze began as it would go on. From the moment she arrived at her first Druze village, in the shadow of Mount Kuleib, she was warmly welcomed and treated with kindness and respect:

The women were filling their earthenware jars ... and at the water stood the most beautiful boy of 19 or 20. I dismounted to water my horse; the boy came up to me, took my hands and kissed me on both cheeks, rather to my surprise. Several others came up and shook hands with me ... Their eyes look enormous, blacked with kohl, men and women alike; they are dark,

straight browed, straight shouldered, with an alert and gentle air
of intelligence which is extraordinarily attractive.

With the boy, Nusr ed Din, to accompany her, she made for the
village of Areh, mentioned in her guidebook as the homeland of the
paramount sheikh of the Druze. In Areh, men came out to greet
her, linked their little fingers with hers, and led her into a house
where she sat on cushions and drank coffee: 'The sense of comfort
and safety and confidence and of being with straight speaking people,
was more delightful than I can tell you,' she told her parents.

She knew by now that it would be courteous to ask to pay her
respects to their chief, Yahya Beg, and in asking if she might meet
him, she took the correct next step in the elaborate desert etiquette
whereby the visitor earns the protection of the tribe. The old
warrior, the first tribal chief that she got to know, had just been
released from five years' imprisonment in a Turkish jail. He was a
splendid figure: 'He is the most perfect type of the Grand Seigneur, a
great big man (40 to 50, I suppose), very handsome and with the most
exquisite manners . . . He's a king, you understand, and a very good king
too, though his kingdom doesn't happen to be a large one.'

He piled up cushions for her on the floor, patted them, then
beckoned her to join him and his men in their meal of meat and
beans, which they ate with their fingers from a central plate. He
asked her about her journey, and told Nusr ed Din and another
Druze to show her all the archaeological ruins in the area, then to
accompany her in safety to her next destination. Before she left, she
asked permission to take his photograph. She learnt how far the
protection of a paramount sheikh could stretch when she heard,
weeks later, that Yahya Beg had continued to monitor her progress,
sending messengers to ask villagers, 'Have you seen a queen
travelling, a consuless?' She already travelled in style, if not as
elaborately as she would later on. The linen, glasses, knives and
forks that were her everyday ware must have been borrowed from
the consulate.

Undoubtedly she was attracted by these courteous warriors:
before she left them she visited another village where, again, she

was overwhelmed by the beauty of the men. Slightly embarrassed, perhaps, at writing of this to her family, she phrased her appreciation carefully: 'They were a group of the most beautiful people you would wish to see. Their average height was about 6 ft 1 in. and their average looks were as though you mixed up Hugo and you, Father.'

She made a short stop in Damascus and travelled on towards Palmyra with three more Turkish soldiers, avoiding the tourist road and making diversions along the route. She learnt to be tough. Until now she had drawn the line at drinking murky water, but after two waterless days she closed her eyes and drank from pools alive with worms and insects, pretending to herself that she was drinking the snow and lemonade mixture you could buy in china bowls from the bazaars. Then: 'We bought a lamb today. He was a perfect love and his fate cut me to the heart. I felt if I looked at him any longer I should be like Byron and the goose,* so I parted from him hastily – and there were delicious lamb cutlets for supper.'

They moved slowly on through the desert, rising before dawn for the sake of the horses. Ahmed the guide rode in front, dressed in white; beside her were the black shadows of her three soldiers; and the mules, their bells tinkling, in her wake. The three camels came on at their own pace – they would all meet up in camp. She was struck again by the total silence of the desert, more intense even than on the mountaintops, she thought: there you heard a sort of echo caused by falling ice and stones. Here you heard nothing at all.

Every day she was learning a new lesson in desert survival: she found that the sun could burn her feet right through her leather boots if she did not cover them, as well, in swathes of fabric. She recognized as mirages the 'immense plaques of water' that never left the horizon; and she sewed herself a sleeping bag of muslin to protect herself from the sandflies at night. 'I'm very proud of this

---

* For food on one of his journeys, Lord Byron bought a couple of geese which accompanied him in a basket. He could never bring himself to have them killed, and so took them home at the end of the journey, where they spent the rest of their lives.

contrivance,' she wrote home, 'but if we have a ghazu [raid] of Arabs I shall certainly be the last to fly, and my flight will be as one who runs a sack race.'

Her Arabic had become good enough for her to discuss desert politics with the notables she met along the way. She began to take her turn with the *narghileh* that was passed around as they talked, the bubble-pipe in which tobacco, marijuana or opium was smoked. She did not enjoy it at first, as she was at pains to tell her parents, but gradually acquired the habit. At one point she discovered that she had been sold leaking water-skins, and mended them, covering the hole with a stone and tying the skin tightly around the neck with a piece of string. She made a note in her diary in future to test the skins before paying.

Her days in the saddle stretched to ten or twelve hours, and she took to passing the time by reading and sleeping as she rode. She would change to a sideways position on the saddle – built for riding astride – and let go of the reins in order to hold her parasol, map and book. When one day her horse suddenly began to trot, she fell off, much to the amusement of the soldiers. She sat in the sand for a moment, wondering whether to be annoyed, and then threw back her head and joined in the laughter. For the last hour or two of these long days, she would sometimes transfer to one of her men's camels:

It's the greatest relief after you have been riding a horse for 8 or 9 hours to feel the long comfy swing and the wide soft saddle of a camel beneath you . . . You ride a camel with only a halter which you mostly tie loosely round the peak of your saddle. A tap with your camel switch on one side of her neck or the other tells her the direction you want her to go, a touch with your heels sends her on, but when you wish her to sit down you have to hit her lightly and often on the neck saying at the same time: 'Kh kh kh kh' . . . The big soft saddle, the 'shedad', is so easy and comfortable that you never tire. You loll about and eat your lunch and observe the landscape through your glasses . . . My camel . . . is the most charming of animals.

In a letter she had collected in Damascus, Florence had asked if she were ever lonely. Gertrude replied that she often wanted her family, particularly her father; then she tried to ameliorate any hurt this might occasion to her stepmother:

> It is at times a very odd sensation to be out in the world quite by myself, but mostly I take it as a matter of course . . . I don't think I ever feel lonely, though the one person I often wish for is Papa . . . I keep wanting to compare notes with him. You, I want to talk to, but not in a tent with earwigs and black beetles around and muddy water to drink! I don't think you would be your true self under such conditions.

As they climbed into the hills, she had to abandon the muslin sleeping bag and wrap herself at night in knickerbockers, gaiters, two coats and a blanket. She slept on the ground: later on her desert travels, she would take a collapsible canvas bed. The going got harder, and the way drier, as they neared Palmyra. On the last day they rose at midnight and rode until sunrise, when on the horizon appeared Palmyra's castle set in its pale bed of sand and salt, ghostly dust clouds whirling over it, and still five thirsty hours away. The towers, the avenues of columns and the immense Temple of Baal were, she thought, the loveliest things she had seen since Petra. She took twenty-four hours to explore the town and pay courtesy calls to its worthies, then turned back, for once, along the tourist route.

On the way back to Damascus, she was joined by a large caravan of camels being brought from the Nejd region to market in the city by a group of ferocious-looking Agail tribesmen, led by their sheikh. Fearing a raid on their camels en route, they wanted the extra protection of Gertrude's three soldiers as witnesses from the Turkish military, should the need arise. She, in turn, wanted to talk to the sheikh and find out more about the feared desert of the Nejd, where she intended to travel one day. Also, she had learnt that in the desert one good turn deserves another: it was no bad thing for the Agail to owe her a favour.

On the way back she happened to meet up with a carriage

containing a couple of tourists, pleasant Englishwomen whom she had met at the consulate in Jerusalem, both very fresh and tidy. The ladies looked askance at her dirty clothes and straggling hair, and shrank back from her escort of scowling Agail with their cartridge belts, knives and twelve-foot lances. Gertrude, however, was delighted to see Miss Blount and Miss Grieve again. She jumped off her horse and swung herself cheerfully into their carriage for a very proper English tea, with Earl Grey and ginger biscuits. 'I wish I could manage to travel on the approved lines,' she wrote afterwards, 'but the fates are against me. I had laid all my plans for coming back from Palmyra like a lady, but no! it was not to be.'

Nearly halfway back to Damascus, beyond Karyatein, she pitched camp and watched a company of Hasineh, with their black tents, come in from their winter quarters. 'Their sheikh, Muhammad, came to call on me, a boy of 20 or younger, handsome, rather thick lipped, solemn, his hair hanging in thick plaits from under his keffiyeh. He carried an enormous sword, the sheath inlaid with silver . . . He owns 500 tents and a house in Damascus, and Heaven knows how many horses and camels.' Later she repaid the call, seating herself on a cushion in his tent to join the circle around the sheikh. As coffee was served, a musician started to play the rubaba, a single-stringed instrument:

> He sang to it long melancholy songs, monotonous, each line of the verse being set to the same time and ending with a drop of the voice which was almost a groan . . . weird and sad and beautiful in its way. All the silent people sat round looking at me, unkempt, half-naked, their keffiyehs drawn up over their faces, nothing alive in them but their eyes . . . Sometimes one would come into the open tent . . . and standing on the edge of the circle, he greeted the Sheikh with a 'Ya Muhammad!' his hand lifted to his forehead and the company with 'Peace be upon you' to which we all answered 'And upon you peace!'

After a while, Gertrude got up and said goodbye. The moment she got back to her tent, her soldiers told her that she had committed a dangerous solecism. A sheep had been killed in her honour, and was being prepared. To walk out before the meal was virtually an insult. And she should have taken the sheikh an offering. What was more, one of Muhammad's standing required to be placated with a gift of considerable value. You can give an Arab nothing, they told her, but a horse or a gun. Perturbed, she took the pistol from one of her crew, wrapped it in a pocket handkerchief, and sent it with a soldier to Muhammad with the message that she had not known that he was intending to honour her by providing meat. The soldier returned with a pressing invitation from the sheikh for her to rejoin the tribesmen. 'Back I went . . . We waited till 9.30! I wasn't bored . . . the talk went round – the politics of the desert: who had sold horses, who owned camels, who had been killed in a raid, how much the blood money would be or where the next battle. It was very difficult to understand, but I followed it more or less . . .'

At last, a slave came round with a long-spouted jug and poured a little water over the hands of all the participants, after which an enormous dish of mutton was carried in. After the meal, hands were washed once more, and Gertrude bowed herself out. It had been, she thought, an expensive dinner; but the evening had been a blueprint for encounters with important sheikhs. In future she would travel with gifts, she would know what to give, how to behave, what to discuss and when to leave. In the morning, she watched the Hasineh move off, and found it an impressive and majestic sight: 'Sheikh Muhammad had only twenty or thirty of his five hundred tents with him, yet the camels filled the plain like the regiments of an army, each household marching with its own detachment of camels . . .'

She returned to Damascus a tried and tested desert traveller. She stayed on in Jerusalem with the Rosens, making further expeditions, and arrived back in England in June. As she left, she wrote a final letter to Hugh, prophetic in its message: 'You know, dearest Father, I shall be back here before long! One doesn't keep away from the East when one has got into it this far.'

Two years after her first adventures, Gertrude went to Haifa, where she spent two months on her own, perfecting her Arabic. It was already nine years since she had started to learn the language. She rented a house on Mount Carmel, filled the rooms with mimosa, jasmine and wild flowers, and did her lessons on the dining-room table under a chandelier in which there was a nest, the birds constantly flying in and out of the open window. Four hours of Arabic a day and two and a half hours of Persian occupied all of her time between riding about the local countryside and involving herself, through her growing circle of contacts, in the politics of the day. She wrote home: 'I am so wildly interested in Arabic that I can think of nothing else. You can understand the joy of at last being able to learn this language that I have been struggling with for so long.' She found, to her surprise, that her first solo expeditions had made her rather famous – a Person with a capital 'P', as she was quick to assure her family: 'I am much entertained to find that I am a Person in this country – they all think I am a Person! . . . Renown is not very difficult to acquire here.'

Once she could speak the language easily, she undertook the first of five extraordinary Middle Eastern expeditions. Her four-month journey on horseback in 1905 started from Jerusalem, traversed the Jebel Druze mountains, then skirted the Syrian desert to Damascus and on north to Aleppo. She crossed Turkey from Antioch in the south through Anatolia to Constantinople, covering only the last few hundred miles by train. In 1907 she landed at Smyrna on the Mediterranean coast of Turkey and travelled on horseback again from one major archaeological site to another, with stops to join her hired railway carriage bringing her luggage. Going gradually eastwards she reached Binbirkilisse, where she worked with Professor Ramsay until taking the train homewards through Constantinople.

Gertrude's longest journey began in February 1909 at Aleppo, taking the northern desert route to meet the Euphrates River in what is now north-western Iraq. She travelled its length to Baghdad. In the nearby desert, and in some danger, she measured and photographed the great palace of Ukhaidir south of the city, then went on to the sites of Babylon and Ctesiphon before joining the Tigris. She followed this river northwards past the western mountains of Iran and over the Turkish border to its source in the high plateau of the Tur Abdin. Reaching Mardin after five months in the saddle, she headed once more for Constantinople.

In February 1911, she set off from Damascus in bad weather. At first camping in deep snow and having to contend with the camels slipping and falling on the frozen ground, she crossed the empty Syrian desert eastwards then south to Ukhaidir. After completing the measurements of the palace that she had first taken in 1909, and visiting Najaf, she started north again, resting in Baghdad and then taking the Tigris valley route into southern Turkey and the Tur Abdin once more. Returning south into Syria, stopping at Carchemish, she arrived in Aleppo at the end of May, going home through Beirut.

Beginning in November 1913, Gertrude made an epic camel journey crossing and recrossing the Arabian desert, with her largest ever caravan complete with servants, crew, pack animals and hangers-on. She passed through the Nejd, the vast waterless desert of gravel and lava, to the feared city of Hayyil at its centre. Once free of the city, she continued on to Baghdad for a short rest, before facing the desert once more. Crossing the Syrian desert for the second time, she reached Damascus in late May, arriving home with little time for recovery before the First World War broke out.

To list these desert journeys one after another does little to convey their phenomenal length and hardship. Taken together, her journeys encompassed most of Syria, Turkey and Mesopotamia – roughly, the broad territory containing Basra, Baghdad and Mosul. She covered more than ten thousand miles on the map, but she went over hills and mountains, searched for fords, took detours to ancient sites and made contact with sheikhs. Over six hundred days she must have journeyed at least 20,000 miles in the saddle.

Her visits were timed at more or less two-year intervals, between which she travelled to other places and pursued her mountain climbing. In 1901, when her grandfather Sir Lowthian, at the age of eighty-five, had decided to amalgamate the Bell companies with Dorman Long, she had a bigger income at her disposal. The six-month journeys for which she would once have needed the funding of her father were now affordable.

Journey by journey, she targeted her Middle Eastern travels on archaeological sites in unmapped territories. Methodically covering the ground, these expeditions resulted in five books, some readable, some indigestibly packed with information. She dreamed that one day she might bring to light a secret citadel, a jewel in the wilderness; meanwhile, she left no ruin along her route unvisited. After journeys endured for the most part in appalling weather, and across territories swept by marauding tribes, often suffering from lack of water and food, she would fastidiously record the day's events by candlelight on the folding table in her tent.

She was very conscious that she lacked the qualifications of an archaeologist – for instance, a knowledge of epigraphy. Between these carefully planned expeditions, she therefore set out to learn new practical skills, so that, passing through uncharted territories, she would be able to pinpoint the sites, make maps, and finally recognize what she found and fit it into the historical and archaeological context as she recorded it. She attended courses that taught her how to measure and draw up accounts of her finds; she became a skilled photographer and a member of the Royal Photographic Society. As such, she was able to have her film professionally printed. She carried two cameras wherever she went. One was a hand camera that took glass plates 6.5 inches high by 4.25 wide, the other designed for panoramic views. When she returned from her travels she used a technique adopted more recently by David Hockney, to scan an entire horizon by combining five or six carefully angled shots. The School of Historical Studies at Newcastle University, which holds seven thousand of her photographs, particularly values her panoramas as of considerable archaeological value to this day, showing as they do precisely how the different monuments relate to each other across the landscape. Her documentary records of the monuments and churches themselves are no less important, depicting the buildings as they were when she photographed them, before twentieth-century erosion and pilfering caused further damage. In view of the scarcity of photographs of Gertrude herself, her shadow, often visible in the foreground of her pictures as she bent over her camera to get the best light on the object, with the sunrise or sunset behind her, holds a particular fascination.

Her 1909 journey would take her down the east bank of the Euphrates, into unmapped territories. For weeks beforehand, she went to Mr Reeves of the Royal Geographical Society to learn surveying and astronomical observation for determining positions.

> Yesterday . . . in the evening I went to Red Hill, getting there at 8. A young man (one of my fellow students) met me at the station and we walked up on to the Common where we met Mr Reeves. Then we took observations on stars for two hours . . . I took a number of observations and shall work them out on Monday . . . this morning I was back at Red Hill before 10 and spent three hours taking bearings for a map with Mr Reeves.

Later, Reeves told Florence that he had never had anyone to teach who learnt more rapidly. He wrote, 'Miss Bell's prismatic compass route traverse made on her remarkable journeys after she left me, was plotted from her field books, and adjusted to her latitudes here by our draughtsmen. I need not say that her mapping has proved of the greatest value and importance.' The RGS still holds those field books.

Gertrude had been interested in archaeology since a holiday in Greece in 1899 with her father and her uncle Thomas Marshall, a classical scholar who had married her mother Mary Shield's sister. There she had met Dr David Hogarth, the scholarly brother of her Oxford friend Janet. He was in the process of excavating the six-thousand-year-old city of Melos, and was pleased to show them his finds. She became so interested in the dig that she stayed for several days near Melos, to watch and help. Hogarth became a friend with whom she corresponded; his later book *The Penetration of Arabia* would go with her as part of her travelling library. Later, in 1915, he would precipitate the most important turning point of her career.

Two years on, after a holiday with her father and Hugo, she went on to join archaeological digs at the ancient sites of Pergamon,

Magnesia and Sardis. She evidently enjoyed the excavation work more than the rather dull cruise that preceded it, chiefly memorable for a day's sightseeing in Santa Flavia with Winston Churchill, who was staying in a villa there in order to paint.

By 1904, Gertrude was immersed in plans for her imminent journey through western Syria and Asia Minor, her first expedition after Jerusalem and the Rosens. To give substance to her archaeological credentials, she had written an essay on the geometry of the cruciform structure, which she wanted to place in an eminent magazine, the *Revue Archéologique*, whose offices were in Paris. She wanted to make herself known to the editor, Professor Salomon Reinach, the scholar who had proselytized for the East as the origin of civilization. He was also the director of the Saint-Germain Museum. She set off with her cousin Sylvia and the Stanleys, ostensibly to do a little clothes shopping and buy Christmas presents. She duly called on Reinach, a plain and kindly man and the father of young children. He welcomed her warmly, taking to her at once and opening up his address book for her. She wrote home on 7 November:

> I went shopping with the Stanleys and bought a charming little fur jacket to ride in in Syria – yes, I did! Then I came in and read till 2 when Salomon fetched me and we went together to the Louvre ... We passed from Egypt through Pompeii and back to Alexandria ... Salomon developed an entirely new theory about eyelids – Greek eyelids, of course, and illustrated it with a Pheidean bust and a Scopas head ... it *was* nice.

With his letters of introduction to scholarly Paris, Gertrude was welcomed in every library and museum that she had time to visit. Reinach also gave her what amounted to a crash course in archaeological history. Under his aegis she examined Greek manuscripts and early ivories, buried herself in the Bibliothèque Nationale, spent a day in the Cluny museum, toured a new Byzantine museum not yet open to the public, and spent evenings poring over books in his library – 'Reinach has simply set all his boundless knowledge at my disposal and I have learnt more in these few days than I should have learnt by myself in a year.'

On her last evening he played a game with her, showing her a photograph or drawing at random from one of his books, and asking her to identify it. She thought she must have passed the test, for at the end of the evening he paid her the compliment of inviting her to write a book review for the magazine. The book was by Josef Strzygowski, the controversial Viennese archaeologist who looked to the Orient for origins and influences on the West. He was noted for a conviction – debatable – that the antecedents of Christian buildings could be traced to Iran. Writing about any book by Strzygowski would require a delicate balance of views, but Gertrude was not daunted. She spoke to Reinach of her forthcoming journey, and he encouraged her to examine Roman and Byzantine ruins and learn about the impact of these civilizations upon the region. Of the two empires, the Byzantine was then the smaller and less developed field: from now on it would become her special field of study. He would publish her essay, Reinach told her, and they parted company warmly. She would meet him again in Paris after her trip, and he promised to unravel for her some of the mysteries of Nabataean and Safaitic inscriptions.

In January 1905 she set off from Beirut, buying herself two strong horses and aiming south along the coast, riding astride. Her crew was small. She took a couple of mules, carrying her own green waterproof tent bought in London, a travelling canvas bath and extra pistols, as well as lesser gifts bought locally to give, as necessary, to sheikhs.

The journey began badly and became much worse before she ended up in Konya in Anatolia, nine hundred miles later. Even before she had covered the 150 miles from Beirut to Jerusalem, 'the mud was incredible. We waded . . . for an hour at a time knee deep, the mules fell down, the donkeys almost disappeared, and the horses grew wearier and wearier.' Fever delayed her, then ice. She had her fur jacket from Paris, but otherwise only two small trunks. In the Jordan Valley the hundred-foot ravines of mud, washed by falling rain, became so slippery that she nearly lost a horse. She arrived twenty miles north of the Dead Sea, in Salt, so saturated that she took shelter in a house: 'My host,' she wrote home, '. . . his nephew and his small boys held it a point of hospitality not to leave me for a moment, and they assisted with much interest while I changed my boots and gaiters and even my petticoat, for I was deeply coated in mud.'

Her declared intention was to revisit the Jebel Druze without contacting the Turkish authorities, who would remember how she had slipped through their fingers before. They would have heard that she was in the area and insist on giving her a military escort, which would herald the end of her plans to travel from sheikh to sheikh and site to site in western Syria. Her now sound knowledge of the language was the only key she needed. Her host in Salt passed her on to his brother-in-law Namoud, a well-to-do merchant east of Madeba, who would take good care of her. To reach him, she would be moving a day's march east, and beyond the Turkish authorities.

Poring over her map with her, Namoud was able to tell her exactly how to get to the Jebel Druze and avoid the Turks. But now came a delay in the form of a phenomenal storm. Like castaways on an island shore, a group of Bedouins of the Beni Sakhr tribe, plus three of the Sherarat, were washed out of their tents and joined Gertrude and her crew, all taking shelter in the enormous cave where Namoud and his people lived with their twenty-three cows. It was a group of Beni Sakhr who had menaced Gertrude on her trip to Petra, before she had learnt how to enlist their friendship and help. Now they made her one of themselves. 'Mashallah! Bint Arab,' they declared – 'As God has willed: a daughter of the desert.'

In the desert, word travels almost by magic. Now a kinsman of the Sheikh of the Daja arrived, to act as escort (*rafiq*) for Gertrude over the four days' journey into Druze territory. As warm as she could make herself in her fur, and smoking Egyptian cigarettes, Gertrude sat by the fire in the damp cave and observed the shades of difference between the three tribes and the complexities of their politics. After a few subsequent questions to Namoud and her crew, she was able to summarize the information in the clearest way. She noted that the Sherarat, though generally considered by the others to be base-born, sold the best camels in Arabia; that there was blood between the Sherarat and the Sakhr, that the Sakhr were allied to the Howeitat tribe, and that both were enemies of the Druze and the Beni Hassan, who were allied in their turn to the Daja.

She was soon the guest of the Sheikh of the Daja, and was struck, in the course of conversation, by the tribe's knowledge of current affairs and of poetry. The recitations accompanied the evening gossip concerning the latest *ghazzus* – tribal raids – and tales of Turkish oppression. Sitting in Sheikh Fellah's goat-hair tent, with his harem curtained off on the far side, she became more than a guest – an equal.

> I produced the Muallakat [pre-Muhammadan poems] and three or four examples for the use of various words. This excited much interest, and we bent over the fire to read the text which was passed from hand to hand . . . I spent a most enjoyable evening . . . telling them how things are in Egypt. Egypt is a sort of Promised Land, you have no idea what an impression our government there has made on the Oriental mind.

A day further on, her Daja guide led her to a camp of Beni Hassan, where they found despondency. They had just missed a *ghazzu* by five hundred riders of combined Sakhr and Howeitat tribesmen, who had carried off two thousand head of cattle and many tents – 'I could not help regretting a little,' she wrote, 'that the ghazu had not waited till today that we might have seen it.' Meanwhile, it was the Feast of Sacrifice. Gertrude drew a veil over the killing of three camels, but joined in with the firing of guns at sunset: 'I too contributed – by request – in a modest way, with my revolver, the first, and I expect the only, time I shall use it.'

A grim ruined castle at Salkhad, a town of black lava built into the southern slope of a volcano, provided compensation for missing the excitement in the Beni Hassan camp. Dining on the evening of her arrival, she heard wild singing and gunfire outside in the darkness. Stepping out of her tent, she saw a fire burning on the castle tower. So she left her supper, scrambled up the mountainside and came upon a *ghazzu* in the making, a retaliation for a Sakhr raid that had recently carried off five thousand sheep belonging to the Druze. She described the scene:

> Tomorrow the Druzes are going forth, 2000 horsemen, to recapture their flocks, and to kill every man, woman and child of the Sakhr that they may come across. The bonfire was a signal to the countryside. There at the top we found a group of Druzes, men and boys, standing in a circle and singing a terrible song. They were all armed and most of them carried bare swords . . .

She approached and listened, spellbound, to the words of the war song:

> 'Oh Lord our God! Upon them! Upon them!' Then half a dozen or so stepped into the circle, each shaking his club or his drawn sword in the face of those standing round. 'Are you a true man? Are you valiant?' . . . the swords glistened and quivered in the moonlight. Then several came up to me and saluted me: 'Upon thee be peace!' they said, 'The English and the Druze are one!' I said: 'Praise be to God! We too are a fighting race.'
>
> And if you had listened to that song you would know that the finest thing in the world is to go out and kill your enemy.

The ceremony ended with a headlong rush down the mountainside. Gertrude, carried away by the thrill of it all, ran with them. In the valley she stopped, let them pass, and stood listening for a few minutes before returning slowly to her tent. She was the first woman who had ever been to the Safeh, that wild territory continually swept at the time by tribal raids from both north and south. For the rest of the journey she would ride fully armed.

Bad as had been the weather throughout, it worsened. Soon they were fighting their way through deep snow and ten degrees of frost:

... it was more abominable than words can say. The mules fell down in snow drifts, the horses reared and bucked, and if I had been on a side-saddle we should have been down half a dozen times, but on this beloved saddle one can sit straight and close. So we plunged on ... till at last we came out on to a world entirely white. The last hour I walked and led my horse for he broke through the deep snow at every step.

At the Druze village of Saleh where she took shelter, she found that the male inhabitants knew the name of the Colonial Secretary, Joseph Chamberlain, and were interested in Lord Salisbury, the former Prime Minister, expressing polite regret to hear that he had died. 'The real triumph of eloquence was when I explained to them the fiscal question, and they all became Free Traders on the spot.'

Leaving Druze territory, she sheltered for two nights with some Ghiath tribesmen, whose tents were smoky and full of fleas. She wrote to Florence that the bath that followed, back in her own tent, was one of the most delightful she had ever had. Arriving in Damascus, she was greeted by an invitation from the Governor, and learnt that there had been three telegrams a day from Salkhad about her disappearance. She had become a Person in Syria too.

She entered the great mosque, leaving her shoes at the door, and was much moved by the evening prayers: 'Islam is the greatest republic in the world, there is neither class nor race inside the creed ... I begin to see dimly what the civilization of a great Eastern city means – how they live, what they think; and I have got on to terms with them.'

Being a Person, she soon saw, was not always an advantage. Later in her journey she was to discover that she had been followed in Damascus, unaware, by a police 'minder'. She arrived in Homs, a hundred miles further on, a celebrity, to find that she could not even take a casual walk through the bazaar because of the interest she excited — 'Tiresome, for I was never without the company of fifty or sixty people. It's one of the most difficult things I know to keep one's temper when one is constantly surrounded and mobbed ... I hereby renounce in despair the hope of ever again being a simple, happy traveller.' She had to employ a soldier to keep the crowd at bay, and then to fend off the authorities who wanted to give her eight watchmen for the night, when she refused to have more than two.

Escorted by travelling Kurds and a couple of handcuffed prisoners, she moved on to Aleppo and the Anatolian border, where floods and broken bridges awaited her. She paused to explore the place where the Syrian hermit Simeon Stylites lived for the last thirty-seven years of his life upon the tops of a series of pillars, and considered how different he must have been from her. In pouring rain she tried to copy carvings, using her cloak to protect her notebook. 'The devil take all Syrian inscriptions!'

The weather suddenly changed. It became so hot that the ground steamed, and mosquitoes plagued her tent. Her new Turkish muleteers were sulky and quarrelsome. For the first time she wished she was a man:

> There was nothing for it but to hold one's tongue, do the work oneself, and having seen that the horses were fed, I went to bed supperless because no one would own that it was his duty to light the fire! ... there are moments when being a woman increases one's difficulties. What my servants needed was a good beating and that's what they would have got if I had been a man – I seldom remember being in such a state of suppressed rage!

A short while later, after a day spent trying to copy inscriptions and take photographs in ruins lying deep in snake-infested grass, she came back to another supperless and tentless camp, lost her temper and lashed out at her muleteers with her riding crop. They infuriated her even more by smiling, and sitting down on another tent pack. She reached Adana and, as if by Providence, she was recommended a new servant: Fattuh, an Armenian Catholic with a wife in Aleppo. Fattuh was destined to become her Jeeves, the man she described as 'the alpha and omega of all'. She hired him as a cook, and it became a shared joke between the two of them that it was the one skill he never mastered — but she never again had to wait for her tent to be put up. He accompanied her on all her travels thereafter. He was clever, a superb manager of muleteers, brave, humorous and devoted to her. She would repay the compliment by her care of him when he fell ill at Binbirkilisse in 1907. Once only, after a most exhausting day's travelling, did she vent her fury on him. Most uncharacteristically, she sought him out a little later and humbly apologized. Two weeks after he had joined her crew, she was writing: 'Fattuh, bless him! The best servant I have ever had, ready to cook my dinner or push a mule or dig out an inscription with equal alacrity . . . and to tell me endless tales of travel as we ride, for he began life as a muleteer at the age of ten and knows every inch of ground from Aleppo to Van and Bagdad.'

From Konya, with great relief, she took the train to Binbirkilisse. Her attention had been drawn to this fortress city of ruined churches and monasteries by Strzygowski's 1903 book *Kleinasien* ('Asia Minor'), in which he concentrated on the early Byzantine monuments. She had brought the book in her saddle-bag all the way from Beirut. Her own explorations there could be undertaken daily, commuting from Konya. Returning one evening to her hotel, she ran into the great ecclesiastical archaeologist Sir William Ramsay, whose books on the Church and the Roman Empire stood on the shelves of her study at home. 'We fell into each other's arms and made great friends,' she told her parents. She had spotted something in a half-obliterated inscription in a cave in Binbirkilisse which she believed was a date. Together, and with Mrs Ramsay, they caught the train and she was able to show it to him. She was correct, and it was not long before they made a pact to return in a year or two to make a thorough investigation of the ruins and to try and date them with the help of the inscription.

The deeper she penetrated into the East, the greater became her respect for the people:

> Race, culture, art, religion, pick them up at any point you please down the long course of history, and you shall find them to be essentially Asiatic . . . Some day I hope the East will be strong again and develop its own civilization, not imitate ours, and then perhaps it will teach us a few things we once learnt from it and have now forgotten, to our great loss.

On her return to Rounton in June, she would write to Valentine Chirol: 'Did I tell you I was writing a travel book? Well I am. It's the greatest fun . . . It's Syria from underneath, what they think of it, the talk I hear round my camp fires, the tales they tell me as they ride with me, the gossip of the bazaar.' *The Desert and the Sown*, published in 1907, is still a classic of travel writing.

By the time of her 1909 journey to the Middle East, Gertrude's copious diaries had become virtually unreadable. They are a mixture of exhaustive archaeological detail, abbreviated notes about people and anything they said to her of a political or economic nature, and myriad details of daily desert life occasionally laced with flashes of adventure.* They sometimes slip into Turkish or Arabic. It would often happen that she wrote these notes around midnight after ten or twelve hours' travel and an evening of multi-lingual conversation in a desert tent or gilded embassy.

Why did she do so? Why did this wealthy young woman spend years of her prime learning some of the most difficult languages in the world and make great efforts in order to pit herself against truly appalling conditions and great dangers and go to places so obscure that they did not figure on any contemporary map? An independent woman of great ability, she inherited the purposeful curiosity of Lowthian Bell, acknowledged worldwide for his scientific breakthroughs and technological achievements. For Gertrude, at first, curiosity predominated over purpose. She was well aware that climbing, for instance, was not an adequate aim in life. Conquering a mountain belonged in the category of human achievement, but it helped no one but yourself. Usually, as soon as she excelled in one project, she moved on to the next. Driven by her

---

* A random example from her visit to Constantinople that year: 'As to the fall of Kiamil: it was quite unconstitutional: Kiamil tried a fall with the Committee and was beaten. As far as Sir A knows Ap 13 was due firstly to the Liberals – Ismail Kemal much to blame, he has not come up to expectation. Not unprobably they themselves founded or helped to found the Muhammidiyyah committee.'

need to test herself, she veered towards challenges tinged with danger and excitement.

When she discovered desert travel, the challenges suddenly proliferated into an all-embracing personal experiment of which she would never reach the end. There were languages to perfect, customs to learn, new kinds of human being to plumb, archaeology and history to explore, the techniques of surveying and navigation, photography and cartography to acquire. There was the risky business of staying alive and reaching her goal; and the intoxication of asserting her own identity far from the world where she would have been recognized first and foremost as a Bell, the spinster daughter of Hugh, heiress granddaughter of Lowthian.

Her adventures were not an attempt to make herself famous, or elevate herself into high society. All her life she rejected publicity, and had less and less interest in the aristocracy unless it came with a high degree of ability. Hugh, while maintaining the respect of government and business, had deliberately decided not to make the conventional follow-up moves – buying a country estate, spending time in London clubs, acquiring a peerage – to take the Bells from successful leaders of industry to members of the upper class. He had no time for men who acquired prestige only through their titles and the privileges that went with them. In an era when he would have counted more as a lord than as a man of achievement, he wanted to be recognized for his expertise, his business acumen and his civil leadership. Similarly, as a member of the third Bell generation, Gertrude was not using her inherited power and position in the enterprises she took on. The only help she accepted was the family money that funded her exploits. For everything else she depended on her intellect, her courage and her thirst for learning.

As the prospect of marriage and children receded, she felt an ever-increasing need for self-fulfilment in diversionary activities. At a certain point, even this would not be enough, but when that moment came, life would present her with a purpose of world importance. For the time being, she was beginning to make her name in the world of affairs. Up to the First World War, affairs of state, domestic and foreign, were conducted as comprehensively at dinner parties, soirées and embassy receptions as in government offices. She accessed this world, and was becoming recognized in it, as an expert in her areas of interest.

When she travelled, she had no hesitation in making herself immediately known to the consulate, or in calling on the ambassador, *mudir* or governor (*vali*) of the district. Wherever she went – Bucharest, Paris, Homs, Antioch – she would announce her arrival. There would follow dinner invitations, lunch parties, receptions, pressure to conduct her affairs from a room in the consulate rather than from a small tent. If you were a 'Person' as she now was – a person who mattered – you knew that it would be discourteous not to call and leave your card. If you were not a duke or an earl you could only maintain this position if you continued to merit it, and if you could prove that you mattered in the milieu of ambassadors and other notables. When Gertrude talked of her discussions with Dr So and So about the plight of the persecuted citizens in Armenia, or the importance of Aqaba as a supply route for oil, or the reasons for extending the railway to Mecca, or the fact that ten regiments were to be sent from Damascus to bring the Druzes of the Hauran to order, the table grew silent. People listened to her, and repeated what she said. Gertrude was not trying to enter the world of men – she was already part of it.

Since the eighteenth century, women such as Georgiana, Duchess of Devonshire, who engineered the success of the Liberal Party – or in America, much more recently, Mrs Harriman, who resurrected the fortunes of the Democrats – had exercised 'salon power' through dinners and house parties. Gertrude was a new and modern phenomenon, a person who exercised influence by delivering first-hand knowledge and opinions based on that knowledge. At home and abroad, she conferred with the greatest men of her day. She was definitively different from other Englishwomen who travelled in the East before and after her: Freya Stark, who said that it was wonderful to be a woman traveller there because you could pretend to be more stupid than you were; Lady Anne Blunt, who accompanied her husband Wilfrid; or the several romantic women profiled in Lesley Blanch's *The Wilder Shores of Love*, such as Lady Burton and Jane Digby.

As a person of affairs, her up-to-the-minute information about what was going on, as well as her perspective on it, was a vital tool. Her diaries stored, in abbreviated form, everything that a computer memory would now encompass. She would jot down what was being said in one circle, and perhaps find later that it threw light on what she heard elsewhere. She would pass her information on to her journalist friend Chirol, and, from home or abroad, face to face or in correspondence, to the statesmen of the day. As with many another archaeologist reporting on local politics in the Middle East, it has been said that she was a 'spy'. She would have regarded the label as both sensational and demeaning. She was a gatherer and disseminator of information, who lost nothing by doing the work without pay, and thereby gained entry into the corridors of power – entry as a fully fledged 'Person'.

As already mentioned, her mode of travelling, from 1909, was nothing short of majestic. It was not only that she liked to travel in style, but she knew that the sheikhs would judge her status by her possessions and her gifts, and treat her accordingly. She did not forget the Druze Yahya Beg's questioning the local villagers, 'Have you seen a queen travelling?' She packed couture evening dresses, lawn blouses and linen riding skirts, cotton shirts and fur coats, sweaters and scarves, canvas and leather boots. Beneath layers of lacy petticoats she hid guns, cameras and film, and wrapped up many pairs of binoculars and pistols as gifts for the more important sheikhs. She carried hats, veils, parasols, lavender soap, Egyptian cigarettes in a silver case, insect powder, maps, books, a Wedgwood dinner service, silver candlesticks and hairbrushes, crystal glasses, linen and blankets, folding tables and a comfortable chair – as well as her travelling canvas bed and bath. She took two tents, one for Fattuh to put up the moment they pitched camp, so that she had a table to write on, the other with her bath, to be filled with hot water once there was a fire, and her bed, to be made up with the muslin sleeping bag laid out under the blankets. 'I need not have hidden the cartridges in my boots!,' she wrote home in January 1909. 'We got through customs without having a single box opened.'

Mapping the Euphrates in 1909, Gertrude examined sites for 450 miles along its banks before arriving in the area of Najaf and her destination, Karbala. Here, at Ukhaidir, she found an immense and beautiful palace in a remarkable state of repair. She would never forget her amazement at first gazing on its formidable walls and vaulted ceilings. For a time, when it was confirmed that her plan of the palace was the first to be made, she believed that she had discovered an unknown citadel: 'No one knows of it, no one has seen it . . . It's the greatest piece of luck that has ever happened to me . . . A subject so enchanting and so suggestive as the Palace of Ukhaidir is not likely to present itself more than once in a lifetime.'

In 1910 she was to publish a preliminary paper on Ukhaidir in the *Journal of Hellenic Studies*, as well as giving a painstaking account of the building in her fifth book, covering her great expeditions of 1909 and 1910, *Amurath to Amurath*, which she copiously illustrated with her own photographs. But returning to the site in 1911, this time straight across the desert from Damascus to Hit, she found to her bitter disappointment that the long monograph she was about to publish, 168 pages of skilfully drawn plans and 166 photographs, would not be the first. In Babylon she discovered that some German archaeologists had been to the site during the two years of her absence, and were about to publish their own book. Her attitude to this setback demonstrated grace under pressure: she wrote in the preface to her book, *The Palace and Mosque at Ukhaidir*, of her admiration for the 'masterly' German volume, and apologized for offering a second version while explaining why she did so: '. . . my work, which was almost completed when the German volume came out, covers not only the ground traversed by my learned friends in Babylon, but also ground which they had neither leisure nor opportunity to explore . . . With this I must take leave of a field of study which formed for four years my principal occupation, as well as my chief delight.'

Gertrude's entry in the *Prolegomena*, the *Who's Who* of archaeology, names her as 'the remarkable pioneer woman of Byzantine architecture'. After publishing *The Thousand and One Churches*, about Binbirkilisse, in 1909, she concentrated on the high Anatolian plateau of the Tur Abdin, publishing the material she gathered there as her seventh book, *The Churches and Monasteries of the Tur Abdin*, in 1913. Gertrude had by now found her own archaeological viewpoint and argued persuasively against some of the convictions of Josef Strzygowski. Far from taking offence, though, he invited her to write an essay on the Tur Abdin in the journal he published with Max van Berchem, *Amida*, which she followed with a second essay in the *Zeitschrift für Geschichte der Architektur*, both illustrated by her plans and photographs.

Leaving the Tur Abdin behind her, on that same trip she had made a small diversion to the archaeological site of Carchemish, the ancient southern capital of the Hittites. There she had hoped to see her old mentor and friend David Hogarth, but he had left. Instead she found a young man who would become part of her future life, as she would of his. On 18 April 1911 Gertrude wrote of him: 'An interesting boy, he will make a traveller.'

His name was T. E. Lawrence; and he was impressed by her, as she was by him. He wrote of the famous traveller to his mother back home in England that she was pleasant, about thirty-six – she was in fact forty-three – and not beautiful.

Miss Gertrude Bell called last Sunday, and we showed her all our finds, and she told us all hers. We parted with mutual expressions of esteem: but she told Thompson his ideas of digging were prehistoric: and so we had to squash her with a display of erudition. She was taken (in 5 minutes) over Byzantine, Crusader, Roman, Hittite, and French architecture . . . and over Greek folk-lore, Assyrian architecture, and Mesopotamian Ethnology . . . prehistoric pottery and telephoto lenses, bronze age metal technique, Meredith, Anatole France and the Octobrists . . . the Young Turk movement, the construct state in Arabic, the price of riding camels, Assyrian burial-customs, and German methods of excavation with the Baghdad railway . . . This was a kind of hors d'oeuvre . . . she was getting more respectful.

To David Hogarth he wrote more flatteringly, in a rather different vein: 'Gerty has gone back to her tents to sleep. She has been a success: and a brave one.'

In every expedition, there is a moment long remembered that catches in memory its essence. For Gertrude in 1911 this came at Ashur, in northern Mesopotamia some sixty miles south of Mosul. Sitting in solitude on a hilltop, she remained there for an hour, while in her mind's eye she watched the history of civilization stream past:

> The whole world shone like a jewel, green crops, and blue waters and far away the gleaming snows of the mountains that bound Mesopotamia to the north ... I considered that the history of Asia was spread out before me. Here Mithridates murdered the Greek generals, here Xenophon began to have his command, and just beyond the Zab the Greeks turned and defeated the archers of Mithridates, marching then on to Larissa, the mound of Nimrud, where Xenophon saw the great Assyrian city of Calah standing in ruins. Nimrud stood out among the cornfields at my feet. A little further and I could see the plain of Arbela where Alexander conquered Asia.
>
> We people of the west can always conquer, but we can never hold Asia – that seemed to me to be the legend written across the landscape.

She was looking down on what would become Iraq, the country of which she would be the uncrowned queen. Curiously, she had also foretold its future, a future extending far beyond her own lifetime.

7

DICK DOUGHTY-WYLIE

A steadfast hero . . . Braver soldier never drew sword
. . . Tenderness and pity filled his heart.

In the summer of 1907, with her latest book just published, Gertrude was at Konya and Binbirkilisse in Turkey, working with Sir William Ramsay. Their association over this project, carried out as promised in 1905, entailed Gertrude willingly taking on the drudgery of the work, measuring and planning the buildings and working twelve-hour days while he supervised and interpreted. The resulting book, *The Thousand and One Churches*, published in 1909, is still the standard work on early Byzantine architecture in Anatolia. The reward, for Gertrude, was a prestige and credibility in the world of archaeology that she could have gained in no other way without years of study, and that many archaeologists would envy.

Gertrude had great advantages as an archaeologist: her willingness to go into dangerous territories, the freedom with which she could pursue her independent and expensive ends, her energy, her enthusiasm. No mountain was too high, no site too well guarded by snakes, spiders or mosquitoes, no journey too far for her, once she was on the scent. Ramsay wrote in the preface of the book, and in a letter to Florence, that the all-important date that she had spotted two years earlier in Binbirkilisse was concealed in a small cave, where it had hitherto been overlooked. He wrote of his admiration for Gertrude's 'thoroughness and alertness' in having noticed it, adding: 'the chronology of the Thousand and One Churches centres round this text'. Compared to Ramsay, Gertrude was a gifted novice in the field. When David Hogarth had applied to work with him, the professor had packed him off to Greece to learn epigraphy. In extending his patronage to the eager student that was Gertrude, Ramsay may not have been entirely ingenuous. She was already famous for her expeditions and it was known that she was an heiress who might contribute financially to excavations.

Gertrude had met up with her beloved servant from Aleppo, Fattuh, having arrived in Asia Minor in April. She wrote on the 28th:

> The seas and the hills are all full of legend and the valleys are scattered over with the ruins of the great rich Greek cities. Here is a page of history that . . . enters into the mind as no book can relate it . . . I don't suppose there is anyone in the world happier than I am or any country more lovely than Asia Minor. I just mention these facts in passing so that you may bear them in mind.

At Miletus she received a telegram from her sister Elsa to say that she was engaged to one Herbert Richmond. Florence's follow-up letter arrived at the site of the ancient Carian city of Aphrodisias, where Gertrude was entranced by doorways decorated with scrolls of fruit and flowers entwined with birds and animals. She made her way along the shores of lakes and past peach and cherry trees under snow-covered mountains, the rough roads crossed by rushing streams which made the going difficult for the baggage animals. At the Lake of Egerdir she bought another horse for ten Turkish pounds, and persuaded a fisherman to row her out to a tiny island: 'It was surrounded by ruined Byzantine walls dropping into the water in great blocks of masonry; here and there there was a bit of an older column . . . and they were densely populated by snakes.' Looking down at the lake below, she could see the glimmer of a fallen stone under the water that seemed to have an inscription on it. Brushing aside the snakes, she climbed down over the rocks and waded in: 'I did all I knew to get the inscription. I tried to scrub the slime off the stone, but . . . the slime floated back and finally I gave up and came out very wet and more than a little annoyed.'

With Fattuh, she crossed into Asia via the Roman roads, noting the many butterflies, and reached Konya. She was already at work in Binbirkilisse, 'digging up churches', when the Ramsays rumbled in on a couple of donkey carts with their son, who had come on a project for the British Museum. Mrs Ramsay made tea while the professor, 'oblivious of all other considerations', immersed himself at once in what Gertrude was doing, as if continuing a conversation they had broken off only a moment or two earlier. 'We think we have a Hittite settlement!' she wrote home on 25 May. 'What gorgeous fun it's being. You should see me directing the labours of 20 Turks and 4 Kurds!'

Although she was now thirty-eight, she was in her prime. Love apart, she was fully realized and still – as Janet Hogarth had noted at Oxford – effervescently alive at all points. So good a time was she having that Florence probably took with a pinch of salt Gertrude's scribbled protestation at the foot of a letter that 'I'm horribly bored at not being at E's wedding.' Happy and absorbed, she had no presentiment that she was about to meet the man who would prove to be the love of her life.

Major Charles Hotham Montagu Doughty-Wylie of the Royal Welch Fusiliers – Richard, or 'Dick' to his friends – was a quiet war hero who had won clasps and medals in battles both during the East African campaign of 1903 and before then. He was the nephew of the traveller Charles Montague Doughty, the poet and geologist who had written the sonorous *Arabia Deserta*. The record of Doughty's wild and dangerous adventures, written in rich majestic prose, the book was a kind of Bible to serious travellers in the Middle East. It was one of the books that Gertrude always took with her when she travelled.

Dick Doughty-Wylie had been educated at Winchester and Sandhurst. In 1889, at twenty-one – he was the same age as Gertrude, almost to the day – he had joined up and gone on to serve in the British Egyptian army in China and in South and East Africa. He had been a transport officer in India, a mounted infantryman in South Africa, and in charge of a camel detachment in Somalia. A military photograph shows him thin and moustached, tanned, taller, broader and more handsome than many of his contemporaries, and with a chestful of medals. He had been badly wounded in the Boer War and again in Tientsin during the Chinese rebellion. He had married only three years before meeting Gertrude, in the year she had climbed the Matterhorn. His volatile and ambitious wife Lilian, known outside the family as Judith, had been the widow of Lt Henry Adams-Wylie of the Indian Medical Service. (She had demanded that both husbands add her surname to theirs.) In a photograph taken in Konya she sits in a garden chair, leaning forward looking pensively at the ground, her hands in her lap, the fingers tightly interlaced. Judith's insistence, combined with Dick's need for a breathing space, had motivated his transfer to the diplomatic field, and he was now the British military consul at Konya. Gertrude made their acquaintance when she knocked at the door to pick up her mail.

To Gertrude, at first, Doughty-Wylie was just the 'charming young soldier' with the 'quite pleasant little wife' who invited her to lunch in the shady garden of their Konya house. Gertrude arrived and was ushered into the garden with the other guests. After weeks of digging in the burning sun, she was tanned; her green eyes sparkled; wisps of her auburn hair, escaping from her straw hat, had faded to blonde. When crossing the desert she would habitually wear a pale-blue veil that she pulled down all round from the brim of her hat, but on the dig she needed to survey and inspect, and the veil got in the way. Judith's skin was pale: she wore white, and tended to frills. She seldom ventured out without a parasol.

Gertrude exuded energy; she talked volubly; she laughed a lot. She was in her element. Six troubled years later, Doughty-Wylie would recall the occasion: 'GB walking in covered with energy and discovery and pleasantness'. By now rather a famous Englishwoman, she was at once the centre of attention. Everyone was curious to meet this traveller and linguist, whose latest book *The Desert and the Sown* was being widely discussed. A brilliant conversationalist and a confident storyteller, she dominated the afternoon, amusing everyone with her descriptions of Ramsay's chaotic mode of travelling. He might have been the prototype of the absent-minded professor, losing track of his luggage and clothes along the way, regularly leaving his drawings and rubbings under a stone somewhere on site. Gertrude had got into the habit of doing a tour of the dig each time they left, picking up the papers and notes he had scattered about, while Mrs Ramsay would run along behind him with his Panama hat and cups of tea. On one occasion he asked Gertrude: 'Remind me, my dear, where are we?' Without his wife or Gertrude he was incapable of remembering the name of his hotel or its location.

'The "Wylies" are dears, both of them,' Gertrude wrote to Florence, adding that it was particularly to the quiet Dick that she had 'talked long' of things and people. He was fascinated by the Middle East and had great affection and respect for the Turks: the previous year he had taken his wife on a tour of Baghdad, Constantinople and the ancient city of Babylon. Gertrude and he had left the table to discuss the Sufi philosopher and theosophist Jalal ad-Din Rumi, whose tomb at Konya is still visited by tens of thousands of disciples each year. The mystic Rumi gave himself to the composition of poetry and the rituals of the whirling dervishes. Doughty-Wylie was profoundly moved by the world of Islam, and was impressed to see that Gertrude knew much of the poetry by heart. She had first read with Henry Cadogan Rumi's lines of yearning for his spiritual home: 'Ah, listen to the reed as it tells its tale;/ Listen, ah listen, to the plaint of the reed./ They reft me from the rushes of my home,/ my voice is sad with longing,/ sad and low . . .'

She was to meet Dick and Judith several times at Konya, and they helped her in many small ways. But that was all there was to their first encounters. This expedition came to an abrupt end because of the worrying condition of her servant Fattuh. On a previous archaeological trip with Gertrude, he had rushed eagerly after her into a ruined building and hit his head on the lintel of a low doorway. He now collapsed, and it transpired that he had been suffering agonizing headaches ever since the accident. Gertrude, who did nothing by halves, telegraphed the British Ambassador in Constantinople and Ferid Pasha the Grand Vizier, explaining that Fattuh needed specialist attention. She prepared to take him to a hospital there without further ado, said her goodbyes to the Wylies, invited them to visit her at Rounton sometime, and departed. No sooner was Fattuh safely in hospital and on the mend than she was cruising the Bosporus on the embassy yacht and meeting the Grand Vizier — 'He is a very great man, and . . . moreover he was kinder to me than words can say.'

She arrived home in August 1907, and was reunited with her French maid Marie Delaire who had come up to London to help her buy a new autumn wardrobe. Soon afterwards she was back at Rounton, sitting in her study with Professor Ramsay, who had arrived with his wife to work with his hostess on *The Thousand and One Churches*.

Knowing as many notables as she did, and since her great friend Chirol wrote regularly for *The Times*, it is not surprising that she kept a cuttings book. Into it she was soon pasting an account of Doughty-Wylie's latest heroic venture. In the volatile mood engendered by the Young Turks' nationalist rebellion, fanatical mobs in the Konya area were now slaughtering Armenian Christians, leaving corpses scattered across roads and railway tracks. Donning his old uniform, Doughty-Wylie had collected together a body of Turkish troops and led them through Mersin and Adana, pacifying the murderous crowds. Wounded by a bullet, he went out on patrol again with a bandaged right arm. His initiative was said to have saved hundreds if not thousands of lives, and he was made a Companion of the Order of St Michael and St George. Most unusually, the Turkish authorities also decorated him for valour, awarding him the rare Order of Majidieh. Gertrude's letter of congratulation was only one of many he received from all over the world, but he must have answered it warmly, for a year later they were in regular correspondence, Gertrude sometimes addressing her letters to them both and sometimes to him alone. It seems that the Doughty-Wylies did visit the Bells at Rounton, in 1908: 'he is very nice,' Gertrude noted almost shyly. Given her usual expansive way of expressing herself, the four words are notable for their brevity, as if she were suppressing whatever else might be said or felt about him.

A new warmth entered their correspondence as it shuttled to and fro between Mesopotamia, where Gertrude was embarking on one of her most important exploratory journeys and archaeological projects – the drawing and measuring of the enormous ruined palace of Ukhaidir – and Addis Ababa, where Dick was now consul. And then, in spring 1912, he arrived in London without Judith, who was visiting her mother in Wales, to take up the appointment of director-in-chief of the Red Cross relief organization. He was staying in his old bachelor flat in Half Moon Street, as he did when his wife was not with him. It is possible that Gertrude and Dick had met once or twice in London during the five years since their first meeting, for it took her no time at all to decide that she had to be in London too. She had been asked to give a lecture, she told Florence, it was high time she saw her cousins, and she needed a lot of new clothes for the summer. She shot up to town and launched herself into one of the happiest times of her life.

Gertrude's large circle of well-heeled friends and vivacious Stanley cousins provided her with a perfect opportunity to absorb the weary soldier into her orbit. He was serious in mind and grave in demeanour. She felt there was little laughter in his life. He met through her a more lively, stimulating group of people than he had ever known, perhaps more intellectual and witty, probably more appreciative of music, books and painting than his army friends at the club. It was known amongst them that his marriage was not entirely congenial; and after all he had been through, he was content for a while to drift, to escape his old friends and colleagues for days and evenings of a thoroughly unpredictable kind. In groups of family or friends, Gertrude and he went to plays, to the music-hall, to museums and exhibitions, listened to bands and concerts in the park and joined in vociferous arguments about art and literature. He went to see Gertrude lecture, something she did with style and confidence, her humour as much as her erudition carrying her audience with her. On a walk in the park or on the way to an 'at home' or restaurant in the West End, Doughty-Wylie would tower over Gertrude; and they would fall behind, deep in conversation, their bursts of laughter sometimes causing her cousins to look back

over their shoulders and wonder what they found so funny. After
dinner, the two of them would tend to draw apart, talking and
laughing late into the night, veiled in the smoke from her long
ivory holder. Seeing Gertrude in her pearls and diamonds, her
green eyes sparkling, her beautiful hair brushed and pinned up, and
wearing one of her new French evening dresses, her family must
have realized with a jolt just how pretty she could be – and how
flirtatious.

She was not just amusing herself any more. This was becoming
the most important relationship in her life. She found in Dick
Doughty-Wylie a combination of irresistible qualities. Like his uncle,
the ascetic Charles M. Doughty whose *Arabia Deserta* was her constant companion, and like the Bedouin she had come to admire and
love, he was both spiritual and unflinching. The flicker and pulse of
sexual attraction between them grew stronger with each meeting.
The bond was growing – she knew he felt it too. She made no plans
to go abroad that year, and by January 1913 she was writing to
Chirol to tell him that she had turned down an invitation to go on
a scientific expedition to the Karakoram mountains in China: 'The
nearer I came to it, the more I could not bear it. I can't face being away
from home for fourteen months. My life now in England is so delightful
that I will not take such a long time out of it.'

She had waited so long for this happiness. And in the excitement
of their mutual attraction and interests she found it easy to forget
the existence of Judith. From her initial meeting with the Doughty-
Wylies in Konya, she had described him in her letters home as 'a
charming young soldier' with 'a quite pleasant little wife'. Any woman
reading this description of the Consul and his wife would have been
alerted by the egregious word 'little'. In Gertrude's system of values,
'little woman' would be a phrase used more frequently as time went
by, and always in a pejorative sense. 'A nice little woman' was one of
her deadliest assessments. The phrase had become family code for
an unimportant, irritating person – often, unfortunately, attached
to a 'useful' man. In the case of Mrs Doughty-Wylie, a trained
nurse, this was wide of the mark indeed. When Dick had undertaken the relief of twenty-two thousand refugees at Konya, Judith

had organized three makeshift hospitals for the sick and injured. But it was no secret that the Doughty-Wylies had a difficult marriage. Judith was surely not unaware of his philandering, but she was no complaisant wife, as she was to prove.

The happiness that Gertrude felt could not last for ever. Judith was expected in London, the date was set, and in due course she arrived. Gertrude returned to Yorkshire, downcast, confused. In the meantime, she threw herself into gardening and archaeological study, and as the summer of 1913 turned into autumn she spent long days hunting – doing anything and everything she could think of to pass the time until she saw him again. The zenith of each day was the arrival of the post which might, and frequently did, contain letters from him.

Writing an article or drawing a church in her study, she would fall into a reverie, chin on hand, then come to with a start. Having ordered the gardeners to get on with their work, she would wander off into the woods leaving them unsupervised, with a drain half dug or planting programme unspecified. She was happy one moment, sad the next. Dick and she had become so important to each other that she was constantly wondering if, and on what terms, she could improve her situation. If only she could persuade him to leave Judith to be with her, she felt that she could withstand the ostracism that would follow. Much as she dreaded Hugh's and Florence's disapproval, if she and Dick could stand firm and constant to each other for long enough, she speculated, her parents would probably capitulate. Then she would fall to considering her lover's situation. Distinguished soldier-statesman that he was, he would lose wife, career and reputation all in one. Her unsatisfied longings always brought her back to this station of the cross: he had never given her any cause for hope on this score. This left her, in the reflective moments that pressed in on her more and more frequently, with a sense of agonizing loneliness and depression. She lived for their next meeting.

A devoted family woman, feminine in her tastes, Gertrude loved the company of children and young people. How unjust that she had never had a happy affair, let alone a husband or child. In her bleakest moments, she would face up to the fact that, despite all her triumphs, she had never come first with anyone – except, perhaps, her father. She knew that her confrontational manner and quick, impatient responses alienated many men, but she didn't mind that. Anyone that she could intimidate could be no life partner for Gertrude. As she had grown older and her list of achievements longer, her requirements grew more exacting – indeed, they were almost unmatchable. She wanted a handsome, clever man who was larger than life, with accomplishments at least the equal of hers; a brave man who could fight and hunt and quote poetry, who had read the great books of civilization, and spoke foreign languages, appreciated the theatre and the National Gallery; someone who was at home in London and in foreign society, who was well travelled, who knew the distinguished politicians and statesmen she herself knew. She was looking for a hero – and why not? She was, after all, a heroine. She felt no doubt that Doughty-Wylie was her true match.

Confused by emotions that she had hardly ever experienced before, she was existing in a state of perpetual impatience. She ended it by deciding to invite him to Rounton.

She rationalized this move to herself time and time again. It would hardly be a social indiscretion for him to stay without his wife. She could ask both of them at a time when Dick had indicated that Judith would be in Wales. Gertrude was constantly entertaining friends and family; every weekend brought a different house party, and he would be just one of the crowd. In the autumn and winter there were hunting and shooting, the races, dances, and the houses of their neighbours to visit. When the lake froze, there were vicious games of ice hockey in which she played a major part. But she would invite Dick in July, when picnics, tennis tournaments, hacking, fishing, seaside visits, boat trips and jaunts to ruined abbeys filled the days. However, while she could bring Dick into this life without comment from friends and neighbours, she was cautious about the attitude of Hugh and Florence. Not for the world would she have upset them, indeed she ached for their approval. And there was not, of course, the faintest hope that those two pillars of society, who adhered to all the rules of social conduct, would approve of her plans. There was also – no mean consideration – her own sense of honour, one so inviolable that it would compromise the affair at every stage. Gertrude was no hypocrite. She did not intend to break the rules. As an outsider looking in, she saw marriage as sacrosanct. She did not intend to start a sexual relationship with him, merely to continue the exquisite mutual delight of his attractive and attracted presence. For once in her life, perhaps, she did not allow her head to rule her heart.

She stopped herself from wondering how far that pleasure might take them in their private moments together, or what the consequences might be for her. By the time she troubled about that, she was too far in to deny herself the rare delight of his company. There must have been, initially, some self-deception as to the depth of her feelings for him, for she was still keeping from Hugh and Florence the fact that she was inviting Dick on the understanding that he would come without his wife. But Gertrude had to admit to herself that her intentions were not what they ought to be. Certainly, consideration for Judith mattered less than her growing intimacy with Dick. If Florence suspected anything, as she probably did, she may have reflected that Gertrude, at forty-four, was not of an age at which she could be told how to behave. And she would probably have looked back with pity at the twenty-four-year-old being separated from her fiancé, then having to come to terms with his death. The young woman's total lack of bitterness or recrimination towards her parents over this tragedy may well have been lovingly recalled by her stepmother, but it may not have relieved her of feelings of remorse. Perhaps, remembering how she had never allowed the teenage Gertrude to visit those aristocratic houses where casual adultery took place, Florence sighed as she decided to look the other way.

There was another woman in the house who may have suspected the truth. Marie Delaire could not have failed to notice her mistress's anxiety about her summer wardrobe. There were a dozen fittings for new dinner dresses, hats to be retrimmed, linen skirts to be taken up, alterations to last year's costumes, and a dozen filmy white blouses to be sewn with pin-tucks and edging: the new fashion was to wear your fine blouses with a string of pearls inside, so that they could be seen through the delicate fabric.

And so Dick came to Rounton for a few days in July 1913. After the day's excursion, the gallop across the fields, the noisy, cheerful dinner followed by coffee and card games in the drawing-room, the babble of voices would gradually diminish by ones and twos as the guests said goodnight and drifted upstairs to their rooms. Gertrude and Dick sat on by the fire together, talking and looking at each other.

To her it was a dream: it would have been like this if they had been married. Her happiness was an intoxication. Here was the man she loved, here was the family she loved, in the house that she loved. Reserve after reserve was breaking down, but there must have been an awkwardness, too, an unspoken question about the night to come. Perhaps, obliquely, she let him know where her room was. At last she went up to bed. Unpinning her hair, she heard him knocking softly at her door, and let him in. They stood, his arms around her, her heart beating fast, then sat a little uncomfortably on the bed. They talked, half in whispers. Grave as ever, he was difficult for her to read, but as always, she found there were no limits to what she could say. She explained her feelings: her happiness to have found the man she could love – and her misery to have found him already married. He pressed her to him, full of affection, and they lay down. Folded in his arms, Gertrude told him that she was a virgin. His warmth and attentive sympathy were boundless, but when he kissed her and moved closer, put his hands on her, she stiffened, panicked, whispered 'No'. He stopped at once, assuring her that it didn't matter, and when tears came into her eyes he comforted her for a few minutes and told her nothing had changed. Then he slipped away and out of the door.

The next day, another jarring round of distractions and entertainments wound to its end. It was impossible to speak to him for long, and then he was gone. His thank you letter, written on 13 August, followed shortly afterwards – she snatched it from the hall table and ran upstairs to read it in private:

My dear Gertrude

I am so very glad you took me to Rounton. I so much enjoyed it, the people, the place, the garden, the woods, everything. They are a vital setting to my friend, however many other frames she fits in. And I am so glad you told me things, and found you could talk to me. It's that I like – just openness and freedom to say and do exactly what one wants to do. In your mind I think there was a feeling, natural at first openings of doors, that it wasn't properly appreciated. But it was – I love openness – I've always ever since those early Turkey days wanted to be a friend of yours – Now I feel as if we had come closer, were really intimate friends – I've gained so much and I want to hold it. The loneliness – why we are all born alone die alone really live alone – and it hurts at times – Is this nonsense or preachments? I don't care – I must write something, something to show you how very proud I am to be your friend. Something to have meaning, even if it cannot be set down, affection, my dear, and gratitude and admiration and confidence, and an urgent desire to see you as much as possible . . .

All the good luck in the world,

Yours ever, R.

'All the good luck in the world'! She was mortified, humiliated. Where did such a letter leave her? She read and reread his words, turning and twisting them to extract the last drop of meaning. She tried to compensate for the coolness of the letter by dwelling on the words 'we all really live alone'. This must be a reference to the unsatisfactory state of his marriage, but it told her nothing new. Her spirits plummeted again. Was he really saying, 'Don't be embarrassed, I appreciate the depth of your feelings, I'm glad you weren't inhibited, let's be friends'?

But she wanted to be so much more than friends. In a flash she saw that the intimate evening at Rounton was momentous for her in a way that it was not for him. He was so much more experienced than she was: he had told her of his numerous encounters with women. Her own love life had not been successful. She felt things too deeply and had suffered too much over Henry Cadogan to lightly repeat the experience. Twenty years had passed, but it remained by far the most important affair in her life, a poetic, heartfelt engagement that had prompted Florence and Hugh to investigate his past and his finances, and turn him down – or at least to counsel several years of waiting. Then had come his death from pneumonia as a result of falling into the icy river, which left a question mark over what had actually happened. It would have been traumatic at any age to have committed yourself to a person you loved, to have had to break that commitment, and then to hear that your lover had died in a way that would always raise agonizing questions.

Cadogan's death had left her wounded: she would flirt, but she would not commit. Attractive as she was in her warmth and energy and perfect health, lovely as she could look with her red hair and slim, strong body, few men could break through her reserve. She had had one particular admirer, one Bertie Crackenthorpe, whom she first noted was 'very devoted' – and then, with mounting irritation, she found him 'always at my elbow listening'. Soon after this, she wrote him off: 'I've seen quite enough of him for the moment!' Then there was the short-lived but deeply felt relationship with Florence's nephew Billy Lascelles, kept on the boil by several family holidays. When that was over and she had grown up, she examined her feelings in a detached way: '. . . how odd it is to realise that those fires are ashes now, no vestiges of spark, thank goodness! No excitement, no regret. All that remains is a memory of sadness that aches curiously at times, but which is far and far from demanding his presence.' Later, she had a flirtation with a charming Yorkshireman, Will Pease. Her watchful half-sister Molly wrote: 'Gertrude flirts awfully with him', and Elizabeth Robins, the family friend, thought that they would become engaged. But whatever Pease intended, Gertrude evaded him. The affair proceeded no further than affectionate banter.

Love came only twice to Gertrude. This time it had moved her to the depths of her soul. The effect it had on her was perhaps due, in part, to her almost complete lack of sentiment and to her

formidable intellect. She was not likely, as another woman might
have been, to confuse affection with passion. As Florence, who
knew Gertrude better than any other woman, was to write: 'In
truth the real basis of Gertrude's nature was her capacity for deep
emotion. Great joys came into her life, and also great sorrows.
How could it be otherwise, with . . . her ardent and magnetic
personality . . . and a temperament so avid of experience?' She had
learnt, long before her thirties, to live without a lover, and no
woman was better equipped to compensate, filling her life with
adventures of so many other kinds. At the same time the longings
that had not been fulfilled were expressed in her extraordinary
aptitude for poetry that she had had since her schooldays, when
reading Milton made her 'want to stand on her head for joy'. The
expression of the most distilled emotions, poetry was the only
dimension in her that her stepmother was disappointed not to see
fully realized. Had the lack of a lover and husband, Florence would
wonder, inhibited this powerful source of feeling in her stepdaughter?

Doughty-Wylie had proceeded from Rounton to Suffolk. From
there he wrote again to add a strange corollary to his letter:

> . . . By the way, talking of dreams – Rounton ghosts visited me
> the next night also. Is there any history of them? Some shadowy
> figure of a woman who really quite bothered me, so that I
> turned on the light. It wasn't your ghost, or anything like you;
> but something hostile and alarming . . . She . . . was a long,
> shadowy woman thing that swept and swept across my bed like
> a hawk, stooping and said nothing, and I didn't know who the
> devil she was, but she meant attack, and I wanted the light . . .

Rounton was only forty-one years old, and had been occupied by
Hugh and Florence since 1905.*

Dick returned to London to find a stack of letters from
Gertrude. Undoubtedly he was flattered by the attentions of this
much respected woman, and didn't want to lose her friendship; but

* Miles Richmond, the last member of the family to live there, knows nothing
of ghosts in the house.

while her letters addressed the issues that tortured her, his responses stopped short of any sense of commitment. '. . . Wonderful letters, my dear, which delight me. Bless you. But there can be no words to answer you with. Well – let's talk about other things . . .'

And then came the hammer blow. A letter from him at his club told her that he had accepted a post in Albania, with the International Boundary Commission. 'My wife is in Wales. She'll come up when I wire to her and go with me – till we see the hows and whys and wheres . . . I have turned into my old bachelor quarters in Half Moon Street, no. 29. Write to me there . . . while I am alone, let's be alone.' Perhaps in recognition of what this news would mean to Gertrude, and to comfort her a little, he signed himself 'Dick' for the first time. Any hope she had of seeing him again soon, or of distancing herself from the despair she felt after his visit to Rounton, was gone at a stroke. His letters were her lifeline. She had read them so many times she knew them all by heart – but now she wondered, had he allowed their correspondence only out of pity, saying to himself, 'I'll soon be gone, and that will be that'?

She expressed her misery to him, and he tried to comfort her. 'My dear, this shall go to speak with you – to give you my love and a kiss as if I were a child or you were.' She was only a beginner where love was concerned. Perhaps she made mistakes, pouring out her longing for him too early, urging him to leave his wife. In his oblique way he tried to communicate to her the link between these longings and the frustrations of self-imposed chastity. From the kindness of his heart, and somewhat clumsily, he was trying to tell her that she should not be ashamed of any of these emotions: 'Last night, a poor girl stopped me – the same old story – and I gave her money and sent her home . . . So many are really like me, or what I used to be, and I'm sorry for them . . . These desires of the body that are right and natural, that are so often nothing more than any common hunger – they can be the vehicle of fire of the mind, and as that only are they great . . .'

Then, a warning: 'Judith knowing you well and having always before seen your letters would find it very odd to be suddenly

debarred them and on voyages our lives are at close quarters.'
Gertrude was frantic. Didn't he want her letters? She would put it
to the test. She stopped writing, and he rose to the bait. Reassur-
ance came from him at once, at the end of August: 'A blank day,
my dear. I am tempted to wonder – did I say too much? Or was it
that you thought the time had passed? Or were you too occupied?
Away with all such things. In the chains we live in – or I live in –
it is wise and right to wear them easily.' She built on her small
victory, by asking how she could best write to him in Albania. He
replied:

> Of course call me Dick in letters, and I shall call you Gertrude
> – there is nothing in that – many people do – my wife doesn't
> see my letters as a rule, but as she often writes to you herself
> we have always passed them across – but oh how I shall miss
> them . . . There is another thing that has to be done – tonight
> I shall destroy your letters – I hate it – but it is right – one
> might die or something, and they are not for any soul but me.

Nothing, she felt, could be worse. It was a goodbye, and it was
followed by another: '. . . if I can't write to you, I shall always
think of you telling me things in your room at Rounton . . . the
subtle book eludes, but our hands met on the cover'. 'The subtle
book' was always, she recognized, his metaphor for sex. '. . . And
you'll go on being the wise and splendid woman that you are, not
afraid of any amazement and finding work and life and the fullness
of it always to your hand. And I shall always be your friend.'
She had reached the crossroads of her life. At an age when it
was realistic to relinquish hopes of meeting a man she could marry
and with whom she could have children, she had met exactly the
kind of man she had always been looking for – one who could not
be belittled by her own achievements, a man she could compare
with pride to her powerful father and grandfather. Less likely than
most women to have an unwise affair, she was still very vulnerable.
Nonconformist, mould-breaking – feeling, being and making it plain
that she was superior to almost all the men she met – she had
hidden for so long behind her lines of defence that she was caught

unawares by his hold on her. In her few melancholy moments hitherto, it was only the lack of a husband and family that gave her pain. There was never the slightest bitterness or jealousy in her references to Elsa's and Molly's children, whom she found enchanting. Valentine Chirol had noticed how, on a holiday visit to Wales, she had reduced a group of lively children in his garden to spellbound silence with a ragbag of stories, some serious, some ridiculous. Children brought out her playful side, and Florence had shown her how to be silly with children in the best possible way. At her Stanley cousin's coming-out dance, there were about twenty little girls with whom she had danced wildly all evening.

With all her erudition Gertrude was still the same person she had been at Oxford when, feeling too hot one day, she had jumped into the river with all her clothes on. She would be the first to leave a lunch table at which the children had been fidgeting and bickering, to chase them into the garden or collect a bat and ball and start a loud and argumentative game. At Mount Grace Priory, she had recently arranged a splendid picnic party for all the children in the family, and her letters are littered with affectionate comments about her little nieces. 'I don't think I ever saw anything more adorable than Moll's children. There's no question about Pauline's being pretty, I think she's quite charming.'

Her last chance of happiness seemed to evaporate as Dick and Judith packed their trunks for Albania. Aching head in hands, Gertrude accepted that she could neither forward the affair nor communicate with him directly. It seemed that her pleasure in all things was at an end. She did not mind, now, if she lived or died. It was not her first reverse, nor would it be her last; but she was, after all, a spoilt heiress who had been denied very few of the things that she had wanted in life. She had rarely heard the word 'No', but it was her fate to meet denial at the very times it was hardest for her to accept it.

With the same courage that characterized her entire life, she decided once and for all to detach herself from the seesaw of hope and despair. Gertrude was no Victorian moralist – she was too intelligent for that – but she accepted that she had broken the rules, and the rules were on the side of the marriage vow. But she would show Dick that the love she felt for him could be diminished by neither time nor distance. To exorcise her anguish, she would undertake some life-threatening project and consecrate it to him. She would go back to the desert and undertake a journey that had killed other travellers before her. He told her that he loved her writing. Well, she would write a book for him of her daily trials and triumphs and send it to him in instalments as she reached each staging post. It would be rigorous in its focus on her journey. He, in Albania, perhaps not getting on very well with Judith, would be forever reminded that she was out there on account of him, loving him, risking her life – she could already be dead – and that he might never see her again. She would follow in his uncle's footsteps, she suddenly thought, her spirit quickening, and take the hard road through warring tribes to Hayyil, a venture that others had not survived.

Gertrude left for the East six weeks after the Doughty-Wylies' departure. Just before her own, she sent Dick a bundle of her books and review articles. He responded:

> I do like your writing – you very clever and charming person – and you in your desert . . . I don't know if this will reach you before you push off – if it does, my dear, it is to wish you all the luck and success, all safety and reasonable comfort (both of those last your fiery soul is apt to despise) . . . Have a good journey – find castles – keep well – and remain my friend. P.S. As to procès verbaux, the great thing is to put in my colleagues and leave out myself.

It was a cool letter and a coded way of reminding her to write to Judith and not to him. She braced herself against the pain. The book, she thought, would be a love letter in itself. Like Scheherazade, she would win his attention and then his love by her spellbinding storytelling and the sheer force of the adventure.

In London Dick had intended to bring the relationship to a close, but he had not been a month in Albania when he was once again writing to Gertrude every few days. Perhaps he had wanted to put more of himself into his marriage, and it had not worked out. Perhaps, with Gertrude out there, he felt more secure from Judith's scrutiny. Perhaps, after dinner and when Judith had gone to bed, after a day of tricky boundary negotiations with the Serbs, the Albanians and the Montenegrins, he sat down with a decanter of port and allowed his inner feelings to surface. He seemed, in one letter, to admit as much, writing of the occasion at Rounton when she had kept him at arm's length: 'It was right . . . and the sober part of me does not regret – the drunk part regrets and remembers until he goes to sleep.' In any case, a new warmth now entered his communications.

'Yes – I'm very fond of you – I think, I have thought for a long time, that you are delightful and wise and strong, and such as my soul loveth. And in thought, on a swifter camel, into the desert I go with you . . . I shall go on writing.' On another occasion:

It's late and I'm all alone, and thinking of . . . love and life – and an evening at Rounton – and what it all meant . . . You are in the desert, I am in the mountains, and in these places much could be said under the clouds. Does it mean that the fence was folly, and that we might have been man and woman as God made us and been happy . . . But I myself answer to myself that it is a lie. If I had been your man to you, in the bodies we live in, would it change us, surely not. We could not be together long, and there's the afterwards sometimes to be afraid of . . . And still it is a great and splendid thing, the birthright of everyone, for woman as for man, only so many of them don't understand the simplicity of it. And I have always maintained that this curious, powerful sex attraction is a thing right and natural and to be gratified, and if it is not gratified, what then; are we any worse?

The Doughty-Wylies did not stay long in Albania, but returned to London for Christmas, when Dick called on Gertrude's parents in Sloane Street and found Hugh at home. In Suffolk for New Year, it seems that things were not well between the Doughty-Wylies. Dick wrote:

Tonight . . . should I want to tell you . . . of the disappointment of my relations and my wife that I have not acquired any
more letters after my name? . . . Where are you? It's like
writing to an idea, a dream . . . Is it that gloom that is so black
tonight? Or is it the regret for things lost, great and splendid
things I find in your book, your mind and body, and the dear
love of you, all lost . . . Would you like me to write you a
love letter – to say how glad and gratified and humble I am
when I think of you . . .

Soon he was writing that he would be going to Addis Ababa,
alone this time: 'There's anarchy out there, complete and beastly
. . . Perhaps I can hear in Cairo. Your father will let me know . . .'
Gertrude, at Ziza, had just been denied protection for her journey
by both the Turkish officials and the British government. She was
to all intents and purposes an outlaw, and as she turned towards
the desert to begin the more hazardous part of her journey, she
began the book she would write exclusively for him. She would
now be parcelling it up and posting it in instalments to Addis
Ababa, together with her letters. She no longer had, at least, to
fear that they would fall into Judith's hands.

She had received, through Dick, wishes for a safe journey from
the author of *Arabia Deserta* himself. Nothing could have meant
more to her at that moment, except the sense she was now getting
from Dick's letters that the emotional tie between them was
intensifying, even if nothing fundamental had changed:

The desert has you [he wrote], you and your splendid courage,
my queen of the desert – and my heart is with you. If I was
young and free, and a very perfect knight, it would be more
fitting to take and kiss you. But I am old and tired and full of
a hundred faults . . . you are right – not that way for you and
me – because we are slaves, not because it is not the right, the
natural way – when the passions of the body flame and melt
into the passions of the spirit – in those dream ecstasies so
rarely found by any human creature, those, as you say, whom
God hath really joined – in some divine moment we might
reach it – the ecstasy. We never shall. But there is left so

much. As you say my dear, wise Queen — all that there is we
will take.

Difficult as his letters were for her to translate into her own
clear perceptions, he was, at least, writing to her every day or two
from London. There was no reserve, no evasion or calculation in
her own communications. She told him again and again what she
wanted. He replied: 'I cannot tell you how much it moves me . . .
to see it written by you, that you might have married me, have
borne my children, have been my life as well as my heart.'

Reminding him that the words for 'garden' and 'paradise' were
the same in Persian, Gertrude had invented the metaphor of a
fantasy garden where only the two of them could enter. There they
could always be alone together:

> You give me a new world, Gertrude, you give me the key to
> your heart, though I have friends, some of them women, even
> a wife, they are as far removed from the garden where we walk
> as east from west . . . I have often loved women as a man like
> me does love them, well and badly, little and much, as the
> blood took me, or the time or the invitation, or simply for the
> adventure — to see what happened. But that is all behind me.

At the end of January 1914 Dick visited Hugh again, then set off
for Addis Ababa. As he left, he wrote a letter that was less rhetorical
and more sensual than any he had sent her: 'Where are you now?
By the Belka castles,* working like ten men, tired and hungry and
sleepy . . . Like that I love to think of you: sometimes, too (but it's
beastly of me), I love to think of you lonely, and wanting me . . .'
Finally, he wrote the words she had waited so long to hear:

> You said you wanted to hear me say I loved you, you wanted it
> plain to eyes and ears . . . I love you — does it do any good out
> there in the desert? Is it less vast, less lonely, like the far edge
> of life? someday perhaps, in a whisper, in a kiss, I will tell you
> . . . love like this is life itself . . . Oh, where are you, where
> are you? . . . Well, I go. Africa draws me; I know I shall have

* The ruins of the Belka plain, near Salt.

> things to try for . . . But of them I scarcely think: it is only that
> I love you, Gertrude, and shall not see you . . .

Sitting in her small tent, she read the words again and again, and her heart leapt. He had made a commitment to her at last. He had admitted to himself as much as to her that he loved her. And yet she had never felt further from him. Could he even remember what she looked like? she wondered. There were terrible moments when she tried to conjure up *his* face, and could not do it. She was nearly at the end of her journey, she could almost say that she had survived it, but facing her was perhaps a vaster loneliness than she had already endured. He was physically as distant from her as ever, and no nearer to leaving his wife. Weeping from sheer exhaustion and sadness, she asked herself what she had gained:

> I try to school myself beforehand by reminding myself how I
> have looked forward . . . to the end, and when it came have
> found it – just nothing. Dust and ashes in one's hand . . . dead
> bones that look as if they would never rise and dance – it's all
> just nothing and one turns away from it with a sigh and tries to
> fix one's eyes on to the new thing before one . . . Whether I can
> bear with England – come back to the same things and do them
> all over again – that is what I sometimes wonder.

She returned to an England without Dick Doughty-Wylie – but not to do the same things all over again. The summer was hot and full of political foreboding. His letters continued, their tone intensifying and becoming less guarded than ever: 'What wouldn't I give to have you sitting opposite in this all-alone house?'

At Rounton on the outbreak of war, on 4 August, she was propelled into war work – at first, temporarily, at Lord Onslow's hospital at Clandon Park near Guildford in Surrey. She had written to the Red Cross asking if they could find a job for her. She had not been at Clandon for more than three weeks when she received a telegram in reply, asking if she would go at once to Boulogne, to work in the Wounded and Missing Office there.

In October the German army had marched through Flanders,

and a British expeditionary force sent to Ypres to stop them had
been virtually massacred. The casualties were huge. There were
still wounded men on stretchers waiting at the docks and at the
station when Gertrude arrived at the end of November.

She checked into her tiny attic room in the town, and went at
once to the office, setting to work filing and indexing, making lists
of the wounded and missing for the War Office. Working eight or
nine hours a day, she would go to a restaurant for her dinner, then
sit down, dead tired, to write to Dick and to her family. She was
less unhappy now that she was at full stretch again, well into her
stride and beginning to work at a pace that her office colleagues
could hardly believe, still less keep up with. His letters were now
as passionate as she could wish; she took them with her to the office
so that she could reread them over her snatched lunch:

> Tonight I should not want to talk [he wrote]. I should make
> love to you. Would you like it, welcome it, or would a hundred
> hedges rise and bristle and divide? — but we would tear them
> down. What is a hedge that it should divide us . . .? You are
> in my arms, alight, afire. Tonight I do not want dreams and
> fancies. But it will never be . . . The first time should I not be
> nearly afraid to be your lover?

Deprived of sex, he could sometimes think of little else.

> So much a thing of the mind is the insistent passion of the body.
> Women sometimes give themselves to men for the man's
> pleasure. I'd hate a woman to be like that with me. I'd want
> her to feel to the last sigh the same surge and stir that carried
> me away. She should miss nothing that I could give her.

She answered him from the depths of her heart:

> Dearest, dearest, I give this year of mine to you, and all the years
> that shall come after it . . . Dearest, when you tell me you love
> me and want me still, my heart sings — and then weeps with
> longing to be with you. I have filled all the hollow places of the
> world with my desire for you; it floods out to creep up the high
> mountains where you live.

But in December came unwelcome news. Judith had arrived in northern France, and was not far away, working in a hospital. All too soon a letter arrived, suggesting they meet for lunch. Panicking, unable to consult Dick, Gertrude decided that it would look odd if she did not respond. She would go through with it.

If Judith already had her suspicions that Dick and Gertrude were in close contact, they were likely to have been confirmed by the encounter. Gertrude was no dissembler. Asked the question, she would have told the truth. It seems, from Gertrude's subsequent letter to Dick, that Judith, trembling with anger and misery, had told her that Dick would always stick to his marriage, and that Gertrude must accept that in the end he would abandon her. She wrote to him: 'I hated it. Don't make me have that to bear . . . You won't leave me? . . . It's torture, eternal torture.'

From the very beginning, each encounter, each letter, had snatched her up to the heights before dropping her once more into the depths. Almost predictably, she now lurched from one extreme of feeling to the opposite. The lunch with Judith had thrown her into turmoil. Now, she suddenly found herself elevated to a state of sublime happiness – Dick had written that he was coming home. He would reach Marseilles in February, call in on Judith on his way through France, then journey on to London. Gertrude could join him there. She should wait for his message, and be ready to go. But he would not stay long. He had volunteered for the front line, 'with joy', and was on his way to Gallipoli.

The message came. Her small bag was packed already. She snatched it up and ran for the car that would take her to the ferry. Arriving in London, she made her way to 29 Half Moon Street, raced up the steps and rang the bell. The door opened, and they were face to face at last. They stood looking at each other for a moment, then he scooped up her suitcase with one hand and drew her inside with the other. They were together and alone for four nights and three days. Then he was gone, to join General Sir Ian Hamilton's staff as the forces gathered for the hopeless quest that was Gallipoli.

With the Great War stuck fast, a whole generation of young

men were being killed in France on the Western Front without any advance being made against the Germans. To try to break the deadlock, British battleships in the Mediterranean were ordered through the narrow Dardanelles to pound Constantinople and Germany's allies, the Turks. If a new battle front could be opened in the south-east, Germany would be forced to divert troops from the Western Front. In the event, tragically, the British ships ran straight into mines. Three battleships sank, and the navy retreated. The hasty fall-back plan for opening the new front was to land the British army on the beaches at Gallipoli. It would become a suicide mission for the men, strafed continuously by Turkish machine-guns as they struggled out of the water and up the beaches.

The happiest romantic moments in Gertrude's life were also the most poignant and painful. A modern woman will find it hard to understand that she still had not consummated her love in the full physical sense, but she had not. It could be argued that her inviolable principles, the same ones that had brought her safely through the desert and a thousand other dangers, would not allow her to become an adulteress. But it is not necessary to make that case. A letter that the distraught Gertrude wrote to Dick a few days after their parting makes it clear that she was not afraid of the consequences in terms of a possible pregnancy, but she had not been able to overcome an inborn prudishness. She so much wanted to consecrate their union in sex, and at the same time she could not prevent herself from recoiling at the last moment. What she really wanted, she had to explain, was that he override her reluctance and her protests and make forceful love to her. But for all his experience, he was a gentle and fatally compromised lover, and could not bring himself to do it.

She sent letters after him, terrified at her inability, panicking, consumed with regret:

> Someday I'll try to explain it to you – the fear, the terror of it – oh you thought I was brave. Understand me: not the fear of consequences – I've never weighed them for one second. It's the fear of something I don't know ... you must know all about it

because I tell you. Every time it surged up in me and I wanted you to brush it aside . . . But I couldn't say to you, Exorcise it. I couldn't. That last word I can never say. You must say it . . . Fear is a horrible thing . . . It's a shadow – I know it's nothing . . . Only you can free me from it – drive it away from me, I know now, but till the last moment . . . I was terribly afraid. Then at the last I knew it was a shadow. I know it now.

He wrote back: 'Was it perhaps some subtle spirit of foreknowledge that kept us apart in London? The risk to you was too great – the risk to your body, and to your peace of mind and pride of soul . . .' She was prepared to 'meet the bill', she replied, however high the cost – pregnancy, disgrace or social exclusion. Now she thought that a baby, far from being the worst of consequences, might have been the best:

And suppose the other thing had happened, the thing you feared – that I half feared – must have brought you back. If I had it now, the thing you feared, I would magnify the Lord and fear nothing . . . Not only the final greatest gift to give you – a greater gift even than love – but for me, the divine pledge of fulfilment, created in rapture, the handing on of life in fire, to be cherished and worshipped and lived for, with the selfsame ardour that cherishes and worships the creator.

Her letters grew out of hours of suffering and regretting, as she promised him that she would never hold back again. 'If I had given more, should I have held you closer, drawn you back more surely? I look back and rage at my reluctance . . . I've had a few resplendent hours. I could die on them and be happy. But you, you've not had what you wanted.'

For Gertrude, intrepid as she was, sex was the final frontier. She should not be judged too harshly – she was certainly punished for her reluctance every day for the rest of her life. She had only really known Dick well since those happy days in London in the spring of 1912. In the three years since then, despite the rising tempo of their letters, she had spent only a handful of days with him. Time and again they would glimpse each other across a crowded, eventful world, stretch out their hands to each other and be snatched apart. Gertrude and Dick were in some ways no different from those many wartime couples who married on the brink of war, were parted when the man left for the front, then reunited long afterwards as husband and wife – and almost complete strangers. They should have got to know each other when they were young, amid family and friends, and drifted towards an intimacy that would have led inexorably to bed; but such gradual progressions rarely happened in the violent, confusing world of 1915. They were thrust together for a moment, barely got to know each other again during those four nights in London, and then he was gone, leaving her even more in love, and even more bereft.

She had not believed her suffering could get any worse, but it had increased tenfold. What she wrote to him was an ultimatum:

I can't sleep – I can't sleep. It's one in the morning . . . You and you and you are between me and any rest . . . out of your arms there is no rest. Life, you called me, and fire. I flame and am consumed . . . Dick, it's not possible to live like this. When it's all over you must take your own. . . . Before all the world, claim me and take me and hold me for ever and ever . . . Furtiveness I hate – But openly to come to you, that I can do and live, what should I lose? It's all nothing to me; I breathe and think and move in you. Can you do it, dare you? When this thing is over, your work well done, will you risk it for me? It's that or nothing. I can't live without you.

The people who love me would stand by me if I did it that way – I know them. But not the other way. Not to deceive and lie and cheat and at the last be found out, as I should be . . . If it's honour you think of, this is honour and the other dishonour. If it's faithfulness you think of, this is faithfulness – keep faith with love . . . Because I held up my head and wouldn't walk by diverse ways perhaps in the end we can marry. I don't count on it, but it would be better, far better for me . . . But don't miss the camp fire that burns in this letter – a clear flame, a bright flame fed by my life.

> Do you think I can hide the blaze of that fire across half the world? Or share you with any other. If you die, wait for me – I am not afraid of that other crossing; I will come to you.

He had told her, when they were together, that Judith had threatened suicide by using the 'morphia tubes' available in the hospitals. He had not dared to explain to his wife about Gallipoli or what it might mean, but he kept no such secrets from Gertrude. He trusted her to be calm and resilient. Now – no doubt, to his horror – he read that she was considering that same way out. She wrote in April 1915:

> I am very calm about the shot and shell to which you go. What takes you, takes me out to look for you. If there's search and finding beyond the border I shall find you. If there's nothingness, as with my reason I think, why then there's nothingness . . . life shrinks from it . . . but I'm not afraid. Life would be gone, how could the fire burn? But I'm brave – you know it – as far as human courage goes.
>
> Oh Dick, write to me. When shall I hear? . . . I trust, I believe, you'll take care of me – let me stand upright and say I've never walked by furtive ways. Then they'll forgive me and you – all the people that matter will forgive . . . But it's you who should be saying this, should be saying it now, not I. I won't say it any more.

Poor Doughty-Wylie, caught between a distraught wife and a lover bent on following him into the afterlife. From Gallipoli he answered Gertrude:

> My dear, don't do what you talked of – it's horrible to me to think of it – that's why I told you about my wife – how much more for you – don't do anything so unworthy of so free and brave a spirit. One must walk along the road to the end of it. When I asked for this ship, my joy in it was half strangled by that thing you said, I can't even name it or talk about it . . . Don't do it. Time is nothing, we join up again, but to hurry the pace is unworthy of us all.

And again, reminding her of her own earlier conviction that death ends all, 'As to the things you say of some future in far places, they are dreams, dream woman. We must walk along the road – such heavenly madness is for gods and poets – not for us except in lovely dreams.' His letters now became a little remote. After all, the time for Gertrude to offer herself was past. He knew very well that the battle ahead was little short of a suicide mission, and he had much to think about.

In the archives of the Imperial War Museum there is a final letter from Dick Doughty-Wylie. Written neither to his lover nor to his wife, it holds the key to the indecisiveness of his attitude to Gertrude. It is a letter written to Judith's mother, Mrs H. H. Coe – Jean – in Llandysul, Wales. It was dated 20 April 1915, six days before he was killed at Gallipoli, and written from General Headquarters Mediterranean Expeditionary Force. A careful and sober letter, it speaks of his concern for his wife and his anxiety about her state of mind.

My dear Jean,

Lily [Judith] tells me that I never wrote to you . . . I wanted to tell how she was when I saw her in France, both coming and going. She was very full of work, and doing I think rather too much herself, as she always is prone to do, but on the whole well. It is a very good work very well done, in the middle of many difficulties of all sorts. Her nursing staff I liked and thought well of, and also her two English doctors. I didn't care so much about the French doctor but he has been changed.

Now I want you to do something for me. I am going to embark tomorrow on what is certainly an extremely dangerous job, namely the wreck ship of which you will see in the papers. If the thing went wrong, Lily would feel intolerably lonely and hopeless after her long hours of work – which tell sorely on anybody's spirits and vitality. She talks about overdoses of morphia and such things. I think that in reality she is too brave and strong minded for such things, but still the saying weighs on my spirits. If you hear I'm killed go over at once to France with H.H. and seek her out. Telegraph to her at once that you are coming and want her to send Frank Wylie and a car to meet you at Boulogne – don't lose any time, but go and look after her. Don't take her away from her work, for it will be best for her to work, but manage to stay somewhere near and see her through. Tell her what is perfectly true that the work cannot go on without her. I haven't told her yet of this wreck ship because I don't want her to know till it's over.

This is only by way of precaution. She has a great friend with her one Sister Isobel Stenhouse, and a Miss Sandford sister of my helper in Abyssinia, a very good girl indeed – and on the whole she is in the best place possible – and I am unduly worried about her.

This is a very interesting show from every point of view – but it runs a great many chances however one looks at it. It may be a really startling success, and is certainly bold enough an idea.

I hope you and H.H. are both well. I was only in England as I think you knew under 3 days and I had no time to see anybody at all – or in fact to get fit of which I stand in need.

So don't be unduly anxious over this business – it's all in the day's work as far as I am concerned – and her hospital is the very best place in the world for Lily if anything did happen.

Love to you both
Yrs. Affectionately Dick

He was not, of course, telling the truth when he told his mother-in-law that he had not been able to see anybody in London. More importantly, the letter casts a new light on him and on his attitudes to the two women in his life. It suggests that the letters that Gertrude had found so hard to understand, seeming to declare his love on the one hand and avoiding any kind of commitment on the other, were compromised by his wife's instability and his continuing responsibility and care for her. Perhaps he knew that Judith would not be able to cope without him. When not losing herself in her demanding hospital work, she was evidently in disarray. As he had not dared to tell her about the 'wreck ship', it is quite likely that she was actually threatening suicide if he abandoned her for Gertrude. In any case, he saw that if he was killed she would probably break down.

It seems that he had come to love Gertrude as much as she could have wished, sex or no sex, but had never been able to bring himself to leave his wife. What is certain is that he now found himself in a terrible dilemma. He could shore up his wife's mental health, and cause Gertrude continued suffering; or he could make his love for Gertrude plain and bring that suffering home to his fragile wife. He was, perhaps, exhausted by the struggle. For the moment, he did not have to make that decision: his own life was in the balance.

His last words to Gertrude as he embarked on the *River Clyde* were: 'So many memories my dear queen, of you and your splendid love and your kisses and your courage and the wonderful letters you wrote me, from your heart to mine – the letters, some of which I have packed up, like drops of blood.' These letters of hers that followed him to Gallipoli he addressed back to her, the day before he expected to storm V beach.

There were two thousand men on the boat – all the Munsters, two companies of Hampshires, one company of Dublins, a few Royal Naval Division troops, Doughty-Wylie and another member of Hamilton's staff, Lieutenant-Colonel Weir de Lancy Williams. That night, before leading the invasion against the Turks, for whom he held such affection, Doughty-Wylie was very quiet. A colleague, Ellis Ashmead-Bartlett, said he seldom spoke but 'seemed to think so much'. Colonel Weir Williams wrote: 'I am firmly of the opinion that poor Doughty-Wylie realised he would be killed in this war.'

The *River Clyde* was run aground on V beach, and the lighters were moved into position for use as a floating bridge. Doughty-Wylie and Williams waited until Captain Garth Walford arrived at midnight with orders from Major-General Aylmer Hunter-Weston that the advance on the castle and village of Sedd-el-Bahr be resumed. Walford went on shore in the morning of 26 April, to fight alongside the Hampshires. The plan was for one party to try to take the castle and village, a second to try and join up with the troops on W beach, while a third would drive through the barbed wire straight ahead towards Hill 141.

The troops took the castle, but Walford was shot. The village was a different proposition. The Turks were hiding in cellars and behind the walls of every house and sniping at the invaders as they emerged from the castle. Sometimes they waited until they had passed, then fired into their backs. Doughty-Wylie had watched from the wreck ship and suffered until late morning. Then, he picked up his cane and headed for the village. His pistol, if he had brought it, was left on the *River Clyde*. Near the back gate of the castle, a bullet knocked off his cap. A Munster officer wrote later that Doughty-Wylie walked into houses that might have been full of Turkish soldiers as casually as though he were walking into a shop: 'I . . . remember being struck by the calm way in which he treated this incident. He was carrying no weapon of any description at the time, only a small cane.' As he walked serenely on, he picked up a rifle lying beside a dead soldier, but within a few seconds, as if changing his mind, dropped it again. The village was eventually won. Doughty-Wylie now went for Hill 141. Carrying his cane and maintaining his eery calm, he walked up the hill leading a cheering crowd of Dublins, Munsters and Hampshires. They reached the top, the Turks retreating before them. At the moment of victory, Doughty-Wylie was shot through the head.

He was buried where he lay, by Williams and other soldiers. Williams said the Lord's Prayer over his grave and bid him goodbye. Later, he had a temporary cross knocked up by a ship's carpenter to mark the grave, and the Munsters' chaplain read the burial service. Dick Doughty-Wylie was the most senior officer to win the VC, the highest military award, during the Gallipoli campaign. His grave remains there to this day, surrounded by lavender bushes and two cypress trees, the only Allied cemetery on Gallipoli with just one grave. As Sir Ian Hamilton wrote, 'Braver soldier never drew sword. He had no hatred of the enemy . . . Tenderness and pity filled his heart . . . He was a steadfast hero . . . Now as he would have wished to die, so he has died.'

His death left questions. Why was he not carrying his pistol? Was he so reluctant to attack his Turkish friends that he was prepared to be shot rather than defend himself? Had he committed a form of suicide, having first counselled those he loved to 'walk along the road to the end . . . to hurry the pace is unworthy'?

Perhaps he thought that if he survived Gallipoli, his life from then on would be untenable. Gertrude had given him a passionate ultimatum: 'Before all the world, claim me . . . It's that or nothing. I can't live without you.' Judith had reached breaking point. Perhaps, like Gertrude when she started for Hayyil, he did not care if he lived or died, and would do nothing to protect himself. Essentially, as Hamilton had said, 'tenderness and pity filled his heart': he would rather walk clear-eyed to his death than hurt either of the two women he loved.

When Judith heard the news she wrote in her diary: 'The shock was terrible. Something seemed to tear at the region of my heart . . . I suppose I shall have to pick up the pieces . . . just a lonely widow.'

Gertrude was to learn of his death in an even more shocking way. She had continued to write to him, for no one had told her what had happened: she was, after all, neither kith nor kin. She was at a lunch party with friends in London when, having no idea of her connection with him, someone at the table remarked what a pity it was that Dick Doughty-Wylie had been killed. They talked on about his courage while she sat there, ashen-faced, and the room whirled around her. Quietly, she rose from the table and excused herself. Hardly knowing what she did, she made her way to Hampstead to the home of her half-sister Elsa, now Lady Richmond. When she opened the door to a devastated Gertrude, she had immediately jumped to the conclusion that it was their brother Maurice who had been killed, and burst into tears herself.

'No,' said Gertrude almost impatiently. 'No – not Maurice.'
She lay down on a sofa, where for a few minutes Elsa stroked her forehead. Then she turned her head away.

Towards the end of 1915, a visitor was seen by soldiers at Dick Doughty-Wylie's grave. There was no doubt that it was a veiled woman, but her identity has always been in doubt. According to L. A. Carlyon:

Gertrude's grandfather, the great iron-master Isaac Lowthian Bell. It appears that the anonymous painter has allowed Lowthian to scratch a diagram of a steel furnace into the wet paint on the right-hand side of the picture.

The long gallery of the house that architect Philip Webb built for Lowthian Bell at the height of the family fortunes. Begun in 1872, Rounton Grange, Northallerton, was decorated and furnished by William Morris and Edward Burne-Jones.

Rounton was inherited by Gertrude's father in 1904, when she was thirty-six. With her stepmother Florence, she hosted many house parties and events there between her travels abroad.

Red Barns, now a hotel, built by Philip Webb as Hugh Bell's first house, was designed on a more modest scale. Despite her mother's death, Gertrude went on to have a happy childhood here with her extended family after Hugh's second marriage.

The red-haired Gertrude, aged eight, and Hugh in the year of his remarriage, 1876. The portrait by Edward Poynter is an early illustration of the deep mutual affection between father and daughter, which Florence said was 'to both the very foundation of existence until the day she died.'

Above. Portrait of Mary Shield, Hugh's first wife and the mother of Gertrude and Maurice. Mary, the pretty daughter of a Newcastle merchant, died not three weeks after the birth of her son in March 1871.

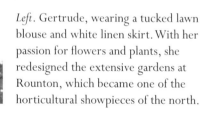

Left. Gertrude, wearing a tucked lawn blouse and white linen skirt. With her passion for flowers and plants, she redesigned the extensive gardens at Rounton, which became one of the horticultural showpieces of the north.

Florence Bell, Gertrude's stepmother, in the grey silk gloves she wore at all times, even indoors and to play the piano. All her life she wore sweeping robes of lace and silk, ignoring changes in fashion. Even in the 1920s, when most women were wearing their hems at the knees, her skirts touched the pavements, so that when one day she fell in the street, her young granddaughter was astonished to see that she had legs.

Hugh Bell in spring 1920 on his visit to Baghdad to see Gertrude. In anticipation of his arrival, she had ordered furniture, chintzes and crockery from the London furniture shop Maples, so that in this picture Hugh could have been in the drawing room of a house in the home counties, instead of an adapted summerhouse in Mesopotamia.

Undated photograph of Gertrude Bell, probably around the time she met 'Dick' Doughty-Wylie.

Gertrude with Ulrich and Heinrich Führer, the mountain guides with whom she climbed from 1900 to 1904.

The 14,022 foot Finsteraarhorn, the highest mountain in the Oberland, with its razor ridge visible for a hundred miles. Gertrude, aged thirty-five, was determined to conquer the unclimbed perpendicular north-east face. She and her guides, the Führers, were caught in a snow blizzard during their attempt in August 1902, and scarcely escaped with their lives.

In Duris, in the Lebanon, in 1900, Gertrude rides with an Arab keffiyeh, or headdress, over her straw hat, a high-collared shirt with mutton-chop sleeves and the wraparound skirt she designed herself for riding in the Middle East. She swept the panel behind her in the saddle, so that when she dismounted it fell decorously forward to hide the divided skirt.

Gertrude and Professor William Ramsay at Binbirkilisse, where they were working together to measure, map and date the archaeological site. In 1909, they would publish *The Thousand and One Churches*, still the standard work on early Byzantine architecture in Anatolia.

The quiet war hero 'Dick' Doughty-Wylie, Major Charles Hotham Montagu Doughty-Wylie of the Royal Welch Fusiliers, with his wife, Lilian. She tended to frills and seldom went out without a parasol. Gertrude described them on her first meeting as 'a charming young soldier with a quite pleasant little wife'.

On November 17 1915, a woman stepped ashore at V Beach, which had become the main French base. She is thought to be the only woman to have landed during the Gallipoli campaign. She left the *River Clyde*, now being used as a pier, walked through the castle . . . past the line of tottery walls and unearthed cellars that had once been Sedd-el-Bahr village, past the fig and pomegranate trees that had survived the bombardment, and began to climb Hill 141. On the summit, she stopped at a lone grave fenced off with barbed wire, placed a wreath on the wooden cross and left . . . We do not know what she was wearing . . . we do not even know for certain who she was. Most likely she was Lilian Doughty-Wylie, who at this time worked for the French hospital service. She may have been Gertrude Bell, the English writer and explorer. We do know the grave she visited . . . [that of] Lieutenant-Colonel Charles 'Dick' Doughty-Wylie, Victoria Cross.

Michael Hickey's history of that fine and futile campaign offers a rather different version of events:

A curious mystery attends this hero's burial; towards the end of 1915, a woman landed from a boat sent ashore from a transport, and laid a wreath on the grave. Speaking to no one, but apparently seen by dozens of British and French troops, she then returned to her boat and departed. It is most likely that it was Mrs Doughty-Wylie, who by then was working for the French Red Cross on the island of Tenedos. She had influence with the authorities and was thus able to arrange for passage to Gallipoli. There is, however, a persistent story that it was his old friend Gertrude Bell, also in the area at the time. She certainly visited the grave in 1919.

Other books note that during the visit of this mysterious woman, not a shot was fired on either side.

Where was Judith on 17 November 1915? According to her diaries, between December 1914 and September 1915 she was serving as director of the Anglo-Ethiopian Red Cross Hospital situated at Frévent, some seventy miles south of Calais, up to May, and then at St-Valery-sur-Somme until September. Her diaries reveal her difficulties with the voluntary staff and the grave short-comings of the French army medical services. In April 1916 she took up work as matron in charge of a hospital at Mudros West on the island of Lemnos.

Doughty-Wylie was killed on 26 April 1915. Probably, Judith's mother did as he had requested and arrived in Frévent after a few days to look after her daughter. He had cautioned Mrs Coe not to take Judith away from her job, but her mother would no doubt have wanted to bring her home to Wales for a break from her difficult and demanding work. That might explain why Judith left Frévent in May and then took up work again at St-Valery-sur-Somme (on an unspecified date). To believe that it was Judith who stepped ashore that November, you would have to assume that she was in the area six months before she needed to be. It is most unlikely that either the army or the French hospital service could or would have seen it their business to bring a widow into the war zone – 39 VCs were awarded in all, and their widows would all have been entitled to the same consideration. It is also very doubtful that either body could or would have organized a ceasefire on the Turkish side during her visit to the grave.

It is not until we consult a book published in 1975, *Gallipoli* by Captain Eric Wheeler Bush DSO, DFC, Royal Navy, that some of the facts can be established:

> The story told by several authors that Lily Doughty-Wylie, 'the only woman to put a foot ashore during the occupation', landed at Sedd-el-Bahr on the 17th November 1915 and laid a wreath on Dick's grave, and that 'the Turks fired neither bullet nor shell during the Ceremony', may only have occurred in one of her dreams. Boatwork was impossible over that period because of gales. Though this visit is not mentioned in any official report, she certainly believed she had made it and there are two eye-witness accounts [Lieutenant Corbett Williamson, RM, and F. L. Hilton, RND] of a woman seen on Cape Hellen about that time. Lily wrote to the British Ambassador in Athens thanking him for 'a success I owe in some measure to you' but never posted the letter . . .

There is a suggestion between the lines that Doughty-Wylie's misgivings about his wife's stability were well founded, and that she had suffered some kind of breakdown. She either believed or wanted to prove that she, not Gertrude, was the woman on V beach. One way to do that would have been to suggest to the Ambassador that it was indeed she who had made that journey; but in the end she was either too honest or too confused to send the letter.

Eric Bush adds that poor Lily got to her husband's grave in 1919. Even in peacetime she needed help from Headquarters British Army of the Black Sea, Constantinople, and from the advance base, Kilia Liman, to make the excursion. She was taken to the beach in a pilot boat and stepped ashore from the same *River Clyde*.

The date of the legendary wreath-laying, 17 November, is vague. Bush, a naval man, says that on that date, boat landing was impossible because of the weather. Hickey, as we see, dates the event no more precisely than 'towards the end of 1915'. In November, Gertrude was summoned to the office of the Director of Naval Intelligence, Captain R. Hall. The Cairo office, he told her, had cabled that they would like her to come out. Her old friend Dr David Hogarth had suggested that her recently acquired knowledge of the tribes of northern Arabia would be invaluable to the Bureau. She responded without hesitation, and on 16 November was writing to Florence:

> I think it more than likely that when I reach Egypt I shall find they have no job that will occupy me more than a fortnight, and I may be back before Christmas. It's all vaguer than words can say.
>
> *As to any further journey nothing definite is said and I think the chances are strongly against it.*

On 17 November Gertrude was at 95 Sloane Street, packing up her kit. On Saturday the 20th she was embarking at Marseilles on board the P&O ship *Arabia*, writing to her father that it would sail at 4 a.m. the next day, and that she expected to arrive at Port Said on Thursday the 25th. But her first letter home from Cairo is dated Tuesday 30 November, and seems to have been written on the day of her arrival. She mentions the 'horrible journey – almost continuous storm' and says 'we reached Port Said after dark on Thursday night . . . Next morning I came up here.' Oddly, she also says: 'I telegraphed to you this morning after my arrival and asked you to send me by Lady B another gown and skirt' — which sounds as if she made two arrivals, one on Friday the 26th and a second the following Tuesday. The rest of her letter describes nothing that happened after dinner on the 26th, when she was taken out by her two new colleagues, Hogarth and T. E. Lawrence. The days and nights of the 27th, 28th and 29th are missing.

The Cairo Bureau was the intelligence base with specific responsibility for the Mediterranean Expeditionary Force sent to Gallipoli. Besides Hogarth and Lawrence — himself in mourning for his much loved brother Will — two other acquaintances of hers were there: Leonard Woolley was the intelligence chief at Port Said, and another Captain Hall, brother of the one who had sent her to Cairo, was in charge of the railway. She was surrounded by friends. Did she, in fact, under their discreet aegis, catch the express train to Port Said early the next morning and board a transport ship carrying supplies for the Dardanelles, then take a lighter to V beach? If the Turkish guns were silenced, was it out of a combination of curiosity and respect both for the mysterious unaccompanied woman and for Doughty-Wylie, for whose grave she was clearly heading?

Was it not Gertrude who, after all, made that 'further journey' she had mentioned to Florence before she left England?

8

LIMIT OF ENDURANCE

Even before his death, Dick Doughty-Wylie had precipitated a significant turning point in Gertrude's life. It was at the end of the summer of 1913, a few weeks after his visit to Rounton, that he burnt her letters and departed for Albania with Judith to take up his new post with the International Boundary Commission.

Their affair, although unconsummated, had given her days of ecstatic happiness such as she had never known. There was the euphoria of sexual attraction that they both felt; and the novelty of being with a man who was not wary of her, nor alienated by her exploits nor anxious to hide his ignorance of the subjects she discussed so knowledgeably. She had long outgrown the complacent English milieu in which she now swam like a rainbow fish among tadpoles. At forty-five, she was annoyed to find that despite the achievements for which she was internationally renowned, the society she inhabited in London and Yorkshire retained its stolidly Edwardian view of her as maiden aunt cum frightening intellectual. It was thirteen years since she had written, in a burst of exuberance, 'I have become a Person!' but outside her large circle of family and friends she was merely a spinster oddity, albeit a beautifully dressed one trailing clouds of glory. Was it for this, she must have asked herself, that she had rocketed through a high-powered education, pioneered travels that would have been exceptional even for a man, and mastered archaeology, cartography, mountaineering and six foreign languages? Dick, on the other hand, was critically aware of the significance of her expeditions and, knowing the Middle East as well as she did, could match her, story for story, adventure for adventure.

Now that he had left for Albania, Gertrude was left utterly desolate. Her family would not be able to countenance her affair with a married man — there could be no doubt about that. Her society friends knew nothing of it. At any moment the name of Dick Doughty-Wylie could come up in the course of conversation, to twist the knife in the wound. Even worse, there was always a chance that at some London charity event or concert party she might suddenly come face to face with his wife. Forthright to the point of eccentricity, Gertrude hated the thought of evasion or subterfuge. She wrote to Chirol: 'If you knew the way I had paced backwards and forwards along the floor of hell for the last few months, you would think me right to try any way out. I want to cut all links with the world . . . This is the best and wisest thing to do . . . I want the road and the dawn, the sun, the wind and the rain, the camp fire under the stars, and sleep, and the road again.'

The last eighteen months had shaken her profoundly. Now there were only his letters to look forward to. Mentally and spiritually she sank into the deepest state of despair, one which might have caused a breakdown in a less robust individual. Now whenever she heard a piece of melancholy music, or read one of the aching poems of Hafiz, or remembered how she would look for him across a crowded drawing-room and count the moments until he reached her side, tears would blur her vision. Castigate herself as she might for behaving like the kind of 'silly little woman' she so despised, she had to admit she couldn't get him out of her mind. The last bastion of her self-respect lay in keeping from her father and Florence just how far she had allowed herself to drift into dependence on a man she could not have. Hugh, a most unusual Victorian, adored her for her independence, intellect, courage and good Geordie sense. Those were the characteristics he most admired in a woman; and if in Mary Shield, Gertrude's mother, he had chosen a beautiful local girl, he had picked for his second wife a woman whose intelligence and thoughtfulness far outweighed her plainer looks and unassertive nature. Gertrude's entire life had been predicated on pleasing him and winning his support for her adventures. God forbid that he should see just how this affair had brought her to her knees.

And so she made every effort to appear normal, putting up as good a show as she could muster over the family dinner, when the Bells renounced gossip for discussion of politics, agriculture or industry, books and plays. Then she would wish them goodnight and go up to her room, where she chain-smoked, sometimes sitting on her bed with her head in her hands, or pacing the floor until the early hours. If there had been another way — if in her loneliness she could have overcome her resistance, dented her pride enough to consent to be Dick's mistress — she might have borne it, but in the end she would tell herself, 'Not in my father's lifetime.' She would put the pain behind her, the only way she could.

She had waited, hoping perhaps that something would change, until Dick left for Albania; and then she acted. She would escape into 'wild travel' again, get away from the kind, half-comprehending regard of family and friends that made it all the harder. Damascus would be her jumping-off point. Again she spoke to herself the lines of Hafiz that had so well expressed her anguish over that earlier, slighter love affair with Henry Cadogan:

> Ah! When he found it easy to depart,
> He left the harder pilgrimage to me!
> Oh Camel-driver, though the cordage start,
> For God's sake help me lift my fallen load,
> And Pity be my comrade of the road!

She did not really care where she went. It was more important to get away; but her state of mind dictated that this should be an epic, momentous journey, and that she should be away a long time. She did not, at the moment, care very much whether she came back at all.

How changed was her mood in this August of 1913 from the way she had felt in the spring — and how different were her shopping expeditions. She would take plenty of luggage this time and be ready for anything. First, there were her two English-made tents, one for bathing and sleeping in, one for eating and writing, both with a loose flap that could be tied back, laced shut or used as a shady canopy. She ordered more of the skirts that she had designed with her tailor for riding horses in the Middle East: neither side-saddle habit nor breeches, but an ankle-length divided skirt with an apron panel. In the saddle, she would sweep this backward and gather the surplus material behind her and to one side, where it looked in profile like a bustle. When she dismounted, the panel fell around her like an apron and concealed the division. She bought lace and tucked-lawn evening gowns for dinners with consuls and sheikhs, for sitting at a dining-table at an embassy or cross-legged on a carpet in a tent. She would take her cigarette holders, silver cigarette cases, evening purses, a score of white or striped cotton shirts with mutton-chop shoulders and high rounded collars, tucked or frilled, with pearl buttons and tight cuffs. At the neck she would wear a man's tie, or an oval pin.

The list was a long one: she would take a dozen linen skirts stopping short of the ankle, nipped in to release fabric from her small waist, and an entire caseful of shoes and boots for scrambling about amongst ruins and rocks – leather ones to the knees, canvas laced ankle-boots; strap-and-button low-heeled shoes for evening; beige lisle stockings, silk underwear and parasols; Purdy revolvers and a crate of rifles; theodolites, and some boxes of the Zeiss telescopes she would give as special gifts to sheikhs who helped her along the way. She bought a dozen shady linen and straw hats: if one blew off it would hardly be worth the trouble of descending from the camel to chase after it. As the temperature soared, a locally bought cotton keffiyeh could be substituted, caught round her head with a bright silk rope and fluttering out behind her to protect her shoulders from the sun.

This time it would be winter in the desert, and she folded a fur coat and jacket into her Wolsey valise. The list continued: tweed travelling costumes, woollen cardigans, and a set of five-foot muslin bags with elastic drawstring necks, like big shoe-bags, into which she would climb beneath the blankets in bed to protect herself from fleas and other insects; then the multiple little leather notebooks which she would use for her archaeological notes and as diaries; her two cameras and her film, reams of writing paper, compasses, cartography paper, pencils, pens and ink; lavender soaps and bottles of eau de toilette, silver hairbrushes and candlesticks, linen sheets and embroidered tablecloths; the surveying and map-projection instruments provided for her by the Royal Geographical Society; the specially made folding canvas bed and chair that would furnish her bedroom tent, and the canvas bath – 'my luxury' – that before the end of the trip would double as a drinking trough for the camels; finally, medical supplies, cosmetics, and the all-important cartridges which she wrapped in white silk evening stockings and hid, pushing them down into the pointed toes of her shoes and boots.

The journey she was undertaking began at last to excite her, not least because she had been seriously warned against it, but also because of the physical demands and geographical difficulties it posed. Her destination would be Hayyil, the almost mythical city at the centre of Arabia described by Charles M. Doughty, Dick's intrepid geologist uncle, in his 1888 book *Arabia Deserta*, the book she had taken with her on every one of her expeditions. He had written grimly of two ill-starred visits there during a daunting two years travelling the border between the Arabian and Syrian deserts. At Hayyil he had been detained and nearly lost his life.

In choosing Hayyil, she would be travelling to one of the most volatile and least known parts of the world. The ostensible purpose of the visit was to provide information for the Foreign Office. War with Germany was increasingly likely, and the attention of the British government was turning to the political situation in central Arabia, where Germany was cementing its ties with the Ottoman Empire by training their army, supplying them with arms and building railways.

For a century the enmity between the two major forces in central Arabia, the Sauds and the Rashids, had been pivotal to the history of the peninsula. Britain was principally supplying arms and money to the charismatic but ferocious chieftain Abdul Aziz Abdurrahman al Saud, Hakim of Nejd – usually known as Ibn Saud.* This leader of the fanatical puritan Wahabi sect of Islam operated from

* Ibn Saud – 'son of Saud'.

the Saud capital Riyadh, his authority growing as he won back the territories his forefathers had lost. The Ottoman government supported the opposing dynasty of Ibn Rashid of the Shammar federation, perhaps the cruellest, most violent tribe of Arabia. Now the Sauds were poised to strike at the Rashids, and it was to the Rashid stronghold Hayyil that Gertrude determined to go first. At this stage, she harboured a second plan, to travel further south, to Riyadh, to collect further information that would be of interest, perhaps to the Foreign Office. Captain William Shakespear, setting out for Riyadh almost neck and neck with Gertrude, would get caught up in a battle between the Sauds and the Rashids fifteen months later, and be killed.

The scope of the journey Gertrude was planning was extraordinary. She proposed to travel sixteen hundred miles by camel, taking a circular route south from Damascus, then east across the northern third of the Arabian peninsula, the landmass bounded by the Red Sea, the Gulf and the Arabian Sea. Geographically and politically, a journey such as this was enough to daunt the most experienced of travellers. On a comparable expedition Charles Huber, most distinguished of Arabian explorers, had lost heart and turned back on his tracks only to be murdered by his own guides; and the Austrian Baron Nolde had been driven to suicide. Reaching Hayyil had become the desert traveller's ultimate challenge. To penetrate this barren country would have been hazardous enough even if the Bedouin could have been relied upon to be friendly. Gertrude was proposing to travel into the arena of Saud–Rashid conflict at a time when events were moving to a climax.

The first part of the journey would take her south to central Arabia and across the vast interior highland of Nejd, which stretches from Syria in the north to Yemen in the south. Then she would cross the shifting sands of the Nefud, becoming the first Westerner to cross that angle of the desert. She would leave the Nefud via the Misma Mountains, a strange and unearthly place not unlike the Gothic visions of Gustave Doré, the nineteenth-century illustrator of Dante's *Inferno*. A landscape littered with rock pinnacles as high as ten-storey buildings, it had another extraordinary property: because of the flint in the rock formations, it was as black as night. She would then descend into the featureless dry plateau of granite and basalt grit, at the heart of which the snow-white medieval city of Hayyil floated like a mirage.

Gertrude had thought about this expedition, and put it off, for a long time. She was by now so experienced a desert voyager that there was little she had not done. This time, for personal reasons, she wanted not only an escape, but a challenge that would test her to the limit – an adventure that would impress Dick Doughty-Wylie, cause him anxiety on her behalf, fix his attention. She wanted his admiration, even if she was never to return. She told her parents that she would leave her destination open and get advice in Damascus, but David Hogarth wrote to remind her that she already had reason to know that her project would not be approved, either by the Ottoman authorities or by the chief representative of Great Britain in Turkey, Sir Louis Mallet. This new ambassador in Constantinople (and friend of the Bell family) had advised her strongly against the journey while he was working at the Foreign Office in London. Four years previously a friend, Richmond Ritchie, had arranged for Gertrude to meet the Indian government's Resident in the Persian Gulf while he was in England, to discuss the route to Hayyil. The Resident was Lieutenant-Colonel Percy Cox, a name that would come to mean much to her later. He too warned her against the journey, and especially against a southern route.

In the book bag, along with the maps, her travelling set of pocket Shakespeare and her well thumbed copy of *Arabia Deserta*, she packed *Pilgrimage to Nejd* by Anne Blunt, who had visited Hayyil with her husband Wilfrid and had fallen foul of the Rashids. Gertrude had met her once at her stables in Cairo, wearing Bedouin costume and surrounded by wolves. She would have perused the book many times, noting Anne Blunt's oracular 'It was a lesson and a warning . . . that we were Europeans still among Asiatics, a warning that [Hayyil] was a lions' den.'

In her present state of mind, it was all one to Gertrude. She almost welcomed the danger and the warnings. This was to be a portentous journey. She did not know it, but it was to be her last desert expedition. Before it was all over she would have learnt the meaning of fear, wonderingly identifying this new sensation. The trip would allow her to provide the Foreign Office with detailed new information at a critical moment, essential data for imperial administrators, policymakers and military geographers. It would also be the hardest and longest she had ever undertaken, bringing her face to face with thieves and murderers. She would come to wonder whether the game was worth the candle.

For now, she wrote to Dick only of her intention of reaching Hayyil, and he was as worried as she could wish. An experienced traveller himself, and although fully comprehending her reasons for going, he was troubled by this perverse choice of destination and the length of time she would be outside the sphere of British influence. His anxiety comes through clearly in letters she received at her first port of call, Damascus. Resonant with the understatement that was *de rigueur* for a man of his class and profession, his letter went: 'God go with you – and the luck of the world . . . I am nervous about you somehow, lest things should go wrong . . . south of Maan and from there to Hayil is surely a colossal trek. For your palaces your road your Baghdad your Persia I do not feel so nervous – but Hail from Maan – Inshallah!'

On 27 November 1913 Gertrude arrived by boat, then train, in the Syrian capital of Damascus. She had travelled straight from Beirut. Because she was accompanied by such a pyramid of luggage, she omitted to visit T. E. Lawrence, spying on the Germans from Carchemish. 'Miss Bell passed straight through,' he wrote to his brother with some disappointment. '[She] will not visit us till Spring.'

Gertrude's arrival at her favourite Damascus Palace Hotel caused the usual stir. She was the most famous British traveller of her day, male or female. Her new and sixth book, *The Palace and Mosque at Ukhaidir*, was soon to be published to much attention from archaeologists and historians of the Middle East. No one had yet heard of T. E. Lawrence, whose reputation did not eclipse hers until 1920, and then only because of a somewhat sensational biography. The hotel manager welcomed her with deep bows, champagne and a basket of apricots in her suite. As the bellboys carried in trunk after trunk, she would have thrown open the windows and looked down on the teeming streets, late-flowering gardens and all-night bazaars. Her melancholy was kept at bay for a while in this familiar city, now pleasantly red and gold in the mellow November sunlight.

There were people to visit, things to do. She would have ordered black coffee and then started to unpack a few of her boxes on the bed and carpets, the room rapidly acquiring a familiar jumble and a miasma of cigarette smoke. As soon as she was settled, she contacted Muhammad al-Bessam, a wily and very wealthy wheeler-dealer currently buying up land around the line of the future Baghdad railway. She knew him, and she knew that he could locate for her the best riding camels and the best guide. He introduced her to Muhammad al-Marawi, who came highly recommended. He had travelled with Douglas Carruthers, the man who was to draw up her maps for the Royal Geographical Society when she returned to London. She had written from England for Fattuh, her old companion of the road, to meet her there. She was delighted to see him again when, on her second day, he arrived from Aleppo. As before, he would be responsible for her personal comfort on the road, putting up her tents, carrying the water for her bath, making up her complicated bed with the muslin bag, cheerfully unpacking her linen, silver and china and setting her candlelit table for dinner before retiring to a respectful and ever-vigilant distance.

Leaving him to continue her unpacking, she began at once to take up her contacts and to find out everything she could about the current state of tribal affairs around Hayyil. Almost immediately, she began writing home to reassure her parents, and almost immediately, the shade of a divergence from the truth began to creep into her letters. She wrote glibly to Florence on 27 November: Muhammad says that it is perfectly easy to go to Nejd this year. It looks as though I have fallen on an exceedingly lucky moment and . . . the desert is almost preternaturally quiet . . . If I found it so I should certainly go. I will let you know anyhow from Madeba.'

If Muhammad al-Marawi had in fact said this to Gertrude, he must have known better. Perhaps, like Bessam, whose advice she had also sought, he was too ready to pocket her money. Perhaps both believed that she would be certain to turn back long before she got to Nejd. It would have been extremely difficult to deter her, of course, but she appealed, next, to Hugh, as the spoilt daughter she had always been. She wrote as though his refusal would have brought her home on the next boat, but knowing that she could always twist him round her little finger: 'I hope you will not say No. It is unlikely that you will because you are such a beloved father that you never say No to the most outrageous demands . . . Dearest beloved Father, don't think me very mad or very unreasonable and remember always that I love you more than words can say.'

Gertrude knew just how to go about organizing a caravan, but this would be the most elaborate she had ever undertaken. She needed seventeen camels, costing an average of £13 each with their saddles and cordage. 'I must reckon to spend £50 on food,' she scribbled in her diary, '. . . £50 for presents such as cloaks, keffeyehs for the head, cotton cloth, etc.' Following the advice of Bessam, she would take £80 with her, and give £200 to the Rashid agent for a letter of credit which would permit her to draw the sum in Hayyil. Adding up her expenses, she was surprised to find them making a total of £601. She would need twice as much as she had brought, and would have to ask her father to telegraph the money through the Ottoman Bank. On 28 November, she wired him for £400 – a not inconsiderable sum, the equivalent of £23,000 in today's money – then hurried back to the hotel to write him a long letter of explanation: 'This is not a gift for which I am asking. I am practically using all my next year's income for this journey, but if I sit very quiet and write the book of it . . . I don't see why I shouldn't be able to pay it all back . . . The desert is absolutely tranquil and there should be no difficulty whatever in getting to Hayyil, that is Ibn al Rashid's capital.'

The fact that she had to explain the significance of Hayyil shows just how little she had told her father. Hugh, as always, poring over maps in the Rounton library with her latest letter in his hand, knew only what Gertrude wished him to know.

As usual, she bared her soul to her friend Domnul, one of the few people she felt able to write to about her relationship with Doughty-Wylie: 'I don't know that it is an ultimate way out, but it is worth trying. As I have told you before it is mostly my fault, but that does not prevent it from being an irretrievable misfortune – for both of us. But I am turning away from it now, and time deadens even the keenest things.' In claiming most of the responsibility for her misery she may have been being disingenuous. It is more likely, given Domnul's affection and respect for her, that she was putting a spin on the facts. It would have been awkward for her to explain that the love of her life would rather live with his wife. She might have preferred to stress what was after all no less than the truth – that she was the one to draw back from adultery.

Meanwhile, she discussed her route with Muhammad. As her chief of staff and the man who would keep her crew in order, he would lead them through the Hamad desert and an uncharted region of the Nefud. In a photograph she took of him, with his moustache and curly Sinbad beard, he sits cross-legged on the ground holding a folded telescope and looking keenly into the camera lens from under his white keffiyeh. This was 'the man of all others who I should have chosen,' she decided. That evening he accompanied her to dinner in the Maidan, the native bazaar quarter, to meet the Rashid agent who would collect Gertrude's £200. In her description of him there is almost a suggestion of ill omen, as if she had a passing premonition of danger awaiting her in Hayyil:

> A curious figure, young, very tall and slight, wrapped in a gold embroidered cloak and his head covered with an immense gold bound camel's hair robe which shadowed his crafty narrow face. He leant back among his cushions and scarcely lifted his eyes, talking in a soft slow voice . . . and told marvellous tales of hidden treasure and ancient wealth and mysterious writings . . . The men on either side of me murmured from time to time 'Oh Beneficent, oh Ever Present!' as they listened . . . Finally we ate together and then – why then we all came back together on the electric tram!

While she waited for the money from home, she bought camels and hired camel drivers with Muhammad, adding to her staff a smiling black African, Fellah, and the first *rafiq* of the trip, an escort from the Ghiyadh tribe. By employing a *rafiq*, travellers gained an ally whose paid companionship would protect them from attack by his own particular tribe. She would hire a score or more, one by one, as she encountered different tribes along the way.

She toured the bazaars, haggling for cheap presents to smooth her way across the desert, and worried about Fattuh, who she had begun to realize was unwell. She hated the thought of starting without him, but suspected that he had malaria. She delayed a few days, by which time he was so much worse that she feared it was typhoid. Leaving him in the care of his wife, she decided to start without him. He could join her along the way. It was the arrangement to meet up with Fattuh that made her alter her planned route. Now she would skirt the Druze mountains northeast of the Dead Sea and make her way to the station at Aziz where, she hoped, he would meet her. It would give him three weeks to recover his health.

Before she left, she received mail from Dick. 'I wonder where in the great desert you might be?' he asked, not knowing she had had to delay. 'I shall miss you more than ever when I get back to London . . . I shall go to see Lady Bell.' As always, he blew hot and cold alternately, writing in his familiar rhetorical manner and prevaricating in a way that must have tortured her. 'Might we have been man and woman as God made us and been happy? I know what you felt, what you would do and why not – but still and after all you don't know – that way lies a great and splendid thing, but for you all sorts of dangers.' He had told her he would burn all of her letters – 'one might die, or something' – and she knew that he had. But she would keep all of his.

And so on Tuesday 16 December 1913 she set off, through orchards of apricots and olives, to meet her party at their staging ground. The cordage complete – the tying on to the camels and donkeys of all the tents, equipment and baggage – the stately procession moved off in the direction of Adhra. The first day's ride was a short one, just to the edge of the Damascus oasis. The next day brought torrential rain and bitter winds and took them across icy volcanic ground — far removed from the baking yellow sand and shimmering mirages of popular imagination. She wrote: 'We struggled on . . . through the mud and irrigation canals – a horrible business with the camels slipping and falling . . . It was horribly cold last night . . . impossible to keep warm in bed. I am not cut out for Arctic exploration. The men's big tent was frozen hard and they had to light fires under it to unfreeze the canvas.'

It was an inauspicious beginning, and about to get worse. Starting at 9.15 a.m. on the 21st, the party soon spotted smoke rising in a thin column on the horizon. The camel drivers became nervous. As Hamad, the new *rafiq*, remarked, 'Every Arab in the desert fears the other.' Full of her usual confidence, Gertrude scoffed and marched to the top of a nearby tor, extending her telescope for a better view. What she saw was a collection of tents surrounded by sheep: just shepherds, she concluded. But she was wrong, and she had been spotted. Nearly half an hour passed, and then, like a whirlwind, a Druze horseman came galloping towards them, firing as he came.

Hamad advanced with his hands in the air; the horseman aimed the rifle at him. Muhammad came forward shouting, 'Stay! God guide you! We are Shawam and Agail and Qanasil', naming three tribes not likely to be enemies. The rider, his long matted hair flying around him, circled the caravan at a gallop, whirling his rifle above his head. Riding up at full speed to Ali, one of the camel drivers, he demanded his gun and fur cloak. Backing away from the stamping horse, Ali threw them to the ground. Now the lone rider was joined by a larger group of equally wild-looking Bedouin, some riding, some running, and firing in all directions. One of them, aiming his gun at Muhammad, seized the guide's sword and hit him across the chest with the flat of the blade. Then, turning, he charged at Gertrude on her camel, hitting the animal across the head in the same way that he had hit Muhammad. He seized the reins and forced the frightened animal to crouch, while a couple of boys pushed her aside and ransacked her saddlebags. At the same time the other men, all half-dressed and one 'stark naked except for a handkerchief', all shouting, began systematically to strip her men of their arms and cartridges while she watched helplessly. It was at this moment that the day was saved by Fellah, the black boy who looked after the men's tents. Bursting into theatrical tears, he yelled out that he knew them and they knew him: he had been a guest amongst them only a year ago, buying camels. There was a sudden silence, a tense moment of hesitation, and then the traditional etiquette of the desert swung slowly into play. Piece by piece, the booty was returned. Before they were finished, a couple of sheikhs rode up, took stock of the situation and greeted Gertrude and her party. They continued, however, to behave menacingly. Gertrude proceeded to pitch camp, and followed the usual custom by paying for a local *rafiq*. But the sheikhs remained immovable until, reluctantly, she handed over more money. At night they returned to her camp, yelling and singing.

In fact, anything could have happened: had her rifles and other possessions been stolen, she would have had to turn back to Damascus. As she had always done when thrown on the hunting field, she remounted and continued, but the experience had come close to the bone. Not a week into the trip she had been forced to confront her own vulnerability. But she did not admit it, particularly when writing to her parents. All she said was 'A preposterous and provoking episode has delayed us today.'

Late the next day, and with the sullen new *rafiq* in tow, the caravan moved off into a desert turned into 'a sticky sop' from heavy overnight rain. Jagged black volcanic rock rose above them, and a black sky above that. She wrote: 'The stony hills draw together in front of us like the gates of an abandoned Hades. A desolate world, cold and grey . . . Ibrahim lighted a fire. It smoked abominably and he was rebuked by Ali. "Smoke is seen far in the morning and sound is heard far."'

Wrapped in fur, Gertrude sat by the fire drinking pints of coffee and listened to the men as they talked of theft, raid and murder, ghosts and superstitions. From the several tribes represented among her crew, she heard of grudges and old scores unsettled, and began to draw in her mind a map of liaisons and enmities that would be crucial to her later. 'The foes of Sukhur are the Fed'an, the Sba' and all the Jebehiyyeh except the 'Isa and the Serdiyyeh,' she wrote one night before she went to bed; another time, she noted the rumour that the Ottoman government had sent seventy camel-loads of arms to Ibn Rashid to help him fight Ibn Saud.

By Christmas Day they were at Burqu, little more than a jumble of rocks surmounted by the ruins of a Roman fort. The weather was icy. Gertrude made her way through freezing fog to copy a Kufic inscription, stepping carefully round a half-eaten human body to do so. She thought of Rounton and of the very different kind of day her family would be having. They wound on in raging winds, the camels slipping on the icy stones, moaning as they went. They were now in the camping grounds of the Ruwalla, one of the Wahabi tribes led by Ibn Saud and one of the largest desert groupings in Arabia, with between five and six thousand tents. Constantly looking over their shoulders, her men pitched camp where they would be hidden from view. As chance would have it, they encountered a group of Beni Sakhr, enemies of the Ruwalla, and she dined in the tent of one Sheikh Ibn Mitab. She wrote home: 'Extremely nasty dinner . . . sheep and bread in a greasy stew which he mixed up for me with his fingers, saying "It is all good. I made it with my hand."'

She completed the formalities by comparing rifles with him, and presented him with a silk under-robe, coffee and sugar. The water they found there was pure mud, caking the men's beards as it dried. Gertrude had to give up washing, as well as the longed-for luxury of sitting down to dinner clean and fresh. Sitting outside her tent, she could hear the silence. At night, Arab fires twinkled in the far distance, and were answered by the stars.

The journey continued full of spooks and portents. At one point, a mob of aggressive villagers stopped her from making a plan of a castle; at another, she came upon a dead man − the second she had encountered on this trip − whose 'horrible presence is not easily for-gotten'. Other villagers insisted she treat a man with gangrene. Around the fire her men talked of *jinnehs*, witches who walk along-side travellers, their eyes set lengthwise in their faces. Sometimes the drinking water was alive with energetic red insects; once her tent pole cracked and broke in the night, bringing wet canvas down on her bed. In the diary she was writing for Dick she noted that she had liked this part of the journey so little that she almost turned back. It had become 'a mountain of evils . . . I do not feel at all like the daughter of kings, which I am supposed to be here. It's a bore being a woman when you are in Arabia.'

On 8 January they arrived at Ziza, the end of the railway and the place where she would wait for Fattuh and more of her luggage. She was happy to see him earlier than expected – still convalescent, but bringing her delicious things to eat and the longed-for mail. Dick had just received a copy of *The Palace and Mosque at Ukhaidir*. 'The book I have read all day,' he said. 'It's perfectly wonderful and I love it and you. I can't write about it yet – and it would take the book of my soul, never written, to answer it. I kiss your hands and your feet, dear woman of my heart.'

She now had to be wary of Turkish military patrols. The Sultan, the head of the Ottoman Empire, did not encourage non-Muslims in his provinces, and his governors-general held the power to grant or refuse permits. Gertrude had so far dodged the bureaucracy, and having no permission from either the British or the Turks, intended to ride on quickly. She could not, however, resist making what turned out to be a fruitless diversion in order to find and photograph an ancient stone niche decorated with a carved shell, said to exist in some ruins at a place called Mshetta. On her return, she saw in the distance three figures moving rapidly towards her tents. Her heart sank. She knew she had been found out.

By the time she got back, Turkish soldiers were installed around her fire, shouting and laughing and generally behaving in a loutish and threatening manner. They were soon joined by more – now ten in all – under the command of an angry captain and his staff sergeant. The authorities had been alerted when Fattuh had applied for a permit to join her. Telegraphs had been sent from Constantinople, and now the soldiers had orders to stop her expedition and take her to Amman. 'I was an idiot to come in so close to the railway,' she commented, '. . . but I was like an ostrich with its head in the sand and didn't know all the fuss there had been about me.'

She was in trouble. Her first impulse was to send her camel driver Abdullah off to Madeba some twenty miles away to telegraph the consuls at Beirut and Damascus. He slipped quietly out of camp but was followed, intercepted en route, and by nightfall was imprisoned at Ziza. Gertrude, head high, maintained her usual aloofness. But there came a moment when she had cause to take herself off a little distance from camp: she had to relieve herself. When she was doggedly followed by an officious soldier, Fattuh put himself between the two of them and told the Turk to allow the lady some privacy. In spite of all that Gertrude could do, Fattuh was arrested and taken away under escort to join Abdullah. It was a wild night. The sky darkened, the wind thundered and sentries were posted around the camp. 'The night was as icy as my demeanour.'

She had to watch while the contents of her luggage were turned out on the ground, and all her arms were confiscated. The soldiers were now awaiting the arrival of the district governor, the *vali*, whose proper title was the Qaimmaqam of Salt. Much depended on this figure, who could grant her a permit. If he did not, she would probably have to turn back under armed guard into Turkish territory. Having summoned this important personage, the captain began to feel alarmed at what he had done and lost a little of his bravado.

Gertrude's chilly restraint combined with her impressive wealth soon facilitated the return of Fattuh and Abdullah. Still, it was an awkward stand-off. She was able to relieve the tension by asking her crew to mend her broken tent pole: even the soldiers joined in. Sheltering at the table in her second tent, she calmly drew out a map of the ruined site of Kharaneh while inwardly resolving that, if permission was refused, she would return to Damascus and start again via the Palmyra route. Then she wrote up the last two days in light ironical vein for her diary and for her parents: 'It's all rather comic; I don't much care. It's a laughable episode in the adventure, but I don't think the adventure is ended; only it must take another turn'. Resorting to the language of the Rounton nursery – 'None of your fancy behaviour, Miss!' – she concluded with a truly Yorkshire 'It is all rather fancy, I must say.'

Her predicament was not in the least comic, of course, but she still ended the day on a light note, which – if they heard her laughter – must have surprised the sentries shivering outside her tents. The joke was Fattuh's, who had remarked: 'I spent the first night of the journey in the railway station, and the second in prison – where next?'

The morning announced itself with driving sleet. Flanked by the staff sergeant and four of his soldiers, she rode to the station to collect the last of her baggage. On the way they spotted a distant group of soldiers. It seemed that the district governor and his party had arrived at last. Gertrude swapped her camel for the staff sergeant's horse and cantered up to them, jumping off to shake hands. She would always rather deal with the man at the top, and immediately hit it off with the Qaimmaqam, describing him later in her letter home as 'a charming, educated man, a Christian, willing and ready to let me go anywhere I like by any road I please ... But there comes in a question of conscience.' She didn't want to get this kind man into trouble by taking advantage of him, she told Hugh and Florence. That was the only reason, she said, why she had telegraphed Damascus for permission to visit some local ruins, in order to relieve him of all responsibility when she left.

Clearly she was protecting her parents from anxiety on her behalf, as she always did. How different was the description of events that she wrote up in her diary, which reveals that she was told to telegraph for permission. Now she had to wait day after day for the response from Damascus and from Constantinople too, knowing all the time what it would be.

Stuck fast for the time being, she spent her time meeting up with friends made on her earlier expedition into the terrain, including a nephew of Abu Namrud, the guide who had helped her on her journey into the Jebel Druze in 1905. Lunching with the Qaimmaqam in the house of Muhammad Beg, the richest inhabitant of Amman, she heard rumours of a Russian countess who had recently left Damascus with twenty camels. Amid much laughter, all three concluded that by a process of Chinese whispers and the usual distortions of verbal desert communication, this countess must be none other than Gertrude. She returned to her tent with a bunch of marigolds and garnet-red carnations.

She had soon been waiting four days, and was getting restive. She busied herself with local affairs and attended a Circassian wedding. The bride was unveiled before her: 'She stood like an image in a room crowded with women and very hot. She stood with downcast eyes looking very tired . . . a pasty heavy complexion, otherwise pretty.' She was a great object of curiosity herself. She noted without comment the remark of a man she met later in the day, about the rest of the men assembled: 'They like to smell your smell.' Lavender water from Bond Street was new to them.

At last she received the expected communication from an irritated Ambassador Mallet, who had warned her not to undertake this journey in the first place. HM Government would disclaim responsibility for her if she went one step further, he told her shortly. There was as yet no response from the Turkish side. She wrote in her diary on 14 January: 'Decided to run away.'

She was now writing parallel diary entries. One continued to be a cursory memorandum written daily while the memory was fresh. Reading these factual, ill-organized jottings, full of Arab words and phrases, gives a vivid picture of Gertrude, tired and dirty after a day's march, her hair falling out of its pins, scribbling away at her folding desk while Fattuh put up her bedroom tent, unpacked and arranged her possessions. These notes contained the information and positions she would pass on to the Foreign Office, and the raw material for her letters home. The second diary,* with entries written a few days apart, was a thoughtful and polished account of her journey and feelings, kept for Dick alone. Though by no means as euphemistic as her letters to her parents, it portrayed her as a shade more robust in her attitude to danger than was perhaps the case.

That night she told her crew that she would wait no longer for permission. There was a stir, a ripple of mutiny. While her faithful servants would have followed her anywhere, three of the Agail

* This diary will be referred to as her 'other' diary.

camel drivers were terrified of repercussions. But she knew that if she waited, the situation would only become worse. Permission would be refused all round. She told the Turkish captain that she intended to visit some local archaeological sites. He may or may not have believed her, but in the end she gave him a signed letter absolving the Turkish authorities from any responsibility for her, and declaring that England had no cause for complaint if anything happened to her. Pocketing the document, he intimated that she could now do as she liked. She swept off to bed without a backward glance, but once in her tent she regretted having signed, and fretted all night. She wrote in her other diary, for Dick: 'There is something in the written word which works on the imagination, and I spent my night sleepless with the thought of it ... The desert looks terrible from without, and even I have a moment when my heart beats a little quicker and my eyes strain themselves to catch a glimpse of the future.'

The first thing she did next day was to try and get her letter back. It had already gone to headquarters, she was told. 'All lies,' she wrote irritably in her diary, 'but could not get it anyway.' Back in camp, she wrote Florence a jaunty letter that was extremely frugal with the truth: 'My troubles are over. I have today permission from the Vali to go where I like. The permission comes just in time for all my plans were laid and I was going to run away tomorrow night. They could not have caught me. However I am now saved the trouble – and amusement! – of this last resource.'

As she well knew, any 'permission' was valueless. She had also received strong discouragement from the British Consul. She would go at her own risk.

The three Agail were paid off and departed angrily, denouncing the 'accursed road' to Hayyil. On 15 January she sent most of her crew on ahead of her and went to collect three replacement camel drivers from friendly Christian farmers whom she had taken into her confidence. She stopped for a moment at the station at Ziza to enquire about a missing letter addressed to Dick, but did not find it, and accepted that, for the moment, there would be no further contact with those she loved. She would continue to write a series of letters that she could not post, hoarding them until she reached another railway line on the other side of the Syrian desert.

She was now fifty-four days into her journey, but only a fifth of the way to Hayyil. She had a long and uncertain road ahead of her, but once she was free again, her serenity returned and once more she fell under the spell of the desert. Terrifying and beautiful, with its roaring silence and jewelled nights, it had become for her more than the ultimate testing ground. It was a symbolic alternative to the divinity in whom she had never believed. In her need for love and support, it had become an escape to another perspective. She told the real truths in her rarer and more poetic letters to her friend Chirol:

> I have known loneliness in solitude now, for the first time, and . . . my thoughts have gone wandering far from the camp fire into places which I wish were not so full of acute sensation . . . Sometimes I have gone to bed with a heart so heavy that I thought I could not carry it through the next day. Then comes the dawn, soft and beneficent, stealing over the wide plain and down the long slopes of the little hollows, and in the end it steals into my dark heart also . . . That's the best I can make of it, taught at least some wisdom by solitude, taught submission, and how to bear pain without crying out.

In her other diary she wrote on 16 January:

> I have cut the thread . . . Louis Mallet has informed me that if I go on towards Nejd my own government washes its hands of me, and I have given a categorical acquittal to the Ottoman Government, saying that I go on at my own risk . . . We turn towards Nejd, inshallah, renounced by all the powers that be, and the only thread which is not cut runs through this little book, which is the diary of my way kept for you.
>   I am an outlaw!

The die was cast, and politically Gertrude had passed the point of no return. From Damascus she had already travelled nearly two hundred miles south to Ziza, and would now direct her caravan south-east to Hayyil. From there, she planned to head north-east to Baghdad before setting out across the Syrian desert from east to west, back to her starting point of Damascus.

The wilderness ahead of her was infinitely varied in its forms and conditions. The summer brought extremes of heat, up to 140 degrees in the desert at midday, but now, in the coldest months of January and February, there could be howling winds, ice, fog and sleet. Cultivation was intermittent, depending on the unpredictable winter rainfall. In the plains and deserts there were occasional underground streams giving rise to pools and thin patches of soil, before giving way again to steppes of rock and gravel with the odd tuft of plant life burnt white by sun and wind. Where and when the rain had come to swell the springs, it was possible for villagers to grow some crops in the oases, but Gertrude was leaving the villagers behind her, travelling where the nomads were making their seasonal migration over hundreds of miles. They were moving great herds of female camels and their young to pasture before pushing north-west to Syria or north-east to Iraq for the annual camel sales. 'The world is full of camels . . . They drift across our path in thousands, grazing. It is like some immense slow river, hours wide.'

Gertrude shared with Lawrence an admiration amounting almost to an addiction for the Bedouin and their powerful mystique. Both admired the independence, mobility and resilience that made these nomads the aristocracy of the desert. Contained in this, perhaps for both of them, was a physical attraction to the type of a warrior ascetic. Lawrence was to write in his introduction to *Arabia Deserta*:

> The Beduin has been born and brought up in the desert, and has embraced this barrenness too harsh for volunteers with all his soul, for the reason . . . that there he finds himself indubitably free. He loses all natural ties, all comforting superfluities or complications, to achieve that personal liberty which haunts starvation and death . . . He finds luxury in abnegation, renunciation, self-restraint. He lives his own life in a hard selfishness.

The Bedouin rejected all authority, and their rules of conduct were their own: they did not answer to Turkish persuasion any more than to British influence. There was, as the Middle Eastern scholar Albert Hourani writes, 'a certain hierarchical conception . . . [the Arab pastoralists] regarded themselves as having a freedom, nobility and honour which were lacking in peasants, merchants and craftsmen'. Gertrude, who had to rely on this sense of tribal honour for her life, enthusiastically subscribed to this view.

Members of each tribe were linked by a supposedly common ancestor. The notion of sharing a family through this ancestor, often an ideal concept rather than a provable fact, was promoted by the sheikhs as the inherited leaders, guardians and judges. While grazing land and water were regarded as common property between the nomads, the tribal groupings engendered constant skirmishes and *ghazzus*, raids whose object was usually the looting of camels, sheep and goats – or sometimes murder, when they would also carry off the women. Gertrude had written of the fatalistic nomadic attitude to this life in *The Desert and the Sown*.

> The Arab is never safe and yet he behaves as though security were his daily bread. He pitches his feeble little camps, ten or fifteen tents together, over a wide stretch of undefended and indefensible country . . . Having lost all his worldly goods, he goes about the desert and makes his plaint, and one man gives him a strip or two of goats-hair cloth, and another a coffee pot, a third presents him with a camel and a fourth with a few sheep till he has a roof to cover him and enough animals to keep his family from hunger.

Slights and grudges resulted in enmities which could continue down through the generations, in a similar way to the self-perpetuating blood feuds of the Italian mafia. By honourable tradition, however, the sheikhs extended their protection and hospitality to those travellers who strictly followed their etiquette. This code of conduct, without which Gertrude could never have travelled in the Middle East, was in fact not so much a matter of etiquette as of obligation. It was written into the Koran, the Word of God as revealed to the Prophet Muhammad in the Arabic language, and the communication of God's commandments to the world of Islam. The Third Pillar of these commandments was the benevolent duty of *zakat*, the giving of help to the poor and the needy, for the relief of debtors, the liberation of slaves and, most importantly in the desert, the giving of welfare to wayfarers. 'I am in the real desert again, with the real desert people, the Bedu, who never touch settled life . . . I have to be voice and tongue for myself. I like it; it amuses me to run my own show,' Gertrude told her parents.

On her travels, Gertrude rode straight to the tent of any sheikh in the vicinity, greeting him in fluent Arabic and with all conventional deferences. She paid for the usual *rafiq*, as any male traveller would have done, but as a woman she had, for her very life, to convince the sheikh that she was his equal. She had to impress him with her importance and wealth, initially by the giving of presents. The gifts she dispensed were carefully graded, but sometimes she misjudged. After giving a minor sheikh a silk under-robe, she noted in her diary: 'He did not think it enough, I fear.' The stock of gifts that she carried included bales of silk, cotton headdresses, coffee and sugar, and the very valuable rifles and collapsible Zeiss telescopes that she had bought in quantity in London.

Because of the sheikh's own position in the tribal hierarchy, she had to make it clear that she was a member of a family as great as his own. In the telling, her father Hugh was transformed from a leading industrialist to the paramount sheikh of northern England. 'Your safest course of action in the desert is to let it be known that you come of great and honoured stock.'

Feminine as she was, Gertrude was not a woman as the sheikh knew women. In the first place, she rode like a man in the saddle, and not like the women of his harem, who rode curled up on small platforms of cushions. He would put together all the evidence she presented and conclude that she was mysteriously independent, rich, powerful and probably royal. She was certainly not his enemy, and might even, with her connections, be his ally. She spoke his language and she could quote more mystical Arab poetry than he knew himself. In the purely oral culture of the nomad, where every poem was lost if not committed to memory, her long study of the subject and her translation of *The Divan of Hafiz* stood her in good stead. Many were the occasions after dinner in a desert tent, when she cast a spell over the company by speaking an entire poem of which the sheikh might know only a line or two. Some of the odes, or *qasidas*, that she could quote from her photographic memory were written before AD 600: her hosts, she noted in *The Desert and the Sown*, had no idea that Arab culture had existed before the Prophet. Equally important, she had up-to-date gossip to impart — information about tribal movements and water sources that she had learnt along the way. Only Gertrude, with her regal bearing and assertive self-confidence protecting her like a suit of armour, could have survived the desert as a woman alone, but she was always close to danger. An important slip in her manner, or an encounter with a sheikh careless of his Koranic duty, or any number of other accidents, could prove fatal.

Safely distant from Ziza, she and her caravan rode across rolling Shammar country. She was getting to know the members of her expedition. There was the chief-of-staff, the elderly Muhammad al-Marawi who knew the Nejd and many of the Rashids of Hayyil from riding and fighting with them as a young man. A camel dealer in his middle years, he had fallen on lean times and now took whatever odd jobs presented themselves — 'He has had few odder jobs than me, I expect,' commented Gertrude drily. Then there was his courteous and educated nephew Salim, 'a capital boy', who helped Fattuh. Ali she knew from a former journey across the Syrian desert. He was, she wrote to Dick borrowing one of his own phrases, 'an 'ole dog', but brave as a lion. Sayyid, the chief camel driver, was another nephew of Muhammad's and 'a treasure'. They had a raw recruit, an Agail — 'but he will learn' — and Mustafa, a farm worker sent with her from her Christian friends near Ziza. There was Fellah, the black camelherd whose histrionics had saved them from the Druze horsemen, the cameleers and two *rafiqs*, and the occasional guest or hanger-on. The first of these, a young sheikh of the Sukhur tribe, 'a nice boy', arrived with his slave and lodged with her caravan for the night.

The desert to the south of them was uninhabited. Her men kept watch for robbers who might take off with her camels. The land here had no landmarks to use as bearings, and they were getting short of water. Gertrude walked behind the caravan, using the direction of the line of camels in conjunction with the compass in her hand. The crew looked back from time to time, when she would correct their course by pointing with her outstretched arm. They marched for three days through a bare, forbidding land littered with flints, then on to a plain with outcrops of rusty volcanic stone. Here the men spotted recent camel prints in the dust, and feared the worst. They turned off into a dip and stretched out silently alongside the camels while Gertrude and two of her men climbed up a tell, rifles in hand, and lay on their stomachs, peering over the rocks. This time there were no warning shots, and after a while they stood up and went cautiously on. She wrote to Dick:

> When we were little, Maurice and I had a favourite game which consisted in wandering all over the house, up and down the staircases, without being seen by the housemaids – I felt exactly as if we were playing that beloved game as we crept up to the shoulder of the tell. But a careful survey through my glasses revealed no housemaids, and we went on boldly.

A little rain fell on the night of 23 January, and the camels hurried to drink from small puddles on the flinty ground as the water drained away. There was no prospect of any more for at least a day ahead. 'There are no words to tell you how bare and forbidding is this land . . . mile after mile of flat black country and nothing grows . . . I found a brave little geranium – the only flower I have seen.'

She delighted in the meagre life of desolate places, and noted down every edible mushroom, each wild geranium or marigold, oryx or cloud of moths that she saw on the journey. These minute notes on the flora and fauna were mixed in with the horrid tales of murder and mutilation that she heard every night around the fire. She had no reason to doubt these stories. Inspecting a ruin on her path two days previously, she had found a dead body: it was roughly buried, but draped over the mound were the corpse's clothes soaked in dried blood. Each day's march took her further from the zone of British influence and in her daily diary there were frequent references to her men's, rather than her own, anxiety about *ghazzus*. For herself, she was occupied with more pedestrian problems. There was no spare water for washing – she hated to go dirty but hardly ever complained about it.

In search of water, they turned away from the flint-strewn plateau into a valley where they found a multitude of fresh prints of camels and men. They did not know whether these were the footprints of friends or enemies, and they no longer knew exactly where they were, but whatever happened they would have to find water by nightfall. Gertrude pored over her map and found a well in the eastern hills. But even if they got there, would these unknown people have used it up? After two hours' driving east, they saw a curl of smoke above the tells, and she put their next move up for democratic vote among the crew. If it was a *ghazzu*, would it be better to make themselves known? The crew thought so. They would be tracked down in any case, and, after all, they could find themselves among friends. They turned towards the smoke, and crept up a low ridge to the south. There below them was a village. Now they knew where they were – at the winter pasturage of the Howeitat, a large and powerful tribe of what is described in *Arabia Deserta* as 'the stout nomad native', with a reputation for courage and devilry. The camels, sniffing water, set off at a bumpy, jingling trot and drank their fill. From shepherds they learnt that numerous Howeitat were some way off with their head sheikh, Audah Abu Tayyi, but that nearer, perhaps a day off, they could find the tents of another important Howeiti sheikh, Harb.

A night passed on the road, and the next morning they came upon the black tents of Sheikh Harb al Daransheh, scattered on the slopes of a high rocky gorge and tucked into the valleys beneath. To her relief, the elderly Harb greeted her caravan with cordiality and killed a sheep in her honour. It was 29 January, thirteen days since Ziza, and at last Gertrude could bathe herself in the folding bath, wash her hair and give her dirty clothes to Fattuh for laundering. In an evening dress and her fur coat – which doubled as a blanket on these cold nights – she went to Harb's tent and enjoyed an excellent dinner. As they ate, another distinguished guest arrived. Muhammad Abu Tayyi was a cousin of Sheikh Audah. Built on the heroic lines that Gertrude admired, he conformed in every way to her ideal man. She described him to Dick in emotional terms: 'A formidable looking person he is, great and stony and flashing eyed . . . all was new and interesting. And very beautiful . . . not least Muhammad's great figure sitting on the cushions beside me, with the white keffiyye falling over his black brows and his eyes flashing in question and answer.'

If she wanted to make Doughty-Wylie just a little insecure, who could blame her? When she asked her men about Muhammad, they told her of his terrifying anger, and how he had cut off the hands and feet of an enemy and left him to die. She preferred to ignore this, or put it down to myth. She progressed from Harb's tents to Muhammad's, a five-pole palace of a nomad dwelling, and dined with him on splendid carpets while a man sang to them of great Arab deeds. They finished the meal with camel's milk from huge wooden bowls. It was the most enjoyable evening of the journey so far, and as she watched him she tried to put the ugly rumour out of her mind. 'I saw his jurisdiction and found it to be just; I heard his tales of the desert and made friends with his women; and I made friends with him. He is a man, and a good fellow, you can lay your head down in his tents, and sleep at night, and have no fear.'

She made her presentation of gifts to both sheikhs, and Muhammad reciprocated. The first present he sent over with his men was exotic, but she found that she was meant to pay for it: an ostrich skin and an egg, 'the price of which I must insinuate delicately into their palms'. The second was even less welcome, the next day's dinner in the form of a charming black and white lamb 'with whom I have come into terms of such intimate friendship that I can scarcely bear the thought of sacrificing it, yet I cannot well carry it with me like Byron's goose'. Seeing her fondness for animals, Muhammad offered her his Arabian oryx, a pet calf that ran around in his tents and that she described as 'the most enchanting little beast'. She sensibly refused it. While she appreciated animals, and would make pets of them when she was settled, she did not allow herself to become sentimental about them. She loved to see the 'preposterous' baby camels, all legs and neck, as she passed the breeding herds, and would join the men in feeding her own animals, three by three, at the end of the day. It was a habit she had learnt in childhood, when at Rounton, after a day's hunting, she and Maurice would help the grooms clean and feed their ponies before having their own baths and suppers. When Fattuh told her that one of her own camels had sat down and would not move, she went back to bring it water and food. They found it rolling and kicking with pain and, diagnosing a disease called *al tair*, Muhammad asked whether he should finish its life. Tight-lipped, Gertrude nodded and watched him draw his knife and cut the camel's throat. 'I am deeply attached to all my camels,' she wrote that night. 'I grieve over her death.'

She stayed a week with the hospitable sheikhs, giving a dinner for them in her own tents before she left. Perhaps Muhammad had a liking for Gertrude himself. He detained her a couple of days in order to show her an only mildly interesting archaeological site seven hours distant: she wanted to get on with her journey, but felt it would be discourteous to refuse.

Her week's sojourn with the Howeitat had allowed her to absorb another dimension of Arab life, until now a mystery to her: she had learnt about the life of the wives. She spent many hours in the harem tents with her camera, and took some of her best photographs. In one, Sheikh Harb, with striped sashes and a belt of cartridges, holds back a tent flap to reveal his women huddled together in the dark with their children, hiding their faces. Although Gertrude was not particularly interested in women's lives, she could not help but be impressed by their stories. One of the four wives of Muhammad, Hilah, told her how women suffered from the heavy physical work and constant moving, especially during and immediately after childbirth. 'We do not rest an hour,' she said: each of her four babies had died while she had carried on with her strenuous work of putting up and taking down the tents, collecting camel dung for the fires and preparing the food. As Gertrude sat at the door of her tent on the frosty night of 30 January, committing

Hilah's tale to paper and reflecting on the difference between their fates, she looked up to see an immense falling star — 'it fell across half heaven'.

Muhammad warned her to avoid the Shammar, who he said would rob her and kill her men, and to go east instead of south, with Harb's brother Awwad and a Sherarat *rafiq*, Musuid, to see her safe into the river valley some days ahead. In the manner of a chess game, the strategy changed again when news came to the Howeitat that their enemies the Ruwalla were camped not far away. Gertrude did not care whether she fell in with Ruwalla or Howeitat, but a substitute was found for Awwad, who would certainly have been the Ruwalla's first victim. And so, on 2 February, she set off south as originally planned. 'Everyone goes in fear except only I, who have nothing to lose that matters . . . Occasionally I wonder whether I shall come out of this adventure alive. But the doubt has no shadow of anxiety in it – I am so profoundly indifferent.'

In traditional desert manner, her caravan had grown as it travelled. She was now the sheikh of the largest expedition she had ever led: some thirty nomads swathed and cloaked to the eyes, her men carrying rifles, all filing silently through the barren landscape and accompanied by a few sheep and goats. She had fallen in with a family of Shammar who begged her protection on their way home out of Howeitat country. The benefit was mutual, as they would not have dared to take the road alone, and they would be useful allies in case of a Shammar raid. She had also picked up two miserable tents of Sherarat with a tiny flock of goats. The inhabitants of these ragged tents were 'as near starvation as can be'. Touchingly, they arrived each evening at her tent with the gift of a small bowl of goat's milk, which she did not like but felt obliged to drink, and in return she gave them small amounts of meat and flour.

They were lucky that the November rains had been plentiful where they were now on the march, and there were rain pools, bushes and sweet-smelling plants. The camels could eat as they went along – a bonus, given that they could only carry sufficient dried grass for five days' march. Soon she had to decide whether to make a detour to the city of Jof, where she could have bought more food, but she was beginning to feel that she would never get to Hayyil if there were any more diversions. And so the caravan wound on, through red sandstone and sand ridges the size of hills. 'Abandoned of God and man, that is how it looks,' she wrote to Dick. 'Noone can travel here and come back the same. It sets its seal upon you, for good or ill.'

One more event delayed them, on 9 February, in the form of a Howeitat party hunting oryx. They warned Gertrude of Wadi Sulaiman Arabs some five hours to the east. As she could be sure that the Sulaiman would already know of her caravan, it was politic to visit their tents and take on another *rafiq*. Gertrude's caravan turned in to a mountain pass in a bitter wind and, sighing, she changed her clothes/direction and set off for the Sulaiman tents. But as soon as she met their sheikh, she assessed the one-eyed Sayyid ibn Murted as 'cursed of his two parents'.

Over the first cup of coffee he was already pressing her rudely as to her route and purpose. When she left, he followed her like a shadow and, arriving at her tents, began to turn over and examine her possessions, while her men stood by powerless to stop him. As soon as he found her telescope, the sheikh demanded that she give it to him. She refused, but by nightfall, after hours of loud argument, it was agreed that she should give him a revolver in return for his nephew as a paid *rafiq*.

The trouble had only begun. In the morning, before she was up, he arrived again and she heard him angrily telling Fattuh and Sayyd her camel driver that no Christian woman had ever travelled in this country before, and that none should travel there now. As she quickly dressed, she heard him trying to incite her crew to mutiny and asked herself how she would ever get rid of him. She hurried out to draw his fire and treated him to her iciest manner. After an hour of gradually mounting threats, he said that if he did not get a gun and the Zeiss glass, he would follow her in the night and take whatever he wanted. Her men took Gertrude aside and whispered that she had better give him what he demanded, for fear of reprisals, and she angrily capitulated. Sayyid ibn Murted grabbed both, and demanded further money from the Shammar family; the Sherarat were too poor for him to bother with. Rid of him at last, she reimbursed the Shammars and restored to them their one precious carpet, that they had entrusted to her for safe keeping.

As she drew closer to Hayyil, she was starting to turn her mind to the uncertainties of her arrival in this most political of cities. What kind of reception would the Rashids – the ruling family of the Shammar tribe – give her? Would they welcome her, or would she be in danger of robbery, or worse? The British were, after all, aiding the Rashid enemy, Ibn Saud. Her well-being would depend entirely on finding favour with the royal family, and now she heard news which disturbed her, concerning the young ruler.

> The Amir, it seems is not at Hayyil, but camping to the north with his camel herds. I fear this may be tiresome for me; I would rather have dealt with him than with his representative. Also report says that he informed all men of my coming but whether to forward me or to stop me I do not know. Neither do I know whether the report is true.

On 11 February, nearly two months since she had set out from Damascus, they rode over a bleak pebbly plain and glimpsed, at last, in the distance, the first great sand hills of the Nefud. The huge unmapped dunes marched ahead of them across the horizon like a mountain range. She would have to take careful topographical measurements and bearings day by day, and would chart the water sources as she travelled.

They entered the Nefud a day later and immediately began to struggle through the deep, soft sand, the camels floundering and slowing. In the deep troughs and rises, they could go no faster than an exhausting one mile an hour. The driving wind had hollowed out huge cavities, perhaps half a mile wide, so that time and again the caravan would toil up a slope only to find itself poised on the brink of a hundred-foot precipice of sand, carved by the wind into a knife edge. The crew were full of stories about camels falling through sand crests like these, plummeting into the ravines below and breaking their legs. The caravan would skirt that horseshoe of sand, only to find itself having to climb up the next slope. And so

it went on, burning hot in the midday sun, with freezing temperatures at night. Clambering up a particularly high dune on foot,
Gertrude stood poised at its peak like a sailor at the prow of a tall
ship, gazing out over these petrified waves of a turbulent ocean,
and saw, still far ahead, the sandstone mountains of the Jebel
Misma.

After five days of this demoralizing landscape, the continual
effort began to take its toll. The camels were exhausted, the men
silent, and Gertrude most unusually succumbed to a severe bout of
depression. She wrote to Dick:

> [It] springs from a profound doubt as to whether the adventure
> is after all worth the candle. Not because of the danger – I don't
> mind that; but . . . It is nothing, the journey to Nejd, so far as any
> real advantage goes, or any real addition to knowledge . . . Here,
> if there is anything to record the probability is that you can't find
> it or reach it, because a hostile tribe bars your way, or the road is
> waterless . . . I fear when I look back I shall say: It was a waste of
> time.

Now another annoyance was added to their troubles: torrential
rain, wrapping the landscape and hiding all landmarks. They could
not move for fear of getting lost in the Nefud. Soaked, Gertrude
attempted to dry her hair and her clothes with the men by the
guttering fire. At a little distance, the Shammars and Sherarat
huddled round their own tiny fires, almost invisible in the grey and
watery night. Fattuh ran from tent to tent, trying to keep her
bedding, now stiff with dirt, as dry as he was able. The tents were
choked with baggage which was normally left outside, and the
demoralized cameleers hurried to feed the animals and get back into
their dripping tents. In the thunder and hail, Gertrude wrapped her
furs around her and shivered in her tent, reading *Hamlet* from
beginning to end. Shakespeare, as always, lifted her spirits a little.
'Princes and powers of Arabia stepped down into their true place. There
rose up above them the human soul conscious and answerable to itself,
made with such large discourse, looking before and after.'

February 20th brought them to the edge of the Nefud, where

they sighted a collection of tents. Yet another new *rafiq*, the elderly and ragged Mhailam, was induced by Gertrude, on payment of £2 and new clothes, to see them through the last stage of their journey to Hayyil. Against his advice, and Muhammad's, she determined to cut the rest of her journey short, leaving behind the comparative safety of the dunes and the desert, and strike out across the plain, where her caravan would be highly visible to any raiders in the vicinity. *Ghazzus* and hunger, she decided, were 'as nothing to the possibility of a hard straight road'. From the last cliff of shifting sand, she stood and caught her breath as she looked upon the black and forbidding terrain to come, its pinnacles like the skeleton of a city gutted by fire. She wrote home:

> This morning we reached the barren sandstone crags of Jebel Misma, which bound here the Nefud, and passed beyond them into Nejd . . . the landscape which opened before us was more terrifyingly dead and empty than anything I have ever seen. The blackened rocks of Misma drop steeply on the E. side into a wilderness of jagged peaks . . . and beyond and beyond, more pallid lifeless plain and more great crags of sandstone mountains rising abruptly out of it. And over it all, the bitter wind whipped the cloud shadows.

From behind her came Muhammad's voice: 'We have come to the gates of hell.' On those words she departed the Nefud, giving the Shammars and Sherarat her last gifts of money and food, and descended into the blackened landscape and the plain.

It was on 22 February, eleven days since entering the Nefud, that she came to a village, the first she had seen since Ziza. Two days later, the caravan finally came to rest within a couple of hours' ride of Hayyil. Early on the twenty-fifth she sent Muhammad and Ali on ahead to announce her coming, and then rode the last part of the clean granite and basalt plain to the picturesque towers of the icing-sugar city as slowly and easily as if she had been 'strolling through Piccadilly'. She had done it, and after all she had been through over the last six hundred miles, it was almost an anticlimax.

Ahead of her, visible now to the naked eye, was the singularly beautiful fortress city washed in the rose pink of the morning sunlight, its mud walls whitened with plaster and crowned with dogstooth battlements, the green fronds of palm trees waving gently over them, and its encircling gardens breaking into pink almond and white plum blossom. Behind the skyline of tall towers ringed with machicolations, distant peaks of azure mountains soared like clouds on the horizon. Nothing could have looked more inviting, innocent or peaceful. Steeped in *Arabia Deserta* as she was, she felt she was on a pilgrimage to a sacred site.

9

ESCAPE

A mile or so from Hayyil, Gertrude was met by three Rashid envoys accompanying her camel driver Ali, and three more outriders, one carrying a lance and all of them mounted on magnificent horses. Coming to a jingling stop, pennants flying, tassels swinging, they welcomed her, surrounded her caravan and guided it to the south gate of the city. Gertrude, flanked by her own armed men and then by Hayyil's sword-bearers, rode into Hayyil feeling for once exactly like 'the daughter of kings'.

As they circled the clay-brick walls, she glanced up at the towers and found them just as Charles Doughty had described them thirty-seven years before, like embattled windmills without sails. The procession turned in through a plain square gate. Gertrude, dismounting, found herself all at once in the world of the *Arabian Nights*. At a white doorway in a windowless inner wall, her guide Muhammad al-Marawi was waiting for her. Inside, she climbed up a dark, steep ramp to an inner court and a shadowy, carpeted columned hall. The pillars were whitened palm trunks, and the ceiling was made of palm fronds. The whitewashed walls were decorated with a high band of intricate, geometrical patterns in red and blue. This summer dwelling of the royal family, reserved for important visitors, was where she was to lodge. Here, in the reception hall, she greeted the two bowing female slaves who had been put at her disposal. She glanced into the coffee rooms and the courtyard with its three little trees – a quince, a lemon and an apple – then ran up another ramp to the roof to look over the city. Below, her men were unloading all the camels and pitching their tents in the great bleak courtyard, where every year the Haj would pause on its seven-hundred-mile journey south. On the other side of the house, the white tower of the castle seemed suspended in the blue air above the town. But immediately she was called below to meet her first visitors.

Two women awaited her. Lulua, an old woman in crimson and black, was the caretaker. The other, with her handsome broad face and darkened eyes hooded by a black and gold embroidered scarf, wore a black visiting robe parting over magenta and violet cotton skirts. From a centre parting, four thick plaits fell to her waist, and around her neck hung 'strings and strings of rough pearls', tangling with a fringed necklace of emeralds and rubies. This was Turkiyyeh, a talkative Circassian, sent by Ibrahim, the Amir of Hayyil's deputy, to greet her.

A slave-girl brought coffee, and Turkiyyeh and Gertrude sat on the cushions to talk. The Circassian's story was extraordinary. She had been a gift from the Sultan in Constantinople to the late Muhammad ibn Rashid, then the Amir, whose favourite wife she had quickly become. With another of his wives, Mudi, he was the father of the present Amir. She began to explain to Gertrude the Hayyil hierarchy. The present Amir, sixteen years old, had been absent for two months now, raiding the Ruwalla camping grounds with eight hundred men. He already had four wives and two baby sons. The highest authority in the Amir's absence was his deputy Ibrahim, brother of the chief adviser and Regent, Zamil ibn Subhan. Ibrahim was nonetheless in awe of the Amir's powerful grandmother, Fatima. This old matriarch could read and write, said Turkiyyeh, and she held the royal purse-strings. The power behind the throne, she had the Amir's ear, and people were terrified of what she might tell him when he returned. She had favourites – and Allah help those who incurred her displeasure! Gertrude made a mental note to visit Fatima as soon as she could. She prompted her companion to further revelations. The jewels she wore, Turkiyyeh explained, belonged communally to the harem and were lent to favoured wives or borrowed for special events – rather like the Bell tiara, thought Gertrude. Turkiyyeh promised to take her to visit Mudi and the other women of the harem.

Gertrude knew less about the royal harem, who would spend the rest of their days inside the walls of the palace, than she did about the lives of Bedouin warriors. She asked questions, which Turkiyyeh was delighted to answer. According to a judgement handed down from the fourteenth century, a woman should leave her house on only three occasions: when conducted to the house of her bridegroom, on the deaths of her parents, and when she went to her own grave. Ordinary women in Hayyil did venture out at night, completely veiled, but only to see female members of their family. The more powerful the family, the more strictly did it interpret the rules. Every woman should have a male guardian, even if this was a boy half her age, and it would be he who contracted her marriage. A husband could have up to four wives, provided he behaved with equal generosity to all, and as many concubines as he wanted. He could divorce a wife without giving a reason, by speaking a simple form of words in the presence of witnesses.

Overseeing the harem were the eunuchs, brought from Mecca or Constantinople. Some had important outside duties: the eunuch Salih, for instance, was also the watchman of Hayyil. Then there were the male slaves, whose importance was far greater than the word suggests. These men, taken in raids along with horses and camels, were divided into two categories. If they were judged ugly or stupid, they would spend the rest of their lives making themselves useful to their owners. If they were intelligent, handsome and presentable, they would be taken into the wealthiest families and given trusted positions. Charles Doughty had called them the 'slave-brothers'. Of these, the elite would become part of the royal household, living in the palace. They were allowed to carry arms. Turkiyyeh led Gertrude to understand that she would do well to make allies of these men if she could. Chief of the slave-brothers was Sayyid, who was also a eunuch, and a direct conduit to the Amir or his deputy Ibrahim. Such was the closed political world that Gertrude had entered; and as she sat there, smoking and listening to the gossip, she reflected that she had never talked to a woman like this before. She concluded that Turkiyyeh was 'a merry lady', and that she would enjoy her company while finding her advice extremely useful.

After the midday meal, the arrival of an even more important guest was announced by one of Turkiyyeh's slaves. Gertrude straightened her skirt, pinned up her hair and hurried back to the reception room where she sat expectantly on a divan, while her guide Muhammad positioned himself at a respectful distance. A slave appeared in the doorway, moved to one side, then a strong scent of attar of rose filled the room as Ibrahim swept in. He arrived 'in state and all smiles', wearing a brilliantly dyed keffiyeh bound with a gold cord, or *agal*, and carrying a sword in a silver scabbard. She noticed his thin face, his feverish black eyes rimmed with kohl, his straggly imperial beard and discoloured teeth. But most of all she noted his 'nervous manner and restless eye'. He uttered the conventional forms of greeting and struck her as well educated — 'for Arabia'. She thanked him, told him her first impressions of Hayyil and briefly described her journey. He stayed until the call to afternoon prayer, but as he left the room came a first note of warning. Pausing at the door, he whispered to Muhammad that there was some discontent among the Muslim clerics at the arrival of a woman alone, and that she would have to be a little discreet — 'In short, I was not to come further into the town till I was invited.'

The next day she regretfully sold some of her camels, in a wretched condition from crossing the Nefud desert, and sent the best back some distance to water and greenery where they could recover their health. Two little bejewelled and brocaded Rashid princes were brought to visit her, hand in hand and accompanied by their slave-boys. They sat silently staring at her with their brilliant kohl-rimmed eyes, eating the apples and biscuits that she gave them. They were, she noted drily, the 'two of the six male descendants who are all that remain of the Rashid stock, so relentlessly have they slaughtered one another'. Over the last eight years, Turki-yyeh had told her, three Amirs had been assassinated. She concluded: 'In Hayil, murder is like the spilling of milk.'

She was longing to explore the city, but having been asked to remain at the house, she could go no further than the courtyard, to visit her men. She felt frustrated. Her habitual strategy in a new place was to walk about, make contacts, pick up the latest news and work her way into the echelons of the community that could be of help to her.

It was time to present her gifts to Ibrahim and she asked Muhammad to take him a message together with the robes, rolls of silk and boxes of sweetmeats. Might she return his call? she asked Ibrahim courteously. He sent back an invitation, but told her not to come before dark: he would send a mare for her, and slaves to guide her. She waited restlessly until nightfall, when the horse arrived with a couple of men, one to lead it and one to carry a lantern and walk in front. She put on her evening dress, slipped a cigarette case and her ivory holder into a purse, and rode side-saddle through winding lanes between blind walls. The horse's hooves made no sound on the dirt lanes. In the light from the lantern, drainpipes and doorways fluttered past and sank again into the velvety blackness. She would never be able to find her way through this maze again by daylight. It was a starlit night, but the huge sparkling heavens of the open desert had been replaced by a narrow channel of sky between the roofs. She passed just a couple of women, scurrying along under the walls, looking neither left nor right.

They came to a halt in front of a stout wooden gate, which was unlocked from inside with much scraping and groaning of hinges. She was taken past a fountain and the mosque, and dismounted before a second locked gate, finally entering a screened antechamber. Here, she heard murmured conversation from the reception gallery ahead, and entered. Blinking in the light of half a dozen hanging lamps, she now found herself in a large colonnaded hall with a central fire, surrounded with cushions and carpets. '[It was] a very splendid place with great stone columns supporting an immensely lofty roof, the walls white-washed, the floor of white juss [sic.], beaten hard and shining as if it were polished.'

The room was filled with men, who now fell silent. They rose to their feet as she entered, looking at her curiously. Ibrahim advanced to meet her, and she was ceremonially seated on a cushion to his right. The conversation was formal and impersonal. He spoke to her of the history of the Shammar, the tribe of which the Rashids were the leaders, and then talked of the royal family themselves. As Gertrude listened, and responded with descriptions of the archaeological sites she had passed, slave-boys served them with glasses of tea and small, sweet lemons to squeeze into them, followed by what she called 'most excellent' strong coffee. Then, swinging sweet-smelling censers in front of each guest, the slaves – very soon, it seemed to her – signalled that the reception was over. Gertrude rose and left.

She felt frustrated. This brief meeting had not allowed her to address any of the issues she wanted to discuss, particularly her need of money. In Damascus she had given £200 to the Rashid agent and had expected to be repaid without delay when she reached Hayyil. The agent had given her the usual letter of credit, and she had carried it with her to present to the Rashids on her arrival. This time-honoured method saved desert travellers from having to carry on them large amounts of money, which might be stolen on the way. She was by now almost penniless. How long should she, could she, wait for an opportunity to present the document?

'And then followed day after weary day with nothing whatever to do,' she wrote in her other diary. Now that the novelty was over, and unable to be her usual active self, Gertrude found the time passed slowly. She was woken every morning before sunrise by the haunting chant of her gate-keeper, Chesb – 'God is great. There is no God but God' – and at midday and evening prayers she went up to the roof to listen to the muezzin calling from the mosque. The mornings dragged, she ate too many sweetmeats, and wrote furiously in her diary that women in Hayyil 'do absolutely nothing all day'. She mapped her route to Baghdad, and when that was done she put the finishing touches to her archaeological drawings.

Like the Arabian king who waited every day for Scheherazade's next tale, her only entertainment was listening to Turkiyyeh's extraordinary and vivid life story. She had been sold as a child and parted from her beloved baby brother, whom she was still trying to locate. When she was of marriageable age, she was sold again and carried off on an overcrowded ship rife with disease. As one by one the passengers died, the crew came on deck, kicked the supine ones so as to check they were dead, then threw them overboard. Gertrude picked up her camera and took photographs as Turkiyyeh talked. Ending up in Mecca, she said, toying with her rubies, she was married to a young Persian that she had grown to love, but all too soon she was abducted again, this time by an agent of the Rashid Amir, and was dragged off screaming while her young husband ran wailing after them. At first she would not look at Muhammad, but he was patient and gentle, she said, and soon she was pleased to make him happy. When Muhammad wanted a younger wife, he followed custom by marrying Turkiyyeh off to a respectable man. But now she was a widow. Her greatest sorrow, she told Gertrude with tears in her dark eyes, was that she had no children alive. Of the seven babies she had borne, six had died at birth and the seventh at one year old. 'Turkiyyeh says the people here think of women as dogs and so treat them,' Gertrude wrote.

Occasionally her men dropped by to tell her of the chatter in the market-place. The whole town was waiting to hear the outcome of the Amir's latest raid. There was nothing to do but talk, and Gertrude had never been fond of gossip. She was unable to think of anything for her slaves to do, so they sat about on cushions, chewing the ends of their plaits and recounting domestic dramas until she lost her temper and sent them packing. She had several migraines, and hated the warm wind that ran around the courtyard, raising wisps of sand as it passed. She was not sleeping well: 'Wind and dust, a little rain . . . At night a little owl cries softly.'

Ever more impatient, she sent a message about her letter of credit to Ibrahim, but his reply, when it arrived, dashed her hopes. He had been with the Amir's grandmother, the tight-fisted Fatima, when her message was delivered, and the reply came back that they had no knowledge of the transaction. 'It is clear they won't give it up,' she concluded bitterly. In any case, they would give her no money until the Amir's return, and who knew when that would be? Was

she to remain here indefinitely? she fretted. She had tried to make
personal contact with Fatima by every means she could devise, but
being deprived of the opportunity to seek out useful intermediaries,
she received no response. In the strange, antiquated society of this
edgy city, was the silence to be interpreted as a personal rejection?
When Ibrahim's men brought back her presents, she was more
worried than ever. Was this an insult or, as her men tried to
reassure her, excessive courtesy?

She did what she could. She counted what money she had left,
sent for her remaining camels, and sold as many as she could spare.
She planned to leave Hayyil with a much reduced caravan. She paid
off all the men she had taken on in Damascus. They would depart
as the opportunity arose for them to join caravans, and leave her
with a party of three: Fattuh, Ali – her guide from Hamad – and
Fellah. She would have to cross the far side of the embattled Nefud,
and she did not like to think how she would manage with so small
a caravan. 'I have just £40, enough if Ibrahim lets us go. I am to see him
tonight. An anxious day.'

There was one ray of hope, in the form of Ali. Ali's uncles,
presently guests in Hayyil, were Anazeh tribesmen and sheikhs.
They were needed as allies by the Rashids, who hoped they would
help capture the city of Jof, where the Amir was heading. These
uncles, Ali told Gertrude, were negotiating for her behind the
scenes, and had protested vigorously against the treatment that
Ibrahim had meted out to her concerning the letter of credit.
Privately, said Ali, his uncles were calling Fatima *kelbeh* – the bitch.

Night fell at last and she set out again, on the same mare, for
the all-important second meeting with Ibrahim. Outside, a hot wind
was rising. The dusty sand circled in the courtyard, and the particles
were blown stinging against her face. She was shown to a smaller
room than before, and waited some time for Ibrahim to join her.
She had taken care to bring her presents back with her, and as soon
as she had greeted him, she told him that she wanted him to keep
them. Now she raised once again the issue of the money, and this
time she did not pull her punches. She would stay in Hayyil no
longer, she said. The withholding of her money had caused her

great inconvenience, and she must now ask for a *rafiq* to go with her on the next stage of her journey. Ibrahim was civil in his response. He smiled and assured her that he was ready to supply her with a *rafiq*, but his eyes avoided her confrontational gaze. She was not reassured. Writing in her diary for Dick that night, for the first time she was close to admitting fear, and, stout atheist as she was, she concluded the letter with a prayer for safety:

> I spent a long night contriving in my head schemes of escape if things went wrong . . . to the spiritual sense the place smells of blood . . . the tales round my camp fire are all of murder and the air whispers murder. It gets upon your nerves when you sit day after day between high mud walls and I thank heaven that my nerves are not very responsive . . . And good, please God! Please God nothing but good.

Her worst fears were realized the next morning, 3 March, with the appearance of the slave-brother Sayyid. Brilliantly dressed and accompanied by his own servant, he brought only a repetition of the information she had already received: that she could not travel, neither could they give her any money until a messenger arrived with permission from the Amir. It was the first confirmation that they were actually detaining her at Hayyil. Gertrude caught her breath, turned on her heel, ran down the ramp to the courtyard, and returned with Muhammad and Ali. She told Sayyid to repeat in front of them what he had said, word for word.

Gertrude's interests were of very minor importance to the Rashids at present. She had arrived in their city at a most inopportune moment. What she did not know – and Ibrahim himself did not know – was that at this very moment the Amir, the sixteen-year-old head of the family, was planning to murder Ibrahim's brother Zamil ibn Subhan. As the Amir's Regent, adviser and uncle, Zamil was accompanying him in the desert at the head of their army of tribesmen. He was urging the Amir to make peace with Ibn Saud, but the Amir wanted absolute rule without interference. A short while later, at a desert post called Abu Ghar, the Amir would order a slave to shoot the Regent in the back. As

Zamil toppled to the ground, his brothers and slaves would be massacred all around him. The Amir and his accomplices, according to reports, would ride past the murder scene without even bothering to turn their heads to look. Ibrahim was probably well aware that his family were out of favour with the Amir, and was especially reluctant to provoke him, either by giving Gertrude her money or by being responsible for her leaving.

Meanwhile, Turkiyyeh had made good her promise that Gertrude would be invited to meet the royal harem. The mother of the Amir, Mudi, sent a message inviting Gertrude to visit her, one evening after dark. Gertrude was deeply interested in the scene so often portrayed by orientalist painters and *New Yorker* cartoonists, with its lush beauties lying around on cushions and attended by slaves and eunuchs. She was particularly impressed by Mudi. In spite of having already been married to three amirs in turn, she was still young; Gertrude described her as very beautiful and charming, as well as intelligent and receptive:

> I passed two hours taken straight from the Arabian Nights with the women of the palace. I imagine that there are few places left wherein you can see the unadulterated East in its habit as it has lived for centuries and centuries – of these few Hayyil is one. There they were, those women – wrapped in Indian brocades, hung with jewels, served by slaves. They pass from hand to hand – the victor takes them . . . and think of it! His hands are red with the blood of their husbands and children. Truly I still feel bewildered by it.

For Mudi, too, Gertrude was a distraction of unique interest. The two women gazed at each other, delighted, each experiencing in the other a new phenomenon. Avid for explanations, full of questions, they talked with increasing intensity as the other wives looked on fascinated, absorbed in both Gertrude's appearance – her pale skin, her green eyes, her red unhennaed hair, her lace evening dress, her buttoned shoes – and her breathtaking masculine freedoms. Here was a woman, undoubtedly a woman, who apparently lived the life of a sheikh and a warrior. Gertrude explained her present predicament; Mudi, with no experience of independence herself, understood that the traveller before her was trapped like a caged bird. The two hours passed in a moment. They looked at each other for the last time, representatives of opposite worlds perfectly understanding each other, and then it was time to part.

By 6 March, Gertrude had effectively been under house arrest for eleven days. There was no disguising it from herself any more. Without permission to leave, and a *rafiq* to ensure her safety, she was a prisoner. She had come to the end of her resources. As she sat biting her lip, half-listening to Turkiyyeh and the caretaker complaining about the price of slave-girls – 'You used to be able to get a good girl for 200 Spanish reals,' complained Lulua, 'now you could not buy one for 500' – a messenger arrived with another royal invitation, this one to visit cousins of the Amir in their garden that afternoon – in the light of day. Her hosts turned out to be five small children, dressed in embroidered gold robes and with painted faces. She sat with them in a summer-house on carpets 'like all the drawings in Persian picture books'. Slaves and eunuchs brought plates of fruit, tea and coffee, and the boys took her round the garden naming for her each tree and flower. Other adults were present, and she soon identified Sayyid sitting among them. Gertrude sat down next to him and spoke without the introductory courtesies. Tersely, she told him of her urgent desire to leave Hayyil. When he responded that 'the going and coming are not in our power', she lost her temper: 'I spoke to him with much vigour and ended the interview abruptly by rising and leaving him . . . to tell you the truth I was bothered,' she wrote in her other diary.

An hour later, she was sitting in the coffee room she used as her bedroom when a slave beckoned her into the reception hall. This time she did not bother to straighten her clothes or brush her hair. There in the doorway stood Sayyid, impassive as ever, holding a bag in his hand. He told her that she had full permission to go where she liked and when she liked. Wonderingly, she took the bag from him and found it full of gold. 'And why they have now given way, or why they did not give way before, I cannot guess,' she wrote. 'But anyhow I am free and my heart is at rest – it is widened.'

She would never know the reason for her unexpected freedom, and she would always wonder. Turning it over in her mind, a new idea came to her. Where Ali's uncles had interceded and failed, where Ibrahim had lied and where Fatima had refused to give up the money, had a nobler spirit interceded on her behalf? Doubtless there were ways in which even harem women could influence male dictates and events. Was it Mudi, effectively the queen of Hayyil, who had unlocked the door of the cage and given her back the liberty she would never have herself?

Anyone else would have packed up and left while the going was good, preferably before dawn. It was characteristic of Gertrude that, having asked so many times to leave, she now asked permission to stay an extra day, pushing her luck, spending eight more hours looking into every corner of Hayyil and taking many photographs. One imagines her request coming by messenger to Ibrahim, cloistered perhaps with Fatima or drinking coffee with his slaves, then their exclamations of surprise giving way to amusement at the pure effrontery of this demand. The lighter mood seems to have reached the city outside. Certainly Gertrude, flaunting herself unveiled in the sunshine despite the disapproval of the clerics, found herself the object of friendly curiosity wherever she walked. 'Everyone was smiling and affable . . . all the people crowded out to see me, but they seemed to take nothing but a benevolent interest in my doings.'

She circled the palace towers that crowned the massive defences, walked through the Medina gate guarded by slaves, delved into the palace kitchens, climbed to the rooftops, then descended to the plain, to take pictures of the fortifications. When she returned there was a message from Turkiyyeh inviting her to tea: 'I went, and took an affectionate farewell of her. She and I are now, I imagine, parted for ever, except in remembrance. And thus it was that my strange visit to Hayyil ended, after 11 days' imprisonment, in a sort of apotheosis!'

The next day, 7 March, she was up before dawn, and was surprised to receive another visitor as she was packing up. He was a palace slave, a man of sinister aspect with henna-dyed beard and blackened eyes, come to tell her to take the western road out of Hayyil as it would be safer for her. She knew she had to follow his instructions because she would be watched, but she was immediately suspicious. 'I fancy they meant to send me to the Amir and thinking he was certain to be on the western road they issued their order,' she noted. The intrigue backfired, for by the time she reached the place where the Amir was expected, he had fortunately passed east of them. She had still not shaken the dust of Hayyil from her feet: on the second day out, Rashid messengers arrived at her tents to say that the Amir was expecting her. They told her that he had taken Jof and driven out the Ruwalla, sparing her few of the details about the capture. They left, and she set off again. Keeping steadfastly to her road, she marched nine or ten hours a day, turning north-west to Baghdad by way of Hayianiya and Najaf: '[The journey is] so wearying to the spirit in this immense monotony that I come into camp every evening giddy with fatigue . . . I am beginning to feel the effects of rather hard camp fare; anyway I shall be glad to reach civilization again.'

She was amused to receive an entirely different version of the 'capture' of Jof from a new *rafiq* who had come to her directly from the Amir's campaign. This innocent, unaware of the official spin that had been issued to her by the Amir's messengers, reported that the Rashids had stopped short of the city, to be turned back by the Ruwalla without even setting eyes on Jof. Mulling over her experiences as she rode, this last lie convinced her that the Rashids were 'moving towards their close':

> Not one grown man of their house remains alive – the Amir is only 16 or 17, and all the others are little more than babes, so deadly has been the family strife . . . Their history is one long tale of treachery and murder. I should say that the future lies with Ibn Sa'ud. He is a formidable adversary . . . I think that his star is in the ascendant and if he combines with Ibn Sha'lan [of the Ruwalla Anazeh tribe] they will have Ibn Rashid between the hammer and the anvil . . . So there! My next Arabian journey shall be to him.

She saw the impossibility, on this journey, of continuing south from Hayyil to gather information at Riyadh, the Saud capital.

Disappointed as she was, she recognized that the road would be impassable for a traveller coming straight from the Rashids. In her exhaustion of body and spirit, she did not know what she had accomplished, and wrote bitterly in her diary to Dick: 'I fear when I look back I shall say: it was a waste of time.'

In March 1914, there was so much that she could not know. The exploration of tribal life that she had undertaken, the mapping of the terrains, the networks of tribal affiliations and enmities that she had uncovered, had culminated in a unique body of knowledge. Her fluency in their language had given her a clear picture of the centuries-old Arab system of government, the ruling cabals of favoured families and tribes. In the years ahead, the knowledge acquired on this, her last expedition, was to prove invaluable. Now, wearily covering the ground to Baghdad, she was treading the boundary line between the future Iraq and the future Saudi Arabia. Her long years of preparation had ended, and the career that was to be her destiny had already begun.

For now, her recognition that the future of Central Arabia lay with Ibn Saud would carry immense weight when she communicated it, in context and with the facts that she had discovered, to the British Ambassador in Constantinople. She would confirm the powerful Saud as the worthy recipient of British aid. She had not been able to meet Ibn Saud, and that disappointed her. How astounded she would have been to know that when he took the unprecedented step of visiting the British administration in his quest for arms a couple of years later, he would be travelling to meet her.

With Hayyil now ten days behind her, she reached the borderlands of the Euphrates and there passed out of Bedouin territory. Now her caravan of camels was particularly conspicuous in a terrain of donkey-riding Shia shepherds of the Riu tribe. There were the usual alarms: approaching camps whose sheikh might decide to welcome them or, equally, rob them; having to hide in hollows with rifles at the ready; having to find replacements for frightened *rafiqs* along the way. At one point they ran out of water and walked into a

group of thieves at the filthy watering hole: here their poker-faced
Ghazalat *rafiq* stepped in and averted disaster. Several times they
were fired on. She wondered if what she was experiencing was fear
– and decided that she could at last identify the feeling. Hayyil had
taught her that. She wrote in her other diary:

> On a careful analysis of my feelings I have come to the conclusion
> that I'm afraid at these times. That must be fear, that little
> restiveness of the mind, like a very fresh horse that keeps on
> straining at the reins and then letting them go abruptly – you
> know the feeling in your hands, like an irregular pulse. One of
> my horses at home does it, a very mad one. And then the
> profound desire to be safely through the next hour! Yes, it's fear.

She was exhausted. At Najaf, Fattuh hired her a carriage. Ahead
lay the high road into Baghdad which would be accomplished much
more quickly by horse. She followed her personal luggage into the
cart, and jolted the six hours to Karbala, with two changes of horses
at the posting stations. Arriving after dark, she left her baggage at
the posting inn and visited an old friend, Muhammad Hussain Khan.
Over dinner, they talked in English, the first time she had done so
for ten weeks. She was amused to write to Dick about what Khan
had said concerning a forthcoming holiday he was to take in Britain.
When she had asked what he would do with his family, he replied
that he would leave them behind, divorcing his wife before he left.
She expressed her feelings about this with a row of exclamation
marks.

For the last leg of the journey, she had to be seated in the post
carriage by 3 a.m. She slept for only a couple of hours. Now that
her letters from home were almost within her grasp, she began to
fret about her family. Anything could have happened in the ten
weeks since she had heard from them. She rattled off again across
this last stretch to Baghdad, passed the new railway and arrived in
the city at lunchtime. Tired and anxious, she found herself snapping
at the faithful Fattuh, then asked him to forgive her. She always
tried hard to be patient, recalling the words of one of her *rafiqs* in
the Nefud:

'In all the years when we come to this place we shall say "Here we came with her, here she camped."' I expect they will, and it makes me dreadfully anxious that they should tell nothing but good, since they will judge my whole race by me. That recollection very often checks the hasty word when I am tired, and feeling cross, or bored – heavens! How bored, cross and tired sometimes!

She went straight to the British Residency and collected her letters from the new incumbent, one Colonel Erskine. She was as sharp as a knife in her dismissal of him:

He does not get up till 12 and he is found playing patience in his room after lunch. He knows no language, not even French and his mind is a complete blank as regards Turkey in general and Turkish Arabia in particular. And this is the man who we send here at the moment when the Baghdad Railway on the one hand and our irrigation schemes on the other are passing . . . into realities. We are an odd nation.

And then she retreated to an inn, smoked cigarette after cigarette, and spent the rest of the day and night reading her letters. Nothing had changed, after all. Her family had survived intact, and so had Dick's cruel and maddening ability, filtered through pages of rhetoric, to raise her expectations one minute and dash them the next. The further off she had been, the fonder he became – on paper. Starved of his love and companionship, she found nothing to comfort her, and yet he could work away at her sensibilities until she could almost convince herself they might have a future together. The agony began again as she read his words: 'I love you – does it do any good out there in the desert? Is it less vast, less lonely, like the far edge of life?' And finally, from Addis Ababa in Abyssinia, where he was now the British representative to the International Boundaries Commission, 'What wouldn't I give to have you sitting opposite in this all-alone house?'

She felt, at the end of it all, worn out and disillusioned. She had tried to remind herself that this sense of 'dust and ashes in my hand' was something she always experienced at the end of an adventure. Here she was, asking herself why she had subjected herself to the last three months, when they had made no difference either to her feelings or to the world in general.

Dick had written of a visit to Sloane Street, where he met her father, referring to the master industrialist as a 'dear old man'. He was full of his own affairs, due to leave for meetings with Lord Kitchener, then Resident in Khartoum, and Sir Reginald Wingate, the High Commissioner in Cairo. He had something to ask of Gertrude: that she would wire him a message to Addis Ababa. He wanted her to send only two words – 'Safe Baghdad' – and to leave them anonymous. She did so from the post office the next morning, and followed it with a package – that other diary that she had kept just for him, which would tell him everything that the telegram would not. She reread it quickly, and found it unaccountably impersonal:

> I think the only things that are worth saying are those that I can't say – my own self in it, how it looked to the eyes of the human being, weak and ignorant and wondering, weary and disappointed, who was in the midst of it. I can't say them because they are too intimate, and also because I haven't the skill ... One doesn't put those things into one's own diary because one is not trying to draw the picture – it is there before one.

Old friends welcomed her back to Baghdad, incredulous about her journey, astonished to find that she was alive, and congratulating her 'in a way which warmed my heart'. These included a figure who would be crucial to the future of Iraq, Sir Sayyid Abdul Rahman. He was known by his title, the Naqib – the figurehead of the Sunnis – and was a religious leader so important that he would receive no woman but Gertrude into his august presence. 'He is too holy to shake hands with me,' she noted, 'but . . . I was vastly amused, as ever, by his talk.'

New friends included Arthur Tod, a director of Lynch Brothers who ran the Tigris ferries, and his 'darling little Italian wife' who, when she saw how tired Gertrude was, immediately invited her to stay with them. Aurelia Tod, who would become one of Gertrude's great friends, saw that the voyager's clothes were laundered and pressed while she slept and before she began to bustle around the town again. This was a much needed holiday break for Gertrude, and she spent much of it sightseeing like any tourist, in spite of temperatures of up to 140 degrees Fahrenheit. She visited the new Turkish German-built railway, so soon to become a threat to Britain's control of the Gulf. From the banks of the Tigris she watched wooden sleepers arriving from Hamburg and being swung ashore from a flotilla of ancient lateen-sailed boats. The efficiency and the scope of the project excited and impressed the ironmaster's daughter. The famous German engineer Heinrich August Meissner, in charge of the railway construction, explained the difficulties. They did not only have to import the sleepers. To make the concrete they needed, they first had to filter the salt out of the water, then crush tons of pebbles for lack of stone and sand; and they had to bring in the necessary wood. 'The muddy waters of Tigris flood, the palms, the ragged singing Arabs – these were the ancient East,' Gertrude noted, 'and in their midst stood the shining faultless engines, the blue eyed, close cropped Germans with smart military bearing – the soldiery of the West, come out to conquer . . .'

She dined out on her tales of Hayyil, and her admiration for Ibn Saud increased when she was told how he had taken Hasa. He had turned the Turks out of the town without a single shot being fired, marched the garrisons down to the coast and appropriated their arms. On the Tods' launch she floated up the river, passing one of the city's palaces, drank tea under tamarisk trees, wandered in the rose gardens and watched the sun set. 'Baghdad shimmered through the heat haze like a fairy city'.

It was, without doubt, her favourite city, built in the Persian style, and she loved the Euphrates. Baghdad epitomized for her the romance of the *Arabian Nights*, the famous cycle of stories that came to light during the eleventh century. A creation of the Abbasid dynasty, it was the survivor of a triad of cities built at the confluence of the Euphrates and the Tigris. Babylon and Ctesiphon had crumbled, but Baghdad had survived in all its rich and varied culture, despite the Mongol invasion of 1258 and the vicissitudes of two Ottoman Empires. It was built on the vast alluvial plain where a system of canals, now fallen into disrepair, channelled the melted snows of Anatolia and made cultivation possible. It was at the hub of the old strategic routes to Iran and thence to China, via Iraq, Syria and Egypt, through Anatolia to Constantinople and Trebizond.

Gertrude would have read the evocation of its glory by the historian al-Khatib al-Baghdadi (1002–71), and his description of the court of the Caliph al-Muqtadir in 917. This splendid court, with its halls and parks, chanceries and treasuries, eunuchs and soldiers, chamberlains and pages, was famous throughout the world. On one occasion a visiting Byzantine embassy was shown the Caliph's famous lifesize treasure tree, its branches covered with leaves and birds, all made of silver and gold. The leaves of the tree moved as if in the wind, and the jewelled birds piped and sang. When the ambassadors were ushered into the presence of the Caliph, they found him enthroned between eighteen ropes of jewels, with his personal executioner standing beside him amongst the courtiers, ready to mete out summary justice.

Gertrude deplored the all-night bars, the gambling dens, the prostitution and corruption of 1914, but saw in them a certain continuation of the exotic past: 'Baghdad has taken to this kind of civilization so quickly and so wholeheartedly because it is a return to what she knew in the gorgeous days of the Khalifate,' she wrote in her other diary.

The holiday over, Gertrude turned towards Damascus. She had 350 miles of Syrian desert still to cross. In her streamlined new caravan there were now eight camels and four people: herself, Fattuh, Fellah and Sayyid the Sherari. They would travel north of the Fertile Crescent, past areas where the nomadic pastoralists had spread from Nejd. It would be a fascinating voyage across history, from the origins of Islam in the east to the margins of the Greek and Roman civilizations in the west. But she wanted this journey to come to an end. She would travel light, and travel hard. She left most of her luggage to be sent back by sea, taking only a new, native tent, smaller and lighter than the ones she had brought from London, and her folding chair; one bag of clothes, provisions for three weeks and a minimum of cooking pots. She clung to her 'one luxury', her canvas bath, but resigned herself to two weeks on the thin roll of bedding that she had substituted for the bulky folding bed in Baghdad. 'Out under the open sky again and at once my heart leaps to it. I shall soon weary of my bed on the ground, I know! Oh Dick! Our poor bones! When we lay them at last in our graves, how they will ache ... The dust, noone can like ... I wonder whether my hair will ever be clean again ... Those who sit at home and think what fun it must be to explore waste places, they do not know the price for it which has to be reckoned in such days as these. Tut, tut! What a fuss I am making about a bad night!'

Despite a dust storm on the third day, which heaped sand over the new tent, they made good progress to a ruined fort at Wizeh. There they discovered an 'immense rocky hole' in the ground. Gertrude, you might think, would have had enough adventures for one journey. The hole, however, exerted the same fascination over her as unclimbed mountains had in previous years. Nothing would satisfy her but to descend into the black tunnel, and so she removed most of her clothing, put a handful of candles and matches in her pocket, and climbed down two hundred feet, accompanied by the no doubt reluctant Fattuh. She recounted:

We went on boldly through this strange crack in the rocks. Sometimes it opened out into a great hall, sometimes it was so low that we had to creep through it, flat on the sand. And at the end we reached a clear, cold pool, fed by a spring in the rock. We waded into it and filled all our flasks ... We had left lights at various points on the way to guide us back, yet the place was so strange and gate-of-the-pit-like, that I was not sorry when we saw daylight again.

The benefits of her brief rest in Baghdad soon evaporated, and her diary gives the picture of a woman so tired that her normal alarm response was barely functioning. She was able to fall asleep on her camel, for the first time, and without falling off. More importantly, the Syrian desert was no longer as safe as she had counted on. Raids – *ghazzus* – were taking place all around, and she soon heard of bodies being left in the desert to be eaten by dogs. In her weariness, the ritual tasks of visiting tents and taking on *rafiqs* began to assume a dreamlike, repetitive quality. She remembered only the unusual things, like her encounter with a baby gazelle in a sheikh's tent:

> They brought it to me and laid it in my lap, where it fell asleep. It lay curled round like a Mycenaean ivory, with one absurd pointed horn stretched out over its ear; it slept through the talk. And I looking at the sharp watchful faces of the men round the coffee hearth, and remembering my own probably anxious face, thought that there was none in that company wholly free from apprehension but the little gazelle asleep upon my knee. Its small confident presence was encouraging.

Ten days out of Baghdad she found herself near a huge encampment of Anazeh tribesmen, and resigned herself with reluctance to the delays of another courtesy visit and the taking on of another *rafiq*. The Anazeh were numerous and widespread enough for her to describe them as a 'nation'. The southern Anazeh belonged to Ibn Saud, while the northern were divided into two, one group ruled by Ibn Shlan, the other by Fahad Beg ibn Hadhdbal, whose three hundred tents were presently spread over the grassy ridges of the Garah just ahead of her. He was 'such a big man that I fear I shall have to camp with him,' she commented. But when she met him, she warmed to him: 'He received me with a kindness almost fatherly and I loved being with him. He spread out beautiful carpets on which we sat, leaning against a camel saddle. His hawk sat on its perch behind us, and his greyhound lay beside it.' It was to be one of the most significant encounters of her life, and of immense value in her later work.

Fahad Beg, some seventy years old, was a man of vision. He was one of the first great sheikhs of the Bedouin to recognize the value of property. He understood that the coming of the railway would mean the end of breeding camels for transport. He had bought land in the settled area of the Hussainiyah Canal west of Karbala, where he cultivated palms, but for half the year he reverted to his Bedouin wanderings with his camels and his clan, while the obligatory raids were carried on by his eldest son Mitab. Much later, in the post-war world, it would amuse Gertrude, in recognition of his early appreciation of mechanical transport, to take him for his first flight in a plane.

She spent that afternoon exploring the ruins of a primitive town an hour away, took copious notes, and returned to a message from Fahad Beg saying that he would like to spend the evening with her. He came to her tent followed by an entourage of men carrying many bowls and cooking pots, and provided what was to Gertrude a true desert luxury: a delicious dinner. In the enjoyment of this, a strong rapport was established between them. 'We ate and the dusk fell and the rain came down again, and still we talked, of the state of the 'Iraq and of the future of Turkey and of our friends in Baghdad, till at 8 o'clock he left me and I went to bed . . . amid a shower of blessings.'

Struggling on the next day against a furious cold wind, she wondered if this journey would ever end. She had what we would probably identify as repetitive strain injury, a pulled muscle from camel-riding that sent shooting pains from her thigh to her instep. She limped about the camp, and wrote in her other diary that she needed to sleep for a year. She was beginning to lose track of the days — 'Yesterday – what happened yesterday? We crossed high plains and wide valleys' — and found the landscape tiresome to map because it had no features. Then, suddenly, out of this wilderness appeared a solitary man, on foot. They rode up to him and tried to communicate in Arabic, Persian and Turkish, but he maintained silence. They gave him a handful of bread, which he accepted, and they rode on. She looked back and watched him, slowly heading for the heart of an uninhabited desert. Later on, she almost wondered whether she had been hallucinating. She was exhausted enough for anything:

There are people camped in the hills above us and I don't care what they do to us . . . Here was such a long day's march ahead of us and my soul shrank from it. I wondered whether I should cry, out of sheer weariness, and what they would think if I dropped tears into the coffee hearth! My reputation as a traveller would never survive these revelations.

In the way that extreme sleep deprivation liberates the mind from stress, taking the edge off imminent predicaments while promoting a more impressionable state of mind, her daily writings took on a bigger and more spiritual perspective. She jotted down a remembered verse of Shelley's 'Spirit of Delight':

> I love snow and all the forms
> of the radiant frost;
> I love wind and rain storms, anything almost
> That is Nature's and may be
> Untouched by man's misery.

And her own description of a storm ahead is as poetic a piece of prose as she ever wrote:

A great storm marched across our path. We, riding in a world darkened by its august presence, watched and heard. The lightning flickered through the cloud masses, the thunder spoke from them and on the outskirts companies of hail, scourged and bent by a wind we could not feel, hurried over the plain and took possession of the mountains.

Then the clouds cleared, revealing a beautiful golden bay of desert with the towers of the medieval castle at its centre. They were within sight of Palmyra. Three more days of ten- or twelve-hour marches, and they came down from the snows of Mount Hermon to the very place where she had picked up her camels, outside Damascus, and pitched their first camp of the journey. On 1 May she rode through the city's outlying vineyards and orchards. She had not seen a green landscape for four and a half months, and the rushing water, the new corn, the abundant olives, the rustling of chestnut leaves, the birdsong and the sun-bleached roses – all blessed her eyes and ears. The first building on the Dumayr road, as she came into Damascus, was the English hospital, where she had a friend, Dr Mackinnon. She heaved herself off the camel and almost fell through the door. In a few minutes Dr Mackinnon was beside her, then his wife. They looked at her – and took charge. Later that day she reflected:

> So here I am in a garden which is one bower of roses, and in a quiet house where no one can bother me and I can lie still and rest. But it isn't much of a success yet, for I go on riding camels through my dreams . . . Now it's all behind me and I must try to forget it for a little, till I am less weary. I'm still too near it – it looms too big, out of all proportion to the world, and too dark, unbelievably menacing.

She rested for a few days, then the visitors began to arrive. Among them, in due course, came the Rashid agent whose 'crafty narrow face' and 'soft slow voice' had filled her with a vague alarm when she had invested her £200 with him in exchange for the letter of credit. He asked her if she had heard the news about Ibrahim. She asked him what he meant. 'He looked at me in silence and drew his fingers across his throat.'

Ibrahim, it has been suggested, died because he had let Gertrude leave Hayyil. In fact, at about the time she had arrived in Baghdad, the young Amir had indeed had his uncle, the Regent Zamil ibn Subhan, murdered at Abu Ghar – in part because Zamil had been in secret communication with Ibn Saud in the hope of reaching a peaceful settlement. The Amir now needed to kill Zamil's brother Ibrahim, together with all the Subhan kinsmen and their slaves, because, if he had not, they would have been honour-bound to kill the Amir and his sons. Thus a fresh blood feud had been initiated. It was not long before the Amir, in his turn, was murdered. And so the Rashids declined, as Gertrude had predicted, moving towards their end in a welter of assassination and intrigue.

Fitting epilogue though this was to the horrors of Hayyil, it was not of Ibrahim's death that she found herself thinking when she fell into a reverie, settling the events of the past four months into some kind of perspective. The muezzin call that had haunted her captivity haunted her now, forming in her mind an indelible impression of Arab fatalism and spirituality:

> 'God is great, God is great. There is no God but God. And Mohammed is the prophet of God. God is great. God is great.' Low and soft, borne on the scented breeze of the desert, the mighty invocation, which is the Alpha and Omega of Islam, sounds through my memory when I think of Hayyil.

10

WAR WORK

The cat and I are the only two not in uniform.

It was a different Gertrude who returned from Hayyil, and it was to a different world that she returned. She had gone to Rounton to recover, and was there at the outbreak of war, writing heart-sore letters to Dick Doughty-Wylie in Addis Ababa. When war was proclaimed on 4 August 1914, she went out on to the estate, climbing on haystacks and carts to address the labourers, encouraging them to do what she would have done if she had been a man – to join up. She went to talk to the workers in the iron ore mines, and bumped through the fields in a car, exhorting the men to go and fight.

The war was expected to last four months, not four years. Since the ravages of Napoleon's total war, Europe had forged treaties binding nation to nation in a grid of obligation. Britain would come to the aid of France, France would intervene for Russia, Germany for Austria, Russia for Serbia, Poland and Italy; Turkey would march with Germany.

Germany had in Kaiser Wilhelm an arrogant aggressor of the military class, busy building surplus battleships for his navy and promoting the power of his army. But the danger came from the most unlikely quarter, the tired old empire of Austria-Hungary. The Emperor deplored change, and ruled with a firm hand as his divided subjects worked for self-determination. The Serbians, particularly, resented their subservience, and militant groups were unwilling to wait for the promised reforms of the Emperor's well intentioned heir, Archduke Ferdinand. As Ferdinand toured Sarajevo in his open carriage on a pleasant summer's day, a shot rang out from the crowd and the Archduke fell dead.

As the dominoes had been stacked, so they fell. Austria marched into Serbia. Russia mobilized in support of Serbia, made threats against Turkey, and called in France. Observing the powers of Europe lining up against her, Germany decided on a pre-emptive strike. To the dismay of the French, the Germans tore through Belgium and in a few weeks were camped within reach of Paris. Britain felt honour-bound to declare war, and sent an expeditionary force of a hundred thousand men to the aid of France. This joint force took the full impact of the onslaught in the north, while two million Frenchmen formed a human barrier as far as Switzerland. Meanwhile, Canada, Australia, New Zealand, India and the African colonies came to the aid of Britain. Soon Japan had invaded China. Country by country, most of the world had slipped into war. That single shot in a remote European capital precipitated the mobilization of 65 million men and would cause 38 million casualties.

Before the end of 1914, Britain's Intelligence Bureau in Cairo was already asking questions about the Arab provinces of the Ottoman Empire. Russia was facing war on two fronts and asking for Britain's support in the Mediterranean. Britain, contemplating a new strategy, was ready to give it. After only three months, the fighting in the trenches of northern France had reached stalemate, with no end in sight. If Britain initiated a south-eastern front in the Dardanelles, they hoped Germany would divide its forces and go to the defence of the Turks. The question was this: if there was to be a south-eastern front, if Turkey joined Germany in all-out war against Great Britain, whose side would the Arabs take? Wyndham Deedes in Cairo asked the War Office if they could get hold of Gertrude Bell, the well known traveller who had so recently covered the ground, and ask for her views.

Gertrude, at Rounton, took the letter from the breakfast table straight into her study, cleared her desk in her time-honoured way by sweeping all the books and papers on to the floor, and sat down to write. The report that she produced, in response to the War Office's request, showed her sensitive grasp of a complicated political situation. The gist was this: Syria was pro-British, with a dislike of the growing French influence in the region. In the circumstances, Syria would be perfectly content to come under British jurisdiction:

> On the Baghdad side we weigh much more heavily in the scale than Germany because of the importance of Indian relations – trade, chiefly. The presence of a large body of German engineers in Baghdad, for railway building, will be of no advantage to Germany, for they are not popular. On the whole I should say that Iraq would not willingly see Turkey at war with us and would not take an active part in it. But out there, the Turks would probably turn . . . to Arab chiefs who have received our protection. Such action would be extremely unpopular with the Arab Unionists who look on Sayid Talib of Basra, Kuwait, and Ibn Saud, as powerful protagonists. Sayid Talib is a rogue, he has had no help from us, but our people (merchants) have maintained excellent terms with him . . .

The import of her report was fully corroborated for the War Office by their inspectors on the ground, who knew their own Arab *vilayets*,* although they could not see the bigger picture that Gertrude could so easily supply after her epic journey to Hayyil. For the first time, Whitehall was recognizing her formidable knowledge and making use of it. From now on, her future was to be bound up with the British government.

The 'Bell Report' was swiftly passed to Cairo and also to the Foreign Secretary, Sir Edward Grey. Grey was already, like so many of the Liberal statesmen and politicians of the day, well known to the Bells. Hugh had sat with him on the board of the London and North Eastern Railway, and Grey's gentle treatise on fly-fishing was one of the books Gertrude had taken with her to the desert in 1911 to remind her of the temperate English countryside

---

* The Turkish word for an administrative region.

— she had told him so on her return from Hayyil, when Grey had been one of the first visitors to Sloane Street.

Life everywhere was changing, for some less than for others. The magazines were full of photographs of society beauties in uniform: Countess Bathurst in her Red Cross outfit, the Marchioness of Londonderry in the uniform of the Women's Service Legion. The new British *Vogue*, of which Gertrude would later become an occasional reader, showed the Duchess of Wellington knitting a sock for a soldier. Mrs Vincent Astor, photographed in a fetching garden hat, was quoted as wishing to open a convalescent home near Paris. Lady Randolph Churchill had 'organized some very beautiful tableaux vivants'. Gertrude, who was well aware of the silliness of this, longed to find work commensurate with her abilities. 'I have asked some of my friends at the Red X to join me in the first suitable job abroad that falls vacant,' she wrote to a friend, '. . . and I have written to friends in Paris asking whether I could be of use to them in any way . . . Arabia can wait.'

For the moment, all she could do was to join the influx of well-born ladies into the workplace, and take a genteel clerking job in a hospital at Lord Onslow's at Clandon Park in Surrey, one of the many grand houses now occupied by the wounded. There were a hundred Belgian soldiers in the wards there but, to her bitter disappointment, she was restricted to the routine paperwork and not allowed to do any nursing. She complained to Florence that she had not got nearly enough to do. Sundays were particularly boring. On one, she went for a walk and stopped for tea with some Surrey friends, the John St Loe Stracheys, who had also filled the bedrooms of their large house with convalescents. At Rounton, Florence was making ready to do the same. She told Gertrude that there would be twenty at first, more later, and Gertrude wondered how they could all be fitted in. She told Florence about one of the Stracheys' first inmates, a Congolese soldier who was parted with difficulty from a large knife he insisted on keeping beside him in bed: he explained that in his part of Africa, prisoners were killed and eaten. 'St Loe remarked "It is a curiously unexpected result of the war to have one's best bedroom occupied by a cannibal."'

It was after only three weeks at Clandon, on 21 November, that she was asked to go at once to Boulogne, to work in the new Red Cross Office for the Wounded and Missing.

The Wounded and Missing Enquiry Department had opened in Paris at the outbreak of war, to help answer the questions of families whose men had gone to war and whose letters had ceased. These families had no idea whether their men were wounded, missing or dead. News only reached them by means of the so-called 'fear telegram' whereby the War Office let them know the man had been killed, or by finding his name among the casualties list published in *The Times*. The War Office being unable to cope with the flood of enquiries, the families' only recourse was to write to the Red Cross for information. The task of the W&MED was to try to trace three categories of men: those who were dead but not yet known to be dead, the men wounded so seriously that they were in hospital and not well enough to write home, and those who had been taken prisoner. At first it concerned itself only with the higher ranks. Not until December was a satellite Enquiry Office opened to deal with letters from the families of non-commissioned officers and men, who were harder to trace.

In the early stages of the conflict, liaison with the French hospitals in Paris was paramount. Since the British were fighting in the north of France, the new Red Cross branch was placed as near to them as possible, alongside the British hospitals that had been set up in Boulogne. When Gertrude arrived, the office was only three weeks old. The German army had recently marched through Flanders, and the British expeditionary force sent to Ypres to stop them had lost some fifteen thousand men. Mired in the trenches, with barbed wire and machine-guns separating them, the protagonists settled into a war of attrition punctuated by intermittent attempts to break through the line. These offensives pitted fifty to a hundred thousand men at the enemy, with no lasting gain. The fighting had reached deadlock, with the hundred yards gained on one day lost a day or a week later. Each Allied offensive brought appalling loss of life and new waves of casualties, with wounded men on stretchers arriving by every ambulance train, and piling up at the station for transfer to hospital.

Gertrude would be taking her place in the W&MED office alongside her childhood friend Flora Russell, who was already employed there, and Flora's sister Diana. The sisters worked turn and turn about, so that one of them was always in the office and the other on leave. Flora was at present in London, and Gertrude was able to meet up with her, to be told of the dreadful chaos and dirt that she was about to encounter. Flora scribbled a list of clothes that Gertrude would need, and went off to enjoy her leave. Given just three days to get herself to Boulogne, Gertrude sent a flurry of letters via Florence to Marie Delaire, her long-suffering maid, demanding underclothes, watches, jackets, and her riding boots to cope with the mud. Her messages to Marie were abrupt, albeit sifted through Florence's tactful intervention. But Marie's affection and loyalty for Gertrude knew no bounds: she would stay with her, through thick and thin, all of her mistress's life.

Naturally impatient, Gertrude was suffering, as always, from Dick's absence. He had now admitted that he loved her, but in Addis Ababa he could hardly be further away. When would she see him? She knew that if he came home, he was likely to offer his services once more to the army, and then he would be gone again. She packed the locked box of his letters at the bottom of her suitcase.

She was almost the only woman on the Folkestone steamer among the crowd of subdued uniformed men returning to the front after their seventy-two hours' leave. She stepped on to the quay at Boulogne in heavy November rain, scarcely recognizing this grey town as the starting point for so many of the Bells' European holidays. There used to be a crowd of eager porters; now there was no one. Turning up her collar, she picked up her case and followed the soldiers, who had shouldered their kit and were making for the station yard. There they climbed aboard the fleet of London omnibuses co-opted to take the troops to the front. Although they had been in France for only four or five weeks, these vehicles were so mud-spattered that barely a trace of the original colour was visible. Those that had broken down had been turned into makeshift shelters from the rain. Under the encrustation

Gertrude could just make out a couple of the original destinations – Putney and Kilburn. She walked past the ranks of Red Cross ambulances to the goods sheds, now converted into a hospital crisply run by the Army Medical Service. The only other women on the street were nurses going to work or leaving after their shifts, wearing the grey ankle-length uniform of the Army Sisters.

She found the office car waiting for her by the rest station, where an ambulance was unloading the wounded. Those able to walk looked as if they were made of clay, their faces and greatcoats, too, plastered with mud. They limped and shuffled like old men, looking neither to left nor right. Others were being carried away on stretchers, or smoking cigarettes while awaiting the next stage of repatriation. The car splashed away through the puddles, and through the smeared windows she saw dirt and discomfort everywhere she looked. They pulled up at the run-down lodging house where she had been assigned a room in the attic, reached by a long, steep staircase smelling of old food. Diana, who shared a room downstairs with Flora, came to find her and agreed that it was an awful hole. Gertrude changed her shoes and the two of them went straight off to get her a passport. She told Dick in a letter: 'I had a hideous interview with the passport people at the Red Cross . . . age 46, height 5 foot 5½ . . . no profession . . . mouth normal . . . face, well . . . I looked at the orderly: "Round" she said.'

She was given a desk and introduced to the volunteers, a group of dedicated but disorganized ladies who staffed the office. The gaunt, high-ceilinged room was darker than the grey view through the windows. The four or five desks, and the floor around them, were almost hidden under heaps of dog-eared papers. Several times a day a messenger would arrive with more boxes of letters and lists, which would throw everyone into feverish activity. Sometimes a name on a letter would strike a chord, and inspire them to burrow through five or six piles. Gertrude noted that they soon gave up and sat down again to pore over a fresh pile of enquiry letters from families and newspaper cuttings.

Everyone tried to explain to her what they were doing, but their explanations varied so much and they themselves seemed so confused that in the end she worked it out for herself. As the letters arrived, the staff took note of the names and tried to trace them through the various listings. She saw at once that they had no system: they had begun the work when there was just a trickle of letters, and they were continuing to tackle it in the same way although the trickle had turned into a torrent. They were trying to match fresh enquiries to names on lists often a month or two old: lists of hospital admissions, reports from the searchers in the hospital wards, lists of prisoners, and casualty and missing lists from the newspapers. When they could verify a name, a rare occurrence, they would write to the families concerned to tell them that their man was either wounded or missing, dead or taken prisoner. Working from scribbled notes and from memory, deluged with documents from so many sources while close to the cutting edge of a battle that no one was winning, the volunteers' morale had slumped and their sense of purpose was being eroded daily. With more than fifteen thousand British men killed, wounded or missing in the recent Mons campaign, the small office was not so much overwhelmed as washed away in the flood.

Gertrude realized that, to put in a workable system, she would have to begin at the beginning. She set her mind to the job and took it up with all her energy. This heiress who had lived her entire life for adventure and self-education, now dedicated her days to working at a modest desk as though her life depended on it: 'I think I have inherited a love of office work! A clerk was what I was meant to be . . . I feel as if I had flown to this work as one might take to drink, for some forgetting.' She proved to be a formidable administrator.

The well-meaning volunteers soon found themselves bossed about by the newcomer, who first interrogated them about their methods and then produced a new way of doing things that they felt obliged to follow. Her first object was to create a database from which the whole office could work. She made an alphabetical card index of all officers admitted to the base hospitals in France, recording dates of admission, transfers to other hospitals, evacuation back to Britain or return to the front. Names from the letters of enquiry could then be quickly checked against it for a match. As soon as she finished the database, she began sorting through the enquiries and finding names on the hospital admissions lists. She then classified the enquiries in another card index, this one divided into wounded or missing, with all available details. She worked on the card stacks in her lunch hour and after work when the office was supposed to be shut. When that had been completed, she was able to cross-reference, so that new information coming in from any source could be compared, corroborated and verified. She was pleased with her efforts: 'I've very nearly cleared away the mountain of mistakes which I found when I came. Nothing was ever verified, and we went on piling error on to error, with no idea of the confusion that was being caused . . . If we are not scrupulously correct we are no good at all.'

She weeded out those names that had been on the books for five months or more. These men would remain in a kind of no-man's-land entitled 'Missing Presumed Dead' until there was verification of their deaths, when their unfortunate families could finally give up hope. Then they would receive the dreaded form from the War Office, and the soldier's name would appear on the official casualty list.

Now, she told Florence, all she had to do was persuade the W&MED in London and Paris to adopt her system and to make sure that all information was constantly updated. When she had time for lunch, she went with Diana or Flora to a tiny restaurant packed with soldiers, everybody taking everybody else for granted. It was, she told her family, the oddest world.

Her office hours, as yet rather less than modern staffers put in in an average week, were considerable for a woman who had never worked in an office before: 'It is fearful the amount of office work there is. We are at it all day from 10 till 12.30 and from 2 to 5 filing, indexing and answering enquiries . . . The more we do, the more necessary it is to keep our information properly tabulated . . . I need not say I'm ready to take it all. The more work they give me the better I like it.' Would Florence, she added, request on her behalf a complete list of the Territorial battalions? And could she have a London address book for the office – an old telephone directory would do nicely.

The Boulogne lists were soon acknowledged to be as complete as they could be made, and Paris began sending its own lists of admissions and discharges there, instead of the other way round. Flora and Diana departed to run a new office in Rouen, along Gertrude's lines. She had also instigated a 'watching list' of some fifteen hundred names registered as 'enquiries', so that hospitals themselves could check their admissions against it as soon as they arrived.

In time, she thought, they would have one of the best-run offices in France. But the job was not being made any easier by those in command. The head of the W&MED, Lord Robert Cecil, had recently asked to have a W&MED representative permanently at the front, only for the army to refuse. The Red Cross had also asked the Army Council to let their searchers go to the front after each offensive and make early enquiries about the dead and missing among the wounded at field hospitals and rest stations. The military authorities did not see their way to permitting this either, and ordered that the W&MED should remain well behind the line. Undeterred, Gertrude cooked up a plan to create their own channels through army chaplains. It was soon understood that the military agenda was to hide from civilians not only the true catastrophic course of the war in the trenches, but also the miscalculations of the commanders, who continued to order escalating offensives when it should have been abundantly clear to them that the strategy was not working. For more obscure reasons, the Red Cross had decided not to let any women make enquiries at the hospitals. 'Very silly,' sniffed Gertrude, determining to make friends with the nurses and go in, albeit unofficially, whenever she liked.

She would walk along the seafront from 8.30 to 9 a.m. At 5, after her work in the office had finished, she began defiantly visiting out-stations and hospitals, talking to the men in the wards. She made a special trip in the office car to Le Touquet, to visit the Secunderabad Hospital for Indian regiments. She was warmly received by the medical staff, who told her how isolated they felt. For her, this short visit was like a home from home. They gave her tea and escorted her around the wards to meet Sikhs, Gurkhas, Jats and Afridis, most sitting cross-legged on their beds and playing cards: 'The cooks [were] preparing Hindu and Mohammadan dinners over separate fires, and the good smell of ghee and the musty aromatic East pervading the whole . . . Every man had the King's Christmas card pinned up above his bed, and Princess Mary's box of spices lying on the table beneath it.'

In the centre of Boulogne itself, the Casino, a riot of bright lights and gilded paintwork, had been taken over by the War Office and turned into a military hospital. The American Bar, she was amused to see, was now an X-ray room, and the Café Bar served as a dispensary for bandages and carbolic lotion. She was interested to find that the British soldiers sharing wards with the wounded Germans were perfectly pleasant and friendly to their former enemies. On 11 December she wrote to Chirol:

> There is a recent order, direct from Kitchener, that no visitor is to go into hospitals without a pass. It's unspeakably silly. The reason given out is that spies get into the hospitals, question the wounded and gain valuable information concerning the position of their regiments! Anyone who has talked to the men in hospital knows how ridiculous that is. They are generally quite vague as to where they were or what they were doing.

In November and December – December being Gertrude's first month in the job – there were 1,838 enquiries from families. Her new card index listed 5,000 names, and she was able to resolve the fate of 127 men. Most of them were traced by the three male 'searchers' attached to the Boulogne office, whose daily job it was to go to the hospitals and question the wounded about their missing colleagues. If these shell-shocked and disabled men could throw any light on their fate, the information was filed with the office. Where death was a certainty, the War Office was informed. The Boulogne section of a Joint War Committee Report, probably penned by Gertrude herself, reads:

> It should be appreciated at home that these enquiries from wounded men about their missing comrades are a most difficult

part of our work. Men reach hospital from the trenches in such a nerve-racked condition that their evidence has to be checked and counterchecked by questioning other men, and thus every 'enquiry case' may necessitate the catechism of four or five men.

When the British fell back, their wounded were overtaken by the Germans, and either killed or taken prisoner. Nothing more would be known about them unless they could be found on one of the lists of prisoners coming from Germany through the Red Cross at Geneva. These lists, as they arrived in Boulogne, enabled the office to determine the fate of at least some of the missing.

This was fighting unlike any that had been known before. The unknown soldier, as A. J. P. Taylor was to write, was the true hero in a war that resulted in nearly 192,000 men from the British Empire missing or taken prisoner. One shell could blow fifty men apart in such a way that they could never be identified. One of the grimmest parts of the work that Gertrude initiated at Boulogne consisted in finding wherever possible the graves of men hastily buried on the battlefield, whose relatives wanted to know whether there was proof of death, and if so, where they were buried. The exhumations were the work of the Red Cross searchers, the same men who normally went into the hospitals to interview the wounded. They often found that the grave which contained the colonel or captain they were trying to find would turn out to be a pit into which a number of other bodies had also been thrown. The most recent that Gertrude had recorded in mid-December contained 98 men. Of the 98, only 66 still wore their identity discs – but at least these deaths could be certified and their graves ascertained. After verification, the grave was lengthened, the bodies laid side by side and the burial service read over them. Gertrude told Valentine Chirol:

Where we are under a cross fire of artillery, we have about 50 casualties a day . . . It's miserable up there now – continuous rain . . . The roads beyond St Omer are in an awful state. The cobbled pavement is giving way . . . and on either side of it is a slough of mud. The heavy motor transport, if it is pushed off the pavement into the mud can't be got out and stays there for ever.

She did not always succeed in putting Dick to the back of her mind, and now she had an extra worry. In the New Year Maurice was to be sent to the front. She dreaded that one day it might be his name that turned up on one of the lists on her desk. As usual she opened her heart only to Chirol, sheltering her family from the knowledge of her misery:

> I can work here all day long – it makes a little plank across the gulf of wretchedness over which I have walked this long long time. Sometimes even that comes near to breaking point . . . I ought not to write of it. Forgive me. There are days when it is still almost more than I can bear – this is one of them, and I cry out to you . . . My dear Domnul, dearest and best of friends.

At the beginning of the war the officers, being career soldiers, would have been older than most of the ranks, and more likely to have wives who would write in to the Red Cross to initiate a search if they disappeared. Since the War Office issued commissions and recorded promotions, they had the lists of officers to hand, while the names of the men in the ranks were known only to their regiments. As the Joint War Committee Report put it, 'With the small staff at its disposal it was obviously impossible to keep a complete record of everybody, and this work was at first confined to officers.' While there is a deplorable aspect to this attitude, it is nonetheless true that the number of soldiers was astronomical. Recruitment offices collapsed under the applications of the two and a half million men who volunteered in response to Kitchener's 'Your Country Needs You' campaign.

Shortly after the new Enquiry Office opened, dealing with non-commissioned officers and men, the army discontinued its practice of issuing the Red Cross with hospital lists, because the hospitals were inundated and worked off their feet. Without that lifeline, and without any searchers on the small staff, it was only a few weeks before the new office closed. The correspondence from the families went instead to Gertrude, whose work had been doubled already with the correspondence that was now re-routed from Paris. She and her staff readily took up the burden of the enquiries about the non-commissioned officers and men – 'Some rather complicated business has been settled up, the result being that we take on privates as well as officers, for which I am very glad' – and brought news, good or bad, to at least some of these British families.

She asked Florence to post to her the latest arrangements about allowances for soldiers and sailors. Having grown up with a keen family awareness of the straitened finances of working families such as those at her father's ironworks, she knew what it would mean to them to lose the breadwinner. When families had to be informed that their husband or father had been disabled or killed, she wanted to be able to explain their entitlements and how they could apply for them.

It was almost Christmas. Hugh had asked her if she wanted a car to help her with the work, but she had turned it down, explaining that she could always borrow one if she wanted. He sent her £50 instead, and hoped she would be back for the holiday. She wrote to thank him and tell him that she wanted to stay in Boulogne, for fear that her new system would fall to pieces if she were not there to enforce it. The great advantage she had over Flora and Diana, she said, was that she could be there all the time; and as long as she was hard at work, it kept her from dwelling on her anxieties.

She told Hugh how she would be spending his £50. Realizing that he had a good lieutenant in Gertrude, Cecil had told her how much he appreciated her reorganization of the work. She was the obvious choice for head of the department, and was invited to take over a room for her private office. She chose one of the empty rooms in the property, all of them gloomy, had it cleaned and repapered, and put in a mat and new chintz curtains. It looked as charming as it could, thanks to Hugh. 'In spite of dirt and gloom I have made my office cheerful enough, with jars of lilac and narcissus which I buy in the market. I wonder they can bring up flowers to Boulogne in war time, and I bless them for it,' she told Chirol. And she still had plenty of money to spend on books and files and ledgers. It was good, she told her father, to feel it all cost the Red Cross nothing.

Her Christmas passed almost unnoticed. On 27 December she sat down to write home about a curious phenomenon that was the talk of the town:

> I hear that on Xmas Day there was almost the peace of God. Scarcely a shot was fired, the men came out of the trenches and mixed together, and at one place there was even a game of football between the enemies . . . Strange, isn't it . . . Sometimes we recover lost ground and find all our wounded carefully bound up and laid in shelter; sometimes we find them all bayoneted – according to the regiment, or the temper of the moment, what do I know? But day by day it becomes a blacker weight upon the mind.

Cecil had at long last managed to persuade the War Office to let him establish a communication line with the front. Major Fabian Ware and his team were to be the new recipients of the enquiry lists from the Red Cross office: it was hoped that they would be able to get information that was beyond the reach of the W&MED.

One of the team, a Mr Cazalet, arrived in Boulogne on New Year's Eve and brought with him a huge bundle of lists and crumpled letters taken from the pockets of the dead, some of them bloodstained. Fresh information coming in from the front line was of great value, with the proviso that all checking had to be done during the next twenty-four hours, after which Cazalet would return to the front. He would then have to hand the letters over, for return to the families, together with any other personal effects. Only Gertrude and Diana were staffing the office over the New Year. They sat down immediately to sort and check and enter the results in a ledger. They worked the rest of the day, then returned to the office after dinner and worked until 2 a.m.: 'At midnight we broke off for a few minutes, wished each other a better year and ate some chocolates.'

Gertrude was back in the office at 8.15 a.m., and the work was finished by 12.30, with just an hour to spare. She took the office car and delivered it in person. Major Ware was impressed, and it was not long before he visited the office. He had a long talk with Gertrude and left promising that in future he would send her all the details he could collect. Then, in January, for the first time Cecil sent her the War Office's monthly list of missing men for her comments. 'It was full of errors, both of commission and omission,' she wrote to Chirol. As the W&MED knew so much more about the missing than the WO did, she wrote back, why didn't she simply take the work over?

But in spite of her limitless capacity for work, she was worn thin. With Maurice now at the front and Dick inclined to return to the fighting, she was trying hard to resist depression. The appalling weather became a metaphor for the constant haemorrhaging of life and the profitless state of the war. Unusually, she had admitted her low spirits to Chirol: 'I feel tired . . . I'm too near the horrible struggle in the mud. It's infernal country, completely under water . . . you can't move for mud.'

As the numbers of the wounded and missing proliferated, the War Office did hand over much of what had originally been their responsibility to the efficient Red Cross operation in Boulogne. Gertrude toiled on – and all aspects of the work now flooded into her capable hands. She asked for, and was given, the task of responding to the enquiries that would entail the Red Cross informing the families of the deaths of their relatives. Her style was in sharp contrast to the dreaded Form B101–82 sent by the War Office:

Madam,

It is my painful duty to inform you that a report has this day been received from the War Office notifying the death of Number 15296 Private Williams, J. D. which occurred at Place Not Stated on the 13th of November, 1915 The cause of death was Killed In Action

The 'fear telegram' was even more succinct:

> Deeply regret to inform you that E. R. Cook British Grenadiers
> was killed in action 26th April Lord Kitchener expresses his
> sympathy Secretary War Office

She did all she could to convey the news in the gentlest and most
sympathetic manner. Having worn out one typewriter with the sad
work, she was awarded a newer model. The Joint War Committee
Report paid tribute to Gertrude's work, without naming her, and
described her approach:

> Official forms and methods should be, as far as possible,
> discarded, so that each enquirer might feel that a certain
> personal interest was taken in his or her case . . . and it was
> abundantly proved that no labour was wasted which might
> convince the families of the missing of the wide and assiduous
> research which had been made on their behalf.

Gertrude wrote to Chirol on 12 January:

> They have put all the correspondence into my hands, Paris,
> Boulogne and Rouen. I am glad because the form in which we
> convey terrible tidings – that is mostly what we have to convey –
> matters very much, and when I have it to do, I know at least that
> no pains will be spared over it . . . I lead a cloistered existence
> and think of nothing but my poor people whose fortunes I am
> following so painfully . . .
>
> The letters I receive and answer daily are heart-rending. At
> any rate, even if we can give these people little news that is good,
> it comforts them I think that something is being done to find out
> what has happened to their beloveds. Often I know myself that
> there is no chance for them, and I have to answer as gently as I
> can and carefully keep from them horrible details which I have
> learnt. That is my daily job.

Now, at her lowest ebb, she received the letter that brought her
back to life. Dick wrote to say that he was on his way back to
London. She should wait for his message and come straight there to
meet him.

Her office colleagues were taken aback: the boss who never took a holiday — who seldom took a lunch-break or left when the office shut — had suddenly gone absent without a word of explanation.

These were the four nights and three days that Gertrude was to spend with the man she loved before he set off for Gallipoli. She knew she might never see him again. When he had gone, she caught the Folkestone steamer in the rain for Boulogne, her heart heavier than she had ever known it. Already depressed, she was now entering one of the darkest periods of her life.

Occasionally, sitting alone at her desk in the empty building after supper, alongside the full ashtray and the jug of spring flowers from a world far away in the sun, she would put her head down on her arms and weep. Every list of wounded and missing might now include the names of Dick or Maurice. She was sure that she would never know happiness again. From now on, her letters home sound a note of enduring pain:

> My work goes on — quite continuous, very absorbing, and so sad that at times I can scarcely bear it. It is as though the intimate dossier of the War passed through my hands. The tales that come in to me are unforgettable; the splendid simple figures that live in them people my thoughts, and their words, brought back to me, ring in my ears. The waste, the sorrow of it all.
>
> Here we sit, and lives run out like water with nothing done. It's unbelievable now at the front — the men knee deep in water in the trenches, the mud impassable. They sink in it up to the knee, up to the thigh. When they lie down in the open to shoot they cannot fire because their elbows are buried in it to the wrist. Half the cases that come down to the hospital are rheumatism and forms of frost bite. They stay in the trenches twenty-one days, sometimes thirty-six days, think of it.

Walking on the beach in the pouring rain, she would think about these soldiers, catapulted into war, each one a lover, a brother, a husband or son. She must have reflected too on her early enthusiasm for the war, and on the probable fate of those young Yorkshiremen she had exhorted to join up. In her three months at Boulogne she had come to understand trench warfare as few people did who were not themselves in the front line. Every day, in her head, she heard the bombardment that was the prelude to an infantry assault, saw the men run out from the shafts and dive for the shell craters, setting up their machine-guns while three or four more waves of men climbed out of the shafts behind them and surged towards the German line. She saw them running forward at a steady pace, the signal rockets being fired, then the lines advancing into a hurricane of shells from the German batteries. She saw figures tossed into the air, limbs going in all directions. She saw the ones that fell motionless to the ground, and she heard the screams of the wounded as they thrashed the ground in their agony. She saw the broken lines regroup, then advance in short rushes until they were at point-blank range of the German trenches. She heard orders being shouted and the shrill cheers as the British charged, the bursting of bombs and the fusillade of machine-guns. And she heard the moans and cries as the remnants of the British line were beaten back yet again. The dead, the wounded, the missing, all of them, all the mud and the blood, to be reduced to names on lists on a desk in Boulogne. 'They reckon the average duration of an officer at the front at about a month, before he is wounded,' she wrote to Chirol on 2 February. '. . . The taking, losing and retaking of a trench is what it comes to; and 4000 lives lost over it in the last 6 weeks. Bitter waste.'

On 24 April, Maurice distinguished himself at the front. A lieutenant-colonel of the Green Howards, he played a major part in the attack on the village of Fortuin, over the Belgian border north-west of Lille, where the Germans had broken through the line. When Lt.-Col. G. H. Shaw commanding the 4th East Yorks was shot, fighting alongside him, Maurice took command of both battalions and attacked the Germans, driving them back more than a mile. He would be wounded in March of the following year. He did not recover quickly from the subsequent operation, but went back to the front after a few months. He was invalided out again in June 1917, almost totally deaf.

The British public were largely kept in the dark about the true numbers of casualties, while Gertrude had a clear view of the reality, and of the duplicity that went on. She knew that entire battalions could be wiped out in a day, down to the last man, following orders from staff officers who might never have been to the front themselves. It was the beginning of a disenchantment with government and with authority in general that she was as yet too loyal to express openly. It informed an attitude she would come to hold later in her life. 'The Pyrrhic victory of Neuve Chapelle showed more clearly than before that we can't break through the lines. Why they concealed our losses it is hard to guess. They were close on 20,000; and the German casualties between 8 and 10,000.'

At the end of March she returned to London. Cecil had set up a new W&MED office in Pall Mall in response to the enormous numbers of unrecorded wounded men now lying in British hospitals throughout the country. This main office would act as the clearing house for all of the enquiries from families, sending them on to the appropriate Red Cross office abroad – the south-eastern front included. Now there would be one central record, one focus for information from all sources, and one office from which to respond to the families. There was no longer any reason for anywhere but London to be the centre of operations – except that the woman who had control of it all was stationed in Boulogne. Having seen what she had achieved in France, Cecil told Gertrude that she was needed to run his new office. She would have a staff of twenty, plus four typists, and he would be on hand, working out of the same office, available at all times for discussion and advice.

Her last letter from Boulogne was to Florence. Her mind was full of Dick and her work: she felt too vulnerable for any kind of social life. 'Don't let anyone know I'm coming. I shall have no time and I don't want to be bothered with people.'

It was, at least, a change. She was out of the dirt and discomfort of Boulogne and living at 95 Sloane Street, being looked after again by Marie Delaire. She walked across Hyde Park four times a day, coming back for lunch and returning to Arlington Street, where the expanding office was soon rehoused. The exercise and the novel comforts of domestic life brought a slight improvement to her spirits, but the state of confusion in the office was beyond anything she had encountered even in Boulogne. Some of her old humour returned, to lighten her letters to Chirol:

> I love Lord Robert. He resembles a very large elf, and elves, as every reader of fairy stories knows, are good colleagues on an uphill job . . . but it's a job for Hercules. I never knew what chaos meant till now.
>
> I go nowhere and see no one, for I am at the office from 9 am till 7 pm . . . I have some 20 ladies under me, 4 type-writers (not near enough) and 2 boy scouts who are an infinite joy.

In spite of the daunting hours she was now working, she tried hard to be stoical and good-humoured, no matter the stress she was under. She had always exhibited grace under pressure, at least to her family. But now her world came to an end.

Predictably, agonizingly, she heard that Dick had died a hero's death in Gallipoli. Her sister Molly wrote: 'It has ended her life – there is no reason now for her to go on with anything she cared for.'

Little was seen of her for a while and then, pale and thin, she returned to work. She had always worked harder and longer than anyone else, but now she had no other life. 'I get rather tired towards the end of the week. But the quiet day in the office on Sunday sets me up again.'

In vain Florence tried to coax her away for a rest, fearful of the consequences of her stepdaughter's personal tragedy combined with her ferocious workload. Gertrude's spontaneous humour and quick intimacies had been completely extinguished under this heaviest of blows, and her uncomprehending staff must have begun to dislike her, even fear her. But instead of breaking down she worked on, for the sake of people like her lover and her brother. She was short-tempered and impatient even with Florence, countering with unusual irritation her attempts to distract her: 'I could not possibly get away next week. I am having a horrible time, with a lot of new people, all to be taught and all making mistakes at every moment. There is no one in whose hands I could leave the office even for a day. It's being rather intolerable altogether. I hate changing and changes.'

In such pain that she often forgot to spare other people's feelings, she would sadly acknowledge her shortcomings. Three months after Doughty-Wylie's death, Florence wrote from Rounton to ask if Gertrude would like her to come up and be with her at this sad time. Gertrude replied: 'It's very dear of you ... but you mustn't do it. Nobody does any good really ... Nothing does any good.'

And now even more work descended on her from the Foreign Office, who requested that the Wounded and Missing Enquiry Department should take on the gathering and tabulating of all information with regard to German prison camps. She wrote home on 20 August:

> It is of vital importance that we should have this knowledge properly arranged, for it shows us how best to help our prisoners who stand in most need of it. But it means more files, more archives, more people working on them.
>
> I've been bitterly alone this month. It's intolerable not to like being alone as I used, but I can't keep myself away from my own thoughts, and they are still more intolerable.

Janet Courtney – Janet Hogarth of her Oxford days – was one of the women who came to help her in the London office. Janet wrote some time later of that period: 'I was greatly struck by her mental weariness and discouragement, little as she ever let either interfere with the work. But she would not, she said she could not, rest. The War obsessed her to the exclusion of every other consideration ... She would let no personal griefs lessen her capacity for doing. She faced a sorrow and put it behind her.'

Janet's brother David had seen Gertrude shortly before going out to Cairo to help organize a branch of the Admiralty Intelligence Service, dealing specifically with Arab peoples. He suggested that she might follow him but, absorbed in her Red Cross work, she had hardly listened. Once in Cairo he wrote again. This time he practically insisted that she join him in his work.

One day, when Janet went in to work as usual at Norfolk House in St James's Square – lent to the constantly expanding W&MED by the Duke of Norfolk – Gertrude immediately seized her arm in her old impulsive way, and drew her aside. 'I've heard from David; he says anyone can trace the missing but only I can map Northern Arabia. I'm going next week.'

As this chapter of her life closed, with all its toil and misery, she could at least look back with satisfaction on a part of the war effort that she had made definitively her own. For hundreds of thousands of families, she had shone a light into the darkness and played some part in enabling them to get on with living. Her work for the W&MED was to be formally acknowledged as beyond value by HRH the Princess Christian and the other members of the War Executive Committee.

Now, the most exciting and rewarding part of her life was about to begin.

11

CAIRO, DELHI, BASRA

In the 1910s the Middle East was rife with intelligence-gathering and crypto-diplomacy. Before 1908, when Britain became suspicious of Germany's ambitions in the area, there had been no international secret service bureau in London. The Foreign Office routinely used unpaid amateurs and adventurers to report on their expeditions. There were few such in the Middle East, where the hazards of travel demanded linguistic ability and a knowledge of desert etiquette, where much of the wilderness was unmapped and where there were no roads and no recourse if things went wrong. Gertrude was skilled in surveillance and drawn to the political flashpoints. Her travels had made her an obvious choice as one of these volunteer informers. She had been in the employment, though unpaid, of the Intelligence Division of the Admiralty, and it was in November 1915 that the director of Naval Intelligence, Captain Hall, sent for her in London and told her that Cairo had cabled for her.

Gertrude's first-hand knowledge of the vast reaches of Arabia and its diverse peoples made her unique, not only because that knowledge was encyclopaedic, but because her information was so recent. She had returned from Hayyil only sixteen months earlier. In all, she had spent nearly two years of her life travelling in the Arabian deserts. On her seven expeditions she had observed the weaknesses of the Ottoman Empire, first as a wealthy tourist and then as explorer, archaeologist and information-gatherer for the British government.

Some of her reports had been solicited, some volunteered. At first they had been sent perhaps via Chirol, then directly by herself to the interested statesmen and diplomats that she knew. It was probably the Foreign Secretary Sir Edward Grey who was responsible for her initial employment. The Foreign Office had asked her to investigate how far German influence had penetrated the Turkish Empire in northern and eastern Arabia, and she had found the answers via the many ways open to a woman who would not be suspected of espionage. On the road she had sipped coffee and exchanged gossip in the tent of every sheikh she came across. She had dressed up and dined out in towns and cities, and she had made it her business to use her many contacts to meet and talk to everyone who counted socially or politically. She had photographed many archaeological sites and noted military installations. Where entry was complicated, as in March 1900 at the crusader castle at Kerak, where German officers were retraining Turkish soldiers, she had used all her natural effrontery and simply walked right in – 'in an affable way, greet[ing] all the soldiers politely'. Her ever-growing directory of contacts, her skill in direction-finding and cartography, and the meticulous methodology of her records now brought her an official title.

Major Miss Bell arrived in Cairo, the first woman officer in the history of British military intelligence. Her rank of Major was a courtesy, but she was immediately accounted a General Staff Officer 2nd Grade in the official pecking order. Had the WRENS existed then, she would have worn their white and navy uniform, with white pips for political service. As it was, she wore blue and white striped cotton dresses with flowers at the waist and large straw hats, which she would park alongside the peaked caps and pith helmets on the office coat-stand; in the evenings, she would change into flowing silk gowns with small cardigan jackets to match. 'The military people here are much put about how she is to be treated and to how much she is to be admitted,' Hogarth, now a lieutenant-commander in the Royal Naval Volunteer Reserve at Cairo, had written to his wife just before Gertrude's arrival, 'I have told them but *she'll* settle that and they needn't worry!' Gertrude wrote home on 3 January 1916: 'I'm getting to feel quite at home as a Staff Officer! It is comic isn't it.'

Sir Gilbert Clayton had been head of military intelligence for the Egyptian army until transferring to work for Sir Henry McMahon, the new High Commissioner and effectively the ruler of Egypt. Lieutenant-Commander Hogarth had exchanged his archaeologist's bow-ties and rumpled linen jackets for a starchy white naval uniform and joined Clayton to form the 'Arab Bureau', the new intelligence organization for Arab affairs. To the staff members – typically fifteen – of the Bureau, Hogarth was the mentor and referee who monitored the vociferous debates and arguments, Clayton the calm centre, quietly working his powerful influence. Its effect, said Lawrence, was like oil 'creeping silently and insistently through everything'.

The Bureau staff were palmily housed in Cairo's Grand Continental Hotel, their offices next door in the even grander Savoy. Fans whirled in the ceiling, bells rang and servants in floor-length robes brought trays of coffee and peppermint tea. Hogarth and Major Lawrence, his own uniform well creased and stained with oil from his Triumph motor-bike, had already lined the walls with reference books on all subjects pertaining to the Middle East. Despite the verandas with their wicker chairs and the palm gardens baking in the midday sun, the atmosphere, permeated with pipe smoke, suggested panelled rooms in Oxford rather than North African tourist luxury. For Gertrude, after her bereavement and her withdrawal from social life, it was almost too convivial. An afternoon spent with Lady Anne Blunt was 'an oasis of peace and quiet after the noise and crowd of Cairo. How I hate hotels and the perpetual living in public which they imply! One loathes it more than ever after months of a hermit's existence.'

Cairo was the secure heart of the British protectorate that was Egypt, the centre of control. Nominally, the Khedive, or King, still answered to the Turks, but when he ran into bankruptcy in 1875 the British had bailed him out and demanded a Residency in return. Britain then infiltrated the administration much as the Turks had done throughout the Middle East.

Gertrude's letters home from Cairo were shorter and less vivid than formerly. She did not describe the clever men by whom she was now surrounded. It was, after all, a secret office. From the military point of view, it was an elitist and possibly subversive entity whose staff were extraordinarily free to pursue their own agendas. The far-reaching international schemes under discussion and the covert aura of their deliberations gave rise to much suspicion, emanating from intelligence staff in India and communicated to London by the Viceroy himself.

After the initial shock of her arrival, Gertrude was quickly drawn into a new and fascinating world. In the office and over dinner she got to know the big personalities of this circle of which she was now a member. 'Gertrude,' as Hogarth remarked before a short trip to London, 'is beginning to pervade the place.' She had much in common with the archaeologist Leonard Woolley, who had stood in for Hogarth as director of operations at Carchemish, which was being excavated in 1911 when she met Lawrence for the first time. Woolley was now the head of intelligence in Port Said, and the man who had first welcomed her to Egypt. He sat in his office writing, according to Lawrence, 'windy concealers of truth for the press'.

Sir Mark Sykes swept through during that first year. A bombastic Catholic landowner and a near-neighbour of the Bells in Yorkshire, Sykes was an excitable, opinionated traveller who had published books on his expeditions in the Middle East. Gertrude had met him in Haifa in 1905 but the two had quarrelled at a dinner, when he called the Arabs 'animals' and described them as 'cowardly', 'diseased' and 'idle'. At the time, both she and Sykes had been intent on visiting the Jebel Druze, and later he was to accuse her of tricking him in order to get there first. He wrote to his wife Edith: 'Confound the silly chattering windbag of conceited, gushing, flatchested, man-woman, globe-trotting, rump-wagging, blethering ass!' His anger was probably justified. Gertrude did get there first, and she may well have used some trick to delay him. It is alleged that, to ensure that Sykes would be refused permission to travel in the desert, she let slip a lie to the *vali* in Damascus, telling him that Sykes was 'brother-in-law to the Prime Minister of Egypt'. Somehow they had managed to patch up their always spiky relationship;

Gertrude wrote to Florence, 'I have seen a good deal of him.' Now the principal adviser to the British government on its wartime relations with the Arabs, his baggage of prejudices was bound to tarnish their image and damage their fortunes and prospects wherever he meddled.

The restless George Lloyd, of the banking family, also passed through. He was a cool customer, an expert in finance, politics and trade and a firm believer in the merits of British imperialism. He did not stay long in Cairo. The myopic and bohemian Aubrey Herbert had crossed Sinai in 1907. His perfect Turkish was a useful Bureau tool. And then there was the Oriental Secretary Sir Ronald Storrs, who had served in turn Sir Eldon Gorst and Kitchener, Residents before McMahon. Storrs was the most entertaining of the sparkling Arab Bureau circle – quick, quizzical and erudite. He was to Lawrence the most brilliant Englishman in the Near East, 'the great man among us', an incomparable linguist and one who could reduce people of any nationality and class to helpless laughter in a matter of minutes. He was also a connoisseur and a fastidious collector of oriental antiques.

T. E. Lawrence was a law unto himself, seldom to be found and a constant aggravation to the military. Scruffy, brilliant, self-absorbed, he was both welcoming and challenging, just as he had been when Gertrude had met him, and liked him, at Carchemish. His habit of grinning to himself, as if at some private joke, was still disconcerting – but Gertrude, or 'Gerty' as he called her, was seldom disconcerted. His own lengthy wanderings had concentrated on the Crusader castles of Syria and northern Mesopotamia. He had a habit, out of the office, of wearing embroidered waistcoats and cloaks, or Arab dress, but his Arabic was by no means as good as hers. Lacking her wealth, and therefore her status among the sheikhs in the desert, he had not yet been accepted by them as an equal. He had been at the Bureau for months, assembling his 'scraps of information', and took a cavalier attitude to map-making. As he admitted in a letter concerning his map of Sinai roads and wells, 'Some of it was accurate, and the rest I invented.' One day, he feared, nemesis would be awaiting him: he would be told to find his way about that desert country with nothing but a copy of his own map.

Such were the individuals with whom Gertrude was now working. At her first dinner there, with Hogarth and Lawrence, she familiarized herself with the question that was currently dividing loyalties amongst the British staff in Cairo: could an Arab revolt, perhaps supported by Britain, do to the Turks what three hundred thousand troops had failed to do in the Dardanelles? Both the military and the old-fashioned colonialists were adamant that all that could conceivably be done was being done. In their view, the warrior tribes – dignified in the officers' mess by the all-encompassing title 'the Frocks' – were incapable of disciplined modern warfare. To this argument the Bureau would have retorted that disciplined modern warfare had failed on three fronts already.

1914 was the year in which the first definite indication of an Arab revolt had surfaced, initially emanating from the shrewd Hashemite Sharif of Mecca, the holiest city of the Hejaz – the region that stretches the length of the Red Sea, on its eastern bank. The title of 'Sharif' implied a descendant of Muhammad through his daughter Fatima. The current Sharif, the seventy-year-old Hussain, had been held an 'honourable' prisoner in Constantinople for eighteen years, until the overthrow of the old Sultan's bureaucracy in 1908, after which the new government known as the Young Turks unwisely sent him back to Mecca as Amir, the most senior of all sharifs. Two of his sons, the well educated and experienced Abdullah and Faisal, stayed on in Constantinople keeping him politically informed until 1914, when they broke with the Turks and headed for Mecca. The outbreak of war had isolated the Hejaz. The pilgrimages ceased, and the supply of food to this arid region depended at present on the goodwill of the Turks and their all-important railway. In the event of a revolt, British food ships would play a vital role.

On the eve of the world war Abdullah, as his father's envoy, had paid a surprise visit to the Oriental Secretary. Sir Ronald Storrs was then acting for the Consul-General in Cairo. The Machiavellian Abdullah, lover of pre-Islamic poetry and player of jocular games, fell to telling ancient tales and reciting the Seven Odes and Laments. Raptly listening, Storrs was moved and impressed by the profundity and the quantity of poetry that Abdullah had committed to memory; so impressed, indeed, that he thought he must have been making a mistake when he was jarred out of his reverie by the discordant word 'machine-guns'. Abdullah, reaching the point of his visit at last, wanted to know whether the British would supply the guns as 'defence' against attack from the Turks, should his father defy them.

The issue was taken up by the then British Resident, Lord Kitchener. With the entry into the war of Ottoman Turkey in prospect, he began a correspondence with Abdullah which, once Kitchener had returned to London as Secretary of State for War, would be continued by his successor McMahon. Kitchener asked whether Abdullah 'and his father and the Arabs of the Hijaz would be with us or against us'. In a subsequent cable he promised British protection in return for the assistance of 'the Arab nation'. He also hinted: 'It may be that an Arab of true race will assume the Khalifate at Mecca or Medina', and went on to talk of 'the good tidings of the freedom of the Arabs and the rising of the sun over Arabia'.

Kitchener's hints were succeeded by McMahon's equally shrewd obfuscations. Carried in elaborate secrecy to the Amir Hussain, in the hilts of daggers and the soles of shoes, the letters continued to explore the likelihood and ramifications of an Arab revolt against the Turks. Nothing definite had been promised, but, nevertheless, Hussain had seized on the idea that he might become the ruler of the Arab nation.

'The Arab Question', as it was called, affected Gertrude particularly in that her initial job was to master the intricacies of Arab politics and personalities in the Hejaz, from Jerusalem as far south as Mecca, where it was hoped the revolt might be initiated. She was to collect together all her tribal information and fill in any gaps, identifying the tribes and their affiliations and enmities, which she would always enliven with entertaining character sketches of the many sheikhs she knew. At the same time she would map the desert tracks, passable ways through the mountains and waterless expanses, transportation facilities and natural resources, together with the positions and influences of racial and religious groupings and minorities. 'My tribe stuff is beginning to be pulled into shape . . . I love doing it . . . I can scarcely tear myself away from it,' she wrote.

The second part of Gertrude's work centred on Mesopotamia, which had become of prime importance as the war commenced. Since the earliest civilization this region, set between its natural boundaries of the Euphrates and Tigris rivers, provided a fertile easterly frame to Arabia's northern deserts and gave a passable route to the Indian Ocean through the waters of the Persian Gulf in the south-east. The Mesopotamian Campaign, begun in 1914, had stemmed from the 1911 decision of the First Sea Lord, Admiral John 'Jacky' Fisher, with the First Lord of the Admiralty, Mr Winston Churchill, to give more speed to the British navy by converting its ships from coal to oil. It became a priority to ensure a reliable British-owned source of crude.

The two largest suppliers of oil until 1908 had been America and Russia, but the yield in Azerbaijan had begun to fall, and was by no means under British control. In that year, Burmah Oil struck lucky in the foothills of the Zagros mountains, on the borders of Mesopotamia and Persia. The company would supply fuel oil to the new Anglo-Persian Oil Company (APOC), piping it the 138 miles down to Abadan, to a new refinery on the east bank of the Shatt al Arab, the great waterway at the southern end of Mesopotamia that carries the Tigris and Euphrates into the Persian Gulf. The British government provided £2.2 million and took a 51 per cent share in APOC, together with a twenty-year contract for the supply of the navy.

Now there were crucial reasons why Britain should fight the Turks in Mesopotamia: to secure the oil and its pipelines; to guard the threshold of India; to draw grain supplies from the valley of the Euphrates; and to prevent the Turks from using the Baghdad–Basra railway link to deliver troops and supplies to the theatre of war.

With the standing Egyptian army in check, its staff officers playing squash in Cairo while the junior officers led doomed campaigns against the Turks in Sinai, and the British government under duress in Europe, the best that Whitehall could do was to send commands to India with a view to preserving Britain's interests in the Middle East. In anticipation of Turkish hostilities, India had already sent a Poona Brigade to the Persian Gulf, which subsequently captured Fao, the Turkish fort and cable station at the mouth of the Basra river, and drove the enemy back up the Tigris. Soon two divisions of the Indian army would make further progress in Mesopotamia, under their commander General Nixon, finally capturing Nasiriyeh.

The British government in India had its own reasons for alienation from Westminster. In his memoirs *My Indian Years*, the then Viceroy, Lord Hardinge, writes of his conviction that it was in Flanders that the war would be won, and there that London should have concentrated its efforts and terminated the war. He describes the continual demands of the home government for the government of India to send troops, war matériel and supplies to France, East Africa, the Dardanelles, Salonica and elsewhere. Enumerating the efforts made in India to meet the increasing demands of the War Office, he cites the recruitment of 300,000 Indian troops, and the supply of 70 million rounds of small-arms ammunition, 60,000 rifles, 550 guns, plus tents, boots, clothing and saddlery. By the time the war reached Mesopotamia, India was, in his words, 'bled white' and had hardly anything more to give. The hint of an Arab uprising sent his blood pressure rocketing. It was quite impossible, and if it ever succeeded, it would bring havoc to India. He would never support the ambitions of the Sunni Muslim Sharif of Mecca, with all the problems his further elevation would bring from the Shia Muslim sheikhdoms and emirates of the Persian Gulf maintained by India.

In India, the Viceroy ruled the largest population of Muslims in the world, and the demands made on him by the War Office were already causing considerable difficulty. The Turkish army was almost entirely Muslim – Turks and Arabs recruited from the desert. Sending Indian army troops, many of them Muslims, to fight the Turks in Mesopotamia meant that the British were effectively pitting

Muslim soldier against Muslim soldier. This was further complicated by the allegiance that Indian Muslims gave to the traditional ruler of Ottoman Turkey, the Caliph. For the Viceroy it was therefore beyond comprehension that Britain should invite even more dissension among Muslims by promoting an Arab revolt against the Turkish Muslim regime. India's prominent pan-Islamic institutions, Kudam-I-kaaba and the Central Committee of All India Muslims, were pro-Turkish. On the North-West Frontier, too, an Arab revolt would bring universal condemnation. At present, as British cipher messages from Simla to London pointed out, they had succeeded in securing a precarious peace and quiet throughout these hotspots of civil unrest and religious fervour. For the moment, the Colonial Office was in agreement with the Viceroy that an Arab revolt would not be helpful; London and Delhi were convinced that in any case it would never materialize, and that if it ever did, it would be doomed to failure.

Nevertheless, by the spring of 1915 Lawrence was itching to leave map-making and return to the sphere of action. He had formulated a plan 'to roll up Syria by way of the Hedjaz in the name of the Sherif . . . we can rush right up to Damascus, and biff the French out of all hope of Syria'. To him 'it felt like morning, and the freshness of the world-to-be intoxicated us'. For Gertrude, with her aching heart, it felt very different. Devastated by the death of the man she had loved, worn thin from reorganizing and running the Wounded and Missing Offices, the Gertrude who had arrived in Cairo was a wounded creature. At the turn of the year she reflected on the emotional turmoil that had been 1915, and wrote first to Florence and then to her father a heartbroken lament for Doughty-Wylie. Sometimes she prayed that she would never have to bear another year like the last, and sometimes she found herself thinking that it had all been worth it for those few days of happiness:

I wonder, if I could choose, whether I would not have the past year again, for the wonder it held, and bear the sorrow again. And dearest, not least of all the wonder would be your kindness and love . . . I don't speak of these things now; it's best to keep silence. But you know that they are always in my mind.

Darling, darling Father . . . there never could be words in which to say to you what you have been to me. No one has helped another as you have helped me, and to tell you what your love and sympathy meant is more than I know how to do . . . I still can't write of it; but you know, don't you?

Her recent depression and overwork resulted, towards the end of January, in a brief physical collapse. Most unusually, she complained of exhaustion, and to remedy it she began getting up early in order to ride out into the desert for a morning gallop. It would be the last time she admitted to looking back. Work, as always, was to be her renaissance, and as always she subordinated her feelings to the job in hand. Keep silence as she might, it is more than likely that she talked of her loss and sorrow with Lawrence, who was also in mourning for his beloved brother Will, a pilot who had joined the Royal Flying Corps and been shot down in September just before Gertrude's arrival. Lawrence, perhaps with Hogarth and Woolley, may have helped her to pay her final respects at Doughty-Wylie's grave. In any case, she now got to know and appreciate the fine qualities, as well as the considerable shortcomings, of this unusual colleague. Gertrude and her 'dear boy' became friends. The two were destined to become the Bureau's most famous recruits, pursuing their dreams and realizing them against all odds. Lawrence would be the first to live his legend, and when she heard of his exploits, she would pause over her mounds of paperwork and long for freedom and action again.

As an agency of the British government, the ultimate aim of the Bureau had to be winning the war. They knew that an Arab rebellion against the Turks was their only hope, and they knew that it was a possibility. By 1914 disaffection was common among the Arabian subjects of the Ottoman Empire. Gertrude in her conversations with the Jebel Druze as early as 1905 had noted the beginnings of a movement towards independence. The people of

Najaf and Karbala had turned against the Turks in Mesopotamia, and the Arab Independence Movement had begun in Basra, although this was being engineered by the unscrupulous Sayyid Talib chiefly for his own ends. At the same time, the Bureau knew perfectly well that pan-Arab independence was impossible. Allegiance amongst all tribes in the Middle East? It was hard enough to get two sheikhs to sit down together! Gertrude set out the reasons in one of her crystal-clear information papers:

> Political union is a conception unfamiliar to a society which is still highly coloured by its tribal origins and maintains in its midst so many strongly disruptive elements of tribal organization ... The conditions of nomad life have no analogy with those of the cultivated areas and not infrequently the direct interests of the tribes are incompatible with those of the settled areas ... It is well to dismiss from the outset the anticipation that there exists any individual who could be set up as a head or a figure-head for the Arab provinces as a whole ... The sole individual who might be regarded as a possible figure-head is the King of the Hejaz, but though he might become the representative of religious union among the Arabs, he would never have any real political significance. Mesopotamia being preponderately Shi'ah, his name carries no weight there ... His religious position is an asset; it is probably the only element of union which can be found. But it cannot be converted into political supremacy.

The fact remained that there was only one inducement for the tribes to unite against the Turks and counter their call to anti-British Jihad – the duty to respond to a call to fight for God – and that was the notion of Arab freedom and independence ... or something like it. There was already the half-promise of that outcome, made by Kitchener, which could not be disowned. The issue was further compromised by the Hussain–McMahon correspondence. Every one of the Arab Bureau personnel knew that in their efforts to raise a revolt they would be living a half-lie. For Lawrence and Gertrude particularly, with their respect and love for the Arabs, it was a dilemma that would occupy them for the rest of their lives. Lawrence would inscribe his legend across the Hejaz with the agonizing sense of betraying his Arab friends, and admit it more than once in *The Seven Pillars of Wisdom*:

> The Arab Revolt had begun on false pretences. To gain the Sherif's help our Cabinet had offered, through Sir Henry McMahon, to support the establishment of native governments . . . the Arabs . . . asked me, as a free agent, to endorse the promises of the British Government . . . I could see that if we won the war the promises to the Arabs were dead paper . . . Yet the Arab inspiration was our main tool in winning the Eastern war . . . but, of course, instead of being proud of what we did together, I was continually and bitterly ashamed.

Gertrude had no intention of taking any action of which *she* would be ashamed. She would use her brilliant intellect and her formidable ability to deliver that promise to the Arabs. She would change hearts and minds, she would explain every aspect and ramification of the issue to its best advantage, she would blend British administration with Arab self-determination and pride and do her best to see good government established. She would find a way to establish an Arab state alongside a benevolent British administration and produce genuine political cohesion.

Gertrude and Lawrence were not alone in their wish for self-determination for the Arabs, bolstered and stabilized by British advisers. While the 'think tank' that was the Arab Bureau believed to a man that the multiplicity of races and tribes and beliefs made it impossible to form a single coherent nation with effective political institutions, they were pragmatic men of integrity. They would resist all attempts by India to annex Mesopotamia and to substitute the Raj for the Ottoman Empire. While the British in India had been able to tap into and dominate a universal Indian system based on the rule of the maharajahs, the Middle East allowed of no such easy entry. The Arab system derived from descent from the Prophet and other figures of religious pre-eminence, and it was from this that the leading families drew their moral and temporal power. Their hold over their sources of wealth was sufficient for them to extend patronage to lesser leaders and their tribes. Gertrude's grasp of the situation and her political acumen, her persuasive clarity in presenting issues of enormous complexity, were most valuable additions to the collective determination of the Bureau to find the way ahead.

Clear thinking, though, was somewhat hard to come by. As one commentator points out, there were around twenty separate government and military departments involved at any one time in the formulation of British policy in the Middle East during the First World War: the War Cabinet, the Admiralty and the War Office each had their own point of view; there were the rival India Office and Foreign Office; then the bureaucracies in India, Egypt and the Sudan, which also had plenty to say on the subject. Three major expeditionary forces were stationed in Mesopotamia, Ismailia and Alexandria, and there were naval and political establishments in four other major areas. No wonder there were crossed lines of communication, and that the promises made to the Arabs should differ in content and intention. Indeed, the Anglo-Arab understanding would be beset with misunderstandings, deriving principally from that initial correspondence between McMahon and Sharif Hussain, and the retrogressive Anglo-French agreement rattled off by the intemperate Sykes and France's Georges-Picot in May 1916, of which Gertrude and her then boss would not be informed for a further two years.

There was the sense, in the Bureau, of a secret agenda. They even gave themselves a name: the 'Intrusives'. Lawrence wrote of their subversive intention of infiltrating the corridors of power to 'foster the new Arabic world'. Their first convert was the High Commissioner himself, the efficient, loyal but unimaginative Sir Henry McMahon. Subjected to the steady seepage of Gilbert Clayton's persuasive influence and already disillusioned by the failure of the military in Sinai, with their complacent and inflexible views, he was the first to understand and approve.

The Intrusives held their views on Arab self-determination in opposition to Delhi. They could hardly move ahead with their plans for an Arab uprising without support from India, and they were not going to get it. The Viceroy and his government in India believed vehemently that British rule should be imposed over all Arabs, and that it would succeed as it had succeeded in the Raj. After all, they had managed to run India with only fifty thousand British troops. The view in Cairo was more realistic. As the war dragged on, Britain would have little hope of financing imperialist governments in a new continent. The Bureau played that card for all it was worth, pointing out that influence cost less than control.

In the intense, lengthy debates that Gertrude now joined, they explored the possibility of defeating the Turks by other, 'non-British' methods of warfare: by funding insurrection, cutting railway lines, hijacking supplies, fostering terrorism, leading guerrilla warfare. Gertrude's participation, and her knowledge of Arab methods and customs, helped them crystallize these ideas. She was, after all, probably the only one among them – explorers, desert travellers all – who had actually taken part in a *ghazzu*. It would be possible to assemble an Arab army against the Turks, she said, if the men's pride in the notion of Arab self-determination was strong enough. There would have to be considerable funds made available. Money would be needed for two reasons: because it was impossible to move through a sheikh's territory without payment, and because neither the Bedouin nor the desert villagers would leave their camel herds or homes to fight, unless the family income they would be losing was replaced from another source. The Arab fighter was a mercenary, not a volunteer.

The Indian government remained determined to extend its authority in Arabia and to annex Mesopotamia. The Viceroy made his feelings clear in a stinging letter to the Foreign Office:

> I devoutly hope that this proposed Arab state will fall to pieces, if it is ever created. Nobody could possibly have devised a scheme more detrimental to British interests in the Middle East than this. It simply means misgovernment, chaos and corruption, since there never can be and never has been any consistency or cohesion among the Arab tribes . . . I cannot tell you how detrimental I think this interference and influence from Cairo has been.

With this letter, he engendered opposition to the Bureau from London as well.

By then Gertrude had finished her initial report on the tribes, which was received by General Headquarters with mounting respect for its completeness and detail. Having supplied what she had been asked for, she might now quite respectably have returned to a depressed wartime England, the Wounded and Missing Office and a London full of sad memory. Instead she reflected on the damaging feud between Cairo and Delhi and on the determinations of the Viceroy. Lord Hardinge, the grand and highly decorated former ambassador at St Petersburg and Paris, personally chosen and officially approved adviser to the King on foreign affairs, was none other than Gertrude's old friend from the days of snowy walks in Bucharest, Charles Hardinge. Knowing him as she did, and understanding the problems as she did, was there anything she could do to improve matters between India and Cairo? 'It is essential India and Egypt should keep in the closest touch since they are dealing with two sides of the same problem,' she would write to Captain Hall, Director of Naval Intelligence in London, on 20 February 1916

Gertrude talked to Clayton: might she go to Delhi? The ostensible reason for her journey would be to complete her tribal data with information that she could get only from India's Foreign Department. Comprehending as the Intrusives did that there could be no pan-Arab nation, but unable to broadcast the fact because it had been held out by Kitchener to Hussain as a possibility, her real agenda would be to reassure Hardinge that Cairo understood just as well as Delhi that such a nation could never exist, but that, as the only reason for the Arab tribes to unite against the Turks, the pretence had to be maintained, however uncomfortable. She would put the case for employing new tactics against the Turks, and try to open the minds of those who ran the Raj to the possibilities of Arab guerrilla warfare. She was already, privately, forming a complicated scheme to foster Arab self-determination despite all.

If Hardinge had a close friend in India with him at the time, it was the distinguished *Times* correspondent Sir Valentine Ignatius Chirol, Gertrude's 'dearest Domnul', to whom she now sent a cable.

The man who understood better than anyone how much she had loved Doughty-Wylie, and whose kindly disposition had caused him much anxiety about her, Chirol had mentioned to Hardinge that she had been ill and depressed and was now working in an official capacity in Cairo. Through Domnul's good auspices, Gertrude now received a warm invitation from the Viceroy.

In a letter written at the end of January, Clayton showed his unqualified approval of her plan, and his confidence in her ability to carry out this complex and crucial piece of diplomacy. He hints at the real purpose of her journey:

> . . . the people in India cling so firmly to the wrong end of the stick that they are hard to deal with. Miss Gertrude Bell is leaving here today for India, partly at my instigation and with the full approval of the High Commissioner. She is, as you know, one of the great authorities on Arabia and Syria and has been working under me for some months. She is fully conversant with the Arab questions and entirely agrees with our policy. As she is an intimate friend of the Viceroy and of Sir Valentine Chirol (who carries much weight), and is going to stay with the Viceroy, I think that she may succeed in inducing a better impression of what the Arab question really means.

Hardinge was to write later, in his memoirs:

> It was at this time that I heard that Miss Gertrude Bell, whom I had known many years before as the niece of Sir Frank Lascelles, and who was employed in the Military Intelligence Department at Cairo, was ill and unhappy on account of the death of a very great friend in the operations at Gallipoli. I asked her to come to pay me a visit at Delhi, where she would have an opportunity of studying the Arab information at the disposal of the Foreign Department.

Gertrude now wrote a letter to her father in which she slightly rearranges the order of events. With her anxiety for Hugh's good opinion in all matters, and in view of the magnitude of the politics which she was proposing to manipulate, she wanted to deflect any impression he might get that his daughter was becoming over-ambitious or self-important:

> When I got Lord H's message through Domnul I suggested that it might be a good plan if I, a quite unimportant and unofficial person were to take advantage of the Viceroy's invitation and go out to see what could be done by putting this side of the case before them . . . My chief has approved . . . So I'm going. I feel a little anxious about it, but take refuge in my own extreme obscurity and the general kindness I find everywhere. The pull one has in being so unofficial is that if one doesn't succeed, no one is any the worse. I shall find Domnul at Delhi which will make everything easy, otherwise I don't think I should have the face to set out on a political mission.

Excitement soon overtook anxiety. On 28 January, as she threw her clothes into a case, she dashed off another letter: 'I'm off finally at a moment's notice to catch a troop ship at Suez. I really do the oddest things. I learnt at 3 pm that I could catch it if I left at 6 pm which did not allow much time for thought. I'm charged with much negotiation – and I hope I may be well inspired.'

An officer who was at Cairo at the time was to tell Florence that he never saw anyone mobilize as quickly as Miss Bell.

The new name 'Intrusive' fitted her perfectly. It was what she had been all her life. She had achieved her purposes in the desert by intruding into the Bedouin camps. She had intruded into the corridors of power by directly approaching the statesmen she knew and supplying the information they required. Now she was planning her most important venture so far: she was about to intrude into the crucial determinations of the British Empire.

Five days on a troop ship gave her time to assemble her ideas. There were so many layers, so many duplicities, to the Arab question. The Bureau were going ahead with Kitchener's policy of engineering an Arab revolt, perhaps the only way left that might change the fortunes of the war. They had to maintain a promise of independence amongst the Arabs that would be impossible to fulfil. Even those in the British administration who thought it worth a try to engineer a revolt were not prepared to consider why the tribes should take the risk, nor what prize they might get out of it. What the Arabs wanted, the British could not give, and would not give even if they could. At one and the same time, the Intrusives had to convince the Arabs that independence was possible, whilst accepting the conviction in the corridors of British and Allied power that it was not. The Bureau could not act alone, although Lawrence would force the issue: to support the Arabs, they would need funds, food, guns, ammunition and military back-up.

Gertrude came to reassure the Viceroy that a pan-Arab nation would never come to pass, that Cairo knew it, and that Hardinge could relax his concerns. She would point out that for the last few months the Sharif and his sons had been engaged in trying to patch up tribal feuds on the northern reaches of the Hejaz railway as a preliminary to what she called 'the smallest measure of combination'. She would agree that the Arab Independence Movement was a mirage if considered as a bond of union in the Arab provinces. She would venture to sketch a possible model of administrative union after the defeat of the Turks, depending on the full cooperation of the British and French Allies at the end of the war, and their inclusion of Arab representatives in their deliberations. Hardinge would undoubtedly tell her that an Arab revolt would cause havoc in India, and to this she would have to find a way of saying the unsayable. Only Kitchener, with no such scruples, would express the sentiment in the most brutal of words: 'Better to lose India than lose the war.'

She took stock and wrote up her memoranda, working all morning and again after dinner in the room that, in the ship's liner days, had been used as the nursery. On board she found a chaplain who knew her half-brother Hugo, and agreed to his request to address the soldiers on board, the 23rd and 24th Rifle Corps. 'They get so bored,' she wrote home on 1 February, '. . . I shall love to do anything to amuse them. The adjutant has also asked me to give a conference on Mesopotamia to the officers which I shall like less.'

*

Disembarking at Karachi, she took the sweltering train to Delhi, arriving white with dust. Domnul was there to meet her at the station, and while they laughed and talked her luggage was put into the shiny flagged staff car which was to take them to the viceregal lodge. Just as had been provided for the important guests at the coronation durbar in 1903, her quarters were three cool canvas rooms in a luxurious tent, one of an avenue of tents in the beautiful viceregal gardens. There were a sitting room, bedroom and bathroom, all carpeted and magnificently furnished, set with flowers and a tea table, and plenty of servants. As she sat catching up with Domnul, the tent flap lifted and in came Charles Hardinge on a welcoming visit and to invite her to dinner. She curtsied to him and remembered to call him 'Your Excellency'.

Over the next few days, Gertrude was shoehorned into Hardinge's schedule for several long conversations. She was invited to peruse the files that she had expressed interest in, and embarked on what she saw as her real job. From his memoirs it appears that Hardinge never quite understood that in his seemingly more casual exchanges with Gertrude lay the true purpose of her visit.

In between these taxing confrontations, she was entertained and escorted by Domnul, and attended a colourful meeting of the Legislative Council. One memorable afternoon, with Hardinge and his party, she was shown around the new Delhi by its architect Edwin Lutyens: 'It was very wonderful seeing it with him who had invented it all, and though I knew the plans . . . I didn't realize how gigantic it is. They have blasted away hills and filled up valleys . . . the roads are laid out that lead from it to the four corners of India, and down each vista you see the ruins of some older imperial Delhi.'

She talked with the foreign affairs officials, scrutinized the files that were her overt reason for being in Delhi, and had secret dossiers opened for her. It was arranged that she should go up to Simla for a few days, to meet and talk to the intelligence staff there. Initially wary, they quickly came to appreciate her grasp of the issues, and after her return to the Viceroy's camp they sent an officer after her to discuss how better to coordinate the work between Egypt and India. She devised a scheme for this, and sent it off for Cairo's approval. At the same time they invited her to help edit their journal, the *Gazetteer of Arabia*. She thought her visit had been profitable, she told her father, but did not go into details. 'I have . . . talked about Arabia till I am weary of the very word . . . I think I have pulled things straight a little as between Delhi and Cairo.'

Back in old Delhi, she was an interested guest at a state dinner given for the Maharajah of Mysore and his suite, a man of such noble caste that the Viceroy had to build a six-room house merely to receive him. The Maharajah could not eat or pray, Hardinge told Gertrude, except in rooms of a certain size and arranged in a certain order.

Hardinge was deeply impressed by her. The blunt-spoken, opinionated young woman whose company he had enjoyed in Bucharest had become a skilful diplomat, able at the same time to promulgate a view and remain receptive to a barrage of counter-opinions. He was impressed by her rigour and her grasp of a situation she had been exploring for only six weeks. Her work for Britain was far from over, he felt. He now made a plan that was to change her life – and, indeed, change the shape of the Middle East. He suggested that she should go to the current hotspot of the war, to Basra on the Shatt al Arab, at the convergence of Mesopotamia, Kuwait, Arabia and Persia. Her job would be to act as liaison between Cairo and Delhi intelligence, and at the same time work up a detailed report on the Mesopotamian tribes and their affiliations. At the most difficult moment in the Mesopotamian advance, she should do her best to convince the local Arabs to cooperate with the British.

It would be, he warned her, a most awkward job for a woman – and a woman in an unofficial position – to pull off. She would be working at General Sir Percy Lake's military headquarters. Lake's chief political officer was Sir Percy Cox, Britain's most distinguished official expert on the Middle East, in the employ of the Indian government. If and when Baghdad was taken, Hardinge did not have to tell Gertrude, Cox would move up there and establish an administration. Gertrude knew Sir Percy and Lady Cox from a couple of meetings through their mutual friends, Sir Richmond and

Lady Ritchie. Cox had been the Resident in the Persian Gulf when, on vacation in London, he had lunched with Gertrude and advised her strongly against the dangers of an expedition to Hayyil, especially from one of the ports of the Gulf, which were under his jurisdiction. Would Cox, she wondered, resent the fact that she had so famously made it to Hayyil four years later, albeit approaching from the north-west instead? She told her parents: 'The V. is anxious that I should stay at Basrah and lend a hand with the Intll. Dept. there, but all depends on what their views are and whether I can be of any use. That hangs on me, I feel – as we have often said, all you can do for people is to give them the opportunity of making a place for themselves. The V. has done that amply.'

There would be, of course, as there always had been, considerable opposition on the part of intelligence and military staff to accepting a woman among them as an equal. As Hogarth had told the Cairo office when they asked how she should be treated and to what she could be admitted, '*She'll* settle that!' Hardinge warned her of the probable difficulties in Basra, pointing out that it was up to her whether she could make a permanent job for herself. He then wrote to Cox, advising him to take Gertrude seriously. The words he chose deserve to be inscribed in the annals of chauvinism, and would have brought an ironic smile to Gertrude's lips had she known of them: 'She is a remarkably clever woman,' he wrote '. . . with the brains of a man.' And writing of her later in his memoirs: 'I warned her that being a woman her presence would be resented by Sir Percy, but that it rested with her by her tact and knowledge to make good her position. As I anticipated, there was serious opposition at Busra, but as is well known she, by her ability and her obvious good sense and tact, overcame it.'

When Gertrude has occasionally been described as unfeminine – and nothing could be further from the truth – it has to be remembered what she was up against in these exclusively male official and military circles. Challenged on their own ground by a woman who was so often right, some of the old buffers she had to work alongside fell back on attacking her sexuality. These were often the same patriots and colonialists who, like Lieutenant-

General Sir George MacMunn, the Inspector-General of Communication in Mesopotamia, referred to the Arabs in private as 'the Frocks'. MacMunn would become friendly with Gertrude, then a critic. He was so wide of the mark generally as to refer to the brilliant and wayward T. E. Lawrence as having 'a simple desert mind', incapable of meaning anything more complex by the word 'Arab' than 'the patriarchal tribes of the desert, the sheik in all his imperative wantonness, with his blood horses, his apparelled camels . . . and the like'. To MacMunn, Lawrence was not attuned to 'the difficult situations' arising in Damascus and Baghdad, and Gertrude was a 'little wisp of a human being, said to be a woman', who became far too important for the good of the administration. In her turn, Gertrude cared not a jot whether someone were gay, eccentric or weirdly motivated, whether they had sixty-four wives or worshipped the devil, but simply drew the best from every personal encounter, and passed on. She did not demean herself by describing these petty prejudices in her letters home, for she always had more interesting things to write about, but let slip the occasional brief remark that suggests how very tired she became of dealing with such misogyny and having to prove herself again and again. 'It's not easy here – some day I'll tell you about it,' she wrote to Hugh, 'I think I have got over most of the difficulties and the growing cordiality of my colleagues is a source of unmixed satisfaction.'

And so Gertrude arrived at the intelligence branch of the General Headquarters at Basra without title, job or pay, not knowing whether the department she was visiting would keep her there or instantly send her away. The town, an ugly jumble of mud-walled houses and palm groves punctuated with irrigation channels, had had to expand into a large army base almost overnight. Every room and office was packed with soldiery, and the atmosphere was charged with the excitement of impending action. Sir Percy Cox was away for a few days, but Lady Cox was welcoming and helpful and put Gertrude in their spare bedroom until she could find a home. There was no office for her, though. She was expected to work in the bedroom of a Colonel Beach, who was in charge of military intelligence. This space was shared during office hours with

Beach's pleasant assistant Campbell Thompson, who had also worked with Hogarth and Lawrence at Carchemish.

She began to read the files she was given, engaged an Arab boy, Mikhail, as her servant, and submitted herself for the time being, but with a raised eyebrow, to the rules: her mail would be censored, she was limited as to where she could go and what she could do, and if she visited Arabs in their homes she had to be accompanied by an officer or chaperone. She tried to be as little trouble to Lady Cox as possible, by lunching at the mess and booking a room at GHQ. It was very different from the stimulating life of the Bureau, and she was tempted to return to Cairo where she knew she was wanted. The days passed monotonously: 'I wish I ever knew how long I was going to stay in any place or what I were likely to do next. I fall to asking myself what I am really doing here,' she wrote. '. . . At the end of a week I look back and think I've perhaps put in one useful word . . . And if I went away it wouldn't matter, or if I stay it wouldn't matter.'

Sir Percy returned and she was no longer bored. Immediately he congratulated her, with some amusement, on her successful expedition to Hayyil. He would not underestimate her again. Tall, with silver hair and a broken aquiline nose, he was fifty-one, four years older than Gertrude. A product of Harrow and Sandhurst, he was much respected, an urbane, persuasive and civilized man who shared Delhi's worries about Cairo's fostering of an Arab revolt. He had served in the region as Agent for the government of India for nearly a decade. Whatever his immediate reaction to this woman's arrival at a military base at this particular juncture, he was far too intelligent a man to advertise his prejudices. With Hardinge's letter in mind, he decided to throw Gertrude in at the deep end. He arranged for her to have lunch, on 9 March, with the four generals in charge of the military advance in Mesopotamia. It was Military Intelligence she was supposed to be working for. If she had 'the brains of a man', he might have told Lady Cox over his morning coffee, then let Gertrude explain herself and convince the military of her use and professionalism.

It was a test, almost an audition. The local command were

dumbfounded and pre-programmed with a hatful of prejudices against the curious interloper who had abruptly appeared amongst them for no apparent reason. Now, they were expected to find something for her to do. Generals Lake, Cowper, Money and Offley Shaw of the India Expeditionary Force would have preferred to continue to ignore her. Asked to entertain her to lunch in the officers' mess, they were generally prepared to assess her both as a woman and as a job applicant. The little woman was, they understood, quite a famous traveller. They had spotted her hat bobbing along the pavement as she passed to and from the room where she was working – whatever she was supposed to be doing there. They had heard that she was a friend of that effeminate and insubordinate excuse for an officer, Lawrence. They leaned back in their chairs and laughed at their little jokes about spinsters. An Arab revolt! As if the Frocks could pose a military challenge! It was tacitly understood between them that they would patronize her, be gallant, make a little quiet fun of her views, then continue to ostracize her.

Challenge brought out the best in Gertrude. She was in her element. She entered briskly, they stood up, they all sat down, and before they could marshal their thoughts she began to talk. And she talked them down, while managing to strike, as she always did, the right note. She spoke their military language, she mastered her facts strategically, she spoke with authority, and above all she knew her stuff. She lightened her lecture with humour, and she dominated the table. Then she listened, took the long view, let slip a few names, flattered them just a little, and outlined a few crucial tactical and administrative differences between the Indian Muslims and the Bedouin independents of the Middle East. The generals were surprised, and a little seduced. They called for cigars, and Gertrude fitted a cigarette into her holder. They began to reflect on why this woman had been sent to Cairo and Delhi in the first place, and then, on the express wish of the Viceroy himself, on to Basra.

She did not let the lunch run on too long. She had, she indicated, plenty to do. She smiled warmly, thanked them pleasantly, and swept out, leaving a faint aura of English lavender in the smoke-filled air. After the lunchtime break she went back to work. As she approached her 'office', she saw to her consternation that her files were being taken out of the house and piled into a cart. A mystified Captain Thompson stood on the porch, remonstrating. The servants explained they had orders from headquarters. Gertrude drew herself up for battle. Together, she and Thompson went along to General Staff to find out why they were being ejected. All affability, a staff officer ushered them through the building on to a spacious wooden veranda overlooking the river through a screen of leaves and flowers. Opening on to this airy space, with its wicker chairs and coffee tables, was a wide, cool room with fans whirling over a couple of large desks. The cases along the walls had already been filled with the books she and Thompson had amassed. Servants passed them, loaded with their files, papers and books. This was to be their new office. She wrote home:

> Today I lunched with all the Generals ... and as an immediate result they moved me and my maps and books on to a splendid great verandah with a cool room behind it where I sit and work all day long. My companion here is Captain Campbell Thompson ... very pleasant and obliging and delighted to benefit with me by the change of workshop.

She had passed the test. She was in. She was about to become a salaried Indian military staff officer.

The generals had decided to like Gertrude, and she quickly became a favourite with the military. In the steaming heat of midsummer, when the floods were up and the whole country was under water, Generals Cowper and MacMunn – the latter to become Commander-in-Chief in Mesopotamia in 1919 – took her off for a few days in a river steamer to north of the Shatt al Arab, to visit the country of the Marsh Arabs. The steamer had rudimentary cabins on deck, made of wooden screens; Gertrude took a servant and her camp furniture. They anchored in the Hawr al Hammar lagoon, where the waters of the Tigris and Euphrates join. She was fascinated by the waterscapes and the strange architectural beauty of the reed-built floating houses and *mudhifs*, or village

centres, imposing buildings some fifty feet long and fifteen wide.
This was the ancient waterborne culture that would obsess Wilfred
Thesiger throughout the early 1950s, and that, in his time, Saddam
Hussein would destroy. She wrote to Chirol on 12 June:

> To the south we could see the high edge of the desert and the
> great ridge of mounds which is Ur of the Chaldaes . . . The villages
> are not stationary, but shift as the flood falls and rises. Many are
> built on a floating foundation of reed mats, with floating farm-
> yards, on which the cows stand contentedly anchored, I must
> suppose, to palm trees . . . over each reed hut village rose the
> square mud tower of the shaikh's fort, like squat church towers
> in a land of flooded fen. The light and colour were beyond belief
> – I never saw a landscape of such strange beauty . . . I am burnt
> to a cinder.

They found that Nasiriyeh, which had just been taken by the
British, had turned into an island three miles long. There she met
General Brooking – 'a fiery little man with a broken heart who lost
his only son four months ago in France' – and a Major Hamilton,
who turned out to be a cousin of the Stanleys. Charming interlude though it was, certain things worried her. Whenever the
local telegraph line was cut, her fiery general was dealing out
indiscriminate punishment to friend and foe alike. Her letter to
Chirol continued:

> I need not say that it is called strafing. The amount of damage
> you can do by shelling from the water is almost negligible, and it
> is always followed by reprisals which get more and more people
> into trouble – an ever widening circle of unrest and hostility.
> That's what I think and I made bold to tell him so. 'You've been
> living with the Politicals', he said, half a snort and half a twinkle.
> I said why yes, I had lived with Politicals all my life.

Back in Basra, there were more problems. Heavy labour
demanded large numbers of men, and these were being levied by
the military without consideration for the families, left without a
man to grow the crops or provide a living. She would write to

Hardinge of their predicament, she decided. Not only did these things trouble her conscience, but how would the future administration in Mesopotamia win the trust and cooperation of the Arabs after such breaches of human consideration?

> There are many things about which I don't feel very happy, first and foremost I think is the labour difficulty. There is a very fine line – I sometimes think an invisible line – between what we are doing here and what the Germans did in Belgium. I would rather import labour for war purposes than impress it, much as I dislike importing Indians. It's not easy, Domnul, you don't know how difficult my job is here.

So far the Mesopotamian Campaign had been an unqualified success, but now there was a serious reverse. After the British-led force under General Nixon had routed the Turks from Nasiriyeh, Major-General Charles Townshend and the 6th Division of some ten thousand troops went on to capture the fortress city of Kut. There they wished to regroup and wait for reinforcements, but Nixon – receiving in his turn orders from India – directed them on. From a flotilla of river steamers they launched themselves into battle at Ctesiphon, whose massive arch, photographed many times by Gertrude, could almost be seen from Baghdad. There twenty thousand Turkish troops were well dug in and lying in wait. The advance ceased, and the casualties were soon so heavy that Townshend and his men had to beat a retreat to Kut. It was the beginning of December. Surrounded by the Turks, the unfortunate survivors of the 6th Division were destined to endure the longest siege in British history. Week after week, month after month, and despite three major relief attempts, the soldiers and citizens remained imprisoned within the walls and were soon reduced to eating cats and dogs, then rats. 'Nothing happens and nothing seems likely to happen at Kut – it's a desperate business, Heaven knows how it will end,' she wrote in April.

Mid-April brought a visit to Basra from Lawrence and Aubrey Herbert on mysterious business from the Cairo Intelligence Bureau. They went straight to Gertrude's office and sat on her veranda, catching up. Because of their strange commission and unmilitary appearance, they were ostracized by the officers' mess. Lawrence and Herbert had been authorised to offer up to £2 million to buy off the Turks and relieve the garrison at Kut. As a last resort they would discuss an exchange of wounded, and appeal for clemency for Kut's Arab population. It was a demeaning exercise, but it was the last effort to stave off an appalling British disaster. Lawrence later described the vehement objections to his mission expressed by the British in Basra, and how two generals had collared him to tell him it was a dishonourable move.

Lawrence and Herbert sat at table with Gertrude, and it was with Gertrude that they talked. For her, it was an immense relief to be exposed once more to the quick intelligence of Cairo's brightest: she could not help comparing them with the dull old generals who were her usual lunch companions: This week has been greatly enlivened by the appearance of Mr Lawrence, sent out as liaison officer from Egypt. We have had great talks and made vast schemes for the government of the universe. He goes up river to-morrow, where the battle is raging these days.'

It was, in fact, too late, and the bribe was humiliatingly rejected by the Turkish commander, Halil Pasha. On 29 April, after 147 days, the Turks finally entered Kut and the soldiers were taken prisoner. Four thousand British troops, weakened by starvation, would subsequently die as a result of the hard labour and forced marches. The Arab citizens, although hapless victims of the situation, were appallingly treated by the victorious, an outcome that understandably decided many sections of Arab society against throwing in their lot with the British. Lawrence and Herbert returned to Basra. They were now even more *personae non gratae*, but Lawrence remained for several days more in Gertrude's company. Full of concern for the reverses in Mesopotamia, Hugh wrote informing her of the criticism prevalent in England that the authorities in Basra and Delhi were merely 'muddling through'. She responded to this with passion, and with an over-arching perspective and an absence of partisanship to be expected of the seasoned stateswoman she was becoming:

. . . we rushed into the business with our usual disregard for a comprehensive political scheme. We treated Mesopotamia as if it were an isolated unit, instead of which it is part of Arabia, its politics indissolubly connected with the great and far reaching Arab question, which presents indeed, different facets as you regard it from different aspects, and is yet always and always one and the same indivisible block. The co-ordinating of Arabian politics and the creation of an Arabia policy should have been done at home . . . there was no one to do it, no one who had ever thought of it, and it was left to our people in Egypt to thrash out, in the face of strenuous opposition from India and London, some sort of wide scheme, which will, I am persuaded, ultimately form the basis of our relations with the Arabs . . . Well, that is enough of politics. But when people talk of our muddling through it throws me into a passion. Muddle through! Why yes so we do – wading through blood and tears that need never have been shed.

She completed her job of collecting tribal information from the Mesopotamian side. She had come to a position of mutual respect with Sir Percy Cox, who wrote of this phase of events:

The military authorities decided that the particular service for which she had been deputed to Basrah had been completed as far as it could be for the time being, and finding a member of her sex a little difficult to place as a permanency in a military GHQ in the field, they offered her services to me in my capacity of Chief Political Officer – services which were gladly accepted.

Gertrude had proved herself to him twice over, in the matter of Hayyil and of the generals, and now he began to find her indispensible. Not only was she indefatigable, but she saved him endless time by screening and entertaining his many sheikhly visitors from all over Mesopotamia. She filtered out the unimportant ones, and sent the rest on to Cox's office with a concise note stating the name of their tribe, where they came from and what they wanted. He gave her official status as assistant political officer, and the job title of Oriental Secretary. She wrote casually to Chirol of this promotion, but her pleasure in it is evident:

> It never occurred to me to tell you that I am an A.P.O. [Assistant Political Officer] because it's quite unimportant ... Sir Percy gave me the title because it is so much more convenient to have a definite official position – though I think at the time his chief motive was to give himself a much firmer hold over me! It would have been quite impossible to be a nondescript with no definite standing. As it is I'm an officer in I.E.F.D [Indian Expeditionary Force D] and have the right to be lodged and fed, and looked after when I'm ill. I'm officially attached ... And do you know I earn a handsome salary – Rs 300 a month – which is a great deal more than I ever expected to earn in the course of my life and times.

She worked not only for Cox, but for his workaholic deputy, Captain, later Lieutenant-Colonel, Sir Arnold Wilson, KCIE, one of the most formidable and eccentric of the Middle East empire-builders. Massively built and with a thick black moustache, he cultivated a lifestyle of Spartan self-denial. In his travels he liked to sleep on the ground without bed or tent, and read the Bible daily. He could ride across country at a hundred miles a day, and on arriving at a river preferred to swim across rather than take the bridge. On one voyage home to England, he saved himself the fare by taking a job as a ship's stoker, shovelling coal for sixteen hours a day. Disembarking at Marseilles, he bought a bicycle and rode the last nine hundred miles to his family home in Worcester. At first, Gertrude and he got on very well: 'He is ... a most remarkable creature, 34, brilliant abilities, a combined mental and physical power which is extremely rare. I'm devoted to him – he is the best of colleagues and he ought to make a wonderful career. I don't think I've ever come across anyone of more extraordinary force.' But his imperialist, dogmatic views were bound to come between them in due course.

Early in 1916, the War Office finally took on the overall control of operations in Mesopotamia, and poured in troops, aeroplanes, guns and transport. It was all too late to prevent the agonies of Kut, but it impressed the next important visitor to Basra, in November, the Amir and Hakim of southern Nejd, Abdul Aziz ibn Saud. He came on what was almost a royal visit, and inspected the modern scientific world of warfare that Basra had become. If there was any Arab leader whom Gertrude had wished to meet and failed to, it was this charismatic and formidable warrior, hereditary imam, judge, ruler and governor combined. He was the uncompromising leader of the fundamentalist Wahabi sect, dedicated to returning to the original Islam of the Prophet under the strict guidance of Sharia law. When he was fifteen, Rashid power had driven the Saud tribe into exile and occupied Riyadh, their capital. At twenty-two, with eighty camel riders supplied by his ally against the Rashid, the Sheikh of Kuwait, Ibn Saud fell on Riyadh at night, and with only eight hand-picked followers scaled the palace walls, stabbed the sleeping Rashid, and, as dawn turned the sky pink, threw open the city gates.

For the next decade, year after year, Ibn Saud made it his business to recover the territories of his fathers. In 1913 he seized the Turkish province of Hasa, formerly an appendage of Riyadh, put the Ottoman garrisons to flight and established himself on the banks of the Persian Gulf. Ibn Saud had become a friend of the British Political Agent at Kuwait, Captain William Shakespear, who had made repeated attempts to convince the British government of the ever-increasing importance of this desert prince. Shortly after the declaration of the First World War, Shakespear went into Nejd and joined the black tents of Ibn Saud, on the march north to repel the latest Rashid attack, backed by the Turks. In that battle Shakespear, though a non-combatant, was killed. Shortly afterwards, Ibn Saud met with Sir Percy Cox, then Chief Political Agent of the Persian Gulf, and concluded a formal agreement with Britain, together with the sheikhs of the Gulf cities of Kuwait and Muhammarah.

In the course of a few hours, on 27 November 1916, the future founder of Saudi Arabia was welcomed by Cox and Gertrude, then trailed glory through Basra as he was shown all the latest machinery of offence. A magnificent figure with his glittering eyes and his hair plaited and finished with hooks, he toyed with his worry beads as he watched the firing of high explosives at an improvised trench and the launching of anti-aircraft shells. Speaking seldom, he travelled by railway for the first time and was driven at speed in a car to nearby Shaaibah to inspect British infantry and Indian cavalry. He witnessed a battery of artillery in action, and watched a plane go through its paces in the sky. In a base hospital, Gertrude put her hand into the X-ray machine; Ibn Saud followed suit and saw revealed the bones of his own hand. He is definitively portrayed by Gertrude in her essay for Lawrence's *Arab Bulletin* — the gazette of secret information circulated to British government offices and edited in Cairo.

Ibn Saud is barely forty, though he looks some years older. He is a man of splendid physique, standing well over six feet, and carrying himself with the air of one accustomed to command. Though he is more massively built than the typical nomad Sheikh, he has the characteristics of the well bred Arab, the strongly marked aquiline profile, full-fleshed nostrils, prominent lips and long narrow chin, accentuated by a pointed beard. His hands are fine with slender fingers, a trait almost universal among the tribes of pure Arab blood, and in spite of his great height and breadth of shoulder he conveys the impression, common enough in the desert, of an indefinable lassitude, not individual but racial, the secular weariness of an ancient and self-contained people, which has made heavy drafts on its vital forces . . . His deliberate movements, his slow sweet smile and the contemplative glance of his heavy-lidded eyes, though they add to his dignity and charm, do not accord with the Western conception of a vigorous personality. Nevertheless reports credit him with powers of endurance rare even in hard-bitten Arabia. Among men bred in the camel saddle he is said to have few rivals as a tireless rider . . . He is of proved daring, and he combines with his qualities as a soldier that grasp of statecraft which is yet more highly prized by the tribesmen.

The impression of Gertrude on Ibn Saud was somewhat more equivocal. Cox had already spoken to him of her pre-war expedition to Hayyil, but he had never before come into contact with a European woman. He was reliably reported, however, to have married and then divorced some sixty-five times, passing his women on after a night or two to his sheikhs and followers. That he should be expected to meet this blatantly unveiled woman on anything like an equal footing was, to him, an insult to his manly dignity, and he was dumbfounded by the way important men stood back to let her go first. Furthermore, not only did Gertrude greet Ibn Saud on the friendliest terms, she was deputed to show him around. Cox was to write in diplomatic tone:

> . . . the phenomenon of one of the gentler sex occupying an official position with a British Expeditionary Force was one quite outside his Bedouin comprehension; nevertheless when the time came he met Miss Bell with complete frankness and sangfroid as if he had been associated with European ladies all his life.

Ibn Saud, too, might have been diplomatic at the time, but later he expressed his real feelings. The political officer Harry St John Philby, no friend of Gertrude's at the time of writing, was to state that 'many a Najdi audience has been tickled to uproarious merriment by his mimicking of her shrill voice and feminine patter: "Abdul Aziz [Ibn Saud]! Abdul Aziz! Look at this, and what do you think of that?" and so forth.' Ibn Saud was, perhaps, the only Arab sheikh who mocked her; revealingly, he was also perhaps the only important sheikh she had met on Western rather than Bedouin terms. Had she come to his tent in the desert, in evening dress, and presented him with binoculars and guns, had she sat on his carpets with him and spoken fluently to him in terms of his own culture, poetry, and the politics of the desert, she would have impressed him as she had so easily impressed Yahya Beg, Muhammad Abu Tayyi, Fahad Beg, and the rest.

The visit over, Gertrude worked on through appalling weather conditions, not knowing if it was preferable in winter, with all roads turned to mud and planks bridging the open drains, or in summer when, to a Yorkshirewoman born and bred, the heat was unbearable: 'Last night I woke at 1 am to find the temperature still over 100 and myself lying in a pool. My silk nightgown goes into the bath with me in the morning, is wrung out and needs no more bother . . . one's bath water, drawn from a tank on the roof, is never under 100 . . . but it doesn't steam – the air's hotter,' she wrote to her parents. With the constant washing, her clothes were dropping to pieces. She was having to get up at 5.30 or 6 in the morning to mend them – something her maid Marie had always done for her in England. Her desperate requests for clothes were sometimes fruitful:

> One wears almost nothing, fortunately, still it's all the more essential that that nothing should not be in holes . . . To think that I was once clean and tidy! . . . Thank you so much – I have a lace evening gown, a white crepe gown, a stripy blue muslin gown, two shirts and a stripy silk gown, all most suitable . . . and the box and umbrella have come too!

But she was often disappointed, as a letter of 20 January 1917 reveals:

> A box has just arrived from Marte – it ought to have contained a black satin gown, but it has been opened and the gown has been abstracted. Isn't it infuriating? All that was left was a small cardboard box inside, containing the little black satin coat Marte sent with the gown, some net, and a gold flower . . .

She missed having a family of her own even more, now, in the almost exclusively male world that she occupied. She felt the lack of a woman friend, but almost the only women she met were Lady Cox, her boss's wife, the occasional temporary teacher or missionary, and 'the notable Miss Jones' – the likeable but very busy matron of the officers' hospital and rest house down river. Gertrude was her grateful patient when, exhausted by temperatures of around 107 degrees combined with Basra's lack of good food, she went down with a bad bout of jaundice in September that year. She wrote to Florence: 'Do you know I've never been so ill as this before. I hadn't an idea what it was like to feel so deadly weak that you couldn't move your body much nor hold your mind at all.'

After her convalescence, she returned to writing her reports. She told Hugh and Florence:

> The amount I've written during the last year is appalling. Some of it is botched together out of reports, some spun out of my own mind and former knowledge, and some an attempt to fix the far corners of the new world we are discovering now, and some dry as dust tribal analyses, dull, but perhaps more useful than most things . . . But it's sometimes exasperating to be obliged to sit in an office when I long to be out in the desert, seeing the places I hear of, and finding out about them for myself . . . One can't do much more than sit and record if one is of my sex, devil take it.

'Botched together . . . dry as dust . . . dull' – never was Gertrude more disingenuous. She knew that her essays were beginning to be celebrated by the high commands in India, Egypt, the Sudan and London for their lively and often humorous clarifications of political situations and for their crisply entertaining character portraits. In another letter home she admits as much: 'Happy to tell you that I hear my utterances receive a truly preposterous attention in London.'

Some reports she wrote as part of her duty to the Arab Bureau, or as contributions to the *Arab Bulletin*. They added to her fame as perhaps the most prominent British personality in the Middle East. Some of her other essays, collected together as *The Arab of Mesopotamia*, were produced as an instruction manual for British officers on arrival in Basra. Forbiddingly entitled *The Pax Britannica in the Occupied Territories of Mesopotamia; or The Basis of Government in Turkish Arabia*, these pieces would turn out to be delightfully easy to enjoy while telling the neophyte officer all he needed to know. Turning to an essay on 'Star Worshippers', he would learn that the tenets of this strange sect entailed living next to running water, practising polygamy and believing that the world is actually a great egg; also, that they had invented a book which could be read simultaneously by two priests sitting on either side of a stream. 'One wonders how

this curious growth will fare in the new soil of British administration,'
Gertrude remarked.

'Officialdom,' wrote Sir Kinahan Cornwallis, director of the
Arab Bureau from 1916, 'could never spoil the freshness and
vividness of her style or the terseness of her descriptions. Throughout them all can be seen the breadth of her knowledge, and her
sympathy and understanding for the people whom she loved so
well.' Tired politicians and hard-pressed political officers working
through their in-trays would have turned with relief and anticipation
to the polished résumés signed 'G.L.B.'. She was in a class of her
own when describing the government of Turkish Arabia as a fiction:
'No country which turned to the eye of the world an appearance of
established rule and centralized Government was, to a greater extent
than the Ottoman Empire, a land of make-believe'; or when detailing
the intricacies of the internal politics of Muscat — 'Sultan Seyyid
Feisal ibn Turki saw in the suppression of the arms trade by the British
Government a distinct advantage to himself, since his rebellious subjects
became unable to furnish themselves with weapons to use against him'
— or when explaining the tribal fights of the Shamiyah, which meant
'the taking of an enemy by a surprise raid . . . the casualties may be in
some cases more, in others rather less, than those of a football match'.

Gertrude's letters to Florence, Hugh and the rest of her family
were as beautifully written, more personal but sometimes as far-
reaching. Writing home two or three times a week was a sacred
commitment, a substitute for spending time with them, subsequently almost an apology for hardly ever returning home. It
became ever more difficult to envisage going back for a visit, what
with the laborious journey and the length of time that she would
have to be away, not to speak of all that she would be missing in
this eastern sphere of the war.

Keeping in touch with the people she loved, most of all her
father, was an escape from the arid, lonely, masculine world of
work and war. The letters centred her, reminding her of who she
was and where she came from. She could always interest herself in
her father's affairs, whether political or commercial, but it sometimes occurred to her that the interests of Florence, Elsa and Molly,

even of Maurice and Hugo, were on a very different scale to her own. We know that she often massaged or omitted the facts, to spare them anxiety, and took trouble not to write too much of Mesopotamian affairs for fear of boring them. Just as when she had worked in the Wounded and Missing Office, Gertrude occasionally had to absorb accounts of atrocities and massacres, without anyone to confide in or distract her from the nightmare scenarios that these events opened out before her. She felt the lack of a husband and family more than ever now. At home Molly, and Elsa to a lesser extent, with their growing families and urgent domestic concerns, smiled over her importance and called her, however affectionately, 'the Great Gertrude'. Meanwhile she wrote back of their preoccupations as if they were as important to her as the affairs of the nation. Only to Chirol did she come close to admitting the truth:

The only interesting letters I have – except yours – are from the Arab Bureau in Egypt. I write to them weekly and they keep me pretty well posted as to Hejaz and Syrian matters ... My family write nothing except about their own affairs, which I like to hear too, bless them.'

Cox and Gertrude, now working hand in hand and alongside Wilson and other staff, had done much to establish order in the Basra *vilayet*, pursuing beneficial policies in relation to agriculture, finance, law and education. They brought local sheikhs into the process of government, and paid them to rule their traditional districts. Unfortunately, this first foray into Arab self-determination was dissipated in corruption and mismanagement. British administrators had to be sent to work alongside the sheikhs in the remoter districts.

The winter campaign under General Maude saw the recovery of Kut and the advance on Baghdad, which was occupied by British forces on 11 March 1917. The centre of gravity moved north, and Gertrude awaited Sir Percy's summons to join him in Baghdad to set up a nucleus for his new Secretariat. She wrote home:

I had a letter from Sir Percy to-day, from the Front, full of exultation and confidence ... It's the first big success of the war,

and I think it is going to have varied and remarkable consequences. We shall, I trust, make it a great centre of Arab civilization, a prosperity; that will be my job partly, I hope, and I never
lose sight of it . . . I can't tell you how wonderful it is to be in at
the birth, so to speak, of a new administration.

The call came, and she went up river on a crowded steamer:
nine days in the humid heat with a couple of nurses and six hundred
troops. At Rounton, the Bells received a two-word telegram:
'Address Bagdad'.

There were many such as Arnold Wilson who remained convinced that only complete British control would secure the oil
supply for the British navy and the Empire. Equally there were
people like Hardinge, who believed that any form of Arab partnership would lead to chaos in the Middle East and deprive the Empire
of its links between Europe, India and the rest of the East. They
were to be proved wrong. By means of the blending of British
administration with Arab self-determination and pride, good
government was about to be established. Stability would go on very
nearly unbroken until 1920, the oil would continue to flow and a
benevolent British interest would be maintained. The sensitivity to
Middle Eastern minds and attitudes that Gertrude brought to the
administration would enable her to achieve what nobody believed
was possible. This was the great task that lay ahead of her in
Baghdad.

12

GOVERNMENT THROUGH GERTRUDE

Gertrude had anticipated her arrival in Baghdad for weeks, and longed to live once more in that great city where she had many friends already. With relief she disembarked from the overloaded boat and made her way through the steamy, crowded quayside to where Cox's car was waiting. At the office she received a warm welcome from her chief and his handful of staff. She did not know where she would be spending the night, but after twelve months in a single room in the Basra headquarters she hoped for something more spacious, and cooler. She was reassured to hear that a house had been allotted to her, and set off in the car again, address in hand.

The car stopped in a dirty, noisy little bazaar. A sycophantic landlord appeared and ushered her into a stifling box of a house without running water or a stick of furniture. She had brought a few pieces from Basra, but they were not yet unloaded; her servant Mikhail had remained with the boat to collect them. However, experienced voyager as she was, she had not parted with her old canvas bed and bath, which she now set up in the grubby rooms: 'I unpacked my box which had been dropped into the Tigris, and hung out all the things to dry on the railings . . . It was breathlessly hot. I hadn't so much as a chair to put things on, and when I wanted water for washing I had to open my front door and call in the help of the bazaar.'

She dined with Sir Percy, then returned to the house to sleep. Later, she was awakened by a hammering on the door. It was Mikhail, arriving with the rest of her luggage. Morning came with all the heat and noise of inner-city Baghdad: 'I confess that after having done my hair and breakfasted on the floor I felt a little discouraged.'

She would not bother Cox: she was here on exactly the same terms as the rest of his staff, and he had more important things to do. She put on her straw hat and set out on foot to find a better house, making her way down to the cooler, tree-shaded spaces by the river, near to the political office in the pre-war Austrian embassy. She came almost at once to an old wall surrounding a large overgrown garden with cool trees and a profusion of pink roses. Peering through the iron gate she saw a stone water-tank at the end of a short drive, and beyond it, not a house, but three run-down summer-houses, with birds perched on the roofs. Part of the property was an extensive date-palm garden – a place where it would be cool to walk in the evening.

Sometimes the places where we live for important parts of our lives seem to find us, and so it was with Gertrude in April 1917. Here was the lovely spot where she would live for the rest of her life. Making enquiries of the neighbours, she discovered that the garden belonged to a wealthy proprietor she knew and liked, Musa Chalabi. A visit to his home resolved all that needed to be resolved, and the next ten days were spent in rapid alterations and repairs. In early May she installed herself in the first of the summer-houses, and then moved from one to the other as a modern kitchen and bathroom were added. She had everything painted white, and employed a gardener, a cook and an old man she knew and trusted, Shamao, to run the household. Sun-blinds were put up at all the windows, plants and wicker furniture installed on the deep wooden verandas. She put up her two writing desks and filled all her vases with flowers. The furthest building she turned over to accommo-dation for the servants, and before long there were women hanging out washing while a baby played in the grass at their feet. She had at last a home and a garden of her own. She planted beds of cottage flowers – iris, verbena, chrysanthemums – violets in pots, yellow hollyhock seeds sent from Darlington, and cabbages. A short while later she was able to boast that she had managed to get daffodils into flower – the first ever seen in Mesopotamia. She wrote home on the 17th:

> Oh my dearest ones it's so wonderful here – I can't tell you how much I'm loving it . . . I wonder what inheritance from Cumbrian farmers can have developed unexpectedly into so compelling an at-home-ness with the East?
>
> I have grown to love this land, its sights and its sounds. I never weary of the East, just as I never feel it to be alien. I cannot feel exiled here; it is a second native country. If my family were not in England I should have no wish to return.

She scarcely missed a day's work. She was needed as never before, but she had to prove herself all over again. In his sketch of this period when government was being established in Iraq, Cox wrote:

> When I told [the GOC] that some of my office staff were coming up from Basra, including Miss Bell, [he] expressed considerable misgiving at the news, as he feared her arrival might form an inconvenient precedent for appeals from other ladies, but I reminded him that her services had been specifically offered to me by his predecessor as an ordinary member of my Secretariat; that I regarded and treated her no differently from any male officer of my Staff, and that her particular abilities could be very useful to me at the present moment. In due course she arrived and was not long in establishing happy personal relations with Sir Stanley Maude.

The forging of these 'happy personal relations' described by Cox, the consummate diplomat, were no doubt much to Gertrude's credit, but she made her real feelings clear to her family after Maude's death from cholera a few months later, when Hugh had written to ask her what she had thought of him. It was Maude's brilliant military campaign that had won Baghdad and almost effaced the tragedy of Kut from the public mind, but he was a man of limited perspective and had made the work of the administrators more difficult. The objection to the presence of a woman in a man's world, even in the rare instance of that woman being supremely well qualified to be there, had several times in her life been couched in terms of a concession to one precipitating some 'monstrous regiment' to follow. This was bound to exasperate Gertrude. Her brief portrait of Maude is scathing and, despite his recent death, unmitigated in its contempt, not so much for the man, but for the type of military mind she had so often had to fight as a woman and as an administrator:

> General Maude was essentially a soldier; he had no knowledge of statecraft and regarded it as totally unnecessary ... He was determined beyond the verge of obstinacy, a narrow intelligence confined to one channel and the more forcible for its concentration. I knew him very little ... If he had lived there would have been a desperate tussle when administrative problems began to become more important than military. The time was near when questions which he had insisted on regarding as purely administrative and therefore of no immediate concern ... could no longer be neglected or treated on purely military lines.

The army wins the territory, and the administration takes over: but in Mesopotamia the struggle to install conditions conducive to peace and eventual prosperity would prove as daunting as the battlefront itself. The prospect for the nucleus British administration in Baghdad was dismal, the future opaque. Roughly half of Mesopotamia was under precarious British control, but the Turks were fighting on in the north. Arabs spoke a common language but were not a common people. Mesopotamia was not a country but a province of a derelict empire. Iraq was not a nation. The very names caused confusion. Mesopotamia, Greek for 'between the rivers', was the historic and archaeological term used in the West for what the Arabs called 'Al Iraq', 'the Iraq'. The Arab term originally referred to the area of the Basra *vilayet* and Kuwait in the south, but when they took over the British used it to describe the territory of the three *vilayets* Basra, Baghdad and Mosul. In 1932, at full independence, the country was officially recognized as 'Iraq'.

In 1917, practical difficulties confronted the British in all directions. Lack of food was the most urgent, for many of the irrigation systems necessary to agriculture had crumbled from neglect, and much of what was left had been destroyed in the war. The two opposing armies had consumed any food surplus, and as the Turks had withdrawn to the north, they had followed what was virtually a scorched-earth policy, taking any valuables and destroying any crops they could not consume. Even the climate had done its worst, and the famously fertile Euphrates basin was facing its third growing season without rain. The population was becoming hungry, and disease was spreading. In the cities the sanitation system had collapsed, and the one hospital in Baghdad – formerly the British Residency – was discovered to be in an indescribable condition, with a few horribly wounded men struggling to maintain life. In the countryside, the farmers were eating their seed grain instead of planting it, for anything they grew had been confiscated, time and again. No one knew who would now own the land, or who would have to pay what taxes. Starvation, disaffection and lawlessness could well be just around the corner. If the administration could not pull the country together at once and get it running, if Basra and Baghdad collapsed into anarchy, the army of some hundred thousand troops would not be able to hold the country down. Administrative problems were compounded by lack of funds from His Majesty's Government and an absence of military cooperation, until the welcome arrival of Maude's more amenable successor, Lieutenant-General Sir William Marshall.

In spite of these massive difficulties, there was a noble determination on the part of Cox and his staff to get it right. They were dedicated to instituting benevolent, effective government and to serving honourably the peoples of the Basra and Baghdad *vilayets* with their multitudinous identities and problems. It was the idea above all that inspired and excited Gertrude:

Nowhere in the war-shattered universe can we begin more speedily to make good the immense losses sustained by humanity . . . It's an immense opportunity, just at this time when the atmosphere is so emotional; one catches hold of people as one will never do again, and establishes relations which won't dissolve. It is not for my own sake, but because it greases the wheels of administration – it really does, and I want to watch it all very carefully almost from day to day, so as to be able to take what I hope may be . . . a decisive hand in [the] final disposition. I shall be able to do that, I shall indeed, with the knowledge I'm gaining. It's so intimate. They are beyond words outgoing to me. What does anything else matter when the job is such a big one? There never was anything quite like this before, you must understand that – it's amazing.

It's the making of a new world.

After the British defeat at Kut, the army, now reinforced and led by General Maude, had begun again to roll back the Turkish mantle. Like the roof being stripped from a derelict house, it exposed to the daylight the rotten timbers, rat-infested rooms and insanitary corners of a moribund empire. For some five hundred years the Turks had exploited Mesopotamia: their officials with sinecures in the Baghdad offices had maintained their comfortable lifestyles by disguising the reality under a sea of paper. The good government that it purported to document was nothing more than make-believe. Corruption was condoned throughout the Empire; most of its operatives, either unsalaried or paid a pittance, lived on bribery and extortion. The building and maintenance of municipal and provincial public works, roads and bridges, sanitation and lighting, houses, hospitals, schools – all had been recorded on paper, but had never been carried out. Infant mortality was as high as ever.

Turkish bureaucracy had imposed its dark empire over the length and breadth of Mesopotamia by a policy of division and dominance. The language of law, business, administration and education was Turkish, not Arabic. The peasant farmers were forced to pay rent in lieu of tax to the new urban owners of their land, selected by the Turks, and very little of that rent found its way back into improvement of their farms. The traders in the towns had had to buy a permit every time they made a sale or a purchase, imported or exported. The chosen few amassed wealth from their privileged positions. A court case was only won in Baghdad by payment to the judge, who might have no qualifications for his position. An appeal against a legal decision could be lost for years, even decades, in the Kafkaesque courts of Constantinople, after which it would be referred back again to Baghdad.

As the Turks retreated they destroyed their paperwork, and their beneficiaries went with them, taking their records and all trace of a system. They left behind only the animosity that they had fostered for so long. In the desert, particularly on either side of the Euphrates valley where they had partitioned the lands of some fifty tribes, they had pitted sheikh against sheikh and built on the destruction of native elements of order.

The vacuum left by the departing power was complicated by the fact that the Turks were Sunni Muslims. They had given preference in almost every aspect of national life to Sunni personnel and culture and had taken into their own hands the immensely wealthy Muhammadan charitable trusts, or *Auqaf*, in the form of property dedicated in perpetuity to pious purposes. Ignoring the intended beneficiaries, the Turks devoted the income accruing from this to the building of new Sunni mosques and to the salaries of those employed in them. The object of the exercise was to remit as much money as possible to Constantinople. One effect of this policy was that Shia mosques and properties were allowed to fall into ruin. The historic enmities between the majority Shia population and the Sunnis were thus deepened.

The British administration would only be able to establish a government of any kind if it won a largely united backing. In a land where there were perhaps more races, creeds and allegiances than anywhere else in the world, it had to identify and engage every prominent man capable of persuading his adherents to cooperate. It had to persuade them of the benefits of the new economic initiatives and regulations. Disparate in character and education, traditionally susceptible to corruption of every sort, jealous of their position to the point of enmity with every neighbour, these leaders came to the Secretariat from ragged tents as well as Baghdad palaces. They had held sway under the Ottoman Empire by reason of wealth or the number of their followers, by land ownership imposed by the Turks or won in tribal wars, or by inheritance and descent from the Prophet. From the most promising of these, Cox and Gertrude hoped against all the odds to find Iraq's future administrators and political leaders.

During the spring and summer of 1917, the British Indian army was fully occupied in consolidating its position round Baghdad, which left no detachments for outlying areas. The Turks were dispensing virulent anti-British propaganda, as well as a flow of money to potential dissidents. It was hard for the tribes to believe that the new occupiers of Baghdad would hold on to their conquest, or that the Turks would not eventually return, ready to exact a horrible revenge on all who had placed their trust in the British. The first overtures of the sheikhs and other Mesopotamian notables were made in the spirit of insurance in case the British should stay. The single incentive for joining forces with the British remained the Arab prize of self-determination, so far the vaguest of concepts. To the Shia *mujtahids*, the religious representatives of the biggest proportion of the population, it meant a theocratic state under Sharia law; to the Sunnis and free-thinkers of Baghdad it meant an independent Arab state under an amir; to the tribes in the deserts and mountains it meant no government at all.

It was shortage of food that brought more tribes over to the administration, now in command of central transport and distribution. They were warmly welcomed by Gertrude, whatever their political or personal past: 'Today there rolled in a whole band of sheikhs from the Euphrates. Most of them I hadn't seen before, though I know them all well by name and by exploit; hard-bitten rogues – but so attractive! – It's all to the good, especially if we can get them to sowing wheat and barley this winter,' she wrote on 2 February.

Once face to face with Gertrude and then Cox, they had to be convinced that British administration would be benevolent, that their rights would be maintained, and that the British were prepared for the huge expenditure in both effort and money that would secure their various ways of life. They were welcomed, listened to, their situations comprehended. Word spread, and enormous numbers now descended on Cox's new Secretariat to lodge their separate interests – nomadic tribesmen, traders, farmers, landowners, owners of wells and watercourses, importers of tobacco and other goods, exporters, businessmen, religious representatives, figureheads of every kind had to be persuaded to support the new regime. Each one had to be met with proper traditional courtesies, such as the giving of small presents, and lengthy discussions had to take place. If they did not make the first approach, they had to be invited, and the most distinguished, particularly the religious leaders, had to be visited.

Who was there, other than Gertrude, who would recognize and be recognized by so many of them, who could identify their status and interests, who could interview them in their own language or dialect, who could assess and reassure them?

Perhaps no other Westerner understood as thoroughly as Gertrude how these people had emerged from their history. She was an expert on the Bedouin who, since before the Prophet, had flowed for centuries out of the meagre lands of the Yemen into the desert, carrying the few dates, clothes and arms that they could trade. She had described their journeys from village to village, oasis to oasis, to the towns, selling off their camels in the northern market-places as they arrived. Reaching the fertile lands of the Euphrates and the Tigris, they had begun to breed a few sheep on the fringes of the grass. She had followed the settlement of those who, having made a little money, had been able to move to watered land and start to farm. She knew the new generations of Bedouin who had begun to trade in grain and goods brought from across the desert, numbering among her friends many who had continued as nomads as well as those who had settled down, and the increasing number who had begun to divide their year between the two ways of life. She had watched the bigger traders, attracted by the markets, learning to manipulate the economy as the cities grew in size and importance. She had been befriended by the Christian professionals, clerks and teachers who had come from southern Russia and the Mediterranean. She had travelled among the mountainous tribes of the north as they adapted from a life of fighting to one of farming.

She had appreciated the hospitality of the Kurds and noted the explosive mix of races and religions in the unmapped northern territory they shared with the historic peoples of Armenia, Assyria, Turkey and northern Persia. She understood the hereditary lines of Arab families. She knew just how to approach a *mujtahid* or a Sunni cleric, a *mullah*, a *mukhtar* or a *mutawalli*.

To the people queuing up outside her office, Gertrude was more than an administrator. She was someone they could trust. She had never lied to them, had respected them and their ways to the point of entrusting her life to them when travelling alone in their lands. To the Arab-speaking visitors demanding interviews, Sir Percy Cox was 'Kokus'; but Gertrude was greeted as 'Khatun' – desert queen – or 'Umm al Muminin', Mother of the Faithful, after Ayishah, the wife of the Prophet. She was the one with whom everyone wanted to make first contact, and whose blessing they sought. She used these overtures not just to win trust for the administration, but for the sake of peace and prosperity, to improve relationships between the people. She was doing the most important work she had ever undertaken.

A boisterous character and tremendous admirer of Gertrude's, Fahad Beg ibn Hadhdbal, now arrived in Baghdad. The paramount sheikh of the confederation of the Anazeh in the north-west of Amara, he was an 'almighty swell' bent with ferocious determination on acquiring a set of false teeth. Ronald Storrs, now a firm friend of Gertrude's, was in Baghdad for a fortnight's visit and coincided with the eruption into the capital of this magnetic figure. He observed the meeting between Fahad Beg and Gertrude, and told Cox that the sheikh's affection for her was 'almost compromising'. As Gertrude wrote, 'Fahad Beg and I had the most tenderly affectionate meeting . . . N.B. Fahad Beg is 75 bien sonné – but a dear, and so wise in desert politics.'

The sheikh was one of those Bedouin prepared to embrace modern life. He owned extensive palm gardens near Karbala, which brought him a good income, but reverted to his nomadic life for six months of the year. She had paid her respects to him in the desert on her way back to Damascus from Hayyil in 1914, narrowly missing one of his many *ghazzus* against the pro-Turkish Shammar tribe. He had received her 'with a kindness almost fatherly and I loved being with him'. They had sat on beautiful carpets in his tent, where she had admired his hawk and the magnificent greyhound stretched out at his feet, and been introduced to his latest wife and baby. The following night he had paid a return visit to her tent, followed by a procession of slaves carrying the best dinner she had enjoyed for months, and they had talked politics under the stars.

He now told Gertrude that parties of Turkish and German officers had been approaching his tribe with bags of gold, attempting to buy Anazeh allegiance. At her request he sent a message to his son in the desert, forbidding the enemy's caravans to cross the territory and ordering that all trade with them should stop. She set up a conference for him with Cox and Wilson, for whose benefit he recalled the powerful effect on him produced by one of her letters:

> '. . . I summoned my sheikhs' he wound up (I feeling more and more of a Person as he proceeded) 'I read them your letter and I said to them Oh Sheikhs' – we hung upon his words – 'This is a woman – what must the men be like!'
>
> This delicious peroration restored me to my true place in the twinkling of an eye.

Complete with new teeth, he made ready to return to the desert. Before he left, she took him to the Baghdad aeroplane base where, for the first time, he saw planes and watched a flying display. Then she led him on to one of the grounded planes to inspect the cockpit. The battle-scarred old warrior took a hesitant step or two inside before exhorting her: '"Don't let it go away!"'

However much she loved Iraq and its people, the climate did not suit Gertrude, and her health suffered. Sometimes in summer the temperature rose above 120 degrees, and in the winter it could be so cold and wet that she had to wear her furs all day. The Secretariat, accordingly, had its summer and its winter quarters. She particularly enjoyed moving into the winter quarters, out of dark, cool rooms into sunny ones open to the air. Gertrude made her offices charming, not only because she liked them that way but because of her constant stream of visitors. She wrote:

> Our office is a wonderful place ... two big houses built round courtyards on the river. Mine is all shielded with mats and blinds against the sun and is wonderfully cool. It has a writing table and a big map table, a sofa and some chairs with white cotton covers and lovely bits of Persian brocade over them, 2 or 3 very good rugs on the brick floor and a couple of exquisite old Persian glass vases on top of the black wood book-case. The walls covered with maps ... Maps are my passion; I like to see the world with which I'm dealing, and everyone comes round to my room for geography.

On the veranda that ran round the courtyard sat a row of kavasses, office servants in khaki uniform, ready to run messages. The office of Major May, the financial adviser, was across the courtyard from Gertrude and next to the cipher room. A tame peacock that had somehow attached itself to the Secretariat liked to sit in his office, but occasionally looked in on Gertrude.

Arnold Wilson, Cox's deputy – or A.T., as Gertrude always called him – occupied the next room to hers. It would be difficult to say which of them was the greater workaholic. Both the rooms were thick with cigarette smoke, stirred into ghostly whirlpools by the slowly turning ceiling fans. A.T., his chair creaking under his Herculean weight, would flail through his paperwork. Sometimes he worked until late at night, snatching a few hours of sleep on the floor before beginning again at first light. Initially he baulked at the inclusion of a woman in what he considered should be a masculine administration. She wrote of him to her family a little later: 'I had a difficult time when I first came out here, you know; it makes me laugh now to think of it ... [A.T.] began by regarding me as "a born intriguer", and I, not unnaturally, regarded him with some suspicion, knowing that that was his opinion of me ... I think I've helped to educate him a little.' Gertrude, between her streams of visitors, wrote end-to-end reports and position papers, now widely acknowledged as the clearest and most readable of all the official documents the Arab Bureau produced.

The half-dozen British running the government with Cox were not Arabists and knew little of Iraq. Unfamiliar with the ways of the locals and their needs, they reported at this stage to the army chief-of-staff in Mesopotamia, then later to the India Office in London. Support was needed in terms of men, supplies and money from the British governments in Delhi, Cairo, Khartoum and London. Friendly relations had to be maintained with the newly emerging kingdom of Ibn Saud and with the sheikhdoms of Kuwait and Muhammarah. The eastern border with Persia and its unstable government was rent with tribal disloyalties, and in the west the British were trying to resolve borders with the territory of Syria. Every department of the new government was engaged in tailoring its policies to local custom and to circumstances on the ground, and at the same time in justifying them to Delhi or London, and to the local military command.

Gertrude was the communicating mastermind. At times she would be writing seven articles at once, and whenever relevant she sought to remind the War Office of the promises made to the Arabs and of the obligation to consider their welfare. Her life was now increasingly dedicated to finding a way in which those obligations could be met with credit and advantage to Britain, the West, and the rest of the world.

In October 1917 she was made a Commander of the new Order of the British Empire, an award that could be made to women as well as to men. The first she heard of it was in a letter from Hugh and Florence. Then followed congratulations from Sir Reginald Wingate, the new High Commissioner in Egypt, and a deluge of good wishes from friends and colleagues. Gertrude's reaction was curmudgeonly. Much as she loved tributes from unusual quarters, the least expected the better, she was entirely self-motivated and pursued her chosen path uninfluenced by praise and undeterred by criticism. Any suggestion that her motive was love of honour or title was abhorrent to her. Brought up in a tradition of public service, even as a schoolgirl she had regretted that her grandfather had seen fit to accept a baronetcy. She looked up the names of the others who had been awarded a CBE, and was unimpressed. 'I don't really care a button . . . It's rather absurd, and as far as I can see from the lists there doesn't appear to be much damned merit about this new order.'

She had, perhaps, seen too much of inept officialdom in Europe and the Middle East to treat this formal recognition of her abilities with anything like awe. The fact that she was a woman, she thought, had nothing to do with it. She showed little interest, again, when she was awarded in March 1918 the Founder's Medal of the Royal Geographical Society for her journey to Hayyil, but in this case she was being recognized for a particularly dangerous achievement and was accordingly more courteous – 'it's far too great an honour'. Though only four years ago, that journey seemed to her already to belong to a distant past, almost to another life. Hugh attended the Geographical Society dinner in London in her place, accepted the medal and wrote her a lively account of the evening. These two honours provoked a surge of new interest in her and in what she was doing in the East, and the Bells were constantly being asked for interviews about her. She still discounted public adulation, and condemned 'the whole advertisement business'. She told Hugh and Florence in no uncertain terms that they were never to cooperate with the press: 'Please, please don't supply information about me or photographs of me to newspaper correspondents. I've said this so often before that I thought you understood . . . I always throw all letters asking for an interview or a photograph straight into the waste paper basket and I beg you to do the same on my behalf.'

Traditionally, where the British Empire had established its rule over newly infiltrated nations, it had superimposed its own concepts of justice, administration, language and military control, including the peculiarly British notion of public service free of corruption. By the time the British moved into Iraq, they no longer had the money, will or manpower to provide an overarching imperial structure, having exhausted all their resources in fighting the world war. Their main objects were the defeat of the Turks and their German allies, and the protection of British oil interests.

Once the Turkish army had been destroyed, the British could have retreated to the stronghold of Basra to secure their oil supplies and left the rest of the population to anarchy and starvation. This economically sound approach was heartily advocated by influential politicians in London and Delhi, including Winston Churchill, then Minister of Munitions and soon to be Secretary of State for the Colonies. But at the same time, amongst the British administration and emanating from the Secretariat, there emerged a strong sense of responsibility for the inhabitants and a pride in securing good government for them after the abuses they had suffered at the hands of the Ottoman Empire. As the British took hold of more and more of Mesopotamia, attitudes towards them changed. Little by little, the population began to see improvements in their conditions, and that the British meant to do well by them. They saw that their taxes were fed back into their communities and not siphoned off to pay the occupying army or to send to London.

America had recently entered the war, with a view to ending the carnage and limiting the devastating impact of the chain reaction that had affected so much of the world. President Woodrow Wilson had the support of his electorate in providing funds and troops to bring the war to an end, but no mandate to prop up old colonial regimes. Many Americans had themselves fled such old discriminatory tyrannies, and endorsed the spirit of self-determination that the President advocated. This spirit would permeate all discussions about the future of the Middle East.

There was vital reconstruction to do. In many towns, public buildings and markets had to be rebuilt. Irrigation systems, roads, bridges and railways had to be repaired and extended, telegraph communication established. Education and justice needed to be made available to all. Police had to be recruited and trained, crime discouraged and the law defined – and applied – with due consideration for local religion and creed. Guns had to be collected: Gertrude describes the collection of fifty thousand rifles as 'making a beginning'.

Crucially, there was a lack of specialist administrators able to do these jobs. The army, India and Egypt were ransacked for the most appropriate and capable man for each post; he would be an expert in his field but would almost certainly be ignorant of Iraq. At last a man would be located in a dusty Sudanese office or remote Indian province, and arrive at the docks or the station in a sweat-stained linen suit, be greeted with open arms and rushed, almost before he had unpacked, to Gertrude's office. There he would remain for some hours, while she explained the job as it would have to be done on the ground in a territory where each district was quite distinct from its neighbours ethnically, religiously, economically and socially. Whatever the common policy, it had to be implemented sensitively and intelligently in ways that would suit the attitudes and skills, or lack of them, of the local people. She would explain the status quo, the problems of the specific community and who was who. The newcomer would enter the debate thinking in terms of British priorities, but come out of it persuaded to think in terms of local needs. As a result, the policy developed in the capital did not, as so often happens, falter in its application to the real world. In the meeting of the two agendas, those of the administration and the population, Gertrude brought about compliance by knowing which benefits would purchase cooperation. As Oriental Secretary, a good part of her day was spent in trading government favours to smooth the path of the administration.

No wonder that she wrote so often to her family that she could not take a holiday. She was holding the administration together. As Percy Cox wrote of Gertrude, '[She] had all the personnel and politics of the local communities at her fingers' end.' Confronting the vacuum out of which he would be required to produce order, the new specialist, whatever his field, would be inspired to create the new world that would be Iraq. Gertrude was to write later:

> Any administration must bring to the task . . . singular integrity and diligence, combined with a just comprehension of the conflicting claims of different classes of the population. It must also command the confidence of the people so as to secure the co-operation of public opinion, without which so complex a tangle could not be unravelled.

Gradually the administrators began to restructure the public life of central and southern Mesopotamia, the half that was under British control. They began with the rebuilding of the deserted ruin that was Kut, as a memorial to those who had given their lives in its defence, both the soldiers and the citizens who had starved to death or been killed after the retaking of the town by the Turks. The mosques and public buildings were repaired or rebuilt, and a splendid arcaded bazaar was erected on the riverbank so that buying and selling could begin again. The families of citizens who had been killed were given funds to rebuild their houses. It was an inspired act of public relations, and within a couple of months the population of Kut numbered two hundred.

The priority was public hygiene. On entering Baghdad, the army had found it littered with corpses and running with rats, the drains in a state of collapse and water infested. Cholera had broken out. Latrines and incinerators were built and butcheries and markets inspected, chlorinated water provided, pest-control started. By mid-1918 there was a civil hospital or dispensary in each military station of any importance. A medical officer and his military assistant headed a small group of sanitary workers for the first year, but by 1919 there was a Secretary of Health running some fifty civil hospitals and dispensaries. That year there was an outbreak of plague. A vaccine depot ensured a supply sufficient to inoculate some eighty thousand people and the plague was checked: a triumph equalled by the success of the medical educators in convincing them of the need for vaccination. A new isolation hospital was built, an x-ray unit, a venereal hospital for women and a dental institute, but the Health Department was burdened with the problem of the 'pilgrim corpses', foreigners imported into the country for burial at the holy cities of Karbala and Najaf. Under Turkish practice, these corpses must have been buried for at least three months before being examined at the frontier. Even Gertrude baulked at the problem, and performed a quick side-step around the issue. 'The question of regulation of pilgrim and corpse traffic is a difficult and delicate one with many side issues, and will demand ... very careful scrutiny and consideration.'

Food was in short supply in the Baghdad and Basra *vilayets*. In the north, around Mosul where the Turks held on, ten thousand people died of starvation in the winter of 1917–18. The summer rains failed, and the closing of the Mosul road until the British occupation in October cut off all supplies of wheat and fruit to Baghdad. On the banks of the Tigris virtually all cultivation had been destroyed. There had been military action around Balad and Istabulat at the time when the crops were ripe: what the Turks had not eaten they burnt. Elsewhere, watercourses had been blocked to facilitate the building of roads and railways for the use of the army. Where canals existed, they were silted up. Karbala had been flooded, and the breaching of the Saqlawiyah dam had reduced the waters of the Euphrates to such a low level that the crops were unsuccessful. In other areas there was no oil for the pumps that put water into the irrigation systems.

The man required to prevent famine and put the country back on its feet, the expert arriving in Basra in the sweat-stained linen suit, was Henry Dobbs the Revenue Commissioner, direct from the fiscal department of the Indian Civil Service. The Revenue Department, wrote Gertrude, could more correctly be considered as the land agent of an estate, represented in this instance by Iraq, the proprietor being the government. Taxes had to be raised to fund all that needed to be done. Without agriculture, there could be no revenue. As virtually all trade had ceased in 1917 and famine was imminent, the only way of acquiring that income would be to tax the landowners, the farmers and, ultimately, the produce. As neither the landowners nor the farmers had any cash for vegetable seed, cereals, animal fodder or ploughs, the system had to be kick-started. Cultivation had to be enforced, seed and cash provided up front, and tax collected when the crops matured and could be sold. Nevertheless, it was decided to reduce the taxes on some holdings, and even entirely suspend them on particularly poor ones.

Initially, the ownership of land had to be established and recorded, no farmer being willing to produce food unless he had security of tenure, either as tenant or as landowner. Under Turkish rule, the provinces of Basra and Baghdad had been taxed by five independent government departments that interfered with the normal life of the people at every step, a system that invited peculation and corruption – an invitation, as Gertrude would drily warn Dobbs's successors in Baghdad, that was seldom refused. Nor were Turkish obfuscations the only source of confusion. Landowners, in registering their land, liked to describe the boundaries in terms so vague that the area could not be assessed, and to submit the names of people who did not exist – 'East, north, west and south, Haji Hasan Beg's garden' was one example. The Sharia law of succession, too, generated ludicrous assessments of property and tax: 'It has resulted in a subdivision of property so minute that there is a case on record where a single date tree and the land just sufficient to support it are owned by 21 persons in partnership,' Gertrude noted.

It fell to Dobbs to gather together and try to make sense of the odd bits of paper left blowing on the floors of the hastily vacated Turkish offices responsible for recording title-deeds, and begin a new system of land registration. It was his job, next, to make cultivation possible by extending and controlling irrigation, clearing the canals and distributing water from rivers that had a spring rise of twenty feet or more.

Even the administrators were on iron rations. The food in the mess, where Gertrude ate during the working week, was rationed and monotonous. However little she complained, and whatever she put up with when she was travelling, she missed good food. A family friend, Colonel Frank Balfour, who later became Military Governor of Baghdad – Gertrude's 'beloved Frank' – tells the story of joining her in the mess one evening for dinner. When, for the fourteenth day running, the meal consisted of bully beef, Gertrude rather surprised him by throwing down her knife and fork in disgust and bursting into tears. She wrote to Chirol on 9 November 1918:

We are put to it to feed ourselves, and it is hard to feel Herculean on biscuits ... we've had no butter all the summer and when we have it it's tinned. I've forgotten what potatoes taste like – the meat is almost too tough to eat, chickens ditto; milk tinned – how sick one gets of it! . . . when one's feeling rather a poor thing one does hate it all . . . Heaven send us a good harvest next year.

The responsibility for implementing the new agricultural policies lay with the political officers in the outlying provinces. Meetings of landowners were held, and the new Agricultural Development Scheme explained. British assistance would be given in terms of seed, cash and irrigation, but if the landowners did not cooperate, they would lose their right to their share in the following harvest. If land was not cultivated over a period of time, it could be taken from them. Local political officers were allowed to dole out small punishments for such transgressions as, for instance, the breaching of irrigation regulations. Gertrude constantly urged caution and leniency, and her guidance was followed. In 1919 irrigation and agriculture were smoothly handed over to the civil authorities staffed by locals who were now in a position to assume those responsibilities. The scheme was, naturally, most successful in the better-controlled areas, but the spring crop of 1918 supplied the civil population as well as providing some 55,000 tons of grain for the army. With forethought, extra seed had been stored against another lean year, but this could now be released to the Bedouin, and to the Kurds on both sides of the frontier. Mesopotamia was safe from starvation.

From the Sudan legal department came Edgar Bonham-Carter, later Sir Edgar, to be appointed Senior Judicial Officer and then Judicial Secretary in Baghdad. Gertrude thought him a polite and formal person, 'just a trifle desiccated', but welcomed him sincerely. When the British had arrived in Baghdad they found the courts had ceased to function, the courtrooms had been looted, the Turkish judges, court staff and records gone. The custom normally followed by an occupying administration is to leave in place, as far as possible, the systems with which the population is used to dealing. Having disappeared into his office for eight weeks of study, scrutinizing the stupendously complex system of Ottoman justice for what could be saved and calling in Gertrude to discuss tribal and religious law, Bonham-Carter emerged with his conclusion: the system failed to work on any level.

The first change was to make Arabic the language for all legal proceedings: civil disputes, criminal cases, and family law with all its religious implications. A court of small causes and a Muhammadan law court were opened at once, providing a civil court alongside a traditional system based on the Koran and following Sharia law. Thirty more Muhammadan law courts were established and operated and used by Sunnis, but the Shias presented a particular problem in that they preferred to submit disputes to their own ecclesiastical leaders, the *mujtahids*. From now on Shia cases were transferred to the new courts of first instance, together with Jewish and Christian cases, where they could be tried by judges chosen by those communities.

The intention was to set up sessions courts composed of British and Arab judges cooperating in the administration of justice. The difficulty was to provide British judges who spoke Arabic, or Arabs who were trained lawyers. Almost none of the Turkish judges had known any more law than the average clerk, and since their salaries were roughly commensurate with a clerk's, they had been eager for bribes. It was said that there were only two honest judges in Mesopotamia – and bribery had remained the only way in which a citizen could obtain a judgement. There had been, before the war, one reputable school of law in Baghdad, and it was now reopened with the proviso that it must be conducted wholly in Arabic. Those students who had been unable to complete their four-year courses were invited back, and some fifty returned to become qualified.

The myriad faults of Turkish law provided a textbook summary of what not to do. The number of judges was now reduced by necessity to those who were qualified, and their salaries increased to a respectable sum. The new criminal procedure code was based on the Sudan model, which had proved to be clear and workable. Four classes of criminal courts were established, with a court of appeal whose word was final. The beauty of the new judicial system lay in the detail and in the consideration for local conditions that it incorporated. Crimes had to be tried locally – and was it Gertrude who insisted that trials be held within camel- and donkey-ride distance of the accused and the witnesses? Cases must be resolved quickly: under the Turks, the law was so complex that in a case such as a load of dates found to be full of worms, the dispute might go on for three years. Punishments were made more lenient, and in remote areas, where tribal or village law was allowed to hold sway, the headman was forbidden to use the death sentence.

For a 'desiccated' administrator from the Sudan, Bonham-Carter displays in his writings an extraordinary grasp of the medieval rules of Iraqi tribal law – Gertrude again? For instance, he explains the ramifications of the family custom of murdering a daughter for sexual activity before marriage or a wife for adultery, and of the male lover going unpunished; or the traditional compensation for a tribal murder, payment of one virgin in addition to the blood money. Few British legal experts at the time could have comprehended the tendency of the tribal witness to be genuinely incapable of distinguishing between what he had himself observed and what he had been told or had been inferred. In cases of murder in which the motive was revenge or blood feud, the end was considered to justify the means. The family and friends of the victim would get together and agree on the identity of the murderer. To men brought up under the custom that the tribe is responsible for a murder committed by any one of its members, he writes, it must seem of comparatively little importance which tribesman did the deed: the tribal duty is revenge, a life for a life. Tribal law, reflected Gertrude, is no deterrent to crime.

The new administrators of such a territory were bound to discover anomalies, some almost comic, as Gertrude pointed out in her *Review of the Civil Administration of Mesopotamia*:

The Turkish educational programme, as set forth in the official Turkish Education Year Book, full of maps and statistics, might have roused the envy . . . of the British . . . but for the knowledge that, provided a school were shown correctly as a dot on the map, the Turk cared not . . . whether the system of education pursued in it was that of Arnold of Rugby or of Mr. Wopsle's great aunt.

In the matter of girls' education, the inevitably male teachers in the handful of schools for girls were regarded with intense suspicion by the community. Initial British sympathy for the teachers evaporated when they were found to be every bit as libidinous as suspected. They were swiftly replaced by women, and five schools opened for girls. In distant provinces, the officers were often confronted with bizarre problems. The only teacher at Diwaniyah was discovered to be unable to read or write, and the Kurdish education project was held up by the absence of a formulated grammar and orthography. It fell to the political officer and the education officer for Sulaimaniyah, Major Soane and Captain Farrell, to sit down and puzzle out an elementary reader. In reversing the Turkish principle that only Sunnis were encouraged to go to school, the Education Department now welcomed boys of every creed into government schools, where they were taught in Arabic. Sunni, Shia, Christian and Jewish communities were invited to send their own religious teachers to the schools so that religious instruction could be included in the syllabus.

The *Auqaf*, or Department of Pious Bequests, was discovered to be the greatest landlord in Mesopotamia, despite which the Turks had left its treasury empty. Now under the auspices of the Judicial Department, its neglected properties and mosques were inspected, registered and repaired, and – to the amazement of the population – its original intentions and obligations to the poor fulfilled. Bequests were used for the purposes intended, financial irregularities prevented, and a committee of leading Sunnis put in charge of the religious and academic aspects. Much of the Oudh bequest, a large sum of money donated to 'deserving persons' in Karbala and Najaf by King Oudh in the mid-nineteenth century, had also found its way to Constantinople, and was now rerouted by the administration to its intended objects.

Humphrey Bowman, the director of education, wrote a fleeting portrait of Gertrude in Baghdad at around this time, which leaves an indelible impression of her social position in Arab society. The occasion was an 'at home' to some fifty Arab notables at the house of Sir Edgar Bonham-Carter. There were only one or two British guests. Bowman recorded:

> We were all sitting on chairs round the room as we do in the East, getting up whenever some special guest arrived. At last the door opened and Gertrude came in. She was beautifully dressed, as always, and looked very queenly. Everyone rose, and then she walked round the room, shaking hands with each Arab in turn and then saying a few appropriate words to each. Not only did she know them all by name . . . but she knew what to say to each.

Being beautifully dressed was increasingly hard. She often had to get up at dawn to sew on buttons and mend her hard-washed clothes, but succeeded in looking well turned out even while working relentlessly, entertaining numbers of people at home and dining out many evenings a week. While Cox, A.T. and all the men around her wore uniforms that were laundered and maintained by their servants daily, she was using up her thin summer dresses at a rate of three a day during the hottest weather. She wrote to Florence that she had been for four years without a maid: what she needed was someone to look after her clothes, tidy her house and make it attractive, a thing she couldn't do when she was always working. 'What I need is a wife!' she argued, like so many business-women after her, and with far more reason than most.

Florence listened, sympathized and began to work out a solution. She was also, perhaps, a little tired of constant clothes-shopping for her stepdaughter, and of finding that Gertrude's requests were increasingly incompatible with what was available in the shops. Every trip that Florence, Elsa or Molly made to central London must have been partly taken up with dress purchases for Gertrude: five striped muslin dresses requested in one post, a new linen riding habit, shoes by Yapp, tortoiseshell combs, chiffon veils, silk blouses in pale pink or ivory, a dozen pairs of thread stockings, flowered straw hats, satin evening gowns, riding boots, silk dressing gowns, all to be boxed up and sent by ship – a high proportion of them to be stolen en route, or lost at sea together with human life on torpedoed ships. Even when the promised clothes arrived, they could disappoint. In one such case, in a letter dated 26 May 1917, she did not mince her words: 'I regret to say that one [of the gowns] which according to Moll's pattern was intended for me to wear in the evening was no more an evening gown than it was a fur coat, and won't do at all . . . It's rather a blow, for I had a vision of some nice trailing muslin gowns with floating sleeves . . . I shall just have not to dine out when it gets hot.'

Poor Moll was not at fault. As Florence adds in a postscript to this rebuke, since Gertrude had left England, fashion had changed. There were no more 'trailing muslin gowns with floating sleeves', for women were preferring narrower, shorter dresses and less cumbersome silhouettes as they shaped up for the roaring twenties.

Gertrude found a partial answer to the problem through a French convent she passed on her early morning rides. One day she jumped off her horse and rang the bell to ask if they had any dressmakers. They had.

> The nuns are making me a muslin gown – it will be a monument of love and care, for I really believe they lie awake at night thinking what new stitches they can put into it . . . The 'essayages' [fittings] are not like any other dressmaking I've ever known. I go in after riding before breakfast and stand in practically nothing but breeches and boots (for it's hot) while the Mother Superior and the darling dressmaking sister, Soeur Renée . . . pin on bits of muslin. At our elbows a native lay sister bearing cups of coffee. We pause often while the Mother Superior and Soeur Renée discuss gravely what really is the fashion. The result is quite satisfactory. Soeur Renée isn't a Frenchwoman for nothing.

Dislike of 'flapper' fashion was not the only way in which Gertrude had parted company with London life. Writing to her father on the third anniversary of the day she had said goodbye to Dick Doughty-Wylie, she found herself reliving their four days together minute by minute, and finding no inclination to return to a life that for her was over: 'O Father Dearest . . . this sorrow at the back of everything deadens me in a way to all else, to whether I go home or whether I stay here . . . the drawback of England is that I don't want to see any of my kind friends.' To Chirol, as always, she wrote the unvarnished truth. It was Christmas, 1917. 'I have been wishing that I had been in Jerusalem this Xmas . . . Yes, I rather long for the grey hills of Judea – never for England, do you know. My England has gone.'

Life in Sloane Street and Rounton, towards the end of the war, was hard enough for Hugh and Florence, too. Maurice had been invalided home from the front, a mixed blessing given that he returned almost totally deaf. He had always been hard of hearing, but now, in conversation with him, people had to shout to be heard. He retreated more and more into his country gentleman's life of hunting, shooting and fishing. The latest death to distress the Bells was that of Sir Cecil Spring-Rice, the husband of Gertrude's cousin Florence Lascelles, while he was British Ambassador in Washington. She wrote to both Florences, reserving for her stepmother a particularly touching expression of her affection and admiration. Florence's patience, constancy and uncomplaining endurance were no longer undervalued by her stepdaughter. Gertrude wrote on 28 March:

Dearest Mother,

I don't think I have ever told you – though it is constantly in my mind, how much I admire your fortitude and your splendid determination to suffer whatever must be suffered and not give way before the end is won. You use no fine phrases and yet there's not one of us who has shown a finer spirit. Your letters scarcely give any hint of the weariness of the long strain which I can guess at. It's your courage which is so splendid and I can't tell you how much I admire and love it.

In 1918 Florence was made a Dame of the British Empire for her Red Cross work. Gertrude wrote at once to congratulate her. There was never a hint in her letters home that she would have liked such an honour herself, and after her reaction to her own CBE, her views on such orders were clear to all; but it is equally obvious that she too should have been made a dame, then or perhaps a little later.

Gertrude was taking increasing pleasure in her garden home, which she was constantly improving. Her landlord Musa Chalabi had become a close friend with whom she could have a conversation about plants or a frank political debate. She sometimes borrowed a staff car and took him and his family out into the country for a weekend picnic, and one day he presented her with the garden in perpetuity, as a gift. Gertrude stipulated that they would always share it between them.

The time came when she could collect a few animals, something she had never been able to do before. She bought a cock and four hens, and fretted because they laid so few eggs. Her old friend Fahad Beg, whose greyhound she had so admired on their first meeting, sent her two of his own: a present, very definitely not a bribe. She called them Richan and Najmah, the Feathered and the Star. On 30 November 1919 she wrote to Hugh and Florence:

> . . . two most beautiful Arab greyhounds . . . They had walked ten days down the Euphrates with two tribesmen to conduct them, and came in half starved. They are sitting beside me on my sofa as I write, after wandering about the room for half an hour whining. They are very gentle and friendly and I hope they will soon get accustomed to living in a garden instead of a tent.

Richan was particularly naughty. Gertrude's letters are peppered with his antics, how he would run off for days at a time, jump up on the pantry table and break the crockery, or roll on the flowerbed and destroy her nasturtiums.

More than one of the sheikhs she met at work had tried to curry favour by presenting her with a gift, along the lines laid down in the days of Turkish administration. When one of them brought her an Arab horse, she gave it back with a smile and a shake of the head, but admitted to Cox that it had been a fine animal, and that she had longed to keep it. Before the week was out she had been 'issued' by the Secretariat with a splendid mare. In 1920 she would add a pony, a little grey Arab: 'He's quite young and needs teaching, so we take nice confidential rides with the dogs before breakfast, and already he is improving. He is as clever as can be, jumps exquisitely and climbs in and out of water courses, his little feet never making a mistake.'

The sheikhs, having got the message that the Khatun would not accept valuables, were put about to find an alternative. Two of them, whose problems she had already solved, now sent her a young gazelle. Nothing could have pleased her more. It ran free in the garden, consuming the dates that fell from the trees, and ate cucumbers from her hand. At night she would find it curled up on the veranda outside her bedroom. 'It's a darling little animal. I'm on the look out now for a mongoose,' she wrote. The mongoose soon arrived, via the young son of the Mayor of Baghdad. 'It's a most attractive little beast. It sat in my hand this morning and ate fried eggs like a Christian.'

Since Cairo, Gertrude had been living in the East on her salary — £20 a month — and her generous annual allowance had been piling up at home, unused. Hugh had written to ask what she wanted done with it. Since the two things she craved — good food and well made European clothing — were unavailable in Iraq, she wrote back with the lack of financial interest that is the prerogative of the very rich: 'Last week you told me of the wealth which was lying at my bank. It's quite preposterous . . . Always do what you think fit with any money of mine, including appropriating it. I don't care, as I've observed before, a damn. It's ever been a subject on which I can contrive no interest . . . If ever I want money I can always ask for some, bless you!'

The climate continued to take its toll on her, and she had to retreat to the officers' hospital, racked with chills and bronchitis in the cold weather and with heat exhaustion in the summer, together with recurring malaria. With the temperature above 120 degrees even at night, she took her bed on to the roof, where she dropped a sheet into a bucket of water and draped it around herself. When it dried, she would wake up and repeat the process. The rooms in the office were sluiced out two or three times a day. In the winter, she was sometimes driven to wearing two dresses, one on top of the other, and her fur coat over the lot. What with constant overwork, cigarettes and heat-stress, she became extremely thin. When illness forced her to go into hospital, she chafed to be back at work. She learnt that if she came home too early, she would only have to return to convalesce. Not that she ever completely stopped working: she wrote position papers continuously, drafted a fortnightly diary for the government and in November 1917 had taken on the editorship of the vernacular paper *Al Arab*. She thought she had now sampled quite enough tropical diseases, she told her parents, and intended to turn over a new leaf. Writing from her hospital bed, she thanked Hugh for a fabulous forty-ninth birthday present: 'One of my few consolations is that your wonderful emerald is pinned on to the brooch which fastens my nightgown and I look at it with immense pleasure and think what a beloved Father you are.'

About a month later, she received a letter from Florence, followed by a large box through the diplomatic bag: 'there arrived a jeweller's shop of brooches and pendants – the loveliest things – how could you reconcile it with your conscience, both of you, to run to such extravagance? Bless you both; they are exquisite and I expect will excite the unbounded admiration of Indian Expeditionary Force D.'

Indian Expeditionary Force D had routed the Turks from Baghdad and southern Mesopotamia. But in mid-1917 the army still faced two hundred square miles of battleground in the north, their task to evict the enemy from the Mosul *vilayet* and from the border with Syria. For another year the Turks fought a rearguard action, stripping the land of food and anything else they could lift as they retreated through the historic breadbasket of Iraq. The advancing British were vulnerable to attacks on their communication and irrigation systems, and the Turks stood ready to flood back into any province that the British army proved insufficient to police.

In Karbala, the local sheikhs who were temporarily running the administration were discovered to be conducting what Gertrude called 'a brisk trade in supplies' to the enemy, through the desert. These individuals were deposed or pulled into line, and Gertrude's friend Fahad Beg and his Bedouin confederation, the Anazeh, saw to the desert supply runners. In the other holy city, Najaf, the pressure of food shortage caused a local disturbance promoted by Turkish provocation. The tide turned in favour of the British, thanks to the Shias, who had been angered by the way the Turkish administration had treated their holy places. One of the political officers, Captain Marshall, was murdered, but the British responded sensitively: not a shot was fired into the town, and the shrine and holy sites were left undisturbed. Peace was restored, but Karbala and Najaf would continue to be the focus of political unrest.

Throughout central and southern Mesopotamia, the British army provided an unlimited market for labour and for local produce – and, unlike their predecessors, they paid for it. The two southern *vilayets* of Baghdad and Basra were enjoying a level of prosperity unknown under the Ottoman Empire.

Only Gertrude amongst the Baghdad staff was able to identify the multitude of races and creeds in the areas north, east and west of Mosul. In the mountains, Arab tribes gave way to Kurdish, while west towards the desert were the Yazidis – devil-worshippers – a strange sect of whom Gertrude was particularly fond. Their sheikhs had the singular ability to pick up vipers, and their diviners were reputed to forecast the future. 'The Devil Worshippers are tractable and amenable, though of loose morals,' she had written on her encounters with them, noting that in 1915 they had given shelter to a number of Armenian refugees. As well as the Kurdish tribes, there were a number of Christian sects of which the foremost were the Chaldeans, Jacobites, Nestorians and Turkomans, who claimed descent from Tamerlane. On the left bank of the Tigris there lived, amongst a variety of bizarre groupings, Shabak and Sarli, the possessors of a secret faith; the Ali-Ilahis, the Tai, and a Jewish community. The pre-eminent Arab tribe were the Anazeh's hereditary enemies, the Shammar, in the pay of the Turkish army and ready to attack convoys, blow up canal heads, raid and loot whatever they could find.

So carefully put together and administered, so successful in its occupation until the end of the war, the British government of

Mesopotamia was about to be undermined by interminable delays while it waited for decisions not only on its future in Iraq, but, more fundamentally, on where the borders of Iraq were to be. Only when the victors assembled to settle the peace could anyone lay the ground for the people of Iraq to govern themselves with a firm prospect of independence. Without that prospect, many strands of minority dissent, often fomented by the Turks, would grow into outright revolt, threatening all the achievements of the previous three years. As Gertrude would write in 1920:

> The underlying truth of all criticism – and it's what makes the critics so difficult to answer – [was] that we had promised self-governing institutions, and not only made no step towards them but were busily setting up something quite different. One of the [news]papers says, quite rightly, that we had promised an Arab government with British advisers, and had set up a British government with Arab advisers. That's a perfectly fair statement.

In September 1918, Cox, this most able of administrators, had been sent from Baghdad to Teheran. At this most explosive moment in the history of Iraq she was shackled to his former deputy A. T. Wilson as Acting Civil Commissioner, a boss whose high-handed tactics, punitive retaliation against dissidents and preference for imperialist policies had brought home to her over the last twenty-four months the appalling truth: he had no sympathy for the policy of self-determination, and would do his best to undermine and prevent it. Where was Gertrude's dream now?

13

ANGER

It was the astute T. E. Lawrence who noted that one of Gertrude's failings was a propensity to admire the people that she liked, only to disparage them later when she had fallen out with them. She had so far enjoyed a reasonably good working relationship with A.T. Wilson, both under the delicate handling of the fair-minded Cox. While he was the deputy, A.T. had conducted the day-to-day running and development of government, and she had been complementary to him in securing the commitment of the locals and in moulding the new regime to the realities on the ground. But A.T. always wanted to run his own show. He did not involve her in policy as Cox had done, nor did he consult her before making decisions. Furthermore, their attitudes to the Arabs could not have been more different. A.T. dealt with their representations brusquely and paid their leaders, however distinguished, scant respect. She found this worse than embarrassing and, far more seriously, found herself radically differing with her 'colonial dinosaur' of a chief (as Lawrence had branded him). The very words 'self-determination' outraged A.T., whereas the principle was enshrined in Gertrude's heart: '. . . I might be able to help to keep things straight – if they'll let me . . . We are having rather a windy time over self-determination . . . I wish very much that Sir Percy were here,' she wrote in January 1919.

The First World War was over at last, and Gertrude, recovering from another bout of malaria, allowed herself some amusement of a characteristic variety. She steamed down the Tigris on a luxurious boat belonging to one of the generals, reading novels; attended a

lecture on Abbasid history; and rode across the desert to view a
ruin, escorted by thirty-two horsemen of the Bani Tamim tribe.
She also flew in a plane for the first time: 'For the first quarter of an
hour I thought it the most alarming thing I had ever done ... It was a
windy day, the aeroplane wobbled a good deal. However, I presently
became accustomed to it and was much interested and excited. I shall
go up whenever I have an opportunity so as to grow quite used to it.'

For the last year Hugh and Florence had been urging Gertrude
to come home for a holiday, for the sake of her health, and avoid
the scorching Baghdad summer. She had replied frequently that she
could not leave while she was so badly needed. Now, excluded
from most of his important meetings, she was forced to face the
fact that A.T. did not depend on her. However, she told her family,
she was needed by the Arabs, perhaps more than ever. Hugh wrote
that he might, then, come to visit her in Baghdad, and the idea of
showing him her world gave her enormous pleasure. As the time of
Hugh's visit came nearer, duty intervened in the shape of the Paris
Peace Conference. It became clear that A.T. wanted her to cover
the conference before his own arrival, to attend meetings, represent
Mesopotamian interests and keep him informed. It was settled that
Gertrude would go to England first, then on to Paris, where Hugh
would join her for a few days. She could hardly bear the thought
of returning to London. She still felt no desire at all to see most of
her friends or visit her old haunts: everything would remind her
of Dick Doughty-Wylie, the poignancy of their last days together
and the misery that followed. She knew her true friends would
understand. She wrote to one of these, Lord Ullswater's daughter
Milly Lowther, that she was one of the few she wanted to meet.
She had become close to Milly at the Wounded and Missing Office
in London, after Doughty-Wylie's death. 'When I come back I shall
want your help and understanding so much. It will be so difficult to pick
up life in England; I dread it. You must give me a hand as you did
before.'

Her father understood her feelings completely, and hatched a
plan that would neatly avoid the social obligations of London. Much
of her time there, he knew, would be taken up with clothes

shopping. When they had spent the few days in Paris, why didn't the two of them then go off by themselves for a motor tour through Belgium and France, and by sea to Algiers? She was immensely relieved and began to look forward to the trip. But what she wanted most, she wrote, was to see the family; and after that, a Yorkshire leg of mutton.

From Paris in March 1919, she wrote to Florence what it meant to her to be with Hugh again: 'I can't tell you what it has been like to have him for these last two days. He has been more wonderfully dear than words can say, and in such good spirits, looking so well. I can scarcely believe that three years of war have passed over his head since I saw him.'

Father and daughter were always able to pick up where they left off, and time had done nothing to diminish their affection for each other. They had an ecstatic reunion, after which they joined up with Domnul and lunched with Lord Robert Cecil — her former chief at the Wounded and Missing Office. After a few days, Hugh departed and Gertrude got down to work.

In March 1918 revolutionary Russia, under the new Bolshevik government, had signed a treaty with Germany leaving the Allies — France, Britain, Italy and America — to continue the war on the front in Western Europe. The British had continued to push the Turks northwards out of Arabia, hoping again to start a new front moving north-west through Austria, to strike Germany at its undefended southern border — a hope that had been abandoned after the Dardanelles disaster of 1915. At first freed from the conflict with Russia, Germany was able to concentrate its efforts on these fronts, and launched six months of furious attacks against the Allies' trenches running all the way from the North Sea coast in Belgium to the Swiss border in the south. The Allies had held on until the German army was exhausted, running out of equipment, boots and even food. By August, German morale was sinking. The British were assembling a secret army of one hundred thousand fresh infantry, spearheaded by a hundred of Churchill's newly invented tanks. They punched through the weak centre of the

Left. Gertrude and T. E. Lawrence taking time out at the Cairo Conference of 1921.

Below. Panorama of Binbirkilisse, photographed by Gertrude. At a time before the wide-angle lens, she produced comprehensive views of archaeological sites by piecing together a composite of photographs. The picture is of considerable archaeological value, recording the relative positions of the churches, which have deteriorated since.

The palace of Ukhaidir, some thirty miles south-west of Karbala, photographed by Gertrude. She came upon this 'father of castles' on her 1909 expedition, in the dangerous tribal territory of the Dulaim, where she had to enlist the protection of armed soldiers while she sketched and measured.

Gertrude's two desert tents, one for writing and eating, one for bathing and sleep ing. Made in England, they had loose flaps that could be tied back or lifted to make shady canopy. Bed, bath and chair were made of folding canvas and wood. She woul sit down to dinner at a table set with linen, silver and crystal.

Left. Dividing the finds at the biblical of Ur, with her old friend and colleag Leonard Woolley. In cloche hat and cardigan à la Chanel, Gertrude was picking out the best of the treasures t keep for her museum in Iraq.

Below. Directing her armed soldiers to take measurements at Ukhaidir, Gertrude wears a hat and keffiyah, a linen skirt with big pockets for instruments, and leather boots.

Fattuh, Gertrude's brave and devoted servant, was an Armenian Christian from Aleppo. She hired him on her 1905 journey as a cook, and from then on she never travelled without him. It became a joke between them that cooking was one craft he never mastered, although he was invaluable as a guide, aide and adroit negotiator. She said that he could put up her tent in an instant, keep her crew in order and make her laugh in dangerous situations.

Sheikhs at the camp of the Howaitat, photographed by Gertrude.

Similar to Hayyil, where Gertrude was held prisoner in 1914, Riyadh was an isolated desert city in central Arabia.

Above. Hayyil, photographed by Gertrude on her arrival there on 25 March 1914. She noted that the rampart towers were like embattled windmills without sails, as Charles Doughty had described them in his book *Arabia Deserta*.

Left. Portrait of Gertrude by John Singer Sargent in 1923, drawn in England while she was visiting her family for her fifty-fifth birthday. She had known him, and admired his work, for twenty years and thought him delightful.

Turkiyyeh, the Circassian woman sent by the Rashid court to greet Gertrude on her arrival at Hayyil.

The visitors' lodge, and summer palace of the Rashids, where Gertrude was held captive in Hayyil. The pillars were palm trunks painted white, the lofty ceiling thatched with palm fronds, the band of geometrical decoration painted in red and blue.

The harem of Sheikh Harb al Daransheh, who is seen here holding back the tent flap so that Gertrude can photograph his women. On this journey, which would culminate in the arrival at Hayyil, she talked to the women of the harems for the first time and was deeply impressed by the tragic stories she heard.

Amir Faisal, army commander, politician, rebel leader and king-in-waiting: the third son of Hussain ibn Ali, Sharif of Mecca.

Gertrude Bell and Sir Percy Cox at Basra in 1916.

Gertrude's servants in the garden of her home in Baghdad, with the two greyhounds given to her by her great friend, Sheikh Fahad Beg ibn Hadbhal, tribal chief of the eastern Anazeh.

At the Cairo Conference in 1921, Gertrude flanked by Winston Churchill and T. E. Lawrence, lined up in front of the Sphinx.

Gertrude with colleagues and Arab ministers at the High Commission in Baghdad in 1924. Seated second from left is Kinahan Cornwallis.

Ibn Saud, leader of the Wahabi sect. Gertrude described the great desert warrior, standing well over six feet, as conveying the impression of an indefinable lassitude. 'His deliberate movements, his slow sweet smile and the contemplative glance of his heavy-lidded eyes . . . do not accord with the Western conception of a vigorous personality. Nevertheless . . . among men bred in the camel saddle he is said to have few rivals as a tireless rider.'

German lines, rooting the troops out of their trenches and following them miles into territory that four years of fighting had failed to gain. Immediately the French in the north and the Americans in the south hammered away at the German trenches while the British advanced in the centre. The German commander-in-chief recognized defeat, and within days the Germans had sued for peace.

Almost within moments of the peace prospect, the Allies began to wrangle amongst themselves; wrangling which would hinder Gertrude for three more years and bring her mission in Arabia almost to disaster. At first the Allies could not agree whether to pursue the Germans all the way to Berlin, which would leave the country devastated but having learnt a lesson never to be forgotten. Marshal Foch, the French overall Allied commander, declared that more death and destruction would benefit nobody. The Allies produced a document of armistice, by which the Germans admitted defeat and would be forced to accept the total demobilization of their army and the handing over of their navy to the British. The Germans signed on the eleventh day of the eleventh month of 1918, and the firing stopped. Meanwhile, the British army had reached the Turkish border. The Turks had fled Arabia, but the trouble they caused would continue.

The Armistice ended hostilities, but the Allied armies remained poised to fight again if Germany, Austria–Hungary and Turkey would not submit to terms for a permanent peace treaty. What were the terms to be? America wanted repayment of the money it had lent to England and to France, and Britain wanted repayment of its loans to France, but both the European countries were bankrupt. France wanted security for evermore from German attack, and it wanted the return of its German-held territory in Alsace Lorraine. Italy, after grim battles fought on behalf of the Allies, demanded more territory carved from the defeated nations. Britain wanted a secure empire, with a navy once more in control of the oceans. Everyone wanted a Germany humbled, disarmed and paying through the nose, although nobody could reach an acceptable figure.

These problems were enough in themselves to fully occupy the exhausted leaders arriving in Paris in the New Year of 1919. The three major contenders at the Conference were President Wilson for America, the British Prime Minister Lloyd George, and the elderly but tough-minded Prime Minister Clemenceau of France. Beyond the grasp of these men, but part of their responsibilities, were the futures of all those peoples who now had no government, no defined boundaries and no recognized identity as nations. With the collapse of such immense empires as the German, Russian, Austrian and Turkish, hundreds of their subject tribes and races in Europe, Africa and the Middle East were left with no administration, no police, army, or money.

The Paris Peace Conference of 1919 was assembled to resolve all of these issues, even if the problems began with the resolution of a language in which to conduct the discussions. Twenty-seven Allied countries were invited. Every nation affected by the war was offered the chance to stake its case against the defeated enemy, and for its own place in the postwar world. Powerful nations like Britain and America arrived early, before the end of 1918, taking over enormous hotels for their representatives. Small ones from the other side of the world took months to arrive. Amongst them were peoples of which the great Allied powers had hardly heard, including several from Arabia and the now-abandoned Turkish Empire for whose future Gertrude would battle.

President Wilson arrived in Paris to declare his fourteen points of principle for the future relations between nations, including the right of every nation to choose its own form of government. Colonial rule was to be consigned to history. A new model was needed to enable powers such as Great Britain and France to teach the new nations to establish good government, with financial aid and trained administrators preparing the way for independence. The answer would be the 'mandate', a legal document binding the chosen established country to govern and assist the fledgling nation until it was ready to stand alone, perhaps twenty years hence. In return, the supervising power gained immediate trading opportunities and strong diplomatic influence in the region of its protectorate.

Believing that the First World War must be the war to end all wars, President Wilson also came determined to create a new forum where the nations could resolve their disputes by discussion, and even impose sanctions on a country showing aggressive intentions. He proposed the League of Nations, to which all independent countries would belong and through which their legal rights relative to other nations would be laid down. Whereas the Paris Peace Conference was meeting to resolve the terms of the treaties to be drawn up between the Allies and their enemies, the League of Nations would approve the boundaries of the new nations, arrange for them to choose their form of government, and, by the issue of mandates, appoint a supervising power over the weaker ones. The idea of an umbrella authority to govern the relationships between countries was ambitious almost beyond belief. There followed a year of work to establish the League of Nations' constitution and to assemble the member states into a body of representatives. Only then could the League begin to examine the state of each of the new nations, and decide whether the country was ready to govern itself or whether a mandate should be imposed. It would also be the body that approved treaties designed to settle border disputes.

Meanwhile, border disputes continued to descend into outright conflict, weak governments continued to collapse into civil strife, and uncertainty about the future exacerbated incipient revolutionary tendencies. Turkey was refusing to sign a peace treaty with the Allies, and still fomenting insurrection among the people of its former colonies. Now too, Arabia had learnt of the secret Sykes–Picot Agreement of 1916, which parcelled up the Middle East between Britain, France and Russia. The news broke just as the Arabs thought they had won an independent future by backing Britain against the Turks. The end of the war brought the Franco-British Declaration on Iraq and Syria, drafted by the tireless Mark Sykes to prove to the United States that the Allies were carrying out President Wilson's intentions regarding self-determination for previously colonized peoples. The statement contained the promise that with British and French support 'indigenous populations should exercise the right of self-determination regarding the form of national government under which they should live'.

But what did the indigenous peoples of Iraq really want? Shortly before leaving Baghdad, Gertrude had written a paper on behalf of A.T. entitled 'Self-Determination in Mesopotamia', largely prompted by Whitehall's demand for a consultation with Arab leaders. This seemingly disingenuous move, apparently ignoring the tangled issues involved, queried whether the population was in favour of a single Arab state, whether it should be headed by an Arab amir, and whether Iraqis had anyone in mind. A.T. had made a half-hearted and rather bad-tempered attempt to respond to the demand: and the answers, as both predicted, were ludicrously inconclusive and unrepresentative, succeeding only in provoking trouble and undermining the government.

The Intrusives had won the day by default. Self-determination was going to come about: America insisted on it, Churchill was intent on minimizing British financial commitments in the Middle East as elsewhere, and the will to expand empires had evaporated. A.T., on the other hand, thought that Iraq could only be run colonially, as India had been, and was outraged by the Franco-British Declaration. He asked Gertrude to write a paper on the prospects for self-government, explaining the insuperable difficulties involved, for the imminent Conference in Paris. The key question in Gertrude's sensitive analysis of the current situation and its prospects was this: 'If we wish to apply the valuable principle of self-determination to the Occupied Territories, how is this to be done?'

The paper sets out to demonstrate the problems so that, whatever policies might be decided upon in far-away capitals for the future of Iraq, they might have some basis in the reality on the ground. Beginning with the impossibility of establishing any pan-Arab government, she progressed to the impossibility of a demo-cratic republic. With 90 per cent of the population innocent of any political views whatsoever, and most of them illiterate, there was practically nothing resembling an Arab national movement. The notion of self-determination aroused more bewilderment than interest. Every family and every tribe was fighting for its own interests in an essentially individualistic society. Gertrude was daily besieged by anxious Arabs coming to her office to demand an explanation of the Franco–British Declaration. Fears were growing that the British would now walk out, lawlessness and even civil war would erupt, and the Turks return to wreak vengeance on those who had collaborated with the British.

With no sense of nationhood, no figurehead and no understanding of democracy, how could a constitution be formed, or a leader found who could hold the country together in the name of the Arabs? Effectively there were only two families in Arabia from the ruling traditions, the Sauds and the Hashemites. Ibn Saud was already too powerful for the liking of the West, and his Wahabi puritanism had no foothold in Mesopotamia. Most Iraqis were ignorant of the Hashemites, who had no history east of the Hejaz. If the Peace Conference were to settle on a Hashemite, there would be a lot of groundwork to do.

Despite all the difficulties, Gertrude believed that the time had come. For Iraq, self-government would have to be a British decision, organized by the British, and supported by the British. The other members of the old Arab Bureau had been equally captivated by the Arabs, and by the civilization they had created and enjoyed before the five hundred years of Turkish misrule. The ambition to restore to them their ancient culture was heartfelt, but pragmatic too. There was no prospect of any outside nation now having the will or the resources to colonize all or even parts of Arabia.

Lord Kitchener had written: 'If the Arab Nation assist England in this war that has been forced on us . . . England will guarantee that no internal intervention takes place in Arabia and will give the Arabs every assistance against external forcing or aggression.' The promise had been made, and as far as Gertrude was concerned, it must be honoured. Suggestions of less worthy political agendas or imperialist intentions in the West roused her to a passionate and majestic anger:

> I propose to assume . . . that the welfare and prosperity of Iraq
> is not incompatible with the welfare and prosperity of any other
> portion of the world. I assume therefore as an axiom that if, in

disposing of the question of the future administration of Iraq, we allow ourselves to be influenced by any consideration whatsoever other than the well being of the country itself and its people we shall be guilty of a shameless act of deliberate dishonesty rendered the more heinous and contemptible by our reiterated declarations of disinterested solicitude for the peoples concerned.

Her protective fury was directed not only at the politicians, but at the military. Soon after their occupation of Baghdad in 1917, British troops had come into contact with the southernmost Kurdish tribes. These had risen in revolt against the impositions of the Turks, partly in response to the cynical dealings of the Young Turks, and partly because of a yearning for racial autonomy in an area that had historically been such a melting-pot of conflicting interests. There were two Kurdish tribes, the Hamawand around Sulaimaniyah on the mountainous Persian border north-east of Baghdad, and the nomadic Jaf, further north and distributed along the western side of the Diyalah river. There was a third Kurdish area concentrated around Kirkuk, roughly halfway between Sulaimaniyah and the Diyalah. These tribes had refused the Turkish demand to preach Jihad against the Allies. Indeed, the Hamawand had welcomed the British army, believing they would become the benevolent occupiers of the important city of Khanikin, south of Sulaimaniyah. The chief of Khanikin was one Mustafa Bajlan.

In describing the dreadful fate that befell Khanikin and the Kurdish tribes, Gertrude's anger is manifest. Also evident is the reason for her contempt for the late commander-in-chief, General Maude. Cox had urged the importance of the army occupying Khanikin, even nominally, in order to maintain British interests and influence. Maude had refused to do so for lack of troops. Meanwhile, a regiment of Cossacks were drawing close to the city. The Russians were allies of the British and, coming with British consent, were not opposed by the Kurds. However, as they drew near, accounts of the excesses they had committed in other areas caused dismay and panic. They occupied Khanikin in April 1917, and almost immediately reports began to circulate that they were laying it waste, raping and looting. Mustafa Bajlan, having retreated to Sulaimaniyah, begged that at the very least a British political officer might be sent to observe and deter the Russians, but General Maude had once again refused. In her *Review of the Civil Administration of Mesopotamia*, Gertrude commented: '[Maude] did not see his way to comply fearing that friction with our allies might result from the inherent difference in our methods of treating the natives of the country.'

Their treatment at the hands of the Cossacks sent the Kurds fleeing back to Turkish occupation, bad as this had been. Mustafa Pasha, the chief of Khanikin, now came to Baghdad in person to report on the devastation there, which included the murder of both women and men and the stealing of herds and flocks. Cox went for the third time to the military command and asked them to reconsider their position. They replied that they 'doubted the accuracy of the Khanikin reports' and refused to create complications between the Allies. They even referred Mustafa Pasha's complaint to the Russian commander, who – not surprisingly – responded that no British interference was needed or required. As soon as the Russians left, the Turks reoccupied Khanikin and took over the canal heads, blocking the flow of water south, where it was vital for crops. Not until December did the British beat the Turks out of the region. Gertrude wrote: 'In no part of Mesopotamia had we encountered anything comparable to the misery which greeted us at Khanikin. The country harvested by the Russians had been sedulously gleaned by the Turks, who, when they retired, left it in the joint possession of starvation and disease.'

Hearing that there was aid to be had, the Kurds poured down the mountains and back into the town, starving and typhus-ridden, to die or recover in British camps and hospitals. The British army distributed its surplus rations and paid in cash for what it took for itself, but Kurdish goodwill had evaporated. As the road to the north-east, the Persian road, was opened up, the deep hostility to the Allies aroused by the conduct of the Cossacks became evident. One village that constituted a continual threat to lines of communication was bombed by British planes. Meanwhile, revolution had overtaken the Russian army, which was no longer under control or fighting alongside the Allies.

The Kurdish tragedy was far from over. A meeting of chiefs and nobles was held at Sulaimaniyah and a provisional Kurdish government set up, but the necessary diversion of British troops from the principal city, Kirkuk, to open the Persian road, had allowed the Turks to reoccupy the territory once again. Fleeing refugees from every district became the objects of revenge, defenceless against any tribe or army that came across them. Gertrude wrote to Chirol in December 1917: 'We have taken on Khanikin . . . The tribes coming down from the North bring quantities of Armenian girls with them – tattooed like Bedouin women; I've seen some of them in Baghdad. Oh, Domnul, the awfulness of it! The rivers of tears, the floods of human misery that these waifs represent.'

Mosul was finally occupied by the British in November 1918. Now once more there was an opportunity to pacify the country: but two years earlier the Sykes–Picot Agreement had decreed that the Mosul *vilayet* was to be in the French 'sphere of influence'. After all they had endured, the Kurds were in a ferment. They did not know, and were not told for another year, who would be granting – or denying – them racial autonomy, or where their borders were to be. Gertrude fumed. Lonely political officers, the unsung heroes of the Mesopotamian administration, were placed in charge of volatile districts with a couple of clerks and two or three armed soldiers for protection, and told to hold the peace. Three were killed in Amidiyah, Zakho and Bira Kapra, together with their parties.

The Paris Peace Conference proved once and for all that the ignorance of the West about the Middle East was equalled only by its lack of interest. A.T. had noted in Paris:

> Experts on Western Arabia, both military and civil were there in force, but not one, except Miss Bell, had any first-hand knowledge of Iraq or Nejd, or, indeed of Persia. The very existence of a Shi'ah majority in Iraq was blandly denied as a

figment of my imagination by one 'expert' with an international reputation, and Miss Bell and I found it impossible to convince either the Military or the Foreign Office Delegations that Kurds in the Mosul vilayet were numerous and likely to be troublesome, [or] that Ibn Saud was a power seriously to be reckoned with.

Travelling among the Kurds on her expeditions, Gertrude had written that she had 'rather lost her heart' to them, but they were, and remain to this day, a particular problem for any administration. Occupants of the northern reaches of Mesopotamia since prehistory, they were constantly at war with their neighbours, the entire area a mix of many races and creeds, Sunni, Shia, and Christian. They were also scattered throughout Turkey and northern Persia. She admitted that an Arab national ideal, if such were possible, would be of no good to the Kurds, and she would struggle for the rest of her life to yoke their inchoate nationalist aspirations to the service of peace and progress. For now, on the Kurdistan question, the Iraq administration was obliged to mark time, partly because they did not have the troops to police the area, and partly because the border between Turkey and Iraq would not be established for many years to come. Neither were the three groups of Mesopotamian Kurds united with each other: the Kirkuk Kurds refused to be connected in any way with the Sulaimani Kurds. Nevertheless, they were of one mind in demanding 'a Kurdish independent state under our protection,' wrote Gertrude, 'but what they mean by that neither they nor anyone else knows . . . So much for Kurdish nationalism . . .'

A small Kurdish contingent attended the Paris Peace Conference to demand their own country, but no one was prepared to listen to them, and few of the delegates seemed to know who they were or where they came from.

After her tour with her father in the spring of 1919, Gertrude dipped into the Conference once more and then spent the early summer with the rest of the family in England, dodging friends' invitations. 'Beloved Mother. Now I want most immensely to see *you*,' she told Florence.

Florence, who had thought carefully about her stepdaughter's domestic problems – 'What I need is a wife!' – had prepared the ground carefully and tactfully, and was able to present her with a solution. Her French servant Marie Delaire was ready, if wanted, to accompany Gertrude to Baghdad and live with her as lady's maid, seamstress and housekeeper. Gertrude had engaged Marie in 1902, seventeen years previously, for '22 pounds [a year] and her washing'. Since then Marie had become a staple component of the Bell household, working for Gertrude whenever she returned to England. Marie's previous employer had written in her reference that the maid had a bad temper, but Gertrude had 'given her a good talking to' early on, and thereafter found her most amenable. Gertrude herself was by no means easy-going, but Marie served her devotedly and was no doubt proud of her fame. After many years of attending to Florence's equally fastidious wardrobe requirements and being just one Bell servant among many, travelling to Iraq with Gertrude must have seemed a great adventure. She would occupy two new rooms that Gertrude was adding to one of the summer-houses, and would become a great help and support to her mistress. At the end of September, after her second visit to the Paris Conference, Gertrude embarked for Port Said with Marie at her side. The Frenchwoman proved to be an admirable traveller and loved every minute of the journey: 'I've never been so well dressed on a ship,' wrote Gertrude in a letter home on 26 September, 'for she digs into the boxes and produces a fresh costume daily.'

Over recent years, Gertrude had wondered about the well-being of Fattuh, her faithful servant from Aleppo who had accompanied her on many trips. She worried that his connections with the English would have caused him mistreatment at the hands of the Turks: 'Heaven knows if [Fattuh] is still living,' she had written in 1917. 'Aleppo has suffered and is suffering most horribly from Turkish persecution and I fear his well-known association with George [Lloyd] and Mr Hogarth and me will put him at a grave disadvantage.' Now, on her way to Baghdad, she decided to travel back via Aleppo and try to find him. But first she would go on a fact-finding tour. She wanted to get a clear and up-to-date picture of the Syrian situation, and of Zionist developments in Palestine, where Jews were being introduced into the country without a great deal of consideration for the Arab population. She predicted much of the trouble that would follow – and apart from Palestine, there were also some fifty thousand Jews in Baghdad. The last thing she wanted was enmity between Jews and Arabs.

Marie, meanwhile, went on by sea to Basra, from where she would take the train to Baghdad to arrive at more or less the same time as her mistress.

Gertrude touched down in Cairo to 'get the hang of things' from Sir Gilbert Clayton, now Minister of the Interior in the new British protectorate of Egypt. Travelling on to Jerusalem, she stayed with the Administrator General, Sir Harry Watson, and saw a great deal of her good friend Sir Ronald Storrs. Now Governor of Jerusalem, a title he described as 'directly in line of succession to Pontius Pilate', he was in reliably comic mode, ready to talk politics or trawl the carpet and antique markets with her. She was surprised at the strength of anti-French feeling in Damascus and Beirut. Moving on to Aleppo, she tracked down Fattuh and found his circumstances every bit as hard as she had feared. A letter dated 17 October 1919 expresses her great affection for her old employee:

> . . . Fattuh looks older and as if he had been through an awful time, as indeed he has. He has lost everything he had – he was beginning to be quite a well-to-do man and now he has only a horse and a small cart with which he brings in wood to sell in Aleppo . . . He used to have two big houses of his own, poor Fattuh . . . He was chiefly suspect because he was known to have been my servant . . . We have had such happy times together – I called to mind joyous departures from Aleppo, and looking at his haggard face I said 'Oh Fattuh before the war our hearts were so light when we travelled, now they are so heavy that a camel could not carry us' . . . My poor Fattuh.

Visiting his wife in the tiny rented house where they now lived, she discovered that he had kept and still cherished her camp kit. He asked after her father in the terminology that had always made her smile – 'His Excellency the Progenitor'. She was able to help him rent a garden for growing his vegetables, and gave him a hundred pounds.

Back in Baghdad, Gertrude began to show, at last, her gratitude for Marie's help and talents, discovering that she was as capable of making a delicious sauce for a dinner party as a set of lampshades. And from now on, Marie became her dedicated dressmaker. It was easier for the Bells to send off lengths of cloth than the finished article, and Marie was kept busy turning these into dresses. The two women would pore over the fashion magazines on quiet evenings, notably the new British *Vogue*, bought by Florence's maid Lizzie and posted to Baghdad so they would 'know the mode'. Fond of animals, Marie was soon being followed about by Gertrude's tame partridge, the latest addition to the garden menagerie, and making winter coats for the two greyhounds. During Gertrude's frequent maladies, the fevers and chills brought on by overwork and the difficult climate, Marie made iced soups and other tempting concoctions. For all the differences between them, the two women became close friends, and maid remained with mistress for the rest of Gertrude's life. She wrote: 'Marie has been invaluable in making curtains and generally seeing to things. She is the greatest comfort – I don't know how I did without her.'

Hugh had not given up his idea of visiting Gertrude in Baghdad, particularly since Hugo was back in England from South Africa and staying with Florence. With this visit in mind, Gertrude had spent much of her accumulated income in London buying furniture from the smart furniture shop Maples. She wanted more dining chairs and tables, armchairs, beds, wardrobes, chests of drawers and a new dinner service. Back in Baghdad, she would wait impatiently for them to follow her by sea.

In the spring of 1920 Hugh made his promised visit, bringing the travelling items that she had stipulated for him: a camp bed, with bedding in a Wolsey valise, flannel and silk suits, a topee and a sun umbrella. In a photograph taken in her house, Hugh composedly reads the newspaper in one of the new armchairs in its William Morris linen cover, a Persian rug under his well polished shoes and an occasional table at his elbow. On the mantelpiece stand framed family photographs. It could be the drawing-room of a comfortable house in the home counties rather than a garden pavilion in the middle of a great Asian city. He was not allowed to rest there long: they set off on a tour of the country, staying with political officers stationed along their route and visiting Arab notables as they went. They covered some of the distance by plane and discussed, besides Iraq, the Depression and its grip on the British economy. For the first time Gertrude became aware of the need for a degree of economy as her father outlined the first indications of looming financial trouble for the Bells. When he had gone, she missed him dreadfully. He remained what he had always been, save for Dick Doughty-Wylie – the love of her life:

> I wonder how anyone can complain about anything when they have a father like you. I can't tell you what it was like to have you here. One takes for granted where you are concerned that no matter how unfamiliar or complex the things may be that you're seeing or hearing, you'll grasp the whole lie of them at once . . . When I got home the house seemed terribly empty without you – my dogs did their best to comfort me but it wasn't quite enough. – Bless you dearest.

If her life in the office had diminished, her social life had expanded. Two years previously she had started her 'Tuesdays': tea in the garden for the wives of Arab notables. Sir Percy had suggested it, as Lady Cox spoke hardly a word of Arabic, and there was no one else who could do it. Soft drinks, cakes and fruit were provided, and as the daylight faded, coloured glass lanterns would be lit among the bushes and trees. Some fifty women, mostly veiled, and glad to break out of their lives of exclusion, came to meet one another and gossip. She recounted to Chirol: 'I had a ladies' tea party the other day, to which all the great ladies came. It was most select – I turned down all the second rate Christians. Nawab . . . who prepared the list of invitees . . . thought it his duty to mention "Sahib! There are no Christians!" I burst out laughing and replied "You forget that I shall be there!"'

But more to her taste were the political soirées – men only –

that she began for young Arab nationalists. These events were regarded with extreme irritation by A.T., but in her view they were enormously valuable in keeping open lines of communication and preparing for an eventual Arab government. She entertained some thirty at a time, in accordance with her sympathies for the cause and her lifelong belief in the exchange of views. Her opinion of the Englishwomen around her, the wives of her colleagues, was unregenerate. She was irritated by their failure to learn Arabic, and by their pressing invitations to her to take part in the social and sporting activities with which they filled their otherwise empty days. She was angry when they did not turn out for events that she considered obligatory, such as the opening of the first girls' school in Baghdad, at which she gave the official speech in Arabic. Her attitude towards them, which was becoming apparent, cannot have endeared her to them.

> I find social duties rather trying. These idle women here have nothing to do all day long and expect me to call and be called on in the one hour of the day when I can get out and think of nothing. The result is I never get out at all, but I'm going to stop this. It makes life too intolerable and it makes me ill. So they can think what they like about me but I won't bother about them any more.

It was not that Gertrude disliked women, but she did not have much time and she was discriminating. Her relations with Arab women were steadily improving. She arranged for a new woman doctor to give them a lecture on female hygiene, and was gratified to find every seat taken. Before long she was encouraging them to form a committee and collect among the rich families for a new project, a women's hospital. To Chirol again:

> I really think I am beginning to get hold of the women here . . . *Pas sans peine*, though they meet one more than half way. It means taking a good deal of trouble . . . Over and above the fact that I like seeing them and get to know a side of Baghdad which I could know no other way, I'm sure it's worth it. One comes and goes

in the houses with intimacy and has a troop of female friends who vastly improve one's personal relations with the men.

She had much enjoyed the company of the Van Esses, a missionary and his interesting wife whom she had met in Basra. She missed Mrs Humphrey Bowman, the wife of the Director of Education, when the couple left for Egypt, and she loved Aurelia, 'the darling little Italian wife' of Mr Tod who worked for Lynch Brothers in Baghdad; she had stayed with them in 1914. Mrs Tod was a willing co-worker for charity with Gertrude, and gave fundraising parties for the hospital. When her husband was away, she came for dinners à deux with Gertrude, who wrote home that she was delighted to have Aurelia in Baghdad, for she felt she was a real friend. Then there was Miss Jones, the wartime matron in Basra, now running the civil hospital in Baghdad; however seldom these two busy women could meet, she became one of Gertrude's closest women friends in Iraq. When Miss Jones died a little later, Gertrude recalled her kindness at the officers' rest home when she had been admitted with jaundice. She walked behind the Union Jack that covered her friend's coffin at the military funeral, and as she listened to the 'Last Post' she hoped that, when one day people walked behind her own coffin, it would be with thoughts not unlike hers for the good matron.

Hugh's visit had coincided with crucial events in Iraq. While he was with her, in April 1920, she had written soberly and presciently to Florence:

> I think we're on the edge of a pretty considerable Arab nationalist demonstration with which I'm a good deal in sympathy. It will, however, force our hand and we shall have to see whether it will leave us with enough hold to carry on here . . . What I do feel pretty sure of is that if we leave this country to go to the dogs . . . we shall have to reconsider our whole position in Asia. If Meso-potamia goes, Persia goes inevitably, and then India. And the place which we leave empty will be occupied by seven devils a good deal worse than any which existed before we came.

Troop reductions had left too few soldiers to hold the country down; A.T.'s repeated requests for reinforcements were ignored or refused. Winston Churchill, as Secretary of State for War and Air, wrote in the summer of 1919: 'We are at our wits' end to find a single soldier.' A.T. was required to govern 150,000 square miles of rebel-filled terrain with just seventy political officers in their remote outposts, each supported by perhaps a couple of gendarmes, a British sergeant and an armoured car, with a few clerks to back them up. There were ever more disturbances, some claiming the lives of these isolated officers. In undefended areas, planes from Baghdad carrying firebombs and mustard gas were often the only means of controlling and limiting an uprising. This much questioned tactic was approved by Churchill, who distinguished between deadly gas and gas causing temporary incapacity. He wrote from the War Office in May 1919:

I do not understand this squeamishness about the use of gas. We have definitely adopted the position at the Peace Conference of arguing in favour of the retention of gas as a permanent method of warfare. It is sheer affectation to lacerate a man with the poisonous fragment of a bursting shell and to boggle at making his eyes water by means of lachrymatory gas.

I am strongly in favour of using poisoned gas against uncivilized tribes . . . the loss of life should be reduced to a minimum. It is not necessary to use only the most deadly gasses: gasses can be used which cause great inconvenience and would spread a lively terror and yet would leave no serious permanent effects on most of those affected.

Fifteen months later, in the worst of the rebellion, he had sanctioned the use in Iraq of two more air squadrons, making four in all. He suggested they should be equipped with mustard-gas bombs 'which would inflict punishment upon recalcitrant natives without inflicting grave injury upon them'. Firebombs were also used, but only as a last resort. In August 1920 Gertrude reflected: 'If only [the rebel tribes] would throw their hands in before we are in a position to take extreme measures it would be an immense relief.

Order must be restored but it's a very doubtful triumph to restore it at the expense of many Arab lives.'

Between the Armistice in November 1918, the leisurely deliberations of the Paris Peace Conference, the forming of the League of Nations and the publishing of the British mandate for Iraq in May 1920, came eighteen months of territorial uncertainty, escalating nationalism, virulent anti-British propaganda, Turkish-funded insurgency and Bolshevik-inspired subversion. Since the Armistice, the name 'Iraq' had taken the place of the vaguer 'Mesopotamia' to denote the three *vilayets* of Basra, Baghdad and Mosul. In no sense was there yet an Iraqi nation, and the northern and western borders were unfixed, but for the first time the country was acquiring an identity. The endless procrastination was infuriating to Gertrude, as she saw all progress slipping away in the teeth of growing anarchy – the jostling ambitions of local leaders, of opportunists angling to replace the British and run Iraq themselves, and the machinations of secret Arab nationalist parties.

The people of Mesopotamia had been presented with powerful indicators that the British would be replaced: Cox had talked of self-determination, President Wilson had insisted that all 'nationalities' should be 'assured . . . an absolutely unmolested opportunity of autonomous development', the Franco-British Declaration had promised it, and the mandate would reinforce it. In contrast to those Arabs seeking power for themselves and the wilder of the tribes who wanted no government at all, was the mass of sober citizens, businessmen, landowners and sheikhs who wanted a continuance of the orderly administration that allowed them to maintain their livelihoods. Their ideal was an Arab government with British support.

To Kurds, Christians, Jews and the residual Turks, this would mean that they would be subservient minorities to whatever Arab majority was put in place. To the Arabs, self-determination brought to the fore the fundamental split between the majority Shias – unworldly, apolitical – and the minority Sunnis – educated, powerful, financially astute. If these two communities were to form a government, they would have to form a united religious front first.

Sunnis and Shias began to attend certain religious meetings together. In May 1920, in every Sunni and Shia mosque, the festival of Ramadhan brought the assemblies known as *mauluds*, held in tribute to the birth of the Prophet. There, political speeches were made and patriotic poetry recited: the excitement was intense and spilled out into the streets. The next month, Gertrude was commenting: 'The Nationalist propaganda increases. There are constant meetings in mosques ... The extremists are out for independence, without a mandate. They play for all they are worth on the passions of the mob and what with the Unity of Islam and the Rights of the Arab Race they make a fine figure. They have created a reign of terror.'

How to reach out to the Shias, those grimly devout citizens of the holy cities, was a major problem for the British administration. The religious leadership in citadels such as Najaf and Kadhimain would never accept rule by the infidels. At a time when the wives of the political officers were being sent back to England out of harm's way, Gertrude was fearless in penetrating these bastions ruled by the *mujtahids*, each of whom had studied for twenty years in order to reach the status of priestly scholar. Their merest word commanded obedience. Gertrude wrote:

> There they sit in an atmosphere which reeks of antiquity and is so thick with the dust of ages that you can't see through it ... And for the most part they are very hostile to us, a feeling we can't alter because it's so difficult to get at them ... Until quite recently I've been wholly cut off from them because their tenets forbid them to look upon an unveiled woman and my tenets don't permit me to veil.

The Sadr of Kadhimain, perhaps the chief Shia family, at last put out sufficient feelers for Gertrude to offer, with all courtesies, to visit them. Escorted by a free-thinking Baghdad Shia, someone she knew well, she made her way through the narrow, crooked streets to the house of the *mujtahid* Sayyid Hassan and stopped before a small archway. She entered a dark, vaulted passage fifty yards long, then emerged into the velvet silence of an ancient courtyard. She was led through shuttered verandas into the presence of the bearded *mujtahid*, who sat on a carpet before her in his black robe and formidably large turban. Formal greetings over, he began to talk in the rolling periods of the book-learned man. 'I was acutely conscious of the fact that no woman before me had ever been invited to drink coffee with a mujtahid and listen to his discourse,' **Gertrude recorded,** 'and really anxious lest I shouldn't make a good impression.'

They discussed Arab libraries, French intentions in the Middle East, and Bolshevism. She stayed two hours, at the end of which the *mujtahid* complimented her on being the most learned woman of her time, and invited her to visit him as often as she liked.

For Gertrude, much of 1919 and 1920 was marked by feelings of anger over the protracted and ill-informed decisions being made in Europe over the Middle East. Prominent moderate Arabs were continually dropping in to remind her that three years had elapsed since Arab government had first been promised, and nothing had yet materialized.

Doubts about the British agenda were matched by confusion over the Iraqi-Syrian border on the upper Euphrates. At the end of 1919, as British troop numbers were being reduced, there was a major incident at Dair al Zor. The inhabitants had requested that a British officer be sent there to maintain law and order. The officer, Captain Chamier, arrived, only to find Arab representatives from Syria already in place. Chamier succeeded in getting the Arabs recalled to Damascus, and was attempting to clarify his orders when a local leader raised a force of two thousand fanatical tribesmen to retaliate by attacking Dair in the name of Arab independence. The leader was Ramadhan al Shallash of the Mesopotamian League, an extremist political club – as opposition parties were banned and political meetings had to be held in secret, such organizations were referred to as 'clubs' in order to deflect suspicion. The petrol depot was blown up, the hospital, church and offices raided, and ninety people were killed. Meanwhile the majority of the town's leaders, having invited Shallash and his tribesmen in, found themselves unable to control the killing and looting, and begged Chamier to restore the peace. Chamier, with only twenty men, walked bravely along the main street side by side with the mayor in order to try to calm the population, but was attacked on his return and only survived thanks to the simultaneous arrival of two planes from Baghdad, which strafed the town.

Shallash was superseded by another member of the League who at once declared Jihad against the British infidel. The border still being in dispute and undecided, orders came from London to withdraw British control closer to Baghdad. The entire area to its north now became a ferment of insurrection and a channel for Iraqi nationalists infiltrating from Syria. Worse still, the retreat of the British convinced the tribesmen of the Shammar and Dulaim that reports of British military weakness had not been exaggerated. Raids on the road between Baghdad and Mosul culminated with the burning of a train. British officers and their staff, four in all, were killed west of Mosul; and had a British column not arrived in the nick of time, Mosul would have been taken and the whole *vilayet* given over to anarchy.

The interminable deliberations of the Paris Peace Conference had also thrown the much divided territories of Kurdistan into chaos. The Mesopotamian Kurds did not know whether they would end up under the rule of the French, the Turks or the British. In an area where each tribe fought its neighbours, the only element of agreement was their rejection of interference of any kind. Some concluded that government by Christians was a worse prospect, because of the likelihood of their retaliating on behalf of the Armenians. At the Peace Conference, pious sentiments had been expressed towards the Armenians and their tragic past. These Christian people, victims of genocide, had suffered under the harsh rule of Russia, Turkey and Persia ever since the end of the fourteenth century. In the 1890s, the Turks, aided by the Kurds, had initiated a programme of atrocities against them and their growing nationalism. In 1915, having lost against the Russians, the Turks ordered that the Armenians be deported from eastern Anatolia on the grounds that they were 'traitors'. If they were not killed before they could leave their homeland, most died of hunger, exhaustion and disease on the forced marches southwards. Those who died numbered between 300,000 and 1,500,000. The Turks were still powerful and dangerously close, and behind Turkey stood Russia and the Bolsheviks, ready to go to the aid of anyone who fought the accepted order. 'We share the blame with France and America for what is happening – I think there has seldom been such a series of hopeless blunders as the West has made about the East since the armistice,' Gertrude wrote.

In Baghdad, meanwhile, the better-educated younger men began a movement for higher education. As only thirty-three people were currently in secondary education in all of Mesopotamia, their ostensible object was irreproachable. They succeeded in collecting financial support from the wealthy families of the city, and a grant from the Education Department. The new school opened at the beginning of 1920, but after only four months it had become the headquarters of extreme nationalist parties. Documents were found later showing that the funds had been used to hire assassins to remove prominent figures opposed to their views.

As anarchy gained ground, order could not be maintained outside the perimeter of the Baghdad defences, and even friendly chiefs warned that they could not answer for their tribesmen unless the British could score some striking success. To the north, on the Diyalah river, the tribes cut railway communications and attacked Baqubah, the British proving unable to protect it from the mob. South of Baghdad, at Shahraban and Kifri, administrative staff were massacred. A train was derailed and the British garrison at Diwaniyah evacuated sixty miles to Hillah by means of lifting the rails from the back of the train and placing them at the front to fill the gaps. The journey to safety of the three thirsty companies of Manchesters took an excruciating eleven days. They collected en route extra engines and carriages on intact sections of the line, and when they pulled into Hillah the train was over a mile long and punctured with bullets from end to end.

The wilder tribes of southern Iraq had a particular grievance. They had never previously paid taxes, and refused to do so now to the British, just as they had with the Turks. Primitive villagers ruled by warlords, they held grazing land and raised crops under the protection of their chieftain in his defensive tower. Unlike the Turks, the British spent all revenue for the benefit of Iraq. The job of the administration was to raise that revenue come what may, and in the face of opposition from some of his colleagues A.T. gave orders that the towers of the most recalcitrant chieftains were to be bombed. Gertrude had grave reservations about these tactics. She urged A.T. to try to negotiate for tribal cooperation by means of a native committee, but he ignored her pleas. Her memo on the subject had probably been thrown straight into the waste paper basket, she reflected. A.T., frustrated by the liberal sentiments of the mandate and as convinced as ever that the country could only be properly run by direct colonial rule, considered that resistance was inevitable and should be quickly isolated and firmly put down. 'The tribes down there are some of the most lawless in Iraq,' Gertrude wrote in July 1920. '. . . They're rogues, I know . . . But I doubt whether we've gone the best way to make them appreciate the benefits of settled government. For months I and others have been telling A.T. that we were pressing them too hard . . .'

A.T. did not change his position, but in spite of the bombings, the British failed to score a resounding victory in southern Iraq. Opposition to the British spread, with special repercussions for Gertrude, whose early influence, under Sir Percy Cox, had helped persuade the formerly friendly sheikhs to hand in a total of some fifty thousand rifles. Now those very tribes were at a peculiar disadvantage under attack from their neighbours, and had a valid grievance against the British.

Alarm grew among the citizens of Baghdad. Two distinguished Sunni magnates, one of them an extreme nationalist, called on Gertrude in her office to see if anything could be done to pacify the tribes. The Baghdadi notables, having initiated and escalated the trouble in the south, now found the problem getting out of hand. The mob was destroying property in an area where many of them owned land, blowing up the roads and railways and cutting off supplies. Interestingly, the two magnates did not call on A.T.: his views were too well known and his manner still brusque to the point of rudeness, even with the most distinguished of Arab visitors.

To Gertrude they suggested sending a deposition to the divines of Karbala and Najaf, asking them to exert their influence and rein back the tribesmen. She responded that their project would be more effective if they were represented by Sunnis and Shias together, shrewdly reminding them of their recent exhortations on the unity of Islam. With some reluctance they conceded her point. She wrote a summary of the plan, with suggested names, and took it in to A.T. 'He was visibly put out and said he could only listen if the matter came to him through Captain Clayton ... I brought in dear Captain Clayton and he sat there as audience while we finished my scheme ... A.T. had to climb down.'

Accumulated British defeats led to further troubles. British installations were being wrecked and communities isolated. By February 1920 she was writing to Florence:

> We are now in the middle of a full-blown Jihad, that is to say we have against us the fiercest prejudices of a people in a primeval state of civilization. Which means that it's no longer a question of reason ... We're near to the collapse of society – the end of the Roman empire is a very close historical parallel ... The credit of European civilization is gone ... How can we, who have managed our own affairs so badly, claim to teach others to manage theirs better?

With the collapse of Arab society seemingly imminent, Gertrude wanted more than ever what she had always wanted: a prosperous and peaceful Arab nation. Even now, she was determined to stay put:

> It's touch and go – another episode like that of the Manchesters would bring the Tigris tribes out immediately below Bagdad. We are living from hand to mouth ... We may at any moment be cut off from the universe if the Tigris tribes rise. It doesn't seem to matter. In fact I don't mind at all ... Well, if the British evacuate Mesopotamia, I shall stay peacefully here and see what happens.

Off-the-cuff remarks like this could have aroused A.T.'s suspicions about his political officer's priorities and allegiances. During the past couple of years, the two of them had engendered an escalating crisis of their own. With A.T. carrying the whole weight of the administration on his admittedly broad shoulders, and 'cross as a bear' in consequence, they were bound to clash, particularly in Cox's absence. Wilson was, after all, doing an impossible job. Implementing government while waiting for the mandate to be declared was a juggling act, and he was trying to run the administration of an entire country with a central staff of five plus fifty-five assistants, in addition to the seventy British officers monitoring the outlying regions. The tribal attacks on roads and railways hampered the movement of troops around the country to where they were needed: principally, to guard the essential installations – the oil terminal, docks, warehouses and government offices. Moreover, at any one time a high proportion of the sixty thousand troops supposedly at his disposal were on leave deferred from wartime, or in army hospitals suffering from heat exhaustion or malaria. Meanwhile London was constantly reminding him that the insurrection was costing the British taxpayer £2 million a month in military expenditure.

'Rather a trying week,' was Gertrude's understatement of events during this period, 'for A.T. has been over-worked – a chronic state – and in a condition when he ought not to be working, which results in making him savagely cross and all our lives rather a burden in consequence.'

Both so rigorous and dynamic, Gertrude and A.T. were poles apart in almost every other respect. He was thirty-four in 1920, and eccentric in a peculiarly British stoical tradition. His father had been headmaster of the empire-oriented Clifton College near Bristol, where he had been educated, so his background was reactionary and chauvinistic. His favourite reading was the Bible, his favourite poet Kipling, his preferred epithets Latin ones. He was built in heroic mould, but his views placed him firmly in the past. Despite the fact that she was all of eighteen years older than him, Gertrude, with her particular intelligence and her whole-hearted dedication to the Arab cause, belonged to the future.

Nevertheless the conflict between them was not so much

personal as professional. A.T. was becoming deeply suspicious of
Gertrude's relations with her numerous important acquaintances
both in the West and in the East, and especially of her rapport with
the Arab nationalists who opposed his government. She looked
among the powerful Iraqi leaders for future representatives and
used their own aspirations to forward the constitutional changes
she envisaged. He had written to a friend at the India Office, 'She
will take some handling . . . she is undoubtedly popular in Baghdad
among the natives, with whom she keeps in close touch, to her
advantage, though it is sometimes dangerous.' He was even,
perhaps, jealous of her influence and intimacy with Arabs in general,
for she did not pursue her enquiries only among the VIPs: she
continually went out into the countryside, by horse or car, making
acquaintance with boat-builders, marsh farmers, fishermen and
villagers, listening and taking in their views. A.T. came to suspect
that her work was undermining his. He was constitutionally unable
to carry out the day-to-day running of the country while preparing
to dismantle British government in favour of an uncertain future.
She, by contrast, worked tirelessly outside the conventional limits
of her job in her effort to show what needed to be done in readiness
for a British-assisted Arab administration. She did not care whether
or not it was British imperial practice for political officers to
entertain the locals in their own houses, or go to places where
women were not supposed to go, or enter into one-to-one
conversations with extremists. Against a background of procrastination and its disastrous results, an impasse was reached. 'My own
feeling is that if, when we set up civil government, we do it on really
liberal lines, and *not be* afraid, we shall have the country with us . . . I
wish I carried more weight. But the truth is I'm in a minority of one in
the Mesopotamian political service – or nearly – and yet I'm sure that
I'm right.'

When A.T. was made a KCIE in May 1920, Gertrude thought
he deserved it and was genuinely glad, but commented: 'I confess I
wish that in giving him a knighthood they could also endow him with
the manners knights are traditionally credited with!' Both of them were
writing to their absent chief, Sir Percy Cox, during this time.

Gertrude kept him in touch with every turn and twist of Iraqi events, fretting at his absence and trusting that he would return before it was too late. 'Sir P.C. is a very great personal asset and I wish the Government would let him come back at once. The job here is far more important than Persia.'

A.T. had begun to complain of Gertrude to Cox, in an attempt to get rid of her. Lest she should discover this correspondence, he employed coded references to his political officer, referring to her as 'the individual' or 'him', and their troubled relationship as 'the problem'. Six months after Cox's departure, A.T. had disbanded the Baghdad branch of the Arab Bureau, under whose auspices she had technically been appointed, and had intimated to Cox that he did not know what there would be for her to do if she returned after the Paris Peace Conference and her protracted leave. Cox played the diplomat: he wanted to get back to Baghdad and he needed Gertrude.

Meanwhile, A.T.'s rages dominated the Secretariat. There was much shouting and slamming of doors, and his brooding presence put a dampener on the office lunches, where Gertrude made a point of talking to other officers in order to avoid his heavy silences. But there was no going back after mid-June, when they had a worse row than usual. She confided in a letter to Hugh:

. . . my own path has been very difficult. I had an appalling scene last week with A.T. We had been having a sort of honeymoon and then most unfortunately I gave one of our Arab friends here a bit of information I ought not, technically, to have given. It wasn't of much importance and it didn't occur to me I had done wrong till I mentioned it casually to A.T. He was in a black rage that morning and he vented it on me. He told me my indiscretions were intolerable, and that I should never see another paper in the office. I apologized for that particular indiscretion, but he continued: 'You've done more harm than anyone here. If I hadn't been going away myself I should have asked for your dismissal months ago – you and your Amir!' At this point he choked with anger.

The underlying differences between them had been brought to the boil by their disagreement over a draft of a Mesopotamian constitution suggested by the nationalist Yasin Pasha, destined to become a future prime minister of Iraq. Gertrude found it quite reasonable and said so. A.T. replied with the now customary blast: anything of the kind was entirely incompatible with British control, he said, and he would never accept it. Obliged, nevertheless, to follow the guidelines from London, he shortly made a speech to a deputation in which he conceded the possibility of an Amir of Iraq. Gertrude wrote:

> Of course we can't prevent it, nor have we any interest in doing so. But I know well that if this attitude had been adopted 8 months ago, we should not now be in the very delicate position in which we find ourselves. And I expect A.T. knows it too. I think myself that he ought to go now, because he never can be in real sympathy with the policy which was laid down from home in 1918 . . . Meantime it may be I who goes. But I shall not send in my resignation. I shall only go if I am ordered.

There was, however, light at the end of the tunnel. Sir Percy Cox was at last requested to return from Teheran. He passed through Baghdad on his way to London in June, stopping off for a long discussion with Gertrude and leaving her to look after his parrot until his return to Iraq in the autumn. A few days previously, A.T. had received a deputation from a committee of Baghdadis, asking that a constituent assembly be formed to decide the future form of government. Cox concurred, in an announcement that Mesopotamia be constituted an independent state under the guarantee of the League of Nations and subject to the British mandate — by which Britain was obliged to govern Iraq until the country qualified for independence and for joining the League of Nations. He announced that he would return to Baghdad in the autumn to establish a provisional Arab government.

When Cox left for London, he took the first half of a paper that would prove to be Gertrude's *magnum opus*. It was a book-length report that she had been writing for months, that would show the spadework that had been done and convince the British government that, in spite of the insurrection, Mesopotamia had been enough of a success to justify the British staying on. The rest of *Review of the Civil Administration of Mesopotamia* by Miss Gertrude Bell, CBE, was dispatched in the diplomatic bag. It had taken her nine months, writing mostly in her spare time, and when the whole document was presented as a White Paper to both Houses of Parliament, Gertrude – in her absence – received a standing ovation, an exceptional accolade. Florence wrote immediately, sending newspaper cuttings with the family's heartfelt congratulations and her own question as to whether Gertrude had written it at Wilson's instigation. She replied in unequivocal fashion:

> I've just got Mother's letter saying there's a fandango about my report. The general line taken by the press seems to be that it's most remarkable that a dog should be able to stand up on its hind legs – i.e. a female write a white paper. I hope they'll drop that source of wonder and pay attention to the report itself . . . By the way, Mother need not think it was A.T. who asked me to write it – it was the India Office, and I insisted, very much against his will, on doing it my own way.

There would be four more difficult months before Cox returned, but they would be the last four months of having to work with A.T., who was now anxious to move on. There had been warnings from London that the state of affairs in Iraq could not be allowed to continue. A.T. had proved incapable of departing from his high-handed colonial methods when dealing with opposition, usually instigated and funded by the Turks, and early demands for Arab control. He would allow the situation to get out of hand, then react over-harshly, provoking yet more defiance. Nor could he bring himself to use Gertrude as Cox had used her, to bargain, persuade and cajole the tribesmen into collaboration. There was so much that she could have done, but A.T. had sidelined her from the start. He intended to resign, but he also knew that he would not be pressed to stay once Cox was back in the saddle. And there would be one final devastating row between him and Gertrude.

Gertrude had always maintained a vigorous political correspondence with the influential people she knew in London, Cairo, Jerusalem and Delhi. Cox had not objected, because he agreed with her aims and knew that her persuasive if maverick style increased understanding and brought beneficial results. It was something that a man, perhaps, would not have done, but Gertrude considered that she had earned the right to speak out, and she was highly respected in social milieux long before she had become a government employee. Her ambitions went far beyond any official promotions she might receive; in fact, there was no post possible for her, although she had been amused when colleagues had voted her second choice for High Commissioner after Cox. After that, when she wrote to Florence, she had signed herself 'High Commissioner'.

To Florence in early 1920:

> I've just written a long letter to Lord Robert [Cecil] giving an exhaustive criticism of the dealings of the [Paris Peace] Conference with Western Asia . . . For from first to last it's radically bad and there can't be any stability in existing arrangements . . . I have written to Edwin Montagu an immense letter about the sort of government we ought to set up here and even sent him the rough draft of a constitution . . . At any rate I've done my best both to find out what should be done and to lay it before him. I sometimes feel that it's the only thing I really care for, to see this country go right . . .

She could hardly have chosen a more prestigious correspondent. Montagu was Secretary of State for India, with ultimate responsibility for Mesopotamia. Did he enquire of A.T. whether the letter was endorsed by him as Acting Civil Commissioner, or did he assume that Gertrude was stepping out of line? In any event, her letter drew a stinging rebuke in the form of a long telegram:

> From Mr Montagu for Miss Bell. Private and Personal.
>
> I hope you will understand from me that in the present critical state of affairs of Mesopotamia when the future of the country hangs in the balance we should all pull together. If you have

views which you wish us to consider, I should be glad if you would either ask the Civil Commissioner to communicate them or apply for leave and come home and represent them. You may always be sure of consideration of your views but Political Officers should be very careful of their private correspondence with those not at present in control of affairs. Apart from all questions of usual practice and convention it may increase rather than diminish difficulties, a result which I know you would deplore.

If he thought this would crush her, he was wrong. She was not prepared to take it lying down. After all, she was pursuing the steps to self-determination that had been sanctioned, while A.T. was ignoring them as far as it was possible to do so. In April, in the teeth of the nationalist uprisings, he had executed a volte face and attempted to diffuse tension by drawing up a provisional constitution for Iraq, including a council of state composed of British and Arab members with an Arab president, to be chosen by the High Commissioner, and a legislative assembly chosen by election. It had been too little and too late.

Smartly, she sent back her own riposte to Montagu (she did not take a copy, but sent her father a duplicate from memory):

> . . . Colonel Wilson gives me every opportunity of telling him any considerations which may occur to me. I am also wholly in agreement with policy which has been pursued since April. You are sufficiently aware of my general attitude towards the Arab question to know that I regret it was not embarked on earlier. To express this view in public would now however be valueless and even harmful. With regard to correspondence, except for private letters to my Father I cannot recall letters on political subjects to unofficial persons which have not been previously submitted to Colonel Wilson. Your remarks are however a useful warning.

A.T. followed Montagu's telegram, of which he would have been sent a copy, with a stiff inter-office note:

Miss Bell. When Sir Percy Cox passed through he asked – *à propos* of events earlier in the year – whether my relations with you were happier. I said that I could not say they were – that your divergence of opinion was marked and a matter of public knowledge and indeed of comment . . . I said the position would be untenable but for the fact that I was hoping before long to be relieved. You have always maintained your right as an individual to write what you like – to whom you like . . . but I do not like their being written and the fact that I am cognizant of them must not be held to include approval. Otherwise I have no comment to make.

It was the breaking point. When they talked the following day, Gertrude reminded him that it had been inevitable that people knew their opinions diverged, because she had always said so – and to A.T. himself first and foremost. He told her that he objected to any private communications with the India Office, and she replied that she thought it preposterous but would comply with his wishes – 'On this we shook hands warmly – you can't shake hands anything but warmly when the temperature is 115.'

In spite of all, A.T. had been a good organizer, and the day-to-day administration had continued to build on the successes detailed by Gertrude in the White Paper. The country had become prosperous, as exemplified by a rise in taxes. The income of the administration had risen by 300 per cent in the three years until 1920. The fact that the tax revenue had balanced out with expenditure was all-important. Churchill's administrative task as Secretary of State for the Colonies was to cut by half the £37 million currently spent ruling Palestine, Iraq and Arabia, and to find an affordable system of government for the Middle East. In Iraq he would try to reduce the £20 million annual military expenditure to £7 million. He was soon to report to Lloyd George on the absolute need of 'appeasing' Arab sentiment – 'Otherwise we should certainly be forced by expense of the garrisons to evacuate the territories which each country had gained in the war.' Every project in the Middle East would now be subject to reducing military expenditure.

The night before A.T. left, at the end of September, he went into Gertrude's office to say goodbye. It was an emotional moment in which the generous impulses of both came to the fore. She rose and moved towards him, saying that she was feeling more deeply discouraged than she could say, and regretting acutely that they had not made a better job of their relations. When he replied that he had come to apologize, she interrupted him – it was as much her fault as his, she said. She then paid him her greatest compliment, inviting him to call on her father and mother in London; he undertook to do so.

A.T.'s official career was soon over. He married a young widow and took up a post with the Anglo-Persian Oil Company as manager of their operations in the Middle East. A private letter he was to write to a friend from Muhammarah, in the Persian Gulf, a couple of years later shows that his anger encompassed Cox as well as Gertrude. He accuses his old boss of dishonesty and incompetence, of 'promising all things and doing nothing', and calls the Mesopotamia of 1922 'pitiful: no guidance – no decision'. He puts his own spin on events: 'I rejoice daily that I took the plunge and left with colours flying, and that so many of the old gang left with me – all who could afford it . . . No-one trusts Cox now – and his reputation has slumped dreadfully.'

On 11 October 1920, Sir Percy returned to Baghdad. The station, beflagged and carpeted, was crowded with the great and the good, Arab and British. Guns were fired, the road was lined with well-wishers, and Sir Percy, in white and gold uniform, stood at the salute while the band played 'God Save the King'.

After the welcoming address, he replied with a speech in Arabic. He had come by order of HMG, he announced, to enter into counsel with the people of Iraq for the purpose of setting up an Arab government under the supervision of Britain. He asked the people to cooperate with him in establishing settled conditions, so that he might proceed at once with his task. It was a new beginning, and as Gertrude made her curtsey to him she struggled not to let her emotions show. In her letter home of a few days later she wrote:

It is quite impossible to tell you the relief and comfort it is to serve under somebody in whose judgment one has complete confidence. To the extraordinarily difficult task which lies before him he brings a single-eyed desire to act in the interests of the people of the country . . .

Oh, if we can pull this thing off; rope together the young hotheads and the Shiah obscurantists, enthusiasts, polished old statesmen and scholars – if we can make them work together and find their own salvation for themselves, what a fine thing it would be. I see visions and dream dreams . . .

14

FAISAL

In May 1885, when Gertrude was sixteen, a baby was born in his father's castle at Taif in the deserts of the Hejaz, and named after the flashing downstroke of the sword: Faisal. What were the odds that a schoolgirl from Yorkshire and a son of the Hashemite Sharif of Mecca should ever meet, or that their lives would become interwoven?

Faisal was the third son of Sharif Hussain ibn Ali, continuing the bloodline of the Prophet Muhammad through his daughter Fatima who married Ali of the Hashemite clan, and her elder son Hassan. Sharif was the family's honorific title. The Prophet's family had held temporal rule in Mecca for the last nine hundred years. Faisal was twice an aristocrat. His mother, Hussain's first wife Abdiyah Hanem, was also his father's cousin and so also sprang from the Prophet's bloodline. Following hallowed tradition, Faisal was taken from his mother at seven days old and carried off to the desert, to be brought up by a Bedouin tribe until he was seven years old. He never saw his mother again. She died when he was three. Gertrude had lost her mother at the same age.

Faisal, like his older brothers Ali and Abdullah, lived in a black tent as a child of the tribe, learning to fight by taking part in rough games, which left him with a scar on his head and, once, a broken arm.

The Hashemites were regarded by the psychopathic Sultan of the Ottoman Empire, Abdul Hamid, with a mixture of suspicion and respect. Lest these Sharifs should become pre-eminent, he periodically rounded up the most powerful and ordered them to

Constantinople, where they were obliged to live in 'honourable captivity' on frugal incomes, under the constant scrutiny of the Sultan's sinister phalanx of spies, guards and black eunuchs. This was the fate of Sharif Hussain, who would remain there with his family for eighteen long years.

In 1891, when he was six, Faisal was parted from his Bedouin foster family a year early, and taken with his brothers to join his father in a house on the Golden Horn in Constantinople. The household included the thirty-two women of his father's harem, with their suites and slaves.

Hussain was a domestic despot, determined that his sons should never enjoy comforts or luxuries. He held several traditional Ottoman posts, but his income remained modest. The household, large as it was, could only afford meat once a week. Discipline was severe: above all, the sons had to learn self-control. The *falaka* was still being used, a rope with which a child's feet were bound together and a cane for beating his soles. On the other hand, Hussain made sure that his sons were given a sound education: he employed tutors, four to begin with and many more as they grew up. The political atmosphere was highly charged and life was full of danger. The city was rife with the plotting of secret societies, and the Sultan, responsible for the deaths of perhaps half a million people over the course of his lifetime, had a nasty habit of ensuring that his victims were dead by getting their heads boxed up and delivered to him.

At eighteen, in 1903, Faisal began to learn the strategy and tactics of the Turkish army, which was trained on German lines and composed of both Turks and Arabs. As Gertrude reached Japan on her world tour with Hugo, Faisal was being sent out into the desert to patrol the sands with the Turkish camel corps. A few years later, he and Abdullah were called back to Constantinople. Hussain had been instructed by the Turks to quell a rebellion of Arab tribesmen in the southern region of Asir. Abdullah commanded the Turkish troops and Faisal led the Arab camel cavalry. They fought a desperate battle at Quz Abu-al-Ir, only to retreat with seventy survivors out of a total of three thousand. A fortnight later, they attacked the rebels again. The battle lasted two days and a night. The rebels broke up, but it was a hollow victory. The Sharif's army had been reduced from seven thousand to seventeen hundred men. Faisal and Abdullah could not prevent the Turkish troops from burning villages and killing innocent people. Nor could they ever forget the mutilation of the dead Arab rebels. Complaints to their Turkish overlords met with disdain. It was then that Sharif Hussain determined to raise a revolt against the Turks: it would become known as the Arab Revolt.

The brothers were given positions in the Turkish parliament: the Amir Abdullah represented the constituency of Mecca, and the Amir Faisal that of Jidda. The fortunes of the family changed again with the revolution of the Young Turks and their Committee of Union and Progress, whose aim was ruthless modernization of the state. In the year 1909, Abdul Hamid was deposed, a new Sultan and Caliph* was put in place, and Hussain gained the important title of Amir of Mecca, prince of the most holy city of Islam. His primary duties were the custody of the holy places in the Hejaz and the supervision of the Haj, the annual pilgrimage. He returned to his palaces in Mecca and Taif, ordering his sons to maintain their posts in Constantinople and to keep him informed of every change of political opinion.

The suggestion that the Arabs and the British might become allies had first been made before the war, when Lord Kitchener wrote to Hussain. Abdullah, as his father's envoy, travelled to and from Mecca and Constantinople, and would stop at Cairo to talk to Lord Kitchener and his Oriental Secretary Ronald Storrs. Matters came to a head with the outbreak of the war, when the Turks demanded that Hussain, as the Amir of Mecca, declare a Jihad of all Muslims against the Christians. Hussain, pious, courageous and autocratic, refused to do so, using as an excuse that the Turks themselves had a Christian ally, Germany.

Faisal now took on a most dangerous role. As a spy for his

---

* The Sultans of Constantinople had appropriated the role of Caliph in the eighteenth century.

father, he was sent to Damascus secretly to propose a military uprising against the Turks in Syria. Meanwhile, his eldest brother Ali was raising Arab troops in the Hejaz in response to Turkish demands, on the pretext that they were to aid the Turks. Faisal and his father communicated in covert ways, by means of trusted retainers who carried messages to and fro in sword-hilts, in cakes, in the soles of their sandals or written in invisible ink on the wrapping paper of gifts. Faisal's friends in the secret societies – the Arab nationalist political 'clubs' – could have betrayed him at any time, and he was particularly vulnerable as he was obliged when in Damascus to live as the guest of one General Mehmed Jemal Pasha. This Turk expected Faisal, as an officer in the Turkish army, to lead the army that his brother Ali was raising in the Hejaz. But Jemal Pasha was suspicious of Faisal because his father had refused to declare Jihad against Turkey's enemies, and continually put him to the test. He would send for Faisal, and make him watch the public hangings of scores of his Syrian friends. These brave men went to their deaths without making any appeal to Faisal, who needed all his training in self-control not to betray his disgust and anger. As Lawrence wrote in *The Seven Pillars of Wisdom*, 'Only once did he burst out that these executions would cost Jemal all that he was trying to avoid; and it took the intercessions of his Constantinople friends, chief men in Turkey, to save him.' In the meantime, the Turkish Prime Minister, responding to Hussain's terms for Arab cooperation, declared that if he wanted to see Faisal again he must tell his son to join the troops in the Hejaz.

Gertrude's and Faisal's lives were drawing closer. While he was risking his life on the secret mission in Damascus, she was visiting Charles Hardinge in India with a secret agenda – to deflect his opposition to the proposed Arab revolt. In January 1916, when a second group of Arab nationalists were being condemned, Jemal Pasha noted that Faisal 'moved heaven and earth' to save them, and remonstrated with men who would not speak in their favour. Those were the only times that Faisal let his feelings show. One false step, he knew, would have meant the end of the mission for Arab independence. Hussain now told him that all was ready for the rebellion, but Faisal believed the time was not yet ripe. His father, obstinate and controlling as always, told him to come to Medina immediately and join the troops he had amassed there.

Faisal was reluctant, but obedient. He asked leave of his Turkish superiors to inspect the troops in Medina, ostensibly as a preliminary to their advance to the Turkish front. To his despair, Jemal Pasha announced that he and Enver Pasha, the Young Turks' acting commander-in-chief, would accompany him in the review of the troops.

The charade began. Faisal, constrained by the immutable laws of Arab hospitality, had to restrain his troops from shooting the two Turks forthwith, all the while reassuring them that the troops were indeed volunteers for the Holy War against the enemies of the Faithful. In his memoirs, Jemal was to say that, had he known all the facts, he would have taken Faisal prisoner then and there, seized Sharif Hussain and his other sons, and nipped the rebellion in the bud.

On 2 June 1916, Sharif Hussain stood on a balcony of his Meccan palace, a rifle to his shoulder, and fired the shot that began the Arab Revolt. While Abdullah and Zaid, a younger brother, were sent to drive the Turks from Taif, Jidda and Mecca, Faisal and Ali were set an incomparably more difficult project: to pit their few thousand ill-equipped troops against the 22,000-strong Turkish garrison of Medina. Having learnt the strength of the garrison with its heavy battery of artillery, they withdrew to the desert and set about raising a larger force of Bedouin.

Medina would never be taken, but by a later strategy would be successfully isolated from the rest of the Turkish army. Meanwhile Amir Faisal emerged from the episode having gained the love of his men, who called him 'Saidna Faisqal' or 'our Lord Faisal', and won their admiration for his courage. When his tribesmen, unused to heavy bombardment, were reluctant to follow him across an open stretch of land while being raked by gunfire from the walls of Medina, Faisal laughed at them, then walked his horse slowly across the valley of death, never once quickening his pace. From the far side, he beckoned his men to follow. Whooping and waving their rifles over their heads, they galloped over the divide.

Turkish revenge was quick and devastating. They surrounded the Arab citizens of the nearby town of Awali and, as Lawrence reported, massacred 'every living thing within its walls. Hundreds of the inhabitants were raped and butchered, the houses fired, and living and dead alike thrown back into the flames.' The shock waves reverberated across Arabia, fanned the tribes' hatred of the Turks and strengthened their resolve. 'The first rule of Arab war was that women were inviolable,' wrote Lawrence, 'the second that the lives and honour of children too young to fight with men were to be spared: the third, that property impossible to carry off should be left undamaged.' While the Turks would slit the throats of their prisoners, Faisal would pay a pound a head for his enemies to be captured alive.

In the autumn of 1916, as Gertrude was entertaining Ibn Saud at Basra, Lawrence was travelling with the egregious Ronald Storrs from Suez to Jidda, where Storrs, as Oriental Secretary to the Cairo government, was to meet Abdullah to discuss the early failure of the revolt. The issue was whether the British Egyptian army should invade Rabegh on the coast, in order to protect nearby Mecca from the Turks. By exercising his gifts of persuasion, Storrs won permission from Hussain for Lawrence to travel into the desert to meet Faisal.

Lawrence describes Faisal as still and watchful, with lowered eyelids giving him a shuttered look. Tall and thin in his white silk robes, he wore a brown keffiyeh bound with a brilliant red and gold cord, and his fine hands were crossed on the hilt of his scimitar. He was surrounded by many sheikhs, standing silently in the shadows of the room behind him. They sat down on the carpet in an unfriendly silence. Faisal then asked very quietly, without looking up, how Lawrence had found the journey – 'and do you like our place here in Wadi Safra?' Lawrence responded, 'Well; but it is far from Damascus.' A shock wave ran around the room, and Faisal lifted his eyes to his visitor for the first time. He looked directly at Lawrence and smiled his slow, sweet smile: 'Praise be to God, there are Turks nearer us than that.'

In a famous passage from *The Seven Pillars of Wisdom*, Lawrence wrote:

> I had believed these misfortunes of the Revolt to be due . . . to the lack of leadership, Arab and English. So I went down to Arabia to see and consider its great men. The first, the Sherif of Mecca, we knew to be aged. I found Abdullah too clever, Ali too clean, Zaid too cool. Then I rode up-country to Faisal, and found in him the leader with the necessary fire . . . I felt at first glance that this was the man I had come to Arabia to seek – the leader who would bring the Arab Revolt to full glory.

Faisal was indeed a born leader. Though at the time glory was a long way off, his patient leadership and charismatic personality dominated the Bedouin tribes who flocked to his standard. From his tent he performed the endless duties that combined to weld together the rival tribes, Billi and Juheina, Ateiba and Agail. He persuaded them to suspend all their blood feuds and paved the way for his army to pass unmolested across the desert, where inter-tribal robbing, looting and killing were the norm. His father Hussain had sent them orders, but little food or money, and British aid had turned out to be a bitter joke: a few men from the Sudan and four Krupp guns almost too old to be used. Faisal had to travel with a locked chest full of stones to convince his men that he had the gold with which to pay them.

Lawrence departed, promising stores and supplies, officer-volunteers and as many mountain guns and light machine-guns as he could raise. The British would land them at Yenbo, the nearest Red Sea port to Medina, and Yenbo would be Faisal's next base. Lawrence hitched a lift from Admiral Wemyss, staunch supporter of the Arab cause, from Jidda to Port Sudan, then travelled on to make contact with Sir Reginald Wingate, Sirdar of the Egyptian army, in command of the British military side of the Arab adventure. He too was a supporter of the revolt, as was General Clayton, now the civil head of the Arab Bureau, Lawrence's second port of call.

The fighting against the Turks had reached stalemate, and at any minute the Turkish garrison at Medina might move south against Mecca, striking a decisive victory and causing reverberations throughout Islam. The British lacked confidence in their plan to land a conventional army at Rabegh, and hold a line between Medina and Mecca. Lawrence had a solution: guerrilla warfare waged by small groups of Arab fighters backed by British expertise and explosives. The plan, though chancy at best and proposed by an archaeologist with no military training, came as a blessed relief after months of indecision. It was worth a try.

In a search for his own personal odyssey, and very much under Faisal's spell, a vehement Lawrence fulfilled his promise to get things moving at the British end. In due course British technical advisers arrived at Yenbo, with money and arms – Lawrence had stressed that the tribesmen preferred guns that made a lot of noise. He deflected the interference of Colonel Bremond, the head of the French military mission at Jidda, and then was ordered back by Clayton to Faisal's side. Lawrence always maintained that he returned to Yenbo and to the Amir with reluctance, that all he wanted was to get back to map-making in Cairo. Reluctance is an emotion hard to associate with his subsequent legendary role. As much as he craved admiration and fame, he yearned even more to give the impression of a man averse to these very things – like his hero Charles Doughty, author of *Arabia Deserta*, whose heart and soul were vested in another world.

Lawrence found Faisal in the wadi behind Yenbo, the valley filled with a wild confusion of Arabs and camels. It was night, and he describes the Amir sitting serenely on a carpet spread out on the stones, dictating to a kneeling secretary who was writing by the light of a lamp held aloft by a slave. The Harb tribe had been routed by the Turks, who had sent Faisal's brother Zaid, their leader, into rapid retreat. Faisal had moved down to cut off the road from Yenbo, where one Captain Boyle was defending the harbour with his ships' guns against any Turkish approach. Faisal finished his letters, addressed to the paramount sheikhs of the tribal territories ahead, bargaining for protection for his army as they passed through and asking for contributions of troops. Then he sat patiently on in the cold of night, settling the private petitions of his tribesmen until 4 a.m. It was said that Faisal's judgements never left a single Arab dissatisfied or disadvantaged. Then the Amir ate half a dozen dates and lay down on the dew-wetted carpet to sleep. As he slept, noted the watchful Lawrence, his guards crept up and quietly spread their cloaks over him. One hour later, he was awake for the call to prayer.

In his constant daily work of settling feuds and other tribal matters, Faisal was, said Lawrence,

> putting together and arranging in their natural order the innumerable tiny pieces which make up Arabian society and combining them against the Turks . . . he was Court of Appeal, ultimate and unchallenged, for western Arabia. He made the Arab [Independence] Movement national and alive by the force of his personality. When the Sheikhs came to him to assert their allegiance, he made them swear on the Koran to 'wait while he waited, march when he marched, to yield obedience to no Turk, to deal kindly with all who spoke Arabic and to put independence above life, family and goods'.

Lawrence was also deeply involved in persuading the tribes to unite against the Turks, and it was Gertrude's advice and knowledge of desert affiliations that guided him. He admitted that he owed to her much of the information that had helped him to rally the tribes in the desert at a critical moment during the Arab Revolt.

Gertrude had last seen Lawrence in April 1916, on his abortive mission to the besieged Kut, when they discussed at length 'the government of the universe'. Now, in Basra, she followed events as best she could and yearned for action. Lawrence, writing letters only to his family, otherwise confined his correspondence to detailed reports and requests for equipment. He was living with Faisal in his tent in Yenbo – an ordinary bell tent, with a camp bed, a couple of rugs and a beautiful prayer carpet. It was here that Faisal first invited Lawrence to wear Arab clothing, in order to prevent any of his eight thousand tribesmen mistaking him, in his khaki uniform, for a Turkish officer. Lawrence was not slow to accept.

British aid dribbled into Yenbo: four British planes and twenty-three obsolete and extremely noisy guns. Lawrence had a landing strip cleared, and light advance parties were being trained in the use of explosives and the art of dynamiting the Meissner-built Hejaz railway. The technical expert, one Garland, was a physicist who had developed his own devices for cutting metal and toppling telegraph poles. Lawrence was an eager student, and soon devised his own method of direct firing by the use of electricity.

The plan was to move up the coast and capture the Turkish garrison of Wejh, an important town on the Red Sea coast between Yenbo and Aqaba. At the same time, Ali, Abdullah and Zaid would move up inland, concentrating their forces on the railway to Medina, and dynamite the line in several places. The Turks would then be isolated by both sea and land, and deprived of all supplies necessary for attacking Mecca.

On 18 January 1917, Faisal moved off at the head of ten thousand troops on the three-week journey to Wejh, in what would be the defining moment of the Arab Revolt. Operations were no longer confined to the southern Hejaz: the tribes of western Arabia were united for the first time against a common enemy. The beginning of the march that would carry the Amir to Damascus, it was to make of Faisal, and Lawrence, international figures. Faisal's success would also incur his father's lasting jealousy, matched only by that of his brother Abdullah.

Faisal, dressed in white, rode up to the front of the army, cheerfully greeting each sheikh while they, standing in a line by their kneeling camels, made the low bow and sweep of the arm to the lips which was the official salute. As he led off, they fell in behind him, swelling the ranks tribe by tribe until they filled the landscape for a quarter of a mile. Drums beat and poets improvised stanzas as they rode, punctuating the roar of the ten thousand voices raised in warsong. Behind Faisal came the purple banners borne on gold spikes, and the 'wild bouncing mass' of his twelve hundred bodyguards mounted on camels caparisoned in crimson and gold.

Behind them marched some five thousand camelry and 5,300 men on foot, with the Krupp mountain guns and machine-guns, and behind them again, three hundred and eighty camels carrying tents and other essentials.

When Faisal and his army arrived, they found that Wejh had already been captured by the Royal Navy. But by proceeding to blow up bridges and destroy trains and railtracks, the Arabs confounded the Turks despite their vastly superior numbers, and captured the attention of the world.

Lawrence left Wejh in company with Sharif Nasir of Medina and Audah Abu Tayyi of the eastern Howeitat, in an epic detour through the desert to Aqaba. Faisal had approved the venture: Lawrence had £22,000 from the Amir's private purse in his saddle-bag. With a camel corps provided by Abu Tayyi, the party reached Aqaba in July, took the garrison and marched into the town with six hundred Turkish prisoners in tow. Surprise had been on the side of the Arabs. No one had expected an attack on Aqaba from the desert. Its huge guns were fixed in the other direction, to repel attack by sea. The victory registered, once and for all, the importance to the British of the Arabs as allies: with Lawrence they had borne the brunt of the fighting in the south and taken the Red Sea, which would allow the Egyptian army to head for Damascus. General Allenby, newly in charge of the British army, now appointed Faisal commander-in-chief of all Arab operations north of Ma'an, and authorized money, munitions and transport along their route to Damascus.

Delays and setbacks on the part of the British and Arabs were offset by the success of guerrilla action against the Turks garrisoned along the railway, and against their trains carrying munitions and money. Faisal's Syrian supporter Jafar Pasha el Askeri was later to describe hundreds of thousands of Turkish banknotes fluttering out of a burning train, and not one tribesman bothering to scoop them up in their passion to reach Damascus.

While Allenby pressed on towards Jerusalem – to be taken in a supreme victory in December 1917 – Faisal was in camp at Aqaba, preparing the army to march north to Damascus. At that moment a bombshell fell into the camp in the form of a copy of the secret Sykes–Picot Agreement. It was delivered to the camp by courtesy of the Bolsheviks via Faisal's old enemy Jemal Pasha, with the aim of showing the Arabs what was in store for them should the Allies win the war. Faisal knew there had been an agreement, but until now had known little more.

The agreement made between Sir Mark Sykes and M. Georges-Picot divided 'Arabia', in the event of victory, into protectorates and administrations for distribution among the British, the French and the Russians. It seemed to ignore a promise previously made by Sir Henry McMahon to give Arab independence in the area that took in the four sacred Muslim cities. The Sykes–Picot agreement – or disagreement, as it was already being called in London – would form the basis of the San Remo Pact, which would settle Arabia under British and French mandates.

Faisal's lack of this vital information had in fact proceeded from his over-controlling father. Hussain had never shown him the years of correspondence between himself and Henry McMahon that he hoarded at Mecca, or thought it necessary to explain his paternal orders. In fact, Sykes and Picot had visited Hussain at Jidda in May, three months earlier, for the express purpose of explaining the changed conditions forced on the British by French demands, and the terms of the agreement: that France should exert influence over Syria and Lebanon, and Britain over Iraq, Transjordan and northern Palestine. Set in his mind by age and force of personality, Hussain had barely listened to them.

There was nothing to mitigate Faisal's disappointment, and it was what Lawrence had dreaded. For a few days it looked as though the Revolt was finished, and Lawrence was torn by conflicting emotions. Faisal immediately telegraphed his father at Mecca, saying that he and his army refused to continue the war against the Turks because their ideal was the independence and unity of the Arab nation. They would not tolerate the replacement of the Turks by yet more foreigners. In response, Hussain telegraphed London, only to receive the glib assurance that the news was based on mere intrigue, and that the British Government had no aim other than that of the liberation of the Arabs. That was good enough for the Sharif, who thereupon ordered his son to carry on with the war – 'or I shall consider you a traitor'. Already calling himself 'King of the Arabs', Hussain was finding Faisal's success intoxicating.

Lawrence, in some torment of mind, nonetheless reassured Faisal that the British would keep to their promises, in spirit as well as in the letter. From then on, he writes, unable any longer to feel proud of what they had achieved together, he was 'continually and bitterly ashamed'. So the Arab army marched on, tribes taking over from tribes as they advanced, their numbers increasing as they homed in on Damascus. They took Der'a, then came to the village of Tafas, whose ruler Tallal was amongst Faisal's most trusted warriors. Here the Turks, on their retreat from Der'a, had taken their monstrous revenge on the villagers: women and children had been grossly tortured and mangled, houses fired. The provocation was unbearable. Tallal, driven mad with the horror of it, pulled his keffiyeh over his face and galloped head on into the retreating army's fire. The scenes of carnage that followed were indescribable. Lawrence was disgusted with himself for the rest of his life.

Damascus, the 'pearl set in emeralds', was besieged by the Arab army. Not long afterwards, the Turks abandoned it, the British divisions taking seventy thousand prisoners. Faisal's Hejaz irregulars marched through the city on 30 September 1918, and flew the Sharifian flag from the Serai, the Turkish administrative offices. Women flung their veils aside and scattered scent and flowers in their path, men threw their fezzes in the air, and the celebrations continued night and day. When, on 3 October, Amir Faisal neared the city centre, there was a breathless hush. The crowds parted, the drumming of hooves was heard and then on he came, alone, galloping at full pelt, his arm raised in salute. The thousands of cheers that greeted him became one universal roar of triumph that echoed throughout Arabia.

Faisal, the probable future ruler of the country, unfurled the flag of the Hejaz and for the first time met General Allenby. The admiration was mutual. In 1933 Allenby was to say of Faisal: 'He combined the qualities of soldier and statesman; quick of vision, swift in action, outspoken and straightforward . . . Picturesque, literally, as well as figuratively! Tall, graceful; handsome – to the point of beauty – with expressive eyes lighting up a face of calm dignity; he looked the very type of royalty.' Faisal's first address to the people stressed Arab unity and independence, the rule of law, and the reason for the Arabs' alliance with Great Britain, France, Italy and America: to put an end to the atrocities of the Turks.

The new administration under Faisal, from Aqaba to Damascus, at first functioned quietly and well. But scarcely had the cheers died away than Syria was once again riven by political differences, exacerbated by the Franco-British Declaration of 7 November 1918, announced almost simultaneously with the Armistice, the end of the war with Germany. Directed at the people of Syria and Iraq, the Declaration seemed to promise the setting up of national governments and administrations that 'shall derive their authority from the free exercise of the initiative and choice of the indigenous population'; but it also established that while eastern Syria would be administered by Lord Allenby, the so-called Occupied Enemy Territory West, the Syrian littoral and the Lebanon would be under French control. The extremists rose up in a body, but the self-determination paragraph seemed to encapsulate a solemn Allied promise, and Faisal was told the partition was a purely temporary expedient. He headed for the Paris Peace Conference with quiet confidence that the promise would be kept.

Among the hundreds of delegates and thousands of advisers, clerks and typists converging on Paris between January and July 1919 were Gertrude, Lawrence and Faisal. Prime ministers, foreign ministers, presidents, princes and kings arrived by every boat and train, together with supplicant peoples wanting to become nations, nations wanting to know their boundaries, suites of administrators and military representatives, the world's press, and lobbyists for a thousand and one causes. As Margaret Macmillan wrote in her book *Peacemakers*, 'For six months . . . Paris was at once the world's government, its court of appeal and parliament, the focus of its fears and hopes.' Under the leadership of Woodrow Wilson, Lloyd

George and Clemenceau, there were also bankrupt empires to wind up and more crucial questions to answer: in particular, should Germany and its allies be punished and made to pay, or reconstituted? Gertrude commented:

> In our own country [Great Britain] was the increasing indifference of a great democracy to problems too remote to be easily understood, coupled with a generous democratic impulse to give all races equal opportunity and an uneasy consciousness that the West could not stand guiltless of the charge of exploiting the East. The war ... called forth the splendid cooperation of India, the gallant effort of the Arabs side by side with Lord Allenby's armies, till the principles of peace pronounced by President Wilson seemed but a recognition of services in a common cause.
>
> In our extremity the forces of Asia had been enlisted in what was primarily the defence of European liberties, the East had been called into councils of war and an Arab kingdom had been counted among the Allies.

The world had exhausted its energies, and was poised at the outbreak of the pandemic of septic influenza that, beginning in Europe, would kill twenty-seven million weakened and debilitated people – twice as many as the war itself. One of the first victims was Sir Mark Sykes, who died at the Conference. It is interesting to speculate whether, as the homeward-bound parties scattered, they took the virus with them.

Gertrude, a third of the way through her last miserable year with A.T., checked into the Hotel Majestic, the largest of the five hotels taken over by the British Empire delegation near the Arc de Triomphe, and the residential and social centre of the Conference. A gilded pre-war favourite of rich South American women buying the new season's couture, the Majestic's normally excellent food and service had been supplanted by the bad coffee and overcooked fare of a British railway hotel: the staff had been replaced by British employees from Midlands hotels, supposedly so as to protect against spies. So much for Gertrude's longing for a delicious leg of lamb. And not only the food reminded the delegates of school: as visitors arrived, each was issued with a book of house rules. Meals were at set hours, drinks had to be paid for, there was to be no cooking in the rooms and the furniture was not to be damaged.

From the moment she arrived, of course, Gertrude was in her element. Her original plans to leave as soon as A.T. arrived were shelved. The projected motor tour with her father would be delayed, but he came to Paris to see her. Gertrude wrote on 7 March:

> I've dropped into a world so amazing that up to now I've done nothing but gape at it without being able to put a word on to paper. Our Eastern affairs are complex beyond all words, and until I came here there was no one to get the Mesopotamian side of the question at first hand. The magnates have been extremely kind ... They have all urged me to stay and I think for the moment that's my business.

Her friend and correspondent Chirol came at once to find her. They fell immediately into a conversation that would go on for weeks.

Lawrence and Faisal suffered a much worse introduction to the Conference. When they arrived at Marseilles, Faisal was informed by the French authorities that he had no official standing at the Conference and that he had been badly advised in making the journey. It took the intervention of the British to have his name included in the list of official delegates – but as a mere representative from the Hejaz. He rented an imposing Louis XVI mansion in Paris – A. T. Wilson described it as 'florid' – where he fumed when French intelligence delivered his letters already opened and delayed his telegrams to the Middle East.

Lawrence, arriving in Marseilles in full Arab dress, was met with incredulous and insulting stares, and informed that he would be welcome only as a British officer. He left France in a fury: subsequently it was rumoured that he took the Croix de Guerre that the French had awarded him and pinned it to a dog's collar. When he turned up in Paris for the start of the Conference, he was wearing a keffiyeh with his khaki uniform. Instead of being allowed to take his place among his acquaintances and friends at the Majestic, he was shunted off to the less illustrious Continental.

Given the inevitable clash of their personalities, it was hardly surprising that A.T. would be enraged no less by Lawrence's Arab headdress than by his strong pro-Arab views: 'Colonel T. E. Lawrence . . . seems to have done immense harm and our difficulties with the French in Syria seem to me to be mainly due to his actions and advice.' Of Faisal he was scarcely less dismissive, calling him 'the self constituted champion of Syria'.

When Hussain had instructed Faisal to represent him at the Conference, Faisal had asked to see the documents that his father had, relating to the promises made by the British. Hussain had refused. Lloyd George now produced the Sykes–Picot Agreement for Faisal's inspection, revealing for the first time the extent of the promises that Britain had also made to France. Faisal was to say later:

> The first deception occurred when Field-Marshal Lord Allenby announced that Syria had been divided into 3 zones under pretext that this arrangement was purely temporary and administrative. The second blow levelled against the Arabs' happiness was the confirmation of the secret Sykes-Picot treaty which had been denied in 1917 . . . In this way we had to face the bitter truth.

If Faisal was betrayed by all, he was least betrayed by the British. The secret minutes of the Paris Conference's Supreme Council, published later, showed that efforts were made to fulfil the promises made to the Arabs, inconsistent as these might be with the Sykes–Picot Agreement. Lloyd George vehemently maintained that the agreement between Hussain and Britain should be respected. M. Picot, for France, declared that British pre-arrangements with the Arabs were nothing to do with France – adding, without shame, that if France were entrusted with the mandate for Syria, they would be ignored. Lloyd George retorted that he would consider the occupation of Damascus by French troops a violation of Britain's agreement with Hussain. The French chose to read the bond between the British and the Hashemites as a conspiracy, by which Britain intended to reserve a monopoly of influence in the Middle East. The recalcitrance of the French and the confused position of the British, who did not propose to keep Syria but had made overlapping promises both to France and to the Arabs, boded ill for Hashemite interests.

On 6 February Faisal had his chance to address the Supreme Council. He spoke in the fluid and ringing periods of his native Arabic, while Lawrence, standing beside him, translated. Faisal said that the Arab world should have its independence. He wanted all Arabic-speaking regions to enjoy individual independence under an Arab suzerain, the whole to be placed under one mandate until they could stand alone. Arab unity, he went on, would not be realized under the proposed 'spheres of influence'. He reminded Britain of the pledges of Arab independence made in the Hussain–McMahon correspondence, and the French of the spirit of self-determination promoted by President Wilson and set out in the 'free choice' clauses of the Franco-British Declaration. Then he invited questions, taking and answering them in fluent French.

The French Foreign Minister, Stéphen Pichon, intending to trick Faisal into an indiscretion, asked what France had done to help him. Faisal adroitly steered clear of the trap, paying due credit to the French for aid while at the same time leaving the audience in no doubt as to its very limited extent. No one missed the point.

Lloyd George asked carefully constructed questions designed to demonstrate the large contribution the Arabs had made to the Allied victory, but President Wilson asked only if the Arabs would prefer to be part of one mandate or several. Faisal exhibited great restraint and diplomacy. Lloyd George had advised him earlier, in London, that should he be asked whose mandate he would prefer, he should 'hitch his chariot to the star of President Wilson' – America being the only nation capable of preventing Syria coming under a French mandate. Faisal followed this advice to the letter, but was again to be disappointed when he and Lawrence visited Wilson afterwards. The American President was noncommittal, and would shortly pull America out of the negotiations altogether. When the American public lost interest in the Middle East – as it soon would – the Arab cause was lost.

If Gertrude was an increasingly intense figure, not suffering fools gladly, so was Lawrence. Both could be charming to those who interested them, whether desert tribesmen or Western statesmen, but could equally be brutally rude. Gertrude had recently frozen a lunch party in Baghdad by remarking in front of a colleague and his young English bride: 'Why will promising young Englishmen marry such fools of women?' When a neighbour of Lawrence's at a dinner during the Peace Conference said nervously, 'I'm afraid my conversation doesn't interest you much,' Lawrence replied that she was much mistaken: 'It doesn't interest me at all.'

The leisurely pace of the Conference irked both Gertrude and Lawrence, and they decided to push on with their own agenda. With Chirol's help, they organized a dinner at the Paris house of the editor of *The Times*, Wickham Steed. The guests were a number of influential French journalists. All spoke French, Lawrence having spent much of his youth in Brittany. Gertrude wrote in a letter of 26 March 1919:

> After dinner T.E.L. explained exactly the existing situations as between Faisal and his Syrians on the one hand and France on the other, and outlined the programme of a possible agreement without the delay which is the chief defect of the proposal for sending in a Commission. He did it quite admirably. His charm, simplicity and sincerity made a deep personal impression and convinced his listeners. The question now is whether it is not too late to convince the Quai d'Orsay and Clemenceau and that is what we are now discussing.

To her old Arab Bureau colleague Aubrey Herbert she wrote from Paris:

> O my dear they are making such a horrible muddle of the Near East, I confidently anticipate that it will be much worse than it was before the war – except Mesopotamia which we may manage to hold up out of the general chaos. It's like a nightmare in which

you foresee all the horrible things which are going to happen and can't stretch out your hand to prevent them.

She was, of course, enormously interested to meet Faisal, as the hero of the Revolt and the man who would be, one way or another, a future player in the Middle East. She had arrived too late to hear his speech, but she was introduced to him by Lawrence, and her sympathy deepened. Dressed in his habitual gold-embroidered white, carrying his ceremonial dagger, and with the air of command and the mystique she had expected, he was of the type of desert Arab to whom she had always been attracted. But he was far more: his warmth and humour, in contrast with the pensive expression of his slanted hazel eyes, took her by surprise. 'Excuse me,' he had said with a smile, when a passing allusion had been made to the fight for the Holy Land, 'but which one of us won the Crusading wars?' A veteran warrior of thirty-three years, experience and betrayal had accentuated his air of melancholy; never quite well, he was lined and drawn from driving himself, many times over, to the limits of his strength. Though his eyebrows and moustache were heavy and dark, his close-cropped beard was already touched with grey. Lawrence told her of Faisal's passion for Arabic poetry, and how they would listen to recitations of the odes for hours together. He spoke of his brilliance at chess, and of the mysterious frailty that sometimes caused him, after taking the lead in battle, to fall unconscious and have to be carried from the field.

Deeply impressed, hopeful that the French would not prevent Faisal becoming King of Syria, Gertrude asked for an interview with him. She spent a couple of hours talking to him one morning as he was sitting for Augustus John, who had taken a studio in Paris to paint the most interesting of the delegates. Among her papers exists an untitled, undated record of two early interviews with Faisal, one of them in Paris:

In John's studio I told him that I believed that no power on earth would make France relinquish the Syrian Mandate. He had received this opinion with surprise and dismay. I had gone straight from this interview to lunch with Mr Balfour and after

lunch when the other guests had left had related my conversation
with Faisal and reiterated my conviction regarding the attitude of
the French. Mr Balfour ... assure[d] me in a purely private
capacity that he was in agreement with me. Thereupon I begged
him to clear Faisal's mind of illusions ... so that he might shape
his course accordingly. Mr Balfour thereupon summoned Ian
Malcolm and said 'Ian, will you make a note of what she says so
that I may not forget to acquaint Lloyd George.' Ian producing an
exquisite notebook from an impeccable pocket had made the
desired entry – and I, feeling that Ian's notebook was the epitome
of all culs de sac, had left Paris a day or two later.

Lord Arthur James Balfour, Lloyd George's languid Foreign Secretary, had issued a Declaration in November 1917 that the British
government approved 'the establishment in Palestine of a national
home for the Jewish people'. As Gertrude, thinking of the Sykes–
Picot treaty and all the trouble that had caused, wrote in a letter to
Sir Gilbert Clayton, former head of the Arab Bureau in Cairo: 'Mr
Balfour's Zionist pronouncement I regard with the deepest mistrust – if
only people at home would not make pronouncements how much
easier it would be for those on the spot!'

Contentious as the declaration would be, the wording had been
watered down somewhat from the original proclamation that 'Palestine should be reconstituted as the national home of the Jewish
people'. When the first draft of the Declaration had been put to
the Cabinet, Sir Edwin Montagu, Secretary of State for India – the
man who had reprimanded Gertrude for having communicated her
views to him over the head of A. T. Wilson – mounted a vehement
opposition despite being Jewish himself, stating that Zionism was a
'mischievous political creed, untenable by any patriotic citizen of
the United Kingdom'. Was his own loyalty, he demanded, to be to
Palestine? And what would be the repercussions for the rights of
Jews living in other countries? Many Jewish leaders in the West
believed that to offer Palestine to the Jews would be a disservice to
Jewry; moreover, the Jews already settled in Palestine anticipated,
and dreaded, the trouble that Zionism was about to cause. In

support of his argument, Montagu had read out to the Cabinet a strongly argued letter from Gertrude, whose persuasive words had resulted in the rephrasing of the document. She was angered by the tendency of the Zionists and the statesmen at the Conference to talk as if Palestine was empty of people; and she could see that Arabs and Jews could not live peaceably side by side. As long ago as January 1918 she had written to Clayton:

> Palestine for the Jews has always seemed to us to be an imposs-
> ible proposition. I don't believe it can be carried out – personally
> I don't want it to be carried out, and I've said so on every possible
> occasion ... to gratify Jewish sentiment you would have to
> override every conceivable political consideration, including the
> wishes of the large majority of the population.

It was not the first time that the Zionists' dream of a homeland would exclude any consideration for the people who already lived there. The first Zionist congress in 1897 had produced the plan to buy Uganda as a home for the Jews. Thirty years on, what about the rights of the existing community in Palestine? There were five hundred thousand Arabs there, four-fifths of the population. How was the protection promised by the Declaration to be delivered, if it became the home of the Jewish nation?

Half the Jews in the world lived in abject misery in the area called the Pale, now Belarus, the Ukraine and eastern Poland. It was stifling in the summer, bitterly cold in the winter, and desperately poor land at any time. The Russian government gave no protection to its seven million Jews, who were continually subjected to pogroms and murderous anti-Jewish riots. Some of them turned to revolution, like Trotsky, and hundreds of thousands left to begin new lives in America and Western Europe. At the start of the war, there were three million Jews in America and three hundred thousand in Britain, many of them refugees.

Nationalist ideas, which grew in popularity throughout the war, led in France, Germany and Austria to a general suspicion of minorities, and particularly of their Jewish minorities. At the same time, Jews' longing for a nation of their own intensified. In Britain, the leading Zionist was Chaim Weizmann, a reader in bio-chemistry at Manchester University and a man of extraordinarily engaging personality. For him Palestine, the last Jewish kingdom to have been destroyed by the Romans, was the only place for a Jewish homeland. He wanted a land where a Jew could be 'one hundred per cent a Jew', not an assimilated Jew obliged to designate himself by another nationality. These he despised – and they included individuals as prominent as Lord Rothschild and Edwin Montagu. Before the war Weizmann interviewed some two thousand people in an attempt to win them over to the cause. His conquests included Lord Robert Cecil, who helped him to convince Balfour. The Zionist dream struck a romantic chord in the Foreign Secretary, who believed that there should be a national home for 'the most gifted race that mankind has seen since the Greeks of the 5th century'. Weizmann had also converted Mark Sykes, Lloyd George and Churchill, Churchill's sympathies having already been enlisted by the support he was given in his first election by the prominent Jewish community of Manchester.

At the beginning of the war, when Balfour was First Lord of the Admiralty and Lloyd George was Minister of Munitions, Weizmann had created an almost indelible debt to himself. At a time when Britain was facing a hopeless shortage of explosives, he had invented a process for making acetone, essential for their manufacture. He presented it to the government without taking a penny for it throughout the war: he asked for nothing but the support of Britain for the Zionist cause, and it was a promise that could not be forgotten.

The Jewish Legion, volunteers within the Royal Fusiliers, fought bravely alongside Allenby in his advance on Damascus. When he set up his administration there, he duly made his pronouncements in both Hebrew and Arabic. A few months later, the Zionists bought an estate in Jerusalem and Weizmann laid there the foundation stone of the Hebrew University. When Weizmann arrived at the Paris Peace Conference, he made impassioned speeches and backed the British claim for the mandate over Palestine. Not surprisingly, when he and Faisal were introduced to each other, they discovered

common ground: neither wanted the French mandate. Faisal, somewhat contemptuous of the Palestinians whom he regarded as bor-
derline Arabs, and much preoccupied with his own problems,
agreed vaguely with Weizmann that there was 'plenty of land to go
around'. Faisal foresaw a beneficial future for the Palestinian Arabs
in partnership with Jewish immigrants, who would be bringing their
Western education and energy to a barren land. On 3 January 1919
they signed an agreement to encourage immigration in return for
the Zionists' support for an independent Arab state.

After the Conference, a commission distinguished by its insignifi-
cance was sent by America to investigate the future of Palestine and
canvass public opinion in Syria. The two individuals carrying out
the commission discovered, as Gertrude could already have told
them, that there was deep opposition to the Zionist programme on
the part of the Palestinian Arabs: they recommended that the notion
of a Jewish homeland be abandoned. Gertrude was well aware that
up to this time the Arabs in Palestine had not regarded themselves
as a nation. 'In one respect Palestine has reason to be grateful to the
Balfour declaration: the country has found itself in opposing it. National
self-consciousness has grown by leaps and bounds . . . The eager desire
of education everywhere manifest has been induced by a jealous wish
to be level with the Jews.'

Nobody paid any attention to the commissioners' findings;
neither was there any chance of reading their report, as it was never
published.

It was unfortunate that, while Weizmann had worked his charm
at the Conference, the Palestinians had not attended. Instead, and
for the first time, they rioted in Jerusalem against the proposal for
Jewish settlement in Palestine. They sent Balfour a stream of letters
and petitions, but these were all destroyed by his private secretary
before he could read them. The truth was that nobody wanted to
turn their minds to the problem. It was the opinion of those who
did spare a thought for the Palestine question that, in the words of
Lord Curzon, the area 'will be a rankling thorn in the flesh of
whoever is charged with its Mandate'. So it was for the High Commissioner of His Majesty's Government in Palestine, Sir Herbert

Samuel. On his inauguration, Gertrude wrote even-handedly of the friction between the Jews and the Arabs: of the Zionists' tactlessness in the free expression of their hopes for the future of Palestine, and the Arabs' deep resentment of the economic and financial powers granted to the newly established Zionist Commission. This, a committee under Weizmann, had been appointed by the British to be resident in Jerusalem, where it would represent Jewish issues to the local British officials. 'The roaring of responsible members of the Commission, as for instance the declaration that Palestine is to be as Jewish as America is American, will continue to echo behind the High Commissioner's dove-like notes, which they effectively drown,' Gertrude commented.

Faisal left France in April 1919, a disappointed man, and visited the Pope in Rome before returning to Syria to put down a guerrilla war along the coastline. In September, Lloyd George and Clemenceau reached a provisional agreement. British troops in Syria would be replaced by French garrisons. Arab troops would be maintained in the eastern region, under French supervision. The British government invited Faisal to discuss the situation in London. Faisal set out again, was again treated with discourtesy in Marseilles and was forced to bypass Paris. At Boulogne and Dover he was received respectfully by a British admiral and a guard of honour, and at the station in London by Foreign Office representatives. He was informed about the recent prime ministers' agreement, but assured that the arrangement would be only temporary.

He returned to Syria to find that his father Hussain refused to acknowledge his negotiations. Neither would Hussain ratify or acknowledge the peace terms encapsulated in the Treaty of Versailles.* When he arrived in Damascus, Faisal was greeted by ten thousand Arabs marching in protest against the forthcoming French mandate. An Arab Congress met the following March to

---

* The Treaty of Versailles, deriving from the Paris Peace Conference, established peace terms with Germany; the Treaty of Sèvres, a year later, settled the peace terms with Turkey.

demand complete Arab independence in Syria. Meanwhile, in
Mesopotamia, along the Euphrates, Arab tribes were making war
against Faisal's only allies, the British. Gertrude describes him at
about this time:

> Faisal, with his high ideals, his fair conception of the Arab cause
> which he alone represented and defended – acutely sensitive to
> sympathy or political antagonism, trying to hold his own against
> the covert hostility of the French and the ardent folly of his own
> adherents; harassed by his family, deserted by the British govern-
> ment . . . without one single person near him from whom he
> could seek affection and impartial guidance . . .

Caught between the priorities of the West and the extremists in
Syria, Faisal was confronted by Arab nationalists demanding that he
accept the crown of Syria. He took time to make his decision. He
cabled Lord Allenby in Cairo, and asked for advice. If he accepted,
he pointed out, it might be possible to fend off an uprising, but
if he refused it might cause one. The answer also took time, and
when it came it was so evasive and vaguely worded that he allowed
himself to be elected King. Neither Great Britain nor France
acknowledged the coronation: Britain because she could not, France
because she would not. Those who perceived Faisal as self-
constituted were able to accuse him of going over to the extremists.

In April 1920, at the San Remo Conference, Syria was officially
put under a French mandate. Faisal had been invited to attend, but
he had grown weary of rushing across the world at the summons of
the West, only to be treated in summary fashion and dismissed. By
inexorable degrees, Syria had arrived at the point where a conflict
was inevitable.

As soon as the Conference had agreed to the French mandate,
Damascus erupted. Faisal's position was impossible. The Syrians
were calling him pro-French, the French were calling him pro-
British, and the British were saying he was backing the cause of Arab
extremism. He could have submitted to the French or stood up for
the Arabs. Choosing the latter course would have been natural for
him, but the matter was taken out of his hands. General Gouraud

arrived in Damascus as the first French High Commissioner, ironically the very general who had awarded Faisal the Légion d'Honneur.

He found rebellion in the air. There were now ninety thousand French troops in Syria, and the French had taken the all-important ports. When Faisal officially protested against the foreign occupation and appealed against the mandate to the Supreme Council, Gouraud made his move. He demanded from Faisal an unconditional recognition of the mandate, the adoption of French as the government language, an immediate reduction in the Syrian army, the abolition of conscription, the free movement of troops on the railways, the French occupation of Aleppo and the punishment of all Arabs who had rebelled against the mandate. Faisal asked for forty-eight hours to consider, but before that time ran out the French produced another battery of ultimatums. Then, on 22 July, Arab tribesmen took the law into their hands and attacked a French outpost. The following day the French routed them and marched on to occupy Damascus. 'The resistance of the Arabs . . . was not led by Faisal,' noted Gertrude, 'and was in fact in defiance of his orders . . . General Gouraud immediately issued a proclamation, beginning "The Amir Faisal, who has brought this country to the brink of ruin, has ceased to reign."' Gouraud sent an order for him to leave Damascus within twenty-four hours.

And so the first experiment in Arab self-determination was stamped out by the French army boot. Faisal and his younger brother Zaid quietly left Damascus, his reign having lasted less than five months. From Der'a, the scene of the Arab Revolt's greatest triumph, he travelled under British auspices to Haifa, then to Egypt and Europe. Ronald Storrs was there to greet him on the platform at al-Qantara station, where he found the ex-King of Syria sitting on his luggage awaiting the train. Storrs saw that 'The tears stood in his eyes and he was wounded to the soul.'

Gertrude reacted with pain and anger. 'In my opinion there were scarcely words strong enough to express my sense of our responsibility for the Syrian disaster. It is impossible to see, nor I think can the French themselves see, where their policy is leading them . . .' Faisal told her in a later interview that he had counted on a firm alliance between the British government and the Hejaz:

You deserted me in Syria – it is therefore incumbent upon me to form a new scheme. You must remember that I stood and I stand, entirely alone. I have never had the support of my father or my brother Abdullah. They were both bitterly jealous of the position which the successful issue of the Arab campaign had given me in Syria . . . I have never had the confidence of my family.

Faisal and Gertrude were by now on close terms, and he was speaking remarkably frankly. He continued:

While I was in Paris in 1919, my father was continually urging me to force the Allies to fulfil their promises to the Arabs. I did not even know what the promises were – I had never seen the correspondence with McMahon. But in any case to force the Allies was out of the question. What power had I? What wealth? I could only reason and negotiate. That was what I did. I continued to do so when I was left face to face with the French.

His hand was forced by his own followers, he said. At the same time as they had nominated him King of Syria, they had nominated Abdullah King of Iraq.

I knew that the whole business was laughable, but I gave it my countenance in order to appease my own brother. He is, as you know, older than I am – I wanted to give him a status in the Arab world in order to disarm his hostility.

Gertrude could see well enough, now, where the French policy in Syria was leading:

. . . the growing hatred of French control which has been the permanent feature in the history of Syria since our evacuation in November 1919, has by recent events been so deeply embittered that no palliative which can be applied by the French government can be of avail.

[Beside the Syrian Muslims and the Christians] another element has taken the field; the Druzes, flawlessly courageous, unassuageably vindictive, ruthlessly cruel, will neither fear to oppose their small numbers to the forces of the French Republic, nor forgive the injuries . . .

It is the French policy which has combined the . . . Druze and Syrian Arab . . . Their cause has become one . . . Sooner or later, the French must go.

In its attempts to subject the Arabs to military rule, France would further fragment Syria. In the summer of 1925, the Druze instigated a nationalist uprising. Once again Damascus exploded into war, and the French indiscriminately bombed the ancient city into a ruin. Syria would continue for years in a state of ungovernable chaos.

Meeting Faisal, getting to know him and watching with horror as events unfolded in Damascus; concerned about violence in Palestine, appalled by the scale of the insurgency breaking out along the Euphrates as A.T. completed his last months in office, it was no wonder that Gertrude described the disintegration of the Middle East as resembling the collapse of the Roman Empire.

As the British mandate in Iraq became official, A.T. was preparing for his own departure. Preparations also began for an Arab Constituent Assembly in Baghdad, but everyone was waiting for the return of the well-respected Sir Percy Cox from London. Gertrude, rejoicing in the imminent arrival of the man she trusted and could work with, now bent her mind to a workable scheme for putting in place some kind of democratic process: 'I'm happy and interested in my work and very happy in the confidence of my chief. When I think of this time last year . . .'

At this most inconvenient moment she fell ill again with bronchitis, and had to resign herself to vacating the office for nearly a week. She was not, however, allowed to disappear altogether. The summer-house in the garden received visitors at all hours, ostensibly to enquire after her state of health, in reality to pour out their fears and aspirations. Gertrude gave up any hopes of a quiet recovery. She donned her dressing gown, and in this most unsuitable of attire received a party of the distinguished Muslims of

Baghdad, including the Mayor and the son of the elderly Naqib, one of the most important religious nobles in Iraq. Neither could Cox do without her. He called a special meeting to discuss the appointment of Arab ministers and British advisers, and held it in Gertrude's drawing-room.

Back at the office, she received a visit from her friend Fahad Beg, now not far short of eighty, who informed her that he had acquired two more wives. She gave a garden party for him at which, at one point, he opened his robes to show off a huge hole in his chest, acquired in a youthful *ghazzu* when a lance was thrust right through his body. The gasps and screams of the ladies were most gratifying.

Meanwhile Cox had made out a list of trusted and representative Arab candidates. The first Cabinet choice, without question, would be the Naqib of Baghdad, His Reverence Sayyid Abdul Rahman Effendi. Elderly and venerated, he was also the head of the Sunni community. He, like Faisal, traced his descent from the Prophet, and was custodian of the holy shrine of Abdul Qadir Gilani. He was a good friend of Gertrude's: he liked to talk with her, and she often visited his wife and sisters. 'Abdul Rahman Effendi's friendship takes an agreeably tangible expression!' she wrote. 'He sends in weekly a great basket of fruit from his estate – at this season it's filled with huge white grapes.' However, the Naqib lived in dignified religious seclusion, and she thought it unlikely that he would accept their suggestion. Cox went to see him, and after a short delay, and to everyone's pleasure, he did agree. He would now undertake the formation of the provisional government.

In no time at all he had invited eighteen men to form the Council of State, and it was installed in the Serai, the grand old Turkish offices. One of the most prominent figures was Faisal's army commander in the Revolt and his supporter in Syria, Jafar Pasha el Askeri. Soon after him came his brother-in-law, Nuri Pasha Said, a more formidable individual whom Gertrude came to admire as she got to know him. These were the first of the pro-independence figures to be repatriated to Baghdad at the government's expense after the collapse of the Arab regime in Damascus.

Jafar Pasha, a Baghdadi Arab with a command of eight languages, was invited by the Naqib to become Minister of Defence, and to focus on forming a native army to relieve the British. It was when he had heard of the public hanging by Jemal Pasha in Damascus of his Syrian nationalist friends that he had changed sides and thrown in his lot with the Arab forces. Gertrude commented: 'I wish there were more people of his integrity and moderation.' After his experiences with Faisal in Syria he had, he admitted to Gertrude, many misgivings in agreeing to join the Cabinet. She promised him that, in the end, complete independence was what the British government hoped to give Iraq. ' "My Lady" he answered – we were speaking Arabic – "complete independence is never given; it is always taken" – a profound saying.'

There was, inevitably, immediate trouble from the Shias, not only because they looked on the Cabinet as of British parentage, but because it contained fewer Shias than Sunnis. Shias, Gertrude pointed out to all protesters, were almost all subjects of Persia, and not eligible for office in a Mesopotamian government. Shortly, a Shia of Karbala accepted the Ministry of Education, which the Naqib had been induced to offer him.

The provisional Cabinet was to run the country while it prepared for the first general election. One of Gertrude's jobs was to suggest some kind of voting system to put before the Electoral Law Committee, one that would be reasonably fair and representative. She noted: 'Cox sent an admirable letter to the Council saying that in the election assembly which was to decide on the future of Iraq every section of the community must be represented and that he must be able to assure his Govt. that this was the case.'

She had to overcome the problem that the big landowners in the Council would do their best to exclude the tribes from the voting process. Sasun Effendi, the head of the Jewish community, and Daud Yusafani of Mosul came to talk the matter over. 'We were all agreed,' she wrote, 'that it would be disastrous if the tribesmen were to swamp the townsmen, but I pressed upon them the consideration that . . . an Arab National Government could not hope to succeed unless it ultimately contrived to associate the tribesmen with its endeavours.'

Her first idea was to include thirty tribal members in the election assembly, one each from the twenty largest tribes, and the other ten representing smaller ones. Jafar Pasha and Sasun came to her with a different scheme: they proposed two tribal representatives for each division of Iraq, but any tribesman who liked to register could vote in the ordinary way. She was delighted, no less that the Cabinet had produced a better scheme than that it had secured a minimum of ten tribal members in the assembly. At the first meeting of the Council of State of the first Arab government in Mesopotamia since the Abbasids, her excitement was intense.

The first job of the Council was to pacify the country. The violence continued along the Euphrates and in the north, where RAF planes were bombing tribesmen who continued to attack outlying British garrisons. Cox was determined to secure peace before taking another step, and to that end put down the disturbances with all the force he could muster – a task made easier by the additional troops from India now at his disposal. A general amnesty was promised for the leaders of this later revolt, but Cox would not grant it until the tribes submitted. Gertrude urged him to proceed with it at once: she wanted the British to have the kudos of taking the step themselves and to avoid looking as though they were giving way to Arab pressure. She wrote to Chirol: 'Sunni opinion [in Iraq] is veering . . . in favour of a Turkish prince. I don't like it, but I'm prepared to accept it. I'm prepared to accept anything which promises immediate stability . . .'

Peace and stability for Iraq was her consistent aim, so that the life of the ordinary people could prosper. The tribal violence against the British was a bitter pill for her to swallow. The blame lay as much with A.T.'s discredited administration as with the Western powers and their interminable delays in delivering the promised self-determination. She had fumed at both, and now had to suffer the consequences. She hated the bombing and the burning. At the same time she agreed with Cox that a debutante Arab government could not have coped with a raging insurgency, and reluctantly supported him in taking tough measures to bring about peace. Her apparent readiness to accept a Turkish prince, if that was the wish of a future democratic Iraq, is less surprising in view of a humorous remark she made in a letter to Hardinge at an exasperated moment: 'I sometimes wonder whether we should not have done better to leave the Arab provinces under the nominal suzerainty of Turkey, the birth of new states is attended with so much travail!'

In any case, democracy meant accepting the expressed wish of the people, without flinching. In a letter to Hugh of 18 December 1920 she wrote: 'I said the matter was entirely in their hands, we didn't care whom they put up as Amir or what kind of Govt. they selected to have, provided we felt sure the choice was freely and fairly made without pressure or intimidation.'

In this she was not being quite honest. She knew exactly the king she wanted for Mesopotamia. Only a week later she wrote to her father: 'I feel quite clear in my own mind that there is only one workable solution, a son of the Sharif and for choice Faisal: very very much the first choice.'

15

CORONATION

In this preference, she had important allies. Churchill, the new Secretary of State for the Colonies, had picked Lawrence as his adviser on Arabian affairs. Lawrence, like Gertrude, had been shaken by the betrayal of Faisal by the French, and wanted to assuage his feelings of guilt and responsibility for what had happened in Syria. Like Gertrude, he thought Faisal the best solution for the crown of Iraq. The French, however, had to be sounded out first. The result, as Lawrence was soon to inform Churchill, then on a painting holiday in the South of France, was a condition: Faisal must give up all claims to Syria and all support for the Syrian nationalists. Faisal had agreed, and was ready to abandon his father's claims to Palestine in return for the throne of Iraq for himself, and that of the newly created Transjordan for his brother Abdullah.

Churchill, however, had a more urgent administrative task: to reduce substantially the taxpayers' £37 million pound bill for the military control of the Middle East, and the enormous cost of policing Iraq. To that end he summoned Iraq's British officials to meet him for a conference in Cairo.

The ten-day conference began on 12 March 1921, its object to consider the Middle East in all its aspects. In Iraq, Cox had to a large extent quelled the uprising of the previous month, and was as determined as Churchill that the next step towards independent Arab government must not be delayed. Air Marshal Hugh Trenchard of the RAF attended, as did Kinahan Cornwallis, the intelligence expert who had lately run the Arab Bureau and was now attached to the finance ministry in Egypt, and Major-General Sir Edmund

Ironside, commander of the troops in Persia. Sir Percy's party of six included Gertrude, Jafar Pasha and Sasun Effendi Eskail, the Jewish businessman who was now the Minister of Finance. Also there would be A. T. Wilson, now working in the oil business – which would not prevent him from taking a prominent seat in the official group photograph, leaving Gertrude to stand in the background.

Lawrence met the Iraq delegation at Cairo station. Since Gertrude had last seen him at the Peace Conference, he had become world-famous, thanks to the efforts of the journalist Lowell Thomas who had written his biography and now toured the world giving lectures and press briefings about his hero. Lawrence was both tortured and flattered by the publicity – reviling it while having been spotted slipping into the back row of a cinema to watch a film feature about himself. For the first time, he was more widely known than Gertrude – not that she could have cared less. They dodged into her room in the Semiramis Hotel, and she began by taking him to task for some of his comments to the press, some praising, some criticizing the work of the civil administration in Baghdad. Just as Cox had been straining every sinew to put down the insurgents, Lawrence had written in an article in the *Sunday Times*: 'The people of England have been led in Mesopotamia into a trap from which it will be hard to escape with dignity and honour. Things have been far worse than we have been told, our administration more bloody and inefficient than the public knows.' She confronted him with this, and with his accusations that the English language had been forced on Iraq: these were lies, she told him, and he knew it. 'Tosh!'

But they were still great friends, still the old Intrusives, both now among the major movers in the Middle East and both determined to see Faisal King of Iraq. When Lawrence left, Gertrude paid a short visit to Churchill and his wife Clementine in their suite, and the next day they got down to work.

Cox told Churchill that the provisional Council of State, which reported to the British, must soon be replaced by a new authority, preferably an Arab ruler. There were several candidates, Gertrude told him: the Sunni leader the Naqib, Sayyid Abdul Rahman, aged and sure to refuse; a Turkish prince; the Sheikh of Muhammarah. Then there were the two strong contenders, Faisal and the less salubrious Sayyid Talib.

Talib, the son of the Naqib of Basra, was a formidable figure, locally popular, politically astute and once described by Gertrude as 'a rogue'. At present Minister of the Interior, he had been very put out not to have been included in the Cairo delegation. He was a known murderer – at least known to have had people murdered – and had attempted to sell his services at an extravagant price to either the Turks or the British during the war. He had been imprisoned in India but was eventually released through the intervention of A. T. Wilson and the British administration in Baghdad: he was, after all, from an important Iraqi family, his father the head of the powerful Sunni faction in southern Iraq. He had recently cooperated with the British in stifling the revolt in Baghdad and Basra, and had attempted to insinuate himself with Gertrude the night before she had left for Cairo, as she recounted afterwards:

> Amid potations of whisky he whispered in my ear in increasingly maudlin tones that he had always regarded me as his sister, always followed my advice and now saw in me his sole support and stay. And I, feeling profoundly that his ambitions never will and never should be fulfilled, could do nothing but murmur colourless expressions of friendship.

Cox, Gertrude and Lawrence put their case for Faisal to the Conference. He was a war hero, a brave ally of the British during the Revolt. He was honourable and inspiring – and available. Churchill also liked the fact that Faisal would give the British leverage over his father Sharif Hussain and his brother Abdullah. He agreed. The vote was cast in Faisal's favour. Churchill cabled home to stress what was for him the chief point: 'Sharif's son Faisal offers hope of best and cheapest solution.' 'We covered more work in a fortnight than has ever before been got through in a year,' Gertrude wrote to Frank Balfour on the 25th, 'Mr Churchill was admirable, most ready to meet everyone halfway and masterly alike in guiding a

big political meeting and in conducting small political committees into
which we broke up.'

Gertrude's Iraq was beginning to take shape. The small committee into which she, Cox, Lawrence and the Iraqi ministers now
formed set themselves to work out the timing and the geography.
As a Sunni ruler in a country with a Shia majority, the Amir's
descent from the Prophet would be his trump card. He should
immediately be invited to Baghdad, before elections for a ruler
started. He would need to go to Mecca first, and have his candida-
ture announced from there. Support would grow as he progressed
east. Churchill wired home: 'Both Cox and Miss Bell agree that if
procedure is followed, appearance of Faisal in Mesopotamia will
lead to his general adoption.'

The second big issue for discussion, as far as Gertrude was
concerned, was Palestine. Churchill was faced with many conflicting
issues: he had to establish with the French a satisfactory border
between Palestine and Syria, and another in the south between
Palestine and Egypt. He had to honour the promise of a homeland
for Jews while sustaining the promise to the half million Arabs
living in Palestine that they would have their own self-determination. Furthermore, whatever government he provided for Palestine
must cost Britain less than the present £6 million a year. As the
conference progressed, he believed a solution had emerged. East of
the river Jordan, a new Arab state would be created. Eventually
called Transjordan, it would have an Arab government and Abdullah
would be invited to be its ruler. West of the Jordan, Jews would
be allowed to settle amongst the Arabs but the British would remain
in control under the mandate. In addition, it was probably Lawrence
who most influenced him to extend the border of the mandate
south to Aqaba and drive a wedge between the ever more threatening Ibn Saud and the British in Egypt.

He instructed Herbert Samuel, High Commissioner in Palestine,
to restrict his responsibilities to the lands to the west of Jordan,
which the Jews would settle, and gave him a Jewish force to defend
it. Gertrude thought this a recipe for disaster. She agreed with the
comments of Sir Wyndham Deedes, an idealistic Zionist who could

not disguise his alarm at the decisions being taken concerning Palestine. In a private conversation, Deedes had been heard to burst out with: 'Have we a policy? Does our Government know where it is going? If you ask Mr Churchill what he thought would be the position in these Arab countries in 20 years' time, could he give you the most shadowy answer? He does not know; he does not think; there is no coordination in what we are doing.'

Gertrude was forthright in her opposition to Zionism from first to last. She wrote to Domnul: 'The French in Syria, Zionism in Palestine, form a stupendous barrier to honest dealing with the Arabs; only in Mesopotamia can we pursue an honest policy . . . The impasse in Palestine differs very considerably from that which has been reached in Syria; there is a quite obvious way out, namely the abandonment of the Zionist policy.' She was right in her predictions. As early as July 1922 the Arabs would refuse to recognize the Balfour Declaration, reject the Palestinian mandate given to Britain by the League of Nations, and Jews would be massacred in their settlements by Arab mobs.

Once the Conference was over, Gertrude was joined for a few days by her father. Like Churchill, he wanted to talk finance. Her grandfather's empire was on the point of collapse. The share values of the Dorman Long Company, in which Sir Hugh and Sir Arthur Dorman owned the most stocks, had begun to fall. To boost the price of the shares, each had begun to buy them up, but the decline of the company only accelerated. For the first time, Gertrude felt that she too had to turn her mind to the subject of money. As ever, her own finances were of peripheral interest to her – work was her life, and she had no interest in luxuries. Still, she felt that she had to make a sacrifice somewhere. On her return to Baghdad, she was soon so immersed in her work that she could think of nothing better than economizing on feathers. She wrote to Florence for blue tricotine, enough for Marie to run up a dress she could wear to the office, and asked her stepmother to send a cutting of the fabric to her hatmaker for a matching hat 'trimmed with reddish brown wings, pheasant would do . . . not ostrich feathers, that's too dear'.

*

Before any public arrangements could be made in regard to Faisal, there followed the inevitable delay while Churchill consulted with the Cabinet and obtained HMG's consent for Faisal to run as a candidate. The period of waiting was by way of a short holiday for the British in Baghdad, who were in a cheerful mood. It had been a long time since jokes had run around the office, but now there was laughter again. Gertrude contributed the remark of a sheikh who had been among a number invited to a concert at which a musician, one Captain Thomas, had performed the Pathétique sonata. 'At the end he asked what they thought of it. "Wallahi" said one "khosh daqqah" – "by God a good thumping"!'

During this interval, Gertrude busied herself with the current debate on what should be done at Ctesiphon, Iraq's most famous archaeological site, to save the great façade wall, which was developing a marked outward tilt. She also saw something of her friend Haji Naji, a fruit and vegetable grower at nearby Karradah, whose pleasant company was the object of many of her rides and drives out into the country – 'Haji Naji . . . is the salt of the earth . . . an odd substitute for a female friend, but the best I can find.' They would walk and sit under the apricot and mulberry trees whose fruit was now ripening, and picnic on fresh salads. Sometimes he would call at her house in town to talk politics, or to deliver a basket of fruit and vegetables topped with a bouquet of flowers. The fruit-farmer was a staunch supporter of the British and wholly in favour of a Sharifian amir. His friendship with Gertrude was both a help and a hindrance to him. Living alone with his family, deep in the country, he was to some extent targeted by nationalist extremists and occasionally had to post guards around the house at night. Unofficially, she began to make use of Haji Naji as her eyes and ears in the countryside. Later, when the Amir arrived at Basra, she gave the elderly man an introduction to Kinahan Cornwallis, who had been appointed Faisal's aide, and Haji Naji and his party gave Faisal an early welcome.

Three months after the Cairo Conference, the holiday ended and events began to move quickly. Faisal set off from Mecca for Iraq, and would arrive in Baghdad at the end of June. Gertrude was consulted about the design for a temporary flag for Iraq, to decorate the streets for his arrival, and began to display uncustomary nerves. 'I believe Faisal is statesman enough to realize that he must capture the older more steady going people while at the same time not chilling over much the enthusiasm of his more ardent supporters.'

In Cairo, Churchill had asked whether the administration could deliver an election vote in favour of Faisal – 'Can you make sure he is chosen locally?' Western political methods, he remarked, 'are not necessarily applicable to the East, and the basis of the election should be framed'. It was more than a recommendation, it was an order. A rejected Faisal would be a disaster and would open up the whole Arab question again. Cox would follow his directive to the letter. There could be no doubt that Faisal presented the best hope for stability in Iraq. Cox and Gertrude would have to see that he came to power as the country's own choice, but he had to be seen to be elected independently of British wishes. 'I don't for a moment hesitate about the rightness of our policy,' Gertrude commented. 'We can't continue direct British control . . . but it's rather a comic position to be telling people over and over again that whether they like it or not they must have Arab not British government.'

Her upbringing and her education, and her experience of Arabia, had given her a pragmatic view of democracy. In her *Review of the Civil Administration of Mesopotamia* she wrote:

> The rank and file of the tribesmen, the shepherds, marsh dwellers, rice, barley and date cultivators of the Euphrates and Tigris, whose experience of statecraft was confined to speculations as to the performances of their next door neighbours, could hardly be asked who should next be the ruler of the country, and by what constitution. They would in any case have done no more but re-echo by command the formula prescribed by their immediate chiefs, and it was just as profitable besides being more expeditious to refer those questions to their chiefs only.

Modern critics of the procedures whereby the British were to gain support for the selection of Faisal as king might reflect on the much vaunted democracy of today. Every European country has its own brand of democracy. At the time of writing, the 'free and fair' election system has produced in Britain a government that only 36 per cent of the voters wanted; in the United States, it is not the weight of numbers that carries an election, but the vote for marginal interests.

It was Gertrude's job to ensure that nobody suffered as a member of an oppressed minority in a country split by racial, religious and economic differences. These people were in safe hands. All of her writing suggests a guiding ambition to protect people, particularly minorities, from discrimination and persecution. So many of her letters express concern for injustice, particularly for the massacres of the Armenians, Kurds and others within the Turkish Empire. She had witnessed the sick and starving stragglers from such slaughter as they limped into Baghdad ('O Domnul, the tide of human misery'). Her year in France at the Wounded and Missing Office had given her daily experience of barbarism on the greatest scale ever committed. And in her offices in Basra and Baghdad she had perforce to absorb reports of other atrocities. Her efforts to resolve boundaries and develop structures for new governments had been devoted to avoiding incompatible conjunctions of races and creeds. In Iraq, most of the population were minorities, either by religion or race. Any simple numerical majority voting system would have left great swathes of the country unrepresented. Had the British democratic system of the day been applied to Iraq the vote would have been the prerogative only of men of property, and the wealthy Sunni minority would have been back in charge as they had been under the Turks.

On their return from Cairo, Cox and she had found that Sayyid Talib had been canvassing hard. At a dinner he gave in honour of a correspondent of the *Daily Telegraph*, he declared that there were officials in the British entourage who were well known to be partisan and who were exercising undue influence on the election. He asked the journalist whether he should appeal to King George to have these officials removed, while issuing a very definite threat: if any attempt should be made to influence the election, he declared, 'here is the Amir al Rabiah, with 30,000 rifles, to know the reason why, and the Sheikh of Chabaish with all his men'. Gertrude, who was present at the dinner, commented: 'It was an incitement to rebellion as bad as anything which was said by the men who roused the country last year, and not far from a declaration of Jihad. It's not beyond the bounds of possibility that Talib may prosecute the electoral campaign so hotly as to find himself landed in gaol.'

Gertrude had heard that Talib was collecting around him the hired assassins that he was believed to have employed at Basra under the Turks. She immediately informed Cox of what he had said. She shared with Cox her own horrific nightmare of Faisal being killed by Talib's hired cut-throats. Cox was impelled into decisive action, of which he did not previously inform Gertrude. It was immediately after a tea party given the next day by Lady Cox, at which he had been a guest, that Talib was arrested. Cox reported to Churchill: 'He was arrested in a public thoroughfare this afternoon and is being sent down river to Fao. I do not anticipate any trouble as I think the great majority of people are relieved. I trust you will be able to support me in my action and authorize me to send him to Ceylon.' Churchill replied that Talib's speech was seditious, and that exile was in order. He would in fact spend most of his remaining days in Europe, subsidized by a British income, which would be withdrawn at once if he entered Iraq.

Although Gertrude had not been consulted about this high-handed and uncharacteristic move on Cox's part, and although removing a contender on the eve of an election was contrary to all democratic principles, she was immensely relieved: the more so, when Talib's going revealed the extent of his fund-raising activities, much of it from blackmail. She argued that Talib's threats had disqualified him from participation in the democratic process. There was only one complaint made to the British about Talib's deportation: that of Harry St John Bridger Philby, political officer at Cox's office, who had been the British adviser to Talib when he was Minister of the Interior. 'Jack' Philby, formerly of the Indian Civil Service and an experienced traveller in the East, was a man of robust opinions, and had always mystified Gertrude and Cox by the extent of his admiration for Talib. Not surprisingly, he was appalled, and marched into the office for a tremendous row with Cox: as far as Gertrude was concerned he refused to speak to her, and cut her dead on all subsequent occasions.

Gertrude returned to the business of welcoming Faisal. She was pleased that it was the Naqib, and not the British, who took it on himself to see that the Amir would be suitably received and appropriately lodged. Unfortunately the committee chosen to arrange his reception caused so much controversy that the members almost came to blows. Gertrude attended the first meeting and, sighing, left it to its arguments and went about arranging the details herself. She called on the railway officials and had a train specially decorated, to fetch Faisal from Basra.* The only rooms suitable for the Amir and his party were the old government offices, the Serai, currently in need of renovation. She approached the Public Works Department, and gave them a timetable. She raised contributions from Baghdad's nobles for the provision of good carpets, furniture and wall hangings. Merchants were asked to produce other furniture, crockery and silver. Competent servants were found, sixty notables directed to greet Faisal on his arrival, and the guard of honour drilled. She wrote home: 'Yesterday we had news of Faisal's arrival in Basra [23 June 1921] and an excellent reception, heaven be praised . . . Faisal has now gone off to Janaf and Karbala and gets here on Wednesday 29th.'

It was fortunate that Faisal was a natural orator. He had already won over hearts and minds at a large function held in his honour in Basra. After spending the night on the train, he was due to arrive in Baghdad on the morning of the 29th. The city was decorated with triumphal arches and Arab flags, and packed with people. There was an immense crowd at the station, a guard of honour and a band. Then it was announced that there was a delay on the line, and that the Amir would be arriving by motor. With everyone wilting in the heat of the day, Cox took command. He dispatched everyone back home, telling them to return to the station at 6 p.m.

* According to Ronald Bodley, a descendant of Gertrude's who wrote a biography of her in the 1940s.

He sent a message to Faisal to wait on the train until the problem on the line was solved, then to resume his journey at such a time as would allow him to arrive in the cool of the evening. The crowd dispersed, and reassembled. Faisal arrived at last.

The reception went according to plan, Faisal crossing the room to shake Gertrude's hand. But, standing by Kinahan Cornwallis, the Amir's Personal Adviser, after the advance party had left, she heard that the visit to Basra had not gone as well as she had hoped. The political officers who had met him there had been discourteously aloof. The most offensive had been Philby. For Cox to have sent Philby to escort Faisal to Baghdad was, on the face of it, an odd decision. By doing so, he hoped to show that the British were even-handed and not already treating Faisal as the candidate. Perhaps he was giving Philby a second chance. He certainly thought that a few hours of exposure to his charm would convince Philby of Faisal's superior qualities. That, unfortunately, had not happened. On the train Philby had angered the Amir by insisting on the merits of his Hashemite enemy Ibn Saud — after the death of Captain Shakespear, Philby had been Britain's contact with Ibn Saud — and on his own conviction that Iraq should be a republic. Faisal had arrived in Baghdad annoyed and confused. Was the Iraq High Commissioner with him or wasn't he, and if so why did his officers adopt a different attitude?

For Cox, it was the last straw. Philby had disembarked from the train early, supposedly unwell, and did not turn up for a few days. When he did, he was summoned to Cox's office and dismissed. In Cox's own diplomatic words: 'I had to part company with Mr Philby because at the stage of development at which we had then arrived his conception of the policy of HM's government began to diverge too much from mine.'

Gertrude was sorry, but felt Cox had been right. She had known Philby since her days in Basra, spent one Christmas with him on a launch among the Marsh Arabs, and had contributed many features to his Arabic newspaper. He had often been a trusted go-between with the Naqib; but clearly, he could no longer be trusted. She visited Philby and his wife, to express her sadness, and

. . . had a most painful interview. Mrs Philby burst into tears,
accused me of having been the cause of her husband's dismissal,
and went out of the room. I then reminded him of our long
friendship and asked him to believe that I had done all I could . . .
How he could embrace the cause of that rogue Talib passes all
belief, but he had identified himself with him.

As soon as she could, Gertrude left her card at Faisal's quarters
in the Serai; she was immediately followed out by his ADC, who
told her that the Amir would like to see her: 'Presently Faisal sent
for me,' she wrote. 'They showed me into a big room and he came
quickly across in his long white robes, took me by both hands and said
"I couldn't have believed that you could have given me so much help as
you have" . . . so we sat down on a sofa.' A glittering banquet in the
Maude Gardens followed. In honour of Faisal's love of poetry, the
poet Jamil Zahawi rose to his feet and recited a tremendous ode,
full of allusions to Faisal as King of Iraq.

And then there stepped forward into the grassy space between
the tables a Shiah in white robes and a black cloak and big black
turban and chanted a poem of which I didn't understand a word.
It was far too long and as I say quite unintelligible but nevertheless it was wonderful. The tall robed figure chanting and marking
time with an uplifted hand, the darkness in the palm trees
beyond the illuminated circle – it hypnotized you . . .

It was not plain sailing. The tribes of the lower Euphrates were
preparing petitions in favour of a republic, and many of the Shia
mujtahids were ranging themselves against Faisal. Gertrude found
the growing tension hard to deal with; she was straining every
nerve – talking, persuading, writing, carrying on the argument even
in her sleep. Baghdad was won over, she thought; she could only
hope the rest of the country would fall into line.

The receptions and dinners continued, most magnificently at the
Naqib's house, the old man tottering to the head of the stairs as
Faisal approached, where they formally embraced, then walked
hand in hand towards the standing guests. Gertrude sat at Faisal's

right. 'It was a wonderful sight, that dinner party,' **she recorded,** '. . . on the open gallery, the robes and their uniforms and the crowds of servants, all brought up in the Naqib's household, the ordered dignity, the real solid magnificence, the tension of spirit which one felt all round one, as one felt the burning heat of the night.'

On 11 July the Council of State, at the request of the Naqib, unanimously declared Faisal King. Cox, though greatly relieved, knew that a referendum must be held, so as to confirm Faisal as the choice of the people. He and Gertrude had already framed the question — 'Do you agree to Faisal as King and leader of Iraq?' — and printed the papers; they would be circulated to a large number of tribal representatives, including three hundred notables.

Gertrude was becoming a frequent visitor at Faisal's apartments. She would be ushered straight in through a thronged waiting-room by his British adviser, the tall and handsome Kinahan Cornwallis, whom she was beginning to regard as 'a tower of strength'. Faisal spent his days in meeting people from all corners of the country, and his evenings attending or hosting dinners, entertaining as many as fifty guests at a time. The important Jewish community honoured the Amir with a large reception in the Grand Rabbi's official house. Many of them had had reservations about an Arab king, but were reassured that night as Faisal rose to his feet and extemporized, delivering a marvellous speech in which he told them warmly that they were of one race with the Arabs. He thanked them for their gifts, a beautifully bound Talmud and a gold facsimile of the Tablets of the Law. Gertrude commented: 'I'm immensely happy over the way this thing is going. I feel as if I were in a dream . . . On our guarantee all the solid people are coming in to Faisal and there is a general feeling that we made the right choice in recommending him. If we can bring some kind of order out of chaos, what a thing worth doing it will be!'

And then came the celebrations at Ramadi. If Faisal's coronation, to be held in Baghdad some weeks later, was a formal European ceremony, Ramadi was the Bedouin equivalent, a tribal gathering in his honour, and the culmination of the gains of the Arab fight for independence. For Gertrude, too, it was the culmination of her long fight for the Arabs, the sensational climax of tribal joy and triumph; and an occasion on which she, though not the only Briton present, took the prime place amongst them as she stood on the dais beside Faisal, Ali Sulaiman, the powerful pro-British Sheikh of the Dulaim, and her great friend Fahad Beg of the Anazeh.

For three weeks, temperatures had been over 115 degrees. Ramadi was seventy miles away, on the Euphrates. Gertrude and her chauffeur had to leave at 4 a.m. Just before the halfway mark, Fallujah, she saw the rising cloud of dust that signalled Faisal's cavalcade just ahead. Drawing level with his car, she asked permission to drive on so that she might photograph his arrival there. A few miles before Fallujah they came to the tents of the Dulaim, and from that point on, the road was lined with tribesmen roaring their salute and waving their rifles above their heads, kicking up a fog of dust like drifting cliffs on either side. As Faisal's car drew ahead of them they wheeled away and galloped on, to form a continuous wild cavalcade alongside the car. Thus they escorted him into Fallujah, where they found every house decorated and the population crowded out into the streets and on the rooftops.

There they stopped for a while, for Faisal to hold court and eat, while the motorcade was taken across the Euphrates by flying bridge. Faisal and a small party, Gertrude included, then stepped into a decorated boat and crossed the river. The far bank rose steeply, and there where the Syrian desert began were ranged the fighting men of the Anazeh, Fahad Beg's tribe, on horse and camel. Faisal stopped his car to salute the huge standard of their tribe. As they drove on north-west, the tribes rode with them, and the Chief Ali Sulaiman came to the outskirts of Ramadi to greet him. On the banks, an extraordinary sight awaited them: before the massed ranks of horse and camel stood a gigantic snow-white camel ridden by a black standard-bearer holding aloft the standard of the Dulaim.

Faisal entered the shadow of the black tent pitched by the Euphrates, two hundred feet square with its sides made of freshly cut branches. Inside, from the entrance to the dais at the far end, the tribesmen stood shoulder to shoulder. Faisal sat on the high divan with Fahad Beg on his right, 'a great tribesman amongst famous tribes and a great Sunni among Sunnis . . . I never saw [Faisal] look so splendid. He wore his usual white robes with a fine black abba [tunic] over them, flowing white headdress and silver bound Aqal [rope band].'

Then he began to speak, leaning forward to beckon the men at the back to come nearer. There was a surge as some five hundred men drew near and sank to the ground before him. He spoke to them as a tribal chief in his strong musical voice.

He spoke in the great tongue of the desert, sonorous, magnificent – no language like it.

'For four years' he said, 'I have not found myself in a place like this or in such company'. He told them how Iraq was to rise to their endeavours with himself at their head. He asked them 'Arabs, are you at peace with one another?' They shouted back 'Yes, we are at peace'.

'From this day – what is the date? And what is the hour?' They answered him. 'From this day' – giving the Muhammadan date – 'and from this hour any tribesman who lifts his hand against a tribesman is responsible to me. I will judge between you calling your Sheikhs in council. I have my rights over you as your Lord . . . and you have your rights as subjects which it is my business to guard.' His speech rolled on, punctuated with tribal cries of 'Yes, by God' and 'The truth, by God, the truth!'

Now came the supreme moment of Gertrude's career, the culmination of all her work. Fahad Beg and Ali Sulaiman stood up on either side of Faisal to swear allegiance. But the words they spoke were 'We swear allegiance to you because you are acceptable to the British government.' Gertrude wrote:

Faisal was a little surprised. He looked quickly round to me smiling and then he said 'No-one can doubt what my relations are to the British, but we must settle our affairs ourselves'. He looked at me again, and I held out my two hands clasped together as a symbol of the union of the Arab and British governments. It was a tremendous moment.

Now Ali Sulaiman brought up his forty or fifty sheikhs, one by one, to lay their hands in Faisal's and swear allegiance. Faisal, followed by Sulaiman and Fahad Beg, emerged into the sunlight. The tribesmen in their thousands circled them, galloping around with wild cries, as they processed to the palace garden where a feast was held. Afterwards, Faisal climbed on to a high dais against a wall hung with carpets. The chiefs and Gertrude sat behind him, and one by one the mayors, *qazis* and other notables of all the cities of Iraq, from Fallujah to Qaim, rose one after another from their chairs beneath the trees to place their hands in his. Gertrude took in the beauty of the setting, the variety of dress and colour, the grave faces of the village elders, white-turbaned or draped in the red keffiyeh, and the dignity with which Faisal accepted the homage.

It was only six weeks since his arrival, and the referendum had proved almost unanimous in his favour. He was to be crowned in Baghdad in a fortnight, and he called on the Naqib to help him form his first Cabinet. Gertrude wanted to show Faisal the great archway of Ctesiphon, which he had never seen. She drove out with her servants soon after dawn to prepare the breakfast they would eat in the cool of the day. There they sat on fine carpets, drank coffee, and ate eggs, tongue, sardines and melons. She wrote home on 6 August:

> It was wonderfully interesting showing that splendid place to Faisal. He is an inspiring tourist. After we had re-constructed the palace and seen Khosroes sitting in it, I took him into the high windows to the South, whence we could see the Tigris, and told him the story of the Arab conquest as Tabari records it . . . You can imagine what it was like reciting it to him. I don't know which of us was the more thrilled . . .
>
> Faisal has promised me a regiment of the Arab Army – 'the Khatun's Own'. I shall presently ask you to have their colours embroidered . . . Oh Father, isn't it wonderful. I sometimes think I must be in a dream.

The regiment did not come to pass. A charming compliment that gave her much pleasure, it would have been a difficult concept to run past Cox.

Returning straight to the office after the Ctesiphon outing, she worked for four hours, took an hour for lunch, then visited the Naqib. Then, in her role as President of the Baghdad Public Library, she attended a committee meeting. She had determined that the library would contain books in three European languages, as well as in Arabic and five other Oriental languages; and that it would issue a magazine for book reviews and a catalogue of all the manuscripts available there. She paid a courtesy call on the sister-in-law of Sasun Effendi Eskail, and went home to host a dinner for Hamid Khan, a cousin of the Aga Khan. Even for her, it was quite a day. It was unbearably hot, but despite the strong currents and the occasional shark – one had bitten a boy only that week – she took a swim in the Tigris, and was amused to write home about Cox's latest addition to his menagerie, the largest eagle she had ever seen: 'It lives on a perch on the shady side of the house and it eats bats. These bats are netted in the dusk . . . the eagle likes to eat them in the morning, so the long-suffering Lady Cox keeps them in a tin in her ice chest.'

She had never been so busy or so happy. It was a bonus that on the rounds of courtesy calls that she regularly made she would often be accompanied by the King's Advisor. Tall and clean-shaven, 'Ken' Cornwallis was tanned and good-looking, with a beaky nose and piercing blue eyes. A man of aggressive integrity, humorous, he had been Faisal's adviser for five years now, and the Amir had asked him to come with him to Baghdad.

And then there was Faisal, with his charm and his humour, his gratitude, and his interest in her. There was an affection between them: he called her his sister.

One hot evening she was riding by the Euphrates enjoying the cool river air, and passed Faisal's new house, still in the process of being restored and redecorated. She saw his car at the door, and leaving her pony with one of his slaves, climbed up to the roof in her breeches and shirt. There she found him sitting with his ADCs, watching the setting sun reflected in the water, the desert beyond merging with the fading red of the sky. He smiled to see her, invited her with a wave of his hand to join them in their picnic and, rising, took her hand. Moving to one side, he spoke to her in

Arabic, using the familiar 'thou': '"Enti Iraqiyah, enti badasiyak" he said to me, "You're a Mesopotamian, a Bedouin."'

At the last minute before the coronation was due to take place, there was a 'flap'; the Colonial Office sent a cable demanding Faisal announce in his speech that the ultimate authority in the land was the High Commissioner. Faisal said that from the first he had made it clear that he was an independent sovereign in treaty with Britain. To declare Cox the ultimate authority would rekindle the opposition of the extremists. Gertrude agreed with him. That he should increase his independence was what he had been asked to do.

On 23 August 1921, Faisal was crowned in the carpeted courtyard of the Serai in Baghdad, where he was currently occupying the reception rooms. Fifteen hundred guests were seated in blocks: the British, the Arab officials, townsmen, ministers and local deputations. The ceremony began in the cool of the early morning, at 6 a.m. Faisal, in uniform, with Sir Percy in ceremonial white with all his ribbons and stars, and General Sir Aylmer Haldane the army chief, followed by several ADCs, made their way past the guard of honour, the Dorsets, to the dais. 'Faisal looked very dignified but much strung up,' Gertrude noted. '. . . He looked along the front row and caught my eye and I gave him a tiny salute.'

One Sayyid Hussain, representing the elderly Naqib, read out Cox's proclamation, which included the fact that Faisal had been elected King by 96 per cent of the people of Mesopotamia. The cry of 'Long Live the King!' rang out, the audience stood, a flag was broken and the band – for lack as yet of a national anthem – played 'God Save the King'. A salute of twenty-one guns followed. Then came hundreds of deputations to greet Faisal:

Basrah and Amarah came on Friday, Hillah and Mosul on Saturday . . . first the Mosul town magnates, my guests and their colleagues, next the Christian Archbishops and Bishops and the Jewish Grand Rabbi . . . The third group was more exciting than all the others; it was the Kurdish chiefs of the frontier who have elected to come into the Iraq state until they see whether an independent Kurdistan develops which will be still better to their liking . . .

The week culminated in an invitation to Gertrude from Faisal to tea, in order to discuss the design of the new national flag and his personal standard, which was to include a gold crown on the red triangle of the Hejaz. His first Cabinet was formed: she had secret reservations about three of the nine members, and rejoiced that it was no longer her decision.

Faisal invited her to the first dinner party in his house on the river. Dressed exquisitely for evening, she floated up the Tigris on his launch. The people of the suburb of Karradah recognized her as she passed, and saluted her, smiling. Her companion Nuri Pasha Said told her that just as Faisal would be remembered in London for his Arab dress, so she would always be remembered: 'There's only one Khatun . . . So for a hundred years they'll talk of the Khatun riding by.'

Have I ever told you what the river is like on a hot summer night? At dusk the mist hangs in long white bands over the water; the twilight fades and the lights of the town shine out on either bank, with the river, dark and smooth and full of mysterious reflections, like a road of triumph through the mist. Silently a boat with a winking headlight slips down the stream, then a company of quffahs, each with his tiny lamp, loaded to the brim with water melons from Samarra . . . And we slow down the launch so that the wash may not disturb them. The waves of our passage don't even extinguish the floating votive candle each burning on its minute boat made out of the swathe of a date cluster, which anxious hands launched above the town – if they reach the last town yet burning, the sick man will recover, the baby will be born safely into this world of hot darkness and glittering lights . . . Now I've brought you out to where the palm trees stand marshalled along the banks. The water is so still that you can see the Scorpion in it, star by star.

. . . and here are Faisal's steps.

16

STAYING AND LEAVING

Gertrude, at fifty-three, found herself drawn more and more to the King's company. Faisal, thirty-six, was a most charming companion, affectionate with those he trusted, and exercising a persuasive influence on everyone around him. The Oriental Secretary and the King shared a sense of the ridiculous which they could enjoy in private, so that aides busy elsewhere in the house would sometimes be curious to know what was causing the laughter they could hear through closed doors.

For his part, the King saw in Gertrude an extraordinary person, a formidable ally, impeccably well informed, and with a personal history of adventure that he – as an Arab man – could hardly believe. A woman of quick movements and quick understanding, her conversation would catch fire as she entered into political debate. Her gaze, as it fixed her interlocutor, was as penetrating as it had ever been, the occasional snap of irritation more than balanced by the frequent twinkle. In spite of the climate and its effects on her health, she still loved a gallop along the banks of the Tigris in the early morning mists, and to join him in the occasional all-day partridge shoot – dressed in breeches with brown leather knee boots and a tweed tunic – and swim in the river in the evenings.

The American journalist Marguerite Harrison, interviewing her in Baghdad for the *New York Times* in 1923, had a rare opportunity to see Gertrude at her office:

I was ushered into a small room with a high ceiling and long French windows facing the river. It was the untidiest room I had ever seen, chairs, tables and sofas being littered with documents, maps, pamphlets and papers in English, French and Arabic. At a desk piled high with documents that had over-flowed on to the carpet sat a slender woman in a smart sports frock of knitted silk, pale tan in colour. As she rose, I noticed that her figure was still willowy and graceful. Her delicate oval face with its firm mouth and chin and steel-blue eyes, and with its aureole of soft grey hair, was the face of a 'grande dame'. There was nothing of the weather-beaten explorer in her looks or bearing. 'Paris frock, Mayfair manners.' And this was the woman who had made sheikhs tremble!

Even now, she was without fear. One morning, as she was breakfasting with Haji Naji in his summer-house, a dervish strode with an iron staff and rudely demanded to be treated as a guest. Haji Naji told him to go. Looking threateningly at Gertrude, he said that he had as much right as she to be there. He then sat down in the entrance, declared, 'I rely on God', and began to read in a loud voice from the Koran. Neither Haji Naji, his son nor the servants could move him, so Gertrude told the Dervish, 'God's a long way off and the police are very near', snatched up his iron staff and struck him with it. He left.

Faisal and Gertrude together bent their hearts and minds to the well-being of the new country they had established, and to an ultimate ideal of a wider Arab independence. Sir Percy Cox would soon be retiring, to be replaced by the one-time chief of the Revenue Department, Sir Henry Dobbs; Gertrude would remain in Baghdad, available to give official or unofficial help and advice. This period of Faisal's and Gertrude's lives was one of great satisfaction and excitement to both, and brought them together in the close confidence of true friends. She was happy and fulfilled in her work:

I'm acutely conscious of how much life has, after all, given me. I've gone back now, after many years to the old feeling of joy in existence, and I'm happy in feeling that I've got the love and confidence of a whole nation. It mayn't be the intimate happiness

which I've missed, but it's a very wonderful and absorbing thing
– almost too absorbing perhaps.

How close, how confident, was not revealed until after Gertrude's death, and then only in a modest British journal, *Everybody's Weekly*, which had the bright idea of obtaining an interview about her with the King. The editor chose to entitle the feature 'Secrets of Great White Woman of the Desert Which Were Not Revealed in Her Book'. How Gertrude would have hated that! However sensational or over-romantic the language – no doubt a paraphrase of Faisal's answers, edited as befitted a magazine for housewives, and published complete with misspellings – the content to which the King gave his name contains some extraordinary assertions.

Faisal began:

Gertrude Bell is a name that is written indelibly on Arab history
– a name which is spoken with awe – like that of Napoleon, Nelson or Mussolini . . . One might say that she was the greatest woman of her time. Without question her claim to greatness is on a footing with women like Joan of Arc, Florence Nightingale, Edith Cavell, Madame Curie and others.

Speaking of her passion for adventure and her unerring loyalty to all that was just and good, he went on to say that it was not only Colonel Lawrence who should be credited with bringing about the uprising of the Arab tribes against the Turks. Like Lawrence,

[Gertrude] could play a man's part in the action . . . She ventured alone and disguised into the remotest districts to carry the message of revolt, and when the chiefs seemed to lack the courage to obey the call she inspired them with her own amazing courage . . . I do not think she knew what fear was. Death held no fears for her. No danger or exploit was too great for her to face. Her personal safety was her last consideration.

He describes her facility for disguise, her ability to make herself up as an Arab of any tribe she chose, and so skilfully that it was undetectable.

Once, my men brought me a picturesque looking Arab camel driver, who answered all my questions in the vernacular as though his whole life had been spent in following this humble occupation. After I had questioned the captive and had obtained from him all the information I sought . . . the camel driver owned to being Miss Bell.

He went on:

I think I may reveal now the fact that in one of the critical phases of our history, when some of our men were wavering, the great white woman herself led them in an attack on the Turks. At least once in her strange career she was at the mercy of her enemies and had before her the certainty of a terrible death.

She had been betrayed to the Turks by a treacherous Arab while on the way back from one of her perilous missions into the desert, and she was seized, disguised as an Arab tribesman, by a Turkish patrol . . . She was told she would be put to fiendish torture if she did not reveal the secrets of the men who were at that moment planning to throw off the Turkish yoke. To all threats she remained deaf, and not one word of her secret did her captors learn. Had she faltered, the lives of some of our best chiefs would have been forfeit, but this woman preferred to face torture . . . rather than betray anyone. Happily, she was able to make her escape before her captors had a chance of carrying out their threats . . .

He continued with the story of her escape, which, he said, she had confided only to him. She had slipped out of the Turkish camp in the dead of night, and wandered without guide, water or food for three days and nights, managing to hide from passing bands of marauders. She finally reached safety more dead than alive. 'A few days later she was about again, as active as ever, engaged in her great task of inspiring our men to revolt against their oppressors.'

Gertrude had a genius for warfare, Faisal concluded, and on occasion had offered tactical advice of the greatest value to the Arabs. Early in the war, the Turks had put a price on her head:

'The price was one that might have tempted the cupidity of men, but such was the esteem in which our people held her that none could be found to denounce her to her enemies.'

Gertrude left no record of these adventures, and if she never revealed them to Sir Percy and Lady Cox, it is perhaps not surprising. It had been the cautious Cox, years before, who had warned her not to attempt the Hayyil journey. And the vision of his Oriental Secretary playing a practical joke on the King by disguising herself as a camel driver might not have amused him. Just as she would omit or slant events in her letters home, to spare her family anxiety, so she would have avoided harassing them with accounts of her near-fatalities. Perhaps one reason for her lifelong hatred of the press was a fear that these sensational incidents might have been uncovered by their researches, rendering her less effective in her work as a serious administrator, or indeed as a spy.

There is one particularly intriguing possibility: that she was complicit with T. E. Lawrence's attempt in 1916 to buy off the Turkish siege at Kut. At that time she was in Basra, and frustrated by lack of a role, wondering whether to stay or to go. She was desperately anxious about the state of the starving army. One week after Lawrence passed through Basra, en route for Kut, on 16 April, she wrote to her father: 'I've suggested that I should go up the Shatt al' Arab with a local man and check the maps and they seem to think it would be a good plan.' Then there was a most unusual gap in her letters home – until the 27th, when she wrote: 'Dearest Mother, I missed the mail last week for I was out for a night at a little place on the edge of the desert called Zubair and when I came in I found that the confounded post had gone a day earlier than usual . . . Nothing happens and nothing seems likely to happen at Kut – it's a desperate business.'

With Kut uppermost in Lawrence's mind and in hers, one may speculate that the 'vast schemes' they discussed concerned the siege and whether there was any chance of getting the soldiers out. It is not impossible, given the kind of people they were, that they considered the idea of creating a diversion on one side in order to attempt a breakthrough on the other. In his *Seven Pillars of Wisdom*

Lawrence is evasive about what he did in Kut: 'our Government . . . sent me to Mesopotamia to see what could be done by indirect means to relieve the beleaguered garrison . . . As a matter of fact it was too late for action, with Kut just dying; and in consequence I did nothing of what it was in my mind and power to do.'

There is a further hint of a similar involvement on Gertrude's part, although without a date or a context. Her old friend Leo Amery, Secretary of State for the Colonies since 1924, wrote in his memoirs *My Political Life*: 'In organising Arab forces against the Turks her field of operations had to some extent overlapped with that of Lawrence, and she was credited with a signal victory in the desert in which her protégés defeated Lawrence's and captured all their machine guns.' Lawrence wrote to Elsa after Gertrude's death: 'She stood out as the one person who, thinking clearly, saw the true ultimate goal of our work with the Arabs and, daunted by nothing, worked unsparing of herself toward it.'

After his coronation, the King reorganized his life. He now moved out of the apartment in the Serai and into a palace on the outskirts of Baghdad, a large but simple building with lofty rooms. From a waiting-room, guests were shown into the main salon, its windows framed by velvet curtains, good rugs on the floor, a divan along one wall of the room and, on winter days, a log fire in the hearth. A couple of sentries guarded the entrance, and except for evenings when Faisal was entertaining, the servant who opened the door also brought in the coffee tray. This room was also Faisal's office, and where he held interviews and conferences with his ministers. In addition, there was his favourite palace, a villa at Harithya, with its steps down to the river, its rose garden and shaded terrace. He had bought the house together with a small farm, which he liked to supervise himself. Further afield, he owned a large farm at Khaniqin near the Persian frontier, where he grew crops according to modern agricultural guidelines. When he learnt to fly, some time later, he would pilot himself to this property.

Gertrude had fought for an independent Arab nation for just as long as Faisal. It had been her inspiration in Cairo, Basra and Baghdad. She had been a lone voice in the days when she worked for A. T. Wilson; she had sat firm while Britain made repeated threats to withdraw from Iraq; she had nearly despaired during the insurgency; she had watched the years go by as the West procrastinated and the Turks put every obstacle in the way of defining a northern border to Iraq. And still she dreamt of a free Arab government.

By 1921, so much had come right. Cox, a wise and subtle negotiator guided by the same principles, had returned; an Arab king was on the throne; and a respected elder of Baghdad, the Naqib, was Prime Minister. The country was in the hands of a Cabinet chosen from an array of representative Iraqis. National pride in the prospect of self-determination, not yet complete, was to be expected, but agitation for it must follow. Gertrude supported the nationalists in spirit and entertained them in her house, while London insisted on official acceptance of the mandate, without which the British must withdraw from Iraq. And then, as she repeatedly warned Faisal, he would not be able to hold the allegiance of his people against the Turks and Ibn Saud. Faisal was walking a knife edge. His hold on Syria had been broken by that other mandate that France had secured. He knew that his credibility as an Arab leader depended on being seen to reject the British mandate, with its insistence on subservience to their control. So he refused to acknowledge its existence, and despite all Gertrude's pleas, was ready to listen to every extremist and opportunist who approached him. She wrote home on 25 September:

> I dined with the King ... After dinner we sat on the balcony overlooking the river and Faisal unburdened his heart. It arose out of my urging him to bring out his wife and children. He said he felt so uncertain of the future ... he didn't know whether the British Government would not insist on terms in the future treaty which he felt he could not accept.

It was Cox's idea that London might accept a treaty in place of the mandate. The League of Nations would have to be satisfied that Britain would still meet its obligations to the fledgling nation; Iraq would have to be satisfied that the relationship with Britain would be one of equals, leading to self-government without British guidance, and with its own Iraqi army.

Work began on the tortuous negotiations. To draft the detail, the Colonial Office sent one Hubert Young. He led a team including Cornwallis, acting for Faisal; the Iraqi Cabinet's judicial adviser, Edward Drower; and Nigel Davidson, the legal secretary to the High Commissioner. An 'instrument of alliance' would be added, spelling out how the two countries would work together, and they would move on to draft the Organic Law, or constitution. An Electorial Law would follow.

London demanded adherence to the mandate as a condition of the treaty. Faisal insisted that the treaty must stand alone, and the Iraqi Prime Minister said that he would refuse to acknowledge it if it did not. But Faisal had a wider agenda. He hoped that his rejection of the British mandate would lead the Syrians to reject theirs, and his mission was still to demonstrate to the world the viability of a Muslim sovereign state.

In and out of the palace every day, Gertrude found Faisal increasingly difficult to deal with. Intransigent, manipulative, even devious, he condoned anti-mandate propaganda in the Hillah division almost to the point of rebellion. When the British sought the arrest of a certain sheikh who had murdered a British officer, he accused them of being his enemies. He told the press that no Arab noble should be asked to take orders from a foreigner. Each time his ministers agreed the wording for the treaty, he found a new fault with it. Each time Cox sent a fresh version to Whitehall for approval, he would discover local opposition to it.

Gertrude was at her wits' end, Cox and Cornwallis hardly less so. Faisal was risking the loyalty of the moderate sheikhs and ministers who had given him their support; he was inviting the resignation of the British civil servants and advisers who kept his government working; and he was tempting Whitehall to abandon Iraq altogether. Relying on the affection that she knew the King had for her, she resolved to make a last personal appeal to him. As she wrote later, she would take advantage of

the emotional atmosphere of which he, with his acute perceptions, was fully conscious. For I was playing my last card, and I
told him so. I began by asking whether he believed in my
personal sincerity and devotion to him. He said he could not
doubt it . . . I said in that case I could speak with perfect freedom
and that I was extremely unhappy. I had formed a beautiful and
gracious snow image to which I had given allegiance and I saw it
melting before my eyes. Before every noble outline had been
obliterated, I preferred to go; in spite of my love for the Arab
nation and my sense of responsibility for the future, I did not
think I could see the evaporation of the dream . . . I saw him,
whom I had believed to be moved only by the highest principles,
a victim to every form of malicious rumour . . . I would not wait
until the villains in whom he put his trust inevitably blackened
me in his eyes.

On this theme we had a terrific discussion – during which he
kissed my hand at intervals, which is very disconcerting! . . . I'm
still *sous le coup* of this interview. Faisal is one of the most lovable
of human beings but he is amazingly lacking in strength of
character . . . I've left him tonight convinced that my one desire is
to serve him; tomorrow he will be full of doubts.

A few days later, she heard that the King had already changed
his mind on one of the issues they had discussed. Sadly, she resigned
herself to what she took to be Faisal's fluctuating loyalties. There
would be more and worse disagreements, but, like Cornwallis, she
was in thrall to Faisal: she could never resign. The King worked
his magic over both of them. He constantly demanded her company, listened calmly to her remonstrances, kissed her hand – and
remained obdurate. She wrote:

Safwat Pasha [the King's old tutor] begged me to drop in to the
palace as often as I could, as it was clear that I was the only
person here who really loved the King or whom the King really
loved. That does scant justice to Mr Cornwallis who has given up
his whole career for him . . . but Safwat held to it that I was

different, and perhaps the King does hold my hand more, though he embraces Mr Cornwallis oftener – we compare notes.

You can do nothing with Faisal unless he feels certain that he has your devoted affection. He has ours.

For once in her life, Gertrude had met her match.

The British gave way repeatedly over the terms of the treaty; but the sticking point remained the mandate. Gertrude summed up: 'The Treaty is in *statu quo ante*. Sir Percy has sent an admirable telegram home strongly advising Mr Churchill to give way.'

But Churchill refused to compromise. He demanded that Cox and Faisal come to London, where they knew he would confront them with an ultimatum. 'My heart died within me.'

The battle was within a hair's breadth of being lost. Faisal would refuse to sign, and Iraq as she knew it would cease to exist. Cox, taking strength from the fact that he was close to retirement, now used his personal authority. He saw no advantage to be gained, he replied to Churchill, from their coming to London. He proposed publishing the treaty in Iraq as agreed with the King, adding a rider that the mandate was the only point of difference. The King could then show his people that he had fought for the best terms possible. 'But will our government accept this suggestion?' Gertrude wondered. 'That's what we want to know, for being all away grouse shooting we can get no answer to any telegrams.'

It was August 1922 and the anniversary of the coronation, preceded for Gertrude by a week of parties and celebrations. There was a day spent at the King's cotton farm riding through the fields with Faisal and his party, followed by the mounted ADCs and a cavalcade of bodyguards; then in the evening they played bridge. She had organized an entertainment for the King in return, a riverside picnic on the shady banks of the Tigris: 'We roasted great fishes on spits over a fire of palm fronds – the most delicious food in the world – I brought carpets and cushions and hung old Baghdad lanterns in the tamarisk bushes . . . in the rosy stillness of the sunset. "This is peace" said the King.'

Then came the reception at Faisal's Baghdad palace, the Residency party arriving together in two cars. Gertrude wore cream lace pinned with miniature orders that she was wearing for the first time, and two diamond tiaras – the Bell heirloom in her hair and the other around her neck as a sparkling choker. This last had just been sent to her by Florence: 'I opened a parcel in the office . . . and out of it rolled a large tiara. I nearly laughed aloud – it was such an unexpected object in the middle of office files. It's too kind of you to let me have it – I had forgotten how fine it is. I fear in wearing it I may be taken for the crowned Queen of Mesopotamia.'

At the palace, they joined a procession of three or four hundred people climbing the steps to the entrance. When they reached the stairs, there were indistinct shouts, and then a storm of clapping from the crowd. At first she thought they were applauding Cox, but everyone was perplexed. 'As soon as we were back in the office the High Commissioner told me to get on to it at once . . . within an hour I had the information. It was a demonstration on the part of two extremist political parties.'

The dissidents were gathering power, and with Faisal refusing to allow any action to be taken against them unless the mandate was quashed, the entire Cabinet had resigned. The Naqib was left in solitary and ineffectual charge as the anti-mandate insurrection spread. But now fate took a hand, and provided Cox with the opportunity to break the impasse. The King developed appendicitis.

In agreeing to surgery, Faisal also, somewhat oddly, let it be known that he had no objection to any number of observers being present to watch the operation. A great number of notables and sheikhs took him up on the offer, and crowded the observation chamber. Meanwhile Cox – with no King and no Cabinet – took brief but sweeping control of the country. He made good use of it. He had seven leaders of the Baghdad insurrection arrested – the rest escaped dressed as women – rounded up the agitators from the regions, and shut down two dissident newspapers as well as the two extremist political parties. Gertrude wrote on the 27th:

For once Providence has behaved like a gentleman . . . the King['s] illness was beyond words fortunate . . . Sir Percy has saved the situation and has given the King a loop-hole through which he can walk when he is able to walk. By that time – his convalescence if necessary can be prolonged – we shall have got a clear line from home . . . the moderates are lifting their heads sky high . . . and in the provinces the extremists will have to build an ark if they want to escape from the political flood.

Any number of witnesses could testify that Faisal was unconscious while Cox set his initiatives under way. For quite a few days after the operation no one was allowed to see him. Cornwallis was the first to inform him of what had happened. When Cox and Gertrude visited him, his relief was visible, and he was fulsome in his appreciation of Cox's actions. He said: 'You have spared me the blame.' The High Commissioner then took the treaty to the Naqib at his home, put a pen in his hand and asked him to sign it. A flustered Naqib demanded that parts of the English version be read to him in Arabic, to make sure that both versions matched, and then he signed. It was 10 October 1922.

Three days later, Faisal proclaimed the treaty in a ringing speech that looked forward to 'the continuance of the friendship of our illustrious ally, Great Britain, and to carrying out the elections for the convening of a Constituent Assembly to frame the Organic Law'. Ratifications would need to follow, but the game was over. It was also the second step towards membership of the League of Nations as an independent country.

Faisal had told Gertrude that after the debacle in Damascus in 1920, he had been cautious about bringing his wife and children with him to Iraq. Now, in 1924, settled into his two palaces and with the Hejaz suffering increasing aggression from Ibn Saud, he began to bring his family to Baghdad, beginning with his favourite and youngest brother, Zaid. He had fought with Faisal in the Revolt, and was to be of great value in Kurdistan; he would leave for a year's study at Balliol College, Oxford, later in the year. After Zaid came the King's only son, the twelve-year-old Amir Ghazi, small for his age, accompanied by his slaves and with a shy dignity that went straight to Gertrude's heart. She felt that he had been neglected, in a household of slaves and unlettered women. He could barely read and write Arabic; he needed good tutors and the company of men. But before she began on his entourage, she was required to help choose his clothes. The King now wore European dress most of the time, and wanted his son to do the same. She told her parents:

> I was called up to the palace to help to choose Ghazi's clothes. There was an English tailor from Bombay with patterns. So we chose his little shirts and suits, the tailor behaving like a tailor in Thackeray. He skipped about, pointed his toe and handed me patterns with one hand on his heart. Ghazi came in to be measured, half shy and half pleased.

Following the young Amir came his mother the Queen, with Ghazi's three sisters, to live in the country villa at Harithya. In accordance with family tradition, Faisal had married his first cousin, the Amira Hussaina, who lived strictly in purdah with her daughters: the youngest had been an invalid from birth, and was never seen. When Gertrude had talked to Faisal about his wife earlier, he had prevaricated. 'I asked him about his wife . . . and said I thought she too ought to be encouraged to make a position and a court. He was rather shy about her – they always are embarrassed about their women, thinking that they are too ignorant to be presentable, but he agreed that we must make a beginning.'

The fact that the Queen lived in seclusion would make the notion of a Western-style court impossible. Male visitors were entertained at dinners and receptions hosted by Faisal alone in the Baghdad palace, after which he would drive to Harithya to spend the night with his family. Gertrude was one of the first to be received by the Queen, who spoke only Arabic, although she understood a little English and French:

> She's charming, I'm so happy to say. She has the delicate, sensitive Hashimi face and the same winning manner that he has. She had on a very nice, long tunicked brown gown . . . a long long

string of pearls, and a splendid aquamarine pendant. I saw the two eldest girls who are just like her, rather shy but eager to be outgoing.

As soon as Faisal's family was settled in Baghdad, Gertrude had the enormous fun of court-making. First, there were clothes to be made, tunics and gowns suitable for a queen and her all-female receptions and tea parties. Out of doors, the royal women and their suites wore the traditional black silk veil, but when they visited the houses of their women friends or relations, the veils would be left with a maid at the door. Gertrude recommended the dressmaker-nuns who had made her own clothes before she had Marie to sew them, and brought the sisters to the palace to introduce them. Later, Elsa and Molly would be dispatched to the London shops to buy suitable Western-style clothes (only ever to be seen in private) for the royal women: 'The King sent for me on Monday,' Gertrude wrote home, 'to discuss what arrangements should be made about the Queen's household. I was very glad he consulted me for there were some terrible pitfalls ahead . . . So I'm busy!'

There had to be a mistress of ceremonies to help the Queen arrange her entertaining and to teach her orders of precedence and other diplomatic protocol. Gertrude suggested that Faisal should appoint the wife of Jaudat Bey, his principal ADC, to perform the role. Mme Jaudat Bey was from a distinguished Circassian family and highly suitable in every way – well educated, greatly respected and a long-time inhabitant of Baghdad. The King was delighted to comply, and Gertrude congratulated herself on having outmanoeuvred the wife of the King's chamberlain, a vulgar and unpopular Syrian who had continually thrust her daughter forward in an attempt to persuade the King to marry her – either, presumably, as a new wife or because she was not aware that he was already married.

At Harithya one morning to help Mme Jaudat Bey arrange the Queen's first reception, Gertrude was introduced to the children's new governess, an appointment she viewed with approval but not entirely without reservations, the latter to do with class distinctions:

'She is a nice, good little girl and I am very much pleased that she has found a permanent place at the palace . . . She is to teach the girls English and tennis and European behaviour. I shall have to unteach them to call a napkin a serviette, which they will certainly do under her guidance.'

She asked the Queen if she might invite Ghazi to tea. In time, the young Amir would come to see her regularly, first accompanied by his slaves Hamid and Farese, later with his tutor and governess. Gertrude gave him marvellous modern toys ordered from London: 'The train and soldiers I had ordered for him from Harrod's had arrived last mail and were presented, with great success. Especially the train. He loves all kinds of machinery and in fact was much cleverer about the engine than any of us . . . we all sat on the floor and watched it running along the rails, following it with shouts of joy!' He would then be driven home to write her a careful thank you letter in English, before going off hand in hand with his father for the sunset prayers. A progressive, modern King, Faisal never failed to observe the traditional call to prayer. Ghazi, being taught to do the same, presumably did so even during his later schooldays at Harrow. For the loss of her son to an English public school the Queen would find it difficult to forgive Gertrude, on whose advice he was sent there.

Soon after the Queen arrived in Baghdad, it seemed likely that Faisal would be receiving another member of his family, one who would not be so welcome. His father the septuagenarian Hussain had been dislodged from Mecca by the forces of his hereditary enemy Ibn Saud, and as the Hejaz was absorbed into Saudi Arabia he had been obliged to abdicate. Gertrude dreaded Hussain's jealous and interfering presence. 'I do pray that Husain won't take refuge here; he would be the centre of every kind of mischief, anti-Faisal, anti-British . . .'

Trouble had been foreseen since Hussain had assumed the title of Caliph of the Muslim world, an appointment that had been abolished by Mustafa Kemal — Ataturk, the modernizing postwar power in Turkey. This provocative move on Hussain's part gave

Ibn Saud an excuse to oust the Sharif as the head of the Nationalist Arab Party. Ibn Saud had taken Hayyil, where Gertrude had been held captive, in 1921, the year of Faisal's coronation, and hostilities broke out when the unbeatable Saud forces began to attack the Hejaz, Transjordan where Abdullah now ruled, and even the borders of Iraq. In the Akhwan* attack there, two hundred tribesmen were killed, and Royal Air Force planes had to come to their rescue. Gertrude had written to her old friend Charles Hardinge early in 1922:

> The capture of Hail by Ibn Saud has altered the whole political balance . . . Ibn Saud's ambition is to be Lord of the Desert, all of it, including the marches where Iraqi shepherds have gone out from time immemorial to their spring pasturages . . .
>
> The day after they had fired on our aeroplanes we bombed their camp. They fled south . . . and next morning our aeroplanes pursued them and bombed them again. They had made a wholly unprovoked attack, looted and killed our peaceful shepherds and carried off our flocks . . . The Akhwan, with their horrible fanatical appeal to a medieval faith, rouse in me the blackest hatred. They are the worst example of that abominable thing, an omnipotent religious sanction.

In the Akhwan sect of Islam simple pleasures were forbidden and strict observance of religious ceremony was obligatory, but destruction and rapine in war were condoned. Taif, the summer home of the Sharif where Faisal had been born, was attacked, and the residents massacred. Hussain telegraphed to London demanding planes and troops, but he had long ago alienated London with his intransigence over Arab self-determination, and Britain remained neutral. When Hussain abdicated on the insistence of his own people, his eldest son Ali briefly took his place as King of the Hejaz. Ali would finally follow the rest of the family to join his younger brother in Iraq.

Faisal was essentially a man of action trapped in a palace and an

* The name by which Ibn Saud's sect the Wahabis were now known.

office, a volatile personality more used to command than to exercising restraint. Surrounded by intractable problems and not always sure whom to trust, his patience was wearing thin. He resisted yet more attempts to force him into compromise with the British, his ministers, the Kurds and others, but grew ever more frustrated. And not even now that he was King could he put a stop to his father's interference. He flew to Transjordan in an attempt to salvage the family fortunes, and on his return told Gertrude that if the British did not take steps to intervene in the Hejaz, he would have to leave Iraq and go back there to die in the defence of his family and womenfolk. She advised caution, but the King no longer followed her counsels, nor did he always take her into his confidence. She shrugged off his explosions and wrote humorously of him as a tiresome diva. But the honeymoon was over. She wrote to her parents that

> The King is in a mighty taking about the Wahhabis . . . the worst thing to do, however, is what we believe HM to be doing – incite our tribes to open the ball by attacking the Wahhabis. That would lead to immediate reprisals and the desert would be a battle-field . . .
>
> The King had violent hysterics on Monday; on Tuesday he formally abdicated in favour of the Amir Ghazi . . . I remember that in 1922 Ken Cornwallis had Faisal's abdication lying about in a drawer for a month.

The 'violent hysterics' consisted of Faisal losing his temper with his Cabinet over their inaction with regard to the Saudi incursions on the border. He promptly told five of his ministers that they must resign. Cox pacified him in masterly fashion. He had already sent a message to Ibn Saud asking for an explanation, and was soon able to produce a telegram from him claiming to have been totally ignorant of the attack by his men on Faisal's tribes.

Gertrude had been planning to go back to England for a holiday, meeting her father halfway, near Jerusalem. She regretfully decided that while the situation was so finely balanced, she could not spare the time. Instead, she would fly to Ziza and meet him there, and they would have a few days together.

She emerged deaf and dizzy from the long bumpy flight over the desert in the official plane, and fell into her father's waiting arms. When she had recovered her hearing, he told her that they had been invited to dinner with the Amir Abdullah, now encamped not far away near Amman, but he had refused the invitation as he had assumed she would be too tired. Gertrude declared herself fresh as a daisy, unpacked her evening clothes, and their first evening was spent as guests of Faisal's brother.

During the dinner she observed Abdullah closely and with fascination, and quickly decided that she could not feel much respect for him; she wrote of him subsequently as 'useless' and 'an expensive excrescence'.

> Nor does Abdullah strike one as a good ally if it came to fighting. His chief asset is a personal charm which is marred less by his lack of vitality than by his inordinate opinion of his own powers . . . He combines with indolence a narrow and almost fanatical outlook . . . he cannot keep his jealousy of his brother Faisal out of his conversations. Every topic . . . reverts to his chagrin at finding himself Amir in Amman while Faisal is King in Baghdad.

Back in Baghdad, she went to tea with the King and thought herself lucky, after all:

> I had come back with the conviction that we were the only Arab province which was set in the right path, and that if we failed here it would be the end of Arab aspirations. [The King] was most affectionate and charming. I'm glad that it's he and not Abdullah! There may be difficulties in dealing with a creature so sensitive and highly strung but his fine and vital qualities and his wonderful breadth of outlook make up for everything.

Hussain would finally descend on Abdullah and Transjordan instead of Faisal and Iraq. Once there, he immediately embarked on a campaign of attack on Abdullah's deference to the British and to the Zionist-led government in Jerusalem. Abdullah, who was being subsidized by London to the tune of £150,000 a year, also needed British support to fight off Ibn Saud. Arguments broke out between father and son. Dislodged again, Sharif Hussain took to his yacht, first in the Red Sea where he lay off Aqaba until asked to move on, and then in the Mediterranean. The Hashemite misfortunes began to resemble the tangled plot of a comic opera. 'The King's family, apparently, are sailing about the Red Sea like so many Flying Dutchmen,' wrote Gertrude wryly.

With his uncanny knack of turning up whenever he was needed, Sir Ronald Storrs now saved the day by finding Hussain a palace on the island of Cyprus, where Storrs was now Governor. There Hussain lived in exile until his death. Ibn Saud, meanwhile, accepted the throne of the Hejaz with pious reluctance, giving way only 'because the people insisted'.

The Treaty of Lausanne in 1923 had been intended to wind up the final peace negotiations between the Allies and Turkey. Almost inevitably, it failed, and Cox wasted two months in Constantinople attempting to bring about a settlement. While the League of Nations went about its slow business of appointing a Boundary Commission to settle border differences between Turkey and northern Iraq, the Turks invaded the traditional border and laid waste once more to the Assyrians. 'We're in the uncomfortable position,' Gertrude wrote in September 1924, 'of not knowing whether we are at war or not. There are some three thousand Turkish regulars inside our administrative frontier busy killing our Assyrians who are fleeing down as refugees once more ... Meantime H.M.G. says nothing and negotiations continue peacefully at Geneva.'

It would be seven years after the end of the war before the League of Nations came to the decision that the Mosul *vilayet* would not revert to Turkey. Once again, the Iraqi government was hopelessly short of troops, and it was the British political officers who stood almost alone against tribal insurrection and Turkish aggression. Churchill vacillated over the future of the north. In 1921 he had ordered withdrawal from Mosul, and then, at the Cairo Conference, he instructed that the Kurds be allowed to decide their own future. Cox carried out the order, and sent back the predictable answer which was no answer: Sulaimaniyah declined to take part in the whole affair; and Kirkuk wanted Kurdish independence but could not define what that would mean, other than its having nothing whatsoever to do with the the Sulaimani. Gertrude commented:

> Arbil and all the Kurdish districts round Mosul have come in, realizing that their political and economic welfare is bound up with Mosul. They . . . will obtain certain privileges . . . Some ask that all the teaching in the schools should be in Kurdish, a reasonable request if it weren't for the fact that there aren't any Kurdish teachers and those can only be trained in Arabic for there are no Kurdish books.

There were few Kurds with any inclination for national leadership. Only one family put itself forward, that of Sheikh Muhammad. He was twice allowed to form governments in Sulaimaniyah, and twice he used Turkish support to foment rebellion against Iraq. In retaliation the RAF bombed his base, and he was evicted in 1924. Gertrude remarked that his Christmas card, signed 'King of Kurdistan', had probably not advanced his cause.

Faisal instigated a holding operation by sending Zaid to Mosul with the seasoned Captain Clayton in support, creating a northern Sharifian court and promising, even as the Turks massed on the border, that once the boundaries were settled he would grant the Kurds a regional government within Iraq. He also gave an undertaking to award land and self-administration to those Assyrians who had been dispossessed of their homes: 'It's possible that the Turkish threat will go a long way to making a nation of us,' Gertrude remarked.

In her daily work and in her occasional differences with the King, Gertrude was growing closer to his adviser, Kinahan Cornwallis. Cornwallis had been known to Hussain and his sons since the start of the Arab Revolt; Faisal, when in Syria, had specifically asked for him as his personal adviser. Cornwallis would devote the rest of his career to the King. It was Lawrence's opinion that he could 'remain for months hotter than other men's white-heat, and yet look cold and hard'. From their first meeting Gertrude assessed him as 'a great standby'. He was married, by coincidence, to a woman called Gertrude, who was with him in Iraq, but they were seldom seen out as a couple. For his part, Cornwallis quickly recognized the Oriental Secretary's formidable abilities, and was not long in offering her a job in the new Iraqi administration, as chief of intelligence in the Ministry of the Interior. Gertrude smiled and replied that she couldn't possibly leave Sir Percy: she might have added that as an Iraqi government employee she would have to relinquish her special status as liaison with the King.

The closer friendship between Gertrude and Cornwallis began just before Christmas 1922 when, returning from the office, she found her cook and her manservant Zaiya in mortal combat amid a sea of broken crockery in her kitchen, wrestling with a carving knife. 'I rated them soundly for celebrating Xmas in so unsuitable a manner. Marie had gone out to dinner so I dined alone, wondering dejectedly what steps I should take to reorganize my household.'

By the end of the month, the issue between the cook and Zaiya had clarified itself:

> I spent last week in acute discomfort on account of Zaiya's having so completely made it up with my cook as to marry his daughter. It's less inconvenient when they beat one another over the head than when they enter into matrimonial alliances, for Zaiya being a bridegroom and the cook having to cook the wedding breakfast there was no one left to cook or wait. I billeted myself on Mr Cornwallis and Sir Aylmer . . .

The friendship of Gertrude and Cornwallis thrived on proximity and their shared loyalty to and fondness – even love – for the King. They discussed his character exhaustively at lunches, and sharing as they did so many social events hosted by the King they were often thrown together in the evenings and at weekends at dinners, shooting parties, card games – the King liked bridge and chemin de fer – and the usual swimming picnics by the river.

More and more she came to love the coolness and buoyancy of swimming, and the picnics provided some of her happiest moments. She teased the King about his poor performance as a swimmer. She would change under the fig trees, helping herself to ripe fruit as she dried her hair, then emerge to eat bonfire-roasted fish under the tamarisk trees. It was, she said, the only meal of the week that she really enjoyed.

Perhaps because of the difference in their ages, she fifty-three, Cornwallis thirty-eight, he felt able one evening to tell her something of his unhappy marriage, and his loneliness within it. A misty, romantic, note entered her descriptions of such evenings.

> I went up river in the last glow of a wonderful sunset to where Mr Cornwallis, Captain Clayton, Colonel MacNiece and the Davidsons were just beginning dinner at the edge of the fig gardens. We lay there in the dark till past 10 o'clock talking . . . while the stars came out one by one. Don't fancy for a moment that we thought of them as constituents of an infinite firmament; for us they were adornments of the skies of Iraq . . .

Soon the group fell into the habit of spending Sundays together. Gertrude was not, for once, the only woman. She liked Iris Davidson and found her intelligent: she had picked up Arabic 'wonderfully fast', unlike so many of the British wives in Baghdad. 'I've added the Davidsons and Mr Cornwallis to my permanent list of friends,' she reported.

In 1923, the never-mentioned Mrs Cornwallis left her husband and sailed for home; and in Gertrude's letters, the frequently mentioned 'Mr Cornwallis' had already become 'Ken'. Christmas was usually the nadir of the year for Gertrude, who missed her family more than ever in a deserted Baghdad. But that year, it was different. She joined Cornwallis, Faisal's brother Zaid and Nigel Davidson for a six-day shooting party in Babylon. As Marie packed her trunk, she made a point of putting in Gertrude's most beautiful silk and lace nightdresses. Gertrude asked her why she was doing that, and reminded her that it was just a hunting party. The French housekeeper had hesitated a moment before replying that Nur al

Din, Ken's Sudanese manservant, might see them. It is unlikely that Ken or his servant were in close enough proximity to Gertrude at night to admire the nightdresses, but she came back from the expedition extraordinarily happy: 'Altogether I think no more delightful expedition has ever been made in Iraq.'

Sadly, after the Christmas highlight there came some sort of a break. That summer Cornwallis would be going on leave to England to deal with his wife's divorce proceedings. By the end of January she wrote to Florence that she was profoundly unhappy, and for some ten weeks after that she did not mention 'Ken' in her letters at all. Subsequently writing to her sister Molly, she briefly outlined her attempts to convince him that she could make him happy, and describes her love for him as that of a mother and sister combined with 'that other love'. An acutely uncomfortable Cornwallis presented a stony façade to these representations, and began to avoid her. She was to him an incomparable woman, a precious confidante, and unique in having so many interests in common with him; but he was fifteen years younger, and not looking for a mother or a sister. Never petty or ungenerous towards those she loved, she continued to think him one of the finest men she had known. When he went to England, she asked Molly to invite him to lunch. The rift between them slowly closed, and their companionship returned with his gift to her of a puppy from his spaniel's litter. Once again, he collected her mail when she was confined to bed, but kept back anything that looked as though it would tax her energies. Such emotional upheavals, however, leave scars: brave as ever, she found herself a little less resilient, more solitary and, since she had relied on him for internal news about what was going on in the palace and the Cabinet, she felt herself to be perhaps a degree less well informed.

Once the Treaty had been proclaimed, and the mandate issue put aside, the King ordered the preparation of elections to the Constituent Assembly. This would ratify the Treaty, approve the Organic Law for the future government of Iraq, and establish an electoral law so that the first parliament could be elected. At this point the Naqib resigned, his place as Prime Minister to be taken by the younger Abdul Mahsin Bey. There was a parallel change of government in London in 1922, when the Conservatives took office under Prime Minister Bonar Law. They brought in a new pledge for the early evacuation of British personnel from Iraq. Once again, Cox was called to London to review Britain's role in Iraq. He returned with yet another addendum to the Treaty, a protocol which limited Britain's involvement to four more years. Nonetheless, it gave Faisal almost more than he had asked for. Now the question was, would Iraq be ready to defend and govern itself in only four years?

At the end of April 1923, Cox finally left Iraq. His last act of kindness to Gertrude was to sanction the cost of an additional drawing-room to her summer-house, in recognition of all the entertaining she did there for the good of the Secretariat. When he had distributed his menagerie and given his last garden party, it not only seemed like the end of an era – it was. Nobody felt his loss more keenly than Gertrude. She wrote to her parents:

> All this time rather tears the heart strings, you understand, it's very moving saying good-bye to Sir Percy . . . What a position he has made for himself here. I think no Englishman has inspired more confidence in the East. He himself was dreadfully unhappy at going – 40 years' service is not a thing one lays down easily . . .
>
> I must tell you something very touching . . . Sir Percy has sent me a photograph of himself in a silver frame and across the corner he has written: 'To the best of comrades'. Isn't that the nicest thing he could possibly have written?

The new High Commissioner, Sir Henry Dobbs, had arrived the previous December to familiarize himself with the job. He had been among the first handful of officials to join Cox in Basra, as a remarkably successful Revenue Officer. Gertrude herself had written of his achievements in her White Paper on the civil administration of the region. Dobbs took firm charge of Britain's responsibilities for security and foreign affairs. Elections could now go ahead. Faisal toured the country encouraging the population to go out and vote.

Dobbs followed not far behind, so that all could see the united commitment to a democratic Iraq. 'As if by magic, the political atmosphere cleared and even the most distant tribesmen of the Euphrates and of the Kurdish hills enrolled themselves as voters with alacrity,' Dobbs recorded later.

Over the six years he had been Civil Commissioner, it had become routine for Cox to talk things over with Gertrude several times a week. Dobbs discontinued that habit – as she acknowledged, there was no reason why he should go on with it. But she liked her new chief well enough, and found Lady Dobbs kind and considerate, dispensing from the Residency much amusing conversation and the most delicious lunches.

Gertrude was looking forward to seeing her sister Elsa and her husband, now Vice-Admiral Sir Herbert Richmond, who were to visit Baghdad on an official cruise on board the flagship *Chatham* in October 1924. Coinciding with their arrival, Molly's elder son George Trevelyan was expected too, and would go on to join the Richmonds at their destination, Ceylon. She had planned all kinds of entertainments for them, and was heartbroken when she became seriously ill with bronchitis just before they arrived. The King's personal physician, 'Sinbad' – Sir Harry Sinderson – called on her twice a day, would not accept a penny for his trouble, and decided that she was not well enough to have George at home; the young man stayed at the Residency instead, and Lady Dobbs put her car at Gertrude's service as she improved just enough to drive the Richmonds around and show them Baghdad. Nevertheless, some of the family had now seen Gertrude when she was seriously unwell, and conveyed to England their deep concerns about her health. She had made light of her illness in letters to Hugh and Florence, but the bronchitis had been complicated by heat exhaustion and a virtual collapse. On top of that, the news that Elsa brought from home was bad. The Depression, combined with strikes, had hit the Bell fortunes hard. Elizabeth Burgoyne, in the second volume of her book on Gertrude based on her personal papers, reveals that she told her friend Nigel Davidson that 'black depression had settled on her like a cloud; she even asked him to pray for her. In his opinion private griefs, as well as loneliness and a sense of frustration, combined to prevent her from ever again being really happy.'

She was further saddened in February 1925, when her much loved dog, and Ken's too, as it was staying with her at the time, died of distemper within twenty-four hours of each other:

> I don't know which of them I loved most, for Sally was with me all the summer while Ken was on leave. I shall now miss Peter most – he was always with us, in the office and everywhere . . . we neither of us had any idea that it was distemper, the very worst kind that ends in pneumonia. Peter caught it and died after agonies of stifled breathing at 4 am this morning . . . and Sally died after the same agonies at 5 pm. So you will understand that I am rather shattered.

This time, Hugh and Florence would brook no excuses. She was in no fit state to go through another summer in Iraq. She was forced to agree; but the King did not: 'Faisal, when I say I'm going home next summer replies with asperity: "You're not to talk of going *home* – your home is here. You may say you are going to see your father."'

Marie accompanied her, and they arrived in London on 17 July. Gertrude, wrote her stepmother, 'in a condition of great nervous fatigue . . . appeared exhausted mentally and physically'. The doctors who were asked to see her, Sir Thomas Parkinson and Dr Thomas Body, took the same view: that she required a great deal of care and ought not to return to the climate of Iraq. It was a serious warning – perhaps even more than that. Her old Oxford friend Janet Courtney was horrified by how thin and white-haired Gertrude had become since the portrait drawn by John Singer Sargent on her trip two years previously.

As soon as she was up and about again, Gertrude started to take an interest in the younger members of the family, and particularly in her nineteen-year-old niece Pauline, Molly's daughter. Pauline Trevelyan was to recall many years later how Gertrude was always cold, wearing a full-length silver fox fur coat all day, even indoors in summer, at both Sloane Street and Rounton: 'She would stand with her back to the fire smoking a Turkish cigarette in a long holder, and discoursing on . . . people past and present, history, letters, art and architecture, her travels, archaeology, our family – and how devoted she was to all at home, above all to her father.'

Frail, but burning with her perennial enthusiasm, Gertrude swept Pauline off to the British Museum to explain the history of the Assyrian exhibits, then to the Victoria and Albert Museum to see the Constables, inspiring her niece with her own passions. She called at the Stanleys, and invited her recently widowed cousin Sylvia Henley to accompany her back to Iraq; then visited the Churchills at Chartwell. When Janet Courtney went for dinner in Sloane Street one night with Gertrude and her father, Gertrude asked her if she could think of anything she could do if she remained in England. Janet suggested a few days later, in a letter, that her friend might stand for parliament. She replied:

You dear and beloved Janet,

No, I'm afraid you will never see me in the House. I have an invincible hatred of that kind of politics . . . I don't cover a wide enough field and my natural desire is to slip back into the comfortable arena of archaeology and history . . . I think I must certainly go back for this winter, though I privately very much doubt whether it won't be the last . . .

Goodbye, my dear . . .

Did she mean the last winter in Iraq, or her last winter?

About this time, Hugh and Florence told her what she had feared to hear: that for financial reasons they were about to shut Rounton up and depart for a small, though beautiful, house on the Bell estate. Mount Grace Priory, the restored abbot's house set in the ruins of an old abbey and monastery, presented an elegant face to the bleak Yorkshire landscape, but contained only a handful of rooms. The knowledge that the Philip Webb mansion, symbol of the great Bell empire, would soon be gone, and everything with it, lent a poignant fatefulness to these few weeks.

Before the end of her visit, Hugh offered to give a dinner at the

Automobile Club for Faisal, who happened to be in London for medical treatment. The party included Cornwallis, who was particularly attentive. He called at 95 Sloane Street, and was on the platform to see her off to Yorkshire at King's Cross station, the day after the dinner.

Accompanied by Sylvia and Marie, Gertrude left London at the end of September, waved off by a collection of devoted friends including Sir Percy, Domnul and Faisal. She wrote a loving letter to each of her parents as she left. Florence commented: 'We all felt after this last visit of Gertrude to England that she had never seemed more glad to be with us all, never more affectionate and delightful to all her Yorkshire surroundings.'

The profound love for her father that Florence called the foundation of Gertrude's existence had always set the two of them slightly apart from Florence, though she had forbidden herself to feel any jealousy or to stand between them in any way. This time, Gertrude had found a Hugh pained and harassed by the Bell misfortunes. Had the doctors told her in private that her heavy smoking had at last taken its toll and that she had only months to live, then she might have spared him that knowledge.

On the other hand, something of significance certainly did pass between Gertrude and her stepmother in those last few weeks at Rounton, and it resulted in a closer bond between the two of them than had ever existed before. Perhaps Gertrude, finding that she now needed support and affection of the kind that she had always half shrugged off, was able to tell her what she had not felt able to tell her father. Florence, with that unflinching contemplation of the verities of life and death natural to an experienced mother and grandmother, would have met Gertrude's revelation calmly and stoically, and perhaps conspired, gratefully, to keep Hugh in ignorance. They talked many times, and it was a changed Gertrude who set off once more for Iraq, writing to Florence of 'this last summer' perhaps in more senses than one:

Darling Mother

. . . I do so love to think that you liked me to come in to the

library [at Rounton] in the mornings, even though I was interrupting you horribly. You know I feel as if I had never known you
really before, not in all the years. It was perhaps because of the
general crisis we were going through and my immense admiration for your courage and wisdom. Whatever it was I feel certain
that I have never loved you so much, however much I may have
loved you, and I am so thankful that we were together this last
summer and that we both have the sense of its having been a
wonderful experience.

In February 1926, after contracting typhoid on his voyage home
from South Africa, Gertrude's half-brother Hugo died, a shattering
blow for the family, and one from which Florence, in particular,
would hardly recover. Gertrude's poignant letter suggests her own
sad and regretful preoccupations. At times of great misery or
danger, she had called out almost involuntarily to God; at all other
times, her pragmatic intellect left her facing an uncompromising
universe. Florence may have pondered the letter for longer than
Hugh.

My darling Father and Mother,

I am writing to you with the heaviest of hearts. It is so dreadful
to think of what you have gone through . . . My mind has been
so full of Hugo but the thing which comes uppermost is that he
had a complete life. His perfect marriage and the joy of his
children and then at the last his seeing you again . . . I wonder if
we should be happier too if we thought we were all to meet
again. I never could bring myself to it even when I lost what was
dearest to me. The spirit without the body would be as strange
as the body without a spirit. One feels the lovely mind behind,
but what one knows are the little gestures, the sweet smile, the
expression of the mind. But it's no good wondering or thinking
why one can't believe in the unbelievable; one just can't.

In Baghdad, she went straight to the office, and immediately a
stream of people queued to see her. She could do no work at all
for two days. Some kissed her hands and called her 'Light of our

eyes'. She admitted to her parents that it went to her head a little
— that she almost began to think she was a Person. But scarcely had
she settled in again than she fell ill. Sylvia, to her disappointment,
had proved unable to stand even the winter climate of Iraq, and had
soon been forced to return to England. Shortly afterwards Gertrude, wrapped from head to toe and with a hot water bottle on
her knees, went up in icy weather to the King's farm at Khaniqin
in a Christmas shooting party that included Ken Cornwallis. With
them travelled some new furniture that she had ordered for the
King from London, and she spent the first evening speculatively
shunting it around the room with him. Exhausted, she went to bed.
The next day she stayed there. Faisal and Cornwallis joined her in
the bedroom in the evening for a game of bridge on the bedspread.
When Ken looked in on her the following morning, he immediately
telegraphed to Baghdad for a doctor. 'By that time I wasn't taking
much notice, except that I had a general feeling that I was slipping into
great gulfs,' Gertrude wrote later. The doctor arrived with a night
nurse, and within twenty-four hours she was in hospital in Baghdad
with pleurisy. She was still unwell when she wrote the letter of
commiseration about Hugo.

As her office duties had diminished during the last few years, a
new source of work presented itself. It had been the King's idea,
before Cox left. Already in August 1922 she had discussed the need
for a 'law of excavations' with him — 'he is going to make me
provisionally Director of Antiquities as there's no one else,' she had
written.

His first job was the writing of an antiquities law giving due
weight to the rights of the nation and the excavator. She constructed
it in careful consultation with the legal authorities, for wholesale
looting stretching back hundreds of years had hugely depleted the
immense archaeological wealth of Iraq. Now scientific expeditions
from many countries were trying to reconstruct the history of the
region.

Once Gertrude had begun to think in terms of establishing an
Iraq Museum she was zealous in exacting the country's rights to its
own past. Very soon she acquired the richest collection in the world

of objects representing Iraq's early history. She came up against an old friend, Sir Leonard Woolley, former intelligence chief at Port Said, who had worked on the Carchemish dig with Lawrence. Now he was heading a joint expedition organized by the British Museum and the University of Pennsylvania to dig Ur of the Chaldaes, with its royal tombs, temple and ziggurat of the Sumerian dynasty. In her official capacity, she felt obliged to claim for Iraq a particular artefact that surfaced at this time – the famous plaque showing a milking scene, found in the temple. She 'broke his heart'. '[Woolley] values it at ten thousand pounds, at least. I'm not going to tell the Iraq Govt. lest they decide to sell it and thereby blacken my face and theirs. The gold scarab is worth one thousand pounds, but Providence (the toss of a rupee) gave it to me!'

She began to make short archaeological expeditions with the architectural adviser to the Ministry of Public Works, J. M. Wilson. These expeditions were at first no more than office excursions, the faintest echoes of her earlier adventures. She would be energised when their car ran into a ditch or her luggage failed to follow her, and often could not resist borrowing a horse from a village elder and travelling on alone into the countryside for a day or two while Wilson went back to Baghdad. Of a trip to Kish, one of many with an Oxford University expedition, she wrote: 'My sole possessions for the night were a cake of soap, a hairbrush from the Professor [Langdon] and a pair of pyjamas from an unknown benefactor. We spent the time before dinner in looking at their wonderful finds, and after dinner in discussing ancient Babylonian sites.' There she bargained to be allowed to send some fine painted pots to Oxford for expert treatment. She also claimed a Semitic statuette of 2800 BC by her favourite expedient of tossing a coin for it.

In 1926, she turned her full attention to archaeology. With the frontier problem solved at last and the Treaty accepted by the Iraqi parliament, she concentrated on her next project: to get her museum lodged in appropriate premises, instead of the Ministry of Works where it had begun. The museum's Babylonian Stone Room was opened by the King in June. As always, once she was committed to a project, she took on even the most uncongenial tasks. Alone or with a clerk, sometimes with an RAF officer who was a keen amateur archaeologist, she laboriously catalogued the finds from Ur and Kish. She sometimes got up at 5 a.m. to do the day's work before midday — the heat in the fanless museum rooms could be overwhelming.

She was still taking on political work, still passionate about the metamorphosis taking place around her. When the League of Nations' Boundary Commission had arrived in January 1925, finally to determine the border between Iraq and Turkey, it was Gertrude who had entertained and briefed the members. These were eminent men from Sweden, Belgium and Hungary — accompanied, however, by a Turkish assessor and three Turkish 'experts': she told Dobbs she feared their expertise would include intrigue and intimidation. In due course, the Commission's report was published. It recommended that the whole of the Mosul *vilayet* should come within the boundaries of Iraq, provided a new treaty kept Britain's partnership with Iraq in operation for twenty-five more years. Britain and Iraq agreed, both sides hoping that Iraq would be an independent member of the League of Nations long before that time had elapsed. Meanwhile, the Turks resumed their atrocities against the Assyrians, and attacked thousands of Kurdish pro-independents.

The Constituent Assembly having been democratically elected, the Organic Law, or constitution, was framed and passed. An electoral law was created so that legitimate political parties could take part in elections to the first parliament. With the assurance to Faisal of a British financial contribution sufficient to establish an effective defence force, voting began, and the results were in by June. On 16 July, Faisal would inaugurate the first genuinely democratic government in Iraq. In a worthy conclusion to that chapter, the British ambassador in Constantinople, working face to face with the Turks, managed to conclude a tripartite treaty between Iraq, Turkey and Britain to bring some hope of a permanent peace on the borders.

It was time for celebration. On 25 June 1926, the King gave a state banquet to mark the signing of the treaty, at which he expressed his profound thanks to the British government and its representatives for all that they had done for Iraq. Henry Dobbs wrote afterwards: 'Miss Gertrude Bell was one of the most prominent of the guests at this banquet and shared conspicuously in the general atmosphere of congratulation which marked the close of the first stage in the existence of Iraq. It was the last State function which she attended.'

Although her letters to her parents reveal her underlying, less positive, feelings at this period, Gertrude was still the spirited and stimulating woman that she had always been. In the early spring Vita Sackville-West came for the weekend. In her subsequent book *A Passenger to Teheran*, she has left an energetic description of Gertrude and her domestic life.

To reach Gertrude's house, the visitor made her way through 'a dusty jumble' of mean buildings and a quagmire:

Then: a door in the blank wall . . . a creaking of hinges, a broadly smiling servant, a rush of dogs, a vista of garden-path edged with carnations in pots, a little verandah and a little low house at the end of the path, an English voice – Gertrude Bell . . . here she was in her right place, in her own house, with her office in the city, and her white pony in a corner of the garden, and her Arab servants, and her English books, and her Babylonian shards on the mantelpiece, and her long thin nose, and her irrepressible vitality. I felt all my loneliness and despair lifted from me in a second . . . I found myself laughing for the first time in ten days. The garden was small, but cool and friendly; her spaniel wagged not only his tail but his whole little body; the pony looked over the loose-box door and whinnied gently; a tame partridge hopped about the verandah; some native babies who were playing in a corner stopped playing to stare and grin . . . Would I like breakfast first, or a bath? and I would like to see her museum, wouldn't I? did I know she was Director of Antiquities in Iraq? wasn't that a joke? and would I like to come to tea with the King? . . . and she must go to her office, but would be back for luncheon. Oh yes, and there were people to luncheon; and so, still talking, still laughing, she pinned on a hat without looking in the glass, and took her departure.

Gertrude had, she wrote, the gift of making everyone feel suddenly eager, of making you feel that life was full and rich and exciting; and it is clear that, whatever her state of health and mind, she utterly refused to languish or complain. She spoke as if the two of them might visit Ctesiphon together in the autumn.

As she worked on in the museum, Gertrude contemplated her existence, the smallness of her income if and when she retired, and the loss of all those friends who had already left Iraq. She wrote to Hugh:

> I think it is extremely unlikely that I can afford to come back and out again this summer – it's a very expensive business . . . I find myself really rather loose on the world. I don't see at all clearly what I shall do, but of course I can't stay here forever . . . I'm not at all necessary in the office . . .
>
> But it is too lonely, my existence here; one can't go on for ever being alone. At least, I don't feel I can . . .
>
> The afternoons, after tea, hang rather heavy on my hands.

On Sunday 11 July, having joined the usual afternoon swimming party, she returned home exhausted by the heat. She went to bed, asking to be woken at 6 a.m. or, perhaps, not to be disturbed before then. Perhaps she had said something unusual to Marie, or was looking ill again. In either case, Marie was worried about her, and looked in during the night. Gertrude was asleep, a bottle of pills beside her. Whether there were any overt signs of suicide, whether the bottle was empty, whether Marie at once called the hospital, is not known. What *is* known is that the day before, she sent a note to Ken Cornwallis to ask if he would look after her dog Tundra, 'if anything happened to her'.

Gertrude had told Domnul, some years before, that death was no longer a thing she feared, that it had been robbed of its sting. 'I wonder . . . what it will be like after, if there's any sort of an "after"' she had said. Now, she had set out one final time into the unknown, and this time she would never wake up.

Her death certificate, made out by the director of the Royal Hospital in Baghdad, one Dr Dunlop, stated that she had died from

'Dial poisoning'. Dial was the name for a preparation of diallylbar-
bituric acid, or allobarbital, used at the time as a sedative and later
discontinued partly because of its frequent use in suicide attempts.
Dunlop writes that death had taken place in the early hours of 12
July. It was a couple of days before her fifty-eighth birthday.

Cornwallis did not look after Tundra. But Florence and Hugh
must have asked Marie to arrange the dog's passage home. It arrived
at Mount Grace, where the Bells soon received a remorseful letter
from Cornwallis, explaining that he had been unwell at the time of
Gertrude's death and had realized only subsequently the significance
of the note she had sent him.

In her *Letters* Florence wrote that Gertrude's death brought 'an
overwhelming manifestation of sorrow and sympathy from all parts
of the earth, and we realized afresh that her name was known in
every continent, her story had crossed every sea'. A legendary
personality had emerged from the Gertrude that her family had
known. One of the first letters to arrive from Iraq was from her
friend Haji Naji, who wrote: 'It was my faith always to send Miss
Bell the first of my fruits and vegetables and I know not now where
I shall send them.' George V wrote:

> The Queen and I are grieved to hear of the death of your
> distinguished and gifted daughter, whom we held in high regard.
> The nation will with us mourn the loss of one who by her
> intellectual powers, force of character and personal courage
> rendered important and what I trust will prove lasting benefit
> to the country and to those regions where she worked with
> such devotion and self-sacrifice . . .

The Colonial Secretary Leo Amery paid her the rare tribute of a
statement in the House of Commons. Sir Valentine Chirol wrote a
moving portrait of her for *The Times*. Lawrence wrote a brilliant if
characteristically cranky letter to Hugh from India. Seeking anonym-
ity and isolation, he had enlisted in the RAF as Aircraftsman Shaw
and obtained a posting far afield, near Karachi. He had not known
of Gertrude's death until Bernard Shaw's wife had sent him
Florence's compilation of her letters. He wrote:

I think she was very happy in her death, for her political work – one of the biggest things a woman has ever had to do – was as finished as mine. That Irak state is a fine monument; even if it only lasts a few more years, as I often fear and sometimes hope. It seems such a very doubtful benefit – government – to give a people who have long done without. Of course it is you who are unhappy, not having Gertrude any more; but there – she wasn't yours really, though she did give you so much.

Her letters are exactly herself – eager, interested, almost excited, always about her company and the day's events. She kept an everlasting freshness; or at least, however tired she was, she could always get up enough interest to match that of anyone who came to see her. I don't think I ever met anyone more entirely civilized, in the sense of her width of intellectual sympathy. And she was exciting too, for you never knew how far she would leap out in any direction, under the stimulus of some powerful expert who had engaged her mind in his direction. She and I used to have a private laugh over that – because I kept two of her letters, one describing me as an angel, and the other accusing me of being possessed by the devil – and I'd show her first one and then another, begging her to be charitable towards her present objects of dislike . . .

. . . her loss must be nearly unbearable, but I'm so grateful to you for giving so much of her personality to the world . . .

David Hogarth, Salomon Reinach, the editor of the *Revue Archéologique*, Leonard Woolley of the British Museum, and hundreds of sheikhs, British officers and Iraqi ministers added their commiserations. In Baghdad King Faisal and his Cabinet designated one of the rooms in the museum the 'Gertrude Bell Room', and Henry Dobbs wrote on behalf of her friends there to say that they had commissioned a brass plaque, to be put up in the Iraq museum:

GERTRUDE BELL
Whose memory the Arabs will ever hold
in reverence and affection
Created this Museum in 1923

Being then Honorary Director of Antiquities for the Iraq
With wonderful knowledge and devotion
She assembled the most precious objects in it
And through the heat of the Summer
Worked on them until the day of her death
On 12th July, 1926
King Faisal and the Government of Iraq
In gratitude for her great deeds in this country
Have ordered that the Principal Wing shall bear her name
And with their permission
Her friends have erected this Tablet

At the time of her death, Faisal was absent from Iraq. Amir Ali was acting as Regent. He immediately ordered a military funeral for her. She was buried the same afternoon in the cemetery outside Baghdad. Her body was driven in a 'Health Service motor car' to the British cemetery from the Protestant church, her coffin draped with the Union Jack and the flag of Iraq and decked with wreaths from Faisal's family, the British High Commission and many others. The cortège drove slowly through streets lined with soldiers of the Iraqi army, and was followed on foot by the Regent, the Prime Minister, the High Commissioner and other state officials, both civil and military. Enormous crowds had assembled from across the country to watch her coffin pass by and to pay her silent homage; Islamic leaders side by side with Jewish merchants, effendis alongside the poor and ragged. It was reported in the newspapers that 'the whole population of the capital participated in the procession of burial'. At the cemetery gates young men of the High Commission, openly grieving, shouldered the coffin to its resting place. The British army chaplain performed the burial rites and senior British officials scattered handfuls of soil over it. Surrounded by 'a huge concourse of Iraqis and British' – including Sir Henry Dobbs and the entire British staff, the Iraqi Cabinet, and many tribal sheikhs – the coffin was laid in the plain stone tomb. Word had gone out across the desert with the habitual mystifying speed, and the tribes had been pouring into Baghdad all afternoon: first the Howeitat and Dulaim, then sheikhs from near and far.

She had for the last ten years of her life [said Dobbs], consecrated all the indomitable fervour of her spirit and all the astounding gifts of her mind to the service of the Arab cause, and especially to Iraq. At last her body, always frail, was broken by the energy of her soul.

Her bones rest where she had wished them to rest, in the soil of Iraq. Her friends are left desolate.

The Times leader wrote of her capacity for work:

Some power in her linked the love of the East with a practical aim that became a dominating purpose . . . that she endured drudgery, was never dismayed by continual disappointment and never allowed her idealism to turn to bitterness, shows a strength of character rare indeed among those of the English for whom the East has become a passion. She was the one distinguished woman among them and her quality was of the purest English mettle.

The many obituaries paid tribute to the fact that, thanks to her, Iraq was better governed than it had been for five hundred years, calmer, more prosperous and evidently more contented, the British and the Arabs working together in friendly collaboration. *The Times of India* obituary offered a masterly summing-up of her character and work. While the British appreciated her as author, traveller and archaeologist, it said, they remained to the end ignorant of the 'astonishing position she had built up for herself in Iraq, a position which has made her responsible, more than any other single individual, for the shape and appearance of modern Iraq as it stands today'. Recognizing that some readily criticized her, her aims and her methods, the writer reflected:

so challenging a personality could hardly escape enemies . . . To match the almost passionate devotion which she inspired in her immediate circle, she had to face a hostility almost as strong on the part of those with whom she differed. To the ordinary outsider – particularly perhaps the journalistic outsider – she was offhand and even rude . . .

Her great design was

> the creation of a free, prosperous and cultivated Iraq, the
> mainspring for a revival of Arab culture and civilization . . . It
> was Gertrude who advocated day in day out the granting of as
> complete a measure of local autonomy as was compatible with
> some British hold on the country – not . . . on the score of
> expediency, but on that of the natural right of the Arab race to
> its 'place in the sun'.

She had persuaded the British Government to take on the financial
risks of Iraq, and had convinced local Iraqi leaders that it meant
well by them; and that there would be no return to colonial
methods.

In *The Times*, Chirol wrote in his obituary: 'With all the qualities
which are usually described as virile, she combined in a high degree
the charm of feminine refinement, and though only revealed to a
few, even amongst her intimates, great depths of tender and even
passionate affection.' For those who loved Gertrude most, Florence's much earlier words remain unforgettable: 'In truth the real
basis of Gertrude's nature was her capacity for deep emotion. Great
joys came into her life, and also great sorrows. How could it be
otherwise, with a temperament so avid of experience? Her ardent
and magnetic personality drew the lives of others into hers as she
passed along.'

Hugh and Florence, bowed under the blows that fate had dealt
them, moved with Maurice into Mount Grace, while Rounton
turned a desolate façade to the winds off the moors.

In time, there would follow inexorably the demolition of the
showpiece house, now too big and too grand for the Bells. All too
soon, the splintering crash of iron on tiles and stone would silence
for ever the Rounton chimes that had rung out on the quarter-hour
from the stable bells, and turn to rubble the arched gallery where
international affairs had been settled, and house guests had eaten
eggs and bacon at midnight. Dead flies collected in the empty study
where Gertrude and Professor Ramsay had once worked on *The*

Thousand and One Churches. Out of the broken windows, the great rock garden that she had created sank back into dark woodland, the pond where children had ice-skated turned green and stagnant, and the tennis court grew high with weeds.

Eddies of draught through the dining room rippled the Morris and Burne-Jones tapestry of the *Romaunt of the Rose*, that allegory of a lover knight battling to overcome all dangers, all obstacles and scruples, at long last to be united with the hitherto unattainable rose. And at the top of the house, the wallpaper dampened and peeled in the room where Dick Doughty-Wylie and she had once lain together, holding hands in the dark.

NOTES

Abbreviations Used in Source Notes and Bibliography

DUL   Durham University Library
RL   Robinson Library, University of Newcastle upon Tyne

Extracts have been taken from Gertrude Bell's letters to her family, held in the Robinson Library, University of Newcastle (RL); these extracts are identified as 'GLB letters'. 'Gertrude hardly ever dated her letters except by the day of the week, sometimes not even that,' wrote her stepmother Florence when she was compiling *The Letters of Gertrude Bell* (London: Ernest Benn, 1927) after her death. A great many of the letters can be found in Lady Bell's book.

Extracts are also taken from Gertrude Bell's diaries, identified as 'GLB diary', also held by the University of Newcastle.

Copies of Gertrude's papers are littered with crossed-out pencilled dates and question marks, evidence of the many attempts by curators to determine their sequence.

The letters and diaries are available on www.gerty.ncl.ac.uk

Occasionally, to make a point more forcefully, two or more quotations from different letters or texts of Gertrude Bell have been brought together in the narrative and occasionally bought forward.

PREFACE

xvi 'She was, I think, the greatest woman of our time': Janet E. Courtney, *An Oxford Portrait Gallery*

1. GERTRUDE AND FLORENCE

1 *'Sharif's son Faisal offers hope'*: Janet Wallach, *Desert Queen*, p. 297

2 *'from a needle to a ship'*: From Sir Hugh Bell's speech of 10 Jan. 1910, during his campaign for a Liberal parliamentary seat

3 *Lowthian wrote several scientific books*: Papers on Sir Isaac Lowthian Bell discovered at Mount Grace Priory

3 *a comprehensive and logical assessment*: *The Iron Trade of the United Kingdom*, Literary and Philosophical Society, Gallery, 669–1/13: 1875

4 *An illustrated family alphabet:* In the possession of Dr William Plowden

4 *'Your scones are lovely'*: Anecdote about Margaret Bell, in conversation with Mrs Susanna Richmond

6 *'Free Trade is like the quality of mercy'*: From Hugh Bell's campaign speech of 10 Jan. 1910

9 *They met the 22-year-old Florence*: Biographical details about Florence Bell from Kirsten Wang, 'Deeds and Words: The Biography of Dame Florence Bell, 1851–1930', unpublished MS in the possession of Dr William Plowden

10 *'looking beautiful, but very sad'*: Florence's daughter Elsa, Lady Richmond, reporting a conversation with her mother, in Wang, 'Deeds and Words'

10 *One biographer of Gertrude*: Anne Tibble, *One Woman's Story*

10 *'succeed in almost excluding'*: R. Russell, *London Fogs*

11 *'What a privilege to be born in Paris'*: Florence Bell, shortly before she died, in Wang, 'Deeds and Words'

11 *'Lady Olliffe . . . I have brought your daughter home'*: Lady Richmond reporting a conversation with her mother Florence Bell, in ibid.

12 *'If you would like to finish your conversation'*: Mrs Susanna Richmond, in conversation

14 *'The girl was ill at ease'*: From Florence Bell, *The Story of Ursula*

15 *'The abiding influence'*: Florence Bell, *The Letters of Gertrude Bell*, introduction

18 *'My poney behaved like a brute'*: GLB letter, 1881, from Gertrude to her cousin Horace Marshall

19 *'I remember as if it were yesterday'*: Letter to her daughter Molly, Lady Trevelyan, in Wang, 'Deeds and Words'

20 *'We now have out some yellow crocus'*: GLB's first diary, 1879

22 *'I cannot remember her speak in a harsh way'*: Molly Trevelyan in Wang, 'Deeds and Words'

23 *'However valuable the intellectual wares'*: Florence Bell, in her essay, 'On the Better Teaching of Manners', in ibid.

25 *'My mother's idea of the equipment required'*: Ibid.

25 *'It was the Trinity ball'*: Virginia Stephen, in a letter to Emma Vaughan, June 1900, in Stephens, *Flight of the Mind*, vol. 1, p. 34

27 *'Gertrude is being rather thorny'*: Molly Bell in Lesley Gordon, *Gertrude Bell 1868–1926*, exhibition booklet, 1994, RL

2. EDUCATION

28 *'My darling, dearest Mother'*: Elsa Richmond, ed., *The Earlier Letters of Gertrude Bell*

28 *His 'deaf and stupid' sister Bessie*: Details of life at 95 Sloane Street as recounted by Lady Richmond, in Wang, 'Deeds and Words'

29 *Queen's College in Harley Street*: From the sesquicentenary leaflet, *Queen's College, 1848–1998*, 1998

29 *'I don't like Rubens'*: GLB letter, in Anne Tibble, *Gertrude Bell*; Tibble had been in service at Rounton

29 *'I wish I could go to the National'*: GLB letter

30 *'I waded through [your letter]'*: GLB letter

30 *'It's a very disagreeable process'*: GLB letter

31 *'I don't believe a word of it!'*: GLB letter

31 *'The fault of my essay'*: GLB letter

31 *'Fancy the amount more books'*: GLB letter

32 *'I've done Milton most of today'*: GLB letter

33 *'I felt rather guilty'*: From Lesley Gordon, *Gertrude Bell 1868–1926*

33 *'I may say to you I suppose'*: GLB letter to her father

36 *the Winter Garden*: From William Lillie, *The History of Middlesbrough*

37 *'I have had enough of these dinners'*: GLB letter

38 *'I am going to a teaparty'*: GLB letter

39 *Herbert Spencer . . . Dean John Burgon*: Wallach, *Desert Queen*, p. 20

39 *'The amount of work is hopeless'*: GLB letter

40 *'I am sorry, but it is on the right bank'*: Josephine Kamm, *Gertrude Bell*, p. 52

40 *'I'm afraid I must differ'*: Incident recalled by Mr Arthur Hassall of Christchurch, Oxford; in Florence Bell, *Letters*

41 *'There's a reading party'*: GLB letter

42 *'She was, I think, the most brilliant creature'*: Courtney, *Oxford Portrait Gallery*

3. THE CIVILIZED WOMAN

44 'The King was': Letter to Horace Marshall, 1889

44 'You can't think how charming': GLB letter

45 'You dance nothing through': GLB letter

46 'Il me semble, Monsieur' [It seems to me, Sir, that you do not understand the German mind]: Florence Bell, *Letters*, p. 21

46 'It was perfectly delicious': GLB letter

47 'I went into the gardens': GLB letter

48 'About the little girls' frocks': GLB letter

48 'Do you remember discussing': GLB letter

50 'Billy and I sat in the garden': GLB letter

50 'I discussed religious beliefs': GLB letter

50 'I don't think many of our watchful acquaintances': GLB letter

50 'I sat on a bench': GLB letter

50 'the critic': GLB letter

52 'Oh the desert around Teheran!': GLB to Horace Marshall, 18 June 1892

53 'Are we the same people': Ibid.

53 'In this country': Ibid.

54 'tall and red and very thin': GLB letter

54 'It certainly is unexpected': GLB letter

55 'Mr Cadogan and I': GLB letter

55 'Before we had gone far': Gertrude Bell, *Persian Pictures*, 'The Tower of Silence'

55 'Here they come to throw off': Ibid.

55 'Life seized us and inspired us . . .': Ibid.

56 Gertrude had been an interested eavesdropper: GLB diary, 30 Oct. 1889

57 'Our position is very difficult': GLB letter

58 'Took a carriage': GLB letter

59 'She had not yet reached the stage': Florence Bell, *Letters*, p. 34

61 'My Pundit': GLB letter

61 'The spirit of poetry': Ibid., p. 36

4. BECOMING A PERSON

65 'It was the most gorgeous show': GLB diary, 29 Dec. 1902

66 'I suppose you don't approve of this plan': Bishop of St Albans to GLB, in Florence Bell, *Letters*

67 *'Please send first hemistich'*: Recounted by E. Denison Ross in the preface to Gertrude Lowthian Bell, trans., *The Teachings of Hafiz*

67 *'We went on a switch-back'*: GLB letter, 1903

69 *'I pitched my camp'*: GLB letter

70 *'When we reached the level'*: GLB letter

70 *'meadows full'*: GLB letter

70 *'I walked over the tiny alp'*: GLB letter

70 *'My Japanese trees'*: GLB to Chirol, 25 Dec. 1900

71 *'I am sending you a little packet'*: GLB letter

71 *'Reginald Farrer, the Colliers, and Mr Herbert'*: GLB letter, 28 May 1903. Details on Reginald Farrer from Nicola Schulman, *A Rage for Rock Gardening*

72 *'I have spent most of the afternoons'*: GLB to Chirol, 22 Apr. 1910

73 *'If you look with the eye of faith'*: GLB to Chirol, 21 Nov. 1912

75 *'Last night I went to a delightful party'*: GLB letter, 28 Oct. 1908

76 *'We have Lady Jersey as chairman'*: GLB letter, Oct. 1908

76 *'Life was nearly wrecked for a month'*: GLB to Chirol, 21 Nov. 1912

5. MOUNTAINEERING

Descriptions of Gertrude's climbs were aided by photographs and information from the following websites: www.summitpost.com, www.clasohm.com, www.peakware.com, www.panoramas.dk, www.skizermatt.com, www.caingram.info, www.womenclimbing.com, www.en.wikipedia.org

78 *'It was awful'*: GLB letter

80 *'Elsa and Papa stayed on'*: GLB diary, 7 Aug. 1897

81 *'I gave my skirt to Marius'*: Gordon, *Gertrude Bell*, 'Gertrude Bell as a mountaineer'

81 *'We had about two hours'*: GLB letter

82 *'There were two little lumps to hold on to'*: GLB letter

83 *'I was now in rags'*: Elizabeth Burgoyne, *Gertrude Bell from her Personal Papers, 1889–1914*, p. 68

84 *'I am a Person!'*: GLB letter

85 *'Ulrich is as pleased as Punch'*: Gordon, *Gertrude Bell*, 'Gertrude Bell as a mountaineer'

86 *'I was beginning to think'*: GLB letter

87 *'We decided on a place'*: GLB letter

88 *'The lower third'*: GLB letter

89 *'He called out'*: GLB letter

89 *'The fact was'*: GLB letter

90 'This proved quite easy': GLB letter

90 'It was an enchanting house': GLB letter

90 'What do you think': GLB letter

91 'There is another climbing woman here': GLB letter

92 'This morning I started out': GLB letter

92 'The great points': GLB letter

92 'I got back on my feet': GLB letter

93 'I shall remember every inch': GLB letter

93 'We were standing': GLB letter

94 'The golden rule': GLB letter

94 'As there was no further precaution': GLB letter

95 'When things are as bad as ever': GLB letter

95 'We managed badly': GLB letter

95 'It was a near thing': GLB letter

96 'That was the only moment': GLB letter

97 'Every night, do you understand': Edward Whymper, *Scrambles among the Alps in the Years 1860–69*

97 'I look back to it': GLB letter

98 'more like sliding down': GLB letter

6. DESERT TRAVEL

99 'Miss Gertrude Bell knows more': Letter from Lord Cromer to Sir Henry McMahon, British High Commissioner in Egypt, 1915

101 'My apartment consists': GLB letter, Hotel Jerusalem, 13 Dec. 1899

102 I spent the morning unpacking': Ibid.

102 'I may say in passing': GLB letter

102 'a charming little horse': GLB letter

103 'The chief comfort of this journey': GLB letter

104 'Rode out in very bad spirits': GLB diary, 23 Jan. 1900

104 'sheets and sheets': GLB letter

105 'The women are unveiled': GLB letter

106 'Don't think I have ever spent': GLB letter

106 'What the people in Wady Musa live on': GLB letter

106 'the charming façade': GLB letter

106 'a surprising lot of long black': GLB letter

106 'the fire of dry thorns flickered up': GLB letter

108 '"Where was I going?"': GLB letter

109 'The women were filling their': GLB letter

110 'The sense of comfort': GLB letter

110 *'He is the most perfect type'*: GLB letter

111 *'They were a group of the most beautiful'*: GLB letter

111 *'We bought a lamb'*: GLB letter

111 *'I'm very proud of this contrivance'*: GLB letter

112 *'It's the greatest relief'*: GLB letter

113 *'It is at times a very odd sensation'*: GLB letter

114 *'I wish I could manage to travel'*: GLB letter

114 *'Their Sheikh, Muhammad'*: GLB letter

114 *'He sang to it'*: GLB letter

115 *'Back I went'*: GLB letter

115 *'Sheikh Muhammad had only twenty'*: GLB letter

115 *'You know, dearest Father'*: GLB letter

116 *'I am so wildly interested'*: GLB letter

116 *'I am much entertained'*: GLB letter

118 *she became a skilled photographer*: Photographic details from Mr Jim Crow, School of Historical Studies, University of Newcastle

119 *'Yesterday . . . in the evening I went'*: GLB letter, one Saturday, Oct. 1907

120 *'I went shopping with the Stanleys'*: GLB letter, Monday 7 Nov. 1904

120 *'Reinach has simply set'*: GLB letter

121 *'the mud was incredible'*: GLB letter, 1 Feb. 1905

122 *'My host'*: GLB letter

123 *'I produced the Muallakat'*: GLB letter

123 *'I could not help regretting'*: GLB letter

123 *'I too contributed'*: GLB letter

124 *'Tomorrow the Druzes are going forth'*: GLB letter

124 *'"Oh Lord our God! Upon them!"'*: GLB letter

125 *'it was more abominable than'*: GLB letter

125 *'The real triumph of eloquence'*: GLB letter

125 *'Islam is the greatest republic'*: GLB letter

125 *'Tiresome, for I was never'*: GLB letter

126 *'The devil take all Syrian inscriptions!'*: GLB letter

126 *'There was nothing for it'*: GLB letter

127 *'Fattuh, bless him!'*: GLB letter

127 *'We fell into each other's arms'*: GLB letter

127 *'Race, culture, art'*: GLB letter

128 *'Did I tell you I was writing'*: GLB to Chirol

131 *'I need not have hidden the cartridges'*: GLB letter, Jan. 1909

132 *'No one knows of it'*: GLB letter

133 *'An interesting boy'*: GLB letter, 18 Apr. 1911

134 *'The whole world shone like a jewel'*: From Gordon, *Gertrude Bell*, 'Desert Journeys and Archaeology', RL

7. DICK DOUGHTY-WYLIE

135 *'A steadfast hero'*: Tribute by Sir Ian Hamilton to Doughty-Wylie, in Diana Condell, *Lieutenant-Colonel Charles Doughty-Wylie VC CMG – Sedd el Bahr and Hill 141*, www.iwm.org.uk

136 *'The seas and the hills'*: GLB letter, 28 Apr. 1907

136 *'It was surrounded by'*: GLB letter, 1 May 1907

136 *I did all I knew'*: Ibid.

137 *'We think we have a Hittite settlement!'*: GLB letter, 25 May

137 *Dick Doughty-Wylie had been educated*: Facts about Doughty-Wylie from Army List

142 *'The nearer I came to it'*: GLB to Chirol, Jan. 1913, DUL

147–66 *'I am so very glad you took me to Rounton'* . . . 13 Aug. 1913 to 24 Apr. 1915, *'So many memories, my dear queen, of you'*: Letters from Doughty-Wylie from the day before he was killed at Gallipoli. There is a smaller number of letters from GLB to him, returned to her on the eve of the battle, RL

164 *'My dear Jean'*: From Doughty-Wylie to Mrs H. H. Coe, in the papers of Mrs L. O. Doughty-Wylie, Department of Documents, Imperial War Museum

168 *Elsa, now Lady Richmond*; Burgoyne, *Bell 1914–1926*

168 *Towards the end of 1915*: For accounts of the missing days: L. A. Carlyon, *Gallipoli*; Michael Hickey, *Gallipoli*; Eric Wheeler Bush, *Gallipoli*

168 *L. A. Carlyon*: In his book *Gallipoli*

169 *different version of events*: Hickey, *Gallipoli*

169 *According to her diaries*: The Department of Documents, Imperial War Museum

171 *'I think it more than likely'*: This letter is excluded from Florence Bell, *Letters*, but appears in Burgoyne, *Bell, 1914–1926*, p. 29

8. LIMIT OF ENDURANCE

On her trip to Hayyil, Gertrude kept two diaries, one for Doughty-Wylie (D-W) and the other as a reminder to herself of dates, facts and events. She was also writing frequent letters to her parents and the occasional letter to Chirol. Her love letters to Doughty-Wylie probably continued, but were destroyed by him later so that they should not fall into the hands of his wife in the event of his death.

174 *'If you knew the way'*: GLB to Chirol, Dec. 1913, DUL

177 *For a century the enmity*: History of the Sauds and Rashids from T. E. Lawrence, *The Seven Pillars of Wisdom*

178 *Charles Huber . . . Baron Nolde*: From H. V. F. Winstone, *Gertrude Bell*; and Zahra Freeth and H. V. F. Winstone, *Explorers of Arabia from the Renaissance to the Victorian Era*

180 *'Miss Bell passed straight through'*: T. E. Lawrence to his brother, 10 Dec. 1913

180 *a somewhat sensational biography*: Thomas Lowell, *With Lawrence in Arabia*

181 *'Muhammad says'*: GLB letter, 27 Nov. 1913

182 *'I hope you will not say No'*: GLB letter

182 *'This is not a gift for which I am asking'*: GLB letter

183 *'I don't know that it is an ultimate'*: GLB to Chirol, Dec. 1913

183 *'A curious figure'*: GLB letter, 12 Dec. 1913

185 *'We struggled on'*: An account of the incident on 21 Dec. GLB letter

186 *'A preposterous and provoking episode'*: GLB letter

186 *'The stony hills'*: GLB letter

187 *'Extremely nasty dinner'*: GLB letter

188 *'I do not feel at all like the daughter'*: GLB diary for D-W, 16 Feb. 1914

188 *'I was an idiot'*: GLB letter, 9 Jan. 1914

189 *'It's all rather comic'*: Ibid.

191 *'Decided to run away'*: GLB (personal) diary, 14 Jan. 1914

192 *'There is something in the written word'*: GLB diary for D-W, 16 Jan. 1914

192 *'My troubles are over'*: GLB letter, 11 Jan. 1914

193 *'I have known loneliness in solitude'*: GLB to Chirol

193 *'I have cut the thread'*: GLB diary for D-W, 16 Jan. 1914

194 *'The Beduin has been born'*: T. E. Lawrence, in preface to *Arabia Deserta* by Charles M. Doughty, p. 15

195 *'a certain hierarchical conception'*: Albert Hourani, *A History of the Arab Peoples*, p. 102

195 *'The Arab is never safe'*: Gertrude Bell, *The Desert and the Sown*, p. 66

196 *'Your safest course of action'*: Ibid., preface, p. xxii

198 *'When we were little'*: GLB's diary for Doughty-Wylie, 24 Jan. 1914

198 *'There are no words to tell you'*: GLB's diary for D-W, 23 Jan. 1914

200 *'A formidable looking person'*: GLB's diary for D-W, 2 Feb. 1914

200 *'I saw his jurisdiction'*: Ibid.

200 *'the price of which . . . enchanting little beast'*: GLB's diary for D-W, 24 Jan. 1914

203 *'Abandoned of God and man'*: GLB's diary for D-W, 2 Feb. 1914

205 *'[It] springs from a profound doubt'*: GLB's diary for D-W, 16 Feb. 1914

205 *'Princes and powers of Arabia'*: Ibid.

206 *'This morning we reached'*: GLB letter, 19 Feb. 1914

9. ESCAPE

211 'In short, I was not to come further': GLB diary for Doughty-Wylie, 2 Mar. 1914

211 'In Hayil, murder': Ibid.

212 '[It was] a very splendid place': Ibid.

213 'And then followed': Ibid.

214 'Turkiyyeh says': GLB (personal diary, 28 Feb.)

214 'Wind and dust, a little rain': GLB (personal) diary

215 'I have just £40': GLB diary for D-W, 2 Mar.

216 'I spent a long night': Ibid.

216 was planning to murder: For the murder of Zamil ibn Subhan, see H. V. F. Winstone, Gertrude Bell, p. 210, and H. V. F. Winstone, The Illicit Adventure, ch. 5

217 'I passed two hours': GLB diary for D-W, 6 Mar.

218 'I spoke to him': Ibid.

218 'And why they have now given way': Ibid.

219 'Everyone was smiling and affable': GLB diary for D-W, 17 Mar.

219 'I went, and took an affectionate farewell': GLB diary for D-W

220 'I fancy they meant': GLB diary for D-W

220 '[The journey is] so wearying': GLB diary for D-W

220 'Not one grown man': GLB diary for D-W

221 'I fear when I look back': GLB diary for D-W, 16 Feb.

222 'On a careful analysis of my feelings': GLB diary for D-W, 26 Mar.

223 'In all the years': GLB diary for D-W, 17 Apr.

223 'He does not get up till 12': GLB diary for D-W, 28 Mar.

224 'I think the only things': GLB diary for D-W, 26 Mar.

224 'He is too holy': GLB diary for D-W, 28 Mar.

225 'The muddy waters of Tigris flood': Ibid.

225 'Baghdad shimmered': GLB diary for D-W, 12 Apr.

226 description of the court of the Caliph: Baghdad in the time of al-Muqtadir, from the account of al-Khatib al-Baghdadi, in Albert Hourani, A History of the Arab Peoples

226 'Baghdad has taken to': GLB diary for D-W, 13 Apr.

227 'Out under the open sky again': Ibid., 13, 15 and 22 Apr.

227 'We went on boldly': GLB diary for D-W, 16 Apr.

228 'They brought it to me': GLB diary for D-W, 19 Apr.

228 'He received me with a kindness': GLB diary for D-W, 22 Apr.

229 'We ate and the dusk fell': GLB diary for D-W

229 'There are people camped in the hills': GLB diary for D-W, 19 Apr.

230 *'A great storm marched across our path'*: GLB diary for D-W, 25 Apr.

231 *'So here I am in a garden'*: GLB diary for D-W, 1 May

231 *'He looked at me in silence'*: Later undated letter from GLB to Doughty-Wylie

10. WAR WORK

235 *'On the Baghdad side'*: Report by GLB to Wyndham H. Deedes of the Military Operations Directorate, sent on to Sir Edward Grey, Under-Secretary of State for Foreign Affairs, WO 33 doc 48014

236 *The magazines were full of photographs*: Georgina Howell, *In Vogue 1916–1975*

236 *'I have asked some of my friends'*: GLB letter, Nov. 1914

236 *'St Loe remarked'*: GLB letter, 17 Nov.

238 *She stepped on to the quay*: Description of Boulogne from *Red Cross* (periodical), Feb. 1915, p. 39

239 *'I had a hideous interview'*: GLB to Doughty-Wylie, in Winstone, *Gertrude Bell*, p. 229

240 *'I think I have inherited'*: GLB letter

240 *Her first object was to create*: The working of the W&MED, from a report to the Joint War Committee, spring 1915

241 *'I've very nearly'*: GLB letter, 16 Dec.

241 *'It is fearful the amount'*: GLB letter, 26 Nov.

243 *'The cooks [were]'*: GLB letter, New Year, 1915

243 *'There is a recent order'*: GLB to Chirol, 11 Dec. 1914

244 *'Where we are under a cross fire'*: GLB to Chirol

245 *'I can work here all day long'*: GLB to Chirol, 16 Dec.

246 *'Some rather complicated business'*: GLB letter

246 *'In spite of dirt and gloom'*: GLB to Chirol, 20 Jan. 1915, in Burgoyne, *Bell, 1914–1926*, p. 23

247 *'I hear that on Xmas Day'*: GLB letter, 27 Dec. 1914

247 *'At midnight'*: GLB letter, 1 Jan. 1915

248 *'It was full of errors'*: GLB to Chirol, 20 Jan. 1915

248 *'I feel tired'*: Ibid., 27 Dec. 1914

249 *'They have put all the correspondence'*: GLB to Chirol, 12 Jan. 1915

250 *'My work goes on'*: Ibid.

251 *'They reckon the average duration'*: GLB to Chirol, 2 Feb.

252 *'The Pyrrhic victory'*: GLB to Chirol, 2 Feb.

252 *'Don't let anyone know I'm coming'*: GLB letter, 22 Mar. 1915

253 *'I love Lord Robert'*: GLB to Chirol, 1 Apr.

253 *'I get rather tired'*: GLB letter

253 *'I could not possibly get away'*: GLB letter, 5 Aug.

254 *'It's very dear of you'*: GLB letter, 25 Aug.

254 *'It is of vital importance'*: GLB letter, 20 Aug.

255 *'I've heard from David'*: Recalled by Janet Courtney in an article on Gertrude in the *North American Review*, Dec. 1926

11. CAIRO, DELHI, BASRA

257 *'I'm getting to feel'*: GLB letter, 3 Jan. 1916

258 *'an oasis of peace and quiet'*: GLB letter, 6 Dec. 1915

261 *the shrewd Hashemite Sharif of Mecca*: History in T. E. Lawrence, *The Seven Pillars of Wisdom*

261 *On the eve of the world war*: Abdullah's visit to Sir Ronald Storrs in Ronald Storrs, *Orientations*; John Keay, *Sowing the Wind: The Mismanagement of the Middle East 1900–1960*, p. 41

265 *'biff the French out of all hope'*: T. E. Lawrence to D. G. Hogarth, 22 Mar. 1915

265 *'I wonder, if I could choose'*: GLB letter, 1 Jan. 1916

267 *'Political union is a conception unfamiliar'*: Undated paper, GLB Archives, Miscellaneous Collection, RL

269 *As one commentator*: John Keay, *Sowing the Wind: The Mismanagement of the Middle East 1900–1960*

270 *'I devoutly hope'*: Charles Hardinge, letter to the Foreign Office, in Wallach, *Desert Queen*, p. 154

271 *'It is essential'*: GLB to Captain R. Hall, 20 Feb. 1916

272 *'the people in India cling'*: Gilbert Clayton, from General Staff Army Headquarters, Cairo, 28 Jan. 1916

272 *'It was at this time'*: Hardinge of Penshurst, *My Indian Years 1910–1916*, p. 136

273 *'When I got Lord H's message'*: GLB letter, 24 Jan.

273 *'I'm off finally at a moment's notice'*: GLB letter, 28 Jan.

274 *'They get so bored'*: GLB letter, 1 Feb.

275 *'It was very wonderful seeing it'*: GLB letter, 18 Feb.

276 *'I have . . . talked about Arabia'*: Ibid.

277 *'The V. is anxious'*: Ibid.

277 *'She is a remarkably clever woman'*: Hardinge, *Old Diplomacy*

277 *'I warned her'*: Hardinge, *My Indian Years*

279 *'I wish I ever knew'*: GLB letter, 18 Mar.

281 *'Today I lunched'*: GLB letter, 9 Mar.

282-3 'To the south' . . . 'I need not say' . . . 'There are many things': GLB to Chirol, 12 June 1916

283 'Nothing happens': GLB letter, 27 Apr.

284 'This week has been greatly enlivened': GLB letter, 9 Apr.

285 'we rushed into the business': GLB letter, 27 Apr.

286 'It never occurred': GLB to Chirol, 13 Sept.

286 'He is . . . a most remarkable creature': GLB letter, 24 May 1918, in Burgoyne, Bell, 1914–1926, p. 87

287 When he was fifteen: Account of the capture of Riyadh from Keay, Sowing the Wind

288 'Ibn Saud is barely forty': GLB, 'A Ruler of the Desert', in The Arab of Mesopotamia

289 'the phenomenon of one of': Sir Percy Cox of GLB's work, in Florence Bell, Letters

290 'Last night I woke': GLB letter, 15 July

290 'one's bath water': GLB letter, 29 July

290 'One wears almost nothing': GLB letter, 27 Apr. 1916

290 'A box has just arrived': GLB letter, 20 Jan. 1917

290 'Do you know': GLB letter, 20 Sept. 1916

291 'The amount I've written': GLB letter, 2 Mar. 1917

291 'Happy to tell you': GLB letter, 13 Jan. 1917

292 'Officialdom . . . could never spoil': Kinahan Cornwallis, introduction to Gertrude Bell, The Arab War: Confidential Information for GHQ Cairo, Dispatches for the Arab Bulletin

293 'The only interesting letters I have': GLB to Chirol, 13 Sept. 1917

293 'I had a letter from Sir Percy': GLB letter, 10 Mar. 1917

12. GOVERNMENT THROUGH GERTRUDE

The descriptions of the rule of the Ottoman Empire and of the British administration derive from Review of the Civil Administration of Mesopotamia prepared by GLB for the India Office, 1920.

295 'I unpacked my box': GLB letter, 20 Apr. 1917

296 'I confess': Ibid.

297 'Oh my dearest ones': GLB letter, May 1917, in Burgoyne, Bell, 1914–1926, p. 60

298 'General Maude': GLB letter, 22 Nov., in ibid., p. 67

299 'Nowhere in the war-shattered universe': GLB letter, 18 May

302 'Today there rolled in': GLB letter, 2 Feb., in Burgoyne, Bell, 1914–1926, p. 54

304 'Fahad Beg and I': GLB letter, 26 May, in ibid., p. 58

305 'I summoned my sheikhs': GLB letter, 1 June

306 'Our office': GLB letter, 24 May 1918

306 'I had a difficult time': GLB letter, 24 Apr. 1917, in Burgoyne, *Bell, 1914–1926*, p. 84

308 'I don't really care': GLB letter, 26 Oct.

308 'Please, please don't supply': GLB letter, 6 Sept.

310 '[She] had all the personnel': Sir Percy Cox, in Florence Bell, *Letters*, p. 428

311 'The question of regulation of pilgrim': Bell, *Review of the Civil Administration of Mesopotamia*

313 'It has resulted': Ibid.

313 'We are put to it': GLB to Chirol, 9 Nov., in Burgoyne, *Bell, 1914–1926*, p. 67

316 'The Turkish educational programme': Bell, *Review of the Civil Administration of Mesopotamia*

318 'We were all sitting': Florence Bell, *Letters*, p. 402

318 'What I need': GLB letter, 25 Jan. 1918, in Burgoyne, *Bell, 1914–1926*, p. 75

319 'I regret to say': GLB letter, 26 May 1917

319 'The nuns are making me': GLB letter, 14 June 1918

320 'O Father Dearest': GLB letter, 15 Feb. 1918, in Burgoyne, *Bell, 1914–1926*, p. 77

320 'the drawback': GLB letter, 22 Feb., in ibid., p. 78

320 'I have been wishing': GLB to Chirol, end 1917, in ibid.

320 'Dearest Mother': GLB letter, 28 Mar. 1918, in ibid., p. 81

321 'two most beautiful Arab greyhounds': GLB letter, 30 Nov. 1919

322 'It's a most attractive little beast': GLB letter, 20 July 1920

322 'Last week you told me': GLB letter, 2 Mar. 1917, in Burgoyne, *Bell, 1914–1926*, p. 55

323 'One of my few consolations': GLB letter, 5 Sept., in ibid., p. 63

323 'there arrived a jeweller's shop': GLB letter, 25 Sept., in ibid., p. 65

324 'The Devil Worshippers': GLB letter, 28 June 1918, in ibid., p. 89

325 'The underlying truth': GLB letter, 10 Oct. 1920

13. ANGER

326 'I might be able': GLB letter, 17 Jan. 1919

327 'For the first quarter of an hour': Ibid.

327 'When I come back': GLB to Hon. Mildred Lowther, 6 July 1918

328 'I can't tell you': GLB letter, 16 Mar. 1919

332 'If we wish to apply': GLB, 'Self Determination as Applied to the Iraq'

333 'If the Arab Nation assist England': Telegram no. 233 from Kitchener, in Winstone, *Gertrude Bell*, pp. 243, 452

333 'I propose to assume': GLB, 'The Political Future of Iraq'

335 '[Maude] did not see his way': And the story of Khanikin, GLB, *Review of the Civil Administration of Mesopotamia*

335 'In no part of Mesopotamia': GLB, ibid.

336 'We have taken on Khanikin': GLB to Chirol, Dec. 1917

336 'Experts on Western Arabia': A. T. Wilson, in Burgoyne, *Bell, 1914–1926*, p. 110

337 'a Kurdish independent state': GLB letter, 14 Aug. 1921

337 'Beloved Mother': GLB letter, 16 Mar. 1919

338 'I've never been so well dressed': GLB letter, 26 Sept. 1919

338 'Heaven knows': GLB letter, 1 June 1917

339 'Fattuh looks older': GLB letter, 17 Oct. 1919

340 'Marie has been invaluable': GLB letter, 7 Dec. 1919

341 'I wonder how anyone can complain': GLB letter, 6 May 1920

341 'I had a ladies' tea party': GLB to Chirol, 10 May 1918

342 'I find social duties rather trying': Gordon, *Gertrude Bell*

342 'I really think I am beginning': GLB to Chirol, 12 Feb. 1920

343 'I think we're on the edge': GLB letter, 10 Apr. 1920

344 'We are at our wits' end': In Margaret MacMillan, *Peacemakers: The Paris Conference of 1919 and Its Attempt to End War*, p. 419

344 'I do not understand this squeamishness': Martin Gilbert, *Winston S. Churchill*, companion vol. 4, part 1

344 'If only [the rebel tribes]': GLB letter, 8 Aug. 1920

346 'The Nationalist propaganda increases': GLB letter, 14 June 1920

346 'There they sit': GLB letter, 14 Mar. 1920

347 'I was acutely conscious': Ibid.

347 At the end of 1919: For the incident at Dair, GLB, Ibid.

349 'We share the blame': GLB letter, 1 Feb. 1920

350 'The tribes down there': GLB letter, 4 July 1920

351 'He was visibly put out': GLB letter, 26 July 1920

351 'We are now in the middle': GLB letter, Feb. 1920

351 'It's touch and go': GLB letter, 2 Aug. 1920

351 'Well, if the British evacuate': GLB letter, 26 July 1920

352 'Rather a trying week': GLB letter, 20 Dec. 1920

353 'She will take some handling': Letter from A. T. Wilson, Oct. 1919

353 'My own feeling': GLB letter, 12 Feb., in Burgoyne, *Bell*, p. 128

353 'I wish I carried more weight': GLB letter, 12 Jan. 1920, in ibid., p. 125

353 *'I confess'*: GLB letter, 23 May 1920

354 *'Sir P.C'*: GLB to Chirol, 28 Dec. 1919

354 *'my own path'*: GLB letter, 14 June 1920, in Burgoyne, *Bell*, p. 140

355 *'Of course we can't prevent it'*: GLB letter, 14 June, in ibid.

356 *'I've just got Mother's letter'*: GLB letter, 17 Jan. 1921

357 *'I've just written'*: GLB letter, 7 Mar. 1920, in Burgoyne, *Bell*, p. 131

357 *'I have written to'*: GLB letter, 14 Jan. 1920, in ibid., p. 124

357 *'From Mr Montagu for Miss Bell'*: 6 Aug. 1920, in ibid., p. 154

358 *'Colonel Wilson gives me every opportunity'*: GLB to Montagu, 6 Aug. 1920, in ibid.

359 *'Miss Bell. When Sir Percy Cox'*: A. T. Wilson, 6 Aug. 1920, in ibid., p. 155

359 *'On this we shook hands'*: GLB letter, 7 Aug. 1920, in ibid.

360 *A private letter*: 17 June 1922

361 *'It is quite impossible to tell you'*: GLB letter, 17 Oct. 1920, in Burgoyne, *Bell*, p. 455

361 *'Oh, if we can pull this thing off'*: GLB letter, 1 Nov. 1920, in ibid., p. 462

14. FAISAL

362 *In May 1885*: For the accounts of Faisal's early life, Mrs Steuart Erskine, *King Faisal of Iraq*, and Philip Graves (ed.), *King Abdullah of Transjordan: Memoirs*

362 *Following hallowed tradition*: From the account of Faisal in the desert, T. E. Lawrence, *The Seven Pillars of Wisdom*

366 *ready for the rebellion*: From the account of the Arab Revolt, ibid.

368 *'I had believed these misfortunes'*: ibid., book 1, *The Discovery of Feisal*

370 *Lawrence was also deeply involved*: Lawrence's admission that on the subject of the Arab Revolt he owed much to Gertrude – from a radio broadcast by Elizabeth Robins of 17 Sept. 1927; nos 14 and 36, Miscellaneous Collection, GLB Archives, RL. Mentioned in Liora Lukitz, *A Quest in the Middle East*, p. 237.

374 *'or I shall consider you a traitor'*: Steuart Erskine, *Faisal*, p. 76

374 *'He combined the qualities'*: In a broadcast of 8 Sept. 1933

376 *'In our own country'*: From an unsigned, undated document, part handwritten, 'Great Britain and the Iraq; an Experiment in Anglo-Asiatic relations', in Miscellaneous Collection, GLB Archives, RL

376 *Gertrude, a third of the way*: Descriptions of the Paris Peace Conference from Margaret MacMillan, *Peacemakers: The Paris Conference*

377 'I've dropped into a world so amazing': GLB letter, 7 Mar. 1919

378 'Colonel T. E. Lawrence . . . seems': John Keay, Sowing the Wind, p. 132

378 'The first deception occurred': Steuart Erskine, Faisal, pp. 96–7

379 On 6 February Faisal: Address to the Supreme Council, MacMillan, Peacemakers, p. 402

380 'After dinner T. E. L. explained': GLB letter, 26 Mar. 1919, in Burgoyne, Bell, 1914–1926, p. 110

380 'O my dear': GLB to Aubrey Herbert, in MacMillan Peacemakers, p. 411

381 'In John's studio': Untitled, undated paper by GLB in Miscellaneous Collection, GLB Archives, RL

382 'the establishment in Palestine': Macmillan, Peacemakers, p. 427

382 'Mr Balfour's Zionist pronouncement': Ibid.

383 'Palestine for the Jews': GLB to General Clayton, 22 Jan. 1918

384 the leading Zionist: For Weizmann, MacMillan, Peacemakers, p. 427

385 'In one respect Palestine': Unsigned, undated document, 'Palestine', in Miscellaneous Collection, GLB Archives, RL

387 'Faisal, with his high ideals': GLB interview with Faisal in Augustus John's studio, in ibid.

387 General Gouraud arrived: Account of Gouraud's ultimatum to Faisal, Steuart Erskine, Faisal, p. 104

388 'The resistance of the Arabs': GLB's undated handwritten notes, item 12, 'French Policy in Syria' in Miscellaneous Collection, GLB Archives, RL

388 'The tears stood in his eyes': Ronald Storrs, Orientations, p. 506

388 'In my opinion': Untitled, undated paper by GLB, Miscellaneous Collection, GLB Archives, RL

389 'the growing hatred of French control': GLB paper, 'The Syrian Situation and Its Bearings on Iraq', typescript enclosed with a letter of 17 Nov. 1925 and marked 'strictly confidential', in Miscellaneous Collection, GLB Archives, RL

389 'the Druzes, flawlessly courageous': Ibid.

392 'I wish there were more people': GLB letter, 18 Dec. 1922

392 '"My Lady" he answered': GLB letter, 1 Nov. 1920

392 'Cox sent an admirable letter': GLB letter, July 1921

392 'We were all agreed': GLB letter, 18 Dec. 1920

393 'Sunni opinion [in Iraq]': GLB to Chirol, 4 Feb. 1921

394 'I said the matter was entirely': GLB letter, 18 Dec. 1920

394 'I feel quite clear in my own mind': GLB letter, Christmas Day 1920, in Burgoyne, Bell, p. 193

15. CORONATION

395 *Churchill, however*: Churchill and expenditure: Martin Gilbert, *Churchill: a Life*, pp. 431, 433

396 *'The people of England'*: T. E. Lawrence, 'Mesopotamia', article for the *Sunday Times*, 22 Aug. 1920

397 *'Amid potations of whisky'*: GLB letter, 24 Feb. 1921, in Burgoyne, *Bell, 1914–1926*, p. 209

397 *'We covered more work'*: GLB to Colonel Frank Balfour, 25 Mar. 1921, in ibid., p. 211

399 *'Have we a policy?'*: Wyndham Deedes's statement recounted by GLB in unsigned, undated paper in Miscellaneous Collection, GLB Archives, RL

399 *'The French in Syria'*: GLB to Chirol, 4 Feb. 1921

400 *'At the end'*: GLB letter, 25 Apr. 1921

400 *'Haji Naji'*: GLB letter, 8 May 1921

401 *'I believe Faisal is statesman enough'*: GLB letter, 19 June 1921

401 *'Can you make sure he is chosen'*: Churchill to Cox, 10 Jan. 1921, Gilbert, *A Life*, p. 431

401 *'I don't for a moment'*: GLB letter, 12 June 1921

401 *'The rank and file of the tribesmen'*: GLB *Civil Administration*, p. 127

403 *'It was an incitement to rebellion'*: GLB letter, 17 Apr. 1921

403 *'He was arrested in a public thoroughfare'*: Cox to Churchill, April 1921, in Winstone, *Gertrude Bell*

404 *'Yesterday we had news'*: GLB letter, 23 June 1921, in Burgoyne, *Bell, 1914–1926*, p. 221

405 *'I had to part company'*: Cox, in Florence Bell, *Letters*, p. 428

406 *'had a most painful interview'*: GLB letter, 7 July 1921, in Burgoyne, *Bell, 1914–1926*, p. 224

406 *'Presently Faisal sent for me'*: GLB letter, 30 June 1921

406 *'And then there stepped forward'*: Ibid.

407 *'It was a wonderful sight'*: GLB letter, 8 July 1921

407 *'I'm immensely happy'*: GLB letter, 27 July 1921

407 *And then came*: Description of Ramadi from GLB letter, 31 July 1921

408 *'a great tribesman'*; *'in the great tongue'* . . . ; *'Faisal was a little surprised'*: Ibid.

410 *'It was wonderfully interesting'*: GLB letter, 6 Aug. 1921

411 *'It lives on a perch'*: GLB letter, 21 Aug. 1921

412 *'"Enti Iraqiyah . . ."'*: Ibid.

412 *'Faisal looked'*: GLB letter. 28 Aug. 1921

412 *'Basrah and Amarah came'*: Ibid.

413 *'Have I ever told you'*: GLB letter, 11 Sept. 1921

16. STAYING AND LEAVING

415 *a dervish*: From GLB letter, 17 July 1922

415 *'I'm acutely conscious'*: GLB letter, 16 Feb. 1920

416 *in a modest British journal*: Faisal's story in *Everybody's Weekly*, 1 Oct. 1927

419 *Lawrence is evasive*: From *Seven Pillars of Wisdom*, pp. 59–60

419 *'She stood out'*: Letter from Lawrence to Elsa Richmond, also mentioned in Elizabeth Robins's radio broadcast of 17 Sept. 1927, nos 14 and 36, Miscellaneous Collection, GLB Archives, RL

420 *'I dined with the King'*: GLB letter, 25 Sept. 1921, Burgoyne, *Bell, 1914–1926*, p. 247

422 *'the emotional atmosphere'*: GLB letter, 4 June 1922, in ibid., p. 271

422 *'Safwat Pasha'*: GLB letter, 16 July 1922

423 *'The Treaty is in statu quo ante'*: GLB letter, 30 July 1922

423 *'My heart died'*: GLB letter, 15 Aug. 1922

423 *'But will our government'*: Ibid.

423 *'We roasted great fishes'*: GLB letter, 27 Aug. 1922

424 *'I opened a parcel'*: GLB letter, 22 Feb. 1922.

424 *'As soon as we were back'*: GLB letter, 27 Aug. 1922

424 *'For once Providence'*: Ibid., in Burgoyne, *Bell, 1914–1926* p. 291

425 *Faisal proclaimed the treaty*: Steuart Erskine, *Faisal* p. 156

426 *'I was called up to the palace'*: GLB letter, 7 Oct. 1924, in Burgoyne, *Bell, 1914–1926*, p. 355

426 *'I asked him about his wife'*: GLB letter, 24 July 1921, in ibid., p. 229

426 *'She's charming'*: GLB letter, 23 Dec. 1924

427 *'The King sent for me'*: GLB letter, 31 Dec. 1924, in Burgoyne, *Bell, 1914–1926*, p. 360

428 *'The train and soldiers'*: GLB letter, 14 Dec. 1924

428 *'I do pray that Husain'*: GLB letter, 7 Oct. 1924

429 *'The capture of Hail . . . religious sanction'*: GLB to Hardinge, 6 Jan. and 16 Mar., 1922, in Burgoyne, *Bell, 1914–1926*, p. 266

430 *'The King is in a mighty taking'*: GLB letter, 10 Dec. 1924, in ibid., p. 359

430 *'The King had violent hysterics'*: GLB letter, 15 Oct. 1924, in ibid., p. 356

431 *'Nor does Abdullah'*: GLB paper, 'Transjordania', marked 'strictly confidential', unsigned, undated, Miscellaneous Collection, GLB Archives, RL

431 *'I had come back with the conviction'*: GLB letter, 18 May 1922

432 *'The King's family, apparently'*: GLB letter, 15 Oct. 1924, in Burgoyne, *Bell, 1914–1926*, p. 356

432 *'We're in the uncomfortable position'*: GLB letter, 24 Sept. 1924

433 *'Arbil and all the Kurdish districts'*: GLB letter, 14 Aug. 1921, in Burgoyne, *Bell, 1914–1926*, p. 234

434 *'I rated them soundly'*: GLB letter, 2 Jan. 1922, in ibid., p. 258

434 *'I spent last week'*: GLB letter, 31 Jan. 1922, in ibid., p. 261

435 *'I went up river'*: GLB letter, 17 July 1924, in ibid., p. 284

436 *'Altogether I think'*: GLB letter, 31 Dec. 1923

436 *Subsequently, writing to*: Confidences about Cornwallis, to Molly Trevelyan, GLB private correspondence, Miscellaneous Collection, GLB Archives, RL

437 *'All this time'*: GLB letters, 24 April, 9 May 1923, in Burgoyne, *Bell, 1914–1926*, p. 539

437 *'I must tell you something'*: GLB letter, 13 Feb. 1924

438 *'As if by magic'*: Sir Henry Dobbs, in Florence Bell, *Letters*, p. 441

438 *'black depression'*: Burgoyne, *Bell, 1914–1926*, p. 352

439 *'I don't know which of them'*: GLB letter, 11 Feb. 1925, in ibid., p. 581

439 *'condition of great nervous fatigue'*: Florence Bell, *Letters*, p. 591

439 *'She would stand with her back'*: Lecture by Mrs Pauline Dower, University of Newcastle upon Tyne, May 1976

440 *'You dear and beloved Janet'*: GLB to Mrs W. Courtney, 4 Aug. 1925

441 *'We all felt'*: Florence Bell, *Letters*, p. 592

441 *'Darling Mother'*: GLB letter, 21 Oct. 1925

442 *'My darling Father and Mother'*: GLB letter, 9 Feb. 1926, in Burgoyne, *Bell, 1914–1926*, p. 384

443 *'By that time I wasn't taking'*: GLB letter, 30 Dec. 1925

443 *'he is going to make me'*: GLB letter, 18 Aug. 1922, in Burgoyne, *Bell, 1914–1926*, p. 290

444 *'[Woolley] values it at ten thousand pounds'*: GLB letter, Jan. 1924, in ibid., p. 333

444 *'My sole possessions'*: GLB letter, Jan. 1924, in ibid., p. 325

446 *'Miss Gertrude Bell was one of the most'*: Henry Dobbs, in Florence Bell, *Letters*, p. 453

447 *'I think it is extremely unlikely'*: GLB letter, 13 May 1926

447 *a note to Ken Cornwallis*: Request that he look after her dog, from a conversation with Mrs Susanna Richmond

448 *'Dial'*: Information from M. Murphy, Association of the British Pharmaceutical Industry, letter to David Bittner

448 *'It was my faith always'*: Haji Naji to Lady Bell, in Florence Bell, *Letters*, p. 623

448 *'The Queen and I'*: King George V to Lady Bell, in ibid., p. 624

449 *I think she was very happy in her death*: T. E. Shaw to Sir Hugh Bell, 4 Nov. 1927, in Malcolm Brown (ed.), *The Letters of T. E. Lawrence: The Years in India 1927–29*

450 *a military funeral*: Account of GLB's funeral, *The Times*, Tuesday 13 July 1926

BIBLIOGRAPHY

GERTRUDE BELL

Unpublished works

Bell, Gertrude, papers and archaeological fieldbooks, Royal Geographical Society, London

— 'The Camel Trade of Arabia' draft paper, Miscellaneous Collection, GLB Archives, RL

— letters to [Sir] Valentine Chirol, DUL

— commonplace books, RL

— 'Confidences re Cornwallis to Molly Trevelyan', private letter, Miscellaneous Collection, GLB Archives, RL

— 'Report of Wyndham Deedes Statement', unsigned, undated, Miscellaneous Collection, GLB Archives, RL

— extract from a letter to W. H. Deedes, forwarded to Under-Secretary of State for Foreign Affairs, WO 33 doc 48014, DUL 303/1/5

— diaries, www.gerty.ncl.ac.uk, RL

— letter to Lord Hardinge, 8 Feb. 1921, Miscellaneous Collection, GLB archives 11, RL

— 'In John's studio', interview with Faisal in Augustus John's studio during Paris Peace Conference, untitled, undated, Miscellaneous Collection, GLB Archives, RL

— letters, RL, www.gerty.ncl.ac.uk

— photographic archive, RL, www.gerty.ncl.ac.uk

— 'The Political Future of Iraq', paper, DUL, 150/7/69

— private papers, RL

— 'The Resistance of the Arabs', undated handwritten notes, item 12, Miscellaneous Collection, GLB Archives, RL

— 'Self Determination as Applied to the Iraq', paper, DUL, 150/7/62

— 'Self Determination in Mesopotamia', memorandum no. S-24, dated Baghdad, 22 Feb. 1919, marked in handwriting 'By G.L.B.', DUL, 303/1/60
— 'Note by Miss Gertrude Bell on the Settlement of the Arab Provinces', undated, RL
— 'The Syrian Situation and its Bearings on Iraq', typescript enclosed with a letter dated 17 Nov. 1925, signed GLB, RL
— 'Transjordania', marked 'strictly confidential', unsigned, undated, Miscellaneous Collection, GLB Archives, RL
— 'Gertrude Bell Archive, Part 2: Miscellaneous 1892–1938', RL, 1961–91

Published works

Bell, Gertrude, 'The Vaulting System at Ukhaidir', *Journal of Hellenic Studies*, xxx (1910)
— *The Palace and Mosque at Ukhaidir*, Oxford: Clarendon Press, 1914
— *Review of the Civil Administration of Mesopotamia*, London: HMSO, 1920
— *Great Britain and Iraq: An Experiment in Anglo-Asiatic Relations*, London: Round Table, published anonymously, 1924
— *Persian Pictures*, New York: Boni & Liveright, 1928
— *The Arab War: Confidential Information for GHQ Cairo, Dispatches for the Arab Bulletin*, London: Golden Cockerel Press, 1940
— Lowthian, *The Teachings of Hafiz*, London: Octagon Press, 1979
— *Arab War Lords and Iraqi Star Gazers, Gertrude Bell's The Arab of Mesopotamia*, USA: Authors' Choice Press, 1992
— *The Hafez Poems of Gertrude Bell*, Bethesda, MD: Iranbooks, 1995
— *The Desert and the Sown*, New York: Cooper Square Press, 2001
— *Amurath to Amurath, A Journey along the Banks of the Euphrates*, Piscataway, NJ: Gorgias Press, 2002
— with Sir William Ramsey, *The Thousand and One Churches*, London: Hodder & Stoughton, 1909

GENERAL

Alpine Club, 'Miss Gertrude Lowthian Bell', *Alpine Journal*, xxxviii (1926), pp. 296–9
Amery, L. S., *My Political Life, England before the Storm 1896–1914*, London: Hutchinson, 1953
The Leo Amery Diaries, vol. 1, *1896–1929*, London: Barnes & Nicolson, 1980

Records of the Women's National Anti-Suffrage League, Archives Hub, Women's Library, GLB 0106 2/WNA

Anon., 'Arab Revolt', report to Secretary of State from Simla, 29 June, DUL, 137/6/102

Balfour, Lord F. C. C., Gertrude Bell Letters, DUL

Bell, Lady Florence, *Alan's Wife*, London: Henry & Co., 1893

— *The Story of Ursula*, London: Hutchinson, 1895

— *Angela*, London: Ernest Benn, 1926

— *The Letters of Gertrude Bell*, London: Ernest Benn, 1927

— *At the Works: A Study of a Manufacturing Town*, London: Virago Press, 1985

Anon., 'Lady [Florence] Bell's Scheme', *North Eastern Daily Gazette*, 10 Sept. 1906

Bell, Sir Hugh, 'High Wages: Their Cause and Effect', address to National Association of Merchants and Manufacturers, repr. in *Contemporary Review*, Dec. 1920

— Speeches in Defence of Free Trade and Sound Finance, delivered to the electors of the City of London, Jan. 1910, Literary and Philosophical Society Library, Newcastle upon Tyne

Bell, Sir Isaac Lowthian, *Chemical Phenomena of Iron Smelting*, London: 1872

— *The Iron Trade of the United Kingdom Compared with that of the Other Chief Iron-making Nations*, Literary and Philosophical Society, Newcastle upon Tyne, 1875

— Obituary, *The Times*, Durham Mining Museum, 21 Dec. 1904

— catalogue entries, Literary and Philosophical Society, Newcastle upon Tyne

Berchem, M. van, Strzygowski, J., and Bell, Gertrude L., *Amida:matériaux pour l'épigraphie et l'histoire musulmane du Diyar-Bekr*, Heidelberg: Amida, 1910 (Berchem)/*Beiträge zur Kunstgeschichte von Nordmesopotamien Hellas und dem Abendlände* (Strzygowski:)/Bell, *The Churches and Monasteries of the Tur Abdin*

Blunt, Lady Anne, *A Pilgrimage to Nejd, the Cradle of the Arab Race*, London: Century Travellers, 1885

Bodley, Ronald, and Hearst, Lorna, *Gertrude Bell*, New York: Macmillan Co., 1940

Brown, Malcolm, *The Letters of T. E. Lawrence*, London: Dent, 1988

Brunner Mond, 'A Profile of Brunner Mond', www.brunnermond.com

Burgoyne, Elizabeth, *Gertrude Bell from Her Personal Papers, 1889–1914*, London: Ernest Benn, 1958

— *Gertrude Bell from Her Personal Papers, 1914–1926*, London: Ernest Benn, 1961

Burke, Catherine, Description of archive of Mrs L.O. Doughty-Wylie, Diaries 1910–20, Imperial War Museum, London

Bush, Eric Wheeler, *Gallipoli*, London: George Allen & Unwin, 1975

Cambon, Paul, letter to M. Balfour, Principal Secrétaire d'État, 19 Oct. 1918, DUL, 693/14/14

Cannadine, David, *The Decline and Fall of the British Aristocracy*, New Haven, Conn.: Yale University Press, 1990

Carlyon, L. A., *Gallipoli*, Australia: Pan Macmillan, 2001

Casualties in the Great War, 'Casualties WWI/Schlachtaffers WOI www. greatwar.nl, and 'The Heritage of the Great War', Rob Ruggenberg, 'It is my painful duty to inform you' www.greatwar.nl

Chapman, Mike, 'Doughty-Wylie, Charles Hotham Montague', www.victoria cross.net, 2000

Chirol, Sir Ignatius Valentine, letters, DUL

Clayton, General Sir Gilbert, letters, DUL

— private letter to 'My dear General', 28 Jan. 1916, DUL, 136/1/183

Condell, Diana, 'Lieutenant Colonel Charles Doughty-Wylie VC CMG – Sedd el Bahr and Hill 141', www.iwm.org.uk/online/gallipoli/hellesHill141.htm

Coppack, Glyn, *Mount Grace Priory*, London: English Heritage, 1996

Courtney, Janet E., *An Oxford Portrait Gallery*, London: Chapman & Hall, 1931

Cowlin, Dorothy, *A Woman in the Desert: The Story of Gertrude Bell*, London: Frederick Muller, 1967

Cox, P. Z., Al Sa'adun and Abdul Mahsin, 'IRAQ. Protocol of the 30th April, 1923 and the Agreements Subsidiary to the Treaty with King Feisal', London: HMSO, 1924

Cromer, Lord, 'Woman Suffrage', speech at Queen's Hall, 26 Mar. 1909, RL

— letter to Wingate, 18 Nov. 1915, DUL, 135/6/12

'Stepney Areas, The Man who Built Cubitts Town', www.website.lineone.net

Daugherty, Leo J., 'The Mesopotamian Front! As observed by Lieutenant Colonel Edward Davis, US Cavalry, 1918', *Armor*, 3 Jan. 2003

Dearden, Seton, 'Gertrude Bell', Cornhill Magazine, winter 1969–70

Denny, C. J., and K. C. Jordan, 'Europe and the Middle East', British Council map no. 1, London: Royal Geographical Society, 1941

Dixon, John, 'Magnificent but not War: The Role of Col. Sir Maurice Bell in the Attack on Fortuin', www.rollofhonour.com

Dolan, Frances E., 'Battered Women, Petty Traitors, and the Legacy of Coverture', *Feminist Studies*, June 2003

Doughty, Charles M., *Arabia Deserta*, London: Bloomsbury, 1989

Doughty-Wylie, Charles H. M., letter to Jean Coe, 20 April 1915, Imperial War Museum, London

Doughty-Wylie memorial window, Theberton Church, Suffolk, www.sylly suffolk.co.uk

Dower, Pauline, Address at the University of Newcastle upon Tyne, May 1976, RL

'An Appeal against Female Suffrage', manifesto statement, National League for Opposing Woman Suffrage, London

King Feisal of Iraq, 'Secrets of Great White Woman of the Desert which were not revealed in her book', interview, *Everybody's Weekly*, 1 Oct. 1927

Feysal, Amir, letter to 'General Clayton Pasha', 24 Shawal 1336, with trans. of Arabic text, DUL, 693/14/7

Flanders, Judith, *The Victorian House*, London: HarperCollins, 2003

Forth Rail Bridge, Heritage Trail Publications, www.theheritagetrail.co.uk

Freeth, Zahra, and H. V. F. Winstone, *Explorers of Arabia from the Renaissance to the Victorian Era*, London: George Allen & Unwin, 1978

Garnett, David, *The Letters of T. E. Lawrence*, Oxford: Alden Press, 1938

Gilbert, Martin, *Churchill: A Life*, London: Pimlico, 2000

— *Winston S. Churchill*, companion vol. 4 (to *Churchill: A Life*), part 1; departmental minute 12 May 1919, Churchill Papers 16/16

Girouard, Mark, *The Victorian Country House*, London: Yale University Press, 1979

Glover, Brian, *Middlesbrough Transporter Bridge*, leaflet, Middlesbrough Council

Gordon, Lesley, *Gertrude Bell 1868–1926*, British Council/University of Newcastle exhibition booklet, 1994

Graves (ed.), Philip, *King Abdullah of Transjordan: Memoirs*, London: Jonathan Cape, 1950

'The Great Eastern Railway, Its Predecessors and Successors' Great Eastern Railway Society, www.gersociety.org.uk

Green, John Richard, *A Short History of the English People*, London: J. M. Dent, 1945

Greenwood, Paul, 'The British Expeditionary Force, August to September 1914', www.geocities.com

Hague, William, *William Pitt the Younger*, London: Harper Perennial, 2005

Hardinge, Lord, letter to Miss Bell, 27 Dec. 1920, signature missing, author assumed, Miscellaneous Collection, GLB Archives, 90, RL

— letter to Miss Bell, 17 Mar. 1921, signature missing, author assumed, Miscellaneous Collection, GLB Archives, 92, RL

— letter to Miss Bell, 3 July 1921, signature missing, author assumed, Miscellaneous Collection, GLB Archives, 94, RL

— letter to Miss Bell, 20 Sept. 1921, signature missing, author assumed, Miscellaneous Collection, GLB Archives, 96, RL

— *Old Diplomacy*, London: John Murray, 1947

— *My Indian Years 1910–1916*, London: John Murray, 1948

Hattersley, Roy, *The Edwardians*, London: Little Brown, 2004

Hickey, Michael, *Gallipoli*, London: John Murray, 1995

Hill, Stephen, *Gertrude Bell (1868–1926): A Selection from the Photographic Archive of an Archaeologist and Traveller*, University of Newcastle, Department of Archaeology, 1977

Hogarth, David, obituary of Gertrude Bell, *Royal Geographical Society Journal*, 1926

— 'Gertrude Bell's Journey to Hayil', speech, Royal Geographical Society, 4 April 1927

— Presidential Lecture on the 1913 journey of Gertrude Bell, Royal Geographical Society, 1927

Hourani, Albert, *A History of the Arab Peoples*, London: Faber & Faber, 1991

Howell, Georgina, *In Vogue 1916–1975*, London: Allen Lane, 1975

Hunter, Sir William Wilson, *Rulers of India*, Oxford: Clarendon Press, 1891

Anon., secret notes, 'The Establishment of an Intelligence Centre in the Near East', with handwritten diagram, to GFC 1918, DUL, 694/6/1

A History of Iraq, BBC2, 17 Sept. 2003

'Iraq and the Heart of the Middle East' map, *National Geographic*, Washington, DC, 2003

Kamm, Josephine, *Gertrude Bell*, New York: Vanguard Press

Keay, John, *Sowing the Wind: The Mismanagement of the Middle East 1900–1960*, London: John Murray, 2003

Kitchener, Lord, telegram to Amir Abdullah, no. 233 L/P&S/18/B222

Kleinbauer, W. Eugene, *Early Christian and Byzantine Architecture*, G. K. Hall, 1992

Lady Margaret Hall, Oxford, www.clients.networks.co.uk/ladymargarethall: history

Lawrence, T. E., 'Mesopotamia', *Sunday Times*, 22 Aug. 1920

— *The Seven Pillars of Wisdom*, London: Jonathan Cape, 1926

— *Letters*, Karachi: 1927

Lewis, Jonathan, *The First World War*, Channel 4 TV series based on book by Hew Strachan, Simon & Schuster, 2003

Lillie, William, *The History of Middlesbrough*, Middlesbrough: the Mayor, aldermen and burgesses of the County Borough of Middlesbrough, 1968

Lowell, Thomas, *With Lawrence in Arabia*, London: Hutchinson

Lukitz, Liora, *A Quest in the Middle East: Gertrude Bell and the Making of Modern Iraq*, London: I. B. Tauris, 2006

Mack, John E., *A Prince of Our Disorder: The Life of T. E. Lawrence*, Cambridge, Mass.: Harvard University Press, 1998

MacMillan, Margaret, *Peacemakers: The Paris Conference of 1919 and Its Attempt to End War*, London: John Murray, 2001

MacMunn, Lt-Gen. Sir George, 'Gertrude Bell and T. E. Lawrence: The Other Side of Their Stories', *The World Today*, Nov. 1927

Mallet, Louis, letter to Sir Edward Grey, 20 May 1914, DUL, 303/1/2

McEwan, Cheryl, 'The Admission of Women Fellows to the Royal Geographical Society', *Geographical Journal*, Jan. 1996

film of opening Middlesbrough Transporter Bridge, by Prince Arthur, 1911, Middlesbrough Council, Transporter Bridge Visitor Centre

Mill, John Stuart, *On the Probable Futurity of the Labouring Classes*, London: 1848

— *The Subjection of Women*, Indianapolis: Hackett Publishing Co., 1988

Montgomery of Alamein, Lord, *A History of Warfare*, London: William Collins, 1968

Moorhead, Alan, *Gallipoli*, Australia: Macmillan, 1975

'The Battle of Neuve Chapelle, 1915', www.firstworldwar.com and www.1914–1918.net

O'Brien, Rosemary, *Gertrude Bell, the Arabian Diaries 1913–1914*, Syracuse University Press, 2000

Officer, Lawrence H., 'Comparing the Purchasing Power of Money in Great Britain from 1264 to 2002', *Economic History Services*, 2004, www.eh.net

Owen, Roger, 'Lord Cromer and Gertrude Bell', *History Today*, vol. 54 (Jan. 2004)

'Women at Oxford', University of Oxford, www.ox.ac.uk

'Persian Poetry', review of *Poems from the Divan of Hafiz*, *Bookman*, Aug. 1928

'Petticoats and Harnesses, Women in the History of Climbing', www.womenclimbing.com: history

Phillips, Melanie, *The Ascent of Woman*, Boston Mass.: Little, Brown, 2003

Pope-Hennessy, Una, *Charles Dickens*, London, 1945

Pugh, Martin, *The March of the Women*, Oxford: Oxford University Press, 2000

Queen's College, 1848–1998, sesquicentenary leaflet Queen's College, London, 1998

Ramsay, Sir W. M., *Studies in the History and Art of the Eastern Provinces of the Roman Empire*, Aberdeen University Press, 1906

Richmond, Lady Elsa (ed.), *The Earlier Letters of Gertrude Bell*, London: Benn, 1937

Robins, Elizabeth, 'Gertrude Bell', typescript of broadcast of 1926, RL

Robson, Eric, *Uncrowned Queen of Iraq*, 'Mysteries' episode 2, Tyne Tees Granada Television

Roosevelt, Kermit, *War in the Garden of Eden*, New York: Scribner's, 1919

Royal Society of Chemistry, 'A Brief History of the RSC', Jan. 2006, www.rsc.org

Russell, Hon. R., *London Fogs*, London: Edward Stanford, 1880

Sackville-West, Vita, *Passenger to Teheran*, New York: Moyerbell, 1990

Schulman, Nicola, *A Rage for Rock Gardening*, London: Short Books, 2001

Sengupta, Ken, 'Pillaging the Gardens of Babylon', *Independent*, 9 Nov. 2005

Simons, Geoff, *Iraq: From Sumer to Saddam*, London: St Martin's Press

Simpson, John, 'Gertrude Bell and the formation of Iraq', News 24, 15 Jan. 2006

Snelling, Stephen, 'Heroes of the Bronze Cross (Norfolk), Charles Hotham Doughty-Wylie (1868–1915)', www.edp24.co.uk

— 'VCs of the First War – Gallipoli', Naval and Military Press, 1995

Solomon, Gwladys Gladstone, Letters to Lloyd George, National League for Opposing Woman Suffrage, Women's Library

Stephen [Woolf], Virginia, Flight of the Mind: The Letters of Virginia Woolf, vol. 1, London: Hogarth Press, 1975

Steuart Erskine, Mrs, King Faisal of Iraq, London: Hutchinson, 1933

Storrs, Ronald, Orientations, London: Nicolson & Watson, 1945

Strzygowski, J., Kleinasien: ein Neuland der Kunstgeschichte, Leipzig, 1903 Account of funeral of Gertrude Bell, The Times, 13 July 1926

Tibble, Anne, Gertrude Bell, London: Adam & Charles Black, 1958

— One Woman's Story, London: Peter Owen, 1976

Treves, Frederick, 'Boulogne under the Red Cross', Red Cross, Feb. 1915, p.39

'A Great Figure, What Miss Bell Has Done for Iraq', Times of India, Bombay, 8 Aug. 1926

'Captain G. N. Walford VC Royal Field Artillery 29th Division', VC citation, London Gazette, 22 June 1915 from V Beach Cemetery, www.battlefields 1418.50megs.com

Walker, Christopher, 'The Foreign Office and Foreign Policy, 1919–1926', History Today, Jan. 1997

Wallach, Janet, Desert Queen, London: Weidenfeld & Nicolson, 1996

Wang, Kirsten, 'Deeds and Words, The Biography of Dame Florence Bell, 1851–1930', unpublished manuscript

Ward, Philip, Ha'il, Cambridge: Oleander Press, 1983

Weintraub, Stanley, The Importance of Being Edward, King in Waiting, London: John Murray, 2000

Weizmann, Chaim, letter to General Clayton, 6 Dec. 1918, DUL, 693/14/9

Whymper, Edward, Scrambles among the Alps in the Years 1860-69: J. P. Lippincott, 1873

Wilson, A. T., letter, 'My Dear Frank', 20 Jan. 1921, DUL, 303/1/95

— letter, 'My Dear Frank', 20 Oct. 1921, DUL, 303/1/99

— letter 'My Dear Frank', 22 July 1922, DUL, 303/1/111

— letter, 17 June 1922, DUL, 303/1/110

— Loyalties: Mesopotamia: A Personal and Historical Record, New York: Greenwood Press, 1930

'Woodrow Wilson', The White House, www.whitehouse.gov

Wingate, General Sir Reginald, letters, DUL

Winstone, H. V. F., The Illicit Adventure, London: Jonathan Cape, 1982

— *Gertrude Bell*, London: Barzan Publishing, 2004

Woolley, C. Leonard, and Lawrence, T. E., *The Wilderness of Zin*, London: Stacey International, 2003

The Working of the Wounded and Missing Enquiry Department, report to the Joint War Committee, spring 1915

Yoltas, Niyazi, *The Whirling Dervishes and the Stories from Mevlana*, Istanbul: Minyatur Publications

CLIMBING WEBSITES

Alpenkalb, climbing information, Finsteraarhorn, 2003, Engelhörner, 2003, www.summitpost.com

— photos and images, Engelhörner, 2003, Schreckhorn, 2002, Les Droites, 2001–3, www.summitpost.com

Ginat, Jackson, climbing information, Brèche des Droites, www.summitpost.com

Liu, Rachel Maria, climbing information, Ulrichshorn, 2003, www.summitpost.com

Matterhorn climb and route photographs, 2004, www.ski-Zermatt.com

Mountaindoc, climbing information, Lauteraarhorn, 2003, www.summitpost.com

Om, climbing information, Barre des Écrins, 2003, La Meije, 2003, www.summitpost.com

Peakware, Matterhorn, Schreckhorn, Bernese Oberland, Finsteraarhorn, Mont Blanc, 2004, www.peakware.com

Sahaguin, Diego, climbing information, Schreckhorn, www.summitpost.com

Schreckhorn, www.summitpost.com, Grindelwald, www.clashohm.com

Taugwalder, Matthias, Matterhorn–Zermatt Switzerland, 2004, www.panoramas.dk

NOTE ON MONEY VALUES

The following notes bring some of the amounts mentioned in this book and other, related, amounts up to today's values in sterling, by adjusting for the changes in the UK Retail Price Index to 2004 (with the US dollar equivalent of $1.80 to the £). Amounts for wages and salaries are also adjusted for the changes in UK average earnings.

Around 1900, when Florence Bell was compiling *At the Works*, a family with two to three children on the lowest wage spent about £50 a year on rent, a limited diet, heat and clothing, insurance and tobacco, but had nothing to spare. A skilled ironworker was paid in basic wages about the same as a clerk in an office, on average £100 a year. This could be increased by overtime pay for working more than eight hours per day, plus bonuses, to above £150. That gives an RPI-adjusted purchasing power today of £9,600 ($17,300). If adjusted by the rise in average earnings that would be £50,000 ($90,000), reflecting the very different standard of living enjoyed by similar workers in developed countries today.

In 1904 Hugh Bell inherited £750,000 from his father's estate; £45 million ($81 million), RPI-adjusted.

Gertrude budgeted her journey to Hayyil in 1913 at £601 (including the cost of travelling back through the Syrian desert), this is £35,000 ($59,477), RPI-adjusted. Her seventeen camels with their equipment at £13 each cost £221, but this was recoverable when they were sold after the journey – about £13,000 ($23,400) today. She described the cost of the journey, a net £22,000 ($40,000) today, as 'the whole of my income for the following year'. This income derived from investments and proceeds from her books as well as an allowance from her father.

Lawrence's offer of £2 million to the Turkish army commander to lift his siege of Kut would be about £100 million ($180 million) today and was about the same amount as Churchill arranged for the British Admiralty to pay for 51 per cent of the Anglo-Persian Oil Company in 1914. In 1921, Churchill aimed to reduce British military expenditure in Iraq from £20 million to £7 million a year, in today's terms a reduction of £287 million ($517 million), RPI-adjusted. By 1921 the British administration of Iraq had spent £8 million governing and developing the country, all raised from local taxes: £200 million ($360 million), RPI-adjusted.

Gertrude's government salary in 1925 was £835 a year: £69,000 ($124,000) RPI-adjusted, but £120,000 ($216,000) if inflated by the change in UK average earnings. Her bequest of £6,000 to found a British Iraq School of Archaeology would be £208,000 ($374,000) today.

CHRONOLOGY

1807 Great-grandfather Thomas Bell, Jarrow alkali manufacturer, opens iron foundry with James Losh and George Wilson at Walker, nr Newcastle upon Tyne

1816 Grandfather (Isaac) Lowthian Bell born to Thomas and Katherine (née Lowthian) at Washington New Hall, elder brother of John and Tom

1832 First Reform Act passed by British parliament

1836 Lowthian joins his father's ironworks at Walker, later becoming a partner

1837 Queen Victoria succeeds William IV

1842 Lowthian marries Margaret Pattinson, daughter of Hugh Lee Pattinson FRS

1844 Gertrude's father (Thomas) Hugh Bell born at Walker, elder brother of Charles, Mary (Maisie), Florence, Ada and Sophie; Gertrude's mother, Maria Shield (Mary), born

1845 Lowthian Bell takes control of Walker ironworks on death of his father

1850 Lowthian opens Washington chemical company with Hugh Pattinson; with Newall, pioneers steel rope and undersea cable manufacture (company becomes Brunner Mond, 1872)

1851 Great Exhibition at Crystal Palace, London; future stepmother Florence born to Dr Sir Joseph and Lady Olliffe (née Cubitt)

1852 Lowthian Bell opens Bell Brothers iron foundry with brothers John and Thomas

1854 Lowthian elected Lord Mayor of Newcastle (and again in 1863); opens Clarence ironworks in Middlesbrough

1857 First Atlantic cable laid, using 1,280 miles of Washington cable

1860 Lowthian pioneers manufacture of aluminium at Washington

1865 Lowthian incorporates his Cleveland Railway into the North Eastern Railway Company (later London and North Eastern Railway)

1867 23 Apr. – Hugh Bell marries Maria (Mary) Shield

1868 14 July – Gertrude Margaret Lowthian Bell (GLB) born at grandfather's home, Washington New Hall, County Durham

1869 Lowthian Bell is founding organizer of the British Iron and Steel Institute

1870 Hugh Bell and family move to newly built Red Barns, Redcar, near Middlesbrough

1871 Franco-Prussian War; Olliffe family evacuate from British Embassy in Paris as Prussians approach

29 Mar. – Brother Maurice Hugh Lowthian Bell born

19 Apr. – Mother Mary Bell dies, aged 27; Hugh's sister Ada manages household

1872 Lowthian Bell starts building Rounton Grange on newly acquired estate near Northallerton

1874 Hugh Bell elected Mayor of Middlesbrough

1875 Lowthian Bell elected Fellow of the Royal Society and elected Liberal MP for Hartlepool

1876 Sir Edward Poynter paints Gertrude and Hugh; Rounton Grange complete

10 Aug. – Hugh Bell marries Florence Eveleen Eleanore Olliffe

1877 Lowthian Bell is founding organizer of the British Institute of Chemistry (later, Royal Institute)

Queen Victoria declared Empress of India

1878 Lowthian Bell awarded Légion d'honneur

GLB's half-brother Hugh (Hugo) born

1879 GLB's half-sister Elsa born

1880 Lowthian Bell resigns from parliament

1881 GLB's half-sister Mary (Molly) born

1882 Forth Bridge Company formed to build world's largest
      bridge; Hugh Bell becomes director

1884 Lowthian Bell appointed High Sheriff of County Durham;
      rebuilds East Rounton church; Hugh again elected
      Mayor of Middlesbrough; Tees ferry *Hugh Bell* launched

      Apr. – GLB attends Queen's College, London, living with
      stepgrandmother Lady Olliffe at 95 Sloane Street

1885 Lowthian Bell accepts Baronetcy; Maurice Bell goes to
      Eton – there until 1889

1886 Apr. – GLB attends Lady Margaret Hall, Oxford Uni-
      versity

      July–Aug. – Lodges with a family in Weilheim, Germany
      Grandmother Dame Margaret Bell dies

1887 Great-uncle John Bell, Sir Lowthian's business partner,
      dies

1888 June – GLB graduates from Oxford with 1st Class Honours
      Dec. – Stays in Bucharest with Sir Frank and Mary
      Lascelles (aunt); meets Valentine Chirol and Charles
      Hardinge; befriended by Queen Elizabeth of Romania
      (aka Carmen Sylva)

1889 Cousin Billy Lascelles accompanies GLB to Constantin-
      ople; they return to England via Paris

      June – Family holiday in Alsace

      GLB acts as housekeeper for her stepmother at Red Barns;
      does social work in Middlesbrough

      GLB 'comes out' in the London season, presented to
      Queen Victoria

      War in South Africa resumes after Boer attack on Cape
      Colony

1890 GLB aids Florence's group studying lives of local working
      families; becomes treasurer of its committee

1891 Washington New Hall given away as an orphanage, named
      Dame Margaret's Hall

1892 Hugh Bell stands for parliament as a Unionist Party candi-
      date, unsuccessful

1892 Apr. – GLB travels to Persia with cousin Florence Lascelles to stay with her parents in Teheran; studies Persian; begins reading the poetry of Hafiz

GLB begins romance in Persia with legation secretary Henry Cadogan; betrothal intended

Dec. – GLB returns to London with cousin Gerald Lascelles; her parents refuse permission to marry Cadogan

1893 Cadogan dies

Jan. – GLB goes to Switzerland and northern Italy with Mary Talbot

Apr. – Travels to Algiers with father to visit Great-uncle John Bell's widow Lizzie

May – Returns to London with Mary Talbot via Switzerland and Weimar, where Maurice is staying

June–Dec. – GLB in England, learning Persian and Latin; starts Arabic studies

1894 Jan.–Feb. – GLB and Hugh tour Italy

Mar.–July – GLB in England; *Safar Nameh: Persian Pictures* published

Aug.–Sept. – Family holiday in Paris, Switzerland and Austria

1895 Aug. – Family holiday in Switzerland

Sept. – GLB in England working on *The Divan of Hafiz*

1896 Mar.–Apr. – visits Italy with Hugh; takes Italian lessons

Sir Lowthian awarded Albert Medal of the Royal Society of Arts

July–Aug. – Family holiday in Switzerland

Sept. – GLB visits Lascelles, Ambassador Sir Frank and Lady Mary, at embassy country house in Potsdam

Oct.–Dec. – Returns to England; continues Persian and Arabic studies

1897 Jan.–Mar. – With sister Florence visits the Lascelles in Berlin; takes tea with the German Emperor and Empress

Apr. – Lady Mary Lascelles dies

June – *The Divan of Hafiz* published

1897 July–Aug. – GLB begins climbing during family visit to La Grave, Switzerland

Dec. – GLB and Maurice go on world tour, visiting the West Indies, Mexico, San Francisco, Honolulu, Japan, China, Singapore, Hong Kong, Burma; then return via Egypt, Greece and Constantinople

1898 Sir Lowthian acquires the estate of Mount Grace Priory and restores the house

June – GLB and Maurice return to England

Aug.–Sept. – Family holiday near Fort William, Scotland

Oct. – GLB in England studying Arabic with Sir Denison Ross

1899 Mar. – Travels to Italy, then meets up with Hugh in Athens; studies Greek antiquities, meets archaeologist David Hogarth; returns alone via Constantinople, Prague and Berlin

Aug. – Visits Bayreuth to attend opera

Aug.–Sept. – Climbs the Meije and Les Écrins

Sept.–Nov. – GLB in England; Bell Brothers becomes a public company

Nov. – Goes to Jerusalem to stay with the Rosens at German Consulate; travels via Damascus, visiting Baalbek and Beirut, Athens and Smyrna; studies Arabic and Hebrew

1900 Jan. – Maurice Bell leaves for Boer War, commanding Volunteer Service of the Yorkshire Regiment; Aunt Ada dies

Feb.–June – GLB's first desert travels, Jerusalem, Palmyra, Damascus, Baalbek, Beirut

June–July – GLB in England

Aug.–Sept. – In the Alps, climbs Mont Blanc, the Grepon and the Dru

Sept.–Dec. – GLB in England

1901 Jan.–Feb. – In London, watches funeral procession of Queen Victoria; Edward VII succeeds to the throne

Mar.–Aug. – GLB in Redcar and London

1901 Sir Lowthian sells majority holdings in the Bell companies and merges steel interests with Dorman Long (in 1902), releasing substantial funds. Hugh takes directorships in all Bell associated companies

Aug. – GLB in Bernese Oberland, climbs Schreckhorn and Engelhorn range; Gertrudspitze named after her

Sept.–Dec. – In England, takes up photographic developing

1902 Jan.–May – Travels with father and Hugo to Malta; then Sicily, to be guided by Winston Churchill; travels on alone to Greece, Turkey, Lebanon and Palestine

Maurice Bell returns from South Africa wounded

Ibn Saud regains Riyadh from Rashid dynasty in night attack

May – Boer War ends

July – GLB in Switzerland; via new route almost reaches summit of Finsteraarhorn; frostbitten

Sept.–Nov. – In England, engages lady's maid Marie Delaire

Nov. – GLB leaves for second world tour with Hugo

Dec. – Attends Delhi durbar as guest of the Viceroy

1903 Dec.–July – Goes to Afghanistan, Himalayas, Burma, Singapore, Hong Kong, China, Korea, Japan, Vancouver, climbing in the Rocky Mountains, Canada, Boston

July – Returns to England with Hugo

1904 Jan. – Sister Molly marries Charles Trevelyan

Feb. – Sir Lowthian gives £5,000 to each of his grandchildren

Apr. – Entente Cordiale established between Britain and France

Aug. – GLB at Zermatt, climbs the Matterhorn

Sept.–Nov. – GLB in England

Dec. – Studies antiquities in Paris with Salomon Reinach

20 Dec. – Sir Lowthian dies aged 88 at London home, Belgravia; Hugh succeeds to baronetcy and inherits £750,000

1904 Dec. – GLB goes on archaeological trip via Paris, Marseilles, Naples, Beirut; Haifa, Jerusalem, then takes desert route to Druze mountains, Damascus, Homs, Baalbek, Orontes valley, Aleppo; continues on horseback to Antioch, Osmaniyeh, Adana, Tarsus, Karaman; then by train to Konya, explores Binbirkilisse

1905 Apr. – Takes on Fattuh, her principal servant on future desert journeys

May – Stays in Constantinople before returning to England

June–Sept. – GLB in England, begins *The Desert and the Sown*; Sir Hugh and family move to Rounton Grange

Oct. – Studies ancient manuscripts in Paris with Reinach; writes essay on the geometry of the cruciform structure

Nov.–Dec. – In England; begins to transform the Rounton Grange gardens

1905–6 Dec.–Feb. – Travels to Gibraltar, Tangier, Spain and Paris with Sir Hugh

1906 Feb.–Dec. – GLB in England; Sir Hugh appointed Lord Lieutenant of the North Riding (25-year tenure)

Dec. – GLB and Sir Hugh arrive in Cairo, joined by Hugo from Australia

1907 Feb. – Return to England, delayed by Sir Hugh's illness

Feb.–Mar. – GLB in England

Mar.–July – In Turkey, travels on horseback across Anatolia visiting ancient sites; works with Professor Sir William Ramsay in Binbirkilisse; meets Dick Doughty-Wylie

July – Sister Elsa marries Hubert, later Admiral Sir Hubert Richmond

Aug. – GLB takes Fattuh to hospital in Constantinople; guest of Grand Vizier

Aug.–Dec. – GLB in England; publication of *The Desert and the Sown*

1908 Young Turks' Committee of Union and Progress rebel against Sultan, taking six more years to achieve full power over Ottoman Empire

1908 GLB in England all year; founding secretary of the Women's National Anti-Suffrage League; drafts *The Thousand and One Churches*; holidays in North Wales with Valentine Chirol and Frank Balfour

Doughty-Wylie unofficially rallies Turkish troops to stop massacre of Armenians; wounded, organizes relief for 22,000 refugees

Sept. – Hugo Bell ordained priest; curate of Guiseley, Leeds

Oct. – GLB trains in surveying and map-making with the Royal Geographical Society

1909 Jan.–July – Travels to Syria and Mesopotamia; on horseback, follows Euphrates to Baghdad, measures Ukhaidir, then follows Tigris to Turkey

July – In England; publication of *The Thousand and One Churches*; draws palace of Ukhaidir; writes on Armenian monasteries for Josef Strzygowski; meets Sir Percy Cox, discusses with him proposed desert journeys; begins *Amurath to Amurath*; continues with Rounton gardens, now becoming a showpiece

Stepmother Florence first president of the North Riding branch of the British Red Cross (until 1930)

1910 Feb. – GLB visits archaeological sites in Italy; pays flying visit to Munich

Hugh Bell stands as Liberal candidate for the City of London – unsuccessful. George V succeeds Edward VII

1911 Jan.–May – GLB goes via Beirut and Damascus across desert to Baghdad to check measurements of Ukhaidir; travels along Tigris

May – Meets T. E. Lawrence at Carchemish in Syria working for David Hogarth

June – Returns to England; publication of *Amurath to Amurath*

1912 GLB in England all year; involved in worldwide fundraising for relief of Constantinople after the great fire;

creates new water garden at Rounton; meets Dick Doughty-Wylie in London

1913 Jan.–Nov. – GLB in England; elected to Fellowship of the Royal Geographical Society; awarded its Gill memorial theodolite, first woman to receive an RGS award; completes *The Palace and Mosque of Ukhaidir*

Woodrow Wilson becomes 28th President of the US

Nov. – GLB travels to Damascus to organize journey to Hayyil, with intention of meeting Ibn Saud in Riyadh

Dec. – GLB and caravan leave for Hayyil

1914 Mar. – GLB arrives in Hayyil, put under house arrest

Mar.–May – Released; continues to Baghdad, through Mesopotamian and Syrian deserts; returns to England

June – Churchill persuades British parliament to approve Admiralty purchase of 51% of Anglo-Persian oil company to secure fuel for navy

14 June – Archduke Ferdinand of Austria shot at Sarajevo

July – GLB awarded Gold Medal by the Royal Geographical Society

Aug. – First World War begins; GLB gives speeches to raise troops; publication of *The Palace and Mosque at Ukhaidir*; Maurice mobilized as Lieut. Col. commanding 4th (territorial) Battalion, Green Howards

Nov. – GLB works at Lord Onslow's Hospital, Clandon Park, Surrey

Oct. – Turkey joins war as ally of Germany

British Indian Army expeditionary force occupies Shatt al Arab and creates a base at Basra

Dec. – GLB takes charge of the Missing and Wounded Office of the Red Cross, Boulogne

1915 Apr. – Maurice Bell on Western Front in France, leads attack at Fortuin

Lady Florence sets up auxiliary convalescent hospital for the Red Cross at Rounton Village Institute

1915 Apr.–Nov. – GLB opens London Missing and Wounded Office of the Red Cross

26 Apr. – Dick Doughty-Wylie dies at Gallipoli

May – British Liberal Prime Minister Asquith invites Bonar Law's Conservatives to join a coalition government; Churchill forced to resign from the Admiralty

Sept. – British win decisive battle against Turkish/Arab army at Kut and advance to Ctesiphon near Baghdad

17 Nov. – GLB leaves Sloane Street

20 Nov. – Embarks at Marseilles

26 Nov. – Dines with Lawrence and Hogarth at Port Said. Probably visits Dardanelles

30 Nov. – GLB travels to Cairo

Nov.–Dec. – Works there for Gilbert Clayton, head of civil and military intelligence

Nov. – British defeated by Turkish force at Ctesiphon, retreat to Kut

Dec. – British encircled at Kut; siege begins

1916 Jan.–Feb. – GLB in India, advises Viceroy; Arab Intelligence Bureau in Cairo authorized

Feb.–Dec. – GLB in Basra as assistant political officer with rank of major under Chief Political Officer Sir Percy Cox, reporting to GOC Indian Expeditionary Force in Iraq

Feb. – Hogarth initiates *Arab Bulletin* as a regular intelligence report; GLB its principal contributor

Mar. – British evacuate Gallipoli; Maurice wounded in France

Apr. – T. E. Lawrence attempts to bribe Turks to free Kut; has long discussions with GLB

– Turks enter Kut, population massacred; many British troops die in forced march north

May – Secret Sykes–Picot Agreement anticipates postwar division of influence in Middle East between France, Britain and Russia

1916 June – GLB appointed head of Iraq branch of the Arab Bureau as an officer of the Indian Expeditionary Force D (based in Basra)

– Maurice invalided out of active service

– Hashemites family lead revolt of Arabs against Turkish rule in western Arabia

Sept. – GLB in hospital with jaundice; then holidays on Euphrates

Oct. – Cox signs treaty with Ibn Saud

Nov. – GLB arranges visit of Ibn Saud to Basra

– Hashemite Amir Hussain, Sharif of Mecca, proclaimed King of the Hejaz

Dec. – Lloyd George becomes Prime Minister

1917 Jan.–Mar. – GLB continues in Basra, Oriental Secretary to the civil administration for Sir Percy Cox, as well as head of the Arab Bureau (Iraq)

Jan. – In western Arabia Amir Faisal with T. E. Lawrence starts march of Arab army northwards

Mar. – Turkish army vacates Baghdad; British occupy

Apr. – President Wilson asks US Congress to declare war on Germany; American troops engaged in France

– GLB moves to Baghdad after 9-day journey up Tigris

May – Occupies her permanent home in Baghdad

July – Lawrence takes Aqaba with Arab irregulars

– Cox appointed Civil Commissioner of Mesopotamia reporting to Secretary of State for India in London

Aug. – British defeat Turkish army in Gaza

Oct. – Bolsheviks take control of the Russian Revolution; Cossack troops commit atrocities in northern Mesopotamia

– British Cabinet approves Balfour Declaration favouring Palestine as a national home for the Jews (announced 2 Nov.)

– GLB awarded CBE; suffering exhaustion, admitted to convalescent hospital

1917   Nov. – Appointed editor of *Al Arab*; writing *The Arab of Mesopotamia*

Dec. – British take Jerusalem

1918   Jan. – President Wilson lists his 14 points of principle, including 'a general association of nations'

Feb. – Russia makes peace with Germany; Allied troops fight Red Army in Russia

Mar. – GLB awarded Founder's Medal of the Royal Geographical Society

July – GLB holidays on horseback in Persian mountains; women over 30 gain the vote in Britain

Sept. – GLB arranges durbar of sheikhs in Iraq

– Cox posted to Teheran; provisionally replaced by Sir Arnold Wilson as Acting Civil Commissioner; GLB's role restricted

– Lady Florence made Dame (DCIE) for her work for the Red Cross; Sir Hugh awarded CB

Oct. – Amir Faisal's army takes Damascus with Lawrence; Turks fight last battle at Sharqat, then withdraw; Turks sign Mudros Armistice, end of Ottoman Empire

Nov. – Allies sign Armistice with Germany

Dec. – GLB starts Tuesday soirées for wives of prominent Arabs; influenza pandemic reaches Baghdad

1919   Mar. – GLB prepares a paper for the Paris Peace Conference on the future of Mesopotamia; attends until A. T. Wilson arrives

Apr.–May – GLB tours France and visits Algiers with Sir Hugh; returns to Peace Conference

May–Sept. – GLB in England

June – Germany signs Treaty of Versailles accepting peace conditions, First World War ends; League of Nations initiated

Sept. – GLB visits Cairo, Jerusalem, Damascus, Beirut, Aleppo

– President Wilson suffers stroke while campaigning for

US to join the League of Nations; permanently inca-
pacitated

1919 Sept. – US Senate fails to ratify its membership of the
League of Nations

Nov.–Dec. – GLB returns to Baghdad, starts writing
Review of the Civil Administration of Mesopotamia; Marie
Delaire joins her permanently in Baghdad

1920 Jan. – Arab Bureau wound up; GLB takes archaeological
trip to Babylon site

Feb. – Organizes funding for a women's hospital in
Baghdad

Mar. – Amir Faisal elected and crowned King of Syria

Mar.–Apr. – Sir Hugh visits Baghdad

Apr. – San Remo Conference agrees terms of British
mandate over Iraq while instituting self-government

– GLB to compile annual reports on the state of Iraq
required by the League of Nations

June – Cox makes official visit to Baghdad; Sir Frank
Lascelles dies

July – French occupy Damascus; King Faisal deposed

Aug. – Treaty of Sèvres between Allies and Turkey

Oct. – Cox returns as High Commissioner for Iraq; Naqib
of Baghdad forms provisional Arab government; A. T.
Wilson leaves public service

– GLB initiates fortnightly reports to Colonial Office on
the progress of the administration in Iraq

Nov. – Resumes duties as Oriental Secretary; first meeting
of Iraq Council of State

Dec. – Publication of *Review of the Civil Administration of
Mesopotamia*, presented to parliament

1921 Feb. – Churchill appointed Secretary of State for Colonies
(including responsibility for the Middle East)

Mar. – GLB attends Cairo Conference; holidays in Egypt
with Sir Hugh; returns to Baghdad

23 June – Amir Faisal arrives in Basra

1921 29 June — Greets GLB on his arrival at Baghdad

GLB elected President of new Baghdad Public Library

Ibn Saud takes Hayyil; Rashid dynasty ends; Shammar tribesmen flee into Iraq; 3-month British miners' strike hits
steel industry

July — GLB announces result of Iraq referendum; Naqib
declares Faisal King-elect on behalf of Iraqi Council

Aug. — Faisal ibn Hussain ibn Ali crowned Faisal I of Iraq

Sept. — King invites Naqib to form Cabinet

Nov. — GLB's brother Hugo marries Frances Morkill

1922 Apr.–May — Iraq's Constituent Assembly passes electoral
law; Sir Hugh joins GLB in Jerusalem

July — GLB drafts antiquities law for Iraq

Aug. — Bell finances diminish during international reces-
sion

Oct. — Aiming to comply with the terms of the mandate,
Cox and Prime Minister Naqib sign a Treaty of Alliance
between Iraq and Great Britain giving 20 years of
British occupation in advisory capacity

13 Oct. — Faisal proclaims Treaty

Oct. — Allies and Turkey sign peace treaty officially ending
war with Turkey

— Macmillan Company donates books to Baghdad Public
Library

— Lloyd George's wartime coalition government collapses;
Bonar Law's Conservatives win election; Duke of Devon-
shire replaces Churchill with responsibility for Middle
East; Charles Trevelyan elected MP for Newcastle upon
Tyne

— Faisal, with Iraq Cabinet approval, appoints GLB Honorary Director of Antiquities for Iraq

— Air Marshall Sir John Salmond takes command of British
forces; RAF tasked with controlling tribal dissension in
Iraq

Dec. — Sir Henry Dobbs arrives as prospective High
Commissioner, in charge while Cox visits London;

GLB asked to continue as Oriental Secretary; Cox signs treaties with Ibn Saud

1923 Feb. – Organic Law (constitution) approved

Apr. – Cox signs treaty reducing British advisory occupation of Iraq to 4 years

May – Cox retires, leaves Iraq

– Transjordan declared independent under Amir Abdullah by treaty with Britain

July–Aug. – GLB travels to England via Haifa, stays with Sir Herbert Samuel, High Commissioner for Palestine; John Singer Sargeant draws her; GLB visits Churchills at Chartwell; corresponds with Lawrence on publication of *Seven Pillars of Wisdom*

July – League of Nations ratifies Turkish Peace Treaty at Conference of Lausanne

Sept. – GLB amends her will, leaving £6,000 to the British Museum for a British Iraq School of Archaeology

Oct. – Returns to Baghdad with Sylvia Henley; initiates the Iraq Museum

1924 Jan. – Ramsay MacDonald forms first Labour government in coalition with Liberals; Charles Trevelyan in Cabinet as President of Board of Education

Feb. – First national elections in Iraq

Mar. – Dorman Long wins contract to build Sydney Harbour Bridge

– King Faisal opens Iraq National Assembly

– King Hussain of the Hejaz proclaims himself Caliph of Islam following abolition of the appointment by Ataturk, but without pan-Islamic acclamation

Sept. – British–Iraq Treaty accepted by League of Nations as meeting the League's covenant

– Ibn Saud's Wahabis raid the Hashemite summer palace of Taif in the Hejaz; townspeople massacred

Oct. – Mecca falls to Ibn Saud; King Hussain abdicates in favour of his son Ali

Dec. – George V and Faisal ratify the British–Iraq Treaty

1925 Jan. – GLB briefs League of Nations' Turkish Boundary Commission

July–Oct. – GLB's last visit to England; returns to Baghdad via Beirut

Autumn – Sir Hugh, Dame Florence and Maurice move to Mount Grace Priory to economize; Rounton Grange closed

1926 Jan. – Ibn Saud ousts Faisal's brother Ali as King of the Hejaz; annexes the territory

2 Feb. – Brother Hugo dies of pneumonia

Mar. – Vita Sackville-West stays with GLB in Iraq

May – British General Strike; 7-month miners' strike cripples steel industry

14 June – First room of Iraq Museum opened

July – Treaty between Britain, Iraq and Turkey defines borders of Mosul district

12 July – GLB dies; military funeral; buried in British Cemetery, Baghdad

July – Memorial service at St Margaret's Church, Westminster; ministers pay tribute to GLB in British parliament

1927 Oil struck in Kirkuk

Dame Florence holds pageant at Mount Grace Priory in presence of Queen Mary, partly financed by sales of signed editions of Dickens's works and letters to the family

Apr. – Tributes paid to GLB at Royal Geographical Society, London

Aug. – Publication of *The Letters of Gertrude Bell* by Dame Florence, who gives celebratory dinner inviting Faisal, Prime Minister Jafar, the Dobbses, the Coxes and the Richmonds

1928 Window dedicated to GLB in St Lawrence's Church, East Rounton

1930 Commemorative bronze plaque unveiled by King Faisal; bust of GLB identifies the Gertrude Bell Principal Wing of the Iraq Museum

1930 Dame Florence Bell dies

1931 Sir Hugh Bell dies; Maurice succeeds to baronetcy

1932 British School of Archaeology in Iraq founded in London (£4,000 donation from Sir Hugh)

Iraq joins League of Nations as independent state

1933 King Faisal dies; succeeded by son Ghazi

1939 King Ghazi dies in motoring accident, succeeded by son Faisal II

1940 Rounton Grange used as a home for Second World War evacuees and for Italian prisoners of war

1947 British Treasury grant enables formation of the British Archaeological Expedition to Iraq under auspices of the School of Archaeology; permanent base in Baghdad established

1950 Rounton Grange demolished

1958 Faisal II of Iraq assassinated in coup; Iraq declared a republic

1991 Jan. – National Museum of Iraq closed during the First Gulf War

2000 Apr. – Iraq Museum reopened

2003 Apr. – Following invasion of Iraq by Americans and British, the museum was looted of some 10,000 items and closed

INDEX

Note: *ill.* following an entry indicates that there is an illustration of the subject in the plate section.

GLB in the index stands for Gertrude Lowthian Bell; WWI for World War I.

Abadan, Iran 263
Abdiyah Hanem (mother of King Faisal) 362
Abdul Hamid, Sultan of Turkey 362–3, 364
Abdul Mahsin Bey, Iraq Prime Minister 437
Abdul Rahman, Sayyid (the Naqib) 224, 391–2, 397, 406–7, 410, 411, 420, 424, 425
Abdullah (camel driver) 189
Abdullah ibn Hussain, Amir: in Constantinople 363–4; visits Storrs 261–2; 362; and Arab Revolt 362, 366, 367, 368, 371, 389; suggested King of Iraq 389; King of Transjordan 395, 398, 431–2; GLB meets 431
Abu Ghar, Iraq 216, 231
Abu Namrud (guide) 190
Adana, Turkey 126
Addis Ababa, Abyssinia 141, 155, 156, 223, 224, 238
Admiralty, British: Intelligence Division 171, 172, 254, 256
Agail tribesmen 113–14
Akhwan sect *see* Wahabi sect
Al Arab 323
al-Muqtadir, Caliph 226

Albania 152, 153–4, 173
Aleppo, Syria 116, 117, 126, 338, 339, 388
Ali (camel driver) 185, 186, 197, 206, 208, 215, 216
Ali ibn Hussain, Emir: in Arab Revolt 362, 365, 366, 368; subsequently 429, 450
Ali Sulaiman, Sheikh, Chief of the Dulaim 408, 409–10
Allenby, Gen. Edmund, 1st Viscount of Megiddo 372, 374–5, 378, 384, 387
Alpine Journal 91, 98
Alps: French 70, 78–84; Swiss 84–90, 91–8
Amery, Sir Leonard ('Leo') 419, 448
Amida (journal) 133
Amman, Jordan 190, 431
Anatolia, Turkey 126, 133, 135
Anazeh tribe 215, 228, 305, 324, 408
Anglo-Persian Oil Company 263, 360
animals 200–1, 321–2, 340; dogs 436, 439, 447, 448; gazelle 228, 322; greyhounds 321, 340; horses 102–3, 321–2; *see also* camels
Anti-Suffrage League 76
Aphrodisias, Turkey 136
Aqaba, Jordan 130, 372

Arab Bulletin 288, 291

Arab Bureau, Cairo Intelligence
Department 258–61, 262–3,
265–72, 274, 291, 292, 293, 333,
368; 'Intrusives' 269–70, 273–4,
332

Arab Independence Movement 267, 274

Arab nationalism 342, 343–51, 365, 373,
386

Arab Revolt 261–2, 265, 266–71, 273–4,
365–75; attitude of Indian
government 265, 269–70

Arabia ('Middle East') 99–101; in Sykes-
Picot Agreement 373; in San Remo
Pact 373; *see also* desert, travelling
in *and place names*

Arabia (ship) 171

Arabic language 102, 108, 112, 115–16,
315, 316

archaeology 76–7, 108, 118, 119–21, 131,
132–3, 135–7; GLB at Carchemish
133; Director of Antiquities in Iraq
443–5, 450

Areh village, Jordan 110

Armenians 130, 348–9

Ashur, Mesopotamia 134

Asir, Saudi Arabia 363

Asquith, Herbert H. 1st Earl of Oxford,
British Prime Minister 75

Auda abu Tayyi, Sheikh 372

Awali, massacre 367

Awwad 202

Babylon, Iraq 116, 132, 139, 225, 435

Baghdad: history 225–6; GLB visits, *1909*
116; under Turkish rule 300–1,
312–13; GLB in, *1914* 222–6;
British occupy, *1917* 293, 297, 311,
314, 334; Indian army surrounds
302; GLB moves to 293–4, 295–7;
GLB working in 297–300, 302–7,
309–19, 321–5, 326–7; *1919* 311;
GLB returns to work in 340–3,
346–7, 349–61; in *1920* 349–51;
Hugh Bell visits, *1920* 340–1; GLB
working in 390–4, 399–407,
411–13, 414–16, 420–8, 430, 431,

433–9; Faisal in, *1921* 404–5,
406–7, 411–12; with Faisal as King
413, 414, 415, 419, 420–31, 433,
434–7, 439; GLB in, *1926* 442–7;
GLB's house in 296–7, 437, 446,
ill.; GLB's office 306, 414–15;
cemetery 450; convent 319; Faisal's
palace 419, 423–4; Iraq Museum in
xvi, 443, 444–5, 449–50; Jews in
339; Public Library 411; GLB's
work for women in 76, 341

Bajlan, Mustafa Pasha, Chief of Khanikin
334, 335

Balad, Iraq 312

Balfour, Arthur James, 1st Earl, British
Foreign Secretary 382, 384, 385

Balfour, Col. Frank 313, 397

Balfour Declaration 382–3, 385, 399

Bani Tamim tribe 327

Baqubah, Iraq 349

Barre des Écrins mountain, France 83

Basra, Iraq 298, 299; Sayyid Talib in 267;
GLB working in 276–7, 278–81,
282–94, 295, 367, 370, 418–19;
under Turkish rule 312–13; *1917*
312, 324; Faisal arrives, *1921* 404,
405

Bayreuth, Bavaria 80

Bedouin 100, 104, 105, 122, 178, 185,
194–7, 270, 302

Beg, Muhammad 190

Beirut 121, 339

Belgrave Terrace, Number 10, London 56

Belka plain, Jordan 156

Bell, Ada (aunt of GLB) 4, 8–9, 11, 12,
104

Bell, Charles (Uncle of GLB) 4, 12–13

Bell, Elsa (later Lady Richmond; half-sister
of GLB) 4, 12, 50, 136, 168,
292–3; childhood 19, 25, 47, 48; in
Baghdad 438

Bell, Florence (*née* Olliffe; stepmother of
GLB): early life 10–11, 23, 24;
career 9, 24; meets Hugh Bell
9–10; marries Hugh 11–12; in
GLB's childhood 12–13, 14–27, 28,
29–32, 42; in GLB's youth 33, 42,

43, 46–50, 56, 58; clothes 14–15; social work 33–7, 74; and Henry James 51; and GLB as adult 144–5, 148, 253, 318–19, 320, 338; in WWI 236; D.B.E. 320; in *1925* 440, 441; after death of GLB 452; correspondence with GLB 20, 28, 30, 39, 45, 48, 57, 58, 101, 104, 113, 125, 137, 139, 171, 181, 192, 241, 247, 250, 252, 254, 260, 265–6, 290–1, 292, 293–4, 297, 308, 318, 319, 320, 323, 328, 337, 343, 351, 356, 357, 361, 399, 411, 418, 424, 427, 436, 437, 438, 441–2; writes of GLB 15, 16, 42, 46, 61, 149, 452; *ill.*:

WORKS: *Alan's Wife* (play) 24; *Angela* (play) 16; *At the Works* 34–6, 73–4; *Bluebeard* (opera) 11; essays 22; *The Letters of Gertrude Bell* 16, 448, 455

Bell, Gertrude: birth 7; childhood 4, 8, 9, 12–13, 14–27, 201; school 28–32; university years 33, 34–37, 38–42; in Bucharest 43–6; as debutante 46, 47–50; in Persia 52–9; in London, *1892–3* 59–60; mountaineering, *1897* 78–80; world tour with Maurice 63; mountaineering, *1899* 78, 80–4; in Jerusalem with Rosens 70, 101–3; travels in desert, *1900* 104–15; mountaineering, *1901–2* 84–97; world tour with Hugo 66–7, 71; at durbar in Delhi 64–5; mountaineering, *1903–4* 97–8; desert travel, *1905* 116, 121–8; archaeological work 118–21, 132–3, 135–7, 444–5; in England, *1907–8* 140–53; desert travel, *1909* 116–17, 119, 128, 132; desert travel, *1911* 117, 133–4; in England, *1912–13* 174–6; desert travels, *1913–14* 117, 177–80, 182–207; in Hayyil 208–20; return to Baghdad 221–6; journey to Damascus 226–32; in England, *1914* 157, 233–8; Wounded and Missing Enquiry Department,

Boulogne 157–9, 238–52; London, *1915* 252–4; in Cairo with British Intelligence Department 171–2, 257–73; visits Doughty-Wylie's grave? 168–9, 171–2, 266; on ship to India 273–4; in India with Viceroy 275–7; in Basra with Chief Political Officer 278–94, 370, 418–19; in Baghdad, *1919* 295–325; in England and France, *1919* 327–8, 337–8; travels 339–40; at Paris Peace Conference 330–3, 336–7, 375–82, 383, 385–6; in Baghdad, *1919–20* 340–61, 388–94; *ill.* 390–1; at Cairo conference 1, 396–9; Baghdad, *1921* 399–407; at Ramadi tribal gathering 407–10; Baghdad, *1921–23* 411–13, 414–16, 419–30; Faisal's stories of 417–18; with father, meets Abdullah 431; Baghdad, *1923–25* 431–9; in England, *1925* 439–41; Baghdad, *1926* 442–7; Director of Antiquities in Iraq 443–5, 450; death 447–9; funeral 450:

PERSONAL: appearance 43–4; character and abilities 26–7, 30, 31, 40–2, 51, 77, 78, 129–30, 145, 149, 152–3, 277–8, 446–7, 448–9, 451; portraits 73, 439; honours and awards 73, 307–8, 320–1; tributes to 448–50, 451; *ill.*:

RELATIONSHIPS: with men 148–9; Cadogan 54–8, 59, 175; Chirol 45–6; Cornwallis 433–6; Doughty-Wylie 137–47, 173–5, 179, 183, 265, 319–20; Faisal 21–2, 27, 434–5; father 15, 42, 113, 174–5, 182, 266, 328, 341, 441; with stepmother Florence 21–2, 27, 42, 265–6, 320, 441–2:

WORKS: *Amurath to Amurath* 132; *The Arab of Mesopotamia* 291–2; *The Churches and Monasteries of the Tur Abdin* 133; *The Desert and the Sown* 128, 138, 195, 197; diaries 65, 128,

Bell, Gertrude (cont.)
  131, 188, 189, 190, 191, 192–3,
  222, 462; The Divan of Hafiz 59–61,
  62; letters see under names of
  recipients; The Palace and Mosque at
  Ukhaidir 132, 180, 188; Persian
  Pictures 58–9; poetry 60–1, 62, 67;
  Review of the Civil Administration of
  Mesopotamia xvii, 316–17, 335, 356,
  401, 467; 'Self-Determination in
  Mesopotamia' 332–3; The Thousand
  and One Churches 133, 135, 140

Bell, Sir Hugh (father of GLB) 3–4, 5, 33,
  56, 104, 144–5, 148, 174, 246,
  308, 320; career 5–6, 7, 19, 34,
  129; speeches 6; first marriage 7–8,
  16; second marriage 8–10, 11–12,
  23, 174; in GLB's childhood 12, 13,
  15–16, 18, 19, 21, 26; in her youth,
  30, 31, 32, 56–7, 58, 61, 64;
  mountaineering with GLB 79–80; in
  France with GLB, 1919 327–8, 377;
  visits Iraq 340–1, 343; in Paris with
  GLB, 1922 399; in Jerusalem 430–1;
  in 1925 440–1; 1926 448, 452;
  correspondence with GLB 33, 82,
  106–7, 182, 247, 272–3, 276, 277,
  278, 284–5, 291, 292, 293–4, 297,
  308, 319–20, 322, 323, 327, 354,
  361, 394, 410, 411, 418, 427, 437,
  438, 442, 447; ill.

Bell, Hugo (half-brother of GLB) 18, 64,
  66–7, 71, 274, 340; death 442

Bell, Sir [Isaac] Lowthian (grandfather of
  GLB) 7, 56, 64, 117; career 2–3;
  made baronet 33; character 4–5,
  128; death 68; ill.

Bell, Mary ('Maisie') (later Stanley; aunt of
  GLB) 4, 8, 9–10, 11, 120

Bell, Mary (née Shield; mother of GLB) 7,
  8, 16, 174; ill.

Bell, Maurice (brother of GLB) 293;
  childhood 8, 12, 13, 15, 16–17, 20,
  21; education 26, 47; travels with
  GLB 63; in Boer War 96, 104; in
  WW1 245, 248, 251, 320; after
  WW1 320, 452

Bell, Mary ('Molly') (later Lady Trevelyan;
  half-sister of GLB) 18, 22, 27, 47,
  48, 50, 85, 148, 292–3, 319, 436;
  quoted 25, 253

Bell Brothers Ironworks 2, 5–6, 7, 34, 64
Beni Hassan tribe 123
Beni Sakhr tribe 105–6, 122–3, 124, 187
Berlin 79
Bethlehem, Palestine 102
Binbirkilisse, Turkey: archaeology 116,
  127, 133, 135; ill.
Blount, Miss (in Arabia) 114
Blunt, Lady Anne 130, 179, 258
Blunt, Wilfrid 130, 179
Bodley, Ronald 404n
Body, Dr Thomas 439
Boer War 96, 104, 138
Bonham-Carter, Sir Edgar, Judicial
  Secretary, Iraq 314–15, 316, 318
Booth, Charles 33
Bosra, Jordan 107, 108
Boulogne, France: Casino 243; Faisal in
  386; Office of Red Cross Wounded
  and Missing Enquiry Department
  157–8, 237–8, 239–42, 243–52,
  402
Bowman, Humphrey 317–18, 343
Boyle, Capt. William H. D. 369
Brémond, Col. Edouard 369
British Empire 6–7, 64, 273, 294, 308
British Museum 64, 137, 440, 444
Brooking, Gen. H. T. 282
Browne, Edward G. 60
Bucharest 43–6
Burgon, John 39
Burgoyne, Elizabeth 438
Burmah Oil 263
Burnett, Dr James 25–6
Burqu, Jordan 187
Bush, Capt. Eric Wheeler 170, 171
Bute, island, Scotland 7
Byron, George Gordon, 6th Baronet 111
Byzantine empire 121, 133, 135, 136, 226

Cabinet, Iraq 391, 392, 393, 420, 424
Cadogan, Henry 54–8, 59, 139, 145, 148,
  175

Cairo, Egypt 179; GLB arrives in 171–2; Hotels 258; British Intelligence Bureau 171, 172, 234, 254–5, 256, 257–63, 265–73, 274, 283–4; *see also* Arab Bureau

Cairo Conference, *1921* 1, 395–9, 401, 432–3

camels 112, 201, 228–9

Carchemish, Syria 117, 133–4, 180, 259, 279

Carlyon, L. A. 168–9

Carol, King of Romania 44

Carruthers, Douglas (cartographer)181

Cecil, Robert, 1st Viscount of Chelwood 242, 246, 247, 248, 252, 253, 328, 357, 384

Chalabi, Musa 296, 321

Chamier, Captain 347–8

Chicago, USA 67

Chirol, Sir Valentine Ignatius ('Domnul') 45–6, 80, 131, 140, 152; in Constantinople 46; in India 64, 271–2, 273, 275; in Paris 328, 377, 380; GLB's letters to 56–7, 70, 72, 128, 142, 174, 182–3, 193, 243, 244–5, 246, 248, 249, 250, 253, 282, 283, 286, 313–14, 320, 336, 341, 342–3, 393, 399; obituary of GLB 448, 452

Christian sects in Mesopotamia 324

Churchill, Winston 34, 263, 309, 332, 359, 384, 440; in Sicily, *1902* 120; on mustard gas 344; at Cairo Conference 1, 395, 396–9, 400, 401, 432–3; subsequently 403, 423; *ill.*

City of Rio de Janeiro (steamship) 63

Clandon Park, Surrey, England: hospital 157, 236–7

Clayton, Gen. Sir Gilbert 258, 269, 271, 272, 339, 351, 368, 369, 382, 383, 433

Coe, Jean 164–5, 170

Collier, Eric and Gerard 85–6

Colonial Office, London 265, 412, 421

Constantinople, Turkey 139, 171, 179, 301; Hashemites in 261, 363–4;

GLB visits, *1889* 46; *1905* 116; *1909* 117, 128n; in WWI 160

Constituent Assembly, Iraq 390, 425, 436, 445

Cooper Abbs, K. E. M. 5

Cornwallis, Sir Kinahan 292, 395, 400, 433–4; in Baghdad 405, 407, 411, 421, 422–3, 425, 430, 434–6, 439; in London 441; in Iraq, *1926* 443, 447, 448; writes of GLB 292; *ill.*

Coronation, King Faisal of Iraq 412

Council of State, Iraq 391, 392, 393, 396, 407

Cox, Sir Percy Z., High Commissioner for Iraq 179, 418; at Basra 276–7, 278, 285–6, 287, 293; in Baghdad 293, 295–6, 297, 299, 302–3, 304, 305, 307, 310, 326, 335, 341, 350, 356–7; moved to Teheran 325, 353–4; in London 355; in Baghdad, *1920* 355, 359, 360–1, 390, 391, 392, 393; at Cairo Conference *1921* 395, 396–8, 401, 433; in Baghdad subsequently 402, 403–5, 407, 411, 412, 415, 420, 421, 423, 430, 438; controls Iraq during Faisal's illness 424–5; *1923* 432; in London 437; leaves Iraq 437; *ill.*

Crackenthorpe, Bertie 148

Cromer, Evelyn Baring, 1st Earl, British Consul-General in Egypt 99

Croudace, Camilla 28–9, 31, 32

Ctesiphon, Mesopotamia 116, 283, 400, 410

Cubitt, Thomas 9

Cubitt, Sir William 9

Curzon, George Nathaniel, 1st Marquess of Kedleston 64–5, 385 Viceroy of India

Cyprus 432

Dair al Zor, Syria 347–8

Daja tribe 122–3

Damascus, Syria 111, 113, 115, 116, 117, 125, 175, 190, 213; GLB in, *1913* 180–4; Maidan 183; Palace Hotel

Damascus, Syria (*cont.*)
　　180–1; Faisal in with Jemal Pasha
　　365; *1914* 230–1; Arabs advance on
　　372–4; British take, *1918* 374, 384;
　　1919 339; under French Mandate
　　386, 387–8, 390, 391
Davidson, Iris 435
Davidson, Nigel 421, 435, 438–9
Deedes, Sir Wyndham 234, 398–9
Delaire, Marie (lady's maid) 140, 145,
　　238, 252, 290, 338, 339, 439, 441;
　　in Baghdad 340, 435, 447, 448
Delhi, India: *1903* 64–5, *1916* 271, 272,
　　275, 276
Der'a, Syria 374
desert, travelling in 128–32; *1900*
　　104–15; *1905* 116, 121–8; *1909*
　　116–17, 119, 128, 132; *1911* 117,
　　133–4; *1913–14* 117, 175–80,
　　182–207, 220–3, 226–32; *The
　　Desert and the Sown* 128, 138, 195,
　　197
Dickens, Charles 24, 35, 47
Director of Antiquities in Iraq (GLB)
　　443–5, 450
Diwaniyah, Iraq 349
Dobbs, Sir Henry 312–13, 415, 437–8,
　　446; after GLB's death 449, 450,
　　451
Dorman Long Company 64, 117, 399
Doughty, Charles Montague 137, 155,
　　369; *Arabia Deserta* 137, 142, 179,
　　194, 199, 207, 208, 210
Doughty-Wylie, Charles ('Dick') 137–9,
　　140–68, 170–1, 173–4, 179, 265,
　　319, 327; career 137–8; in Young
　　Turks' rebellion 140; at Rounton
　　146–7, 149; in London 141–2,
　　149–50, 154, 159–62, 165, 250;
　　letters to GLB 147, 149–51,
　　153–4, 155–7, 158, 163–4, 165,
　　166, 180, 188, 223, 249; GLB's
　　letters to and diary entries for 140,
　　160–1, 162–3, 166, 180, 184, 188,
　　191, 192–3, 198, 200, 203, 205,
　　216, 221, 222, 223, 227, 228, 230,
　　231, 462; letter to his mother-in-

law 164–5; at Gallipoli 166–7;
　　death 164, 167–8, 253; visitor to
　　grave 168–72, 266; *ill.*
Doughty-Wylie, Lilian ('Judith') 138, 139,
　　141, 142–3, 144, 145, 150–1, 153,
　　154; in France 159; threatens suicide
　　163, 164–6; widowed 168, 170–1;
　　visits husband's grave 169–71; *ill.*
Drower, Edward 421
Druze, Jebel (mountains), Jordan 105,
　　116, 122, 184, 259
Druze tribes: GLB visits, *1900* 108,
　　109–11; *1905* 122, 124–5, 266;
　　1913 185–6; rebel, *1925* 389–90
Dulaim tribe 408, 450
Duris, Lebanon *ill.*

East Rounton church 98
education: Florence Bell's ideas 24–6; in
　　Iraq 316–17, 342, 349; Turkish
　　316–17
Egypt 123, 258, 275–6, 339; *see also* Cairo
electoral systems 401–3
Engelhörner mountain range, Switzerland
　　86, 87–90
Enver Pasha Gen. Ismael, Turkish Minister
　　of War 366
Erskine, Col. 223
Euphrates River 116, 119, 225, 263, 299,
　　300, 303, 408; mapping, *1909* 132;
　　1917 312
Everybody's Weekly 416

Fahad Beg ibn Hadhdbal, Sheikh 228–9,
　　289, 321, 304–5, 324, 391, 408,
　　409–10
Faisal ibn Hussain, Sharif, King of Iraq:
　　early life 362, 363; in
　　Constantinople 261, 363, 364; with
　　Turkish army 363–4; in Arab
　　Revolt 364–75; TEL first meets
　　367–8; Allenby meets 374–5; GLB
　　first meets 381–2, describes GLB
　　416–18; at Paris Peace Conference
　　375, 377, 379, 381, 384–5, 389; in
　　London, *1919* 386; returns to Syria,
　　1919 386–7; King of Syria 387–8;

leaves Syria 388–9; prospects of throne of Iraq 1, 395, 396, 397–8, 400–1; in Baghdad, *1921* 404–5, 406–7, 411–12; at Ramadi gathering 407–10; coronation 412; in Baghdad as King 413, 414, 415, 419, 420–31, 433, 434–6, 437, 439; appendicitis 424; family 425–8; in London, *1925* 441; in Iraq, *1926* 443, 445–6; after GLB's death 449, 450; *ill.*

Fallujah, Iraq 408

Fao, Kuwait 264

Farrer, Reginald 71, 72

Fatima (of Hayyil) 209, 214–15, 219

Fattuh (Armenian servant) 126–7, 136, 137, 181, 184, 188, 189, 190, 191, 199, 201, 203, 205, 215, 222, 226, 338; hospitalized 139–40; in *1919* 339–40; *ill.*

Fellah (camelherd) 184, 186, 197, 215, 226

Ferdinand, Archduke of Austria 234

Ferid Pasha, Grand Vizier 139, 140

Finsteraarhorn mountain, Switzerland 91–7; *ill.*

Fisher, Admiral of the Fleet John, 1st Baron Kilverstone, British First Sea Lord 263

Foch, Marshal of France 329

Foreign Office, British 177, 178, 180, 191, 254, 256, 257, 269, 270–1

Fortuin, Belgium 251

franchise 24, 73–6

Franco-British Declaration, *1918* 331, 332, 333, 345, 375, 379

Führer, Heinrich and Ulrich (mountain guides) 84, 85, 86–90, 91–8; *ill.*

Furse, Revd Michael 66

Gallipoli: campaign 159–60, 163, 166–8; D-W's grave 167, 168–71, 172

Garah 228

gardening 69, 70, 71–2

Gardiner, Prof. S. R. 40

Garland, Maj. H. G. 371

gas, mustard 344

gazelle 228, 322

Gazetteer of Arabia 276

George V, King of England 448

Georges-Picot, François 269, 373, 378

Germany: in WW1 233–4; after WW1 376

Ghanimat tribe 105

Ghazi, Amir (son of King Faisal) xvii, 425–6, 428

Ghiath tribe 125

Glion, Switzerland 70

Gouraud, Gen. Henri J. E. 387–8

Greece 119

Green, J. R. 20, 31

Grey, Edward, 1st Viscount Falloden, British Foreign Secretary 235–6, 257

Grieve, Miss (in Arabia) 114

Hafiz (Persian poet) 55, 59–61, 62, 174, 175

Haifa, Israel 115–16, 259

Haldane, Gen. Sir Aylmer 412

Halil Pasha, Gen. 284

Hall, Capt. R. 171, 256, 271

Hamad (*rafiq*) 185

Hamawand tribe 334

Hamid Khan 411

Hamilton, Gen. Sir Ian C. in C. Mediterranean Expeditionary Forces 167, 168

Harb al Daransheh, Sheikh 199–200, 201; *ill.*

Harb tribe 369

Hardinge, Charles, 1st Baron Penshurst, Viceroy of India 45, 264–5, 270–1, 272–3, 274, 277, 294, 365; GLB meets 275, 276; GLB's letters to 283–4, 394, 429

harems 201, 209–10, 217, 363; *ill.*

Harithya, Baghdad 419, 426, 427–8

Harrison, Marguerite 414–15

Hasa Province, Saudi Arabia 225, 287

Hashemites 261, 333, 362–3, 405, 432; *see also* Hussain ibn Ali el-Aun, Sharif

Hasineh tribe 114

Hassan, Sayyid, mujtahid 346–7, 412

Hawr al Hammar lagoon, Iraq 281–2

Hayyil, Saudi Arabia 117, 153, 177, 178, 179, 181, 182, 204, 206–7; GLB in 208–20, 222, 231; Ibn Saud takes, 1921 429; ill.

Hejaz: and Arab Revolt 261–2, 268, 274, 362, 365, 371, 374; Sauds attack 428–9, 430; see also place names

Henley, Sylvia (née Stanley) 120, 440, 441, 443

Herbert, Aubrey 71, 260, 283–4, 380

Hickey, Michael 169, 171

Hilah (wife of Muhammad Abu Tayyi) 201–2

Hogarth, David 41; archaeology 119, 133, 134, 136; with Arab Bureau 171, 172, 179, 254–5, 257, 258, 259, 261; after GLB's death 449

Hogarth, Janet (later Courtney) xvi, 41–2, 76, 137, 254–5, 439, 440

Homs, Syria 125–6

horse riding 103, 112

Hourani, Albert 195

Howeitat tribe 123, 199–202, 203, 450; ill.

Huber, Charles 178

Hussain ibn Ali el-Aun, Emir, Sharif of Mecca 362; detained in Constantinople 261, 363; as father 363; McMahon correspondence 262, 267–8, 269, 373, 389; and Arab Revolt 261, 262, 274, 364–8, 373–4; subsequently 378, 386; abdication 428–9; and Faisal 389, 428, 430; last years 431–2

Hussaina, Amira, Queen of Iraq (wife of King Faisal) 426–7, 428

Ibn Mutab, Sheikh 187

Ibn Rashid, Amir 178, 187, 220

Ibn Saud, Abdul Aziz, King of Saudi Arabia 177–8, 187, 204, 221, 225, 287–9, 307, 333, 405; in Basra 287–9; described by GLB 288; his view of GLB 289; takes Hayyil 429; attacks

Hejaz and Hashemites 428–9, 430, 432; ill.

Ibrahim (of Hayyil) 210, 211, 212–13, 214–17, 219, 231

India 99: Lord Curzon's durbar 64–5; and Mesopotamia 263, 264, 268, 270; government attitude to Arabia 264–5, 268, 269–70; GLB visits Viceroy 271–2, 274, 275–6

India Office, London 269, 307, 356, 359

Indian Army Expeditionary Force D 264–5, 280, 286, 302, 323

Intrusives 269–70, 273–4, 332

Iraq 116, 345; borders 325, 347, 348, 432, 445; taxation 312–13, 349–50, 359; After WWI 332–3, 345; Franco-British Declaration, 1918 331, 332–3, 345, 375, 379; British Mandate 345, 355, 390, 398, 420–3; elections, 1921 401–3; referendum, 1921 407; British-Iraq Treaty, 1922 420–1, 423, 425, 436–7, 444; elections, 1923 437–8; Organic Law 425, 436, 445; tripartite treaty with Britain and Turkey 445; see also Baghdad; Mesopotamia

Iraq Museum xvi, 443, 444–5; 'Gertrude Bell Room' 449–50

Ironside, Gen. Sir Edmund, C in C. British Forces, Persia, later C.I.G.S. and 1st Baron 395–6

Istabulat, Iraq 312

Jaf tribe 334

Jafar Pasha el Askeri, Iraq Minister of Defence, Ambassador to Great Britain 372, 391, 392, 393, 396

Jamal Zahawi 406

James, Henry 50–1: The Awkward Age 51

Jaudat Bey 427

Jemal Pasha, Gen. Turkish Governor-General of Syria 365, 366, 373, 392

Jerusalem 100–1; GLB's early visits 70, 99, 101–4, 114, 115; Hotel Jerusalem 101–2; Jews in 101, 384, 385; 1919 339

Jewish Legion 384
Jews 100, 101, 339, 382–6, 398–9
Jidda, Saudi Arabia 364, 366, 367, 369, 373
Jof, Saudi Arabia 202, 215, 220
John, Augustus 381
Jones, Miss (hospital matron) 290, 343
Jordan Valley 104–5, 121–2
Judicial System, Iraq 314–16

Kadhimain, Iraq 346–7
Karbala, Iraq 132, 222, 267, 304, 317; pilgrim burial at 311; 1917 312, 323–4
Kemal, Ismail 128n
Kemal, Mustafa (Ataturk) President of Republic of Turkey 428
Kerak, Jordan 105, 257
Khanikin (Khaniqin, Khanakin), Iraq 334–6; King Faisal's farm 419, 443
Kharaneh castle, Jordan 189
Kiamil 128n
Kiepert, Heinrich (map-maker) 102
Kifri, Iraq 349
Kirkuk, Iraq 334, 336, 337, 433
Kish, Iraq 444
Kitchener, Field Marshal Horatio H., 1st Earl of Khartoum 224; and Arab Revolt 262, 267, 271, 273, 274, 333, 364
Klug, Miss (governess) 17, 18, 26
Konya, Anatolia: GLB in, 1905 121, 127; 1907, 135, 137, 138–9; Young Turks in 140; refugees in 142–3
Kuntze, Helene 91
Kurdistan 337, 348, 412, 425, 432–3
Kurds 304, 324, 337, 348, 412; revolt against Turks, 1917 334–6; at Paris Peace Conference 337; after Cairo Conference 432–3
Kut (Kut el Amara), Mesopotamia: siege and capture 283–4, 293, 418–19; rebuilt 311

Lady Margaret Hall, Oxford 32–3, 38–42, 43, 152

Lake, Gen. Sir Percy C. in C. Indian Expeditionary force D 276
Lake of Egerdir, Turkey 136
Langridge, Edith 41
Lascelles, Billy 43, 44, 46, 50, 148
Lascelles, Florence 20, 43, 52, 80, 320
Lascelles, Sir Frank, British Ambassador to Germany 12, 52, 79, 80
Lascelles, Gerald 43, 56
Lascelles, Mary (née Olliffe) 12, 43–6, 52, 54; death 60, 79
Laurence, Alec 75
Lausanne, Treaty of 432
Law, Andrew Bonar, British Prime Minister 437
Lawrence, T. E. xiv, xvi, 194, 278, 280, 326; at Carchemish 133–4, 180; in Cairo 172, 258, 260–1, 265, 266, 267–8, 269, 274; in Basra, and siege of Kut 283–4, 418–19; and Arab Revolt 365, 367–72, 373–4, 416; at Paris Peace Conference 375, 377–8, 379, 380; subsequently 395, 396; at Cairo Conference 1, 396–8; later career 448; writes of GLB 419, 448–9; Seven Pillars of Wisdom 365, 368, 370, 418–19, 433–4; ill.
Lawrence, Will (brother of T. E.) 172, 266
League of Nations 331, 355, 399, 420, 425; Boundary Commission 432, 445
Library, Baghdad Public 411
Lloyd, George Ambrose, 1st Baron 260
Lloyd George, David, 1st Earl of Dwyfor, British Prime Minister 34, 75, 378, 379, 382, 384, 386
London: No. 10 Belgrave Terrace 56; GLB visits 1898 63–4; 1907 140; 1912–13 141–2; 1919 327; 1925 439–40; Half Moon Street 141, 150, 159, 250; National Portrait Gallery 73; parks 72; No. 95 Sloane Street 9, 11, 63, 69, 154, 171, 224, 252, 439, 440; Red Cross Wounded and Missing Enquiry Department 252, 253, 254; School of Oriental Studies 52, 59
Louis of Orléans, Prince 83

Lowther, Milly 327
Lulua (of Hayyil) 209, 218
Lutyens, Sir Edwin (architect) 275

Macmillan, Margaret 375
MacMunn, Gen. Sir George 277–8, 281
Madeba, Jordan 189
Mahan, Alfred Thayer 99
Mackinnon, Dr 231
Malcolm, Ian 382
Mallet, Sir Louis, British Ambassador to
    Turkey 179, 191, 193
mandrake 70–1
Manners for Women 63
Marius (mountain guide) 80, 81, 82
Marshall, Captain: murdered 324
Marshall, Herbert (cousin of GLB) 32
Marshall, Horace (cousin of GLB) 20, 21,
    32; GLB's letters to 44, 52–3
Marshall, Thomas 20, 119
Marshall, Lt. Gen. Sir William 299
Mathon (mountain guide) 80, 81–2
Matterhorn mountain, Switzerland 97–8
Maude, Gen. Sir Stanley 293, 297–8, 299,
    334–5; GLB writes of 298
May, Major 306
McMahon, Sir Henry, High Commissioner
    for Egypt 258, 269; correspondence
    with Hussain 262, 267, 268, 373,
    389
Mecca, Saudia Arabia 261, 262, 362, 364,
    366
Medina, Saudia Arabia 366, 369
Meije mountain, France 78, 80–3
Meissner, Heinrich August (railway
    engineer) 225
Melos, Greece 119
Mesopotamia: definition 263, 298; and
    India 263, 264, 268, 270; under
    Turkish rule 300–1; British rule
    311; Department of Pious Bequests
    317; judicial system 314–16; The
    Arab of Mesopotamia 291–2; Review of
    the Civil Administration of Mesopotamia
    xvii, 316–17, 335, 356, 401, 467;
    'Self-Determination in Mesopotamia'
    332–3; see also place names

Mesopotamian Campaign 263–5, 276, 283
Mesopotamian League 347–8
Mhailam (rafiq) 206
Middlesbrough, Yorkshire 6, 7, 10, 11, 19,
    36, 76; Port Clarence 2, 5, 7, 8,
    63, 68; railway station 12;
    Washington New Hall 3, 4–5, 7, 8;
    Winter Garden 36–7
Miletus, Turkey 136
Mill, John Stuart 65, 73, 77
Misma Mountains, Saudi Arabia 178–9,
    205, 206
Missing Sewell, Elizabeth 26
Moab hills, Jordan 104
Mons campaign 240
Mont Blanc mountain France 84–5
Montagu, Sir Edwin, British Secretary of
    State for India 357–8, 382–3, 384
Montessori, Maria 25
Morris, William 2, 3, 17, 68
Mosul, Mesopotamia 323, 348, 412,
    432–3, 445; 1917 312; 1918 336
Mount Grace Priory, Nr Northallerton,
    Yorkshire 4, 5, 152, 440, 448, 452
Mount Hermon, Israel 230
mountaineering 78–98, 128
Mshetta, Jordan 188
Mudi (wife of Muhammad ibn Rashid) 209,
    217–18, 219
Muhammad (Druze muleteer) 105, 108
Muhammad (Hasineh Sheikh) 114–15
Muhammad (Kurdish Sheikh) 433
Muhammad Abu Tayyi, Sheikh 200–1, 202
Muhammad al-Bessam 181–2
Muhammad al-Marawi (guide) 181–2,
    183–4, 185, 197, 206, 208, 211,
    212, 216
Muhammad Beg (of Amman) 190
Muhammad Hussain Khan 222
Muhammad ibn Rashid 209, 214
Musa, Wady 106
Mustafa (farm worker) 197
Mustafa Pasha, Khanikin chief 335

Najaf, Iraq 117, 220, 222, 267, 317, 346;
    pilgrim burial at 311; in 1917 324
Naji, Haji 400, 415, 448

Namoud (merchant) 122–3
Namrud, Abu 190
Naqib see Abdul Rahman, Sayyid
National Portrait Gallery 73
Nasiriyeh, Iraq 282, 283
Nefud desert 178, 204–6, 211, 222–3
Nejd desert 113, 117, 178, 181–2, 183, 193, 205, 206, 226, 287
New York Times 414
Newcastle upon Tyne 2–3, 5, 7
Nîmes, France 58
Nixon, Gen. Sir John 283
Nolde, Baron Emmanuel 178
North Eastern Railway (Britain) 2, 6, 12, 64, 235
Nuri Pasha Sayyid 391, 413
Nusr ed Din 110

oil 263, 294, 308–9
Olliffe, Florence see Bell
Olliffe, Dr Sir Joseph 9, 24
Olliffe, Lady 11, 24, 28, 47, 69
Olliffe, Mary see Lascelles
Olliffe, Tommy 28, 33
Ottoman Bank 182
Ottoman Empire 100, 177, 178, 187, 188, 193, 226, 234, 256, 292, 300, 301–2
Oxford University: GLB a student 32–3, 38–42, 43, 152; archaeological expedition 444

Palestine 339, 382–6; Balfour Declaration 382–3, 385, 399; discussed at Cairo Conference 398–9; see also place names
Palmyra, Syria 113, 230
Pankhurst, Christabel (Suffragette) 74
Paradis, Marie (climber) 84
Paris, France: Florence Olliffe's early life in 9, 10, 11; GLB in, 1904 120–1; Office of Wounded and Missing Enquiry Department 237, 241, 242; GLB in with father, 1919 328; Hotel Majestic 376–7, 378
Paris Peace Conference, 1919 327, 329–33, 336–7, 344, 345, 348,

357, 375–6, 384–5, 389; Treaty of Versailles 386
Parkinson, Dr Sir Thomas 439
Parliament, British 2, 356, 440
Pattinson, Margaret (later Lady Bell; grandmother of GLB) 3, 4, 33, 68
Pease, Will 148
Pergamon, Turkey 119
Persia 52–7, 58–9, 307
Persian language 52, 59, 102, 116
Petra, Jordan 105, 106
Philby, Harry St John Bridger 289, 403–6
photography 118–19, 201
Pichon, Stéphen 379
Picot, François Georges 269, 373, 378
'pilgrim corpses' 311
Port Said 171, 172, 259, 338
Poynter, Sir Edward 16

Queen's College, London 29–32
Quz Abu-al-Ir, battle 363–4

Rabegh, Saudi Arabia 367, 369
Railway, North Eastern (in Britain) 2, 6, 12, 64, 235
railway, Turkish (in Mesopotamia) 228, 235, 261, 263; construction 25; attacked 349, 372
Ramadi, tribal gathering at 407–10
Ramsay, Sir William 116, 127, 135–6, 137, 138–9, 140
Rashids 177–8, 204, 220, 221, 231, 287
Red Barns, Redcar 3, 8, 9, 12–13, 17, 18–19, 20, 21–2, 56, 68; ill.
Red Cross 239; Wounded and Missing Enquiry Department see under Boulogne; London; Paris
Redcar, North Yorkshire 3, 10, 33–4; beach 17, 21; park 21; railway stop 12;
Reeves, Mr (of Royal Geographical Society) 119
Reichenbach Falls, Switzerland 86
Reinach, Prof. Salomon 120–1, 449
religion 31, 65, 66–7
Revue Archéologique 120, 121
Richmond, Admiral Sir Herbert 136, 438

Ritchie, Anne, Lady 30, 276–7

Ritchie, Sir Richmond, British Permanent Under-secretary of State for India 179, 276

Riu tribe 221

River Clyde (ship) 166, 167, 168, 171

Riyadh 178, 220; Ibn Saud takes 287

Robins, Elizabeth (actress) 24, 50, 73, 148

Robinson, William 72

Rocky Mountains, Canada 67, 97

Romania 43–5

Rosen, Friedrich (German Consul in Jerusalem) and Nina 101, 102, 103, 107, 108, 115

Ross, Sir Edward Denison, Director, School of Oriental Studies, London 59–60, 61, 67

Rounton, Yorkshire 6; East Rounton church 98

Rounton Grange 3, 4, 5, 56, 68–9, 140, 143, 144, 149, 441–2; garden 69, 70–1, 72–3, 453; described 68; tapestry 68, 453; Doughty-Wylie's visit 146–7; in WWI 233, 236; Bells leave 440, 452; demolished 452–3; *ill.*

Royal Air Force 344, 429, 433

Royal Flying Corps 266

Royal Geographical Society 119, 177, 181; Founder's Medal 308; Gill Memorial Award 73

Royal Photographic Society 118

Rumi, Jalal ad-Din 139

Russell, Bertrand, 3rd Earl 8

Russell, Diana 238, 239, 241, 247

Russell, Flora 48, 69, 73, 238, 241; GLB's letters to 58–9

Russia: *1914* 234; and Kurds, *1917* 334–5; *1918* 328

Ruwalla tribe 187, 202, 209, 220

Sackville-West, Vita 446–7

Saddam Hussein, President of Iraq 282

Safeh territory, Syria 124

Safwat Pasha, Treasurer to King Faisal 422

Saleh village, Syria 125

Salih (watchman of Hayyil) 210

Salim (nephew of Muhammad al-Marawi) 197

Salisbury, Robert Cecil, 3rd Marquis of, British Prime Minister 125

Salkhad, Syria 108, 109, 123–4, 125

'salon power' 130

Salt, Jordan 122

Samuel, Sir Herbert, High Commissioner for Palestine 386, 398

San Remo Pact 373, 387–8

Santa Flavia, Sicily 120

Sargent, John Singer 439

Sasun Effendi Eskail 392, 393, 396

Saudi Arabia 221, 428

Sayyid (of Hayyil) 210, 216, 218

Sayyid ibn Murted, Sheikh 203–4

Sayyid the Sherari (camel driver) 197, 203, 226

School of Oriental Studies, London 52, 59

Schreckhorn mountain, Switzerland 85–6

Secunderabad Hospital, Le Touquet, France 242–3

Sedd-el-Bahr village, Iraq 166–7, 168

Shahraban, Iraq 349

Shakespear, Capt. William H. I. 178, 287, 405

Shalash, Ramadhan al 347

Shamiyah tribe 292

Shammar tribe 178, 197, 202, 203–4, 205, 213, 324, 348

Shatt-al-Arab 263, 276, 281, 418

Shaw, Lt.-Col. G. H. 251

Shelley, Percy Bysshe 230

Sherarat tribe 122–3, 202, 203–4, 205

Shia tribes 301, 302, 315, 324, 345, 346, 406

Shield, Mary (later Bell; mother of GLB) 7, 8, 16, 174; *ill.*

Simeon Stylites 126

Simla, India 275

Sinderson, Dr Sir Harry, Dean, Baghdad Medical College 438

Spencer, Herbert 39

Spring-Rice, Sir Cecil, British Ambassador to the US 320

Stanley, Sylvia (*née* Henley) 120, 440, 441, 443

Stanley of Alderley, Lady 8, 11, 33
Stanley of Alderley, Lord 52
Stark, Freya 130
Steed, Wickham, Editor, *The Times* 380
Storrs, Sir Ronald 260, 261–2, 304, 339,
    364, 367, 388, 432
Strachey, John St Loe 236
Strong, S. Arthur 61
Strutt, E. L. 98
Strzygowski, Josef 121, 127, 133
Sudan 314, 315
Suez Canal 99
suffrage and suffragettes 24, 73–6
suicide 163, 164, 168, 447–8
Sulaiman tribe 203
Sulaimaniyah, Iraq 317, 334, 335, 336,
    337, 433
Sunday Times 396
Sunni sect 224, 301, 302, 345–6, 391
Sykes, Sir Mark 259–60, 269, 331, 373,
    384; death 376
Sykes-Picot Agreement 331, 336, 373,
    382; Faisal learns of 373, 378
Syria: and WWI outbreak 235; in Sykes-
    Picot Agreement 373, 378; and
    Franco-British Declaration, *1918*
    331, 375, 379; *1919* 386; Faisal as
    King 387–8, 389; under French
    Mandate 386–90; *see also* place names

Tafas village, Hejaz, Saudi Arabia 374
Taif, Hejaz, Saudi Arabia 364, 366, 429
Talbot, Mary 41, 49
Talib, Sayyid, Iraq Interior Minister 235,
    267, 397, 402–3
Tallal, Sheikh of Tafas 374
taxation, Iraq 312–13, 349–50, 359
Taylor, A. J. P. 244
Thesiger, Wilfred 282
Thomas, Capt. (musician) 400
Thomas, Lowell J. 396
Thompson, Campbell 279, 281
Tigris River 263, 264, 295, 303: GLB at,
    1909 116–17; *1914* 224, 225; *1917*
    312; journey down, *1919* 326; GLB
    describes, *1921* 413; picnic by, *1922*
    423

Times, The 43, 45, 140, 237; GLB's
    obituary notices 448, 451, 452
Times of India 451–2
Tod, Arthur 224–5
Tod, Aurelia 225, 343
Tokyo 71
Townshend, Maj.-Gen. Charles 283
Transjordan 395, 398, 429, 430, 431
Treaty of Lausanne 432
Treaty of Versailles 386
Trenchard, Air Marshal Sir Hugh M. 1st
    Viscount Trenchard 395
Trevelyan, George 438
Trevelyan, Pauline 439–40
Tur Abdin plateau, Anatolia 133
Turkey and Turks: army 264–5; GLB's
    prewar travels in 116, 117; Faisal
    with army 363, 365, 366; and
    Armenians 348–9; and Arab Revolt
    364, 365, 366–7, 369–74; on
    outbreak of WWI 234, 235; *1917*
    323–4; at Kut 283–4; at Tafal 374;
    after WWI 331; Treaty of Lausanne
    432; *1924* invasion 432; tripartite
    treaty with Britain and Iraq 445; *see
    also* Constantinople; Ottoman
    Empire; Young Turks
Turkiyyeh (of Hayyil) 209–11, 213–14,
    217, 218, 219

Ukhaidir palace, Iraq 116, 117, 132, 141;
    ill.
Ur of the Chaldaes, Iraq 282, 444
utilitarianism 65–6, 67

Versailles, Treaty of 386
Victoria, Queen 7
Vogue 236, 340

Wahabi sect (Akhwan) 177, 187, 287, 333,
    429, 430
Wales 152
Walford, Capt. Garth 166–7
Wallington Hall, Northumberland 70
Wang, Kirsten 13
War Office 234–5, 243, 245, 247, 248,
    264, 269, 307, 344; 'fear telegram'

War Office (*cont.*)
  237, 248–9; Joint War Committee
  Report, *1914* 243–4, 245, 249; and
  Mesopotamian Campaign 286–7
Ware, Major Fabian 247, 248
Washington New Hall, Nr Newcastle upon
  Tyne 3, 4–5, 7, 8
water, in desert 111, 112, 187, 198, 199,
  221–2
Watson, Sir Harry 339
Webb, Philip (architect) 17, 68
Weizmann, Chaim Azriel, President of
  Israel 384–5, 386
Wejh, Saudi Arabia 371, 372
Wemyss, Admiral of the Fleet Rosslyn, 1st
  Baron Wester-Wemyss 368
Whymper, Edward (climber) 83, 97
Williams, Col. Weir 166, 167
Wilson, Sir Arnold (A. T.): Civil
  Commissioner for Iraq, character
  and career 286, 352; at Basra 286,
  293, 294; in Baghdad 305, 306–7,
  325, 326, 327, 332, 342, 344, 350,
  351–5, 356, 357, 358–9, 397; view
  of GLB 352–4; leaves Baghdad 360;
  subsequent career 360; at Paris
  Peace Conference 336, 377, 378; at
  Cairo Conference 396
Wilson, J. M. 444
Wilson, Thomas Woodrow, US President
  330–1, 345, 375–6, 379
Wingate, Gen. Sir Reginald F. Governor-
  general of the Sudan, Sirdar of the
  Egyptian Army 224, 307, 368
Wizeh, Iraq 227

women: in Baghdad 341, 342–3; Howeitat
  201–2; suffrage and suffragettes 24,
  73–6; *see also* harems
Woolf, Virginia 25
Woolley, Leonard 172, 259, 444, 449; *ill.*
Wordsworth, Elizabeth 38–9, 40
World War I 99, 117, 157–8, 159–60,
  233, 237; trench warfare 237,
  250–1; US enters 309; *1918* 328–9;
  Armistice 329; *see also* Gallipoli
Wounded and Missing Enquiry
  Department: Boulogne office 157,
  237–8, 239–42, 243–52, 255, 402;
  London 252, 253, 254; Paris office
  237, 241, 242

Yahya Beg 110, 131, 289
Yasin Pasha, Gen. al-Hashimi, Prime
  Minister of Iraq 355
Yazidi sect 324
Yenbo, Saudi Arabia 368, 369, 370–1
Young, Hubert W. 421
Young Turks 140, 261, 334, 364, 366
Ypres, battle 158, 237

Zagros mountains, Iran 263
Zaid ibn Hussain, Emir: in Arab revolt
  366, 368, 369; subsequently 388,
  425, 433, 435
Zaiya (servant) 434
Zamil ibn Subhan 209, 216–17, 231
Zionism 339, 382–6, 399
Zionist Commission 386
Ziza, Jordan, GLB in, *1914* 155, 188, 189,
  192, 194

PERMISSIONS

Many of Gertrude Bell's letters, diaries and papers are reproduced here by kind permission of the Robinson Library, University of Newcastle upon Tyne. Her letters to Valentine Chirol; letters from Sir Gilbert Clayton, Lord Cromer and F. C. C. Balfour about her; and the letter from Sir Louis Mallet to Sir Edward Grey concerning her journey to Hayyil, are reproduced by kind permission of Durham University Library.

Dick Doughty-Wylie's last letter to Mrs Jean Coe is reproduced by kind permission of the executor of the will of the late Mrs M. Inaund; and thanks to Tyne Tees Television for providing the tape *Gertrude Bell: The Uncrowned Queen of Iraq*, programme 2, 'Mysteries' series.

Picture Acknowledgements

John Cleare/Mountain Camera Picture Library: 16; Country Life: 2, 6; Gertrude Bell Photographic Archive, Newcastle University: 1, 3, 4, 8, 9, 10, 11, 12, 13, 14, 15, 17, 18, 19, 20, 21, 22, 23, 25, 27, 28, 29, 31, 32, 33, 34; Getty Images: 5; Royal Geographical Society: 24, 35; Topfoto: 30; courtesy the author: 7.

www.panmacmillan.com